W9-BZR-653

# The Cross-Platform Prep Course

Welcome to the Cross-Platform Prep Course! McGraw-Hill Education's multi-platform course gives you a variety of tools to help you raise your test scores. Whether you're studying at home, in the library, or on-the-go, you can find practice content in the format you need—print, online, or mobile.

## Print Book

This print book gives you the tools you need to ace the test. In its pages you'll find smart test-taking strategies, in-depth reviews of key topics, and ample practice questions and tests. See the Welcome section of your book for a step-by-step guide to its features.

## Online Platform

The Cross-Platform Prep Course gives you additional study and practice content that you can access *anytime, anywhere*. You can create a personalized study plan based on your test date that sets daily goals to keep you on track. Integrated lessons provide important review of key topics. Practice questions, exams, and flashcards give you the practice you need to build test-taking confidence. The game center is filled with challenging games that allow you to practice your new skills in a fun and engaging way. And, you can even interact with other test-takers in the discussion section and gain valuable peer support.

## *Getting Started*

To get started, open your account on the online platform:

**Go to www.xplatform.mhprofessional.com**

↓

**Enter your access code, which you can find on the inside back cover of your book**

↓

**Provide your name and e-mail address to open your account and create a password**

↓

**Click "Start Studying" to enter the platform**

It's as simple as that. You're ready to start studying online.

## *Your Personalized Study Plan*

First, select your test date on the calendar, and you'll be on your way to creating your personalized study plan. Your study plan will help you stay organized and on track and will guide you through the course in the most efficient way. It is tailored to *your* schedule and features daily tasks that are broken down into manageable goals. You can adjust your test date at any time and your daily tasks will be reorganized into an updated plan.

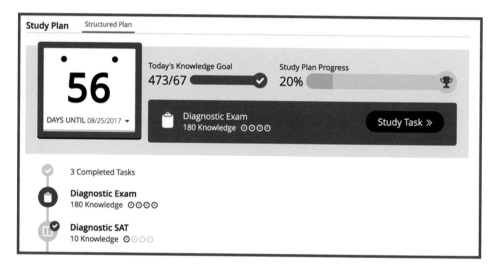

You can track your progress in real time on the Study Plan Dashboard. The "Today's Knowledge Goal" progress bar gives you up-to-the minute feedback on your daily goal. Fulfilling this every time you log on is the most efficient way to work through the entire course. You always get an instant view of where you stand in the entire course with the Study Plan Progress bar.

*If you need to exit the program before completing a task, you can return to the Study Plan Dashboard at any time. Just click the Study Task icon and you can automatically pick up where you left off.*

## *Practice Tests*

One of the first tasks in your personalized study plan is to take the Diagnostic Test. At the end of the test, a detailed evaluation of your strengths and weaknesses shows the areas where you need the most focus. You can review your practice test results either by the question category to see broad trends or question-by-question for a more in-depth look.

The full-length tests are designed to simulate the real thing. Try to simulate actual testing conditions and be sure you set aside enough time to complete the full-length test. You'll learn to pace yourself so that you can work toward the best possible score on test day.

## *Lessons*

The lessons in the online platform are divided into manageable pieces that let you build knowledge and confidence in a progressive way. They cover the full range of topics that you're likely to see on your test.

After you complete a lesson, mark your confidence level. (You must indicate a confidence level in order to count your progress and move on to the next task.) You can also filter the lessons by confidence levels to see the areas you have mastered and those that you might need to revisit.

> *Use the bookmark feature to easily refer back to a concept or leave a note to remember your thoughts or questions about a particular topic.*

## What's new in the redesigned SAT?

Beginning in spring 2016, the redesigned SAT features ten major changes.

**1. More time per question**

The redesigned SAT gives you more time per question, making it less likely that you will underperform due to time restrictions.

| Section | Old SAT Time Per Question | New SAT Time Per Question |
|---|---|---|
| Writing and Language | 43 seconds (49 questions, 35 mins) | 48 seconds (44 questions, 35 mins) |
| Mathematics | 78 seconds (54 questions, 70 mins) | 84 seconds (57 questions, 80 mins) |
| Reading | 63 seconds (67 questions in 70 mins) | 75 seconds (52 questions, 65 mins) |

## *Practice Questions*

All of the practice questions are reflective of actual exams and simulate the test-taking experience. The "Review Answer" button gives you immediate feedback on your answer. Each question includes a rationale that explains why the correct answer is right and the others are wrong. To explore any topic further, you can find detailed explanations by clicking the "Help me learn about this topic" link.

**Quantitative-Data Sufficiency**

Question 1 of 24

**Direction:** The following data sufficiency problem consist of a question and two statements, labeled (1) and (2), in which certain data are given. You have to decide whether the data given in the statements are *sufficient* for answering the question.

A. Statement (1) ALONE is sufficient, but statement (2) alone is not sufficient.
B. Statement (2) ALONE is sufficient, but statement (1) alone is not sufficient.
C. BOTH statements TOGETHER are sufficient, but NEITHER statement ALONE is sufficient.
D. EACH statement ALONE is sufficient.
E. Statements (1) and (2) TOGETHER are NOT sufficient.

**Q.** Is $x$ an integer?

(1) $x$ is evenly divisible by $\frac{1}{2}$

(2) $x$ is evenly divisible by 2.

**Solution:**
**The correct answer is B.**
A reminder: The question stem starts with *is*, so this is a *yes* or *no* problem. The first step is to determine whether statement (1) is sufficient, which we can do by trying out some real numbers. If $x$ is 2, which is evenly divisible by $\frac{1}{2}$ then the answer would be *yes*. But if $x$ were 1.5, which is also evenly divisible by $\frac{1}{2}$ then the answer would be *no*. Since you can get either *yes* or *no*, statement (1) is not sufficient and you should cross off A and D. Now let's move on to statement (2). There are no non-integer numbers that are divisible by 2, so *yes* is the only possibility. Statement (2) is sufficient, so we can eliminate C and E. Thus the answer is **B**.

You can go to the Practice Dashboard to find an overview of your performance in the different categories and sub-categories.

**Practice**     ▦ Dashboard    ✍ Confidence Levels    ✏ Notes    🔖 Bookmarks

Dashboard                  Reset All Questions

**77%** Correct

Questions Taken
159 of 491

Avg. Answer Time
2 min 52 sec

Avg. Correct Answer Time
2 min 20 sec

Avg. Incorrect Answer Time
3 min 6 sec

Avg. Session Duration
18 min 41 sec

Question Categories

| Category Name | Completion | % Correct |
|---|---|---|
| Quantitative-Problem Solving | 94 of 297 | 72% |
| Arithmetic | 75 of 75 | 84% |
| Elementary Algebra | 35 of 189 | 60% |
| Geometry | 0 of 49 | -- |
| Quantitative-Data Sufficiency | 49 of 49 | 81% |
| Arithmetic | 6 of 6 | 75% |
| Elementary Algebra | 30 of 30 | 86% |
| Geometry | 13 of 13 | 82% |
| Verbal | 0 of 129 | -- |
| Reading Comprehension | 0 of 46 | -- |
| Critical Reasoning | 0 of 64 | -- |
| Sentence Correction | 0 of 19 | -- |

# *Dashboard*

The dashboard is constantly updating to reflect your progress and performance. The Percentile Rank icon shows your position relative to all the other students enrolled in the course. You can also find information on your average scores in practice questions and exams.

A detailed overview of your strengths and weaknesses shows your proficiency in a category based on your answers and difficulty of the questions. By viewing your strengths and weaknesses, you can focus your study on areas where you need the most help.

**Strengths & Weaknesses** ❶

**Writing and Language**

Beginner    Basic    [Intermediate]    Proficient    Advanced    Expert

**Reading**

Beginner    [Basic]    Intermediate    Proficient    Advanced    Expert

**Math**

[Beginner]    Basic    Intermediate    Proficient    Advanced    Expert

| | N/A | Beginner | Basic | Intermediate | Proficient | Advanced | Expert |
|---|---|---|---|---|---|---|---|
| The Heart of Algebra | N/A | [Beginner] | Basic | Intermediate | Proficient | Advanced | Expert |
| Advanced Mathematics | N/A | [Beginner] | Basic | Intermediate | Proficient | Advanced | Expert |
| Additional Topics | N/A | Beginner | [Basic] | Intermediate | Proficient | Advanced | Expert |

🔒 Riding dolphins
🔒 What doesn't kill yo...
🔒 Good Karma
🔒 Stenographer

**Top Performers**
- 👤 David Flores
- 👤 Jenny
- 👤 Elle
- 👤 Shadaj L
- 👤 Grant Foray
- 👤 Coco Ma
- 👤 Angela Jeon
- 👤 Sarah Kim
- 👤 Madison McClane
- 👤 Gabi Kreuscher
- ...
- 👤 Tenant Admin

## *Flashcards*

The hundreds of flashcards are perfect for learning key terms quickly, and the interactive format gives you immediate feedback. You can filter the cards by category and confidence level for a more organized approach. Or, you can shuffle them up for a more general challenge.

Another way to customize the flashcards is to create your own sets. You can either keep these private or share or them with the public. Subscribe to Community Sets to access sets from other students preparing for the same exam.

# Game Center

Play a game in the Game Center to test your knowledge of key concepts in a challenging but fun environment. Increase the difficulty level and complete the games quickly to build your highest score. Be sure to check the leaderboard to see who's on top!

# Social Community

Interact with other students who are preparing for the same test. Start a discussion, reply to a post, or even upload files to share. You can search the archives for common topics or start your own private discussion with friends.

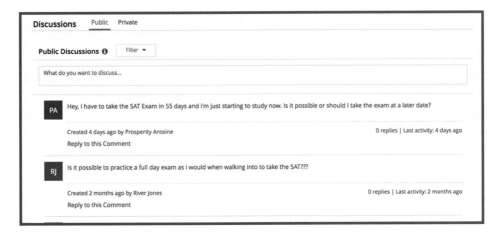

# Mobile App

The companion mobile app lets you toggle between the online platform and your mobile device without missing a beat. Whether you access the course online or from your smartphone or tablet, you'll pick up exactly where you left off.

Go to the iTunes or Google Play stores and search "McGraw-Hill Education Cross-Platform App" to download the companion iOS or Android app. Enter your e-mail address and the same password you created for the online platform to open your account.

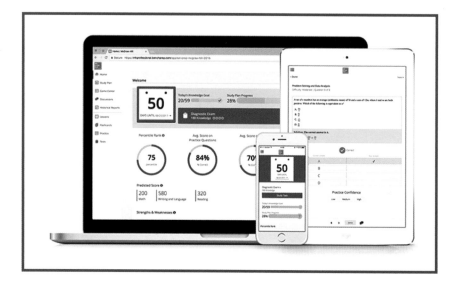

## *Now, let's get started!*

**ELITE** STUDENT EDITION

# 5 STEPS TO A 5

# AP Biology

## 2019

**Mark Anestis • Kellie Ploeger Cox, PhD**

Mc Graw Hill Education

New York  Chicago  San Francisco  Athens  London  Madrid
Mexico City  Milan  New Delhi  Singapore  Sydney  Toronto

Copyright © 2018 by McGraw-Hill Education. All rights reserved. Printed in the United States of America. Except as permitted under the United States Copyright Act of 1976, no part of this publication may be reproduced or distributed in any form or by any means, or stored in a database or retrieval system, without the prior written permission of the publisher.

1 2 3 4 5 6 7 8 9   LHS   23 22 21 20 19 18
1 2 3 4 5 6 7 8 9   LHS   23 22 21 20 19 18 (Elite Student Edition)

ISBN 978-1-260-12281-7
MHID 1-260-12281-6

e-ISBN 978-1-260-12282-4
e-MHID 1-260-12282-4

ISBN 978-1-260-12283-1 (Elite Student Edition)
MHID 1-260-12283-2

e-ISBN 978-1-260-12284-8 (Elite Student Edition)
e-MHID 1-260-12284-0

**Trademarks:** McGraw-Hill Education, the McGraw-Hill Education logo, *5 Steps to a 5*, and related trade dress are trademarks or registered trademarks of McGraw-Hill Education and/or its affiliates in the United States and other countries and may not be used without written permission. All other trademarks are the property of their respective owners. McGraw-Hill Education is not associated with any product or vendor mentioned in this book.

*AP, Advanced Placement Program*, and *College Board* are registered trademarks of the College Board, which was not involved in the production of, and does not endorse, this product.

The series editor was Grace Freedson, and the project editor was Del Franz.

Series design by Jane Tenenbaum.

McGraw-Hill Education products are available at special quantity discounts to use as premiums and sales promotions, or for use in corporate training programs. To contact a representative, please visit the Contact Us pages at www.mhprofessional.com.

# CONTENTS

**STEP 5**      **Build Your Test-Taking Confidence**

**ELITE**      **5 Minute to a 5**
**STUDENT**
**EDITION**

Hello, and welcome to the new edition of the AP Biology review book that promises to be the most fun you have ever had!!!! Well, OK. . . . It will not be the most fun you have ever had . . . but maybe you will enjoy yourself a little bit. If you let yourself, you may at least learn a lot from this book. It contains the major concepts and ideas to which you were exposed over the past year in your AP Biology classroom, written in a manner that, we hope, will be pleasing to your eyes and your brain.

Many books on the market contain the same information that you will find in this book. However, we have approached the material a bit differently. We have tried to make this book as conversational and understandable as possible. We have had to review for countless standardized tests and cannot think of anything more annoying than a review book that is a total snoozer. In fact, we had this book "snooze-tested" by more than five thousand students, and the average reader could go 84 pages before falling asleep. This is better than the "other" review books whose average snooze time fell within the range of 14–43 pages. OK, we made up those statistics . . . but we promise that this book will not put you to sleep.

While preparing this book, we spoke to 154,076 students who had taken the AP exam and asked them how they prepared for the test. They indicated which study techniques were most helpful to them and which topics in this book they considered *vital* to success on this test. Throughout the book there are notes in the margins with these students' comments and tips. Pay heed to these comments because these folks know what they are talking about. They have taken this test and may have advice that will be useful to you.

We are not going to mislead you into thinking that you do not need to study to do well on this exam. You will actually need to prepare quite a bit. But this book will walk you through the process in as painless a way as possible. Use the study questions at the end of each chapter in Step 4 to practice applying the material you just read. Use the study tips listed in Step 3 to help you remember the material you need to know. Take the two practice tests in Step 5 as the actual exam approaches to see how well the information is sinking in.

Well, it's time to stop gabbing and start studying. Begin by setting up your study program in Step 1 of this book. Take the diagnostic test in Step 2 and look through the answers and explanations to see where you stand before you dive into the review process. Then look through the hints and strategies in Step 3, which may help you finally digest all the information that comes at you in Step 4. Then, we suggest that you kick back, relax, grab yourself a comfortable seat, and dig in. There is a lot to learn before the exam. Happy reading!

# ACKNOWLEDGMENTS

This project would not have been completed without the assistance of many dear friends and relatives. To my wife, Stephanie, your countless hours of reading, rereading, and reading once again were of amazing value. Thank you so much for putting in so much time and energy to my cause. You have helped make this book what it is. To my parents and brothers who likewise contributed by reading a few chapters when I needed a second opinion, I thank you. I would like to thank Chris Black for helping me edit and clarify a few of the chapters. I would like to thank Don Reis, whose editing comments have strengthened both the content and the flow of this work. Finally, a big thank-you to all the students and teachers who gave me their input and thoughts on what they believed to be important for this exam. They have made this book that much stronger. Thank you all.

—Mark Anestis

# ABOUT THE AUTHORS

MARK ANESTIS was born in Pittsburgh, Pennsylvania, and has lived in Connecticut since the age of six. He graduated from Weston High School in Weston, Connecticut, in 1993 and attended Yale University. While taking science courses in preparation for medical school, he earned a bachelor's degree cum laude in economics. He attended the University of Connecticut School of Medicine for two years and passed the step 1 boards, then chose to redirect his energy toward educating students in a one-on-one environment. He is the founder and director of The Learning Edge, a tutoring company based in Hamden, Connecticut (www.thelearningedge.net). Since January 2000, he has been tutoring high school students in math, the sciences, and standardized test preparation (including the SAT, ACT, and SAT Subject Tests). In addition to this review book, he has coauthored *McGraw-Hill's SAT, McGraw-Hill's PSAT/NMSQT*, and *McGraw-Hill's 12 SAT Practice Tests and PSAT*. He lives with his wife and sons in Hamden, Connecticut.

The author also created the PERFECT SCORE app (perfect-score.com), which allows students to prepare for the SAT while competing against other students. The app is available on the App Store.

KELLIE PLOEGER COX is originally from Spokane, Washington, and earned her PhD in Microbiology from the University of Idaho. She now lives in Connecticut, where she has been a member of the science department at Hopkins School since 1999. Kellie teaches Introductory Biology, AP Biology, and Contemporary Issues in Biology, and loves all things nerdy. Her favorite science experiments are her two daughters, Raina Faith and Kenley Piper.

# INTRODUCTION: THE FIVE-STEP PROGRAM

## Welcome!

If you focus on the beginning, the rest will fall into place. When you purchase this book and decide to work your way through it, you are beginning your journey to the Advanced Placement (AP) Biology exam. We will be with you every step of the way.

## Why This Book?

We believe that this book has something unique to offer you. We have spoken with many AP Biology teachers and students and have been fortunate to learn quite a bit. Teachers helped us understand which topics are most important for class, and students described what they wanted from a test-prep book. Therefore, the contents of this book reflect genuine student concerns and needs. This is a student-oriented book. We did not attempt to impress you with arrogant language, mislead you with inaccurate information and tasks, or lull you into a false sense of confidence through ingenious shortcuts. We have not put information into this book simply because it is included in other review books. We recognize the fact that there is only so much that one individual can learn for an exam. Believe us, we have taken our fair share of these tests—we know how much work they can be. This book represents a realistic approach to studying for the AP exam. We have included very little heavy technical detail in this book. (There *is* some . . . we had to . . . but there is not very much.)

Think of this text as a resource and guide to accompany you on your AP Biology journey throughout the year. This book is designed to serve many purposes. It should:

- Clarify requirements for the AP Biology exam
- Provide you with test practice
- Help you pace yourself
- Function as a wonderful paperweight when the exam is completed
- Make you aware of the Five Steps to Mastering the AP Biology Exam

## Organization of the Book

We know that your primary concern is to learn about the AP Biology exam. We start by introducing the five-step plan. We then give an overview of the exam in general. We follow that up with three different approaches to exam preparation and then move on to describe some tips and suggestions for how to approach the various sections of the exam. The Diagnostic Exam should give you an idea of where you stand before you begin your preparations. We recommend that you spend 45 minutes on this practice exam.

The volume of material covered in AP Biology is quite intimidating. Step 4 of this book provides a comprehensive review of all the major sections you may or may not have covered in the classroom. Not every AP Biology class in the country will get through the same amount of material. This book should help you fill any gaps in your understanding of the course work.

Step 5 of this book is the practice exam section. Here is where you put your skills to the test. The multiple-choice questions provide practice with the types of questions you may encounter on the AP exam. Keep in mind that they are *not* exact questions taken directly from past exams. Rather, they are designed to focus you on the key topics that often appear on the actual AP Biology exam. When you answer a question we've written in this book, do not think to yourself, "OK . . . that's a past exam question." Instead, you should think to yourself, "OK, the authors thought that was important, so I should remember this fact. It may show up in some form on the real exam." The essay questions are designed to cover the techniques and terms required by the AP exam. After taking each exam, you can check yourself against the explanations of every multiple-choice question and the grading guidelines for the essays.

The material at the end of the book is also important. It contains a bibliography of sources that may be helpful to you, a list of websites related to the AP Biology exam, and a glossary of the key terms discussed in this book.

# Introducing the Five-Step Program

The five-step program is designed to provide you with the skills and strategies vital to the exam and the practice that can help lead you to that perfect "Holy Grail" score of 5.

## Step 1: Set Up Your Study Program

Step 1 leads you through a brief process to help determine which type of exam preparation you want to commit yourself to:

1. Full-year prep: September through May
2. One-semester prep: January through May
3. Six-week prep: the six weeks prior to the exam

## Step 2: Determine Your Test Readiness

Step 2 consists of a diagnostic exam, which will give you an idea of what you already know and what you need to learn between now and the exam. Take the test, which is broken down by topic, look over the detailed explanations, and start learning!

## Step 3: Develop Strategies for Success

Step 3 gives you strategy advice for the AP Biology exam. It teaches you about the multiple-choice questions and the free-response questions you will face on exam day.

## Step 4: Review the Knowledge You Need to Score High

Step 4 is a big one. This is the comprehensive review of all the topics on the AP exam. You've probably been in an AP Bio class all year, and you've likely spent hours upon hours reading through the AP Biology textbooks. These review chapters are appropriate both for quick skimming (to remind yourself of salient points that may have slipped your mind) and for in-depth study (to teach yourself broader concepts that may be new to you.)

## Step 5: Build Your Test-Taking Confidence

Ahhhh, the full-length practice tests—oh, the joy! This book has three of them. If you purchased the cross-platform version of this book, you will find three more practice tests online. One of the most effective ways to improve as you prepare for any exam is to take as many practice tests as you can. Sit down and take these tests fully timed, see what you get wrong, and learn from those mistakes. Remember . . . it's good to make mistakes on these exams because if you learn from those mistakes now, you won't make them again in May!

## The Graphics Used in This Book

To emphasize particular skills and strategies, we use several icons throughout this book. An icon in the margin will alert you that you should pay particular attention to the accompanying text. We use three icons:

**1.** This icon points out a very important concept or fact that you should not pass over.

**2.** This icon calls your attention to a problem-solving strategy that you may want to try.

**3.** This icon indicates a tip that you might find useful.

**Boldfaced** words indicate terms that are included in the Glossary at the end of the book. Boldface is also used to indicate the answer to a sample problem discussed in the test. Throughout the book you will find marginal notes, boxes, and starred areas. Pay close attention to these areas because they can provide tips, hints, strategies, and further explanations to help you reach your full potential.

# THE FOUR "BIG IDEAS" OF AP BIOLOGY

The College Board has identified four key concepts, called "big ideas," that form the basis for the AP Biology curriculum. All the topics covered in the AP Biology course and all the questions on the AP Biology exam are linked to at least one of these big ideas.

The outline that follows provides a basic summary of the four "big ideas" of AP Biology. Each of the four ideas is subdivided into topics, and under each topic are statements that identify essential knowledge. You won't need to memorize this—you won't be asked to list even the big ideas—but you will need to be sure you have a good understanding of them. They are the fundamental concepts on which the course and the exam are based.

As you work through the content review chapters of this book, you'll find icons in the margin with cryptic numbers and letters. Don't let these confuse you! Those icons are there to help you understand how the subject matter in the review chapters fits into the big ideas of the AP Biology course. Look at the example in the left margin.

> **BIG IDEA 4.A.1**
> *The subcomponents of a molecule determine its properties.*

In this example, the number 4 refers to the fourth big idea, "Interactions" (see outline). The letter A refers to topic A under big idea number 4, which is "Biological systems (from cells to ecosystems) contain parts that interact with each other." The number 1 refers to the first point of essential knowledge under topic A, "The properties of biological molecules are determined by their components (monomers and polymers)." As you make your way through the subject review in this book, it is very helpful to keep an eye on the big picture and keep in mind how all the content you review relates to these four big ideas.

## Big Idea 1: Evolution

A. Evolution is change over time.
   1. Evolution occurs because of natural selection.
   2. Natural selection acts on phenotypic variations in populations.
   3. Evolutionary change is random.
   4. Evolution is supported by scientific evidence.

B. Descent from common ancestry links organisms.
   1. Many features are widely conserved (found in all sorts of organisms).
   2. Phylogenetic trees and cladograms are visual representations of these relationships.

C. Evolution continues in a changing environment.
   1. Speciation increases diversity and extinction reduces diversity; both have occurred throughout history.
   2. Speciation is often a result of reproductive isolation.
   3. Organisms continue to evolve.

D. Natural processes explain the origin of life.
   1. There are different hypotheses, each supported by evidence, about how life began.
   2. Different hypotheses of how life began are supported by scientific evidence from many disciplines.

# Big Idea 2: Cellular Processes: Energy, Communication, and Homeostasis

A.  Free energy and matter are required for life processes.
1.  All living things need a constant source of energy.
2.  Autotrophs (through photosynthesis) and heterotrophs (through cellular respiration) capture and store free energy.
3.  Organisms exchange matter with the environment.

B.  Cells maintain an internal environment that is different from their surroundings.
1.  The structure of cell membranes results in selective permeability.
2.  Homeostasis is maintained by movements through cell membranes.
3.  Internal membranes compartmentalize cells (organelles).

C.  Organisms rely on feedback mechanisms to grow, reproduce, and survive.
1.  Organisms use positive and negative feedback.
2.  Feedback mechanisms allow organisms to respond to changes in their environments.

D.  Growth and homeostasis are influenced by environmental changes.
1.  Biotic and abiotic interactions affect everything from cells to ecosystems.
2.  Both common ancestry and divergence (due to different environments) are reflected in homeostatic mechanisms.
3.  Disruptions to homeostasis affect the health of the organism and the balance of the ecosystem.
4.  Plants and animals have defense systems against infection (immune systems).

E.  Temporal (time-based) coordination is involved in homeostasis, growth, and reproduction.
1.  The correct timing of events is necessary for the proper development of an organism.
2.  The timing and coordination of the events is regulated in different ways for different organisms.
3.  Various mechanisms are used to time and coordinate behavior.

# Big Idea 3: Genetics and Information Transfer

A.  The continuity of life is made possible through heritable information.
1.  DNA and RNA provide heritable information from one generation to the next.
2.  The cell cycle, mitosis, and meiosis are processes that transmit heritable information.
3.  The transmittal of genes from parent to child shows the chromosomal basis of inheritance.
4.  The inheritance of traits is more complex than can be explained by simple Mendelian models.

B.  Cellular and molecular mechanisms are involved in gene expression.
1.  Differential gene expression is a result of gene regulation.
2.  Signal transmissions influence gene expression.

C.  Imperfect processing of genetic information creates genetic variation.
1.  Changes in genotype create new phenotypes.
2.  Many biological mechanisms can increase variation.
3.  Viral infections can produce genetic variation in their host organisms.

D.  Cells communicate with other cells through the transmission of chemical signals.
1.  Cell communication is based on common features (which show a common ancestry).

2. Cells can communicate through direct contact or long-distance signaling.
3. Signal transduction pathways begin with the recognition of a signal by a cell and ends with the cellular response.
4. A blocked or defective signal transduction pathway can change the cellular response.

E. Information transmission results in changes in biological systems.
1. Organisms communicate and exchange information.
2. Animal nervous systems perform a key role in the reception, transmittal, and processing of information to produce a response.

# Big Idea 4: Interactions

A. Biological systems (from cells to ecosystems) contain parts that interact with each other.
1. The properties of biological molecules are determined by their components (monomers and polymers).
2. Organelles are essential to cell processes.
3. Interactions between external stimuli and gene expression produce specialized cells, tissues, and organs.
4. Complex properties in organisms are the result of interactions among their constituent parts.
5. Populations of organisms interact in communities.
6. The movement of matter and flow of energy are a result of interaction between communities and their environment.

B. Biological systems are characterized by competition and cooperation.
1. The structure and function of a molecule are influenced by its interaction with other molecules.
2. Cooperative interaction within organisms promotes efficiency.
3. Interactions within and between populations affect species distribution and abundance.
4. Ecosystem distribution changes over time (human impact accelerates change).

C. Diversity within biological systems influences interactions with the environment.
1. Variation in molecular units (e.g., different chlorophyll molecules, antibody proteins, or alleles of a gene) provides cells with a broad range of functions.
2. Gene expression is influenced by environment.
3. Variation influences population dynamics.
4. Diversity affects ecosystem stability.

# STEP 1

# Set Up Your Study Program

# CHAPTER 1

# What You Need to Know About the AP Biology Exam

**IN THIS CHAPTER**

**Summary:** Learn what topics are tested, how the test is scored, and basic test-taking information.

**Key Ideas**

✪ Some colleges will award credit for a score of 4 or 5.

✪ Multiple-choice and grid-in questions account for 50 percent of your final score.

✪ Points are no longer deducted for incorrect answers to multiple-choice questions. You should try to eliminate incorrect answer choices and then guess; there is no penalty for guessing.

✪ Free-response questions account for 50 percent of your final score.

✪ Your composite score on the two test sections is converted into a score on the 1-to-5 scale.

## Background of the Advanced Placement Program

The Advanced Placement program was begun by the College Board in 1955 to construct standard achievement exams that would allow highly motivated high school students the opportunity to be awarded advanced placement as first-year students in colleges and universities in the United States. Today, more than a million students from every state in the nation and from foreign countries take the annual AP exams in May.

The AP programs are designed for high school students who wish to take college-level courses. In our case, the AP Biology course and exam are designed to involve high school students in college-level biology studies.

## Who Writes the AP Biology Exam

After extensive surfing of the College Board website, here is what we have uncovered. The AP Biology exam is created by a group of college and high school biology instructors known as the AP Development Committee. The committee's job is to ensure that the annual AP Biology exam reflects what is being taught and studied in college-level biology classes at high schools.

This committee writes a large number of multiple-choice questions, which are pretested and evaluated for clarity, appropriateness, and range of possible answers. The committee also generates a pool of essay questions, pretests them, and chooses those questions that best represent the full range of the scoring scale, which will allow the AP readers to evaluate the essays equitably.

It is important to remember that the AP Biology exam is thoroughly evaluated after it is administered each year. This way, the College Board can use the results to make course suggestions and to plan future tests.

## The AP Grades and Who Receives Them

Once you have taken the exam and it has been scored, your test will be graded with one of five numbers by the College Board:

- A 5 indicates that you are extremely well qualified.
- A 4 indicates that you are well qualified.
- A 3 indicates that you are adequately qualified.
- A 2 indicates that you are possibly qualified.
- A 1 indicates that you are not qualified to receive college credit.

A grade of 5, 4, 3, 2, or 1 will usually be reported by early July.

## Reasons for Taking the AP Biology Exam

Why put yourself through a year of intensive study, pressure, stress, and preparation? Only you can answer that question. Following are some of the reasons that students have indicated to us for taking the AP exam:

- For personal satisfaction.
- To compare themselves with other students across the nation.
- Because colleges look favorably on the applications of students who elect to enroll in AP courses.
- To receive college credit or advanced standing at their colleges or universities.
- Because they love the subject.
- So that their families will be really proud of them.

There are plenty of other reasons, but no matter what they might be, the primary reason for enrolling in the AP Biology course and taking the exam in May is to feel good about yourself and the challenges you have met.

# Questions Frequently Asked About the AP Biology Exam

Here are some common questions students have about the AP Biology exam and some answers to those questions.

### If I Don't Take an AP Biology Course, Can I Still Take the AP Biology Exam?

Yes. Although the AP Biology exam is designed for students who have had a year's course in AP Biology, some high schools do not offer this type of course. Many students in these high schools have also done well on the exam, although they had not taken the course. However, if your high school does offer an AP Biology course, by all means take advantage of it and the structured background it will provide you.

### How Is the Advanced Placement Biology Exam Organized?

The exam has two parts and is scheduled to last three hours. The first section is a set of 63 multiple-choice questions and six grid-in (calculation-based) questions. You will have 90 minutes to complete this part of the test.

After you complete the multiple-choice section, you will hand in your test booklet and scan sheet, and you will be given a brief break. The length of this break depends on the particular administrator. You will not be able to return to the multiple-choice questions when you return to the examination room.

The second section of the exam is a 90-minute essay-writing segment consisting of two long free-response questions and six short free-response questions. This section will be split into a 10-minute reading period followed by an 80-minute writing period. All of the questions will test your understanding of the four big ideas in biology and how science investigators actually work.

### Must I Check the Box at the End of the Essay Booklet That Allows AP Staff to Use My Essays as Samples for Research?

No. This is simply a way for the College Board to make certain they have your permission if they decide to use one or more of your essays as a model. The readers of your essays pay no attention to whether or not that box is checked. Checking the box will not affect your grade.

### How Is the Multiple-Choice Section Scored?

The scan sheet with your answers is run through a computer, which counts the number of correct answers. The AP Biology questions usually have four choices. A question left blank receives a zero. The very complicated formula for this calculation looks something like this (where $N$ = the number of answers):

$$N_{right} = \text{raw score}$$

OK, that is not complicated at all.

### How Are My Free-Response Answers Scored?

Each of your essays is read by a different, trained AP reader called a *faculty consultant*. The AP/College Board members have developed a highly successful training program for their readers, providing many opportunities for checks and double checks of essays to ensure a fair and equitable reading of each essay.

The scoring guides are carefully developed by a chief faculty consultant, a question leader, table leaders, and content experts. All faculty consultants are then trained to read and score just *one* essay question on the exam. They actually become experts in that one essay question. No one knows the identity of any writer. The identification numbers and names are covered, and the exam booklets are randomly distributed to the readers in packets of 25 randomly chosen essays. Table leaders and the question leader review samples of each reader's scores to ensure that quality standards are constant.

Each essay is scored on a scale from 1 to 10. Once your essay is graded on this scale, the next set of calculations is completed.

## How Is My Composite Score Calculated?

This is where fuzzy math comes into play. The folks at the College Board are constantly adjusting the exact formula used to determine your composite score. Here is an example of a conversion they have used in the past, and this will be the conversion you will use to score any tests you do in this book.

The composite score for the AP Biology exam is 138. The free-response section represents 50 percent of this score, which equals 69 points. The multiple-choice section makes up 50 percent of the composite score, which equals another 69 points.

Take your multiple-choice results and plug them into the following formula (keep in mind that this formula was designed for a previous AP Biology exam and could be subject to some minor tweaking by the AP Board):

Number multiple-choice correct + number of grid-in correct = ——————

Take your essay results and plug them into this formula:

Total free-response points × 1.57 = ——————

Your total composite score for the exam is determined by adding the score from the multiple-choice section to the score from the essay section and rounding that sum to the nearest whole number.

## How Is My Composite Score Turned into the Grade That Is Reported to My College?

Keep in mind that the total composite scores needed to earn a 5, 4, 3, 2, or 1 change each year. These cutoffs are determined by a committee of AP, College Board, and Educational Testing Service (ETS) directors, experts, and statisticians. The same exam that is given to the AP Biology high school students is given to college students. The various college professors report how the college students fared on the exam. This provides information for the chief faculty consultant on where to draw the lines for a 5, 4, 3, 2, or 1 score. A score of 5 on this AP exam is set to represent the average score received by the college students who scored an A on the exam. A score of a 3 or a 4 is the equivalent of a college grade B, and so on.

Over the years there has been an observable trend indicating the number of points required to achieve a specific grade. Data released from a particular AP Biology exam show that the approximate range for the five different scores are as follows (this changes from year to year—just use this as an approximate guideline):

- Mid 80s to 138 points = 5
- Mid 60s to lower 80s points = 4
- Upper 40s to lower 60s points = 3
- Mid 20s to upper 40s points = 2
- 0 to mid 20s points = 1

## What Should I Bring to the Exam?

Here are some suggestions:

- A simple calculator
- Several pencils and an eraser
- Several black pens (black ink is easier on the eyes)
- A watch
- Something to drink—water is best
- A quiet snack, such as Lifesavers
- Your brain
- Tissues

## What Should I *Avoid* Bringing to the Exam?

You should not bring:

- A jackhammer
- Loud stereo
- Pop rocks
- Your parents

## Is There Anything Else I Should Be Aware Of?

You should:

- Allow plenty of time to get to the test site.
- Wear comfortable clothing.
- Eat a light breakfast or lunch.
- Remind yourself that you are well prepared and that the test is an enjoyable challenge and a chance to share your knowledge. Be proud of yourself! You worked hard all year. Once test day comes, there is nothing further you can do. It is out of your hands, and your only job is to answer as many questions correctly as you possibly can.

## What Should I Do the Night Before the Exam?

Although we do not vigorously support last-minute cramming, there may be some value to some last-minute review. Spending the night before the exam relaxing with family or friends is helpful for many students. Watch a movie, play a game, gab on the phone, and then find a quiet spot to study. While you're unwinding, flip through your notebook and review sheets. As you are approaching the exam, you might want to put together a list of topics that have troubled you and review them briefly the night before the exam. If you are unable to fall asleep, flip through our chapter on taxonomy and classification (Chapter 13). Within moments, you're bound to be ready to drift off. Pleasant dreams.

# CHAPTER 2

# How to Plan Your Time

**IN THIS CHAPTER**

**Summary:** What to study for the AP Biology exam, depending on how much time you have available, plus three schedules to help you plan your course of study.

**Key Ideas**

✪ Focus your attention and spend time on those topics that are most likely to increase your score.

✪ Study the topics that you are *afraid* will appear, and relax about those that you know best.

✪ Do not study so widely that you forget to learn the important details of some of the more heavily detailed topics that appear on the AP Biology exam.

## Three Approaches to Preparing for the AP Biology Exam

### Overview of the Three Plans

No one knows your study habits, likes, and dislikes better than you do. So you are the only one who can decide which approach you want or need to adopt to prepare for the Advanced Placement Biology Exam. Look at the brief profiles below. These may help you determine a prep mode.

**You're a Full-Year Prep Student** (Plan A) if

1. You are the kind of person who likes to plan for everything very far in advance.

2. You arrive at the airport two hours before your flight because "you never know when these planes might leave early."

3. You like detailed planning and everything in its place.

4. You feel that you must be thoroughly prepared.

5. You hate surprises.

**You're a One-Semester Prep Student** (Plan B) if

1. You get to the airport one hour before your flight is scheduled to leave.

2. You are willing to plan ahead to feel comfortable in stressful situations, but are okay with skipping some details.

3. You feel more comfortable when you know what to expect, but a surprise or two is cool.

4. You're always on time for appointments.

**You're a Six-Week Prep Student** (Plan C) if

1. You get to the airport just as your plane is announcing its final boarding.

2. You work best under pressure and tight deadlines.

3. You feel very confident with the skills and background you've learned in your AP Biology class.

4. You decided late in the year to take the exam.

5. You like surprises.

6. You feel okay if you arrive 10–15 minutes late for an appointment.

**General Outline of Three Different Study Plans**

| MONTH | PLAN A: FULL SCHOOL YEAR | PLAN B: ONE SEMESTER | PLAN C: SIX WEEKS |
|---|---|---|---|
| September–October | Introduction to material | — | — |
| November | Chapters 5–7 | — | — |
| December | Chapters 8–9 | — | — |
| January | Chapters 10–11 | Chapters 5–7 | — |
| February | Chapters 12–13 | Chapters 8–10 | — |
| March | Chapters 14–16 | Chapters 11–14 | — |
| April | Chapters 17–19; Practice Exam 1 | Chapters 15–19; Practice Exam 1 | Skim Chapters 5–14; all Rapid Review sections; Practice Exam 1 |
| May | Review everything; Practice Exam 2 | Review everything; Practice Exam 2 | Skim Chapters 15–19; Practice Exam 2 |

# Calendar for Each Plan

## Plan A: You Have a Full School Year to Prepare

Although its primary purpose is to prepare you for the AP Biology exam you will take in May, this book can enrich your study of biology, your analytical skills, and your scientific essay-writing skills.

**SEPTEMBER–OCTOBER** (Check off the activities as you complete them.)
— Determine the study mode (A, B, or C) that applies to you.
— Carefully read Steps 1 and 2 of this book.
— Pay close attention to your walk-through of the Diagnostic Exam.
— Get on the web and take a look at the AP website(s).
— Skim the comprehensive review section (Step 4). (Reviewing the topics covered in this section will be part of your yearlong preparation.)
— Buy a few color highlighters.
— Flip through the entire book. Break the book in. Write in it. Toss it around a little bit . . . highlight it.
— Get a clear picture of what your own school's AP Biology curriculum is.
— Begin to use the book as a resource to supplement your classroom learning.

**NOVEMBER** (the first 10 weeks have elapsed)
— Read and study Chapter 5, Chemistry.
— Read and study Chapter 6, Cells.
— Read and study Chapter 7, Respiration.

**DECEMBER**
— Read and study Chapter 8, Photosynthesis.
— Read and study Chapter 9, Cell Division.
— Review Chapters 5–7.

**JANUARY** (20 weeks have elapsed)
— Read and study Chapter 10, Heredity.
— Read and study Chapter 11, Molecular Genetics.
— Review Chapters 5–9.

**FEBRUARY**
— Read and study Chapter 12, Evolution.
— Read and study Chapter 13, Taxonomy and Classification.
— Review Chapters 5–11.

**MARCH** (30 weeks have now elapsed)
— Read and study Chapter 14, Plants.
— Read and study Chapter 15, Human Physiology.
— Read and study Chapter 16, Human Reproduction.
— Review Chapters 5–13.

**APRIL**
— Take Practice Exam 1 in the first week of April.
— Evaluate your strengths and weaknesses.
— Study appropriate chapters to correct your weaknesses.
— Read and study Chapter 17, Behavioral Ecology and Ethology.
— Read and study Chapter 18, Ecology in Further Detail.
— Read and study Chapter 19, Laboratory Review.
— Review Chapters 5–16.

**MAY** (first 2 weeks) (THIS IS IT!)
— Review Chapters 5–19—all the material!
— Take Practice Exam 2.
— Score yourself.
— Get a good night's sleep before the exam. Fall asleep knowing that you are well prepared.

GOOD LUCK ON THE TEST!

## Plan B: You Have One Semester to Prepare

Working under the assumption that you've completed one semester of biology studies,
the following calendar will use those skills you've been practicing to prepare
you for the May exam.

**JANUARY**
— Carefully read Steps 1 and 2 of this book.
— Take the Diagnostic Exam.
— Pay close attention to your walk-through of the Diagnostic Exam.
— Read and study Chapter 5, Chemistry.
— Read and study Chapter 6, Cells.
— Read and study Chapter 7, Respiration.

**FEBRUARY**
— Read and study Chapter 8, Photosynthesis.
— Read and study Chapter 9, Cell Division.
— Read and study Chapter 10, Heredity.
— Review Chapters 5–7.

**MARCH** (10 weeks to go)
— Read and study Chapter 11, Molecular Genetics.
— Read and study Chapter 12, Evolution.
— Review Chapters 8–10.
— Read and study Chapter 13, Taxonomy and Classification.
— Read and study Chapter 14, Plants.

**APRIL**
— Take Practice Exam 1 in the first week of April.
— Evaluate your strengths and weaknesses.

— Study appropriate chapters to correct your weaknesses.
— Read and study Chapter 15, Human Physiology.
— Review Chapters 5–9.
— Read and study Chapter 16, Human Reproduction.
— Read and study Chapter 17, Behavioral Ecology and Ethology.
— Review Chapters 10–14.
— Read and study Chapter 18, Ecology in Further Detail.
— Read and study Chapter 19, Laboratory Review.

**MAY** (first 2 weeks) (THIS IS IT!)
— Review Chapters 5–19, all the material!
— Take Practice Exam 2.
— Score yourself.
— Get a good night's sleep before the exam. Fall asleep knowing that you are well prepared.

GOOD LUCK ON THE TEST!

## Plan C: You Have Six Weeks to Prepare

At this point, we assume that you have been building your biology knowledge base for more than six months. You will, therefore, use this book primarily as a specific guide to the AP Biology exam. Given the time constraints, now is not the time to try to expand your AP Biology curriculum. Rather, you should focus on and refine what you already know.

**APRIL 1–15**
— Skim Steps 1 and 2 of this book.
— Skim Chapters 5–9.
— Carefully go over the Rapid Review sections of Chapters 5–9.
— Complete Practice Exam 1.
— Score yourself and analyze your errors.
— Skim and highlight the Glossary at the end of the book.

**APRIL 16–MAY 1**
— Skim Chapters 10–14.
— Carefully go over the Rapid Review sections of Chapters 10–14.

— Carefully go over the Rapid Review sections for Chapters 5–9.
— Continue to skim and highlight the Glossary.

**MAY** (first 2 weeks) (THIS IS IT!)
— Skim Chapters 15–19.
— Carefully go over the Rapid Review sections of Chapters 15–19.
— Complete Practice Exam 2.
— Score yourself and analyze your errors.
— Get a good night's sleep. Fall asleep knowing that you are well prepared.

GOOD LUCK ON THE TEST!

# STEP 2

# Determine Your Test Readiness

CHAPTER 3 Take a Diagnostic Exam

# CHAPTER 3

# Take a Diagnostic Exam

**IN THIS CHAPTER**

**Summary:** In the following pages you will find a diagnostic exam. It is intended to give you an idea of your level of preparation in biology. After you have completed the test, check your answers against the given answers.

**Key Ideas**

- ✪ Practice the kind of multiple-choice questions you might be asked on the real exam.
- ✪ Answer questions that approximate the coverage of themes on the real exam.
- ✪ Check your work against the given answers.
- ✪ Determine your areas of strength and weakness.
- ✪ Highlight the concepts to which you must give special attention.

# Answer Sheet for Diagnostic Exam in AP Biology

## PART A: MULTIPLE-CHOICE QUESTIONS

| | | |
|---|---|---|
| 1 Ⓐ Ⓑ Ⓒ Ⓓ | 22 Ⓐ Ⓑ Ⓒ Ⓓ | 43 Ⓐ Ⓑ Ⓒ Ⓓ |
| 2 Ⓐ Ⓑ Ⓒ Ⓓ | 23 Ⓐ Ⓑ Ⓒ Ⓓ | 44 Ⓐ Ⓑ Ⓒ Ⓓ |
| 3 Ⓐ Ⓑ Ⓒ Ⓓ | 24 Ⓐ Ⓑ Ⓒ Ⓓ | 45 Ⓐ Ⓑ Ⓒ Ⓓ |
| 4 Ⓐ Ⓑ Ⓒ Ⓓ | 25 Ⓐ Ⓑ Ⓒ Ⓓ | 46 Ⓐ Ⓑ Ⓒ Ⓓ |
| 5 Ⓐ Ⓑ Ⓒ Ⓓ | 26 Ⓐ Ⓑ Ⓒ Ⓓ | 47 Ⓐ Ⓑ Ⓒ Ⓓ |
| 6 Ⓐ Ⓑ Ⓒ Ⓓ | 27 Ⓐ Ⓑ Ⓒ Ⓓ | 48 Ⓐ Ⓑ Ⓒ Ⓓ |
| 7 Ⓐ Ⓑ Ⓒ Ⓓ | 28 Ⓐ Ⓑ Ⓒ Ⓓ | 49 Ⓐ Ⓑ Ⓒ Ⓓ |
| 8 Ⓐ Ⓑ Ⓒ Ⓓ | 29 Ⓐ Ⓑ Ⓒ Ⓓ | 50 Ⓐ Ⓑ Ⓒ Ⓓ |
| 9 Ⓐ Ⓑ Ⓒ Ⓓ | 30 Ⓐ Ⓑ Ⓒ Ⓓ | 51 Ⓐ Ⓑ Ⓒ Ⓓ |
| 10 Ⓐ Ⓑ Ⓒ Ⓓ | 31 Ⓐ Ⓑ Ⓒ Ⓓ | 52 Ⓐ Ⓑ Ⓒ Ⓓ |
| 11 Ⓐ Ⓑ Ⓒ Ⓓ | 32 Ⓐ Ⓑ Ⓒ Ⓓ | 53 Ⓐ Ⓑ Ⓒ Ⓓ |
| 12 Ⓐ Ⓑ Ⓒ Ⓓ | 33 Ⓐ Ⓑ Ⓒ Ⓓ | 54 Ⓐ Ⓑ Ⓒ Ⓓ |
| 13 Ⓐ Ⓑ Ⓒ Ⓓ | 34 Ⓐ Ⓑ Ⓒ Ⓓ | 55 Ⓐ Ⓑ Ⓒ Ⓓ |
| 14 Ⓐ Ⓑ Ⓒ Ⓓ | 35 Ⓐ Ⓑ Ⓒ Ⓓ | 56 Ⓐ Ⓑ Ⓒ Ⓓ |
| 15 Ⓐ Ⓑ Ⓒ Ⓓ | 36 Ⓐ Ⓑ Ⓒ Ⓓ | 57 Ⓐ Ⓑ Ⓒ Ⓓ |
| 16 Ⓐ Ⓑ Ⓒ Ⓓ | 37 Ⓐ Ⓑ Ⓒ Ⓓ | 58 Ⓐ Ⓑ Ⓒ Ⓓ |
| 17 Ⓐ Ⓑ Ⓒ Ⓓ | 38 Ⓐ Ⓑ Ⓒ Ⓓ | 59 Ⓐ Ⓑ Ⓒ Ⓓ |
| 18 Ⓐ Ⓑ Ⓒ Ⓓ | 39 Ⓐ Ⓑ Ⓒ Ⓓ | 60 Ⓐ Ⓑ Ⓒ Ⓓ |
| 19 Ⓐ Ⓑ Ⓒ Ⓓ | 40 Ⓐ Ⓑ Ⓒ Ⓓ | 61 Ⓐ Ⓑ Ⓒ Ⓓ |
| 20 Ⓐ Ⓑ Ⓒ Ⓓ | 41 Ⓐ Ⓑ Ⓒ Ⓓ | 62 Ⓐ Ⓑ Ⓒ Ⓓ |
| 21 Ⓐ Ⓑ Ⓒ Ⓓ | 42 Ⓐ Ⓑ Ⓒ Ⓓ | 63 Ⓐ Ⓑ Ⓒ Ⓓ |

## PART B: GRID-IN QUESTIONS

# DIAGNOSTIC EXAM: AP BIOLOGY: SECTION I

## PART A: MULTIPLE-CHOICE QUESTIONS

Time—1 hour and 30 minutes (for Parts A and B)
For the multiple-choice questions that follow, select the best answer and fill in the appropriate letter on the answer sheet.

1. A pH of 10 is how many times more basic than a pH of 7?

   A. 10
   B. 100
   C. 1,000
   D. 10,000

2. Destruction of microfilaments would most adversely affect which of the following?

   A. Cell division
   B. Cilia
   C. Flagella
   D. Muscular contraction

3. Imagine that for a particular species of moth, females are primed to respond to two types of male mating calls. Males who produce an in-between version will not succeed at obtaining a mate and will therefore have low reproductive success. This is an example of

   A. directional selection.
   B. stabilizing selection.
   C. artificial selection.
   D. disruptive selection.

4. Crossover occurs during

   A. prophase of mitosis.
   B. prophase I of meiosis.
   C. prophase II of meiosis.
   D. prophase I and II of meiosis.

5. Which of the following is a specialized feature of plants that live in hot and dry regions?

   A. Stomata that open and close
   B. Transpiration
   C. Photophosphorylation
   D. $C_4$ photosynthesis

6. A virus that carries the reverse transcriptase enzyme is

   A. a retrovirus.
   B. a prion.
   C. a viroid.
   D. a DNA virus.

7. Ants live on acacia trees and are able to feast on the sugar produced by the trees. The tree is protected by the ants' attack on any foreign insects that may harm the tree. This is an example of

   A. parasitism.
   B. commensualism.
   C. mutualism.
   D. symbiosis.

8. In which of the following structures would one most likely find smooth muscle?

   A. Biceps muscle
   B. Digestive tract
   C. Quadriceps muscle
   D. Gluteus maximus muscle

9. Halophiles would be classified into which major kingdom?

   A. Monera
   B. Protista
   C. Plantae
   D. Fungi

10. A reaction that breaks down compounds by the addition of water is known as

    A. a hydrolysis reaction.
    B. a dehydration reaction.
    C. an endergonic reaction.
    D. an exergonic reaction.

11. In humans, the developing embryo tends to attach to this structure.

    A. Fallopian tube
    B. Oviduct
    C. Endometrium
    D. Cervix

12. Plants that produce a single spore type that gives rise to bisexual gametophytes are called

    A. heterosporous.
    B. gymnosperms.
    C. homosporous.
    D. angiosperms.

**13.** In humans, spermatogenesis, the process of male gamete formation, occurs in the

   A. seminiferous tubules.
   B. epididymis.
   C. vas deferens.
   D. seminal vesicles.

**14.** Which of the following is an example of aneuploidy?

   A. Cri-du-chat syndrome
   B. Chronic myelogenous leukemia
   C. Turner syndrome
   D. Achondroplasia

**15.** Among the following choices, which one would most readily move through a selectively permeable membrane?

   A. Small, uncharged polar molecule
   B. Large, uncharged polar molecule
   C. Glucose
   D. Sodium ion

**16.** Which of the following is not a lipid?

   A. Steroid
   B. Fat
   C. Phospholipid
   D. Glycogen

**17.** Which of the following hormones is *not* released by the anterior pituitary gland?

   A. Follicle-stimulating hormone (FSH)
   B. Antidiuretic hormone (ADH)
   C. Growth hormone (GH or STH)
   D. Adrenocorticotropic hormone (ACTH)

**18.** Which of the following is the *least* specific taxonomic classification category?

   A. Division
   B. Order
   C. Family
   D. Genus

**19.** These cells control the opening and closing of a plant's stomata:

   A. Guard cells
   B. Collenchyma cells
   C. Parenchyma cells
   D. Mesophyll cells

**20.** Imagine that 9 percent of a population of anteaters have a short snout (recessive), while 91 percent have a long snout (dominant). If this population is in Hardy–Weinberg equilibrium, what is the expected frequency (in percent) of the heterozygous condition?

   A. 30.0
   B. 34.0
   C. 38.0
   D. 42.0

**21.** The situation in which a gene at one locus alters the phenotypic expression of a gene at another locus is known as

   A. incomplete dominance.
   B. codominance.
   C. pleiotropy.
   D. epistasis.

**22.** The oxygen produced during the light reactions of photosynthesis comes directly from

   A. $H_2O$.
   B. $H_2O_2$.
   C. $C_2H_3O_2$.
   D. $CO_2$.

**23.** An organism that alternates between a haploid and a diploid multicellular stage during its life cycle is most probably a

   A. shark.
   B. human.
   C. pine tree.
   D. amoeba.

**24.** The presence of which of the following organelles or structures would most convincingly indicate that a cell is a eukaryote and not a prokaryote?

   A. Plasma membrane
   B. Cell wall
   C. Lysosome
   D. Ribosome

**25.** Traits that are similar between organisms that arose from a common ancestor are known as

   A. convergent characters.
   B. homologous characters.
   C. vestigial characters.
   D. divergent characters.

26. The process by which a huge amount of DNA is created from a small amount of DNA in a very short amount of time is known as

A. cloning.
B. transformation.
C. polymerase chain reaction.
D. gel electrophoresis.

27. A compound contains a COOH group. What functional group is that?

A. Carbonyl group
B. Carboxyl group
C. Hydroxyl group
D. Phosphate group

28. Which of the following forms of cell transport requires the input of energy?

A. Diffusion
B. Osmosis
C. Facilitated diffusion
D. Active transport

29. Homologous chromosomes are chromosomes that

A. are found only in identical twins.
B. are formed during mitosis.
C. split apart during meiosis II.
D. resemble one another in shape, size, and function.

30. Which of the following is an incorrect statement about DNA replication?

A. It occurs in the nucleus.
B. It occurs in a semiconservative fashion.
C. Helicase is the enzyme that adds the nucleotides to the growing strand.
D. DNA polymerase can build only in a 5′-to-3′ direction.

31. Warning coloration adopted by animals that possess a chemical defense mechanism is known as

A. cryptic coloration.
B. deceptive markings.
C. aposematic coloration.
D. batesian mimicry.

32. In a large pond that consists of long-finned fish and short-finned fish, a tornado wreaks havoc on the pond, killing 50 percent of the fish population. By chance, most of the fish killed were short-finned varieties, and in the subsequent generation there were fewer fish with short fins. This is an example of

A. gene flow.
B. bottleneck.
C. balanced polymorphism.
D. allopatric speciation.

33. Which of the following structures would not have developed from the mesoderm?

A. Muscle
B. Heart
C. Kidneys
D. Liver

34. Which of the following is not a characteristic of bryophytes?

A. They were the first land plants.
B. They contain a waxy cuticle to protect against water loss.
C. They package their gametes into gametangia.
D. The dominant generation is the sporophyte.

35. The cyclic pathway of photosynthesis occurs because

A. the Calvin cycle uses more ATP than NADPH.
B. it can occur in regions lacking light.
C. it is a more efficient way to produce oxygen.
D. it is a more efficient way to produce the NADPH needed for the Calvin cycle.

36. Which of the following conditions is an X-linked condition?

A. Hemophilia
B. Tay-Sachs disease
C. Cystic fibrosis
D. Sickle cell anemia

37. The uptake of foreign DNA from the surrounding environment is known as

    A. generalized transduction.
    B. specialized transduction.
    C. conjugation.
    D. transformation.

38. Most of the digestion of food occurs in the

    A. esophagus.
    B. stomach.
    C. small intestine.
    D. large intestine.

39. You have just come back from visiting the redwood forests in California and were amazed at how *wide* those trees were. What process is responsible for the increase in width of these trees?

    A. Growth of guard cells
    B. Growth of collenchyma cells
    C. Growth of apical meristem cells
    D. Growth of lateral meristem cells

40. The trophoblast formed during the early stages of human embryology eventually develops into the

    A. placenta.
    B. embryo.
    C. hypoblast.
    D. morula.

41. What biome is known for having the greatest diversity of species?

    A. Taiga
    B. Temperate grasslands
    C. Tropical forest
    D. Savanna

42. In hypercholesterolemia, a genetic condition found in humans, individuals who are HH have normal cholesterol levels, those who are hh have horrifically high cholesterol levels, and those who are Hh have cholesterol levels that are somewhere in between. This is an example of

    A. dominance.
    B. incomplete dominance.
    C. codominance.
    E. epistasis.

43. The light-dependent reactions of photosynthesis occur in the

    A. nucleus.
    B. cytoplasm.
    C. thylakoid membrane.
    D. stroma.

44. Which of the following is a characteristic of an R-selected strategist?

    A. Low reproductive rate
    B. Extensive postnatal care
    C. Relatively constant population size
    D. J-shaped growth curve

45. Which of the following statements about mitosis is correct?

    A. Mitosis makes up 30 percent of the cell cycle.
    B. The order of mitosis is prophase, anaphase, metaphase, telophase.
    C. Single-cell eukaryotes undergo mitosis as part of asexual reproduction.
    D. Cell plates are formed in animal cells during mitosis.

46. A vine that wraps around the trunk of a tree is displaying the concept known as

    A. photoperiodism.
    B. thigmotropism.
    C. gravitropism.
    D. phototropism.

47. This hormone is known for assisting in the closing of the stomata, and inhibition of cell growth.

    A. Abscisic acid
    B. Cytokinin
    C. Ethylene
    D. Gibberellin

48. Antigen invader → B-cell meets antigen → B-cell differentiates into plasma cells and memory cells → plasma cells produce antibodies → antibodies eliminate antigen. The preceding sequence of events is a description of

    A. cell-mediated immunity.
    B. humoral immunity.
    C. nonspecific immunity.
    D. cytotoxic T-cell maturation.

For questions 49–51, please use the following answers:

    A. Abscisic acid
    B. Cytokinins
    C. Ethylene
    D. Gibberellins

**49.** This hormone is known to promote cell division in plant roots and shoots.

**50.** This hormone is known to regulate stem elongation, germination, flowering, and other developmental processes.

**51.** This hormone is produced in the roots of a plant in response to decreased soil water potential and other situations in which the plant may be under stress.

For questions 52–55, please use the following answers:

    A. Glycolysis
    B. Oxidative phosphorylation
    C. Chemiosmosis
    D. Fermentation

**52.** This reaction occurs in the mitochondria and involves the formation of ATP from NADH and FADH$_2$.

**53.** The coupling of the movement of electrons down the electron transport chain with the formation of ATP using the driving force provided by the proton gradient.

**54.** This reaction occurs in the cytoplasm and has as its products 2 ATP, 2 NADH, and 2-pyruvate.

**55.** This reaction is performed by cells in an effort to regenerate the NAD$^+$ required for glycolysis to continue.

For questions 56–59, please use the following answer choices:

    A. Associative learning
    B. Insight learning
    C. Imprinting
    D. Altruistic behavior

**56.** The ability to reason through a problem the first time through with no prior experience.

**57.** Action in which an organism helps another, even if it comes at its own expense.

**58.** Process by which an animal substitutes one stimulus for another to get the same response.

**59.** Innate behavior learned during a critical period early in life.

For questions 60–63, please use the information from the following laboratory experiment:

You are working as a summer intern at the local university laboratory, and a lab technician comes into your room, throws a few graphs and tables at you, and mutters, "Interpret this data for me . . . I need to go play golf. I'll be back this afternoon for your report." Analyze the data this technician so kindly gave to you, and use it to answer questions 60–63. The reaction rates reported in the tables are relative to the original rate of the reaction in the absence of the enzymes. The three enzymes used are all being added to the same reactants to determine which should be used in the future.

**Room Temperature (25°C), pH 7**

| ENZYME | REACTION RATE |
| --- | --- |
| 1 | 1.24 |
| 2 | 1.51 |
| 3 | 1.33 |

**Varying Temperature, Constant (pH 7)**

| ENZYME | 0°C | 5°C | 10°C | 15°C | 20°C | 25°C | 30°C | 35°C | 40°C |
|---|---|---|---|---|---|---|---|---|---|
| 1 | 1.00 | 1.02 | 1.04 | 1.19 | 1.20 | 1.24 | 1.29 | 1.27 | 1.22 |
| 2 | 1.01 | 1.12 | 1.35 | 1.39 | 1.65 | 1.51 | 1.40 | 1.12 | 1.01 |
| 3 | 1.06 | 1.21 | 1.55 | 1.44 | 1.35 | 1.33 | 1.15 | 1.10 | 1.06 |

**Varying pH, Constant Temperature = 25°C**

| ENZYME | 4 | 5 | 6 | 7 | 8 | 9 | 10 |
|---|---|---|---|---|---|---|---|
| 1 | 1.54 | 1.51 | 1.33 | 1.24 | 1.20 | 1.08 | 1.05 |
| 2 | 1.75 | 1.71 | 1.62 | 1.51 | 1.32 | 1.10 | 1.01 |
| 3 | 1.52 | 1.45 | 1.40 | 1.33 | 1.20 | 1.09 | 1.04 |

60. If you had also been given a graph that plotted the moles of product produced versus time, what would have been the best way to calculate the rate for the reaction?

    A. Calculate the average of the slope of the curve for the first and last minute of reaction.
    B. Calculate the slope of the curve for the portion of the curve that is constant.
    C. Calculate the slope of the curve for the portion where the slope begins to flatten out.
    D. Add up the total number of moles produced during each time interval and divide by the total number of time intervals measured.

61. Over the interval measured, at what temperature does enzyme 2 appear to have its optimal efficiency?

    A. 10°C
    B. 15°C
    C. 20°C
    D. 25°C

62. Which of the following statements about enzyme 3 is incorrect?

    A. At a pH of 6 and a temperature of 25°C, it is more efficient than enzyme 2 but less efficient than enzyme 1.
    B. It functions more efficiently in the acidic pH range than the basic pH range.
    C. At 30°C and a pH of 7, it is less efficient than both enzymes 1 and 2.
    D. Over the interval given, its optimal temperature at a pH of 7 is 10°C.

63. Which of the following statements can be made from review of these data?

    A. Enzyme 1 functions most efficiently in a basic environment and at a lower temperature.
    B. Enzyme 1 functions more efficiently than enzyme 2 at 10°C and a pH of 7.
    C. The pH does not affect the efficiency of enzyme 3.
    D. All three enzymes function more efficiently in an acidic environment than a basic environment.

## PART B: GRID-IN QUESTIONS

Calculate the correct answer and enter it on the top line of the grid-in area with each number/symbol in a separate column. Then fill in the correct circle below each number/symbol you entered (only one filled-in circle per column).

1. Sickle cell anemia is a mutation in hemoglobin that affects the shape of red blood cells during periods of low oxygenation. Sickle cell anemia displays recessive inheritance. An expecting mother and father visit a geneticist for counseling. Both parents are carriers of the sickle cell trait. Calculate the likelihood that their child is a carrier.

2. Dwarfism is an autosomal dominant disease. A couple has sought out genetic counseling as they prepare to start a family. They want to have two biological children. One parent has been diagnosed with dwarfism (Dd); the second parent is healthy (dd). Calculate the probability that *both* children will have dwarfism.

3. A population of mice is in Hardy-Weinberg equilibrium. The recessive phenotype is found in 1 out of every 2500 mice. Calculate the percentage of the heterozygous phenotype.

4. A population of fruit flies is in Hardy-Weinberg equilibrium. The allele for black eyes (B) is dominant to the red allele (b). The recessive phenotype is seen in 36% of the population. Calculate the frequency of the dominant allele.

5. In a certain breed of dog, the allele for red-colored tongue (T) is dominant to the allele for purple tongue (t). A researcher collected data on 48 dogs bred from a cross between a red-tongued dog and a purple-tongued dog. Of the 48 offspring, 36 had red tongues and 12 had purple tongues. Calculate the chi-squared value for the null hypothesis, assuming that the red-tongued dog was heterozygous for the tongue-color gene.

**Chi-Square Significance Table**

| DEGREE OF FREEDOM (n) | 5% PROBABILITY VALUE (P) |
|---|---|
| 1 | 3.84 |
| 2 | 5.99 |
| 3 | 7.81 |
| 4 | 9.49 |

6. **pH and Hydrogen ion calculation**

The pH of liquid A is 3. Calculate the hydrogen ion concentration.

$$pH = -\log [H+]$$

# AP Biology Diagnostic Exam: Section II

## FREE-RESPONSE QUESTIONS

Time—1 hour and 30 minutes

(The first 10 minutes is a reading period. Do not begin writing until the 10–minute period has passed.)
Questions 1 and 2 are long free-response questions that should require about 20 minutes each.
Questions 3–8 are short-response questions that should require about 6 minutes each.
Outline form is not acceptable. Answers should be in essay form.

1. **Inheritance, Pedigrees, and Calculations**
   Huntington's disease is a genetic illness that leads to degeneration of the central nervous system. Symptoms typically do not present until between 30 and 40 years of age.

   A. A pedigree is shown at the left. The grey marks indicate that the individual has Huntington's. What type of inheritance pattern is suspected? Explain your reasoning.
   B. The couple indicated by the arrow are planning to have a child. Assume the husband is healthy. Create a Punnett square to demonstrate the risk of inheritance for their offspring.
   C. A randomized trial is run to examine whether "Drug Lauder" delayed the emergence of symptoms among individuals who carried the genetic trait for inheritance. Age at first emergence of symptoms is shown under the patient.

| DRUG STATUS | PATIENT 1 | PATIENT 2 | PATIENT 3 | PATIENT 4 | PATIENT 5 | PATIENT 6 |
|---|---|---|---|---|---|---|
| Control | 32 | 29 | 41 | | | |
| Lauder, 50mg | | | | 47 | 46 | 42 |

On the axis provided below, create an appropriately labeled bar graph of the average age of symptom onset of the two populations.

Average age of symptom onset by years of age

_____

_____

_____

_____

_____

2. **Digestion, Cellular Respiration, and Evolution**
   Adequate nutritional intake, along with absorption of nutrients, is necessary for bodily functioning.

   A. Cellular respiration, comprised of glycolysis, the Krebs cycle, and the electron transport chain, utilizes the glucose from food in order to synthesize ATP. The majority of ATP is created in the electron transport chain. Briefly explain how the electron transport chain creates ATP.

   A researcher is interested in the small and large intestines. He has recognized a new syndrome that significantly reduces nutrient absorption.

B. Briefly differentiate the functions of the small and large intestines.

C. If a patient's small intestine is completely removed, hypothesize the impact that this could have on his weight.

| DRUG STATUS | PATIENT 1 | P2 | P3 | P4 | P5 | P6 | P7 | P8 | MEAN NUTRIENT ABSORPTION LEVEL |
|---|---|---|---|---|---|---|---|---|---|
| Control | 50 | 43 | 76 | 34 | | | | | 50.75 |
| New Drug | | | | | 100 | 78 | 76 | 87 | 85.25 |

The researcher runs a pilot study to determine whether a newly developed drug is effective in treating patients with significantly reduced nutrient absorption. Nutrient absorption levels for each patient and the means are shown above.

D. Interpret the preliminary results shown.

E. Suggest one limitation of the above study, or propose one variable that should be controlled if the study is repeated.

3. Meiosis is a form of cell division in all sexually reproducing organisms during which the nucleus divides during the production of spores or gametes.

A. What are two aspects of meiosis that contribute to genetic diversity?

B. The mating of two individuals who are closely related is termed *consanguineous*. How would consanguinity decrease the genetic diversity of offspring, and why might this decreased diversity be harmful to the offspring?

4. Homeostasis, or the maintenance of balance within the body, is necessary to normal functioning.

A. Explain how insulin and glucagon provide an example of homeostasis.

B. How do the concepts of blood glucose level, insulin, and negative feedback relate?

5. Scientists have recently discovered that the raccoon population in rural New York communicates using chemical signals, via pheromones. The scientists consequently developed four pheromones in an attempt to replicate the natural pheromone. They measured the response time of five raccoons to the developed chemical compounds as an indication of chemical similarity between the developed and natural pheromones. The response times are provided, along with the average response time and standard error of the mean for each developed pheromone.

A. Animals communicate through several mechanisms. Briefly describe TWO methods of communication.

B. Based on the mean response times and the standard error of the mean, explain which pheromone most closely aligned to the raccoon's naturally produced pheromones.

C. A follow up study on raccoon pheromone response time is planned to determine whether response to pheromones is an innate or learned response. Response times will be compared between baby raccoons, young raccoons, and adult raccoons. Hypothesize what the data will show if the response to pheromones is an innate response.

| PHEROMONE | RACCOON 1 | RACCOON 2 | RACCOON 3 | RACCOON 4 | RACCOON 5 | MEAN RESPONSE TIME | STANDARD ERROR OF THE MEAN (SEM) |
|---|---|---|---|---|---|---|---|
| I | 15 | 13 | 16 | 7 | 8 | 11.8 | 1.8 |
| II | 10 | 8 | 7 | 11 | 15 | 10.2 | 1.4 |
| III | 3 | 6 | 5 | 9 | 4 | 5.4 | 1.0 |

6. A young girl presents to the emergency department with symptoms suggesting the effects of a bacterial pathogen. Her parents report that they did not vaccinate their daughter against this particular pathogen.
   A. Briefly describe TWO components of the innate/primary immune response.
   B. If the child had received a vaccination for this particular pathogen, how would the adaptive/secondary immune response differ? Reference the graph shown below.

7. A population of foxes and rabbits in Environment A exhibits the expected predator–prey population curve seen below.
   A. Explain the relationship represented by the curve.

   B. A bacterial pathogen completely wipes out the population of foxes. Researchers closely watch the rabbit population and notice a new population curve. Explain this new curve. In your explanation, be sure to explain the fluctuations seen at the new carrying capacity.

8. A population of wild cats lives in a temperate environment with four seasons. The cats have three main fur colors—white, light brown, and black.

   A scientist decides to transplant a random sample of these cats to an environment covered in snow throughout the full year. He notices that as time passes, the cats with one fur color tend to live longer and evade predators better than those with the other two fur colors.
   A. Identify the cats with the fur color you expect to live longer in this new environment and explain your reasoning.
   B. The scientist is also interested in better understanding the evolutionary relationships between the wild cats and several other wild species. He collected data on various traits. Construct a visual representation of the evolutionary relationships from the data provided.

| Species | TRAIT A | TRAIT B | TRAIT C |
|---------|---------|---------|---------|
| Animal 1 | + | − | − |
| Animal 2 | + | − | + |
| Animal 3 | + | + | + |
| Animal 4 | − | − | − |

# › Answers and Explanations

## PART A: MULTIPLE-CHOICE QUESTIONS

1. **C**—This question deals with the concept of pH: acids and bases. The pH scale is a logarithmic scale that measures how acidic or basic a solution is. A pH of 4 is 10 times more acidic than a pH of 5. A pH of 6 is $10^2$ or 100 times more basic than a pH of 4, and so on. Therefore, a pH of 10 is $10^3$ or 1000 times more basic than a pH of 7.

2. **D**—This question deals with the cytoskeleton of cells. Cell division, cilia, and flagella would be compromised if the *microtubules* were damaged. Microfilaments, made from actin, are important to muscular contraction. Chitin is a polysaccharide found in fungi.

3. **D**—This is a prime example of disruptive selection. Take a look at the material from Chapter 12 on the various types of selection. The illustrations there are worth reviewing.

4. **B**—You have to know this fact. We don't want them to get you on this one if they ask it. ☺

5. **D**—$C_4$ photosynthesis is an adaptive photosynthetic process that attempts to counter the problems that hot and dry weather causes for plants. Be sure that you read about and understand the various forms of photosynthesis for the exam.

6. **A**—Retroviruses are RNA viruses that carry with them the reverse transcriptase enzyme. When they take over a host cell, they first use the enzyme to convert themselves into DNA. They next incorporate into the DNA of the host, and begin the process of viral replication. The HIV virus of AIDS is a well-known retrovirus.

7. **C**—Mutualism is the interaction in which both parties involved benefit.

8. **B**—Smooth muscle is found in the digestive tract, bladder, and arteries, to name only a few. Answer choices A and D are skeletal muscles.

9. **A**—Halophiles are a member of the archaebacteria subgroup of the monerans.

10. **A**—This question deals with five types of reactions you should be familiar with for the AP Biology exam. A hydrolysis reaction is one in which water is added, causing the formation of a compound.

11. **C**—Fertilization tends to occur in the oviduct, also known as the *fallopian tube*. The ovum is produced in the ovary, and the cervix is the passageway from the uterus to the vagina.

12. **C**—Homosporous plants, such as ferns, give rise to bisexual gametophytes.

13. **A**—You should learn the general processes of spermatogenesis and oogenesis in humans for the AP Biology exam.

14. **C**—Turner syndrome (XO) is an example of aneuploidy—conditions in which individuals have an abnormal number of chromosomes. These conditions can be monosomies, as is the case with Turner, or they can be trisomies, as is the case with Down, Klinefelter, and other syndromes.

15. **A**—The selectively permeable membrane is a lipid bilayer composed of phospholipids, proteins, and other macromolecules. Small, uncharged polar molecules and lipids are able to pass through these membranes without difficulty.

16. **D**—Glycogen is a carbohydrate. The three major types of lipids you should know are fats, phospholipids, and steroids. Cholesterol is a type of steroid.

17. **B**—This hormone, which is involved in controlling the function of the kidney, is released from the posterior pituitary.

18. **A**—The stupid phrase we use to remember this classification hierarchy is "Karaoke players can order free grape soda"—kingdom, phylum, class, order, family, genus, and species. This question is sneaky because it requires you to know that a division is the plant kingdom's version of the phylum. The kingdom is the least specific subdivision, and the species the most specific. Therefore, A is the correct answer.

19. **A**—Guard cells are the cells responsible for controlling the opening and closing of the stomata of a plant.

20. **D**—If 9 percent of the population is recessive (ss), then $q^2 = 0.09$. Taking the square root of 0.09 gives us $q = 0.30$. Knowing as we do that $p + q = 1$, $p + 0.30 = 1$, and $p = 0.70$. The frequency of the heterozygous condition $= 2pq = 2(0.30)(0.70) = 42\%$.

21. **D**—Epistasis exists when a gene at one locus affects a gene at another locus.

22. **A**—The inputs to the light reactions include light and water. During these reactions, photolysis occurs, which is the splitting of $H_2O$ into hydrogen ions and oxygen atoms. These oxygen atoms from the water pair together immediately to form the oxygen we breathe.

23. **C**—This life cycle is the one known as "alternation of generations." It is the plant life cycle. Pine trees are the only ones among the choices that would show such a cycle.

24. **C**—Prokaryotes are known for their simplicity. They do not contain a nucleus, nor do they contain membrane-bound organelles. They do have a few structures to remember: cell wall, plasma membrane, ribosomes, and a nucleoid. Lysosomes are found in eukaryotes, not prokaryotes.

25. **B**—Traits are said to be homologous if they are similar because their host organisms arose from a common ancestor. For example, the bone structure in bird wings is homologous in all bird species.

26. **C**—Polymerase chain reaction is the high-speed cloning machine of molecular genetics. It occurs at a much faster rate than does cloning.

27. **B**—Functional groups are a pain in the neck. But you need to be able to recognize them on the exam. Most often, the test asks students to identify functional groups by structure.

28. **D**—Active transport requires energy. The major types of cell transport you need to know for the exam are diffusion, osmosis, facilitated diffusion, endocytosis, exocytosis, and active transport.

29. **D**—Homologous chromosomes resemble one another in shape, size, and function. They pair up during meiosis and separate from each other during meiosis I.

30. **C**—DNA polymerase is the superstar enzyme of the replication process, which occurs during the S phase of the cell cycle in the nucleus of a cell. The process does occur in semiconservative fashion. You should learn the basic concepts behind replication as they are explained in Chapter 11.

31. **C**—Learn the defense mechanisms well from predator–prey relationships in Chapter 18. They will be represented on the exam.

32. **B**—A bottleneck is a specific example of genetic drift: the sudden change in allele frequencies due to random events.

33. **D**—You should learn the list of structures derived from endoderm, mesoderm, and ectoderm. (This could be an easy multiple-choice question for you if you do.)

34. **D**—The dominant generation for bryophytes is the gametophyte (n) generation. They are the only plants for which this is true.

35. **A**—The Calvin cycle uses a disproportionate amount of ATP relative to NADPH. The cyclic light reactions exist to make up for this disparity. The cyclic reactions do not produce NADPH, nor do they produce oxygen.

36. **A**—Tay-Sachs disease, cystic fibrosis, and sickle cell anemia are all autosomal recessive conditions. It will serve you well to learn the most common autosomal recessive conditions, X-linked conditions, and autosomal dominant conditions.

37. **D**—It will serve you well for this exam to be reasonably familiar with biotechnology laboratory techniques. Lab procedures show up often on free-response questions and the later multiple-choice sections of the exam.

38. **C**—The small intestine hosts the most digestion of the digestive tract.

39. **D**—This is known as *cambium*.

40. **A**—The inner cell mass gives rise to the embryo, which eventually gives rise to the epiblast and hypoblast. The morula is an early stage of development.

41. **C**—Biomes are annoying and tough to memorize. Learn as much as you can about them without taking up too much time. . . . More often than not there will be two to three multiple-choice questions about them. But you want to make sure you learn enough to work your way through a free-response question if you were to be so unfortunate as to have one on your test.

42. **B**—Incomplete dominance is the situation in which the heterozygous genotype produces an "intermediate" phenotype rather than the dominant phenotype; neither allele dominates the other.

43. **C**—The light-dependent reactions occur in the thylakoid membrane. The dark reactions, known as the *Calvin cycle*, occur in the stroma.

44. **D**—A J-shaped growth curve is characteristic of exponentially growing populations. That is a characteristic of R-selected strategists.

45. **C**—Mitosis makes up 10 percent of the cell cycle; the correct order of the stages is prophase, metaphase, anaphase, telophase; mitosis is not performed by prokaryotic cells; and cell plates are formed in plant cells.

46. **B**—Thigmotropism, phototropism, and gravitropism are the major tropisms you need to know for plants. Thigmotropism, the growth response of a plant to touch, is the least understood of the bunch.

47. **A**—There are five plant hormones you should know for the exam. Auxin seems to come up the most, but it would serve you well to know the basic functions of all five of them.

48. **B**—Humoral immunity is another name for antibody-mediated immunity. Cell-mediated immunity involves T-cells and the direct cellular destruction of invaders such as viruses.

49. **B**

50. **D**

51. **A**

52. **B**—Each NADH is able to produce up to 3 ATP. Each $FADH_2$ can produce up to 2 ATP.

53. **C**—You have to know the concept of chemiosmosis for the AP exam. Make sure you study it well in Chapter 7.

54. **A**—Glycolysis is the conversion of glucose into pyruvate that occurs in the cytoplasm and is the first step of both aerobic and anaerobic respiration.

55. **D**—Fermentation is anaerobic respiration, and it is the process that begins with glycolysis and ends with the regeneration of $NAD^+$.

56. **B**—Chapter 17 is fairly short and concise. We left it to the bare bones for you to learn. We would suggest you learn this chapter well because it could be worth a good 5–7 points for you on the exam if you are lucky. ☺

57. **D**

58. **A**

59. **C**

60. **B**—The rate of reaction for an enzyme-aided reaction is best estimated by taking the slope of the constant portion of the moles–time plot.

61. **C**—They will test your ability to interpret data on this exam. You should make sure that you are able to look at a chart and interpret information given to you. This enzyme does indeed function most efficiently at 20°C. Above and below that temperature, the reaction rate is lower.

62. **A**—At a pH of 6 and a temperature of 25°C, enzyme 3 is actually LESS efficient than enzyme 2 and MORE efficient than enzyme 1.

63. **D**—This question requires you to know that a pH below 7 (pH < 7) is acidic and a pH above 7 (pH > 7) is basic. It is true that all three enzymes increase the rate of reaction more when in acidic environments than basic environments.

## PART B: GRID–IN QUESTIONS

**1. 0.50**

Let $H^A$ = healthy and $H^C$ = sickle cell trait

|  | $H^A$ | $H^C$ |
|---|---|---|
| $H^A$ | $H^A\ H^A$ | $H^A\ H^C$ |
| $H^C$ | $H^A\ H^C$ | $H^C\ H^C$ |

The child will have a 25% chance of being healthy, a 50% chance of being a carrier, and a 25% chance of having sickle cell anemia.

**2. 0.25**

First, determine the risk for one child of inheriting dwarfism. Since this is an autosomal dominant disease, the child needs to inherit only one dominant allele (Dd) to express the disease.

|  | D | d |
|---|---|---|
| d | Dd | dd |
| d | Dd | dd |

The Punnett square demonstrates that each child has a 50% (or ½) chance of inheriting the dominant allele. The couple wants to know the probability that their two children BOTH will have dwarfism. To calculate the probability that both children inherit the dominant allele, multiply the probability of each individual event.

$$½ * ½ = ¼$$

Thus the probability of both children being diagnosed with dwarfism is 25%, or ¼.

**3. .04**

There are two main Hardy–Weinberg equations: $p + q = 1$ AND $p^2 + 2pq + q^2 = 1$

$p$ and $q$ represent the frequency of the dominant and recessive alleles respectively. $p^2$ and $q^2$ represent the frequency of the homozygous dominant and homozygous recessive phenotypes respectively. Lastly, $2pq$ represents the frequency of the heterozygous phenotype.

Hardy–Weinberg problems often start by providing information about the recessive phenotype. In this case, we know that the recessive phenotype is in 1 out of every 2500 mice; we can turn this into a frequency by creating a fraction: $1/2500 = 0.0004$. This frequency is the homozygous recessive phenotype; thus we can equate $q^2 = 0.0004$.

The question asks for the frequency of the heterozygous phenotype (represented by $2pq$ above). Using our finding $q^2 = 0.0004$, we can determine the value of $2pq$.

$$q^2 = 0.0004$$

so $q = 0.02$

To calculate $p$, we can use the equation: $p + q = 1$
Plugging in $q = 0.02 \rightarrow p + 0.02 = 1 \rightarrow p = 0.98$

Now to calculate *2pq* (frequency of the heterozygous phenotype), plug in the known values: $2(0.98)(0.02) = 0.04$. In other words, 4% of the population is heterozygous.

The frequency of the dominant allele is thus 40%.

**4.** 0.40

Much of the logic from the previous problem will apply here. To reiterate, there are two main Hardy–Weinberg equations: $p + q = 1$ AND $p^2 + 2pq + q^2 = 1$. *p* and *q* represent the frequency of the dominant and recessive alleles respectively. $p^2$ and $q^2$ represent the frequency of the homozygous dominant and homozygous recessive phenotypes respectively. Lastly, *2pq* represents the frequency of the heterozygous phenotype.

If 36% of the population is the recessive phenotype, $q^2 = .36$; thus, $q = 0.6$

We want the value of *p*, the dominant allele. We can use: $p + q = 1$

With $q = 0.6 \rightarrow p + 0.6 = 1 \rightarrow p = 0.4$

**5.** 12

We are given the observed values in the question prompt. Now you need to calculate the expected phenotypes utilizing a Punnett square. The question stem has provided that the cross is between a heterozygous red–tongued dog (Tt) and a purple–tongued dog (tt).

|  |  | T | t |
|---|---|---|---|
|  | t | Tt | tt |
|  | t | Tt | tt |

The Punnett square suggests that this cross would lead to 50% red tongue, 50% white tongue. Out of 48 dogs, 24 would have a red tongue, and 24 would have a purple tongue.

| Phenotype | # Observed (o) | # Expected (e) | o − e | $\dfrac{(o - e)^2}{e}$ |
|---|---|---|---|---|
| Red tongue | 36 | 24 | 12 | $\dfrac{(12)^2}{24} = 6$ |
| Purple tongue | 12 | 24 | −12 | $\dfrac{(-12)^2}{24} = 6$ |
| TOTAL | 48 | 48 |  | SUM = 12 |

For two options, the degree of freedom is 1. Since the chi–squared value of 12 is larger than the 5% probability value of 3.84, the data does not follow predicted values and is statistically significant. Discard the null hypothesis.

**6.** .001

$$pH = -\log [H+]$$
$$3 = -\log [H+]$$
$$10{-}3 = [H+]$$
$$0.001 = [H+]$$

| | | | | 1 | 2 |
|---|---|---|---|---|---|
| ⊖ | | ⊘ | ⊘ | ⊘ | |
| | ⊙ | ⊙ | ⊙ | ⊙ | ⊙ |
| | | ⓪ | ⓪ | ⓪ | ⓪ |
| | ① | ① | ① | ● | ① |
| | ② | ② | ② | ② | ● |
| | ③ | ③ | ③ | ③ | ③ |
| | ④ | ④ | ④ | ④ | ④ |
| | ⑤ | ⑤ | ⑤ | ⑤ | ⑤ |
| | ⑥ | ⑥ | ⑥ | ⑥ | ⑥ |
| | ⑦ | ⑦ | ⑦ | ⑦ | ⑦ |
| | ⑧ | ⑧ | ⑧ | ⑧ | ⑧ |
| | ⑨ | ⑨ | ⑨ | ⑨ | ⑨ |

| | | . | 0 | 0 | 1 |
|---|---|---|---|---|---|
| ⊖ | | ⊘ | ⊘ | ⊘ | |
| | ⊙ | ● | ⊙ | ⊙ | ⊙ |
| | | ⓪ | ● | ● | ⓪ |
| | ① | ① | ① | ① | ● |
| | ② | ② | ② | ② | ② |
| | ③ | ③ | ③ | ③ | ③ |
| | ④ | ④ | ④ | ④ | ④ |
| | ⑤ | ⑤ | ⑤ | ⑤ | ⑤ |
| | ⑥ | ⑥ | ⑥ | ⑥ | ⑥ |
| | ⑦ | ⑦ | ⑦ | ⑦ | ⑦ |
| | ⑧ | ⑧ | ⑧ | ⑧ | ⑧ |
| | ⑨ | ⑨ | ⑨ | ⑨ | ⑨ |

# › Free–Response Grading Outline

1. A. Autosomal dominance inheritance is suspected. Looking at the pedigree, each generation is affected by the illness, which supports dominant as opposed to recessive inheritance. Recessive inheritance would instead show frequent skipping of generations in the pedigree. Autosomal as opposed to sex–linked inheritance is suspected, since males and females are equally affected.

   B. To create the Punnett square, we need to determine whether the individual in row 5 is homozygous or heterozygous for the trait. Since one of her parents is unaffected, we can assume she is heterozygous. We are also told that her husband is healthy and, thus, homozygous recessive.

   |   | H  | h  |
   |---|----|----|
   | h | Hh | hh |
   | h | Hh | hh |

   The Punnett square above suggests that each offspring maintains a 50% chance of inheriting the disease.

   C. First calculate the average age of symptom onset for each of the two conditions:

   $$\text{Control} = \frac{32 + 29 + 41}{3} = 34 \text{ yrs old}$$

   $$\text{Drug} = \frac{47 + 46 + 42}{3} = 45 \text{ yrs old}$$

   Average age of symptom onset by years of age

2. A. The electron transport chain creates a proton gradient which sends protons ($H^+$) out of the mitochondrial matrix using the energy–carrying NADH and $FADH_2$. This proton is then allowed to flow back down through the ATP synthase and create the ATP necessary for bodily function.

   B. The small intestine, comprised of the duodenum, jejunum, and ileum, is where the bulk of digestion and absorption occurs. The large intestine, comprised of the cecum, colon, and rectum, has the function of reabsorbing water from digested material and working to eliminate waste.

   C. Since the small intestine is the primary site of nutrient absorption, if the small intestine is completely removed, the patient would consequently experience inadequate nutrition. Subsequently, we would be worried that the patient's weight would decrease.

   D. The preliminary results suggest that the drug has higher levels of absorption than the control.

   E. A limitation of the study is the small sample size. A few variables that should be controlled include age/sex/ethnicity of patients, time that the study drug is administered, dosage of the study drug, etc.

3. A. Two processes in meiosis that contribute to genetic diversity:
   1. *Crossing over* between homologous chromosomes during prophase I. Complementary DNA strands are exchanged between the chromosomes.
   2. *Random assortment* of homologous chromosomes at the metaphase plate. Homologous chromosomes are divided in half to become haploid cells. It is by chance on which side each pair of chromosomes from the mother and father align.

B. Impact of consanguinity:
   1. Genetic diversity would decrease since the mother and father maintain a more similar genetic makeup than a nonconsanguineous pairing.
   2. Decreased diversity in this case could prove harmful in the case of recessive traits. For example, a trait could be rare, but since the mother and father are related, they could be more likely to both be carriers. If both parents are carriers, the probability that the child inherits one or two recessive alleles is increased.

4. A. Insulin and glucagon are hormones produced in the pancreas that work to control the level of glucose in the blood. Insulin is released from the pancreatic beta cells when glucose levels are higher in the blood—insulin stimulates cellular uptake of glucose for utilization or glycogen production. On the other hand, glucagon is released from the pancreatic alpha cells when glucose levels are lower in the blood. Glucagon stimulates the release of glycogen from the liver to raise glucose levels in the blood. The opposing effects of insulin and glucagon maintain the homeostasis of blood glucose.

   B. Negative feedback occurs when a hormone inhibits further release of a hormone. Concerning the question, when blood glucose levels are high, insulin is released by the pancreas to stimulate cellular uptake of the glucose. The pancreas recognizes the consequent decrease in blood glucose and responds by decreasing or stopping the release of further insulin.

5. A. Communication types include:
   • Visual: the use of visual cues to relay meaning. Examples include peacock feather coloring, bared teeth, rolling over on back.
   • Tactile: the use of touch to relay meaning. For example, monkeys will groom each other as a sign of affection.
   • Auditory: the use of various sounds to relay meaning. For example, the frog chirp to attract a mate.

• Chemical: the use of chemical signals via pheromones. Pheromones play a significant role in animal mating.

   B. Pheromone III demonstrated the fastest mean of the three pheromones tested and thus would be more likely to resemble the natural raccoon pheromones.

   C. An innate response is a behavior that does not need to be taught. Thus if the response to pheromones is innate, the response time of the young raccoons to the pheromones will be similar to the response time of the older raccoons.

6. A. Components of the innate immune response:
   • Physical barriers like the skin, GI tract, respiratory tract, nose hairs
   • Broad defenses like mucous secretions, stomach acid, saliva, tears
   • Aspects of the general immune response like the complement system, phagocytosis of pathogens via macrophages and neutrophils, inflammation to call in additional immune support, NK cells

   B. Secondary exposure
   • Response time would be faster
   • Indicated by the presence of memory cells
   • Production of antibodies is greater in quantity, and they demonstrate higher affinity.

7. A. The curve demonstrates that the population concentrations are correlated. The foxes rely on the rabbits for food. As the foxes consume more rabbits, the fox population will grow due to higher supply levels. At some point, the rabbit population will have a higher death rate than birth rate, and thus the population will diminish. Consequently, the fox population will too decrease. Then with decreased predation by the foxes, the rabbit population will be able to rejuvenate.

   B. With the fox population and predation removed, the rabbits will be able to sustain exponential population growth. At some point, the rabbit population will reach a new carrying capacity, the maximum population size that the environment can support, and thus will level off.

**8.** A. This is a type of directional selection, where one extreme of the phenotype is "safer" or more adaptive in the environment. In this situation, the environment has snow year around. Thus the cats that have white fur are able to blend into their environment better than the cats with black or brown fur and evade predation more successfully.

B. To create a cladogram, it is often easier to determine outliers for each trait. Beginning with Trait A, Animals 1–3 all have the trait, but Animal 4 does not.

Animal 4 also does not have Traits B and C. Next with Trait C, Animals 2 and 3 share the trait, but Animal 1 does not. Lastly with Trait B, only Animal 3 has the trait.

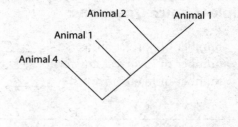

# Scoring and Interpretation
# AP BIOLOGY DIAGNOSTIC EXAM

## Multiple–Choice Questions:

number of correct answers: _____
number of incorrect answers: _____
number of blank answers: _____

_____ + _____ = _____
multiple–choice        grid–in              Section I
number correct      number correct      raw score

## Grid–In Questions:

number of correct answers: _____
number of incorrect answers: _____
number of blank answers: _____

## Free–Response Questions:

1. ____ / 10          3. ____ / 4          6. ____ / 4
2. ____ / 10          4. ____ / 4          7. ____ / 4
                      5. ____ / 4          8. ____ / 4

Add up the total points accumulated in the eight questions and multiply the sum by 1.57 to obtain the free–response raw score: _____ × 1.57 = _____
free–response points          Section II raw score

## CALCULATE YOUR SCORE

Now combine the raw scores from the multiple–choice and free–response sections to obtain your new raw score for the entire practice exam. Use the ranges listed below to determine your grade for this exam. Don't worry about how we arrived at the following ranges, and remember that they are rough estimates on questions that are not actual AP exam questions . . . do not read too much into them.

| Raw Score | Approximate AP Score |
|-----------|---------------------|
| 83–138    | 5                   |
| 63–82     | 4                   |
| 48–62     | 3                   |
| 26–47     | 2                   |
| 0–25      | 1                   |

If this test went amazingly well for you . . . rock and roll . . . but as we just said, your journey is just beginning, and that means you have time to supplement your knowledge even more before the big day! Use your time well.

If this test went poorly for you, don't worry; as has been said twice now, your journey is just beginning and you have plenty of time to learn what you need to know for this exam. Just use this as an exercise in focus that has shown you what you need to concentrate on between now and early May. Good luck!

**STEP** 3

# Develop Strategies for Success

CHAPTER **4** How to Approach Each Question Type

# CHAPTER 4

# How to Approach Each Question Type

**IN THIS CHAPTER**

**Summary:** Become familiar with the types of questions on the exam: multiple-choice and free-response. Pace yourself and know when to skip a question that you can come back to later.

**Key Ideas**

✪ On multiple-choice questions, you no longer lose any points for wrong answers. So you should bubble in an answer for *every* question.

✪ On multiple-choice questions, don't "out-think" the test. Use common sense because that will usually get you to the right answer.

✪ Free-response answers must be in essay form. Outline form is not acceptable.

✪ Free-response questions tend to be multi-part questions—be SURE to answer each part of the question or you will not be able to get the maximum possible number of points for that question.

✪ Make a quick outline before you begin writing your answer.

✪ The free-response questions are graded using a positive-scoring system, so wrong information is ignored.

# Multiple-Choice Questions

You have approximately 90 seconds per question on the multiple-choice section of this exam. Remember that to be on pace for a great score on this exam, you need to correctly answer approximately 42 multiple-choice questions or more. Here are a few rules of thumb:

**1.** *Don't out-think the test.* It is indeed possible to be too smart for these tests. Frequently during these standardized tests we have found ourselves overanalyzing every single problem. If you encounter a question such as, "During what phase of meiosis does crossover (also referred to as *crossing over*) occur?" and you happen to know the answer immediately, this does not mean that the question is too easy. First, give yourself credit for knowing a fact. They asked you something, you knew it, and *wham*, you fill in the bubble. Do not overanalyze the question and assume that your answer is too obvious for that question. Just because you get it doesn't mean that it was too easy.

**2.** *Don't leave questions blank.* The AP Biology exam used to take off one-fourth point for each wrong answer. This is no longer the case. You should bubble in an answer for each multiple-choice question.

**3.** *Be on the lookout for trick wording!* Always pay attention to words or phrases such as "least," "most," "not," "incorrectly," and "does not belong." Do not answer the wrong question. There are few things as annoying as getting a question wrong on this test simply because you didn't read the question carefully enough, especially if you know the right answer.

**4.** *Use your time carefully.* Some of these questions require a lot of careful reading before you can answer them. If you find yourself struggling on a question, try not to waste too much time on it. Circle it in the booklet and come back to it later if time permits. Remember—you are looking to answer approximately 42 multiple-choice questions correctly to be on pace for a great score—this test should be an exercise in window shopping.

It does not matter *which* questions you get correct. What is important is that you answer enough questions correctly. Find the subjects that you know the best, answer those questions, and save the others for review later on.

**5.** *Be careful about changing answers!* If you have answered a question already, come back to it later on, and get the urge to change it . . . make sure that you have a real *reason* to change it. Often an urge to change an answer is the work of exam "elves" in the room who want to trick you into picking a wrong answer. Change your answer only if you can justify your reasons for making the switch.

**6.** *Check your calculations!* The math required in the grid-in section isn't overly complicated. That said, it would be unfortunate to lose points because of a silly calculation error. Make sure to work carefully and check your math. Happily, any equations you need will be provided for you.

# Free-Response Questions

The free-response section consists of eight broad questions. It is important that your answers to these questions display solid reasoning and analytical skills. The two long essays together carry approximately the same weight as the six short-response questions combined. Expect to often use data or information from your laboratory exercises as you answer some of the questions.

Answers for the free-response questions must be in essay form. Outline form is not acceptable. Labeled diagrams may be used to supplement discussion, but in no case will a diagram alone suffice. It is important that you read each question completely before you begin to write. Write all of your answers on the pages following the questions in the booklet.

## Free-Response Tips

Some important tips to keep in mind as you write your essays:

- The free-response questions tend to be multipart questions. You can't be expected to know everything about every topic, and the test preparers sometimes throw you a bone by writing questions that ask you to answer *two* of three parts or *three* of four parts. This gives you an opportunity to focus in on the material that you are most comfortable with. It is very important that you read the question carefully to make sure you understand exactly what the examiners are asking you to do.

- You are given 80 minutes to complete eight free-response questions. The two long free-response questions should take 20 minutes each, and the six short questions should take about six minutes each. This may not seem like a lot of time, but if you write a bunch of practice essays before you take the exam and budget your time wisely during the exam, you will not have to struggle with your timing. Below are suggestions for budgeting your time:

  - Read the question carefully and make sure you know what it is asking you to do.
  - Construct an outline that will help you organize your answer. Don't write the world's most elaborate outline. You won't get points for having the prettiest outline in the country—so there is no reason to spend an excessive amount of time putting it together. Just develop enough of an outline so that you have a basic idea of how you will construct your essay. Your essay is not graded based on how well it is put together, but it certainly will not hurt your score to write a well-organized and grammatically correct response.
  - If the long essay is a two-part question, spend 10 minutes on each part. If it is a three-part question, spend 6–7 minutes on each part. Keep your eye on the clock and make sure you give yourself enough time to address each part of the question.

- Both of the long free-response questions on the AP Biology exam are worth the same number of points. But each question is not created equal. Some questions ask you to answer two sub-questions. Some questions ask you to answer three sub-questions, and some questions ask you to answer four sub-questions. The free-response questions are graded in a way that forces you to provide information for *each* section of the question. There are a maximum number of points that you can get for each subsection. For example, in a question that asks you to answer *three* sub-questions, most likely the grader's guidelines will say something along the lines of:

> Part A — worth a maximum of 3 points
> Part B — worth a maximum of 4 points
> Part C — worth a maximum of 3 points

This is a very important thing for you to know heading into the exam. This means that it is *far* more important for you to attempt to answer every *part* of the question than to try to stuff every little fact that you know about part A into that portion of the essay at the expense of part B. Based on the grading guideline above, no matter how well you write your answer for part A, you can receive at most 3 points for that section. At the risk of being repetitive, we'll say it again because it is so important: no matter how great your essay may be, the grader can only give you the maximum possible number of points for each subsection.

- The free-response section is graded using a "positive scoring" system. This means that wrong information in an essay is ignored. You do not lose points for saying things that are incorrect. (Unfortunately you do not *get* points for saying things that are incorrect either . . . if only!) The importance of this fact is basically that if you are unsure about something and think you may be right, give it a shot and include it in your essay. It's worth the risk.

# STEP 4

# Review the Knowledge You Need to Score High

# CHAPTER ▶ 5

# Chemistry

## IN THIS CHAPTER

**Summary:** This chapter introduces the chemical principles that are related to the AP Biology topics covered throughout the course.

**Key Ideas**

❂ Organic compounds contain carbon; important examples include lipids, proteins, and carbohydrates.

❂ Enzymes are catalytic proteins that react in an induced-fit fashion with substrates to speed up a reaction.

❂ The five types of chemical reactions you should learn include hydrolysis reactions, dehydration synthesis reactions, endergonic reactions, exergonic reactions, and redox reactions.

## Introduction

What is the name of the test you are studying for? The AP Biology exam. Then why in tarnation are we starting your review with a chapter titled *Chemistry*?!?!? Because it is important that you have an understanding of a few chemical principles before we dive into the deeper biological material. We will keep it short, don't worry. ☺

## Elements, Compounds, Atoms, and Ions

By definition, **matter** is anything that has mass and takes up space; an **element** is defined as matter in its simplest form; an **atom** is the smallest form of an element that still displays its particular properties. (Terms boldfaced in text are listed in the Glossary at the end of the book.)

For example, sodium (Na) is an element mentioned often in this book, especially in Chapter 15, Human Physiology. The element sodium can exist as an atom of sodium, in which it is a neutral particle containing an equal number of protons and electrons. It can also exist as an ion, which is an atom that has a positive or negative charge. Ions such as sodium that take on a positive charge are called **cations,** and are composed of more protons than electrons. Ions with a negative charge are called **anions,** and are composed of more electrons than protons.

Elements can be combined to form **molecules,** for example, an oxygen molecule ($O_2$) or a hydrogen molecule ($H_2$). Molecules that are composed of more than one type of element are called **compounds,** for example $H_2O$. The two major types of compounds you need to be familiar with are **organic** and **inorganic** compounds. Organic compounds contain carbon and usually hydrogen; inorganic compounds do not. Some of you are probably skeptical, at this point, as to whether any of what we have said thus far matters for this exam. Bear with me because it does. You will deal with many important organic compounds later on in this book, including **carbohydrates, proteins, lipids,** and **nucleic acids**.

Before moving onto the next section, where we discuss these particular organic compounds in more detail, we would like to cover a topic that many find confusing and therefore ignore in preparing for this exam. This is the subject of **functional groups.** These poorly understood groups are responsible for the chemical properties of organic compounds. They should not intimidate you, nor should you spend a million hours trying to memorize them in full detail. You should remember one or two examples of each group and be able to identify the functional groups on sight, as you are often asked to do so on the AP exam.

The following is a list of the functional groups you should study for this exam:

*John (11th grade):*
*"My teacher wanted me to know these structures . . . she was right!"*

> **BIG IDEA 4.A.1**
> *The subcomponents of a molecule determine its properties.*

1. *Amino group.* An amino group has the following formula:

$$R-N\begin{matrix}H\\H\end{matrix}$$

The symbol R stands for "rest of the compound" to which this $NH_2$ group is attached. One example of a compound containing an amino group is an **amino acid.** Compounds containing amino groups are generally referred to as **amines.** Amino groups act as bases and can pick up protons from acids.

2. *Carbonyl group.* This group contains two structures:

**ketone**          **aldehyde**

If the C=O is at the end of a chain, it is an **aldehyde.** Otherwise, it is a **ketone.** (*Note:* in *aldehydes,* there is an H at the end; there is no H in the word *ketone.*) A carbonyl group makes a compound **hydrophilic** and **polar.** *Hydrophilic* means water-loving, reacting well with water. A *polar* molecule is one that has an unequal distribution of charge, which creates a positive side and a negative side to the molecule.

3. **Carboxyl group.** This group has the following formula:

A *carboxyl group* is a carbonyl group that has a hydroxide in one of the R spots and a carbon chain in the other. This functional group shows up along with amino groups in amino acids. Carboxyl groups act as acids because they are able to donate protons to basic compounds. Compounds containing carboxyl groups are known as *carboxylic acids*.

4. *Hydroxyl group*. This group has the simplest formula of the bunch:

$$R — OH$$

A hydroxyl group is present in compounds known as **alcohols.** Like carbonyl groups, hydroxyl groups are polar and hydrophilic.

5. *Phosphate group*. This group has the following formula:

Phosphate groups are vital components of compounds that serve as cellular energy sources: ATP, ADP, and GTP. Like carboxyl groups, phosphate groups are acidic molecules.

6. *Sulfhydryl group*. This group also has a simple formula:

$$R — SH$$

This functional group does not show up much on the exam, but you should recognize it when it does. This group is present in the amino acids methionine and cysteine and assists in structure stabilization in many proteins.

# Lipids, Carbohydrates, and Proteins

## Lipids

**BIG IDEA 4.C.1**
*These various molecules provide the cell with a wide range of functions.*

**Lipids** are organic compounds used by cells as long-term energy stores or building blocks. Lipids are hydrophobic and insoluble in water because they contain a hydrocarbon tail of $CH_2S$ that is nonpolar and repellant to water. The most important lipids are **fats, oils, steroids,** and **phospholipids.**

Fats, which are lipids made by combining **glycerol** and three **fatty acids** (Figure 5.1), are used as long-term energy stores in cells. They are not as easily metabolized as carbohydrates, yet

**Figure 5.1   Structure of glycerol and fatty acids.**

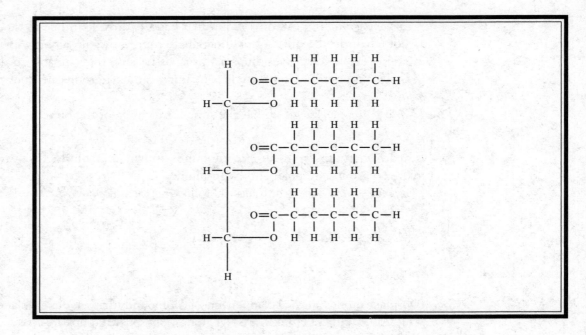

**Figure 5.2  Fat structure (glycerol plus three fatty acids).**

they are a more effective means of storage; for instance, one gram of fat provides two times the energy of one gram of carbohydrate. Fats can be **saturated** or **unsaturated**. Saturated fat molecules contain no double bonds. Unsaturated fats contain one (mono-) or more (poly-) double bonds, which means that they contain fewer hydrogen molecules per carbon than do saturated fats. Saturated fats are the bad guys and are associated with heart disease and atherosclerosis. Most of the fat found in animals is saturated, whereas plants tend to contain unsaturated fats. Fat is formed when three fatty-acid molecules connect to the OH groups of the glycerol molecule. These connecting bonds are formed by dehydration synthesis reaction (Figure 5.2).

**Steroids** are lipids composed of four carbon rings that look like chicken-wire fencing in pictorial representations. One example of a steroid is cholesterol, an important structural component of cell membranes that serves as a precursor molecule for another important class of steroids: the sex hormones (testosterone, progesterone, and estrogen). You should be able to recognize the structures shown in Figure 5.3 for the AP exam.

**Figure 5.3  Steroid structures.**

**Figure 5.4   Structure of phospholipid.**

A **phospholipid** is a lipid formed by combining a glycerol molecule with two fatty acids and a phosphate group (Figure 5.4). Phospholipids are bilayered structures; they have both a hydrophobic tail (a hydrocarbon chain) and a hydrophilic head (the phosphate group) (Figure 5.5). They are the major component of cell membranes; the hydrophilic phosphate group forms the outside portion and the hydrophobic tail forms the interior of the wall.

## Carbohydrates

**Carbohydrates** can be simple sugars or complex molecules containing multiple sugars. Carbohydrates are used by the cells of the body in energy-producing reactions and as structural materials. Carbohydrates have the elements C, H, and O. Hydrogen and oxygen are present in a 2:1 ratio. The three main types of carbohydrates you need to know are monosaccharides, disaccharides, and polysaccharides.

**Figure 5.5   Bilayered structure of phospholipids.**

**Figure 5.6   Glucose structure.**

A **monosaccharide,** or simple sugar, is the simplest form of a carbohydrate. The most important monosaccharide is glucose ($C_6H_{12}O_6$), which is used in cellular respiration to provide energy for cells. Monosaccharides with five carbons ($C_5H_{10}O_5$) are used in compounds such as genetic molecules (RNA) and high-energy molecules (ATP). The structure of glucose is shown in Figure 5.6.

A **disaccharide** is a sugar consisting of two monosaccharides bound together. Common disaccharides include sucrose, maltose, and lactose. Sucrose, a major energy carbohydrate in plants, is a combination of fructose and glucose; maltose, a carbohydrate used in the creation of beer, is a combination of two glucose molecules; and lactose, found in dairy products, is a combination of galactose and glucose.

A **polysaccharide** is a carbohydrate containing three or more monosaccharide molecules. Polysaccharides, usually composed of hundreds or thousands of monosaccharides, act as a storage form of energy and as structural material in and around cells. The most important carbohydrates for storing energy are **starch** and **glycogen**. Starch, made solely of glucose molecules linked together, is the storage form of choice for plants. Animals store much of their carbohydrate energy in the form of glycogen, which is most often found in liver and muscle cells. Glycogen is formed by linking many glucose molecules together.

*Julie (11th grade): "Remembering these four came in handy on the test!"*

Two important structural polysaccharides are **cellulose** and **chitin**. Cellulose, a compound composed of many glucose molecules, is used by plants in the formation of their cell walls. Chitin is an important part of the exoskeletons of arthropods such as insects, spiders, and shellfish (see Chapter 13, Taxonomy and Classification).

## Proteins

A **protein** is a compound composed of chains of amino acids. Proteins have many functions in the body—they serve as structural components, transport aids, enzymes, and cell signals, to name only a few. You should be able to identify a protein or an amino acid by sight if asked to do so on the test.

An amino acid consists of a carbon center surrounded by an amino group, a carboxyl group, a hydrogen, and an R group (See Figure 5.7). Remember that the R stands for "rest" of

**Figure 5.7  Structure of an amino acid.**

**Figure 5.8  Amino acid structure exhibiting peptide linkage.**

the compound, which provides an amino acid's unique personal characteristics. For instance, acidic amino acids have acidic R groups, basic amino acids have basic R groups, and so forth.

Many students preparing for the AP exam wonder if they need to memorize the 20 amino acids and their structures and whether they are polar, nonpolar, or charged. This is a lot of effort for perhaps one multiple-choice question that you might encounter on the exam. We think that this time would be better spent studying other potential exam questions. If this is of any comfort to you, we have yet to see an AP Biology question that asks something to the effect of "Which of these 5 amino acids is nonpolar?" (*Disclaimer:* This does not mean that it will never happen ☺.) It is more important for you to identify the general structure of an amino acid and know the process of protein synthesis, which we discuss in Chapter 15.

A protein consists of amino acids linked together as shown in Figure 5.8. They are most often much larger than that depicted here. Figure 5.8 is included to enable you to identify a peptide linkage on the exam. Most proteins have many more amino acids in the chain.

The AP exam may expect you to know about the structure of proteins:

*Primary structure.* The order of the amino acids that make up the protein.

*Secondary structure.* Three-dimensional arrangement of a protein caused by hydrogen bonding at regular intervals along the polypeptide backbone.

*Tertiary structure.* Three-dimensional arrangement of a protein caused by interaction among the various R groups of the amino acids involved.

*Quaternary structure.* The arrangement of separate polypeptide "subunits" into a single protein. Not all proteins have quaternary structure; many consist of a single polypeptide chain.

Proteins with only primary and secondary structure are called *fibrous* proteins. Proteins with only primary, secondary, and tertiary structures are called *globular* proteins. Either fibrous or globular proteins may contain a quaternary structure if there is more than one polypeptide chain.

# Enzymes

*CT teacher: "The topic of enzymes is full of essay material. Know it well."*

**Enzymes** are proteins that act as organic catalysts and will be encountered often in your review for this exam. **Catalysts** speed up reactions by lowering the energy (activation energy) needed for the reaction to take place, but are not used up in the reaction. The substances that enzymes act on are known as **substrates**.

Enzymes are selective; they interact only with particular substrates. It is the shape of the enzyme that provides the specificity. The part of the enzyme that interacts with the substrate is called the **active site.** The **induced-fit model** of enzyme-substrate interaction

**BIG IDEA 4.B.1**
*The shape of enzymes and their active sites are important to their function.*

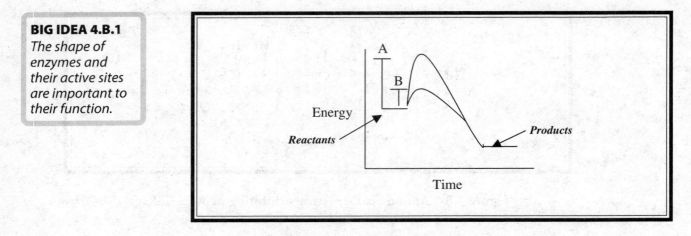

**Figure 5.9** **Plot showing energy versus time. Height A represents original activation energy; height B represents the lowered activation energy due to the addition of enzyme.**

describes the active site of an enzyme as specific for a particular substrate that fits its shape. When the enzyme and substrate bind together, the enzyme is *induced* to alter its shape for a tighter active site–substrate attachment. This tight fit places the substrate in a favorable position to react, speeding up (accelerating) the rate of reaction. After an enzyme interacts with a substrate, converting it into a product, it is free to find and react with another substrate; thus, a small concentration of enzyme can have a major effect on a reaction.

Every enzyme functions best at an optimal temperature and pH. If the pH or temperature strays from those optimal values, the effectiveness of the enzyme will suffer. The effectiveness of an enzyme can be affected by four things:

**1.** The temperature
**2.** The pH
**3.** The concentration of the substrate involved
**4.** The concentration of the enzyme involved

You should be able to identify the basic components of an activation energy diagram if you encounter one on the AP exam. The important parts are identified in Figure 5.9.

The last enzyme topic to cover is the difference between competitive and noncompetitive inhibition. In **competitive inhibition** (Figure 5.10), an inhibitor molecule resembling

**Figure 5.10** **Competitive inhibition.**

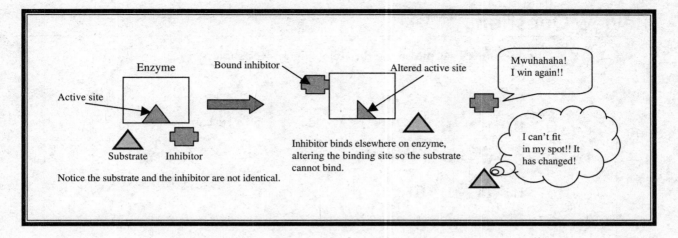

**Figure 5.11   Noncompetitive inhibition.**

the substrate binds to the active site and physically blocks the substrate from attaching. Competitive inhibition can sometimes be overcome by adding a high concentration of substrate to outcompete the inhibitor. In **noncompetitive inhibition** (Figure 5.11), an inhibitor molecule binds to a different part of the enzyme, causing a change in the shape of the active site so that it can no longer interact with the substrate.

# pH: Acids and Bases

The pH scale is used to indicate how acidic or basic a solution is. It ranges from 0 to 14; 7 is neutral. Anything less than 7 is acidic; anything greater than 7 is basic. The pH scale is a logarithmic scale and as a result, a pH of 5 is 10 times more acidic than a pH of 6. Following the same logic, a pH of 4 is 100 times more acidic than a pH of 6. Remember that as the pH of a solution *decreases*, the concentration of hydrogen ions in the solution increases, and vice versa. For the most part, chemical reactions in humans function at or near a neutral pH. The exceptions to this rule are the chemical reactions involving some of the enzymes of the digestive system. (See Chapter 15, Human Physiology.)

# Reactions

**KEY IDEA**

There are five types of reactions you should know for this exam:

1. *Hydrolysis reaction.* A reaction that breaks down compounds by the addition of $H_2O$.
2. *Dehydration synthesis reaction.* A reaction in which two compounds are brought together with $H_2O$ released as a product.
3. *Endergonic reaction.* A reaction that requires input of energy to occur.

$$A + B + energy \rightarrow C$$

4. *Exergonic reaction.* A reaction that gives off energy as a product.

$$A + B \rightarrow energy + C$$

5. *Redox reaction.* A reaction involving the transfer of electrons. Such reactions occur along the electron transport chain of the mitochondria during respiration (Chapter 7).

# › Review Questions

For questions 1–4, please use the following answer choices:

(A)

(B)

(C)

(D)

1. Which of the structures shown above is a polypeptide?

2. Which of these structures is a disaccharide?

3. Which of these structures is a fat?

4. Which of these structures is an amino acid?

5. Which of the following has both a hydrophobic portion and a hydrophilic portion?

   A. Starch
   B. Phospholipids
   C. Proteins
   D. Steroids

6. A solution that has a pH of 2 is how many times more acidic than one with a pH of 5?

   A. 5
   B. 10
   C. 100
   D. 1,000

7. The structure below contains which functional group?

$$CH_3-CH_2-\overset{\overset{\textstyle O}{\|}}{C}-CH_3$$

   A. Aldehyde
   B. Ketone
   C. Amino
   D. Hydroxyl

8. Which of the following will least affect the effectiveness of an enzyme?

   A. Temperature
   B. pH
   C. Concentration of enzyme
   D. Original activation energy of system

9. Which of the following is similar to the process of competitive inhibition?

   A. When you arrive at work in the morning, you are unable to park your car in your (assigned) parking spot because the car of the person who parks next to you has taken up just enough space that you cannot fit your own car in.
   B. When you arrive at work in the morning, you are unable to park your car in your parking spot because someone with a car exactly like yours has already taken your spot, leaving you nowhere to park your car.
   C. As you are about to park your car in your spot at work, a giant bulldozer comes along and smashes your car away from the spot, preventing you from parking your car in your spot.
   D. When you arrive at work in the morning, you are unable to park your car in your parking spot because someone has placed a giant cement block in front of your spot.

10. All the following are carbohydrates except

    A. starch.
    B. glycogen.
    C. chitin.
    D. glycerol.

11. An amino acid contains which of the following functional groups?

    A. Carboxyl group and amino group
    B. Carbonyl group and amino group
    C. Hydroxyl group and amino group
    D. Carboxyl group and hydroxyl group

## > Answers and Explanations

1. **D**

2. **C**

3. **A**

4. **B**

5. **B**—A phospholipid has both a hydrophobic portion and a hydrophilic portion. The hydrocarbon portion, or tail, of the phospholipid dislikes water, and the phosphate portion, the head, is hydrophilic.

6. **D**—Because the pH scale is logarithmic, 2 is 1,000 times more acidic than 5.

7. **B**—This functional group is a carbonyl group. The two main types of carbonyl groups are ketones and aldehydes. In this case, it is a ketone because there are carbon chains on either side of the carbon double-bonded to the oxygen.

8. **D**—The four main factors that affect enzyme efficiency are pH, temperature, enzyme concentration, and substrate concentration.

9. **B**—Competitive inhibition is the inhibition of an enzyme–substrate reaction in which the inhibitor resembles the substrate and physically blocks the substrate from attaching to the active site. This parking spot represents the active site, your car is the substrate, and the other car already in the spot is the competitive inhibitor. Examples A and D more closely resemble noncompetitive inhibition.

10. **D**—Glycerol is not a carbohydrate. It is an alcohol. Starch is a carbohydrate stored in plant cells. Glycogen is a carbohydrate stored in animal cells. Chitin is a carbohydrate used by arthropods to construct their exoskeletons. Cellulose is a carbohydrate used by plants to construct their cell walls.

**11. A**

## › Rapid Review

Try to rapidly review the following material:

*Organic compounds*: contain carbon; examples include lipids, proteins, and carbs (carbohydrates).

*Functional groups*: amino ($NH_2$), carbonyl (RCOR), carboxyl (COOH), hydroxyl (OH), phosphate ($PO_4$), sulfhydryl (SH).

*Fat*: glycerol + 3 fatty acids.

*Saturated fat*: bad for you; animals and some plants have it; solidifies at room temperature.

*Unsaturated fat*: better for you, plants have it; liquifies at room temperature.

*Steroids*: lipids whose structures resemble chicken-wire fence; include cholesterol and sex hormones.

*Phospholipids*: glycerol + 2 fatty acids + 1 phosphate group; make up membrane bilayers of cells; have hydrophobic interiors and hydrophilic exteriors.

*Carbohydrates*: used by cells for energy and structure; monosaccharides (glucose), disaccharides (sucrose, maltose, lactose), storage polysaccharides (starch [plants], glycogen [animals]), structural polysaccharides (chitin [fungi], cellulose [arthropods]).

*Proteins*: made with the help of ribosomes out of amino acids; serve many functions (e.g., transport, enzymes, cell signals, receptor molecules, structural components, and channels).

*Enzymes*: catalytic proteins that react in an induced-fit fashion with substrates to speed up the rate of reactions by lowering the activation energy; effectiveness is affected by changes in pH, temperature, and substrate and enzyme concentrations.

*Competitive inhibition*: inhibitor resembles substrate and binds to active site.

*Noncompetitive inhibition*: inhibitor binds elsewhere on enzyme; alters active site so that substrate cannot bind.

*pH*: logarithmic scale <7 acidic, 7 neutral, >7 basic (alkaline); pH 4 is 10 times more acidic than pH 5.

*Reaction types*:

  *Hydrolysis reaction*: breaks down compounds by adding water.

  *Dehydration reaction*: two components brought together, producing $H_2O$.

  *Endergonic reaction*: reaction that requires input of energy.

  *Exergonic reaction*: reaction that gives off energy.

  *Redox reaction*: electron transfer reactions.

# CHAPTER 6

# Cells

**IN THIS CHAPTER**

**Summary:** This chapter discusses the different types of cells (eukaryotic and prokaryotic) and the important organelles, structures, and transport mechanisms that power these cells.

**Key Ideas**

✪ Prokaryotic cells are simple cells with no nuclei or organelles.
✪ Animal cells do not contain cell walls or chloroplasts and have small vacuoles.
✪ Plant cells do not have centrioles.
✪ The fluid mosaic model states that a cell membrane consists of a phospholipid bilayer with proteins of various lengths and sizes interspersed with cholesterol among the phospholipids.
✪ Passive transport is the movement of a particle across a selectively permeable membrane down its concentration gradient (e.g., diffusion, osmosis).
✪ Active transport is the movement of a particle across a selectively permeable membrane against its concentration gradient (e.g., sodium-potassium pump).

## Introduction

A cell is defined as a small room, sometimes a prison room, usually designed for only one person (but usually housing two or more inmates, except for solitary-confinement cells). It is a place for rehabilitation—whoops! We're looking at the wrong notes here. Sorry, let's start again. A cell is the basic unit of life (that's more like it), discovered in the seventeenth century by Robert Hooke. There are two major divisions of cells: prokaryotic and eukaryotic.

This chapter starts with a discussion of these two cell types, followed by an examination of the organelles found in cells. We conclude with a look at the fluid mosaic model of the cell membrane and a discussion of the different types of cell transport: diffusion, facilitated diffusion, osmosis, active transport, endocytosis, and exocytosis.

## Types of Cells

The **prokaryotic** cell is a *simple* cell. It has no nucleus, and no membrane-bound organelles. The genetic material of a prokaryotic cell is found in a region of the cell known as the **nucleoid.** Bacteria are a fine example of prokaryotic cells and divide by a process known as *binary fission*; they duplicate their genetic material, divide in half, and produce two identical daughter cells. Prokaryotic cells are found only in the kingdom Monera (bacteria group).

*Steve (12th grade): "Five questions on my test dealt with organelle function—know them."*

The **eukaryotic** cell is much more complex. It contains a nucleus, which functions as the control center of the cell, directing DNA replication, transcription, and cell growth. Eukaryotic organisms may be unicellular or multicellular. One of the key features of eukaryotic cells is the presence of membrane-bound organelles, each with its own duties. Two prominent members of the "Eukaryote Club" are animal and plant cells; the differences between these types of cells are discussed in the next section.

## Organelles

**BIG IDEA 1.B.2**
*Cell structure is an example of a widely conserved feature.*

You should familiarize yourselves with approximately a dozen organelles and cell structures before taking the AP Biology exam:

### Prokaryotic Organelles

You should be familiar with the following structures:

*Plasma membrane.* This is a selective barrier around a cell composed of a double layer of phospholipids. Part of this selectivity is due to the many proteins that either rest on the exterior of the membrane or are embedded in the membrane of the cell. Each membrane has a different combination of lipids, proteins, and carbohydrates that provide it with its unique characteristics.

*Cell wall.* This is a wall or barrier that functions to shape and protect cells. This is present in all prokaryotes.

*Ribosomes.* These function as the host organelle for protein synthesis in the cell. They are found in the cytoplasm of cells and are composed of a large unit and a small subunit.

### Eukaryotic Organelles

You should be familiar with the following structures:

**BIG IDEA 2.B.3**
*Eukaryotic cells have organelles to partition such cells into specialized regions.*

*Ribosomes.* As in prokaryotes, eukaryotic ribosomes serve as the host organelles for protein synthesis. Eukaryotes have *bound* ribosomes, which are attached to endoplasmic reticula and form proteins that tend to be exported from the cell or sent to the membrane. There are also *free* ribosomes, which exist freely in the cytoplasm and produce proteins that remain in the cytoplasm of the cell. Eukaryotic ribosomes are built in a structure called the **nucleolus.**

**BIG IDEA 4.A.2**
*The structure and function of organelles provide essential processes for the cell.*

*Smooth endoplasmic reticulum.* This is a membrane-bound organelle involved in lipid synthesis, detoxification, and carbohydrate metabolism. Liver cells contain a lot of **smooth endoplasmic reticulum** (SER) because they host a lot of carbohydrate metabolism (glycolysis). It is given the name "smooth" endoplasmic reticulum because there are no ribosomes on its cytoplasmic surface. The liver contains much SER for another reason—it is the site of alcohol detoxification.

*Rough endoplasmic reticulum.* This membrane-bound organelle is termed "rough" because of the presence of ribosomes on the cytoplasmic surface of the cell. The proteins produced by this organelle are often secreted by the cell and carried by vesicles to the **Golgi apparatus** for further modification.

*Golgi apparatus.* Proteins, lipids, and other macromolecules are sent to the Golgi to be modified by the addition of sugars and other molecules to form **glycoproteins.** The products are then sent in vesicles (escape pods that bud off the edge of the Golgi) to other parts of the cell, directed by the particular changes made by the Golgi. We think of the Golgi apparatus as the post office of the cell—packages are dropped off by customers, and the Golgi adds the appropriate postage and zip code to make sure that the packages reach proper destinations in the cell.

*Mitochondria.* These are double-membraned organelles that specialize in the production of ATP. The innermost portion of the mitochondrion is called the *matrix,* and the folds created by the inner of the two membranes are called *cristae.* The mitochondria are the host organelles for the Krebs cycle (matrix) and oxidative phosphorylation (cristae) of respiration, which we discuss in Chapter 7. We think of the mitochondria as the power plants of the cell.

*Lysosome.* This is a membrane-bound organelle that specializes in digestion. It contains enzymes that break down (hydrolyze) proteins, lipids, nucleic acids, and carbohydrates. This organelle is the stomach of the cell. Absence of a particular lysosomal hydrolytic enzyme can lead to a variety of diseases known as **storage diseases.** An example of this is **Tay-Sachs disease** (discussed in Chapter 10), in which an enzyme used to digest lipids is absent, leading to excessive accumulation of lipids in the brain. Lysosomes are often referred to as "suicide sacs" of the cell. Cells that are no longer needed are often destroyed in these sacs. An example of this process involves the cells of the tail of a tadpole, which are digested as a tadpole changes into a frog.

*Nucleus.* This is the control center of the cell. In eukaryotic cells, this is the storage site of genetic material (DNA). It is the site of replication, transcription, and posttranscriptional modification of RNA. It also contains the nucleolus, the site of ribosome synthesis.

*Vacuole.* This is a storage organelle that acts as a vault. Vacuoles are quite large in plant cells but small in animal cells.

*Peroxisomes.* These are organelles containing enzymes that produce hydrogen peroxide as a by-product while performing various functions, such as breakdown of fatty acids and detoxification of alcohol in the liver. Peroxisomes also contain an enzyme that converts the toxic hydrogen peroxide by-product of these reactions into cell-friendly water.

*Chloroplast.* This is the site of photosynthesis and energy production in plant cells. Chloroplasts contain many pigments, which provide leaves with their color. Chloroplasts are divided into an inner portion and an outer portion. The inner fluid portion is called the **stroma,** which is surrounded by two outer membranes. Winding through the stroma is an inner membrane called the **thylakoid membrane system,** where the light-dependent reactions of photosynthesis occur. The light-independent (dark) reactions occur in the stroma.

*Cytoskeleton.* The skeleton of cells consists of three types of fibers that provide support, shape, and mobility to cells: microtubules, microfilaments, and intermediate filaments. **Microtubules** are constructed from tubulin and have a lead role in the separation of cells during cell division. Microtubules are also important components of cilia and flagella, which are structures that aid the movement of particles (Chapter 19). **Microfilaments,** constructed from actin, play a big part in muscular contraction. **Intermediate filaments** are constructed from a class of proteins called *keratins* and are thought to function as reinforcement for the shape and position of organelles in the cell.

### Remember me!

Of the structures listed above, animal cells contain *all except* cell walls and chloroplasts, and their vacuoles are small. Plant cells contain *all* the structures listed above, and their vacuoles are large. Animal cells have centrioles (cell division structure); plant cells *do not*!

## Cell Membranes: Fluid Mosaic Model

As discussed above and in Chapter 5, a cell membrane is a selective barrier surrounding a cell that has a phospholipid bilayer as its major structural component. Remember that the outer portion of the bilayer contains the hydrophilic (water-loving) head of the phospholipid, while the inner portion is composed of the hydrophobic (water-fearing) tail of the phospholipid (Figure 6.1).

The **fluid mosaic model** is the most accepted model for the arrangement of membranes. It states that the membrane consists of a phospholipid bilayer with proteins of various lengths and sizes interspersed with cholesterol among the phospholipids. These proteins perform various functions depending on their location within the membrane.

The fluid mosaic model consists of **integral proteins,** which are implanted within the bilayer and can extend partway or all the way across the membrane, and **peripheral proteins,** such as receptor proteins, which are not implanted in the bilayer and are often attached to integral proteins of the membrane. These proteins have various functions in cells. A protein that stretches across the membrane can function as a channel to assist the passage of desired molecules into the cell. Proteins on the exterior of a membrane with

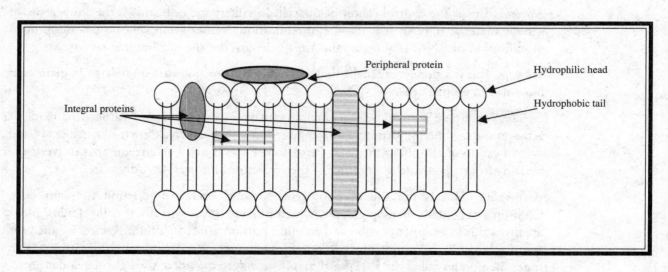

**Figure 6.1    Cross-section of a cell membrane showing phospholipid bilayer.**

binding sites can act as receptors that allow the cell to respond to external signals such as hormones. Proteins embedded in the membrane can also function as enzymes, increasing the rate of cellular reactions.

The cell membrane is "selectively" permeable, meaning that it allows some molecules and other substances through, while others are not permitted to pass. The membrane is like a bouncer at a popular nightclub. What determines the selectivity of the membrane? One factor is the size of the substance, and the other is the charge. The bouncer lets small, uncharged polar substances and hydrophobic substances such as lipids through the membrane, but larger uncharged polar substances (such as glucose) and charged ions (such as sodium) cannot pass through. The other factor determining what is allowed to pass through the membrane is the particular arrangement of proteins in the lipid bilayer. Different proteins in different arrangements allow different molecules to pass through.

# Types of Cell Transport

KEY IDEA

**BIG IDEA 2.B.2**
*Cells maintain their internal environment by transporting materials across their membranes.*

There are six basic types of cell transport:

1. **Diffusion:** the movement of molecules down their concentration gradient without the use of energy. It is a *passive* process during which substances move from a region of higher concentration to a region of lower concentration. The rate of diffusion of substances varies from membrane to membrane because of different selective permeabilities.

2. **Osmosis:** the *passive* diffusion of water down its concentration gradient across selectively permeable membranes. Water moves from a region of *high* water concentration to a region of *low* water concentration. Thinking about osmosis another way, water will flow from a region with a *lower* solute concentration (hypotonic) to a region with a *higher* solute concentration (hypertonic). This process does not require the input of energy. For example, visualize two regions—one with 10 particles of sodium per liter of water; the other with 15. Osmosis would drive water from the region with 10 particles of sodium toward the region with 15 particles of sodium.

3. **Facilitated diffusion:** the diffusion of particles across a selectively permeable membrane with the assistance of the membrane's transport proteins. These proteins will not bring any old molecule looking for a free pass into the cell; they are specific in what they will carry and have binding sites designed for molecules of interest. Like diffusion and osmosis, this process does not require the input of energy.

4. **Active transport:** the movement of a particle across a selectively permeable membrane *against* its concentration gradient (from low concentration to high). This movement requires the input of energy, which is why it is termed "active" transport. As is often the case in cells, adenosine triphosphate (ATP) is called on to provide the energy for this reactive process. These active-transport systems are vital to the ability of cells to maintain particular concentrations of substances despite environmental concentrations. For example, cells have a very high concentration of potassium and a very low concentration of sodium. Diffusion would like to move sodium in and potassium out to equalize the concentrations. The all-important **sodium-potassium pump** actively moves potassium *into* the cell and sodium *out of* the cell against their respective concentration gradients to maintain appropriate levels inside the cell. This is the major pump in animal cells.

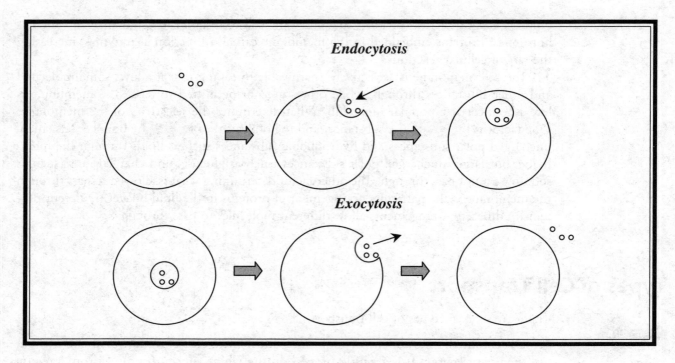

**Figure 6.2   Endocytosis and exocytosis.**

5. **Endocytosis:** a process in which substances are brought into cells by the enclosure of the substance into a membrane-created vesicle that surrounds the substance and escorts it into the cell (Figure 6.2). This process is used by immune cells called **phagocytes** to engulf and eliminate foreign invaders.

6. **Exocytosis:** a process in which substances are exported out of the cell (the reverse of endocytosis). A vesicle again escorts the substance to the plasma membrane, causes it to fuse with the membrane, and ejects the contents of the substance outside the cell (Figure 6.2). In exocytosis, the vesicle functions like the trash chute of the cell.

## ❯ Review Questions

For questions 1–4, please use the following answer choices:

   A.  Cell wall
   B.  Mitochondrion
   C.  Ribosome
   D.  Lysosome

1. This organelle is present in plant cells, but not animal cells.

2. Absence of enzymes from this organelle can lead to storage diseases such as Tay-Sachs disease.

3. This organelle is the host for the Krebs cycle and oxidative phosphorylation of respiration.

4. This organelle is synthesized in the nucleolus of the cell.

5. Which of the following best describes the fluid mosaic model of membranes?

   A. The membrane consists of a phospholipid bilayer with proteins of various lengths and sizes located on the exterior portions of the membrane.
   B. The membrane consists of a phospholipid bilayer with proteins of various lengths and sizes located in the interior of the membrane.
   C. The membrane is composed of a phospholipid bilayer with proteins of uniform lengths and sizes located in the interior of the membrane.
   D. The membrane contains a phospholipid bilayer with proteins of various lengths and sizes interspersed among the phospholipids.

6. Which of the following types of cell transport requires energy?

   A. The movement of a particle across a selectively permeable membrane down its concentration gradient
   B. The movement of a particle across a selectively permeable membrane against its concentration gradient
   C. The movement of water down its concentration gradient across selectively permeable membranes
   D. The movement of a sodium ion from an area of higher concentration to an area of lower concentration

7. Which of the following structures is present in prokaryotic cells?

   A. Nucleus
   B. Mitochondria
   C. Cell wall
   D. Golgi apparatus

8. Which of the following represents an *incorrect* description of an organelle's function?

   A. *Chloroplast:* the site of photosynthesis and energy production in plant cells
   B. *Peroxisome:* organelle that produces hydrogen peroxide as a by-product of reactions involved in the breakdown of fatty acids, and detoxification of alcohol in the liver
   C. *Golgi apparatus:* structure to which proteins, lipids, and other macromolecules are sent to be modified by the addition of sugars and other molecules to form glycoproteins
   D. *Rough endoplasmic reticulum:* membrane-bound organelle lacking ribosomes on its cytoplasmic surface, involved in lipid synthesis, detoxification, and carbohydrate metabolism

9. The destruction of which of the following would most cripple a cell's ability to undergo cell division?

   A. Microfilaments
   B. Intermediate filaments
   C. Microtubules
   D. Actin fibers

10. Which of the following can easily diffuse across a selectively permeable membrane?

   A. $Na^+$
   B. Glucose
   C. Large uncharged polar molecules
   D. Lipids

## ❯ Answers and Explanations

1. **A**—Cell walls exist in plant cells and prokaryotic cells, but not animal cells. They function to shape and protect cells.

2. **D**—The lysosome acts like the stomach of the cell. It contains enzymes that break down proteins, lipids, nucleic acids, and carbohydrates. Absence of these enzymes can lead to storage disorders such as Tay-Sachs disease.

3. **B**—The mitochondrion is the power plant of the cell. This organelle specializes in the production of ATP and hosts the Krebs cycle and oxidative phosphorylation.

4. **C**—The ribosome is an organelle made in the nucleolus that serves as the host for protein synthesis in the cell. It is found in both prokaryotes and eukaryotes.

5. **D**—The fluid mosaic model says that proteins can extend all the way through the phospholipid bilayer of the membrane, and that these proteins are of various sizes and lengths.

6. **B**—Answer choice B is the definition of active transport, which requires the input of energy. Simple diffusion (answer choices A and D) and osmosis (answer choice C) are all passive processes that do not require energy input.

7. **C**—Prokaryotes do not contain many organelles, but they do contain cell walls.

8. **D**—This is the description of the *smooth* endoplasmic reticulum. We know that this is a tricky question, but we wanted you to review the distinction between the two types of endoplasmic reticulum.

9. **C**—Microtubules play an enormous role in cell division. They make up the spindle apparatus that works to pull apart the cells during mitosis (Chapter 9). A loss of microtubules would cripple the cell division process. Actin fibers (answer choice D) are the building blocks of microfilaments (answer choice A), which are involved in muscular contraction. Keratin fibers are the building blocks of intermediate filaments (answer choice B), which function as reinforcement for the shape and position of organelles in the cell.

10. **D**—Lipids are the only substances listed that are able to freely diffuse across selectively permeable membranes.

# ❯ Rapid Review

Try to rapidly review the materials presented in the following table and list:

| ORGANELLE | PROKARYOTES | ANIMAL CELLS EUKARYOTES | PLANT CELLS EUKARYOTES | FUNCTION |
|---|---|---|---|---|
| Cell wall | + | – | + | Protects and shapes the cell |
| Plasma membrane | + | + | + | Regulates what substances enter and leave a cell |
| Ribosome | + | + | + | Host for protein synthesis; formed in nucleolus |
| Smooth ER* | – | + | + | Lipid synthesis, detoxification, carbohydrate metabolism; no ribosomes on cytoplasmic surface |
| Rough ER* | – | + | + | Synthesizes proteins to secrete or send to plasma membrane; contains ribosomes on cytoplasmic surface |
| Golgi | – | + | + | Modifies lipids, proteins, etc., and sends them to other sites in the cell |
| Mitochondria | – | + | + | Power plant of cell; hosts major energy-producing steps of respiration |
| Lysosome | – | + | – | Contains enzymes that digest organic compounds; serves as cell's stomach |
| Nucleus | – | + | + | Control center of cell; host for transcription, replication, and DNA |
| Peroxisome | – | + | + | Breakdown of fatty acids, detoxification of alcohol |
| Chloroplast | – | – | + | Site of photosynthesis in plants |
| Cytoskeleton | – | + | + | Skeleton of cell; consists of microtubules (cell division, cilia, flagella), microfilaments (muscles), and intermediate filaments (reinforcing position of organelles) |
| Vacuole | – | +, small | +, large | Storage vault of cells |
| Centrioles | – | + | – | Part of microtubule separation apparatus that assists cell division in animal cells |

*Endoplasmic reticulum

*Fluid mosaic model*: plasma membrane is a selectively permeable phospholipid bilayer with proteins of various lengths and sizes interspersed with cholesterol among the phospholipids.

*Integral proteins*: proteins implanted within lipid bilayer of plasma membrane.

*Peripheral proteins*: proteins attached to exterior of membrane.

*Diffusion*: passive movement of substances down their concentration gradient (from high to low concentrations).

*Osmosis*: passive movement of water from the side of low solute concentration to the side of high solute concentration (hypotonic to hypertonic).

*Facilitated diffusion*: assisted transport of particles across membrane (no energy input needed).

*Active transport*: movement of substances against concentration gradient (low to high concentrations; requires energy input).

*Endocytosis*: phagocytosis of particles into a cell through the use of vesicles.

*Exocytosis*: process by which particles are ejected from the cell, similar to movement in a trash chute.

# CHAPTER > 7

# Respiration

## IN THIS CHAPTER

**Summary:** This chapter covers the basics behind the energy-creation process known as respiration. This chapter also teaches you the difference between aerobic and anaerobic respiration and takes you through the steps that convert a glucose molecule into ATP.

**Key Ideas**

✪ Aerobic respiration: glycolysis → Krebs cycle → oxidative phosphorylation → 36 ATP.

✪ Anaerobic respiration: glycolysis → regenerate $NAD^+$ → much less ATP.

✪ Oxidative phosphorylation results in the production of large amounts of ATP from NADH and $FADH_2$.

✪ Chemiosmosis is the coupling of the movement of electrons down the electron transport chain with the formation of ATP using the driving force provided by the proton gradient.

# Introduction

**BIG IDEA 2.A.1**

*All living things require constant input of energy.*

In this chapter, we explore how cells obtain energy. It is important that you do not get lost or buried in the details. You should finish this chapter with an understanding of the basic process. The AP Biology exam will not ask you to identify by name the enzyme that catalyzes the third step of glycolysis, nor will it require you to name the fourth molecule in the Krebs cycle. But it *will* ask you questions that require an understanding of the respiration process.

There are two major categories of respiration: **aerobic** and **anaerobic.** Aerobic respiration occurs in the presence of oxygen, while anaerobic respiration occurs in situations where oxygen is not available. Aerobic respiration involves three stages: glycolysis, the Krebs cycle, and oxidative phosphorylation. Anaerobic respiration, sometimes referred to as *fermentation,* also begins with glycolysis, and concludes with the formation of $NAD^+$.

# Aerobic Respiration

## Glycolysis

**BIG IDEA 2.A.2**

*Heterotrophs capture free energy present in the food they eat through cellular respiration.*

**Glycolysis** occurs in the cytoplasm of cells and is the beginning pathway for both aerobic and anaerobic respiration. During glycolysis, a glucose molecule is broken down through a series of reactions into two molecules of pyruvate. It is important to remember that oxygen plays no role in glycolysis. This reaction can occur in oxygen-rich and oxygen-poor environments. However, when in an environment lacking oxygen, glycolysis slows because the cells run out (become depleted) of $NAD^+$. For reasons we will discuss later, a lack of oxygen prevents oxidative phosphorylation from occurring, causing a buildup of NADH in the cells. This buildup causes a shortage of $NAD^+$. This is bad for glycolysis because it requires $NAD^+$ to function. Fermentation is the solution to this problem—it takes the excess NADH that builds up and converts it back to $NAD^+$ so that glycolysis can continue. More to come on fermentation later . . . be patient. ☺

To reiterate, the AP Biology exam will not require you to memorize the various steps of respiration. Your time is better spent studying the broad explanation of respiration, to understand the basic process, and become comfortable with respiration as a whole. Major concepts are the key. We will explain the specific steps of glycolysis because they will help you understand the big picture—but do not memorize them all. Save the space for other facts you have to know from other chapters of this book.

Examine Figure 7.1, which illustrates the general layout of glycolysis. The beginning steps of glycolysis require energy input. The first step adds a phosphate to a molecule of glucose with the assistance of an ATP molecule to produce *glucose-6-phosphate* (G6P). The newly formed G6P rearranges to form a molecule named *fructose-6-phosphate* (F6P). Another molecule of ATP is required for the next step, which adds another phosphate group to produce fructose 1,6-biphosphate. Already, glycolysis has used two of the ATP molecules that it is trying to produce—seems stupid . . . but be patient . . . the genius has yet to show its face. F6P splits into two 3-carbon-long fragments known as **PGAL** (glyceraldehyde phosphate). With the formation of PGAL, the energy-producing portion of glycolysis begins. Each PGAL molecule takes on an inorganic phosphate from the cytoplasm to produce 1,3-diphosphoglycerate. During this reaction, each PGAL gives up two electrons and a hydrogen to molecules of $NAD^+$ to form the all-important NADH molecules. The next step is a big one, as it leads to the production of the first ATP molecule in the process of respiration—the 1,3-diphosphoglycerate molecules donate one of their two phosphates to molecules of ADP to produce ATP and 3-phosphoglycerate (3PG). You'll notice that there are *two* ATP molecules formed here because before this step, the single molecule of glucose divided into *two* 3-carbon fragments. After 3PG rearranges to form 2-phosphoglycerate, phosphoenolpyruvate (PEP) is formed, which donates a phosphate group to molecules of ADP to form another pair of ATP molecules and pyruvate. This is the final step of glycolysis. In total, two molecules each of ATP, NADH, and pyruvate are formed during this process. Glycolysis produces the same result under anaerobic conditions as it does under aerobic conditions: two ATP molecules. If oxygen is present, more ATP is later made by oxidative phosphorylation.

Figure 7.1    Glycolysis.

If you are going to memorize one fact about glycolysis, remember that one glucose molecule produces two pyruvate, two NADH, and two ATP molecules.

One glucose → 2 pyruvate, 2 ATP, 2 NADH

### The Krebs Cycle

The pyruvate formed during glycolysis next enters the **Krebs cycle,** which is also known as the *citric acid cycle.* The Krebs cycle occurs in the matrix of the **mitochondria.** The pyruvate enters the mitochondria of the cell and is converted into acetyl coenzyme A (CoA) in a step that produces an NADH. This compound is now ready to enter the eight-step Krebs cycle, in which pyruvate is broken down completely to $H_2O$ and $CO_2$. You do not need to memorize the eight steps.

As shown in Figure 7.2, a representation of the Krebs cycle, the 3-carbon pyruvate does not enter the Krebs cycle per se. Rather, it is converted, with the assistance of CoA and $NAD^+$, into 2-carbon acetyl CoA and NADH. The acetyl CoA dives into the Krebs cycle and reacts with oxaloacetate to form a 6-carbon molecule called *citrate.* The citrate is converted to a molecule named isocitrate, which then donates electrons and a hydrogen to $NAD^+$ to form 5-carbon α-ketoglutarate, carbon dioxide, and a molecule of NADH. The α-ketoglutarate undergoes a reaction very similar to the one leading to its formation and produces 4-carbon succinyl CoA and another molecule each of NADH and $CO_2$. The succinyl CoA is converted into succinate in a reaction that produces a molecule of ATP. The succinate then transfers electrons and a hydrogen atom to FAD to form $FADH_2$ and fumarate. The next-to-last step in the Krebs cycle takes fumarate and rearranges it to another 4-carbon molecule: malate. Finally, in the last step of the cycle, the malate donates electrons and a hydrogen atom to a molecule of $NAD^+$ to form the final NADH molecule of the Krebs cycle, at the same time regenerating the molecule of oxaloacetate that helped kick off the cycle. One turn of the Krebs cycle takes a single pyruvate and produces one ATP, four NADH, and one $FADH_2$.

If you are going to memorize one thing about the Krebs cycle, remember that for each glucose dropped into glycolysis, the Krebs cycle occurs twice. Each pyruvate dropped into the Krebs cycle produces

4 NADH, 1 $FADH_2$, 1 ATP, and 2 $CO_2$

Therefore, the *pyruvate* obtained from the original glucose molecule produces:

8 NADH, 2 $FADH_2$, and 2 ATP

Up to this point, having gone through glycolysis and the Krebs cycle, one molecule of glucose has produced the following energy-related compounds: 10 NADH, 2 $FADH_2$, and 4 ATP. Not bad for an honest day's work . . . but the body wants more and needs to convert the NADH and $FADH_2$ into ATP. This is where the electron transport chain, chemiosmosis, and oxidative phosphorylation come into play.

### Oxidative Phosphorylation

After the Krebs cycle comes the largest energy-producing step of them all: **oxidative phosphorylation.** During this aerobic process, the NADH and $FADH_2$ produced during the first two stages of respiration are used to create ATP. Each NADH leads to

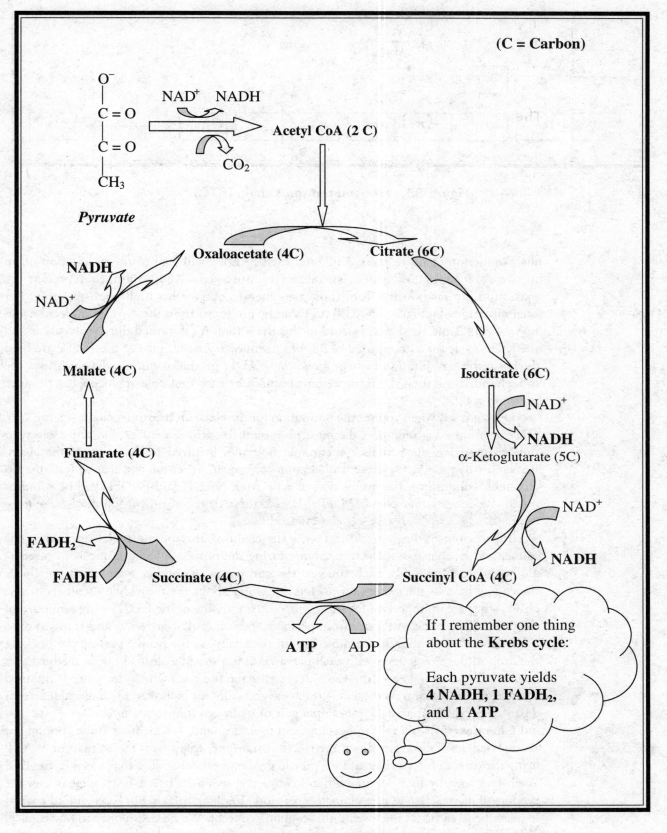

**Figure 7.2   The Krebs cycle.**

**Figure 7.3    Electron transport chain (ETC).**

the production of up to three ATP, and each $FADH_2$ will lead to the production of up to two ATP molecules. This is an inexact measurement—those numbers represent the maximum output possible from those two energy components if all goes smoothly. For each molecule of glucose, up to 30 ATP can be produced from the NADH molecules and up to 4 ATP from the $FADH_2$. Add to this the 4 total ATP formed during glycolysis and the Krebs cycle for a grand total of 38 ATP from *each glucose.* Two of these ATP are used during aerobic respiration to help move the NADH produced during glycolysis into the mitochondria. All totaled, during aerobic respiration, each molecule of glucose can produce up to 36 ATP.

Do not panic when you see the illustration for the **electron transport chain** (Figure 7.3). Once again, the big picture is the most important thing to remember. Do not waste your time memorizing the various cytochrome molecules involved in the steps of the chain. Remember that the ½ $O_2$ is the final electron acceptor in the chain, and that without the $O_2$ (anaerobic conditions), the production of ATP from NADH and $FADH_2$ will be compromised. Remember that each NADH that goes through the chain can produce three molecules of ATP, and each $FADH_2$ can produce two.

The *electron transport chain* (ETC) is the chain of enzyme molecules, located in the mitochondria, that passes electrons along during the process of chemiosmosis to regenerate $NAD^+$ to form ATP. Each time an electron passes to another member of the chain, the energy level of the system drops. Do not worry about the individual members of this chain—they are unimportant for this exam. When thinking of the ETC, we are reminded of the passing of a bucket of water from person to person until it arrives at and is tossed onto a fire. In the ETC, the various molecules in the chain are the people passing the buckets; the drop in the energy level with each pass is akin to the water sloshed out as the bucket is hurriedly passed along, and the ½ $O_2$ represents the fire onto which the water is dumped at the end of the chain. As the ½ $O_2$ (each oxygen atom, or half of an $O_2$ molecule) accepts a pair of electrons, it actually picks up a pair of hydrogen ions to *produce* water.

**Chemiosmosis** is a very important term to understand. It is defined as the coupling of the movement of electrons down the electron transport chain with the formation of ATP using the driving force provided by a proton gradient. So, what does that mean in English? Well, let's start by first defining what a coupled reaction is. It is a reaction that uses the product of *one* reaction as part of *another* reaction. Thinking back to our baseball card collecting days helps us better understand this coupling concept. We needed money to buy baseball cards. We would babysit or do yardwork for our neighbors and use that money to buy cards. We coupled the money-making reaction of hard labor to the money-spending reaction of buying baseball cards.

Let's look more closely at the reactions that are coupled in chemiosmosis. If you look at Figure 7.4a, a crude representation of a mitochondrion, you will find the ETC embedded within the inner mitochondrial membrane. As some of the molecules in the chain accept and then pass on electrons, they pump hydrogen ions into the space between the inner and outer membranes of the mitochondria (Figure 7.4b). This creates a proton gradient that drives the production of ATP. The difference in hydrogen concentration on the two sides of the membrane causes the protons to flow back into the matrix of the mitochondria through ATP synthase channels (Figure 7.4c). **ATP synthase** is an enzyme that uses the flow of hydrogens to drive the phosphorylation of an ADP molecule to produce ATP. This reaction completes the process of oxidative phosphorylation and chemiosmosis. The proton gradient created by the movement of electrons from molecule to molecule has been used to form the ATP that this process is designed to produce. In other words, the formation of ATP has been coupled to the movement of electrons and protons.

Chemiosmosis is not oxidative phosphorylation per se; rather, it is a major *part* of oxidative phosphorylation. An important fact we want you to take out of this chapter is that chemiosmosis is not unique to the mitochondria. It is the same process that occurs in the

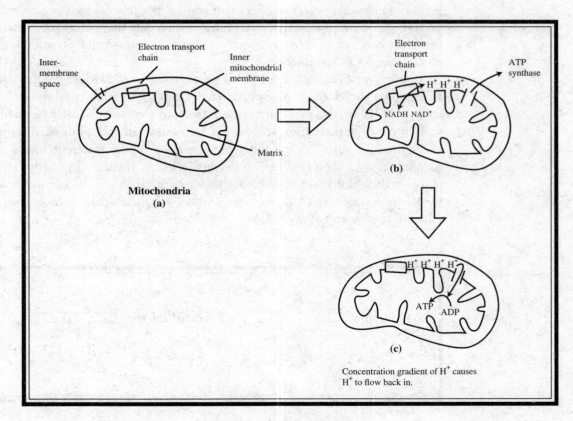

**Figure 7.4    Chemiosmosis.**

chloroplasts during the ATP-creating steps of photosynthesis (see Chapter 8). The difference is that light is driving the electrons along the ETC in plants. Remember that chemiosmosis occurs in both mitochondria and chloroplasts.

Remember the following facts about oxidative phosphorylation (Ox-phos):

1. Each NADH → 3 ATP.
2. Each $FADH_2$ → 2 ATP.
3. ½ $O_2$ is the final electron acceptor of the electron transport chain, and the chain will not function in the absence of oxygen.
4. Ox-phos serves the important function of regenerating $NAD^+$ so that glycolysis and the Krebs cycle can continue.
5. Chemiosmosis occurs in photosynthesis as well as respiration.

# Anaerobic Respiration

*Anaerobic respiration,* or *fermentation,* occurs when oxygen is unavailable or cannot be used by the organism. As in aerobic respiration, glycolysis occurs and pyruvate is produced. The pyruvate enters the Krebs cycle, producing NADH, $FADH_2$, and some ATP. The problem arises in the ETC—because there is no oxygen available, the electrons do not pass down the chain to the final electron acceptor, causing a buildup of NADH in the system. This buildup of NADH means that the $NAD^+$ normally regenerated during oxidative phosphorylation is not produced, and this creates an $NAD^+$ shortage. This is a problem, because in order for glycolysis to proceed to the pyruvate stage, it needs $NAD^+$ to help perform the necessary reactions. **Fermentation** is the process that begins with glycolysis and ends when $NAD^+$ is regenerated. A glucose molecule that enters the fermentation pathway produces two net ATP per molecule of glucose, representing a tremendous decline in the efficiency of ATP production.

Under aerobic conditions, $NAD^+$ is recycled from NADH by the movement of electrons down the electron transport chain. Under anaerobic conditions, $NAD^+$ is recycled from NADH by the movement of electrons to pyruvate, namely, fermentation. The two main types of fermentation are **alcohol fermentation** and **lactic acid fermentation.** Refer to Figures 7.5 and 7.6 for the representations of the different forms of fermentation. Alcohol fermentation (Figure 7.5) occurs in fungi, yeast, and some bacteria. The first step involves the conversion of pyruvate into two 2-carbon acetaldehyde molecules. Then, in the all-important step of alcohol fermentation, the acetaldehyde molecules are converted to ethanol, regenerating two $NAD^+$ molecules in the process.

**Figure 7.5   Alcohol fermentation.**

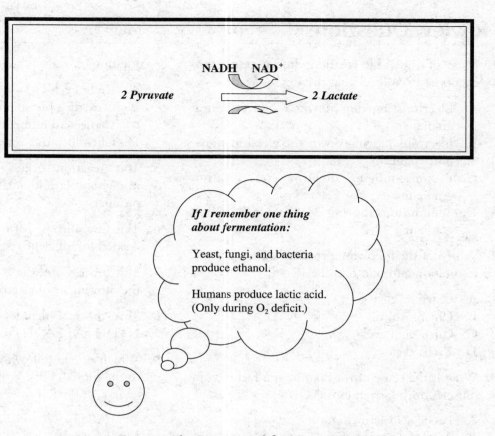

**Figure 7.6   Lactic acid fermentation.**

Lactic acid fermentation (Figure 7.6) occurs in human and animal muscle cells when oxygen is not available. This is a simpler process than alcoholic fermentation—the pyruvate is directly reduced to lactate (also known as lactic acid) by NADH to regenerate the $NAD^+$ needed for the resumption of glycolysis. Have you ever had a cramp during exercise? The pain you felt was the result of lactic acid fermentation. Your muscle was deprived of the necessary amount of oxygen to continue glycolysis, and it switched over to fermentation. The pain from the cramp came from the acidity in the muscle.

# › Review Questions

1. Most of the ATP creation during respiration occurs as a result of what driving force?

   A. Electrons moving down a concentration gradient
   B. Electrons moving down the electron transport chain
   C. Protons moving down a concentration gradient
   D. Sodium ions moving down a concentration gradient

2. Which of the following processes occurs in both respiration and photosynthesis?

   A. Calvin cycle
   B. Chemiosmosis
   C. Citric acid cycle
   D. Krebs cycle

3. What is the cause of the cramps you feel in your muscles during strenuous exercise?

   A. Lactic acid fermentation
   B. Alcohol fermentation
   C. Chemiosmotic coupling
   D. Too much oxygen delivery to the muscles

4. Which of the following statements is *in*correct?

   A. Glycolysis can occur with or without oxygen.
   B. Glycolysis occurs in the mitochondria.
   C. Glycolysis is the first step of both anaerobic and aerobic respiration.
   D. Glycolysis of one molecule of glucose leads to the production of 2 ATP, 2 NADH, and 2 pyruvate.

For questions 5–8, use the following answer choices:

   A. Krebs cycle
   B. Oxidative phosphorylation
   C. Lactic acid fermentation
   D. Chemiosmosis

5. This reaction occurs in the matrix of the mitochondria and includes $FADH_2$ among its products.

6. This reaction is performed to recycle $NAD^+$ needed for efficient respiration.

7. This process uses the proton gradient created by the movement of electrons to form ATP.

8. This process includes the reactions that use NADH and $FADH_2$ to produce ATP.

9. Which of the following molecules can give rise to the most ATP?

   A. NADH
   B. $FADH_2$
   C. Pyruvate
   D. Glucose

10. Which of the following is a proper representation of the products of a single glucose molecule after it has completed the Krebs cycle?

   A. 10 ATP, 4 NADH, 2 $FADH_2$
   B. 10 NADH, 4 $FADH_2$, 2 ATP
   C. 10 ATP, 4 $FADH_2$, 2 NADH
   D. 10 NADH, 4 ATP, 2 $FADH_2$

## › Answers and Explanations

1. **C**—This is the concept of chemiosmosis: the coupling of the movement of electrons down the electron transport chain and the formation of ATP via the creation of a proton gradient. The protons are pushed out of the matrix during the passage of electrons down the chain. They soon build up on the other side of the membrane, and are driven back inside because of the difference in concentration. ATP synthase uses the movement of protons to produce ATP.

2. **B**—This is an important concept to understand. The AP examiners love this topic!

3. **A**—Lactic acid fermentation occurs in human muscle cells when oxygen is not available. Answer choice B would be incorrect because alcohol fermentation occurs in yeast, fungi, and some bacteria. During exercise, if your muscle becomes starved for oxygen, glycolysis will switch over to fermentation. The pain from the cramp is due to the acidity in the muscle caused by the increased concentration of lactate.

4. **B**—Glycolysis occurs in the cytoplasm. All the other statements are correct.

5. **A**

6. **C**

7. **D**

8. **B**

9. **D**—A glucose molecule can net 36 ATP, an NADH molecule can net 3, an $FADH_2$ molecule can net 2, and a pyruvate molecule can net 15.

10. **D**—During glycolysis, a glucose molecule produces 2 ATP, 2 NADH, and 2 pyruvate. The 2 pyruvate then go on to produce 8 NADH, 2 $FADH_2$, and 2 ATP during the Krebs cycle to give the total listed in answer choice D.

## › Rapid Review

Try to rapidly review the material presented below.

There are two main categories of respiration: aerobic and anaerobic.

*Aerobic respiration*: glycolysis → Krebs cycle → oxidative phosphorylation → 36 ATP per glucose molecule

*Anaerobic respiration* (*fermentation*): glycolysis → regenerate $NAD^+$ → 2 ATP per glucose molecule

*Glycolysis*: conversion of 1 glucose molecule into 2 pyruvate, 2 ATP, and 2 NADH; occurs in the cytoplasm, and in both aerobic *and* anaerobic respiration; *must* have $NAD^+$ to proceed.

Total energy production to this point → 2 ATP + 2 NADH

*Krebs cycle*: conversion of 1 pyruvate molecule into 4 NADH, 1 $FADH_2$, 1 ATP, $H_2O$, and $CO_2$; occurs *twice* for each glucose to yield 8 NADH, 2 $FADH_2$, and 2 ATP; occurs in mitochondria.

Total energy production per glucose molecule to this point → 4 ATP + 10 NADH + 2 $FADH_2$

*Oxidative phosphorylation*: production of large amounts of ATP from NADH and $FADH_2$.

- Occurs in the mitochondria; requires presence of oxygen to proceed.
- NADH and $FADH_2$ pass their electrons down the electron transport chain to produce ATP.
- Each NADH can produce up to 3 ATP; each $FADH_2$ up to 2 ATP.
- ½ $O_2$ is the final acceptor in the electron transport chain.
- Movement of electrons down the chain leads to movement of $H^+$ out of matrix.
- Ox-phos *regenerates $NAD^+$* so that glycolysis and the Krebs cycle can continue!

*Chemiosmosis*: coupling of the movement of electrons down the ETC with the formation of ATP using the driving force provided by the proton gradient; occurs in *both* cell respiration *and* photosynthesis to produce ATP.

*ATP synthase*: enzyme responsible for using protons to actually produce ATP from ADP.

Total energy production per glucose molecule to this point → 38 ATP (use 2 in process) → 36 ATP total

*Fermentation* (*general*): process that regenerates $NAD^+$ so glycolysis can begin again.

- Occurs in the absence of oxygen.
- Begins with glycolysis: 2 ATP, 2 pyruvate, and 2 NADH are produced from 1 glucose molecule.
- Because there is no oxygen to accept the electron energy on the chain, there is a shortage of $NAD^+$, which prevents glycolysis from continuing.

*Fermentation* (*alcohol*): occurs in fungi, yeast, and bacteria; causes conversion of pyruvate to ethanol.

*Fermentation* (*lactic acid*): occurs in human and animal muscle cells; causes conversion of pyruvate → lactate; causes cramping sensation when oxygen runs low in muscle cells.

# CHAPTER 8

# Photosynthesis

**IN THIS CHAPTER**

**Summary:** This chapter discusses the basics behind the energy-creation process known as photosynthesis. It also teaches you how plants generate their energy from light. You will learn to differentiate between the two stages—the light-dependent and the light-independent reactions.

**Key Ideas**

✪ Overall photosynthesis reaction: $H_2O + CO_2 + light \rightarrow O_2 + glucose + H_2O$.

✪ Light-dependent reactions: inputs are water and light; products are ATP, NADPH, and $O_2$.

✪ The oxygen produced in photosynthesis comes from the water.

✪ The carbon in the glucose produced in photosynthesis comes from the $CO_2$.

✪ Light-independent reactions (dark reactions): inputs are NADPH, ATP and $CO_2$; products are ADP, $NADP^+$, and sugar.

## Introduction

In Chapter 7, we discussed how human and animal cells generate the energy needed to survive and perform on a day-to-day basis. Now we are going to look at how plants generate their energy from light—the process of **photosynthesis.** We stress again in this chapter what we said about respiration—do not get caught up in the memorization of every fact. Make sure that you understand the basic, overall concepts and the major ideas. Remember that most of plant photosynthesis occurs in the plant's leaves. The majority of the chloroplasts of a plant are found in mesophyll cells. Remember that there are two stages to photosynthesis:

the light-dependent reactions and the light-independent reactions, commonly called the "dark reactions." The simplified equation of photosynthesis is

$$H_2O + CO_2 + light \rightarrow O_2 + glucose + H_2O$$

# The Players in Photosynthesis

The host organelle for photosynthesis is the **chloroplast,** which is divided into an inner and outer portion. The inner fluid portion is called the **stroma,** which is surrounded by two outer membranes. In Figure 8.1, you can see that winding through the stroma is an inner membrane called the **thylakoid membrane system.** This is where the first stage of

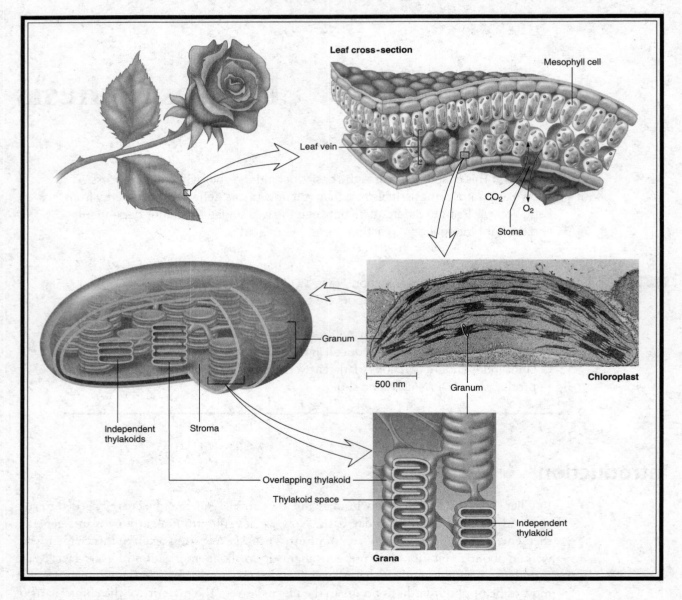

**Figure 8.1 An overall view of photosynthesis.** (*From* Biology, *8th ed., by Sylvia S. Mader, © 1985, 1987, 1990, 1993, 1996, 1998, 2001, 2004 by the McGraw Hill Companies, Inc. Reproduced with permission of The McGraw-Hill Companies.*)

photosynthesis occurs. This membrane consists of flattened channels and disks arranged in stacks called **grana.** We always remember the thylakoid system as resembling stacks of poker chips, where each chip is a single thylakoid. It is within these poker chips that the light-dependent reactions of photosynthesis occur.

Before we examine the process of photosynthesis, here are some definitions that will make things a bit easier as you read this chapter.

*Autotroph:* an organism that is self-nourishing. It obtains carbon and energy without ingesting other organisms. Plants and algae are good examples of autotrophic organisms—they obtain their energy from carbon dioxide, water, and light. They are the producers of the world.

*Bundle sheath cells:* cells that are tightly wrapped around the veins of a leaf. They are the site for the **Calvin cycle** in $C_4$ plants.

*$C_4$ plant:* plant that has adapted its photosynthetic process to more efficiently handle hot and dry conditions.

*Heterotroph:* organisms that must consume other organisms to obtain nourishment. They are the consumers of the world.

*Mesophyll:* interior tissue of a leaf.

*Mesophyll cells:* cells that contain many chloroplasts and host the majority of photosynthesis.

*Photolysis:* process by which water is broken up by an enzyme into hydrogen ions and oxygen atoms; occurs during the light-dependent reactions of photosynthesis.

*Photophosphorylation:* process by which ATP is produced during the light-dependent reactions of photosynthesis. It is the chloroplast equivalent of oxidative phosphorylation.

*Photorespiration:* process by which oxygen competes with carbon dioxide and attaches to RuBP. Plants that experience photorespiration have a lowered capacity for growth.

*Photosystem:* a cluster of light-trapping pigments involved in the process of photosynthesis. Photosystems vary tremendously in their organization and can possess hundreds of pigments. The two most important are photosystems I and II of the light reactions.

> **BIG IDEA 4.C.1**
>
> *Molecular variation in pigment molecules allows plants to absorb a greater range of wavelengths.*

*Pigment:* a molecule that absorbs light of a particular wavelength. Pigments are vital to the process of photosynthesis and include **chlorophyll, carotenoids,** and **phycobilins.**

*Rubisco:* an enzyme that catalyzes the first step of the Calvin cycle in $C_3$ plants.

*Stomata:* structure through which $CO_2$ enters a plant and water vapor and $O_2$ leave.

*Transpiration:* natural process by which plants lose $H_2O$ via evaporation through their leaves.

# The Reactions of Photosynthesis

> **BIG IDEA 2.A.1**
>
> *All living things require input of energy.*

The process of photosynthesis can be neatly divided into two sets of reactions: the light-dependent reactions and the light-independent reactions. The light-dependent reactions occur first and require an input of water and light. They produce three things: the oxygen we breathe, NADPH, and ATP. These last two products of the light reactions are then consumed during the second stage of photosynthesis: the dark reactions. These reactions, which need $CO_2$, NADPH, and ATP as inputs, produce sugar and recycle the $NADP^+$ and ADP to be used by the next set of light-dependent reactions. Now, we would be too kind if we left the discussion there. Let's look at the reactions in more detail. Stop groaning . . . you know we have to go there.

## Light-Dependent Reactions

**BIG IDEA 2.A.2**

*Autotrophs capture free energy present in sunlight through photosynthesis.*

Light-dependent reactions occur in the thylakoid membrane system. The thylakoid system is composed of the various stacks of poker chip look-alikes located within the stroma of the chloroplast. Within the thylakoid membrane is a photosynthetic participant termed **chlorophyll.** There are two main types of chlorophyll that you should remember: chlorophyll *a* and chlorophyll *b*. Chlorophyll *a* is the major pigment of photosynthesis, while chlorophyll *b* is considered to be an accessory pigment. The pigments are very similar structurally, but the minor differences are what account for the variance in their absorption of light. Chlorophyll absorbs light of a particular wavelength, and when it does, one of its electrons is elevated to a higher energy level (it is "excited"). Almost immediately, the excited electron drops back down to the ground state, giving off heat in the process. This energy is passed along until it finds chlorophyll *a*, which, when excited, passes its electron to the primary electron acceptor; then, the light-dependent reactions are under way.

The pigments of the thylakoid space organize themselves into groups called *photosystems.* These photosystems consist of varying combinations of chlorophylls *a*, *b*, and others; pigments called **phycobilins;** and another type of pigment called **carotenoids.** The accessory pigments help pick up light when chlorophyll *a* cannot do it as effectively. An example is red algae on the ocean bottom. When light is picked up by the accessory pigments, it is fluoresced and altered so that chlorophyll *a* can use it.

Imagine that the plant represented in Figure 8.2 is struck by light from the sun. This light excites the **photosystem** of the thylakoid space, which absorbs the photon and transmits the energy from one pigment molecule to another. As this energy is passed along, it loses a bit of energy with each step and eventually reaches chlorophyll *a*, which proceeds to kick off the process of photosynthesis. It initiates the first step of photosynthesis by passing the electron to the primary electron acceptor.

Before we continue, there are two major photosystems we want to tell you about—you might want to get out a pen or pencil here to jot this down, because the names for these photosystems may seem confusing. They are photosystem I and photosystem II. The only difference between these two **reaction centers** is that the main chlorophyll of photosystem I absorbs light with a wavelength of 700 nm, while the main chlorophyll of photosystem II absorbs light with a wavelength of 680 nm. By interacting with different thylakoid membrane proteins, they are able to absorb light of slightly different wavelengths.

Now let's get back to the reactions. Let's go through the rest of Figure 8.2 and talk about the light-dependent reactions. For the sole purpose of confusing you, plants start photosynthesis by using photosystem II before photosystem I. As light strikes photosystem II, the energy is absorbed and passed along until it reaches the P680 chlorophyll. When this chlorophyll is excited, it passes its electrons to the primary electron acceptor. This is where the water molecule comes into play. **Photolysis** in the thylakoid space takes electrons from $H_2O$ and passes them to P680 to replace the electrons given to the primary acceptor. With this reaction, a lone oxygen atom and a pair of hydrogen ions are formed from the water. The oxygen atom quickly finds another oxygen atom buddy, pairs up with it, and generates the $O_2$ that the plants so graciously put out for us every day. This is the first product of the light reactions.

The light reactions do not stop here, however. We need to consider what happens to the electron that has been passed to the primary electron acceptor. The electron is passed to photosystem I, P700, in a manner reminiscent of the electron transport chain. As the electrons are passed from P680 to P700, the lost energy is used to produce ATP

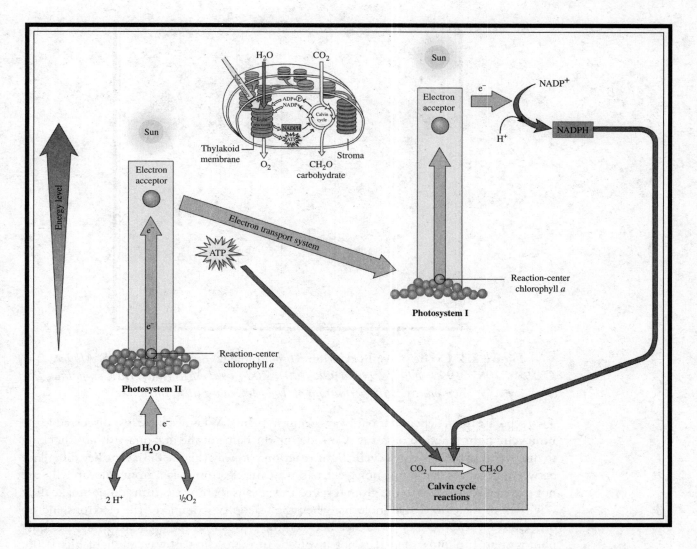

**Figure 8.2    Light-dependent reactions.** (*From* Biology, *8th ed., by Sylvia S. Mader,* © *1985,*
*1987, 1990, 1993, 1996, 1998, 2001, 2004 by the McGraw Hill Companies, Inc.*
*Reproduced with permission of The McGraw-Hill Companies.*)

(remember chemiosmosis). This ATP is the second product of the light reactions and is
produced in a manner mechanistically similar to the way ATP is produced during oxidative phosphorylation of respiration. In plants, this process of ATP formation is called
**photophosphorylation.**

After the photosystem I electrons are excited, photosystem I passes the energy to its
own primary electron acceptor. These electrons are sent down another chain to **ferredoxin,**
which then donates the electrons to $NADP^+$ to produce NADPH, the third and final
product of the light reactions. (Notice how in photosynthesis, there is NADPH instead of
NADH. The symbol P can help you remember that it relates to photosynthesis. ☺)

Remember the following about the light reactions:

**1.** The light reactions occur in the thylakoid membrane.
**2.** The inputs to the light reactions are water and light.
**3.** The light reactions produce three products: ATP, NADPH, and $O_2$.
**4.** The oxygen produced in the light reactions comes from $H_2O$, not $CO_2$.

**Figure 8.3  Cyclic phosphorylation.** (*From* Biology, *8th ed., by Sylvia S. Mader,*
© *1985, 1987, 1990, 1993, 1996, 1998, 2001, 2004 by the McGraw Hill Companies, Inc.*
*Reproduced with permission of The McGraw-Hill Companies.*)

Two separate light-dependent pathways occur in plants. What we have just discussed is the
**noncyclic light reaction** pathway. Considering the name of the first one, it is not shocking
to discover that there is also a **cyclic light reaction** pathway (Figure 8.3). One key difference
between the two is that in the noncyclic pathway, the electrons taken from chlorophyll *a* are
not recycled back down to the ground state. This means that the electrons do not make their
way back to the chlorophyll molecule when the reaction is complete. The electrons end up
on NADPH. Another key difference between the two is that the cyclic pathway uses only
photosystem I; photosystem II is not involved. In the cyclic pathway, sunlight hits P700,
thus exciting the electrons and passing them from P700 to its primary electron acceptor. It
is called the *cyclic pathway* because these electrons pass down the electron chain and eventually back to P700 to complete the cycle. The energy given off during the passage down the
chain is harnessed to produce ATP—the only product of this pathway. Neither oxygen nor
NADPH is produced from these reactions.

   A question that might be forming as you read this is: "Why does this pathway continue
to exist?" or perhaps you are wondering "Why do they insist on torturing me by writing
about all of this photosynthesis stuff?" We will answer the first question and ignore the
second one. The cyclic pathway exists because the Calvin cycle, which we discuss next, uses
more ATP than it does NADPH. This eventually causes a problem because the light reactions produce equal amounts of ATP and NADPH. The plant compensates for this disparity
by dropping into the cyclic phase when needed to produce the ATP necessary to keep the
light-independent reactions from grinding to a halt.

   Before moving on to the Calvin cycle, it is important to understand how ATP is
formed. We know, we know . . . you thought we were finished . . . but we want you to be
an expert in the field of photosynthesis. You never know when these facts might come in
handy. For example, just the other day one of us was offered $10,000 by a random person
on the street to recount the similarities between photosynthesis and respiration. So, this
stuff *is* useful in everyday life. As the electrons are passing from the primary electron acceptor to the next photosystem, hydrogen ions are picked up from outside the membrane and

brought back into the thylakoid compartment, creating an H⁺ gradient similar to what we saw in oxidative phosphorylation. During the light-dependent reactions, when hydrogen ions are taken from water during photolysis, the proton gradient grows larger, causing some protons to leave, leading to the formation of ATP.

You'll notice that this process in plants is a bit different from oxidative phosphorylation of the mitochondria, where the proton gradient is created by pumping protons from the matrix *out* to the intermembrane space. In the mitochondria, the ATP is produced when the protons move back *in*. But in plants, photophosphorylation creates the gradient by pumping protons in from the stroma to the thylakoid compartment, and the ATP is produced as the protons move back *out*. The opposing reactions produce the same happy result—more ATP for the cells.

## Light-Independent Reactions (Calvin Cycle)

After the light reactions have produced the necessary ATP and NADPH, the synthesis phase of photosynthesis is ready to proceed. The inputs into the Calvin cycle are NADPH (which provides hydrogen and electrons), ATP (which provides energy), and $CO_2$. From here on, just so we don't drive you *insane* switching from term to term, we are going to call the dark reactions of photosynthesis the *Calvin cycle* (Figure 8.4). The Calvin cycle occurs

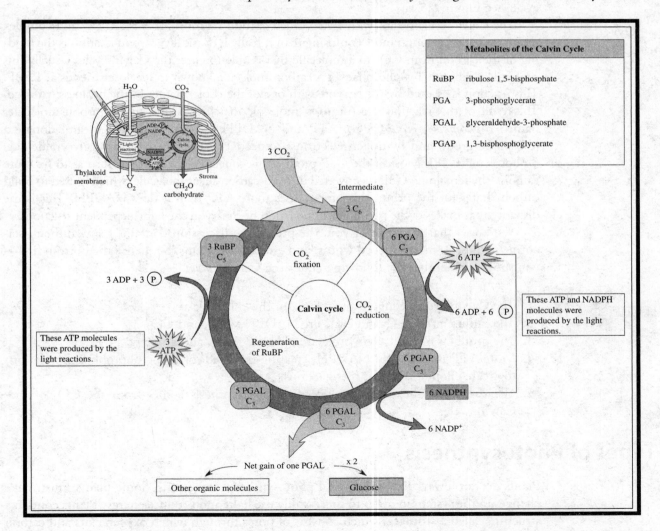

**Figure 8.4  The Calvin cycle.** (*From* Biology, *8th ed., by Sylvia S. Mader, © 1985, 1987, 1990, 1993, 1996, 1998, 2001, 2004 by the McGraw Hill Companies, Inc. Reproduced with permission of The McGraw-Hill Companies.*)

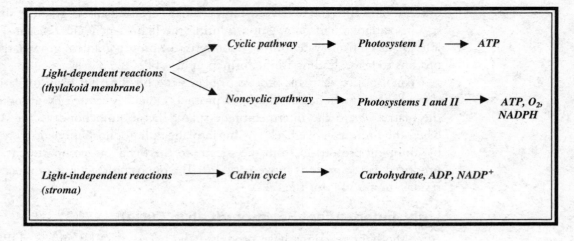

**Figure 8.5 Summary of photosynthesis.**

in the stroma of the chloroplast, which is the fluid surrounding the thylakoid "poker chips." (For further distinctions among the cyclic pathway, the noncyclic pathway, and the Calvin cycle, see Figure 8.5.)

The Calvin cycle begins with a step called **carbon fixation.** This is a tricky and complex term that makes it sound more confusing than it really is. Basically, carbon fixation is the binding of the carbon from $CO_2$ to a molecule that is able to enter the Calvin cycle. Usually this molecule is ribulose bis-phosphate, a 5-carbon molecule known to its closer friends as RuBP. This reaction is assisted by the enzyme with one of the cooler names in the business: **rubisco.** The result of this reaction is a 6-carbon molecule that breaks into two 3-carbon molecules named *3-phosphoglycerate* (3PG). ATP and NADPH step up at this point and donate a phosphate group and hydrogen electrons, respectively, to (3PG) to form glyceraldehyde 3-phosphate (G3P). Most of the G3P produced is converted back to RuBP so as to fix more carbon. The remaining G3P is converted into a 6-carbon sugar molecule, which is used to build carbohydrates for the plant. This process uses more ATP than it does NADPH. This is the disparity that makes cyclic photophosphorylation necessary in the light-dependent reactions.

We know that for some of you, the preceding discussion contains many difficult scientific names, strangely spelled words, and esoteric acronyms. So, here's the bottom line—you should remember the following about the Calvin cycle:

1. The Calvin cycle occurs in the stroma of the chloroplast.
2. The inputs into the Calvin cycle are NADPH, ATP, and $CO_2$.
3. The products of the Calvin cycle are $NADP^+$, ADP, and a sugar.
4. More ATP is used than NADPH, creating the need for cyclic photophosphorylation to create enough ATP for the reactions.
5. The carbon of the sugar produced in photosynthesis comes from the $CO_2$ of the Calvin cycle.

# Types of Photosynthesis

Plants do not always live under ideal photosynthetic conditions. Some plants must make changes to the system in order to successfully use light and produce energy. Plants contain a structure called a **stomata,** which consists of pores through which oxygen exits and carbon dioxide enters the leaf to be used in photosynthesis. **Transpiration** is the natural process by which plants lose water by evaporation from their leaves. When the temperature is very high, plants have to worry about excess transpiration. This is a potential problem for plants because they need the water to continue the process of photosynthesis. To combat this evaporation problem, plants must close their stomata to conserve water. But this solution leads to two different problems: (1) how will they bring in the $CO_2$ required for photosynthesis? and (2) what will the plants do with the excess $O_2$ that builds up when the stomata are closed?

When plants close their stomata to protect against water loss, they experience a shortage of $CO_2$, and the oxygen produced from the light reactions is unable to leave the plant. This excess oxygen competes with the carbon dioxide and attaches to RuBP in a reaction called **photorespiration.** This results in the formation of one molecule of PGA and one molecule of phosphoglycolate. This is not an ideal reaction because the sugar formed in photosynthesis comes from the PGA, not phosphoglycolate. As a result, plants that experience photorespiration have a lowered capacity for growth. Photorespiration tends to occur on hot, dry days when the stomata of the plant are closed.

A group of plants called **$C_4$ plants** combat photorespiration by altering the first step of their Calvin cycle. Normally, carbon fixation produces two 3-carbon molecules. In $C_4$ plants, the carbon fixation step produces a 4-carbon molecule called **oxaloacetate.** This molecule is converted into malate and sent from the mesophyll cells to the bundle sheath cells, where the $CO_2$ is used to build sugar. The **mesophyll** is the tissue of the interior of the leaf, and **mesophyll cells** are cells that contain bunches of chloroplasts. **Bundle sheath cells** are cells that are tightly wrapped around the veins of a leaf. They are the site for the Calvin cycle in $C_4$ plants.

What is the difference between $C_3$ plants and $C_4$ plants? One difference is that $C_4$ plants have two different types of photosynthetic cells: (1) tightly packed bundle sheath cells, which surround the vein of the leaf, and (2) mesophyll cells. Another difference involves the first product of carbon fixation. For $C_3$ plants, it is PGA, for $C_4$ plants, it is oxaloacetate. $C_4$ plants are able to successfully perform photosynthesis in these hot areas because of the presence of an enzyme called PEP (*phosphoenolpyruvate*) *carboxylase*. This enzyme really wants to bind to $CO_2$ and is not tricked by the devious oxygen into using it instead of the necessary $CO_2$. PEP carboxylase prefers to pair up with $CO_2$ rather than $O_2$, and this cuts down on photorespiration for $C_4$ plants. The conversion of PEP to oxaloacetate occurs in the mesophyll cells; then, after being converted into malate, PEP is shipped to the bundle sheath cells. These cells contain the enzymes of photosynthesis, including our good pal rubisco. The malate releases the $CO_2$, which is then used by rubisco to perform the reactions of photosynthesis. This process counters the problem of photorespiration because the shuttling of $CO_2$ from the mesophyll cells to the bundle sheath cells keeps the $CO_2$ concentration high enough so that it is not beat out by oxygen for rubisco's love and attention.

One last variation of photosynthesis that we should look at is the function performed by **CAM** (Crassulacean acid metabolizing) plants—water-storing plants, such as cacti, that close their stomata by day and open them by night to avoid transpiration during the hot days, without depleting the plant's $CO_2$ reserves. The $CO_2$ taken in during the night is stored as organic acids in the vacuoles of mesophyll cells until daybreak when the stomata close. The Calvin cycle is able to proceed during the day because the stored $CO_2$ is released, as needed, from the organic acids to be incorporated into the sugar product of the Calvin cycle.

To sum up these two variations of photosynthesis:

*$C_4$ photosynthesis:* photosynthetic process that first converts $CO_2$ into a 4-carbon molecule in the mesophyll cells, converts that product to malate, and then shuttles the malate into the bundle sheath cells. There, malate releases $CO_2$, which reacts with rubisco to produce the carbohydrate product of photosynthesis.

*CAM photosynthesis:* plants close their stomata during the day, collect $CO_2$ at night, and store the $CO_2$ in the form of acids until it is needed during the day for photosynthesis.

## ❯ Review Questions

Questions 1–4 refer to the following answer choices—use each answer only once.

   A.  Transpiration
   B.  Calvin cycle
   C.  CAM photosynthesis
   D.  Cyclic photophosphorylation

1. Plants use this process so that they can open their stomata at night and close their stomata during the day to avoid water loss during the hot days, without depleting the plant's $CO_2$ reserves.

2. Uses NADPH, ATP, and $CO_2$ as the inputs to its reactions.

3. Photosynthetic process that has ATP as its sole product. There is no oxygen and no NADPH produced from these reactions.

4. The process by which plants lose water via evaporation through their leaves.

5. The photosynthetic process performed by some plants in an effort to survive the hot and dry conditions of climates such as the desert is called

   A.  carbon fixation.
   B.  $C_3$ photosynthesis.
   C.  $C_4$ photosynthesis.
   D.  cyclic photophosphorylation.

6. Which of the following is the photosynthetic stage that produces oxygen?

   A.  The light-dependent reactions
   B.  Chemiosmosis
   C.  The Calvin cycle
   D.  Carbon fixation

7. Which of the following reactions occur in both cellular respiration and photosynthesis?

   A.  Carbon fixation
   B.  Fermentation
   C.  Reduction of NADP$^+$
   D.  Chemiosmosis

8. Which of the following is *not* a product of the light-dependent reactions of photosynthesis?

   A.  $O_2$
   B.  ATP
   C.  NADPH
   D.  Sugar

9. Which of the following is an advantage held by a $C_4$ plant?

   A.  More efficient light absorption
   B.  More efficient photolysis
   C.  More efficient carbon fixation
   D.  More efficient uptake of carbon dioxide into the stomata

10. Carbon dioxide enters the plant through the

   A.  Stomata
   B.  Stroma
   C.  Thylakoid membrane
   D.  Bundle sheath cell

11. Which of the following is the source of the oxygen released during photosynthesis?

   A.  $CO_2$
   B.  $H_2O$
   C.  Rubisco
   D.  PEP carboxylase

12. Which of the following is an *incorrect* statement about the Calvin cycle?

   A. The main inputs to the reactions are NADPH, ATP, and $CO_2$.
   B. The main outputs of the reactions are $NADP^+$, ADP, and sugar.
   C. More NADPH is used than ATP during the Calvin cycle.
   D. Carbon fixation is the first step of the process.

13. Which of the following is the source of the carbon in sugar produced during photosynthesis?

   A. $CO_2$
   B. $H_2O$
   C. Rubisco
   D. PEP carboxylase

14. The light-dependent reactions of photosynthesis occur in the

   A. stroma.
   B. mitochondrial matrix.
   C. thylakoid membrane.
   D. cytoplasm.

## › Answers and Explanations

1. **C**—CAM plants open their stomata at night and close their stomata during the day to avoid water loss due to heat. The carbon dioxide taken in during the night is incorporated into organic acids and stored in vacuoles until the next day, when the stomata close and $CO_2$ is needed for the Calvin cycle.

2. **B**—The Calvin cycle uses ATP, NADPH, and $CO_2$ to produce the desired sugar output of photosynthesis.

3. **D**—Cyclic photophosphorylation occurs because the Calvin cycle uses more ATP than it does NADPH. This is a problem because the light reactions produce an equal amount of ATP and NADPH. The plant compensates for this disparity by dropping into the cyclic phase when needed to produce the ATP necessary to keep the light-independent reactions from grinding to a halt.

4. **A**—Transpiration is the process by which plants lose water through their leaves. Not much else to be said about that. ☺

5. **C**—One of the major problems encountered by plants in hot and dry conditions is of photorespiration. In hot conditions, plants close their stomata to avoid losing water to transpiration. The problem with this is that the plants run low on $CO_2$ and fill with $O_2$. The oxygen competes with the carbon dioxide and attaches to RuBP, leaving the plant with a lowered capacity for growth. $C_4$ plants cycle $CO_2$ from mesophyll cells to bundle sheath cells, creating a higher concentration of $CO_2$ in that region, thus allowing rubisco to carry out the Calvin cycle without being distracted by the $O_2$ competitor.

6. **A**—The light-dependent reactions are the source of the oxygen given off by plants.

7. **D**—Chemiosmosis occurs in both photosynthesis and cellular respiration. This is the process by which the formation of ATP is driven by electrochemical gradients in the cell. Hydrogen ions accumulate on one side of a membrane, creating a proton gradient that causes them to move through channels to the other side of that membrane, thus leading, with the assistance of ATP synthase, to the production of ATP.

8. **D**—Sugar is a product not of the light-dependent reactions of photosynthesis but of the Calvin cycle (the dark reactions). The outputs of the light-dependent reactions are ATP, NADPH, and $O_2$.

9. **C**—$C_4$ plants fix carbon more efficiently than do $C_3$ plants. Please see answer 5 above for a more detailed explanation of this answer.

10. **A**—The stomata is the structure through which the $CO_2$ enters a plant and the oxygen produced in the light-dependent reactions leaves the plant.

11. **B**—The source of the oxygen produced during photosynthesis is the water that is split by the process of photolysis during the light-dependent reactions of photosynthesis. In this reaction, two hydrogen ions and an oxygen atom are formed from the water. The oxygen atom immediately finds and pairs up with another oxygen atom to form the oxygen product of the light-dependent reactions.

12. **C**—This is a trick question. We reversed the two compounds (NADPH and ATP) in this one. More ATP than NADPH is used in the Calvin cycle. It is for this reason that cyclic photophosphorylation exists—to produce ATP to make up for this disparity.

13. **A**—The carbon of $CO_2$ is used to produce the sugar created during the Calvin cycle.

14. **C**—The light-dependent reactions occur in the thylakoid membrane of the chloroplast. Remember, the thylakoid system resembles the various stacks of poker chips located within the stroma of the chloroplast. The light-independent reactions occur in the stroma of the chloroplast.

## ❯ Rapid Review

The following terms should be thoroughly familiar to you:

*Photosynthesis*: process by which plants use the energy from light to generate sugar.

- Occurs in chloroplasts
- Light reactions (thylakoid)
- Calvin cycle (stroma)

*Autotroph*: self-nourishing organism that is also known as a *producer* (plants).

*Heterotroph*: organisms that must consume other organisms to obtain energy—*consumers* (humans).

*Transpiration*: loss of water via evaporation through the stomata (natural process).

*Photophosphorylation*: process by which ATP is made during light reactions.

*Photolysis*: process by which water is split into hydrogen ions and oxygen atoms (light reactions).

*Stomata*: structure through which $CO_2$ enters a plant, and water vapor and oxygen leave a plant.

*Pigment*: molecule that absorbs light of a particular wavelength (chlorophyll, carotenoid, phycobilins).

There are three types of photosynthesis reactions:

*(Noncyclic) light-dependent reactions*

- Occur in thylakoid membrane of chloroplast.

- Inputs are light and water.

- Light strikes photosystem II (P680).

- Electrons pass along until they reach primary electron acceptor.

- Photolysis occurs—$H_2O$ is split to $H^+$ and $O_2$.

- Electrons pass down an ETC to P700 (photosystem I), forming ATP by chemiosmosis.

- Electrons of P700 pass down another ETC to produce NADPH.

- Three products of light reactions are NADPH, ATP, and $O_2$.

- Oxygen produced comes from $H_2O$.

*(Cyclic) light-dependent reactions*

- Occur in thylakoid membrane.

- Only involves photosystem I; no photosystem II.

- ATP is the only product of these reactions.

- No NADPH or oxygen are produced.

- These reactions exist because the Calvin cycle uses more ATP than NADPH; this is how the difference is made up.

*Light-independent reactions (Calvin cycle)*

- Occurs in stroma of chloroplast.

- Inputs are NADPH, ATP, and $CO_2$.

- First step is carbon fixation, which is catalyzed by an enzyme named rubisco.

- A series of reactions lead to the production of $NADP^+$, ADP, and sugar.

- More ATP is used than NADPH, which creates the need for the cyclic light reactions.

- The carbon of the sugar product comes from $CO_2$.

Also:

$C_4$ *plants*—plants that have adapted their photosynthetic process to more efficiently handle hot and dry conditions.

$C_4$ *photosynthesis*—process that first converts $CO_2$ into a 4-carbon molecule in the mesophyll cells, converts *that* product to malate, and then shuttles it to the bundle sheath cells, where the malate releases $CO_2$ and rubisco picks it up as if all were normal.

*CAM plants*—plants that close their stomata during the day, collect $CO_2$ at night, and store the $CO_2$ in the form of acids until it is needed during the day for photosynthesis.

# CHAPTER 9

# Cell Division

**IN THIS CHAPTER**

**Summary:** This chapter teaches you what you need to know about cell division in prokaryotes (binary fission), the cell cycle, and cell division in eukaryotes (mitosis and meiosis). In addition, it discusses the life cycles of various organisms.

**Key Ideas**

- ✪ There are four main stages in the cell cycle—$G_1$, S, $G_2$, and M.
- ✪ The stages of mitosis are: prophase, metaphase, anaphase, telophase, and cytokinesis.
- ✪ Crossing over occurs during prophase I of meiosis.
- ✪ Examples of cell division control mechanisms: growth factors, checkpoints, density-dependent inhibition, and cyclins/protein kinases.
- ✪ Sources of cell variation: crossover, $2^n$ possible gametes, and random pairing of gametes.

## Introduction

Cell division, the process by which cells produce more of their kind, can occur in several ways. In this chapter, we discuss cell division in prokaryotes (binary fission), the cell cycle, and cell division in eukaryotes (mitosis and meiosis). After comparing mitosis and meiosis, we will touch on the life cycles of various organisms.

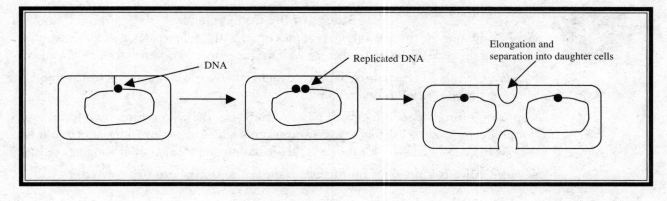

Figure 9.1    Binary fission.

# Cell Division in Prokaryotes

Prokaryotes are simple single-celled organisms without a nucleus. Their genetic material is arranged in a single circular chromosome of DNA, which is anchored to the cell membrane. As in eukaryotes, the genetic material of prokaryotes is duplicated before division. However, instead of entering into a complex cycle for cell division, prokaryotes simply elongate until they are double their original size. At this point, the cell pinches in and separates into two identical daughter cells in a process known as **binary fission** (Figure 9.1).

# The Cell Cycle

> **BIG IDEA 3.A.2**
>
> *In eukaryotes, information is passed to the next generation via the cell cycle.*

Eukaryotic cell reproduction is a bit more complicated. The cell cycle functions as the daily planner of growth and development for the eukaryotic cell. It tells the cell when and in what order it is going to do things, and consists of all the necessary steps required for the reproduction of a cell. It begins after the creation of the cell and concludes with the formation of two daughter cells through cell division. It then begins again for the two daughter cells that have just been formed. There are four main stages to the cell cycle, and they occur in the following sequence: **phases $G_1$, $S$, $G_2$,** and **M** (Figure 9.2). Phases $G_1$ and $G_2$ are growth stages; S is the part of the cell cycle during which the DNA is duplicated; and the M phase stands for mitosis, the cell division phase.

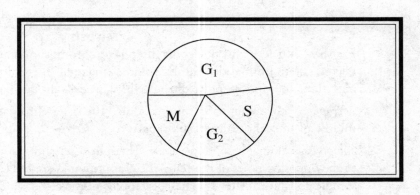

Figure 9.2    Pie chart showing the four main stages of the cell cycle.

### Stages of the Cell Cycle

*$G_1$ phase.* During the first growth phase of the cell cycle, the cell prepares itself for the synthesis stage of the cycle, making sure that it has all the necessary raw materials for DNA synthesis.

*S phase.* The DNA is copied so that each daughter cell has a complete set of chromosomes at the conclusion of the cell cycle.

*$G_2$ phase.* During the second growth phase of the cycle, the cell prepares itself for mitosis (for producing body cells) and/or meiosis (for producing gametes), making sure that it has the raw materials necessary for the physical separation and formation of daughter cells.

*M phase.* Mitosis is the stage during which the cell separates into two new cells.

The first three stages of the cycle ($G_1$, S, and $G_2$) make up the portion of the cell cycle known as **interphase.** A cell spends approximately 90 percent of its cycle in this phase. The other 10 percent is spent in the final stage, mitosis.

The amount of time that a cell requires to complete a cycle varies by cell type. Some cells complete a full cycle in hours, while others can take days to finish. The rapidity with which cells replicate also varies. Skin cells are continually zipping along through the cell cycle, whereas nerve cells do not replicate—once they are damaged, they are lost for good. This is one reason why the death of nerve cells is such a problem—these cells cannot be repaired or regenerated through mitotic replication.

## Mitosis

During mitosis, the fourth stage of the cell cycle, the cell actually takes the second copy of DNA made during the S phase and divides it equally between two cells. Single-cell eukaryotes undergo mitosis for the purpose of asexual reproduction. More complex multicellular eukaryotes use mitosis for other processes as well, such as growth and repair.

Mitosis consists of four major stages: prophase, metaphase, anaphase, and telophase. These stages are immediately followed by **cytokinesis**—the physical separation of the newly formed daughter cells. During interphase, chromosomes are invisible. The **chromatin**—the raw material that gives rise to the chromosomes—is long and thin during this phase. When the chromatin condenses to the point where the chromosome becomes visible through a microscope, the cell is said to have begun mitosis. The AP Biology exam is not going to ask you detailed questions about the different stages of mitosis; just have a *general* understanding of what happens during each step.

### Mitosis

*Prophase.* Nucleus and nucleolus disappear; chromosomes appear as two identical, connected sister chromatids; mitotic spindle (made of microtubules) begins to form; centrioles move to opposite poles of the cell (plant cells do not have centrioles).

*Metaphase.* For metaphase, think middle. The sister chromatids line up along the middle of the cell, ready to split apart.

*Anaphase.* For anaphase, think apart. The split sister chromatids move via the microtubules to the opposing poles of the cell—the chromosomes are pulled to opposite poles by the spindle apparatus. After anaphase, each pole of the cell has a complete set of chromosomes.

*Telophase.* The nuclei for the newly split cells form; the nucleoli reappear, and the chromatin uncoils.

*Cytokinesis.* Newly formed daughter cells split apart. Animal cells are split by the formation of a cleavage furrow, plant cells by the formation of a cell plate.

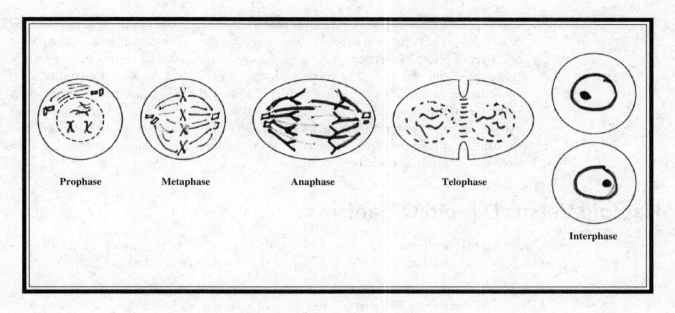

Prophase    Metaphase    Anaphase    Telophase    Interphase

**Figure 9.3    The stages of mitosis.**

Figure 9.3 is a pictorial representation of the stages of mitosis.

Here are the definitions for words you may need to know:

*Cell plate:* plant cell structure, constructed in the Golgi apparatus, composed of vesicles that fuse together along the middle of the cell, completing the separation process.

*Cleavage furrow:* groove formed (in animal cells) between the two daughter cells that pinches together to complete the separation of the two cells after mitosis.

*Cytokinesis:* the actual splitting of the newly formed daughter cells that completes each trip around the cell cycle—some consider it part of mitosis; others regard it as the step immediately following mitosis.

*Mitotic spindle:* apparatus constructed from microtubules that assists the cell in the physical separation of the chromosomes during mitosis.

# Control of Cell Division

Control of the cell cycle is important to normal cell growth. There are various ways in which the cell controls the process of cell division:

*Sam (12th grader): "Control mechanisms are an important theme for this test. Be able to write about them."*

1. *Checkpoints.* There are checkpoints throughout the cell cycle where the cell verifies that there are enough nutrients and raw materials to progress to the next stage of the cycle. The $G_1$ checkpoint, for example, makes sure that the cell has enough raw materials to progress to and successfully complete the S phase.
2. *Density-dependent inhibition.* When a certain density of cells is reached, growth of the cells will slow or stop because there are not enough raw materials for the growth and survival of more cells. Cells that are halted by this inhibition enter a quiescent phase of the cell cycle known as $G_0$. Cancer cells can lose this inhibition and grow out of control.
3. *Growth factors.* Some cells will not divide if certain factors are absent. Growth factors, as their name indicates, assist in the growth of structures.

4. *Cyclins and protein kinases.* **Cyclin** is a protein that accumulates during $G_1$, S, and $G_2$ of the cell cycle. A **protein kinase** is a protein that controls other proteins through the addition of phosphate groups. Cyclin-dependent kinase (CDK) is present at all times throughout the cell cycle and binds with cyclin to form a complex known as MPF (maturation or mitosis promoting factor). Early in the cell cycle, because the cyclin concentration is low, the concentration of MPF is also low. As the concentration of cyclin reaches a certain threshold level, enough MPF is formed to push the cell into mitosis. As mitosis proceeds, the level of cyclin declines, decreasing the amount of MPF present and pulling the cell out of mitosis.

# Haploid Versus Diploid Organisms

One thing that is often a major source of confusion for some of my students is the distinction between being haploid and being diploid. Let's start with a definition of the terms:

A *haploid* (*n*) organism is one that has only one copy of each type of chromosome. In humans, this refers to a cell that has one copy of each type of homologous chromosome.

A *diploid* (2*n*) organism is one that has two copies of each type of chromosome. In humans, this refers to the pairs of homologous chromosomes.

During the discussion of meiosis below, the terms *haploid* and *diploid* will be used often. Whenever we say "2*n*," or diploid, we are referring to an organism that contains two full *sets* of chromosomes. The letter *n* is used to represent the number of sets of chromosomes. So if an organism is said to have 4*n* chromosomes, this means that it has four complete sets of chromosomes. Humans are diploid, and consist of 2*n* chromosomes at all times except as gametes, when they are *n*. Humans have 23 *different* chromosomes; there are two full *sets* of these 23 chromosomes, one from each parent, for a total of 46 chromosomes. Human sex cells have 23 chromosomes each.

# Meiosis

Now that we have armed you with the knowledge of the distinction between haploid and diploid, it is time to dive into the topic of meiosis, which occurs during the process of sexual reproduction. A cell destined to undergo meiosis goes through the cell cycle, synthesizing a second copy of DNA just like mitotic cells. But after $G_2$, the cell instead enters meiosis, which consists of *two* cell divisions, not one. The second cell division exists because the gametes to be formed from meiosis must be haploid. This is because they are going to join with another haploid gamete at conception to produce the diploid zygote. Meiosis is like a two-part made-for-TV miniseries. It has two acts: meiosis I and meiosis II. Each of these two acts is divided into four steps, reminiscent of mitosis: prophase, metaphase, anaphase, and telophase.

**Homologous chromosomes** resemble one another in shape, size, function, and the genetic information they contain. In humans, the 46 chromosomes are divided into 23 homologous pairs. One member of each pair comes from an individual's mother, and the other member comes from the father. Meiosis I is the separation of the homologous pairs into two separate cells. Meiosis II is the separation of the duplicated sister chromatids into chromosomes. As a result, a single meiotic cycle produces *four* cells from a single cell. The cells produced during meiosis in the human life cycle are called **gametes.**

Again, the AP Biology exam is not going to test your mastery of the minute details of the meiotic process. However, a general understanding of the various steps is important:

## Meiosis I

*Prophase I.* Each chromosome pairs with its homolog. Crossover (synapsis) occurs in this phase. The nuclear envelope breaks apart, and spindle apparatus begins to form.

*Metaphase I.* Chromosomes align along the metaphase plate matched with their homologous partner. This stage ends with the separation of the homologous pairs.

*Anaphase I.* Separated homologous pairs move to opposite poles of the cell.

*Telophase I.* Nuclear membrane reforms; the process of cytoplasmic division begins.

*Cytokinesis.* After the daughter cells split, the two newly formed cells are haploid (*n*).

As discussed earlier, meiosis consists of a single synthesis period during which the DNA is replicated, followed by two acts of cell division. With the completion of the first cell division, meiosis I, the cells are haploid because they no longer consist of two full *sets* of chromosomes. Each cell has one of the duplicated chromatid pairs from each homologous pair. The cell then enters meiosis II.

## Meiosis II

*Prophase II.* The nuclear envelope breaks apart, and spindle apparatus begins to form.

*Metaphase II.* Sister chromatids line up along the equator of the cell.

*Anaphase II.* Sister chromatids split apart and are called *chromosomes* as they are pulled to the poles.

*Telophase II.* The nuclei and the nucleoli for the newly split cells return.

*Cytokinesis.* Newly formed daughter cells physically divide.

Figure 9.4 is a pictorial representation of the stages of meiosis I and II.

**Figure 9.4    The stages of meiosis.**

In humans, the process of gamete formation is different in women and men. In men, **spermatogenesis** leads to the production of four haploid sperm during each meiotic cycle. In women, the process is called **oogenesis.** It is a trickier process than spermatogenesis, and each complete meiotic cycle leads to the production of a single ovum, or egg. After meiosis I in females, one cell receives half the genetic information and the majority of the cytoplasm of the parent cell. The other cell, the **polar body,** simply receives half of the genetic information and is cast away. During meiosis II, the remaining cell divides a second time, and forms a polar body that is cast away, and a single haploid ovum that contains half the genetic information and nearly all the cytoplasm of the original parent cell. The excess cytoplasm is required for proper growth of the embryo after fertilization. Thus, the process of oogenesis produces two polar bodies and a single haploid ovum.

To review, why is it important to produce haploid gametes during meiosis? During fertilization, a sperm ($n$) will meet up with an egg ($n$), to produce a diploid zygote ($2n$). If either the sperm or the egg were diploid, then the offspring produced during sexual reproduction would contain more chromosomes than the parent organism. Meiosis circumvents this problem by producing gametes that are haploid and consist of one copy of each type of chromosome. During fertilization between two gametes, each copy will match up with another copy of each type of chromosome to form the diploid zygote.

Before moving on, there are a few important distinctions between meiosis and mitosis that should be emphasized.

|  | **MITOSIS** | **MEIOSIS** |
|---|---|---|
| Resulting daughter cells | Two diploid ($2n$) daughter cells | Four haploid ($n$) daughter cells |
| Crossover? | No | Yes—prophase I |
| Types of cells in which it occurs for humans | All cells of the body other than the cells of the gonads | Cells of gonads to produce gametes |

In meiosis during prophase I, the homologous pairs join together. This matching of chromosomes into homologous pairs does not occur in mitosis. In mitosis, the 46 chromosomes simply align along the metaphase plate alone.

An event of major importance that occurs during meiosis that does not occur during mitosis is known as **crossover** (also known as *crossing over*) (Figure 9.5). When the homologous pairs match up during prophase I of meiosis, complementary pieces from the two homologous chromosomes wrap around each other and are exchanged between the chromosomes. Imagine that chromosome A is the homologous partner for chromosome B. When they pair up during prophase I, a piece of chromosome A containing a certain stretch

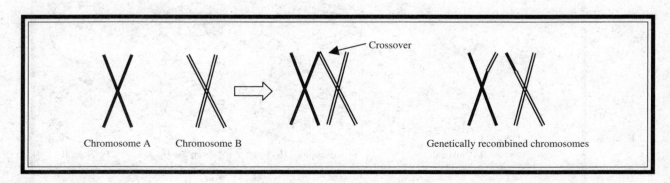

**Figure 9.5   Crossover.**

of genes can be exchanged for the piece of chromosome B containing the same genetic information. This is one of the mechanisms that allows offspring to differ from their parents. Remember that crossing over occurs between the homologous chromosome pairs, *not* the sister chromatids.

## Life Cycles

The AP Biology exam characteristically will ask a question or two about the various types of life cycles for plants, animals, and fungi. A **life cycle** is the sequence of events that make up the reproductive cycle of an organism. Let's take a quick look at the three main life cycles.

The most complicated life cycle of the three is that of plants, also called the **alternation of generations** (Figure 9.6). It is referred to by this term because during the life cycle, plants sometimes exist as a diploid organism and at other times as a haploid organism. It alternates between the two forms. Similar to the other life cycles, two haploid gametes combine to form a diploid zygote, which divides *mitotically* to produce the diploid multicellular stage: the **sporophyte.** The sporophyte undergoes *meiosis* to produce a haploid spore. *Mitotic division* leads to the production of haploid multicellular organisms called **gametophytes.** The gametophyte undergoes *mitosis* to produce haploid gametes, which combine to form diploid zygotes . . . and around and around they go.

The human life cycle (Figure 9.7) is pretty straightforward. The only haploid cells present in this life cycle are the gametes formed during meiosis. The two haploid gametes combine during fertilization to produce a diploid zygote. Mitotic division then leads to formation of

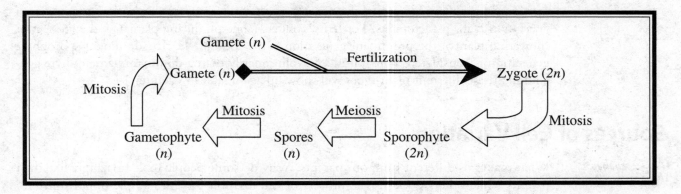

**Figure 9.6    Plant life: alternation of generations.**

**Figure 9.7    Human life cycle.**

**Figure 9.8   Fungus life cycle.**

the diploid multicellular organism. Meiotic division later produces haploid gametes, which continue the cycle.

The life cycle of fungi (Figure 9.8) is different from that of humans. Fungi are haploid organisms, with the zygote being the only diploid form. Like humans, the gametes for fungi are haploid (*n*), and fertilization yields a diploid zygote. But in this life cycle, instead of dividing by mitosis, the zygote divides by meiosis to form a haploid organism. Another difference in this life cycle is that the gametes are formed by *mitosis,* not meiosis—the organism is *already* haploid, before forming the gametes.

Here is some trivia about life cycles that might come in handy on the exam. The only diploid stage for a fungus is the zygote. The only haploid stage for a human is the gamete. Of the plant life cycles, the moss (bryophyte) is an exception in that its prominent generation is the gametophyte. For ferns, conifers (cone-producing plants), and angiosperms (flowering plants), the prominent generation is the sporophyte. The dominant sporophyte generation is considered more advanced evolutionarily than a dominant gametophyte generation. These different plant types will show up again later in Chapter 14.

# Sources of Cell Variation

*NYC teacher: "Knowing the sources of variation is important."*

**BIG IDEA 3.C.2**

*Crossing over and random assortment during meiosis increase variation.*

What makes us different from our parents? Why do some people look amazingly like their parents while others do not? The process of cell division provides ample opportunity for variation. Remember that during meiosis, homologous chromosome pairs align together along the metaphase plate. This alignment is a completely random process, and there is a 50 percent chance that the chromosome in the pair from the individual's mother will go to one side, and a 50 percent chance that the chromosome in the pair from the individual's father will go to that side. This is true for all the homologous pairs in an organism. This means that $2^n$ possible gametes can form from any given set of *n* chromosomes. For example, in a 3-chromosome organism, there are $2^3 = 8$ possible gametes. In humans, there are 23 homologous pairs. This comes out to $2^{23}$ (8,388,608) different ways the gametes can separate during gametogenesis.

Another source of variation during sexual reproduction is the random determination of which sperm meets up with which ovum. In humans, the sperm represents one of $2^{23}$ possibilities from the male gamete factory; the ovum, one of $2^{23}$ possibilities from the female gamete factory. All these factors combine to explain why siblings may look nothing like each other.

A third major source of variation during gamete formation is the **crossover** (or *crossing over*) that occurs during prophase I of meiosis. It is very important for you to remember that this process happens *only* during that stage of cell division. It does not occur in mitosis.

# › Review Questions

1. Which of the following plant types has the gametophyte as its prominent generation?

   A. Angiosperms
   B. Bryophytes
   C. Conifers
   D. Gymnosperms

2. During which phase of the cell cycle does crossing over occur?

   A. Metaphase of mitosis
   B. Metaphase I of meiosis
   C. Prophase I of meiosis
   D. Prophase of mitosis

For questions 3–6, please use the following answer choices:

   A. Prophase
   B. Metaphase
   C. Anaphase
   D. Cytokinesis

3. During this phase, the split sister chromatids, now considered to be chromosomes, are moved to the opposite poles of the cell.

4. During this phase the nucleus deteriorates, and the mitotic spindle begins to form.

5. During this phase, the two daughter cells are actually split apart.

6. During this phase, the sister chromatids line up along the equator of the cell, preparing to split.

7. Which of the following organisms is diploid ($2n$) only as a zygote and is haploid for every other part of its life cycle?

   A. Humans
   B. Bryophytes
   C. Fungi
   D. Bacteria

8. Which of the following statements is true about a human meiotic cell after it has completed meiosis I?

   A. It is diploid ($2n$).
   B. It is haploid ($n$).
   C. It has divided into four daughter cells.
   D. It proceeds directly to meiosis II without an intervening intermission.

9. Which of the following is *not* true about cyclin-dependent kinase (CDK)?

   A. It is present only during the M phase of the cell cycle.
   B. When enough of it is combined with cyclin, the MPF (mitosis promoting factor) formed initiates mitosis.
   C. It is a protein that controls other proteins using phosphate groups.
   D. It is present at all times during the cell cycle.

10. Which of the following statements about meiosis and/or mitosis is incorrect?

   A. Mitosis results in two diploid daughter cells.
   B. Meiosis in humans occurs only in gonad cells.
   C. Homologous chromosomes line up along the metaphase plate during mitosis.
   D. Crossover occurs during prophase I of meiosis.

## › Answers and Explanations

1. **B**—Bryophytes, or mosses, are the plant type that has the gametophyte (haploid) as its dominant generation. The others in this question have the sporophyte (diploid) as their dominant generation.

2. **C**—Crossover occurs in humans only in prophase I. Prophase I is a major source of variation in the production of offspring.

3. **C**

4. **A**

5. **D**

6. **B**

7. **C**—The life cycle for fungi is different from that of humans. Fungi exist as haploid organisms, and the only time they exist in diploid form is as a zygote. Like humans, the gametes for fungi are haploid (*n*) and combine to form a diploid zygote. Unlike in humans, the fungus zygote divides by meiosis to form a haploid organism.

8. **B**—Human cells start with 46 chromosomes arranged in 23 pairs of homologous chromosomes. At this time they are 2*n* because they have two copies of each chromosome. After the S phase of the cell cycle, the DNA has been doubled in preparation for cell division. The first stage of meiosis pulls apart the homologous pairs of chromosomes. This means that after meiosis I, the cells are *n*, or haploid—they no longer consist of *two* full sets of chromosomes.

9. **A**—CDK is present at all times during the cell cycle. It combines with a protein called *cyclin*, which accumulates during interphase of the cell cycle, to form MPF. When enough MPF is formed, the cell is pushed to begin mitosis. As mitosis continues, cyclin is degraded, and when the concentration of MPF drops below a level sufficient to maintain mitotic division, mitosis grinds to a halt until the threshold is reached again next time around the cycle.

10. **C**—Answer choices A, B, and D, are all correct. C is incorrect because homologous pairs of chromosomes pair together only during meiosis. During mitosis, the sister chromatid pairs align along the metaphase plate, separate from the homologous counterpart.

## › Rapid Review

You should be familiar with the following terms:

*Binary fission*: prokaryotic cell division; double the DNA, double the size, then split apart.

*Cell cycle*: $G_1 \rightarrow S \rightarrow G_2 \rightarrow M$ should be familiar with the following growth$_1$ $\rightarrow$ synthesis $\rightarrow$ growth$_2$ $\rightarrow$ mitosis $\rightarrow$ etc.

*Interphase*: $G_1 + S + G_2 = 90$ percent of the cell cycle.

| STAGE | MITOSIS | MEIOSIS |
|---|---|---|
| Prophase | Nucleus, nucleolus disappear; mitotic spindle forms | — |
| Metaphase | Sister chromatids line up at middle | — |
| Anaphase | Sister chromatids are split apart | — |
| Telophase | Nuclei of new cells reform; chromatin uncoils | — |
| Prophase I | — | Each chromosome pairs with its homolog; there is crossover |

| STAGE | MITOSIS | MEIOSIS |
|-------|---------|---------|
| Metaphase I | — | Chromosome pairs align along middle of cell, ready to split apart |
| Anaphase I | — | Homologous chromosomes split apart |
| Telophase I | — | Nuclear membrane reforms; daughter cells are now haploid ($n$) |
| Prophase II | — | Nucleus disappears, spindle apparatus forms |
| Metaphase II | — | Sister chromatids line up at middle |
| Anaphase II | — | Sister chromatids are split apart |
| Telophase II | — | Nuclei of new cells reform; chromatin uncoils |

*Cytokinesis*: physical separation of newly formed daughter cells of cell division.

Cell division control mechanisms:

1. *Growth factors*: factors that when present, promote growth, and when absent, impede growth.
2. *Checkpoints*: a cell stops growing to make sure it has the nutrients and raw materials to proceed.
3. *Density-dependent inhibition*: cell stops growing when certain density is reached—runs out of food!!!
4. *Cyclins and protein kinases*: cyclin combines with CDK to form a structure known as MPF that pushes cell into mitosis when enough is present.

*Haploid* ($n$): one copy of each chromosome.

*Diploid* ($2n$): two copies of each chromosome.

*Homologous chromosomes*: chromosomes that are similar in shape, size, and function.

*Spermatogenesis*: the process of male gamete formation (four sperm from one cell).

*Oogenesis*: the process of female gamete formation (one ovum from each cell).

*Life cycles*: Sequence of events that make up the reproductive cycle of an organism.

- *Human*: zygote ($2n$) → multicellular organism ($2n$) → gametes ($n$) → zygote ($2n$)

- *Fungi*: zygote ($2n$) → multicellular organism ($n$) → gametes ($n$) → zygote ($2n$)

- *Plants*: zygote ($2n$) → sporophyte ($2n$) → spores ($n$) → gametophyte ($n$) → gametes ($n$) → zygote ($2n$)

*Sources of variation*: crossover, $2^n$ possible gametes that can be formed, random pairing of gametes.

# CHAPTER 10

# Heredity

## IN THIS CHAPTER

**Summary:** This chapter examines Mendel's fundamental laws (law of segregation, law of independent assortment, and law of dominance) as well as some classic exceptions to these laws (intermediate inheritance, multiple alleles, polygenic traits, epistasis, and pleiotropy). This chapter also covers linkage (sex linkage, gene linkage, and linkage maps), and chromosomal errors such as nondisjunction, deletions, duplications, translocations, and inversion.

### Key Ideas

- ✪ Law of segregation: the two alleles for a trait separate during the formation of gametes—one to each gamete.
- ✪ Law of independent assortment: inheritance of one trait does not interfere with the inheritance of another trait.
- ✪ Law of dominance: if two opposite pure-breeding varieties are crossed (BB × bb), all offspring resemble the BB parent.
- ✪ Linked genes that lie along the same chromosome do not follow the law of independent assortment.
- ✪ Autosomal recessive disorders: Tay-Sachs, cystic fibrosis, sickle cell anemia, phenylketonuria.
- ✪ Autosomal dominant disorders: Huntington, achondroplasia.
- ✪ Nondisjunction errors: Down, Klinefelter, Turner syndromes.

## Introduction

How many times have you heard someone say as they look at a baby, "Awwww, he looks like his daddy" or "She has her mother's eyes"? What exactly is it that causes an infant to look like his or her parents? This question is the basis of the study of heredity—the study of the passing of traits from generation to generation. Its basic premise is that offspring are more like their parents than less closely related individuals.

In this chapter, we begin by discussing some terms that will prove important to your study of heredity. This is followed by an examination of Mendel's *law of segregation* and the *law of independent assortment,* including how they were discovered and how they can be applied. We will examine the *law of dominance,* which arose from Mendel's work, and we will also discuss some exceptions to Mendel's fundamental laws such as intermediate inheritance (incomplete dominance and codominance), multiple alleles, polygenic traits, epistasis, and pleiotropy.

In the next section, we will examine Thomas Morgan's work on fruit flies, which paved the way for the discovery of linked genes, genetic recombination, and sex-linked inheritance. This discussion concludes with a look at gene linkage and linkage maps.

Finally, since chromosomes carry the vital genes necessary for proper development and passage of hereditary material from one generation to the next, it is important to discuss the types of chromosomal errors that can occur during reproduction. This includes the various forms of nondisjunction, or the improper separation of chromosomes during meiosis (which leads to an abnormal number of chromosomes in offspring). The chapter concludes with an examination of the other major types of chromosomal errors: deletions, duplications, translocations, and inversions.

## Terms Important in Studying Heredity

The following is a list of terms that will help in your understanding of heredity:

*Allele:* a variant of a gene for a particular character. For example, two alleles for fur color could be B (dominant) and b (recessive).

$F_1$: the first generation of offspring, or the first "filial" generation in a genetic cross.

$F_2$: the second generation of offspring, or the second "filial" generation in a genetic cross.

*Genotype:* an organism's genetic makeup for a given trait. A simple example of this could involve fur color where B represents the allele for brown and b represents the allele for black. The possible genotypes include homozygous brown (BB), heterozygous brown (Bb), and homozygous black (bb).

*Heterozygous (hybrid ):* an individual is heterozygous (or a hybrid) for a gene if the two alleles are different (Bb).

*Homozygous (pure):* an individual is homozygous for a gene if both of the given alleles are the same (BB or bb).

*Karyotype:* a chart that organizes chromosomes in relation to number, size, and type.

*Nondisjunction:* the improper separation of chromosomes during meiosis, which leads to an abnormal number of chromosomes in offspring. A few classic examples of nondisjunction-related syndromes are Down, Turner, and Klinefelter syndromes.

$P_1$: the parent generation in a genetic cross.

*Phenotype:* the physical expression of the trait associated with a particular genotype. Some examples of the phenotypes for Mendel's peas were round or wrinkled, green or yellow, purple flower or white flower.

# Mendel and His Peas

The person whose name is most often associated with heredity is Gregor Mendel. Mendel spent many years working with peas. It was a very strange hobby, indeed, but it proved quite useful to the world of science. He mated peas to produce offspring and recorded the phenotype results in order to determine how certain characters are inherited. A **character** is a genetically inherited characteristic that differs from person to person.

Before he began his work in the 1850s, the accepted theory of inheritance was the **"blending" hypothesis,** which stated that the genes contributed by two parents mix as colors do. For example, a blue flower mixed with a yellow flower would produce a green flower. The exact genetic makeup of each parent could never be recovered; the genes would be as inseparable as the blended colors. Mendel used plant experiments to test this hypothesis and developed his two fundamental theories: the law of segregation and the law of independent assortment.

When Mendel was observing a single character during a mating, he was doing something called a **monohybrid cross**—a cross that involves a single character in which both parents are heterozygous (Bb × Bb). A monohybrid cross between heterozygous gametes gives a 3:1 phenotype ratio in the offspring (Figure 10.1). As you can see in Figure 10.1, an offspring is three times more likely to express the dominant B trait than the recessive b trait.

|   | B | b |
|---|---|---|
| B | BB | Bb |
| b | Bb | bb |

**Figure 10.1    Monohybrid cross.**

Mendel also experimented with multiple characters simultaneously. The crossing of two different hybrid characters is termed a **dihybrid cross** (BbRr × BbRr). A dihybrid cross between heterozygous gametes gives a 9:3:3:1 phenotype ratio in the offspring (Figure 10.2).

|   | **BR** | **Br** | **bR** | **br** |
|---|--------|--------|--------|--------|
| BR | BBRR | BBRr | BbRR | BbRr |
| Br | BBRr | BBrr | BbRr | Bbrr |
| bR | BbRR | BbRr | bbRR | bbRr |
| br | BbRr | Bbrr | bbRr | bbrr |

**Figure 10.2  Dihybrid cross.**

From his experiments, Mendel developed two major hereditary laws: the law of segregation and the law of independent assortment.

*The law of segregation.* Every organism carries pairs of factors, called *alleles,* for each trait, and the members of the pair segregate (separate) during the formation of gametes. For example, if an individual is Bb for eye color, during gamete formation, one gamete would receive a B, and the other made from that cell would receive a b.

*The law of independent assortment.* Members of each pair of factors are distributed independently when the gametes are formed. Quite simply, inheritance of one trait or characteristic does not interfere with inheritance of another trait. For example, if an individual is BbRr for two genes, gametes formed during meiosis could contain BR, Br, bR, or br. The B and b alleles assort *independently* of the R and r alleles.

*The law of dominance.* Also based on Mendel's work, this states that when two opposite pure-breeding varieties (homozygous dominant vs. homozygous recessive) of an organism are crossed, all the offspring resemble one parent. This is referred to as the *dominant* trait. The variety that is hidden is referred to as the *recessive* trait.

It is time for you to answer a question for us (of course, we have no way of knowing whether or how you will answer this question): Can the phenotype of an organism be determined from simple observation? Yes—just look at the organism and determine whether it is tall or short, has blue eyes or brown eyes, and so on. However, the genotype of an organism *cannot* always be determined from simple observation. In the case of a recessive trait, the genotype is known. If a person has blue eyes (recessive to brown), the genotype is bb. But if that person has brown eyes, you cannot be sure if the genotype is Bb or BB—the individual can be either homozygous dominant or heterozygous dominant. To determine the exact genotype, you must run an experiment called a **test cross.** Geneticists breed the organism whose genotype is unknown with an organism that is homozygous recessive for the trait. This results in offspring with observable phenotypes. If the unknown genotype is heterozygous, probability indicates one-half of the offspring *should* express the recessive phenotype. If the unknown genotype is homozygous dominant, *all* the organism's offspring *should* express the dominant trait. Of course, such experiments are not done on humans.

**Remember me!**

Mendel discovered many statistical laws of heredity. He learned that a monohybrid cross such as Yy × Yy will result in a phenotype ratio of 3:1 in favor of the dominant trait. He learned that a dihybrid cross, such as YyRr × YyRr, will result in a phenotype ratio of 9:3:3:1 (9 RY, 3 rY, 3 Ry, 1 ry). These two ratios, when they appear in genetic analysis problems, imply mono- and dihybrid crosses.

# Intermediate Inheritance

*Marcy (college freshman): "Understanding this concept is worth 2 points on the exam."*

The inheritance of traits is not always as simple as Mendel's pea experiments seem to indicate. Traits are not always dominant or recessive, and phenotype ratios are not always 9:3:3:1 or 3:1. Mendel's experiments did not account for something called **intermediate inheritance,** in which an individual heterozygous for a trait (Yy) shows characteristics not exactly like *either* parent. The phenotype is a "mixture" of both of the parents' genetic input. There are two major types of intermediate inheritance:

1. Incomplete dominance or "blending inheritance"
2. Codominance

### Incomplete Dominance ("Blending Inheritance")

In **incomplete dominance** ("blending inheritance") the heterozygous genotype produces an "intermediate" phenotype rather than the dominant phenotype; neither allele dominates the other. A classic example of incomplete dominance is flower color in snapdragons— crossing a snapdragon plant that has red flowers with one that has white flowers yields offspring with pink flowers.

One genetic condition in humans that exhibits incomplete dominance is **hypercholesterolemia**—a recessive disorder (hh) that causes cholesterol levels to be many times higher than normal and can lead to heart attacks in children as young as two years old. Those who are HH tend to have normal cholesterol levels, and those who are Hh have cholesterol levels somewhere in between the two extremes. As with many conditions, the environment plays a major role in how genetic conditions express themselves. Thus, people who are HH do not necessarily have normal cholesterol levels if, for example, they have poor diet or exercise habits.

One important side note—try not to confuse the terms blending "hypothesis" and blending "inheritance." The latter is another name for incomplete dominance, whereas the former was the theory on heredity before Mendel worked his magic. The blending "hypothesis" says that the HH and hh extremes can never be retrieved. In reality, and according to blending inheritance, if you were to cross two Hh individuals, the offspring could still be HH or hh, which the blending "hypothesis" says cannot happen once the blending has occurred.

### Codominance

**Codominance** is the situation in which both alleles express themselves fully in a heterozygous organism. A good example of codominance involves the human blood groups: M, N, and MN. Individuals with group M blood have the M glycoprotein on the surface of the blood cell; individuals with group N blood have N glycoproteins on the blood cell; and those with group MN blood have *both*. This is not incomplete dominance because both alleles are fully expressed in the phenotype—they are codominant.

## Other Forms of Inheritance

### Polygenic Traits

Another interesting form of inheritance involves **polygenic traits,** or traits that are affected by more than one gene. Eye color is an example of a polygenic trait. The *tone* (color), *amount* (blue eyes have less than brown eyes), and *position* (how evenly distributed the pigment is) of pigment *all* play a role in determining eye color. Each of these characteristics is determined by separate genes. Another example of this phenomenon is skin color, which is determined by at least three different genes working together to produce a wide range of possible skin tones.

### Multiple Alleles

Many monogenic traits (traits expressed via a single gene) correspond to two alleles, one dominant and one recessive. Other traits, however, involve more than two alleles. A classic example of such a trait is the human blood type. On the most simplistic level, there are four major blood types: A, B, AB, and O. They are named based on the presence or absence of certain antigens on the surface of the red blood cells. The gene for blood type has three possible alleles (multiple alleles): $I^A$, which causes antigens A to be produced on the surface of the red blood cell; $I^B$, which causes antigens B to be produced; and i, which causes *no* antigens to be produced. The following are the possible genotypes for human blood type: $I^A i$ (type A), $I^A I^A$ (type A), $I^B i$ (type B), $I^B I^B$ (type B), $I^A I^B$ (type AB), ii (type O). Type AB blood displays the *codominance* of blood type. As we saw in MN blood groups, both the A and the B alleles succeed in their mission—their antigens appear on the surface of the red blood cell (Figure 10.3). Analyzing blood type can be really complex because human blood types involve not only multiple alleles ($I^A$, $I^B$, and i) and codominance (type AB blood), but classic dominance of $I^A$ and $I^B$ over i as well.

| Blood Type | Antigens on surface of RBC | Antibodies produced by the body | Can be transfused with which types of blood? | Can be donated to individuals of which type? |
|---|---|---|---|---|
| A | Antigen A | Anti B | Type A, O | Type A, AB |
| B | Antigen B | Anti A | Type B, O | Type B, AB |
| AB | Antigens A & B | None | All Types | Type AB |
| O | No Antigens | Anti A and Anti B | Only O | All Types |

**Figure 10.3  Several human blood type characteristics.**

If you have ever watched an episode of *ER* on television, you have heard one of the doctors frantically scream, "We need to type her and bring some O blood down here *stat*!" Why is it important for the physician to determine what type of blood the patient has, and why is it okay to give the patient O blood in the meantime? People with type A blood produce anti-B antibodies because the B antigen that is present on type B and type AB blood is a foreign molecule to someone with type A blood. This is simply the body's defense mechanism doing its job. Following the same logic, those with type B blood make anti-A antibodies, and those with type O blood make anti-A *and* anti-B antibodies. People who are type AB make none, and are therefore the universal acceptor of blood. It is important to find out what kind of blood a person has because if you give type B blood to a person with type A blood, the recipient will have an immune response to the transfused blood. Why is O blood given while they wait to see what blood type the patient is? This is because type O blood has neither antigen on the surface of red blood cells. People with type O blood are universal donors because few people will have an adverse reaction to type O blood. Immune reactions are discussed in further detail in Chapter 15, Human Physiology.

## Epistasis

In **epistasis** the expression of one gene affects the expression of another gene. A classic example of epistasis involves the coat color of mice. Black is dominant over brown, and brown fur has the genotype bb. There is also another gene locus independent of the coat color gene that controls the deposition of pigment in the fur. If a mouse has a dominant allele of this pigment gene (Cc or CC), it leads to pigment deposition and the coloring of the fur according to the coat color gene's instructions. If a mouse is double recessive for this trait (cc), it will have white fur no matter what the coat color gene wants because it will not put any pigment into the fur. It is almost as if the pigment gene were overruling the coat color gene. If you mate two black mice that are BbCc, the ratio of phenotypes in the offspring would not be the 9:3:3:1 ratio that Mendel predicts, but rather 9:4:3 black:white:brown because the epistatic gene alters the phenotype.

## Pleiotropy

In **pleiotropy** a single gene has multiple effects on an organism. A good example of pleiotropy is the mutation that causes sickle cell anemia. This single gene mutation "sickles" the blood cells, leading to systemic symptoms such as heart, lung, and kidney damage; muscle pain; weakness; and generalized fatigue. The problems do not stop there; these symptoms can lead to disastrous side effects such as kidney failure. The mutation of a single gene wreaks havoc on the system as a whole.

# Sex Determination and Sex Linkage

Mendel was not the only one to make progress in the field of heredity. In the early 1900s, Thomas Morgan made key discoveries regarding sex linkage and linked genes.

In human cells, all chromosomes occur in structurally identical pairs except for two very important ones: the sex chromosomes, X and Y. Women have two structurally identical X chromosomes. Men have one X and one Y.

## Sex-Linked Traits

Morgan experimented with a quick-breeding fruit fly species. The fruit flies had four pairs of chromosomes: three autosomal pairs and one sex chromosome pair. An **autosomal chromosome** is one that is not directly involved in determining gender. In fruit flies, the more common phenotype for a trait is called the **wild-type phenotype** (e.g., red eyes). Traits that are different from the normal are called **mutant phenotypes** (e.g., white eyes). Morgan crossed a white-eyed male with a red-eyed female, and all the $F_1$ offspring had red eyes. When he bred the $F_1$ together, he obtained Mendel's 3:1 ratio. But, there was a slight difference from what Mendel's theories would predict—the white trait was restricted to the males. Morgan's conclusion was that the gene for eye color is on the X chromosome. This means that the poor male flies get only a single copy, and if it is abnormal, they are abnormal. But, the lucky ladies have two copies and are normal even if one copy is not.

> **BIG IDEA 3.A.4**
>
> *The inheritance of sex-linked traits cannot be explained by simple Mendelian genetics.*

It is this male–female sex chromosomes difference that allows for sex-linked conditions. If a gene for a recessive disease is present on the X chromosome, then a female must have two defective versions of the gene to show the disease while a male needs only one. This is so because males have no corresponding gene on the Y chromosome to help counter the negative effect of a recessive allele on the X chromosome. Thus, more males than females show recessive X-linked phenotypes. In a pedigree (see Figure 10.6 later in this chapter), a pattern of sex-linked disease will show the sons of carrier mothers with the disease.

The father plays no part in the passage of an X-linked gene to the male children of a couple. Fathers pass X-linked alleles to their daughters, but not to their sons. Do you understand why this is so? The father does not give an X chromosome to the male offspring because he is the one who provides the Y chromosome that makes his son a male. A mother can pass a sex-linked allele to both her daughters *and* sons because she can pass only X chromosomes to her offspring.

> *Emily (12th grader):*
> *"Be able to categorize diseases for this exam!"*

Three common sex-linked disorders are Duchenne's muscular dystrophy, hemophilia, and red-green colorblindness. **Duchenne's muscular dystrophy** is a sex-linked disorder that is caused by the absence of an essential muscle protein. Its symptoms include a progressive loss of muscle strength and coordination. **Hemophilia** is caused by the absence of a protein vital to the clotting process. Individuals with this condition have difficulty clotting blood after even the smallest of wounds. Those most severely affected by the disease can bleed to death after the tiniest of injuries. Females with this condition rarely survive. People afflicted with **red-green colorblindness** are unable to distinguish between red and green colors. This condition is found primarily in males.

## X Inactivation

Here is an important question for you to ponder while preparing for this exam: "Are all the cells in a female identical?"

The answer to this question is "No." Females undergo a process called **X inactivation.** During the development of a female embryo, one of the two X chromosomes in each cell remains coiled as a **Barr body** whose genes are not expressed. A cell expresses the alleles only of the active X chromosome. X inactivation occurs separately in each cell and involves random inactivation of one of a female's X chromosomes. But not all cells inactivate the same X. As a result, different cells will have different active X chromosomes.

Why don't females always express X-linked diseases when this X inactivation occurs? Sometimes they do, but usually they have enough cells with a "good" copy of the allele to compensate for the presence of the recessive allele.

One last sex-related inheritance pattern that needs to be mentioned is **holandric traits,** which are traits inherited via the Y chromosome. An example of a holandric trait in humans is ear hair distribution.

# Linkage and Gene Mapping

Each chromosome has hundreds of genes that tend to be inherited together because the chromosome is passed along as a unit. These are called **linked genes.** Linked genes lie on the same chromosome and do not follow Mendel's law of independent assortment.

Morgan performed an experiment in which he looked at body color and wing size on his beloved fruit flies. The dominant alleles were G (gray) and V (normal wings); the recessive alleles were g (black) and v (vestigial wings). GgVv females were crossed with ggvv males. Mendel's law of independent assortment predicts offspring of four different phenotypes in a 1:1:1:1 ratio. But that is not what Morgan found. Because the genes are linked, the gray/normal flies produce only GV or gv gametes. Thus, Morgan expected the ratio of offspring to be 1:1, half GgVv and half ggvv. Morgan found that there were more wild-type and double-mutant flies than independent assortment would predict, but surprisingly, some Gv and gV were also produced.

How did those other combinations result from the cross if the genes are linked? **Crossover** (also known as *crossing over*), a form of genetic recombination that occurs during prophase I of meiosis, led to their production. The less often this recombination occurs, the closer the genes must be on the chromosome. The farther apart two genes are on a chromosome, the more often crossover will occur. Recombination frequency can be used to determine how close two genes are on a chromosome through the creation of linkage maps, which we will look at next.

## Linkage Maps

A **linkage map** is a genetic map put together using crossover frequencies. Another unit of measurement, the **map unit** (also known as *centigram*), is used to geographically relate the genes on the basis of these frequencies. One map unit is equal to a 1 percent crossover frequency. A linkage map does not provide the *exact* location of genes; it gives only the relative location. Imagine that you want to determine the relative locations of four genes: A, B, C, and D. You know that A crosses over with C 20 percent of the time, B crosses over with C 15 percent of the time, A crosses over with D 10 percent of the time, and D crosses over with B 5 percent of the time. From this information you can determine the sequence (Figure 10.4). Gene A must be 20 units from gene C. Gene B must be 15 units from C, but B could be 5 or 35 units from A. But, because you also know that A is 10 units from D and that D is 5 units from B, you can determine that B must be 5 units from A as well, if A is also to be 10 units from D. This gives you the sequence of genes as ABDC.

**Figure 10.4   A genetic linkage map.**

# Heads or Tails?

*Probability* is a concept important to a full understanding of heredity and inheritance. What is the probability that a flipped coin will come up heads? You can answer that easily: ½. What is the probability that two coins flipped simultaneously will *both* be heads? This is a little harder—it is ½ × ½ = ¼. Take a look at Figure 10.5. The first time you toss the coin, there is a probability of ½ that it will land heads and ½ that it will land tails. When you toss it again, it again has a probability of ½ that it will land heads, and ½ that it will land tails. So in the figure, just concentrate on the ½ of the tosses that land heads. Of those, ½ of them will land heads the second time—or ½ of ½. Multiplied together, this results in the ¼ chance of getting heads twice with two coin tosses. This example illustrates the **law of multiplication** with probabilities. This law states that to determine the probability that two random events will occur in succession, you simply multiply the probability of the first event by the probability of the second event.

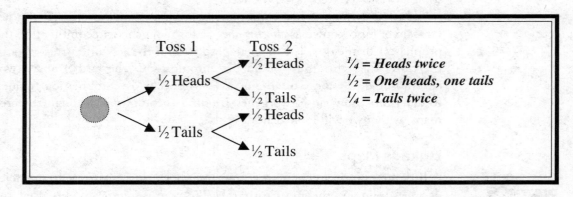

**Figure 10.5   Probability in the law of multiplication.**

This is the same thought process that we follow to understand Mendel's law of segregation. If you are Aa for a trait, what is your chance or passing on the A? That's right—½. If you are AaBb, what is the chance you pass on both A and B? Clever you are—you multiply ½ × ½ to get ½.

# Pedigrees

**Pedigrees** are family trees used to describe the genetic relationships within a family. Comprehension of the probability concept is important for a full understanding of pedigree analysis. Squares represent males, and circles are used for females. A horizontal line from

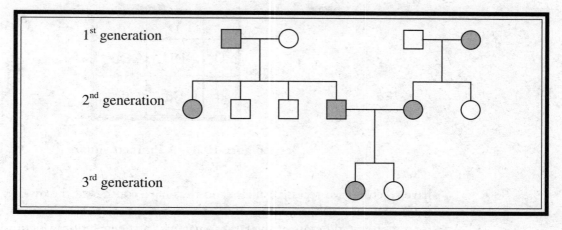

**Figure 10.6    Schematic of a pedigree.**

male to female represents mates that have produced offspring. The offspring are listed below their parents from oldest to youngest. A fully shaded individual possesses the trait being studied. If the condition being studied is a monogenic recessive condition (rr), then those shaded gray have the genotype rr. If the condition being studied is a dominant condition (Rr or RR), then those that are *un*shaded have the genotype rr. A line through a symbol indicates that the person is deceased. A sample pedigree is shown in Figure 10.6.

Pedigrees can be used in many ways. One use is to determine the risk of parents passing certain conditions to their offspring. Imagine that two people want to have a child, and they both have a family history of a certain autosomal recessive condition (dd). Neither has the particular condition, but the man has a brother who died of the disease and the woman's mother died of the disease at an older age. They want to know the probability of having a child with the condition. You must first determine the probability that each parent is a carrier, and then determine the probability of the parents having a child with the disease, given that they are carriers. See the pedigree in Figure 10.7.

*CT teacher: "Test almost always has two to three questions about this topic."*

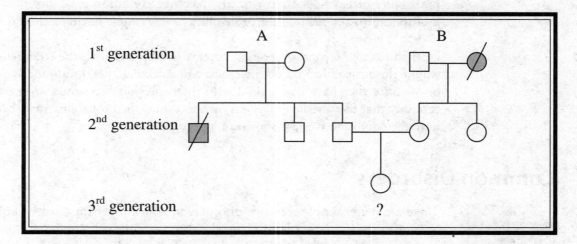

**Figure 10.7    Three-generation pedigree indicating probability of inheriting a particular disease.**

First, we can determine the father's (second generation) probability of being a carrier. We know that both of his parents must be carriers with a genotype of Dd. Why is this the case? Although neither parent has the condition, they must both be carriers for his brother to

|   | D | d |
|---|---|---|
| D | DD | Dd |
| d | Dd | dd |

**Figure 10.8    A Punnett square.**

have received two recessive alleles and thus have contracted the disease. How can we calculate the potential probability of the father being a carrier? We construct a Punnett square for a monohybrid cross of the father's parents (first generation) (Figure 10.8).

We know with certainty that he is not dd, otherwise, he would have the condition. This leaves three equally likely possible genotypes for the father, two of which are "carrier" genotypes (Dd). Thus, the probability of his being a carrier is ⅔.

What is the probability that the mother (second generation) is a carrier? We don't even need a Punnett square to determine this one. Her mother (first generation) died of the condition, which means that she must have been dd, and thus must have passed along a d to each of her children. The mother in question does not have the condition, so she must have a D as well. Therefore her genotype *must* be Dd.

To determine the probability that *both* parents are carriers, apply the law of multiplication with probabilities (similar to tossing a coin) and use the following formula:

$$PF \times PM = ⅔ \times 1 = ⅔$$

(where PF, PM = probabilities of father, mother being carriers).

Now that we have determined the probability that they are both carriers, we need to determine the probability that one of their offspring will have the condition. Their Punnett square would be the same as that shown in Figure 10.8, and we can see that the probability of having a child with the recessive condition is ¼. Again, we use the law of multiplication and see that the probability of this couple having a child with the condition is ⅔ × ¼ = ⅙.

If these two second-generation parents had a child with the recessive condition, what would the probability be of their next child having the condition? It would no longer be ⅙; once they have had a child with the condition, we would know with 100 percent certainty that they are heterozygous carriers. Thus, the probability that their next child will have the condition is ¼, as shown in Figure 10.8.

# Common Disorders

There are many simple recessive disorders in which a person must be homozygous recessive for the gene in question to have the disease. Some of the most common examples are Tay-Sachs disease, cystic fibrosis, sickle cell anemia, phenylketonuria, and albinism. These diseases are commonly used as examples on the AP Biology exam and could also aid you in constructing a well-supported essay answer to a question about heredity and inherited disorders.

**Tay-Sachs disease** is a fatal genetic disorder that renders the body unable to break down a particular type of lipid that accumulates in the brain and eventually causes blindness and brain damage. Individuals with this disease typically do not survive more than a few years. Carriers of this disease do not show any of the effects of the disease, and thus the allele is preserved in the population because carriers usually live to reproduce and potentially pass on the recessive copy of the allele. This disease is found in a higher than normal percentage of people of eastern European Jewish descent.

**Cystic fibrosis (CF)**, a recessive disorder, is the most common fatal genetic disease in this country. The gene for this disease is located on chromosome 7. The normal allele for this gene is involved in cellular chloride ion transport. A defective version of this gene results in the excessive secretion of a thick mucus, which accumulates in the lungs and digestive tract. Left untreated, children with CF die at a very young age. Statistically, one in 25 Caucasians is a carrier for this disease.

**Sickle cell anemia** is a common recessive disease that occurs as a result of an improper amino acid substitution during translation of an important red blood cell protein called *hemoglobin.* It results in the formation of a hemoglobin protein that is less efficient at carrying oxygen. It also causes hemoglobin to deform to a sickle shape when the oxygen content of the blood is low, causing pain, muscle weakness, and fatigue.

Sickle cell anemia is the most common inherited disease among African Americans. It affects one out of every 400 African Americans, and one out of 10 African Americans is a carrier of the disease. The recessive trait is so prevalent because carriers (who are said to have sickle cell "trait") have increased resistance to malaria. In tropical regions, where malaria occurs, the sickle cell trait actually increases an individual's probability of survival, and thus the trait's presence in the population increases (heterozygote advantage).

**Phenylketonuria (PKU)** is another autosomal recessive disease caused by a single gene defect. Children with PKU are unable to successfully digest phenylalanine (an amino acid). This leads to the accumulation of a by-product in the blood that can cause mental retardation. If the disease is caught early, retardation can be prevented by avoiding phenylalanine in the diet.

Dominant disorders are less common in humans. One example of a dominant disorder is **Huntington disease,** a fatal disease that causes the breakdown of the nervous system. It does not show itself until a person is in their 30s or 40s, and individuals afflicted with this condition have a 50 percent chance of passing it to their offspring.

Why are lethal dominant alleles less common than lethal recessive alleles? Think about how recessive alleles often are passed on from generation to generation. An individual can be a carrier of a recessive condition and pass it along without even knowing it. On the other hand, it is impossible to be an unaffected carrier of a dominant condition, and many lethal conditions have unfortunately killed the individual before reproductive maturity has been achieved. This makes it more difficult for the dominant gene to be passed along. To remain prevalent in the population, a dominant disorder must not kill the individual until reproduction has occurred.

# Chromosomal Complications

We have spent a lot of time discussing how genes are inherited and passed from generation to generation. It is also important to discuss the situations in which something goes wrong with the chromosomes themselves that affects the inheritance of genes by the offspring. **Nondisjunction** is an error in homologous chromosome separation. It can occur during meiosis I or II. The result is that one gamete receives too many of one kind of chromosome, and another gamete receives none of a particular chromosome. The fusing of an abnormal gamete with a normal one can lead to the production of offspring with an abnormal number of chromosomes (**aneuploidy**).

**BIG IDEA 3.A.3**

*Certain genetic disorders can provide understanding of how genes are passed from parent to offspring.*

**Down syndrome** is a classic aneuploid example, affecting one out of every 700 children born in this country. It most often involves a trisomy of chromosome 21, and leads to mental retardation, heart defects, short stature, and characteristic facial features. Most people with trisomy 21 are sterile.

Trisomy 21 is not the only form of nondisjunction caused by error in the chromosome separation process. Trisomy 13, also known as **Patau syndrome,** causes serious brain and circulatory defects. Trisomy 18, also known as **Edwards syndrome,** can affect all organs. It is rare for a baby to survive for more than a year with either of these two conditions. There are also syndromes involving aneuploidy of the sex chromosomes. Males can receive an extra Y chromosome (XYY). Although this nondisjunction does not seem to produce a major syndrome, XYY males tend to be taller than average, and some geneticists believe they display a higher degree of aggressive behavior. A male can receive an extra X chromosome, as in **Klinefelter syndrome** (XXY). These infertile individuals have male sex organs but show several feminine body characteristics. Nondisjunction occurs in females as well. Females who are XXX have no real syndrome. Females who are missing an X chromosome (XO) have a condition called **Turner syndrome.** XO individuals are sterile females who possess sex organs that fail to mature at puberty.

Trisomies are not the only kind of chromosomal abnormalities that lead to inherited diseases. A **deletion** occurs when a piece of the chromosome is lost in the developmental process. Deletions, such as **cri-du-chat syndrome,** can lead to problems. This syndrome occurs with a deletion in chromosome 5 that leads to mental retardation, abnormal facial features, and a small head. Most affected individuals die very young.

**Chromosomal translocations,** in which a piece of one chromosome is attached to another, nonhomologous chromosome, can cause major problems. **Chronic myelogenous leukemia** is a cancer affecting white blood cell precursor cells. In this disease, a portion of chromosome 22 has been swapped with a piece of chromosome 9.

A **chromosome inversion** occurs when a portion of a chromosome separates and reattaches in the opposite direction. This can have no effect at all, or it can render a gene nonfunctional if it occurs in the middle of a sequence. A **chromosome duplication** results in the repetition of a genetic segment. A **chromosome duplication** results in the repetition of a genetic segment . . . whoops . . . sorry. . . . Duplications often have serious effects on an organism.

These are the major concepts of heredity with which the AP Biology exam writers would like you to be familiar. Try the practice problems that follow and be sure you are able to construct, read, and analyze both Punnett squares and pedigrees, keeping in mind the laws of probability.

# › Review Questions

1. The following crossover frequencies were noted via experimentation for a set of five genes on a single chromosome:

   A and B → 35%
   B and C → 15%
   A and C → 20%
   A and D → 10%
   D and B → 25%
   A and E → 5%
   B and E → 40%

Pick the answer that most likely represents the relative positions of the five genes.

**A.** |------|------------|------------|------------------|
　　 E　 A　　　 D　　　 C　　　　 B

**B.** |------|------------|------------|------------------|
　　 A　 E　　 C　　　 D　　　　 B

**C.** |------|------------|------------|------------------|
　　 E　 A　　 C　　　 D　　　　 B

**D.** |------------|------------|------|------|
　　 B　　　 C　　 D　 E　 A

2. Imagine that in squirrels, gray color (G) is dominant over black color (g). A black squirrel has the genotype gg. Crossing a gray squirrel with which of the following would let you know with the most certainty the genotype of the gray squirrel?

A. GG
B. Gg
C. gg
D. Cannot be determined from the information given

3. From a cross of AABbCC with AaBbCc, what is the probability that the offspring will display a genotype of AaBbCc?

A. ½
B. ⅓
C. ¼
D. ⅛

Use the following pedigree of an autosomal recessive condition for questions 4–6.

4. What is the genotype of person A?

A. Bb
B. BB
C. bb
D. Cannot be determined from the given information

5. What is the most likely genotype of person B?

A. Bb
B. BB
C. bb
D. Cannot be determined from the information given

6. What is the probability that persons C and D would have a child with the condition?

A. ½
B. ¼
C. ⅙
D. ⅛

7. Which of the following disorders is X-linked?

A. Tay-Sachs disease
B. Cystic fibrosis
C. Hemophilia
D. Albinism

8. A court case is trying to determine the father of a particular baby. The mother has type O blood, and the baby has type B blood. Which of the following blood types would mean that the man was definitely *not* the father of the baby?

A. B and A
B. AB and A
C. O and B
D. O and A

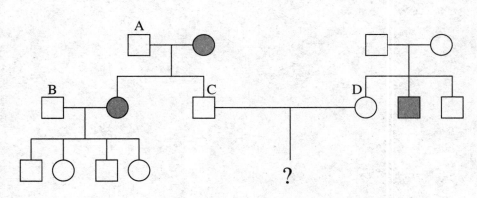

**9.** Assume that gray squirrel color results from a dominant allele G. The father squirrel is black, the mother squirrel is gray, and their first baby is black. What is the probability that their second baby is also black?

A. 1.00
B. 0.75
C. 0.50
D. 0.25

**10.** Imagine that tulips are either yellow or white. You start growing tulips and find out that if you want to get yellow tulips, then at least one of the parents must be yellow. Which color is dominant?

A. White
B. Yellow
C. Neither; it is some form of intermediate inheritance
D. Cannot be determined from the given information

**11.** Suppose that 200 red snapdragons were mated with 200 white snapdragons and they produced only pink snapdragons. The mating of two pink snapdragons would most likely result in off-spring that are

A. 50 percent pink, 25 percent red, 25 percent white
B. 100 percent pink
C. 25 percent pink, 50 percent red, 25 percent white
D. 75 percent red, 25 percent white

**12.** Which of the following represents the number of possible gametes produced from a genotype of RrBBCcDDEe?

A. 2
B. 4
C. 8
D. 16

**13.** Which of the following diseases is *not* caused by trisomy nondisjunction?

A. Down syndrome
B. Klinefelter syndrome
C. Turner syndrome
D. Patau syndrome

**14.** The pedigree below is most likely a pedigree of a condition of which type of inheritance?

A. Autosomal dominant
B. Autosomal recessive
C. Sex-linked dominant
D. Sex-linked recessive

## › Answers and Explanations

**1. A**—The crossover frequencies are an indication of the distance between the different genes on a chromosome. The farther apart they are, the greater chance there is that they will cross over during prophase I of meiosis. You are first told that A and B cross over with a frequency of 35 percent, so imagine that they are 35 units apart on a chromosome map.

A    (35)    B    B    (15)    C    A    (20)    C

We can then tell you that B and C have a frequency of 15 percent. They are 15 units apart on the map,

but you cannot yet be sure what side of gene A that C is on. Gene A and C cross with 20 percent frequency. This means that gene C must be in between A and B.

A (20) C (15) B    A (10) D    D (25) B

Gene A crosses over with D 10 percent of the time, and D crosses with B 25 percent of the time; therefore, D must also be in between A and B. It is closer to A than it is to B. You can use this knowledge to eliminate answer choices B and C.

A (10) D (10) C (15) B

Gene A crosses over with E with a frequency of 5 percent. You do not know which side of A gene E is on until you know its crossover frequency with B. Because the question tells you that it has a 40 percent frequency with B, you know that it must be on the *left* of A. This completes your map, leaving A as the correct answer.

**2. C**—This is a test cross. To determine the genotype of an individual showing the dominant phenotype, you cross that individual with a homozygous recessive individual for the same trait. If they have no offspring with the recessive phenotype, then the individual displaying the dominant phenotype is most likely GG. If approximately one-half of the offspring have the

recessive phenotype, you know the individual has the genotype Gg.

**3. D**—The Punnett square shown below shows all the possible gamete combinations from this cross. Two-sixteenths or one-eighth of the possible gametes will be AaBbCc. A quick way to determine the number of possible gametes that an individual can produce given a certain genotype is to use the formula $2^n$. For example, an individual who is AABbCc can have $2^2 = 4$ possible gametes because Bb and Cc are heterozygous.

|      | **ABC** | **AbC** | **ABc** | **Abc** | **aBC** | **abC** | **aBc** | **abc** |
|------|---------|---------|---------|---------|---------|---------|---------|---------|
| ABC  | AABBCC  | AABbCC  | AABBCc  | AABbCc  | AaBBCC  | AaBbCC  | AaBBCc  | AaBbCc  |
| AbC  | AABbCC  | AAbbCC  | AABbCc  | AAbbCc  | AaBbCC  | AabbCC  | AaBbCc  | AabbCc  |

**4. A**—Person A must have genotype Bb because he has some children that have the recessive condition and some that do not. Because his wife is pure recessive, she can contribute only a b. The father must therefore be the one who contributes the B to the child who does not have the condition, and the second b to the one with the condition.

**5. B**—Person B most likely has a genotype of BB. Because he does not have the condition, we know that his genotype is either BB or Bb. If it were Bb, then when crossed with his wife who has a genotype of bb, 50 percent of his children would be expected to have the recessive condition. None of the children have the condition, which leads you to believe that he is most likely BB. (This test is, of course, not 100 percent accurate. Answer choice B is not certain, but is the most probable conclusion.)

**6. C**—We know that neither parent in the question has the recessive condition. We therefore need to calculate the probability that each of them is Bb. The probability that person C is Bb is 1. Because his mother has the condition, she *must* pass a b to him during gamete formation. So the only possible genotypes he can have are Bb and bb. Since he does not have the condition, he must be Bb with a probability of 1. The probability that person D is Bb is 0.67. Neither of her parents has the condition, but she has a brother who is bb. This means that each of her parents must be a carrier for the condition (Bb). You know that this woman is not bb, because she does not have the condition. As a result, there are only *three* possible genotypes from the cross remaining. Two of these three are Bb, giving her a probability of ⅔, or 0.67, of being Bb. The probability that *both* person C and person D are Bb is (1) × (0.67) = (0.67). Now it is necessary to calculate the probability that two Bb parents will produce a kid who is bb. The Punnett square says that there is a 0.25 chance of this result. To calculate the probability that they will have a child with the recessive condition, you multiply the probability that they are both Bb (0.67) times the probability that two individuals Bb will produce a bb child (0.25). Thus, the probability of an affected child being produced from these two parents is ⅙.

7. **C**—Hemophilia is an X-linked condition. An XY male with hemophilia gets his Y chromosome from his father, and his X chromosome from his mother. All that is needed for the hemophilia condition to occur is a copy of the defective recessive allele from his mother.

8. **D**—Types O and A would prove that he was not the father of this particular child. If the mother has type O blood, this means that her genotype is ii and she *must* pass along an i allele to her child. The baby has type B blood, and her genotype could be $I^Bi$ or $I^BI^B$. Since the mother must give an i, then the baby's genotype must be $I^Bi$. It follows that the father must provide the $I^B$ allele to the baby to complete the known genotype. If he is type O, he won't have an $I^B$ to pass along since his genotype would be ii. This would also be the case if he were type A, because his genotype would be either $I^AI^A$ or $I^Ai$. Therefore, those two blood types would prove that he is not the father of this child.

9. **C**—To figure out this problem, you need to know the genotype of the mother. The father is black, meaning that his genotype is gg. The two of them produced a squirrel that is also black, which means that the gray mother gave a g to the baby. The mother's genotype is Gg. A cross of Gg × gg produces a phenotype ratio of 1:1 gray:black. They have a 0.5 chance of producing another black baby.

10. **B**—According to this scenario, yellow and white are the only colors possible. If white were dominant, and both parents were Ww, you *could* produce a yellow offspring if the two recessive w's combined. If it were intermediate inheritance, you probably would not produce a straight yellow tulip in the offspring because they would either meet halfway (incomplete dominance), or both express fully (codominance). If yellow were dominant, then you could produce a yellow offspring only if there were a Y allele in one of the parents. A cross of yy × yy would produce only white tulips if white were recessive.

11. **A**—This problem involves incomplete dominance. The genotype of the pink offspring from the first generation is RW. When the two RW snapdragons are mated together, they produce the following results:

|   | R  | W  |
|---|----|----|
| R | RR | RW |
| W | RW | WW |

The offspring will be 25 percent red (RR), 50 percent pink (RW), and 25 percent white (WW).

12. **C**—In a problem like this, you will save time by thinking about the laws of probability. The genotype is RrBBCcDDEe. How many possible combinations of the R gene are there? There are two: R and r. How many for B? Only one: B. Following the same logic, C has two and D has one. Now you multiply the possibilities: (2 × 1 × 2 × 1 × 2) = 8. There are 8 possible gametes from this genotype. Another way to arrive at this answer is by use of the expression $2^n$, where *n* is the number of hybrid traits being examined. In this case it would be $2^3$ or 8 possible gametes.

13. **C**—Down syndrome is most often due to a trisomy of chromosome 21. Klinefelter syndrome is a trisomy of the sex chromosomes (XXY). Patau syndrome is a trisomy of chromosome 15. Edwards syndrome is a trisomy of chromosome 18. Turner syndrome, the only nontrisomy listed in this problem, is a *monosomy* of the sex chromosomes (XO).

14. **D**—This is most likely a sex-linked recessive disease. The father in the first generation does not have the condition, so his genotype would be $X^N Y$. The original couple has four children, two boys with the condition, and one girl and one boy without the condition. The genotype of the boys with the condition would be $X^n Y$. This means that the original mother's genotype would be $X^N X^n$—thus she is a carrier. One of the children who inherited the condition has children with a woman from a different family, and neither of their two children displays the condition. However, the daughter of son A has three children with a man who is $X^n Y$, and she has a daughter and a son who show the recessive condition and one normal son. This means that the daughter of son A is most likely $X^N X^n$—another carrier of the condition. This disease is a condition that is, according to the pedigree, more often seen in men, and passed along to men by the X chromosome from the mother. However, it is important to note that if a father who has the X-linked condition has a child with a female carrier for the condition, that couple can indeed produce a female with the condition.

## ❯ Rapid Review

You should be familiar with the following terms:

*Character*: heritable feature, such as flower color.

*Monohybrid cross*: cross involving one character (Bb × Bb) → (3:1 phenotype ratio).

*Dihybrid cross*: cross involving two different characters (BbRr × BbRr) → (9:3:3:1 phenotype ratio).

*Law of segregation*: the two alleles for a trait separate during the formation of gametes—one to each gamete.

*Law of independent assortment*: inheritance of one trait does not interfere with the inheritance of another trait.

*Law of dominance*: if two opposite pure-breeding varieties (BB × bb) are crossed, all offspring resemble BB parent.

*Intermediate inheritance*: heterozygous (Yy) individual shows characteristics unlike *either* parent.

- *Incomplete dominance*: Yy produces an intermediate phenotype between YY and yy (snapdragons).

- *Codominance*: both alleles express themselves fully in a Yy individual—(MN blood groups).

*Polygenic traits*: traits that are affected by more than one gene (eye color, skin color).

*Multiple alleles*: traits that correspond to more than two alleles (ABO blood type: $I^A$, $I^B$, i).

*Epistasis*: a gene at one locus alters the phenotypic expression of a gene at another locus (coat color in mice).

*Pleiotropy*: a single gene has multiple effects on an organism (sickle cell anemia).

*Sex determination*: males are XY, females are XX.

*Autosomal chromosome*: not involved in gender.

*Fruit flies*: wild-type traits are the normal phenotype; mutant traits are those that are different from normal.

*Sex-linked traits*: passed along the X chromosome; more common in males than females (males have only one X) (e.g., hemophilia [can't clot blood], Duchenne's muscular dystrophy [muscle weakness], colorblindness).

*X inactivation*: one of two X chromosomes is randomly inactivated and remains coiled as a Barr body.

*Holandric trait*: one that is inherited via the Y chromosome.

*Linked genes*: genes that lie along the same chromosome and do not follow the law of independent assortment.

- *Crossover*: a form of genetic recombination that occurs during prophase I of meiosis.
- The further apart two genes are along a chromosome, the more often they will cross over.

*Linkage map*: genetic map put together using crossover frequencies.

- Can determine the relative location of a set of genes according to how often they cross over.
- If two genes cross over in 20 percent of the crosses, they are 20 map units apart, etc.

*Law of multiplication*: To determine the probability that two random events will occur in succession, multiply the probability of the first event by the probability of the second event. (Useful in pedigree analysis!)

*Pedigree*: family tree used to describe genetic relationships (use pedigree diagram in review question 14 for clearer understanding). To calculate the risk a couple faces of having a child that has a recessive (bb) condition, first determine the probability that *both* parents are Bb (if neither have the condition), or the probability that one is Bb (if one *has* the condition). Once determined, multiply this probability times the probability that a Bb × Bb cross will produce a bb (¼) or that a bb × Bb will produce a bb (½).

**Autosomal Recessive Disorders**

*Tay-Sachs*: fatal, storage disease, lipid builds up in brain, mental retardation, increased incidence in eastern European Jews.

*Cystic fibrosis*: increased mucus buildup in lungs; untreated children die at young age; one in 25 Caucasians are carriers.

*Sickle cell anemia*: caused by error of single amino acid; hemoglobin is less able to carry $O_2$, and sickles when $O_2$ content of blood is low; one in 10 African Americans is a carrier. Heterozygous condition protects against malaria.

*Phenylketonuria*: inability to digest phenylalanine, which can cause mental retardation if not avoided in diet.

*Autosomal dominant disorders*: Huntington disease (nervous system disease) and achondroplasia (dwarfism).

*Nondisjunction*: error in which homologous chromosomes do not separate properly.

- *Monosomy*: (one copy): Turner syndrome.

- *Trisomy*: (three copies): Down syndrome (21), Patau syndrome (13), Edwards syndrome (18).

*Klinefelter syndrome*: XXY; XYY males, XXX females.

*Chromosome disorders*: deletion (cri-du-chat), inversions, duplications, and translocations (leukemia).

# CHAPTER > 11

# Molecular Genetics

## IN THIS CHAPTER

**Summary:** This chapter describes the various processes in cells that take DNA from gene to protein: replication, transcription, posttranscriptional modification, and translation. It also discusses the regulation of these processes before concluding with a discussion about viruses, bacteria, and genetic engineering.

### Key Ideas

**KEY IDEA**

○ DNA: adenine-thymine, cytosine-guanine—arranged in a double helix.
○ RNA: adenine-uracil, cytosine-guanine—single stranded.
○ DNA replication occurs during the S-phase in a semi-conservative fashion and in a 5′ to 3′ direction.
○ Types of DNA replication mutations: frameshift, missense, nonsense.
○ Transcription: mRNA is formed from a DNA template.
○ Translation: process by which mRNA specified sequence of amino acids is lined up on a ribosome for protein synthesis.
○ Operons act as on-off switches for transcription—allow for production of genes only when needed.
○ Types of genetic recombination: transformation, transduction, and conjugation.

## Introduction

Genetics has implications for all of biology. We begin our study of this subject with an introduction to DNA and RNA, followed by a description of the various processes in cells that take DNA from gene to protein: replication, transcription, posttranscriptional modification, translation, and the regulation of all these processes. The genetics of viruses and bacteria follows, and the chapter concludes with a discussion of genetic engineering.

# DNA Structure and Function

**BIG IDEA 3.A.1**

*DNA (and sometimes RNA) is the primary source of heritable information.*

Deoxyribonucleic acid, known to her peers as DNA, is composed of four **nitrogenous bases:** adenine, guanine, cytosine, and thymine. Adenine and guanine are a type of nitrogenous base called a **purine,** and contain a double-ring structure. Thymine and cytosine are a type of nitrogenous base called a **pyrimidine,** and contain a single-ring structure. Two scientists, James D. Watson and Francis H.C. Crick, spent a good amount of time devoted to determining the structure of DNA. Their efforts paid off, and they were the ones given credit for realizing that DNA was arranged in what they termed a **double helix** composed of two strands of nucleotides held together by hydrogen bonds. They noted that adenine always pairs with thymine (A=T) held together by two hydrogen bonds and that guanine always pairs with cytosine (C≡G) held together by three hydrogen bonds. Each strand of DNA consists of a sugar-phosphate backbone that keeps the nucleotides connected with the strand. The sugar is deoxyribose. (See Figure 11.1 for a rough sketch of what purine–pyrimidine bonds look like.)

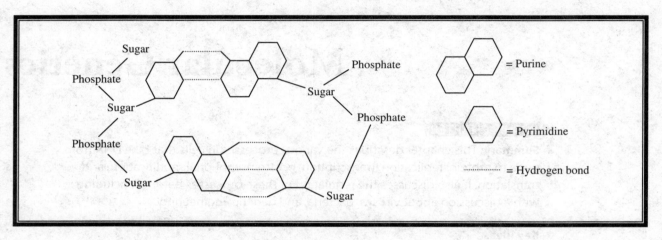

**Figure 11.1   Purine–pyrimidine bonds.**

One last structural note about DNA that can be confusing is that DNA has something called a 5′ end and a 3′ end (Figure 11.2). The two strands of a DNA molecule run antiparallel to each other; the 5′ end of one molecule is paired with the 3′ end of the other molecule, and vice versa.

**Figure 11.2   The 5′ and 3′ ends in DNA structure.**

# RNA Structure and Function

Ribonucleic acid is known to the world as RNA. There are some similarities between DNA and RNA. They both have a sugar-phosphate backbone. They both have four different nucleotides that make up the structure of the molecule. They both have three letters in their nickname—don't worry if you don't see that last similarity right away, . . . remember that we have been studying these things for years. These two molecules also have their share of differences. RNA's nitrogenous bases are adenine, guanine, cytosine, and **uracil.** There is no thymine in RNA; uracil beat out thymine for the job (probably had a better interview during the hiring process). Another difference between DNA and RNA is that the sugar for RNA is ribose instead of deoxyribose. While DNA exists as a double strand, RNA has a bit more of an independent personality and tends to roam the cells as a single-stranded entity.

There are three main types of RNA that you should know about, all of which are formed from DNA templates in the nucleus of eukaryotic cells: (1) messenger RNA (mRNA), (2) transfer RNA (tRNA), and (3) ribosomal RNA (rRNA).

# Replication of DNA

Human cells do not have copy machines to do the dirty work for them. Instead, they use a system called **DNA replication** to copy DNA molecules from cell to cell. As we discussed in Chapter 9, this process occurs during the S-phase of the cell cycle to ensure that every cell produced during mitosis or meiosis receives the proper amount of DNA.

The mechanism for DNA replication was the source of much debate in the mid-1900s. Some argued that it occurred in what was called a "conservative" (**conservative DNA replication**) fashion. In this model, the original double helix of DNA does not change at all; it is as if the DNA is placed on a copy machine and an exact duplicate is made. DNA from the parent appears in only one of the two daughter cells. A different model called the **semiconservative DNA replication** model agrees that the original DNA molecule serves as the template but proposes that before it is copied, the DNA unzips, with each single strand serving as a template for the creation of a new double strand. One strand of DNA from the parent goes to one daughter cell, and the second parent strand to the second daughter cell. A third model, the **dispersive DNA replication model,** suggested that every daughter strand contains *some* parental DNA, but it is dispersed among pieces of DNA not of parental origin. Figure 11.3 is a simplistic sketch showing these three main theories. Watson and Crick would not be pleased to see that we did not draw the DNA as a double helix . . . but as long as you realize this is not how the DNA truly looks, the figure serves its purpose.

An experiment performed in the 1950s by Meselson and Stahl helped select a winner in the debate about replication mechanisms. The experimenters grew bacteria in a medium containing $^{15}N$ (a heavier-than-normal form of nitrogen) to create DNA that was denser than normal. The DNA was denser because the bacteria picked up the $^{15}N$ and incorporated it into their DNA. The bacteria were then transferred to a medium containing normal $^{14}N$ nitrogen. The DNA was allowed to replicate and produced DNA that was half $^{15}N$ and half $^{14}N$. When the first generation of offspring replicated to form the second generation of offspring, the new DNA produced was of two types—one type that had half $^{15}N$ and half $^{14}N$, and another type that was completely $^{14}N$ DNA. This gave a hands-down victory to the semi-conservative theory of DNA replication. Let's take a look at the mechanism of semi-conservative DNA replication.

During the S-phase of the cell cycle, the double-stranded DNA unzips and prepares to replicate. An enzyme called **helicase** unzips the DNA just like a jacket, breaking the hydrogen

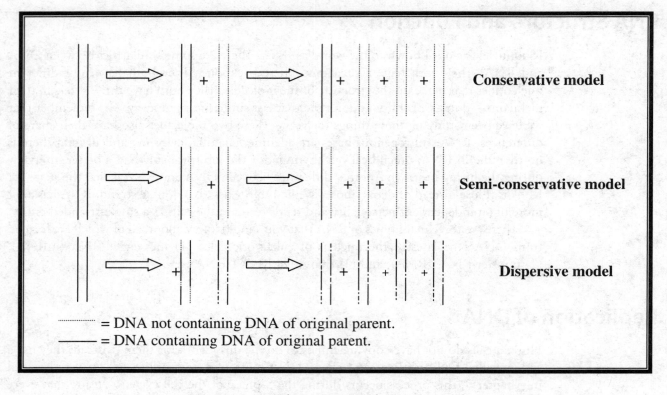

Figure 11.3 Three DNA replication models.

bonds between the nucleotides and producing the **replication fork.** Each strand then functions as a template for production of a new double-stranded DNA molecule. Specific regions along each DNA strand serve as **primer sites** that signal where replication should originate. Primase binds to the primer, and **DNA polymerase,** the superstar enzyme of this process, attaches to the primer region and adds nucleotides to the growing DNA chain in a 5′-to-3′ direction. DNA polymerase is restricted in that it can only add nucleotides to the 3′ end of a parent strand. This creates a problem because, as you can see in Figure 11.4,

Figure 11.4 Semi-conservative DNA replication.

this means that only one of the strands can be produced in a continuous fashion. This continuous strand is known as the **leading strand.** The other strand is affectionately known as the **lagging strand.** You will notice that in the third step of the process in Figure 11.4, the lagging strand consists of tiny pieces called **Okazaki fragments,** which are later connected by an enzyme called DNA ligase to produce the completed double-stranded daughter DNA molecule. This is the semi-conservative model of DNA replication.

Unliek are worck, DNA replication is not a perfect process—mistakes are made. A series of proofreading enzymes function to make sure that the DNA is properly replicated each time. During the first run-through, it is estimated that a nucleotide mismatch is made during replication in one out of every 10,000 basepairs. The proofreaders must do a pretty good job since a mismatch error in replication occurs in only one out of every *billion* nucleotides replicated. DNA polymerase proofreads the newly added base right after it is added on to make sure that it is the correct match. Repair is easy—the polymerase simply removes the incorrect nucleotide, and adds the proper one in its place. This process is known as **mismatch repair.** Another repair mechanism is **excision repair,** in which a *section* of DNA containing an error is cut out and the gap is filled in by DNA polymerase. There are other proteins that assist in the repair process, but their identities are not of major importance. Just be aware that DNA repair exists and is a very efficient process.

Here is a short list of mutation types that you should know:

1. *Frameshift mutations.* Deletion or addition of DNA nucleotides that does not add or remove a multiple of three nucleotides. mRNA is produced on a DNA template and is read in bunches of three called **codons,** which tell the protein synthesis machinery which amino acid to add to the growing protein chain. If the mRNA reads: THE FAT CAT ATE HER HAT, and the F is removed because of an error somewhere, the frame has now *shifted* to read THE ATC ATA THE ERH AT . . . (gibberish). This kind of mutation usually produces a nonfunctional protein unless it occurs late in protein production.
2. *Missense mutation.* Substitution of the wrong nucleotides into the DNA sequence. These substitutions still result in the addition of amino acids to the growing protein chain during translation, but they can sometimes lead to the addition of *incorrect* amino acids to the chain. It could cause no problem at all, or it could cause a big problem as in sickle cell anemia, in which a single amino acid error caused by a substitution mutation leads to a disease that wreaks havoc on the body as a whole.
3. *Nonsense mutation.* Substitution of the wrong nucleotides into the DNA sequence. These substitutions lead to premature stoppage of protein synthesis by the early placement of a **stop codon,** which tells the protein synthesis machinery to grind to a halt. The stop codons are UAA, UAG, and UGA. This type of mutation usually leads to a nonfunctional protein.
4. *Thymine dimers.* Result of too much exposure to UV (ultraviolet) light. Thymine nucleotides located adjacent to one another on the DNA strand bind together when this exposure occurs. This can negatively affect replication of DNA and help cause further mutations.

# Transcription of DNA

*NY teacher: "Know the basic principles. They'll ask you about this process."*

Up until this point, we have just been discussing DNA *replication,* which is simply the production of more DNA. In the rest of the chapter, we discuss transcription, translation, and other processes involving DNA. While DNA is the hereditary material responsible for the passage of traits from generation to generation, DNA does not directly produce the

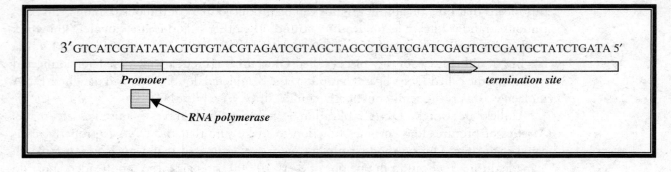

3′GTCATCGTATATACTGTGTACGTAGATCGTAGCTAGCCTGATCGATCGAGTGTCGATGCTATCTGATA 5′

*Promoter*

*RNA polymerase*

*termination site*

**Figure 11.5   Transcription.**

---

**BIG IDEA 3.B.1**
*Gene regulation results in differential gene expression, leading to cell specialization.*

proteins that it encodes. DNA must first be transcribed into an intermediary: mRNA. This process is called *transcription* (Figure 11.5) because both DNA and RNA are built from nucleotides—they speak a similar language. DNA acts as a template for mRNA, which then conveys to the ribosomes the blueprints for producing the protein of interest. Transcription occurs in the nucleus.

Transcription consists of three steps: initiation, elongation, and termination. The process begins when **RNA polymerase** attaches to the promoter region of a DNA strand (initiation). A **promoter region** is simply a recognition site that shows the polymerase where transcription should begin. The promoter region contains a group of nucleotides known as the **TATA box,** which is important to the binding of RNA polymerase. As in DNA replication, the polymerase of transcription needs the assistance of helper proteins to find and attach to the promoter region. These helpers are called **transcription factors.** Once bound, the RNA polymerase works its magic by adding the appropriate RNA nucleotide to the 3′ end of the growing strand (elongation). Like DNA polymerase of replication, RNA polymerase adds nucleotides 5′ to 3′. The growing mRNA strand separates from the DNA as it grows longer. A region called the **termination site** tells the polymerase when transcription should conclude (termination). After reaching this site, the mRNA is released and set free.

## RNA Processing

In bacteria, mRNA is ready to rock immediately after it is released from the DNA. In eukaryotes, this is not the case. The mRNA produced after transcription must be modified before it can leave the nucleus and lead the formation of proteins on the ribosomes. The 5′ and the 3′ ends of the newly produced mRNA molecule are touched up. The 5′ end is given a guanine cap, which serves to protect the RNA and also helps in attachment to the ribosome later on. The 3′ end is given something called a *polyadenine tail,* which may help ease the movement from the nucleus to the cytoplasm. Along with these changes, the **introns** (noncoding regions produced during transcription) are cut out of the mRNA, and the remaining **exons** (coding regions) are glued back together to produce the mRNA that is translated into a protein. This is called **RNA splicing.** We admit that it does seem strange and inefficient that the DNA would contain so many regions that are not used in the production of the gene, but perhaps there is method to the madness. It is hypothesized that introns exist to provide flexibility to the genome. They could allow an organism to make different proteins from the same gene; the only difference is which introns get spliced out from one to the other. It is also possible that this whole splicing process plays a role in allowing the movement of mRNA from the nucleus to the cytoplasm.

# Translation of RNA

Now that the mRNA has escaped from the nucleus, it is ready to help direct the construction of proteins. This process occurs in the cytoplasm, and the site of protein synthesis is the ribosome. As mentioned in Chapter 5, proteins are made of amino acids. Each protein has a distinct and particular amino acid order. Therefore, there must be some system used by the cell to convert the sequences of nucleotides that make up an mRNA molecule into the sequence of amino acids that make up a particular protein. The cell carries out this conversion from nucleotides to amino acids through the use of the **genetic code.** An mRNA molecule is divided into a series of codons that make up the code. Each **codon** is a triplet of nucleotides that codes for a particular amino acid. There are 20 different amino acids, and 64 different combinations of codons. This means that some amino acids are coded for by more than one codon. For example, the codons GCU, GCC, GCA, and GCG all call for the addition of the amino acid alanine during protein creation. Of these 64 possibilities, one is a **start codon,** AUG, which establishes the reading frame for protein formation. Also among these 64 codons are three **stop codons:** UGA, UAA, and UAG. When the protein formation machinery hits these codons, the production of a protein stops.

Before we go through the steps of protein synthesis, we would like to introduce to you the other players involved in the process. We have already spoken about mRNA, but we should meet the host of the entire shindig, the **ribosomes,** which are made up of a large and a small subunit. A huge percentage of a ribosome is built out of the second type of RNA mentioned earlier, rRNA. Two other important parts of a ribosome that we will discuss in more detail later are the **A site** and the **P site,** which are tRNA attachment sites. The job of tRNA is to carry amino acids to the ribosomes. The mRNA molecule that is involved in the formation of a protein consists of a series of codons. Each tRNA has, at its attachment site, a region called the **anticodon,** which is a three-nucleotide sequence that is perfectly complementary to a particular codon. For example, a codon that is AUU has an **anticodon** that reads UAA in the same direction. Each tRNA molecule carries an amino acid that is coded for by the codon that its **anticodon** matches up with. Once the tRNA's amino acid has been incorporated into the growing protein, the tRNA leaves the site to pick up another amino acid just in case its services are needed again at the ribosome. An enzyme known as **aminoacyl tRNA synthetase** makes sure that each tRNA molecule picks up the appropriate amino acid for its anticodon.

Uh-oh . . . there is a potential problem here. There are fewer than 50 different types of tRNA molecules. But there are more codons than that. Oh, dear . . . but wait! This is not a problem because some tRNA are able to match with more than one codon. How can this be? This works thanks to a phenomenon known as **wobble,** where a uracil in the third position of an anticodon can pair with A or G instead of just A. There are some tRNA molecules that have an altered form of adenine, called inosine (I), in the third position of the anticodon. This nitrogenous base is able to bind with U, C, *or* A. Wobble allows the 45 tRNA molecules to service all the different types of codons seen in mRNA molecules.

We have met all the important players in the translation process (see also Figure 11.6), which begins when an mRNA attaches to a small ribosomal subunit. The first codon for this process is always AUG. This attracts a tRNA molecule carrying methionine to attach to the AUG codon. When this occurs, the large subunit of the ribosome, containing the A site and the P site, binds to the complex. The elongation of the protein is ready to begin. The P site is the host for the tRNA carrying the growing protein, while the A site is where the tRNA carrying the next amino acid sits. Think of the A site as the on-deck circle of a baseball field, and P site as the batter's box. So, AUG is the first codon bound, and in the P site is the tRNA carrying the methionine. The next codon in the sequence determines

Large ribosomal subunit

mRNA

A site

tRNA

P site

Small ribosomal subunit

**(a)**

Random amino acids

**(b)**

♦ To start, the P site lies over the AUG codon of the mRNA and the tRNA carrying the appropriate amino acids binds to the site.

The tRNA carrying the <u>next</u> amino acid arrives at the A site.

AUG   CGG

**(c)**

♦ A peptide bond forms between the two amino acids. The amino acid from the P site hops onto the A site amino acid, freeing the tRNA in the P site to leave and find another amino acid to carry.

Old P site

New P site    New A site

**(d)**

**Translocation**: The ribosome slides along the mRNA in such a way that the A site becomes the new P site, and the next tRNA comes into the new A site carrying the next amino acid.

**(e)**

**(f)**

♦ This process continues until the stop codon is reached and the protein is complete.

**Figure 11.6   A pictorial representation of translation.**

which tRNA binds next, and that tRNA molecule sits in the A site of the ribosome. An enzyme helps a peptide bond form between the amino acid on the A site tRNA and the amino acid on the P site tRNA. After this happens, the amino acid from the P site moves to the A site, setting the stage for the tRNA in the P site to leave the ribosome. Now a step called translocation occurs. During this step, the ribosome moves along the mRNA in such a way that the A site becomes the P site and the next tRNA comes into the new A site carrying the next amino acid. This process continues until the stop codon is reached, causing the completed protein to leave the ribosome.

# Gene Expression

Let's cover some vocabulary before diving into this section:

*Promoter region:* a base sequence that signals the start site for gene transcription; this is where RNA polymerase binds to begin the process.

*Operator:* a short sequence near the promoter that assists in transcription by interacting with regulatory proteins (transcription factors).

*CT teacher: "Be able to write about operons."*

*Operon:* a promoter/operator pair that services multiple genes; the **lac operon** is a well-known example (Figure 11.7).

*Repressor:* protein that prevents the binding of RNA polymerase to the promoter site.

*Enhancer:* DNA region, also known as a "regulator," that is located thousands of bases away from the promoter; it influences transcription by interacting with specific transcription factors.

*Inducer:* a molecule that binds to and inactivates a repressor (e.g., lactose for the lac operon).

**BIG IDEA 4.C.2**
*Environmental factors (e.g., lactose in a bacterial culture) can influence gene expression.*

The control of gene expression is vital to the proper and efficient functioning of an organism. In bacteria, operons are a major method of gene expression control. The lactose operon services a series of three genes involved in the process of lactose metabolism. This contains the genes that help the bacteria digest lactose. It makes sense for bacteria to produce these genes only if lactose is present. Otherwise, why waste the energy on unneeded enzymes? This is where operons come into play—in the absence of lactose, a repressor binds to the promoter region and prevents transcription from occurring. When lactose is present, there is a binding site on the repressor where lactose attaches, causing the repressor to let go of the promoter region. RNA polymerase is then free to bind to that site and initiate transcription of the genes. When the lactose is gone, the repressor again becomes free to bind to the promoter, halting the process.

**Figure 11.7   General layout of an operon.**

Because gene expression in eukaryotes involves more steps, there are more places where gene control can occur. Here are a few examples of eukaryotic gene expression control:

*Transcription:* controlled by the presence or absence of particular transcription factors, which bind to the DNA and affect the rate of transcription.

*Translation:* controlled by factors that tend to prevent protein synthesis from starting. This can occur if proteins bind to mRNA and prevent the ribosomes from attaching, or if the initiation factors vital to protein synthesis are inactivated.

*DNA methylation:* addition of $CH_3$ groups to the bases of DNA. Methylation renders DNA inactive. **Barr bodies,** discussed in Chapter 10, are highly methylated.

These are only a few of the examples of gene expression control that occur in eukaryotes. Do not get lost in the specifics.

# The Genetics of Viruses

A **virus** is a parasitic infectious agent that is unable to survive outside of a host organism. Viruses do not contain enzymes for metabolism, and they do not contain ribosomes for protein synthesis. They are completely dependent on their host. Once a virus infects a cell, it takes over the cell's machinery and uses it to produce whatever it needs to survive and reproduce. How a virus acts after it enters a cell depends on what type of virus it is. Classification of viruses is based on many factors:

**BIG IDEA 3.A.1**
*DNA (and sometimes RNA) is the primary source of heritable information.*

*Genetic material:* DNA, RNA, protein, etc.?

*Capsid:* type of capsid?

*Viral envelope:* present or absent?

*Host range:* what type of cells does it affect?

All viruses have a genome (DNA or RNA) and a protein coat (capsid). A **capsid** is a protein shell that surrounds the genetic material. Some viruses are surrounded by a structure called a **viral envelope,** which not only protects the virus but also helps the virus attach to the cells that it prefers to infect. The viral envelope is produced in the endoplasmic reticulum (ER) of the infected cell and contains some elements from the host cell and some from the virus. Each virus has a **host range,** which is the range of cells that the virus is able to infect. For example, the HIV virus infects the T cells of our body, and bacteriophages infect only bacteria.

A special type of virus that merits discussion is one called a retrovirus. This is an RNA virus that carries an enzyme called **reverse transcriptase.** Once in the cytoplasm of the cell, the RNA virus uses this enzyme and "reverse transcribes" its genetic information from RNA into DNA, which then enters the nucleus of the cell. In the nucleus, the newly transcribed DNA incorporates into the host DNA and is transcribed into RNA when the host cell undergoes normal transcription. The mRNA produced from this process gives rise to new retrovirus offspring, which can then leave the cell in a lytic pathway. A well-known example of a retrovirus is the HIV virus of AIDS.

Once inside the cell, a DNA virus can take one of two pathways—a lytic or a lysogenic pathway. In a **lytic cycle,** the cell actually produces many viral offspring, which are released from the cell—killing the host cell in the process. In a **lysogenic cycle,** the virus falls dormant and incorporates its DNA into the host DNA as an entity called a **provirus.** The viral

DNA is quietly reproduced by the cell every time the cell reproduces itself, and this allows the virus to stay alive from generation to generation without killing the host cell. Viruses in the lysogenic cycle can sometimes separate out from the host DNA and enter the lytic cycle (like a bear awaking from hibernation).

Viruses come in many shapes and sizes. Although many viruses are large, **viroids** are plant viruses that are only a few hundred nucleotides in length, showing that size is not the only factor in viral success. Another type of infectious agent you should be familiar with is a **prion**—an incorrectly folded form of a brain cell protein that works its magic by converting other normal host proteins into misshapen proteins. An example of a prion disease that has been getting plenty of press coverage is "mad cow" disease. Prion diseases are degenerative diseases that tend to cause brain dysfunction—dementia, muscular control problems, and loss of balance.

# The Genetics of Bacteria

Bacteria are prokaryotic cells that consist of one double-stranded circular DNA molecule. Present in the cells of many bacteria are extra circles of DNA called **plasmids,** which contain just a few genes and have been useful in genetic engineering. Plasmids replicate independently of the main chromosome. Bacterial cells reproduce in an asexual fashion, undergoing **binary fission.** Quite simply, the cell replicates its DNA and then physically pinches in half, producing a daughter cell that is identical to the parent cell. From this description of binary fission, it seems unlikely that there could be variation among bacterial cells. This is not the case, thanks to mutation and genetic recombination. As in humans, DNA mutation in bacteria occurs very rarely, but some bacteria replicate so quickly that these mutations can have a pronounced effect on their variability.

> **BIG IDEA 3.C.1**
> *Bacteria have multiple ways to increase genetic variation.*

## Transformation

An experiment performed by Griffith in 1928 provides a fantastic example of **transformation**—the uptake of foreign DNA from the surrounding environment. Transformation occurs through the use of proteins on the surface of cells that snag pieces of DNA from around the cell that are from closely related species. This particular experiment involved a bacteria known as *Streptococcus pneumoniae,* which existed as either a rough strain (R), which is nonvirulent, or as a smooth strain (S), which is virulent. A virulent strain is one that can lead to contraction of an illness. The experimenters exposed mice to different forms of the bacteria. Mice given live S bacteria died. Mice given live R bacteria survived. Mice given heat-killed S bacteria survived. Mice given heat-killed S bacteria combined with live R bacteria died. This was the kicker . . . all the other results to this point were expected. Those exposed to heat-killed S combined with live R bacteria contracted the disease because the live R bacteria underwent transformation. Some of the R bacteria picked up the portion of the heat-killed S bacteria's DNA, which contained the instructions on how to make the vital component necessary for successful disease transmission. These R bacteria became virulent.

> **BIG IDEA 3.C.3**
> *Viral infection can introduce genetic variation into the host.*

## Transduction

To understand transduction, you first need to be introduced to something called a **phage** (Figure 11.8)—a virus that infects bacteria. The mechanism by which a phage (otherwise known as bacteriophage) infects a cell reminds me of a syringe. A phage contains within its capsid the DNA that it is attempting to deliver. A phage latches onto the surface of a cell and like a syringe, fires its DNA through the membrane and into the cell. **Transduction** is the movement of genes from one cell to another by phages. The two main forms of transduction you should be familiar with are generalized and specialized transduction.

**Figure 11.8    A phage.**

**Generalized Transduction**    Imagine that a phage virus infects and takes over a bacterial cell that contains a functional gene for resistance to penicillin. Occasionally during the creation of new phage viruses, pieces of host DNA instead of viral DNA are accidentally put into a phage. When the cell lyses, expelling the newly formed viral particles, the phage containing the host DNA may latch onto another cell, injecting the host DNA from one cell into another bacterial cell. If the phage attaches to a cell that contains a nonfunctional gene for resistance to penicillin, the effects of this transduction process can be observed. After injecting the host DNA containing the functional penicillin resistance gene, crossover could occur between the comparable gene regions, switching the nonfunctional gene with the functional gene. This would create a new cell that is resistant to penicillin.

**Specialized Transduction**    This type of transduction involves a virus that is in the lysogenic cycle, resting quietly along with the other DNA of the host cell. Occasionally when a lysogenic virus switches cycles and becomes lytic, it may bring with it a piece of the host DNA as it pulls out of the host chromosome. Imagine that the host DNA it brought with it contains a functional gene for resistance to penicillin. This virus, now in the lytic cycle, will produce numerous copies of new viral offspring that contain this resistance gene from the host cell. If the new phage offspring attaches to a cell that is not penicillin resistant and injects its DNA and crossover occurs, specialized transduction will have occurred.

### Conjugation

This is the raciest of the genetic recombinations that we will cover . . . the bacterial version of sex. It is the transfer of DNA between two bacterial cells connected by appendages called **sex pili**. Movement of DNA between two cells occurs across a cytoplasmic connection between the two cells and requires the presence of an **F-plasmid**, which contains the genes necessary for the production of a sex pilus.

## Genetic Engineering

DNA technology is advancing at a rapid rate, and you need to have a basic understanding of the most common laboratory techniques for the AP Biology exam.

    **Restriction enzymes** are enzymes that cut DNA at specific nucleotide sequences. When added to a solution containing DNA, the enzymes cut the DNA wherever the enzyme's particular sequence appears. This creates DNA fragments with single-stranded ends called "**sticky-ends**," which find and reconnect with other DNA fragments containing the same ends (with the assistance of DNA ligase). Sticky ends allow DNA pieces from different sources to be connected, creating **recombinant DNA**. Another concept important to genetic engineering is the **vector**, which moves DNA from one source to another. Plasmids can be removed from bacterial cells and used as vectors by cutting the DNA of interest and the DNA of the plasmid with the same restriction enzyme to create DNA with similar sticky ends. The DNA can be attached to the plasmid, creating a vector that can be used to transport DNA.

## Gel Electrophoresis

KEY IDEA

*Steve (12th grade): "Know this cold. It was all over my exam!"*

This technique is used to separate and examine DNA fragments. The DNA is cut with our new friends, the restriction enzymes, and then separated by electrophoresis. The pieces of DNA are separated on the basis of size with the help of an electric charge. DNA is added to the wells at the negative end of the gel. When the electric current is turned on, the migration begins. Smaller pieces travel farther along the gel, and larger pieces do not travel as far. The bigger you are, the harder it is to move. This technique can be used to sequence DNA and determine the order in which the nucleotides appear. It can be used in a procedure known as **Southern blotting** (after Edwin M. Southern, a British biologist) to determine if a particular sequence of nucleotides is present in a sample of DNA. Electrophoresis is used in forensics to match DNA found at the crime scene with DNA of suspects. This requires the use of pieces of DNA called *restriction fragment length polymorphisms* (RFLPs). DNA is specific to each individual, and when it is mixed with restriction enzymes, different combinations of RFLPs will be obtained from person to person. Electrophoresis separates DNA samples from the suspect and whatever sample is found at the scene of the crime. The two are compared, and if the RFLPs match, there is a high degree of certainty that the DNA sample came from the suspect. In Figure 11.9, if well A is the DNA from the crime scene, then well C is the DNA of the guilty party.

**Figure 11.9    A sample gel electrophoresis.**

## Cloning

Sometimes it is desirable to obtain large quantities of a gene of interest, such as insulin for the treatment of diabetes. The process of cloning involves many of the steps we just mentioned. Plasmids used for cloning often contain two important genes—one that provides resistance to an antibiotic, and one that gives the bacteria the ability to metabolize some sugar. In this case, we will use a galactose hydrolyzing gene and a gene for ampicillin resistance. The plasmid and DNA of interest are both cut with the same restriction enzyme. The restriction site for this enzyme is right in the middle of the galactose gene of the plasmid. When the sticky ends are created, the DNA of interest and the plasmid molecules are mixed and join together. Not every combination made here is what the scientist is looking for. The recombinant plasmids produced are transformed into bacterial cells. This is where the two specific genes for the plasmid come into play. The transformed cells are allowed to reproduce and are placed on a medium containing ampicillin. Cells that have taken in the ampicillin resistance gene will survive, while those that have not will perish. The medium also contains a special sugar that is broken down by the galactose enzyme present in the vector to form a colored product. The cells containing the gene of interest will remain white since the galactose gene has been interrupted and rendered nonfunctional. This allows the experimenter to isolate cells that contain the desired product. Now, it is time for us to quit cloning around and move onto another genetic engineering technique.

## Polymerase Chain Reaction

Think of this technique as a high-speed copy machine. It is used to produce large quantities of a particular sequence of DNA in a very short amount of time. If the cloning reaction is the 747 of copying DNA, then polymerase chain reaction (PCR) is the Concorde. This process begins with double-stranded DNA containing the gene of interest. DNA polymerase, the superstar enzyme of DNA replication, is added to the mixture along with a huge number of nucleotides and primers specific for the sequence of interest, which help initiate the synthesis of DNA. PCR begins by heating the DNA to split the strands, followed by the cooling of the strands to allow the primers to bind to the sequence of interest. DNA polymerase then steps up to the plate and produces the rest of the DNA molecule by adding the nucleotides to the growing DNA strand. Each cycle concludes having doubled the amount of DNA present at the beginning of the cycle. The cycle is repeated over and over, every few minutes, until a huge amount of DNA has been created. PCR is used in many ways, such as to detect the presence of viruses like HIV in cells, diagnose genetic disorders, and amplify trace amounts of DNA found at crime scenes.

## › Review Questions

1. Which of the following statements is *incorrect*?

   A. Messenger RNA must be processed before it can leave the nucleus of a eukaryotic cell.
   B. A virus in the lysogenic cycle does not kill its host cell, whereas a virus in the lytic cycle destroys its host cell.
   C. DNA polymerase is restricted in that it can add nucleotides only in a 5′-to-3′ direction.
   D. During translation, the A site holds the tRNA carrying the growing protein, while the P site holds the tRNA carrying the next amino acid.

2. The process of transcription results in the formation of

   A. DNA.
   B. proteins.
   C. lipids.
   D. RNA.

3. Which of the following codons signals the beginning of the translation process?

   A. AGU
   B. UGA
   C. AUG
   D. AGG

4. Which of the following is an improper pairing of DNA or RNA nucleotides?

   A. Thymine-adenine
   B. Guanine-thymine
   C. Uracil-adenine
   D. Guanine-cytosine

5. Which of the following is responsible for the type of diseases that includes "mad cow" disease?

   A. Viroids
   B. Plasmids
   C. Prions
   D. Provirus

6. Which of the following is the correct sequence of events that must occur for translation to begin?

   A. Transfer RNA binds to the small ribosomal subunit, which leads to the attachment of the large ribosomal subunit. This signals to the mRNA molecule that it should now bind, with its first codon in the correct site, to the protein synthesis machinery, and translation begins.

   B. Messenger RNA attaches to the small ribosomal subunit, with its first codon in the correct site, thus attracting a tRNA molecule to attach to the codon. This signals to the large subunit that it should now bind to the protein synthesis machinery, and translation can begin.

   C. Messenger RNA attaches to the large ribosomal subunit with its first codon in the correct site, attracting a tRNA molecule to attach to the codon. This signals to the small subunit that it should now bind to the protein synthesis machinery, and translation can begin.

   D. Transfer RNA binds to the large ribosomal subunit, which leads to the attachment of the small ribosomal subunit. This signals to the mRNA molecule that it should now bind with its first codon in the correct site to the protein synthesis machinery, and translation begins.

7. All the following are players involved in the control of gene expression *except*

   A. episomes.
   B. repressors.
   C. operons.
   D. methylation.

8. Which of the following does *not* occur during RNA processing in the nucleus of eukaryotes?

   A. The removal of introns from the RNA molecule
   B. The addition of a string of adenine nucleotides to the 3′ end of the RNA molecule
   C. The addition of a guanine cap to the 5′ end of the RNA molecule
   D. The addition of methyl groups to certain nucleotides of the RNA molecules

9. Which of the following statements is *not* true of a tRNA molecule?

   A. The job of transfer RNA is to carry amino acids to the ribosomes.
   B. At the attachment site of each tRNA, there is a region called the *anticodon*, which is a three-nucleotide sequence that is perfectly complementary to a particular codon.
   C. Each tRNA molecule has a short lifespan and is used only once during translation.
   D. The enzyme responsible for ensuring that a tRNA molecule is carrying the appropriate amino acid is aminoacyl tRNA synthase.

For questions 10 and 11, please use the following gel:

10. Which of the DNA pieces in the gel is smallest in size?

    A.  A
    B.  B
    C.  C
    D.  D

11. If well 1 is DNA from a crime scene, which individual should contact a lawyer?

    A.  Person 2
    B.  Person 3
    C.  Person 4
    D.  Person 5

## ❯ Answers and Explanations

1. **D**—During translation, the **P site** holds the tRNA carrying the growing protein, while the **A site** holds the tRNA carrying the next amino acid. When translation begins, the first codon bound is the AUG codon, and in the P site is the tRNA with the methionine. The next codon in the sequence determines which tRNA binds next, and the appropriate tRNA molecule sits in the A site of the ribosome. A peptide bond forms between the amino acid on the A site tRNA and the amino acid on the P site tRNA. The amino acid from the P site then moves to the A site, allowing the tRNA in the P site to leave the ribosome. Next the ribosome moves along the mRNA in such a way that the A site is now the P site and the next tRNA comes into the A site carrying the next amino acid. Answer choices A, B, and C are all true.

2. **D**—The process of transcription leads to the production of RNA. RNA is not immediately ready to leave the nucleus after it is produced. It must first be processed, during which a 3′ poly-A tail and a 5′ cap are added and the introns are spliced from the RNA molecule. After this process, the RNA is free to leave the nucleus and lead the production of proteins.

3. **C**—AGG codes for the amino acid arginine. AGU codes for the amino acid serine. UGA and UAG are stop codons, which signal the end of

the translation process. AUG is the start codon, which also codes for methionine.

4. **B**—Guanine does not pair with thymine in DNA or RNA. Watson and Crick discovered that adenine pairs with thymine (A=T) held together by two hydrogen bonds and guanine pairs with cytosine (C≡G) held together by three hydrogen bonds. One way that RNA differs from DNA is that it contains uracil instead of thymine. But in RNA, guanine still pairs with cytosine and adenine instead pairs with uracil. Watson and Crick also discovered that for the structure of DNA they discovered to be true, a purine must always be paired with a pyrimidine. Adenine and guanine are the purines, and thymine and cytosine are the pyrimidines.

5. **C**—Prions are the culprit for mad cow disease. *Viroids* are tiny viruses that infect plants. *Plasmids* are small circles of DNA in bacteria that are separate from the main chromosome. They are self-replicating and are vital to the process of genetic engineering. A *provirus* is that which is formed during the lysogenic cycle of a virus when it falls dormant and incorporates its DNA into the host DNA. A *retrovirus* is an RNA virus that carries an enzyme called reverse transcriptase. A classic example of a retrovirus is HIV.

**6. B**—Translation begins when the mRNA attaches to the small ribosomal subunit. The first codon for this process is always AUG. This attracts a tRNA molecule carrying methionine to attach to the AUG codon. When this occurs, the large subunit of the ribosome, containing the A site and the P site, binds to the complex. The elongation of the protein is ready to begin after the complex has been properly constructed. Answers A, C, and D are all in the incorrect order.

**7. A**—Episomes are not involved in gene expression regulation. *Episomes* are plasmids that can be incorporated into a bacterial chromosome. *Repressors* are regulatory proteins involved in gene regulation. They work by preventing transcription by binding to the promoter region. *Operons* are a promoter-operator pair that controls a group of genes, such as the lac operon. Methylation is involved in gene regulation. Barr bodies, discussed in Chapter 10, are found to contain a very high level of methylated DNA. Methyl groups have been associated with inactive DNA that does not undergo transcription. Hormones can affect transcription by acting directly on the transcription machinery in the nucleus of cells.

**8. D**—The mRNA produced after transcription must be modified before it can leave the nucleus and lead the translation of proteins in the ribosomes. Introns are cut out of the mRNA, and the remaining exons are ligated back together to produce the mRNA ready to be translated into a protein. Also, the 5′ end is given a guanine cap, which serves to protect the RNA and also helps the mRNA attach to the ribosome. The 3′ end is given the poly-A tail, which may help ease the movement from the nucleus to the cytoplasm. Methylation does not occur during posttranscriptional modification—it is a means of gene expression control.

**9. C**—tRNA does not have a short lifespan. Each tRNA molecule is released and recycled to bring more amino acids to the ribosomes to aid in translation. It is like a taxicab constantly picking up new passengers to deliver from place to place. Answer choices A, B, and D are all true.

**10. C**—Gel electrophoresis separates DNA fragments on the basis of size—the smaller you are, the farther you go. Because C went the farthest in this gel, this must be the smallest of the four selected DNA pieces. Of the four labeled, piece A must be the largest because it moved the least.

**11. C**—Person 4 should contact a lawyer. The DNA from the crime scene seems to match the DNA fingerprint from person 4. Electrophoresis is a very useful tool in forensics and can very accurately match DNA found at crime scenes with potential suspects.

## › Rapid Review

Briefly review the following terms:

*DNA*: contains A and G (purines), C and T (pyrimidines), arranged in a double helix of two strands held together by hydrogen bonds (A with T, and C with G).

*RNA*: contains A and G (purines), C and U (pyrimidines), single stranded. There are three types: mRNA (blueprints for proteins), tRNA (brings acids to ribosomes), and rRNA (make up ribosomes).

*DNA replication*: occurs during S-phase, semi-conservative, built in 5′-to-3′ direction. Helicase unzips the double strand, DNA polymerase comes in and adds on the nucleotides. Proofreading enzymes minimize errors of process.

*Frameshift mutation*: deletion or addition of nucleotides (not a multiple of 3); shifts reading frame.

*Missense mutation*: substitution of wrong nucleotide into DNA (e.g., sickle cell anemia); still produces a protein.

*Nonsense mutation*: substitution of wrong nucleotide into DNA that produces an early stop codon.

*Transcription*: process by which mRNA is synthesized on a DNA template.

*RNA processing*: introns (noncoding) are spliced out, exons (coding) glued together: 3′ poly-A tail, 5′ G cap.

*Translation*: process by which the mRNA specified sequence of amino acids is lined up on a ribosome for protein synthesis.

*Codon*: triplet of nucleotides that codes for a particular amino acid: **start codon** = AUG; **stop codon** = UGA, UAA, UAG. (For specifics on translation, please flip to text for a good description.)

*Promoter*: base sequence that signals start site for transcription.

*Repressor*: protein that prevents the binding of RNA polymerase to promoter site.

*Inducer*: molecule that binds to and inactivates a repressor.

*Operator*: short sequence near the promoter that assists in transcription by interacting with transcription factors.

*Operon*: on/off switch for transcription. Allows for production of genes only when needed. Remember the lac operon—lactose is the inducer, when present, transcription on; when absent, it is off.

*Viruses*: Parasitic infectious agent unable to survive outside the host; can contain DNA or RNA, or have a viral envelope (protective coat).

* *Lytic cycle*: one in which the virus is actively reproducing and kills the host cell.
* *Lysogenic cycle*: one in which the virus lies dormant within the DNA of the host cell.

*Retrovirus*: RNA virus that carries with it reverse transcriptase (HIV).

*Prion*: virus that converts host brain proteins into misshapen proteins (mad cow disease).

*Viroids*: tiny plant viruses.

*Phage*: virus that infects bacteria.

*Bacteria*: prokaryotic cells; consist of one double-stranded circular DNA molecule; reproduce by binary fission (e.g., **plasmid**—extra circle of DNA present in bacteria that replicate independently of main chromosome).

### Genetic Recombination

*Transformation*: uptake of foreign DNA from the surrounding environment (smooth vs. rough pneumococcus).

*Transduction*: movement of genes from one cell to another by phages, which are incorporated by crossover.

* *Generalized*: lytic cycle accidently places host DNA into a phage, which is brought to another cell.
* *Specialized*: virus leaving lysogenic cycle brings host DNA with it into phage.

*Conjugation*: transfer of DNA between two bacterial cells connected by sex pili.

## Genetic Engineering

*Restriction enzymes*: enzymes that cut DNA at particular sequences, creating sticky ends.

*Vector*: mover of DNA from one source to another (plasmids are good vectors).

*Cloning*: somewhat slow process by which a desired sequence of DNA is copied numerous times.

*Gel electrophoresis*: technique used to separate DNA according to size (small = faster). DNA moves from: − to +.

*Polymerase chain reaction (PCR)*: produces large quantities of sequence in short amount of time.

# CHAPTER 12

# Evolution

**IN THIS CHAPTER**

**Summary:** This chapter discusses evolution and the four major modes in which it occurs. It introduces you to the various forms of selection: natural, directional, stabilizing, disruptive, sexual, and artificial. It discusses the two main forms of speciation (allopatric and sympatric) and briefly touches on the theory behind how life on this planet emerged many years ago.

**Key Ideas**

- ✪ The four major modes of evolution are genetic drift, gene flow, mutation, and natural selection.
- ✪ Natural selection is based on three conditions: variation, heritability, and differential reproductive success.
- ✪ There are four basic patterns of evolution: co-evolution, convergent evolution, divergent evolution, and parallel evolution.
- ✪ Sources of variation within populations: mutation, sexual reproduction, and balanced polymorphism.
- ✪ Hardy-Weinberg conditions: no mutations, no gene flow, no genetic drift, no natural selection, and random mating.
- ✪ Hardy-Weinberg equations: $p + q = 1$ and $p^2 + 2pq + q^2 = 1$.
- ✪ Evidence for evolution: homologous characters, embryology, and vestigial structures.

# Introduction

This chapter begins with an introduction to the concept of evolution and the four major modes in which it occurs. From there we focus more closely on natural selection and the work of Lamarck and Darwin. We then briefly touch on adaptations before looking at the various types of selection: directional, stabilizing, disruptive, sexual, and artificial selection. This is followed by a quick look at the sources of variation within populations followed by a look at the two main types of speciation: allopatric and sympatric. Next will come the yucky math portion of the chapter: the Hardy-Weinberg equation and the conditions necessary for its existence. The chapter concludes with a look at the existing evidence in support of the theory of evolution and a discussion of how life on this planet emerged so many years ago.

# Definition of Evolution

How often have you heard executives report that "the idea evolved into a successful project" or popular science show narrators describe how a star "has been evolving for millions of years"? *Evolution* is no longer strictly a biological term since every academic field and nonacademic industry uses it. Such uses of the verb *evolve* reveal its meaning in its simplest form—to evolve means to change. For the AP Biology exam, however, you should remember the biological definition of evolution: *descent with modification.* Don't let the general uses of the word mislead you; a key part of this definition is *descent,* which can happen only when one group of organisms gives rise to another. When you see the word *evolution,* think of something that happens in populations, not in individuals.

More specifically, evolution describes change in allele frequencies in populations over time. When one generation of organisms (whether algae or giraffes or ferns) reproduces and creates the next, the frequencies of the alleles for the various genes represented in the population may be different from what they were in the parent generation. Frequencies can change so much that certain alleles are lost or others become fixed—all individuals have the same allele for that character. Over many generations, the species can change so much that it becomes quite different from the ancestral species, or a part of the population can branch off and become a new species (**speciation**). Why do we see this change in allele frequencies with time?

Allele frequencies may change because of random factors or by natural selection. Let's consider chance events first. Imagine a population of fish in a large pond that exhibits two alleles for fin length (short and long) and is isolated from other populations of the same species. One day a tornado kills 50 percent of the fish population. Completely by chance, most of the fish killed possess the long-fin allele, and very few of these individuals are left in the population. In the next generation, there are many fewer fish with long fins because fewer long-finned fish were left to reproduce; that allele is much more poorly represented in the pond than it was in the original parent generation before the catastrophe. This is an example of **genetic drift:** a change in allele frequencies that is due to chance events. When drift dramatically reduces population size, we call it a **bottleneck.**

Now imagine that the same pond becomes connected to another pond by a small stream. The two populations mix, and by chance, all the long-finned fish migrate to the other pond, and no long-finned fish migrate in. Again, which individuals migrated was random in this example; thus, there will be a change in the allele frequencies in the next generation. This is an example of **gene flow,** or the change in allele frequencies as genes from one population are incorporated into another.

Gene flow (also more loosely known as *migration* when the individuals are actively relocating) is random with respect to which organisms succeed, but keep in mind that we

**BIG IDEA 4.C.4**
*The diversity of species within an ecosystem may influence the stability of the ecosystem.*

could think of situations in which migration is not random. For example, if only the short-finned fish could fit in the stream connecting the two ponds, the alleles represented in the subsequent generation would *not* be random with respect to that allele. We also have not stated that the short-finned fish have an advantage by swimming to the other pond—if they did, this would be an example of natural selection, which we'll discuss below.

Finally, let's consider **mutation,** the third random event that can cause changes in allele frequencies. Mutation is *always* random with respect to which genes are affected, although the changes in allele frequencies that occur as a result of the mutation may not be. Let's say that a mutation occurs in the offspring of a fish in our hypothetical pond. The mutation creates a new allele. As a result, the allele frequencies in the offspring generation has changed, simply because we have added a new allele (remember that allele frequencies for a given gene always add up to one). As you can imagine, one mutation on its own does not have the potential to dramatically alter the allele frequencies in a population, unless this is a *really* small pond! But mutation is extremely important because it is the basis of the variation we see in the first place and it is a very strong force when it is paired with natural selection.

The four major modes of evolution are

1. Genetic drift
2. Gene flow (also called *migration*)
3. Mutation
4. Natural selection

Remember that the first three factors act randomly with respect to the alleles in the population—which alleles increase and which decrease in frequency are determined by chance events, not because some alleles are inherently better than others. We'll now turn to the fourth mode or process of evolution, natural selection, where the modification that occurs with descent is *nonrandom*.

# Natural Selection

**BIG IDEA 1.A.1**
*Natural selection is a major mechanism of evolution.*

Probably the biggest mistake people make when thinking about natural selection is thinking that it is synonymous with evolution. **Natural selection** is only one process by which evolution occurs (the others are discussed in the previous section). However, it is an important process because it has been instrumental in shaping the natural world. Because of the theory of natural selection, we can explain why organisms look and behave the way they do.

Natural selection is based on three conditions:

1. *Variation:* for natural selection to occur, a population must exhibit phenotypic variance—in other words, differences must exist between individuals, even if they are slight.
2. *Heritability:* parents must be able to pass on the traits that are under natural selection. If a trait cannot be inherited, it cannot be selected for or against.
3. *Differential reproductive success:* this sounds complicated, but it's a simple concept. **Reproductive success** measures how many offspring you produce that survive relative to how many the other individuals in your population produce. The condition simply states that there must be variation between parents in how many offspring they produce as a result of the different traits that the parents have.

**BIG IDEA 1.A.2**
*Natural selection acts on phenotypes.*

It is easiest to illustrate natural selection with an example. Let's revisit our pond before the tornado came, where short- and long-finned fish inhabit murky waters. A new predator invades the pond. Fin length determines swimming speed (longer fins allow a fish to swim faster), and only the fastest fish can escape the predator. How would you expect the allele frequencies to change under these conditions? Fish with what length fin would be eaten the most? Because the short-finned fish would be the slowest, they would be featured on the menu. But the long-finned fish, able to escape this new predator, would survive and reproduce, and the frequency of the long-fin allele would increase relative to the short-fin allele. We have created a situation in which allele frequencies change as a result of a nonrandom event; the predator's presence results in a predictable decrease in the short-fin allele and a consequent increase in the long-fin allele. Remember that allele frequencies always add up to 100 percent, so the long-finned fish don't have to do particularly well for the long-fin allele to increase—they only have to do well *relative* to the short-finned fish. The actual numbers of fish could decrease for both variants of this fish species.

**BIG IDEA 1.A.3**
*Evolutionary change is driven by random processes.*

Why aren't organisms perfectly adapted to their environments? Since natural selection increases the frequencies of advantageous alleles, why don't we get to a point where all individuals have all the best alleles? For one, different alleles confer different advantages in different environments. Furthermore, remember that the environment—which includes everything from habitat, to climate, to competitors, to predators, to food resources—is constantly changing. Species are therefore also constantly changing as the traits that give them an advantage also change. In cases where a trait becomes unconditionally advantageous, we do in fact see fixed alleles; for example, all spiders have eight legs because the alternatives just aren't as good under any circumstances. But where there are heritable characters that both vary and confer fitness advantages (or disadvantages) on their host organisms, natural selection can occur.

## Lamarck and Darwin

The two key figures whose research you should know for the evolution section of the AP Biology exam are Jean-Baptiste Lamarck and Charles Darwin. Lamarck proposed the idea that evolution occurs by the inheritance of acquired characters. The classic example is giraffe necks: Lamarck proposed that giraffes evolved long necks because individuals were constantly reaching for the leaves at the tops of trees. A giraffe's neck lengthened during its lifetime, and then that giraffe's offspring had a long neck because of all that straining its parents did. The key here is that change happened within organisms during their lifetimes and then the change in the trait was passed on.

What's wrong with Lamarck's theory? Try explaining to yourself how the changed character could be passed on to the offspring. The answer is that it couldn't—the instructions in the sex chromosomes that direct the production of offspring cannot be changed after they are created at the birth of an organism. Lamarck confused genetic and environmental (postconceptive) change, which is not surprising because no one had discovered genes yet.

Darwin had another idea, one that ended up being entirely consistent with Mendelian genetics (although Mendel had already written his thesis during Darwin's time, it is rumored that his book sat on Darwin's shelf, with the pages still uncut, until Darwin's death). Darwin suggested the idea of natural selection described above and coined the phrase "survival of the fittest." Although he didn't call them *genes,* he proposed a hypothetical unit of heredity that passed from parent to offspring. Incidentally, a man named Wallace also came up with the idea of natural selection during the same time, but Darwin got the publication out first and has become famous as a result.

# Adaptations

An **adaptation** is a trait that if altered, affects the fitness of the organism. Adaptations are the result of natural selection and can include not only physical traits such as eyes, fingernails, and livers but also the intangible traits of organisms. For example, lifespan length is an adaptation, albeit a variable one. Mating behavior is also an adaptation—it has been selected by natural selection because it is an effective strategy. An individual with a different form of mating behavior may do better or worse than the average, but a change is likely to have some effect on reproductive success. For example, individuals whose mating strategy is to attempt to court women by running at them, arms flailing while screaming wildly, and salivating heavily, do worse than the average male.

Let's take a look at how such a behavioral adaptation can evolve. Reproductive maturity is a good example. Female chimpanzees become reproductively mature at around the age of 13. Females that mature at age 12 spend less time growing and may therefore be more susceptible to problems with pregnancy. Females that mature at 14 have lost valuable time—their earlier-maturing peers have gained a year on them. You can imagine that from generation to generation, females that matured at age 13 became better represented in the population compared to faster and slower maturers. Although there will always be individuals that differ from the mode, we can view age at reproductive maturation as an adaptation.

# Types of Selection

Natural selection can change the frequencies of alleles in populations through various processes. The most commonly described are the following three:

*Mike (freshman in college): "Learn these selection types . . . they make good multiple-choice questions."*

1. **Directional selection.** This occurs when members of a population at one end of a spectrum are selected against, while those at the other end are selected for. For example, imagine a population of elephants with various-sized trunks. In this particular environment, much more food is available in the very tall trees than in the shorter trees. Elephants with what length trunk will survive and reproduce the most successfully? Those with the longest trunks. Those with shorter trunks will be strongly selected against (and those in the middle will also be in the middle in terms of success). Over time we expect to see an increasing percentage of elephants with long trunks (how quickly this change occurs depends on the strength of selection—if all the short-trunked elephants die, we can imagine that the allele frequencies will change very quickly). (See Figure 12.1.)
2. **Stabilizing selection.** This describes selection for the mean of a population for a given allele. A real example of this is human infant birth weight—it is a disadvantage to be really small *or* really big, and it is best to be somewhere in between. Stabilizing selection has the effect of reducing variation in a population (see Figure 12.1).
3. **Disruptive selection.** Also known as *diversifying selection,* this process can be regarded as being the opposite of stabilizing selection. We say that selection is disruptive when individuals at the two extremes of a spectrum of variation do better than the more common forms in the middle. Snail shell color is an example of disruptive selection. Imagine an environment in which snails with very dark shells and those with very light shells are best able to hide from predators. Those with an in-between shell color are gulped up like escargot at a cocktail party, creating the double-hump curve seen in Figure 12.1.

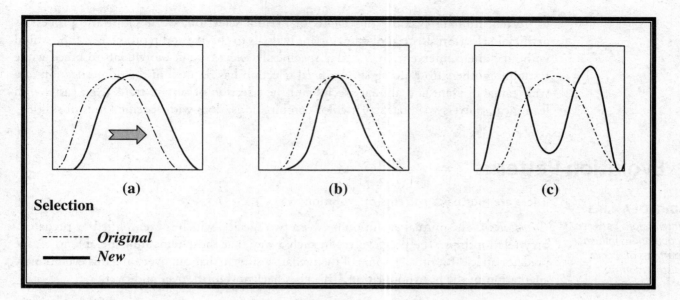

**Selection**

------- *Original*
——— *New*

**Figure 12.1    Three types of selection: (a) directional; (b) stabilizing; (c) disruptive.**

These three processes describe the way in which allele frequencies can change as a result of the forces of natural selection. It is also important to remember two other types of selection that complement natural selection: sexual selection and artificial selection.

**Sexual selection** occurs because individuals differ in mating success. In other words, because not all individuals will have the maximum number of possible offspring, there must be some reason why some individuals have greater reproductive success than others. Think about how this is different from natural selection, which includes both reproduction and survival. Sexual selection is purely about access to mating opportunities.

Sexual selection occurs by two primary processes: **within-sex competition** and **choice.** In mammals and many nonmammalian species, females are limited in the number of offspring they can produce in their lifetimes (because of internal gestation), while males are not (because sperm are cheap to produce and few males participate in offspring care). Which sex do you think will compete, and which sex will be choosier? In most mammals for instance, males compete and females choose. It makes sense that males have to compete because females are a limiting resource, and it makes sense that females are choosy because they invest a lot in each reproductive effort. This leads to the evolution of characters that are designed for two main functions: (1) as weaponry or other tools for male competition (e.g., large testes for sperm competition) and (2) as traits that increase mating opportunities because females prefer to mate with males who have them (e.g., colorful feathers in many birds).

On what do females base their choices? While you need not become an expert on this matter, it is important to remember that female mate choice for certain characters is not random. One hypothesis for why females choose males with colorful feathers, for example, is that colorful feathers indicate good genes, which is important for a female's offspring. Bright colors are costly, so a male with brightly colored feathers is probably healthy (which may, in turn, indicate an ability to reduce parasite load, for example). We call such sexually selected traits that are the result of female choice **honest indicators.** Keep in mind that selecting a mate for particular features does not necessarily involve conscious thought, and in most animals never does; the female does not think, "Oh! What nice feathers. He must come from good genes." Rather, females who choose males that display honest indicators have more surviving offspring than do females who don't, and as a result, the "choosing males with colorful feathers" trait increases in the population.

When humans become the agents of natural selection, we describe the process as **artificial selection.** Instead of allowing individuals to survive and reproduce as they would without human intervention, we may specifically select certain individuals to breed while restraining others from doing so. Artificial selection has resulted in the domestication of a wide range of plant and animal species and the selection of certain traits (e.g., cattle with lean meat, flowers with particular color combinations, dogs with specific kinds of skill).

# Evolution Patterns

**BIG IDEA 4.B.3**
*Interactions between populations influence patterns of species distribution.*

There are four basic patterns of evolution:

*Coevolution.* The mutual evolution between two species, which is exemplified by predator–prey relationships. The prey evolves in such a way that those remaining are able to escape predator attack. Eventually, some of the predators survive that can overcome this evolutionary adaptation in the prey population. This goes back and forth, over and over.

*Convergent evolution.* Two unrelated species evolve in a way that makes them *more* similar (think of them as converging on a single point). They are both responding in the same way to some environmental challenge, and this brings them closer together. We call two *characters* **convergent characters** if they are similar in two species, even though the species do *not* share a common ancestor. For example, birds and insects both have wings in order to fly, despite the fact that insects are not directly related to birds.

*Divergent evolution.* Two related species evolve in a way that makes them *less* similar. Divergent evolution can lead to speciation (allopatric or sympatric).

*Parallel evolution.* Similar evolutionary changes occurring in two species that can be related or unrelated. They are simply responding in a similar manner to a similar environmental condition.

# Sources of Variation

Remember that one of the conditions for natural selection is variation. Where does this variation within populations come from?

1. **Mutation.** We already discussed mutations as a mechanism by which evolution occurs. Random changes in the DNA of an individual can introduce new alleles into a population.
2. **Sexual reproduction.** Refer to Chapter 16, Human Reproduction, and the discussion of why offspring are not identical to their parents (crossover, independent assortment of homologous pairs, and the fact that all sperm and ova are unique and thus create a unique individual when joined).
3. **Balanced polymorphism.** Some characters are fixed, meaning that all individuals in a species or population have them: for example, all tulips develop from bulbs. However, other characters are polymorphic, meaning that there are two or more phenotypic variants. For example, tulips come in a variety of colors. If one phenotypic variant leads to increased reproductive success, we expect directional selection to eventually eliminate all other varieties. However, we can find many examples in the natural world where variation is prominent and one allele is not uniformly better than the others. The various ways in which balanced polymorphism is maintained are presented in Figure 12.2.

**BIG IDEA 3.C.1**
*Heterozygote advantage is one way biological systems can increase genetic variation.*

| Mechanism | Description | Example |
|---|---|---|
| **Heterozygote advantage** | The heterozygous condition has an advantage over either homozygote, so both alleles are maintained (AA is worse off than Aa). | Sickle cell trait, a heterozygous condition, gives people in malarial environments an advantage because they are resistant to this disease. |
| **Hybrid vigor and outbreeding** | Two unrelated individuals are less likely to have the same recessive, deleterious allele than are relatives; therefore, their offspring are less likely to be homozygous for that allele; in addition, outbreeding increases the number of heterozygous alleles, increasing heterozygote advantage. | Artificially selected plants are carefully outbred in order to increase hybrid vigor; mating two inbred strains of potato will increase the number of heterozygous loci and increase the species' resistance to disease. |
| **Frequency-dependent selection** | The least common phenotype is selected for, while common phenotypes have a disadvantage. | In some fruit flies, females choose to mate with males that have the rarer phenotype, resulting in selection against the more common variants. |

**Figure 12.2    How balanced polymorphism is maintained.**

# Speciation

**BIG IDEA 1.C.1**
*Speciation (and extinction) have occurred throughout Earth's history.*

A **species** is a group of interbreeding (or potentially interbreeding) organisms. **Speciation,** the process by which new species evolve, can take one of several forms. You should be familiar with the two main forms of speciation:

1. **Allopatric speciation.** Interbreeding ceases because some sort of barrier separates a single population into two (an area with no food, a mountain, etc.). The two populations evolve independently (by any of the four processes discussed earlier), and if they change enough, then even if the barrier is removed, they cannot interbreed.

2. **Sympatric speciation.** Interbreeding ceases even though no physical barrier prevents it. This may take several forms.

Two other important terms are **polyploidy** and **balanced polymorphism:**

*Polyploidy.* A condition in which an individual has more than the normal number of sets of chromosomes. Although the individual may be healthy, it cannot reproduce with nonpolyploidic members of its species. This is unusual, but in some plants, it has resulted in new species because polyploidic individuals are only able to mate with each other.

**BIG IDEA 1.C.2**
*Speciation may occur when two populations become reproductively isolated.*

*Balanced polymorphism.* This condition (described above) can also lead to speciation if two variants diverge enough to no longer be able to interbreed (if, e.g., potential mates no longer recognize each other as possible partners).

One more term to mention before moving on is **adaptive radiation,** which is a rapid series of speciation events that occur when one or more ancestral species invades a new environment. This process was exemplified by Darwin's finches. If there are many ecological niches (see Chapter 18, Ecology in Further Detail), several species will evolve because each can fill a different niche.

# When Evolution Is Not Occurring: Hardy-Weinberg Equilibrium

**BIG IDEA 4.C.3**
*Allelic variation in a population can be modeled by the Hardy-Weinberg equation.*

Evolutionary change is constantly happening in humans and other species; this seems sensible because evolution is the change in allele frequencies over time. It makes sense that these frequencies are highly variable and subject to change as the environment changes. However, biologists use a theoretical concept called the **Hardy-Weinberg equilibrium** to describe those special cases where a population is in stasis, or not evolving.

Only if the following conditions are met can a population be in Hardy-Weinberg equilibrium:

**KEY IDEA**

### Hardy-Weinberg Conditions

1. No mutations
2. No gene flow
3. No genetic drift (and for this, the population must be large)
4. No natural selection (so that the traits are neutral; none gives an advantage or disadvantage)
5. Random mating

Notice items 1–4 in this list are the four modes of evolution, which makes sense—if we are trying to establish the conditions under which evolution does *not* occur, we must keep these processes of evolution from occurring! The fifth condition, random mating, is included because if individuals mated nonrandomly (e.g., if individuals mated with others that looked like them), the allele frequencies could change in a certain direction, and we would no longer be in equilibrium.

**KEY IDEA**

### Determining Whether a Population Is in Hardy-Weinberg Equilibrium

Unfortunately for you, there is an equation associated with the Hardy-Weinberg equilibrium that the test writers love to put on the exam. Don't let it scare you!

$$p + q = 1$$

This equation is used to determine if a population is in Hardy-Weinberg equilibrium. The symbol $p$ is the frequency of allele 1 (often the *dominant allele*), and $q$ is the frequency of allele 2 (often the recessive allele). Remember that the frequency of two alleles always adds up to 1 *if the population is in Hardy-Weinberg equilibrium*. For example, if 60 percent of the alleles for a given trait are dominant ($p$), then $p = 0.6$, and $q$ (the recessive allele) = 1 − 0.6, or 0.4 (40 percent).

There is a second equation that goes along with this theory: $p^2 + 2pq + q^2 = 1$, where $p^2$ and $q^2$ represent the frequency of the two homozygous conditions (AA and aa). The frequency of the heterozygotes is $pq$ plus $qp$ or $2pq$ (Aa and aA). Since $p$ represents the dominant allele, it makes sense that $p^2$ represents the homozygous dominant condition. By the same logic, $q^2$ represents the homozygous recessive condition.

Let's say that you are told that a population of acacia trees is 16 percent short (which is a, recessive) and 84 percent tall (which is A, dominant). What are the frequencies of

*CT teacher: "Knowing how to do Hardy-Weinberg problems is worth 2 points to you . . . easy points."*

the two alleles? Remember that it is not 0.16 and 0.84 because there are also the heterozygotes to consider!

In a problem like this, it is important to determine the value of $q$ first because we know that all individuals with the recessive phenotype must be aa ($q^2$). You cannot begin by calculating the value of $p$ because it is not true that all the individuals with the dominant phenotype can be lumped into $p^2$. Some folks displaying the dominant phenotype are heterozygous Aa ($pq$).

We know that $q^2 = 0.16$, so we find $q$ by calculating $\sqrt{0.16} \rightarrow q = 0.400$. Now remember that they do not let you use a calculator. So these problems will give numbers that are fairly easy to work with. Do not despair.

What about $p$? Since $p + q$ is 1, and we know $q = 0.40$, then $p$ must equal $1 - 0.40$ or 0.600.

You may also be asked to go a step further and give the percentages of the homozygous dominant and heterozygous conditions (remember, we know that the recessive condition is 16 percent—all these individuals must be aa in order to express the recessive trait). This is simple—just plug in what you know about $p$ and $q$:

$$2pq = (2)\,(0.6)\,(0.4) = 0.48 \text{ or } 48\%$$
$$p^2 = (0.6)\,(0.6) = 0.36 \text{ or } 36\%$$

Now check your math: do the frequencies add up to 100 percent?

$$16 + 48 + 36 = 100$$

Why do we ever use the Hardy-Weinberg equation if it rarely applies to real populations? This can be an excellent tool to determine whether a population is evolving or not; if we find that the allele frequencies do not add up to one, then we need to look for the reasons for this (perhaps the population is too small and genetic drift is a factor, or perhaps one of the alleles is advantageous and is therefore being selected for and increasing in the population). Therefore, although the Hardy-Weinberg equilibrium is largely theoretical, it does have some important uses in evolutionary biology.

# The Evidence for Evolution

Support for the theory of evolution can be found in varied kinds of evidence:

1. **Homologous characters.** Traits are said to be homologous if they are similar because their host organisms arose from a common ancestor (which implies that they have evolved). For example, the bone structure in bird wings is homologous in all bird species.

2. **Embryology.** The study of embryos reveals remarkable similarities between organisms at the earliest stages of life, although as adults (or even at birth) the species look completely different. Human embryos, for example, actually have gills for a short time during early development, hinting at our aquatic ancestry. Darwin used embryology as an important piece of evidence for the process of evolution. In 1866, the scientist Ernst Haeckel uttered the phrase, "Ontogeny recapitulates phylogeny." **Ontogeny** is an *individual's* development; **phylogeny** is a **species'** evolutionary history. What Haeckel meant was that during an organism's embryonic development, it will at some point resemble the adult form of all its ancestors before it. For example, human embryos at some point look a lot like fish embryos. The important conclusion from this is that Haeckel and others thought that embryologic similarity between developing individuals could be used to

deduce phylogenetic relationships. By the end of the nineteenth century, it was clear this law rarely holds. The real development of organisms differs in several important ways from Haeckel's schemes.

3. **Vestigial characters.** Most organisms carry characters that are no longer useful, although they once were. This should remind you of our short discussion about why organisms are not perfectly adapted to their environments (because the environment is constantly changing). Sometimes an environment changes so much that a trait is no longer needed, but is not deleterious enough to actually be selected against and eliminated. Darwin used vestigial characters as evidence in his original formulation of the process of evolution, listing the human appendix as an example.

Keep in mind that the kinds of evidence we've described are often found in the **fossil record**—the physical manifestation of species that have gone extinct (including things like bones as well as imprints). The most important thing to remember is that adaptations are the result of natural selection.

# Macroevolution

Biologists distinguish between microevolution and macroevolution. **Microevolution** includes all of what we have been discussing so far in this chapter—evolution at the level of species and populations. Think of **macroevolution** as the big picture, which includes the study of evolution of groups of species over very long periods of time.

There are disagreements in the field as to the typical pattern of macroevolution. Those who believe in **gradualism** assert that evolutionary change is a steady, slow process, while those who think that evolution is best described by the **punctuated equilibria model** believe that change occurs in rapid bursts separated by large periods of stasis (no change) (see comparison in Figure 12.3). Because the fossil record is

**Figure 12.3    Gradualism versus punctuated equilibrium.**

incomplete, it is very hard to test the two theories—if we find no fossils for a species over a contested period, how can we determine whether change was occurring? The debate therefore continues.

## How Life Probably Emerged

The AP Biology exam often includes questions on how life originated. It is therefore wise to learn the steps of the **heterotroph theory** (Figure 12.4), so named because it posits that the first organisms were **heterotrophs,** organisms that cannot make their own food.

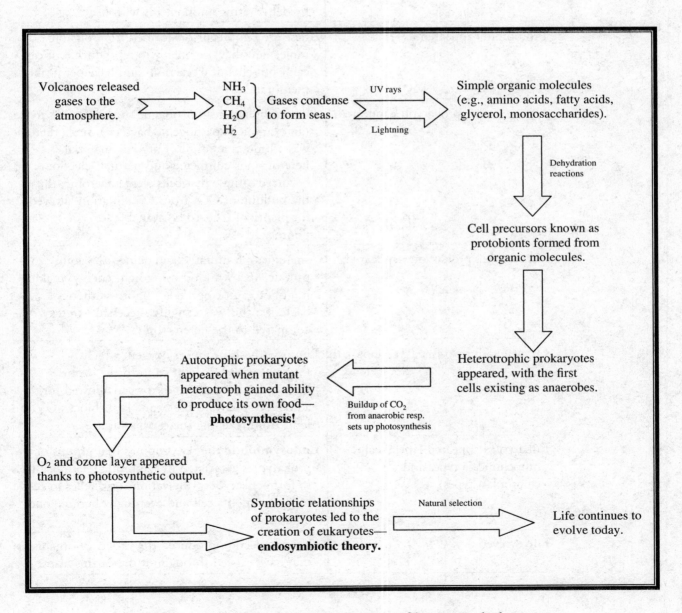

**Figure 12.4  Flowchart representation of heterotroph theory.**

| STEP | DESCRIPTION |
|---|---|
| The earth's atmosphere formed. | Emerging from volcanoes, gases such as $NH_3$, $CH_4$, $H_2O(g)$, and $H_2$ (but not oxygen) invaded the atmosphere. |
| The seas formed. | The gases condensed to form the seas as the earth cooled. |
| Simple organic molecules appeared. | Energy (from UV light, lightning, heat, radioactivity) transformed inorganic molecules to organic ones, including amino acids. |
| Polymers and self-replicating molecules appeared. | These may have been formed through dehydration, or the removal of water molecules; e.g., proteinoids can be produced from polypeptides by dehydrating amino acids with heat. |
| Protobionts appeared. | These are cell precursors formed from organic molecules; they are unable to reproduce, but can carry out chemical reactions and have permeable membranes. |
| Heterotrophic prokaryotes appeared. | Heterotrophs consume organic substances to survive (an example is pathogenic bacteria); since there was a limited amount of organic material, heterotrophs competed and natural selection occurred—these first cells were anaerobic; thus, the buildup of $CO_2$ from fermentation allowed for plenty of $CO_2$ to be available for photosynthesis. |
| Autotrophic prokaryotes appeared. | A heterotroph mutated and gained the ability to produce its own food using light energy, making it a photo autotroph (e.g., photosynthetic bacteria); this was a highly successful strategy compared to the heterotroph's. |
| Oxygen and the ozone layer appeared. | Photosynthesis produces oxygen, which interacts with UV light to form the ozone layer—this production of oxygen allowed for aerobic respiration; the ozone layer blocks UV light from reaching the earth's surface. |
| Eukaryotes appeared (specifically mitochondria types and chloroplast types). | **Endosymbiotic theory** proposes that groups of prokaryotes associated in symbiotic relationships to form eukaryotes (the various organelles in cells today invaded a cell and eventually became one organism). |
| Life evolved. | Natural selection produced the variety of organisms that have existed throughout the earth's history. |

**BIG IDEA 1.D.1**
*There are several hypotheses about the origin of life, each with evidence to support it.*

Why is it important that there was no oxygen to start? Alexander Oparin and J. B. S. Haldane hypothesized that oxygen would have prevented the formation of simple molecules because it is too reactive, and would have taken the place of any other element in chemical reactions. Stanley Miller and Harold Urey tested this hypothesis by simulating a primordial environment, and found that in the absence of oxygen, they were able to form organic molecules (including amino acids).

## ❯ Review Questions

**1.** Which of the following is an evolutionary process *not* based on random factors?

   A. Genetic drift
   B. Natural selection
   C. Mutation
   D. Gene flow

**2.** Which of the following is not a sexually selected trait?

   A. Fruit fly wings
   B. A male baboon's canine teeth
   C. Peacock tail feathers
   D. Male/female dimorphism in body size in many species

**3.** An adaptation

   A. can be shaped by genetic drift.
   B. cannot be altered.
   C. evolves because it specifically improves an individual's mating success.
   D. affects the fitness of an organism if it is altered.

**4.** Which of the following is *not* a requirement for natural selection to occur?

   A. Variation between individuals
   B. Heritability of the trait being selected
   C. Sexual reproduction
   D. Differences in reproductive success among individuals

**5.** Why can Hardy-Weinberg equilibrium occur only in large populations?

   A. Large populations are likely to have more variable environments.
   B. More individuals means less chance for natural selection to occur.
   C. Genetic drift is a much stronger force in small versus large populations.
   D. Large populations make random mating virtually impossible.

**6.** A population of frogs consists of 9 percent with speckles (the recessive condition) and 91 percent without speckles. What are the frequencies of the $p$ and $q$ alleles if this population is in Hardy-Weinberg equilibrium?

   A. $p = 0.49$, $q = 0.51$
   B. $p = 0.60$, $q = 0.40$
   C. $p = 0.70$, $q = 0.30$
   D. $p = 0.49$, $q = 0.30$

**7.** Frequency-dependent selection is

   A. particularly important during speciation.
   B. one way in which multiple alleles are preserved in a population.
   C. possible only when there are two alleles.
   D. most common in bacteria.

**8.** All of the following provide evidence for evolution *except*

   A. vestigial characters.
   B. Darwin's finches.
   C. homologous characters.
   D. mutations.

9. Why do we assume that oxygen was not present in the original atmosphere?

   A. The presence of $O_2$ would have resulted in the evolution of too many species too fast.
   B. Oxygen would have slowed down the rate of evolution.
   C. We know the ozone layer, which is formed by oxygen, has not been around that long.
   D. Inorganic molecules could not have formed in the presence of oxygen.

10. All these are examples of random evolutionary processes *except:*

    A. An earthquake divides a single elk species into two populations, forcing them to no longer interbreed.
    B. A mutation in a flower plant results in a new variety.
    C. An especially long winter causes a group of migrating birds to shift their home range.
    D. A mutation results in a population of trees that spread their seeds more widely than their peers, causing their population to grow.

## ❯ Answers and Explanations

1. **B**—Natural selection is the selective increase in certain alleles because they confer an advantage to their host organism. All other factors are random with respect to the alleles (a "bottleneck" is a type of genetic drift where a population is drastically reduced in size).

2. **A**—All fruit flies need to fly not only to find mates but also to survive. All the other characters listed are sexually selected, meaning that they have evolved because they confer specific advantages in mating (and not survival).

3. **D**—Adaptations are defined as traits that affect fitness if they are altered. Although adaptations may have evolved to increase mating success (answer C), they are not always intended for that function (e.g., they may have remained because they increase survival).

4. **C**—Natural selection can occur in asexually reproducing organisms, as long as the other three necessary conditions are met.

5. **C**—Genetic drift is change in allele frequencies as a result of random factors (e.g., natural disasters or environmental change). In small populations, genetic drift is a much more powerful force because each individual represents a greater percentage of the population's total genes than that person would in a much larger population.

Think of it this way—if you have a population of 10 cheetahs, and 3 die, you have lost 30 percent of the genes in that pool. If you have a population of 100 cheetahs, and 3 die, you have lost only 3 percent. Since Hardy-Weinberg equilibrium depends on no genetic drift, it is much more likely to occur in very large populations.

6. **C**—Remember that $p$ and $q$ must add up to 1 for a population to be in Hardy-Weinberg equilibrium (this eliminates answer D). Calculate $q$ first by taking the square root of 0.09, which is 0.30. Then simply subtract 0.30 from 1 to get $p = 0.70$.

7. **B**—Frequency-dependent selection is one process by which multiple alleles are preserved in a population. For traits that are selected for or against on the basis of frequency, an allele becomes more advantageous when it is rare, and therefore increases. In this way, it is impossible for the allele to become extinct (because as soon as it gets that low, it increases again). When it gets too high, the other allele is low, and that one then increases. Frequency-dependent selection often exhibits itself in this kind of seesaw effect.

8. **D**—Mutations in and of themselves are not evidence for evolution, although they are necessary if evolution is going to occur.

9. **D**—Inorganic molecules could not have formed in the presence of oxygen because oxygen would have taken the place of other elements in every chemical reaction (because it is such a highly reactive element).

10. **D**—This is the only answer that shows evidence of natural selection, which is the *nonrandom* process by which evolution occurs. The two elk species splitting (answer A) is an example of allopatric speciation caused by a random factor (a geologic event). A mutation is also a random event (answer B); for example, if we had said that the new variety became the dominant allele in a population because it had an advantage over other variants, then that *would* be natural selection. A home range shift (answer C) is not evolution, but rather a behavioral change within an organism's lifetime.

## › Rapid Review

There are four modes of *evolution*:

1. *Genetic drift*: change in allele frequencies because of chance events (in small populations).

2. *Gene flow*: change in allele frequencies as genes move from one population to another.

3. *Mutation*: change in allele frequencies due to a *random genetic change* in an allele.

4. *Natural selection*: process by which characters or traits are maintained or eliminated in a population based on their contribution to the differential survival and reproductive success of their "host" organisms.

There are three requirements for *natural selection* to occur:

1. *Variation*: differences must exist between individuals.

2. *Heritability*: the traits to be selected for must be able to be passed along to offspring. Traits that are not inherited cannot be selected against.

3. *Differential reproductive success*: there must be variation among parents in how many offspring they produce as a result of the different traits that the parents have.

*Adaptation* is a trait that, if altered, affects the fitness of an organism. Includes physical or intangible traits.

*Selection types* are as follows:

1. *Directional*: members at one end of a spectrum are selected against, and population shifts toward that end.

2. *Stabilizing*: selection for the mean of a population; reduces variation in a population.

3. *Disruptive (diversifying)*: selects for the two *extremes* of a population; selects against the middle.

4. *Sexual*: certain characters are selected for because they aid in mate acquisition.

5. *Artificial*: human intervention in the form of selective breeding (cattle).

Sources of *variation within populations* are

1.  *Mutation*: random changes in DNA can introduce new alleles into a population.

2.  *Sexual reproduction*: crossover, independent assortment, random gamete combination.

3.  *Balanced polymorphism*: the maintenance of two or more phenotypic variants.

*Speciation* is the process by which new species evolve:

1.  *Allopatric speciation*: interbreeding stops because some physical barrier splits the population into two. If two populations evolve separately and change so they cannot interbreed, speciation has occurred.

2.  *Sympatric speciation*: interbreeding stops even though no physical barrier prevents it.

    • *Polyploidy*: condition in which individual has higher than normal number of chromosome sets. Polyploidic individuals cannot reproduce with nonpolyploidics.

    • *Balanced polymorphism*: two phenotypic variants become so different that the two groups stop interbreeding.

Other terms to remember are

*Adaptive radiation*: rapid series of speciation events that occur when one or more ancestral species invades a new environment.

*Hardy-Weinberg equilibrium*: $p + q = 1$, $p^2 + 2pq + q^2 = 1$. Evolution is *not* occurring. The *rules* for this are no mutations, no gene flow, no genetic drift, no natural selection, and random mating.

*Homologous character*: traits similar between organisms that arose from a common ancestor.

*Vestigial character*: character contained by organism that is no longer functionally useful (appendix).

*Gradualism*: evolutionary change is a slow and steady process.

*Punctuated equilibria*: evolutionary change occurs in rapid bursts separated by large periods of no change.

*Heterotroph theory*: theory that describes how life evolved from original heterotrophs.

*Convergent character*: traits similar to two or more organisms that do *not* share common ancestor; parallel evolution.

*Convergent evolution*: two unrelated species evolve in a way that makes them *more* similar.

*Divergent evolution*: two related species evolve in a way that makes them *less* similar.

# CHAPTER 13

# Taxonomy and Classification

**IN THIS CHAPTER**

**Summary:** This chapter discusses Linnaeus's binomial system of classification and taxonomy in general. It gives information about each of the kingdoms (Monera, Protista, Plantae, Fungi, and Animalia).

**Key Ideas**

✪ Do not spend countless hours memorizing every detail about these various kingdoms. If you have time to burn and really want to learn all the details—go for it. If you are pressed for time, focus in on the basic and important information about each kingdom.

✪ The seven categories of classification listed from broadest to most specific: kingdom–phylum–class–order–family–genus–species.

✪ Autotrophs are the producers of the world; heterotrophs are the consumers.

✪ The endosymbiotic theory states that eukaryotic cells originated from a symbiotic partnership of prokaryotic cells.

✪ Be sure to learn the evolutionary relationships within each kingdom—this is fair game for a free-response question.

# Introduction

Taxonomy is the brainchild of Linnaeus, who came up with a **binomial system of classification** in which each species was given a two-word name. The first word describes the **genus**—the group to which the species belongs. The second word is the name of the particular *species*. For example, *Homo sapiens* is the binomial system name for humans.

**Taxonomy** is the field of biology that classifies organisms according to the presence or absence of shared characteristics in an effort to discover evolutionary relationships among species. A *taxon* is a category that organisms are placed into and can be any of the levels of the hierarchy. There are seven common categories of classification; listed from broadest to most specific, they are kingdom, phylum, class, order, family, genus, species. A way to remember this sequence is through the use of a silly sentence such as this:

"**K**araoke **p**layers **c**an **o**rder **f**ree **g**rape **s**oda" or

"**K**ing **P**hillip **c**ame **o**ver **f**or **g**ood **s**paghetti."

Kingdom–phylum–class–order–family–genus–species.

> **BIG IDEA 1.B.2**
>
> *Phylogenetic trees are visual representations of ancestry.*

A **kingdom** consists of organisms that share characteristics such as cell structure, level of cell specialization, and mechanisms to obtain nutrients. Kingdoms are split into *phyla,* which are split into *classes*, which are further divided into *orders*. Orders are split into *families,* which are made up of the different *genera.* The final and most specific division is the *species.* This is the only naturally occurring taxon. These seven categories apply to many but not *all* organisms. The plant kingdom has **divisions** instead of phyla. Bacterial species tend to be placed into groups called **strains.**

# Five or Six Kingdoms?

The current system of classification is a five-kingdom system that divides all the organisms of the planet into one of five kingdoms: Monera, Protista, Plantae, Fungi, and Animalia. Do not be confused or alarmed if you hear mention of a six-kingdom system. The difference in the six-kingdom system is that the kingdom Monera is split into Eubacteria and Archaebacteria. Other than that, the kingdom delineations are similar. Let's begin the tour of the various kingdoms with the kingdom Monera.

# Kingdom Monera

The members of this kingdom are prokaryotes: single-celled organisms that have no nucleus or membrane-bound organelles. Since this chapter is an exercise in painful amounts of classification, subclassification, and further classification based on the previous classification of classifications, and so on, we thought we would point out a few of the many different ways that the kingdom Monera can be subdivided. The Monera kingdom can be further classified by nutritional class, reactivity with oxygen, and whether they are eubacteria or archaebacteria.

### Nutritional Class

Moneran organisms can be classified as either autotrophs or heterotrophs. **Autotrophs** are the producers of the world:

1. *Photoautotrophs:* photosynthetic autotrophs (used to be called blue-green algae) that produce energy from light.
2. *Chemoautotrophs:* produce energy from inorganic substances (e.g., S bacteria).

**Heterotrophs** are the consumers of the world. Examples of prokaryotic heterotrophs, including parasitic bacteria that feed off hosts, and **saprobes,** such as bacteria of decay, which feed off dead organisms.

### Reactivity with Oxygen

A second way to classify moneran organisms is by their ability to react with oxygen: whether they *must* react with oxygen to survive, whether they must be *without* oxygen to survive, or if they can survive with or without oxygen. There are three classes of oxygen reactivity: obligate aerobes and obligate anaerobes at the two extremes of the spectrum, and facultative anaerobes somewhere in between. **Obligate aerobes** require oxygen for respiration—they must have oxygen to grow; **obligate anaerobes** must avoid oxygen like the plague—oxygen is a poison to them; **facultative anaerobes** are happy to use $O_2$ when available, but can survive without it.

### Archaebacteria Versus Eubacteria

There are two major branches of prokaryotic evolution: Eubacteria and Archaebacteria. **Archaebacteria** tend to live in extreme environments and are thought to resemble the first cells of the earth. The major examples you should be familiar with include (1) **extreme halophiles**—these are the "salt lovers" and live in environments with high salt concentrations, (2) **methanogens**—bacteria that produce methane as a by-product, and (3) **thermo acidophiles**—bacteria that love hot, acidic environments.

   **Eubacteria** are categorized according to their mode of acquiring nutrients, their mechanism of movement, and their shape, among other things. The following is a list of the names of a few groups of bacteria that you should be familiar with for the AP exam:

1. Proteobacteria
2. Gram-positive bacteria
3. Cyanobacteria
4. Spirochetes
5. Chlamydias
6. Chemosynthetic bacteria
7. Nitrogen-fixing bacteria

The three basic shapes of bacteria you might want to be familiar with include:

1. *Rod-shaped bacteria:* also known as *bacilli* (e.g., *Bacillus anthracis,* the bug that causes anthrax).
2. *Spiral-shaped bacteria:* also known as *spirilla* (e.g., *Treponema pallidum,* the bug that causes syphilis).
3. *Sphere-shaped bacteria:* also known as *cocci* (e.g., *Streptococcus,* the fine bug that gives us strep throat).

To summarize, the kingdom Monera can be subdivided according to the following characteristics:

| | |
|---|---|
| Nutrition type? | Autotroph versus heterotroph |
| Oxygen preference? | Obligate aerobes versus obligate anaerobes versus facultative anaerobes |
| Evolutionary branch? | Archaebacteria versus Eubacteria |

# Endosymbiotic Theory

*Bill (11th grade): "Important concept to know."*

**The endosymbiotic theory** states that eukaryotic cells originated from a symbiotic partnership of prokaryotic cells. This theory focuses on the origin of mitochondria and chloroplasts from aerobic heterotrophic and photosynthetic prokaryotes, respectively.

We can see why scientists examining these two organelles would think that they may have originated from prokaryotes. They share many characteristics: (1) they are the same size as eubacteria, (2) they also reproduce in the same way as prokaryotes (binary fission), and (3), if their ribosomes are sliced open and studied, they are found to more closely resemble those of a prokaryote than those of a eukaryote. They are prokaryotic groupies living in a eukaryotic world.

The eukaryotic organism that scientists believe most closely resembles prokaryotes is the **archezoa,** which does not have mitochondria. One phylum grouped with the archezoa is the **diplomonads.** A good example of a diplomonad you should remember is *Giardia*—an infectious agent you would do well to avoid. *Giardia* is a parasitic organism that takes hold in your intestines and essentially denies your body the ability to absorb any fat. This infection makes for very uncomfortable and unpleasant GI (gastrointestinal) issues and usually results from the ingestion of contaminated water.

# Kingdom Protista

The evolution of protists from prokaryotes gave rise to the characteristics that make eukaryotes different from their prokaryotic predecessors. Protists were around a long time before fungi, plants, or animals graced our planet with their presence. Most protists use aerobic metabolism. Since this is a chapter on classification, it would be silly, if not too kind of us, to not mention how these different protists are organized. They are usually grouped into three major categories:

1. *Animal-like protists:* heterotrophic protists, also called *protozoa*
2. *Funguslike protists:* protists that resemble fungi; also called *absorptive protists*
3. *Plantlike protists:* photosynthetic protists, also called *algae*

Protists are usually unicellular or colonial. This is why they are *not* considered plants, animals, or fungi. All protists are capable of asexual reproduction. Some reproduce only asexually, and others can reproduce sexually as well. This variability in the life cycles found among various members of the protist kingdom is just one reason why they are considered to be one of the most diverse kingdoms in existence.

## Animal-Like Protists (Protozoa)

This division includes protists that *ingest* foods—as do animals. As with the rest of this chapter, you do not need to become an expert on protozoans and know everything about every member. But the following is a list that contains basic information about some names that may help you on the multiple-choice section of the test. We will italicize the most important things to remember about each of them.

1. *Rhizopoda.* These *unicellular* and *asexual* organisms are also known as *amoebas.* They get from place to place through the use of **pseudopods,** which are extensions from their cells. Every living creature has to eat, and they do so through *phagocytosis.*
2. *Foraminifera.* These *marine* protists live attached to structures such as rocks and algae. Their name is derived from the word *foramen* because of the presence of calcium carbonate ($CaCO_3$) shells full of holes. Some of these protists obtain nutrients through *photosynthesis* performed by symbiotic algae living in their shells.
3. *Actinopoda.* These organisms move by *pseudopodia* and make up part of plankton, the organisms that drift near the surface of bodies of water. The two divisions of actinopoda include heliozoans and radiozoans. Just recognize the names; do not worry about anything more than that.

4. *Apicomplexa.* These *parasites* are the protists formerly known as sporozoans. They spread from place to place in a small infectious form known as a **sporozoite.** They have both *sexual* and *asexual* stages, and their life cycle requires two different host species for completion. An example of an apicomplexa is **plasmodium,** the causative agent of malaria (two hosts—mosquitoes, then humans).

5. *Zooflagellates.* These *heterotrophic* protists are known for their *flagella,* which they use to move around. Like rhizopoda, they eat by *phagocytosis* and can range from being *parasitic* to their hosts to living *mutualistically* with them. A member of this group is *trypanosoma,* which is known to cause African sleeping sickness.

6. *Ciliophora.* Their name is fitting because these protists use *cilia* to travel from place to place. They live in *water* and contain *two types of nuclei:* a **macronucleus** (which controls everyday activities) and many **micronuclei** (a function in **conjugation**). A ciliaphora you may recognize is paramecium.

## Fungus-Like Protists (Slime Molds and Water Molds)

This division includes protists that resemble fungi. Once again, we are going to provide a list that contains basic information about some names that may help you on multiple-choice questions. The most important things to remember are **boldfaced** or *italicized.*

1. *Myxogastria.* These *heterotrophic,* brightly colored protists include the **plasmodial slime molds** and are not photosynthetic. Unlike the acrasidae, they do not like to eat alone—they eat and grow as a single clumped *unicellular* mass known as a **plasmodium** (same name as the causative agent of malaria, but this entity does not cause malaria). This mass ingests food by *phagocytosis.* When Mother Hubbard's cupboard is bare and there is no more food, the plasmodium stops growing and instead produces spores that allow the protist to reproduce.

2. *Acrasidae.* Known to their closer friends as **cellular slime molds,** these protists have a bit of a strange eating strategy. When there is plenty of food around, these organisms eat alone as solitary beings, but when food becomes scarce, they clump together in a manner similar to slime molds and work together as a unit.

3. *Oomycota.* These *water-mold* protists can be *parasites* or *saprobes.* They are able to munch on their surrounding environment owing to the presence of *filaments* known as *hyphae,* which release digestive enzymes. They are often multicellular, or *coenocytic.* One difference between these organisms and actual fungi is that their cell wall is made of *cellulose,* and not *chitin* as seen in fungi.

## Plant-Like Protists

This division includes protists that are mostly photosynthetic. All of these organisms contain chlorophyll *a.* Focus your attention on the italicized points.

1. *Dinoflagellata.* Protists known for having *two flagella* that rest perpendicular to each other, and which allow them to swim with a funky spinning motion that makes them the envy of all other protist observers (or at least makes them really dizzy). Most dinoflagellates are *unicellular.* These protists are very important producers in many aquatic food chains.

2. *Golden algae.* Known as the *chrysophyta,* these protists move through the use of *flagella* and can also be found swimming among plankton.

3. *Diatoms.* These yellow and brown protists are also known as bacillariophyta and are a major component of plankton. They mostly reproduce in an *asexual* fashion, although they do rarely enter a *sexual* life cycle. They have ornate *walls* made of *silica* to protect them.

4. *Green algae.* Known as *chlorophyta,* they have chlorophyll *a* and *b.* Most of these protists live in freshwater and can be found among the algae that are part of the mutualistic

*lichen* conglomerate. Most have both *asexual* and *sexual* reproductive stages. These organisms are considered to be the ancestors of plants.

5. *Brown algae.* Known as *phaeophyta,* most of these protists are *multicellular* and live in *marine* environments. Two members to know are *kelp* and *seaweed.*

6. *Red algae.* Known as rhodophyta, they get their color from a pigment called *phycobilin.* Most of these *multicellular* protists live in the ocean and produce gametes that do not have flagella. Many live in deep waters and absorb nonvisible light via accessory pigments.

# Kingdom Plantae

Classification of plants is very similar to classification of the animal kingdom, except that plants are divided into divisions instead of phyla. So, instead of "Karaoke players can order free grape soda," remember "Karaoke *dancers* can order free grape soda."

Reality again, folks . . . you do not need to become experts in the evolutionary history of plants, but you should be able to understand a phylogenetic representation of how the various plant types evolved.

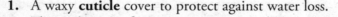
Chlorophytes→bryophytes→seedless vascular plants→gymnosperms→angiosperms

**Chlorophytes** are green algae. Scientists have found enough evidence to conclude that they are the common ancestors of land plants. Plants are said to have experienced four major evolutionary periods since the dawn of time, described in the following sections.

*CT teacher: "Know plant evolution very well. There are a lot of potential questions here. Including essays."*

## Bryophytes

**Bryophytes** were the first land plants to evolve from the chlorophytes. They include mosses, liverworts, and hornworts. Prior to bryophytes, there was no reason for these organisms to worry about water loss because they lived in water and had unlimited access to the treasured resource. But in order to survive on land, where water was no longer unlimited, two evolutionary adaptations in particular helped them survive:

1. A waxy **cuticle** cover to protect against water loss.
2. The packaging of gametes in structures known as **gametangia.**

Bryophyte sperm is produced by the male gametangia, the **antheridia.** Bryophyte eggs are produced by the female gametangia, the **archegonium.** The gametangia provide a safe haven because the fertilization and development of the zygote occur within the protected structure.

Because they lack xylem and phloem, bryophytes are also known as *nonvascular plants.* This lack of vascular tissue combined with the existence of flagellated sperm results in a dependence on water. For this reason, bryophytes must live in damp areas so they do not dry out. There are three nonvascular plants you should know about: mosses, liverworts, and hornworts. Mosses are special in that, unlike all other plants, the dominant generation in their life cycle is the haploid gametophyte. The moss sporophyte is tiny, short lived, and reliant on the gametophyte for nutritional support. One interesting fact about liverworts is that in addition to the alternation of generations life cycle, they are able to reproduce asexually.

## Seedless Vascular Plants

The transition for plants from water to land was a tricky one. They needed to find a way to use the nutritional resources of the minerals and water found in soil, while not denying themselves access to the light needed for photosynthesis. Another problem facing these early land plants was the need to find a way to distribute water and nutrients throughout the plant—not as much of an issue when the plant was submerged in water. The solution to this issue was the development of the xylem and phloem, which you will read about in Chapter 14, Plants. The **xylem** is the water superhighway for the plant, transporting water throughout the plant. The **phloem** is the sugar food highway for the plant, transporting sugar and nutrients to the various plant structures.

The first vascular plants (also referred to as **tracheophytes**) to evolve did not have seeds. Two major evolutionary changes occurred that allowed the transition from bryophytes to seedless vascular plants:

1. The switch from the gametophyte to the sporophyte as the dominant generation of the life cycle.
2. The development of branched sporophytes, increasing the number of spores produced.

The major seedless vascular plants you should know are **ferns,** which are **homosporous plants** that produce a single spore type that gives rise to bisexual gametophytes. The spores tend to exist on the underside of the fern leaves. A **heterosporous plant** produces two types of spores, some of which yield male gametophytes (**microspores**), and others produce female gametophytes (**megaspores**). The dominant generation for ferns is the sporophyte.

## Seed Plants

### Gymnosperm

The third major plant category to branch off the phylogenetic tree is the seed plant. Three major evolutionary changes occurred between the seedless vascular plants and the birth of seed plants:

1. Further decline in the prominence of the gametophyte generation of the life cycle.
2. The birth of pollination.
3. The evolution of the seed.

A seed is a package containing an embryo and the food to feed the developing embryo that is surrounded by a nice protective shell. The first major seed plants to surface were the **gymnosperms.** These plants are heterosporous and usually transport their sperm through the use of **pollen**—the sperm-bearing male gametophyte. Not all gymnosperms have pollen; some have motile sperm. The major gymnosperms you should remember are the **conifers,** plants whose reproductive structure is a cone. Members of this division include pine trees, firs, cedars, and redwoods. These plants survive well in dry conditions and keep their leaves year-round. They are evergreens and usually have needles for leaves.

### Angiosperm

The final major plant evolutionary category to branch off the phylogenetic tree is the flowering plant. Today there are more **angiosperms** around than any other kind of plant. There are two major classes of angiosperms to know: monocots (**monocotyledons**) and dicots (**dicotyledons**). A **cotyledon** is a structure that provides nourishment for a developing plant. One distinction between monocots and dicots is that monocots have a single cotyledon, while dicots have two.

One interesting evolutionary change from the gymnosperm to the angiosperm is the adaptation of the xylem. In gymnosperms, the xylem cells in charge of water transport are the **tracheid cells,** whereas in angiosperms, the xylem cells are the more efficient **vessel elements.** Don't worry too much about this distinction, but store away in the back of your mind that vessel elements are seen in angiosperms, while tracheid cells are seen in gymnosperms.

What are flowers, really? Are they just another visually pleasing structure? No . . . they are so much more. Flowers are the main tools for angiosperm reproduction. Do not waste too much time learning every little part of a flower. Here are the most important parts to remember:

*Stamen:* male structure composed of an **anther,** which produces pollen.

*Carpel:* female structure that consists of an *ovary,* a **style,** and a **stigma.** The stigma functions as the receiver of the pollen, and the style is the pathway leading to the ovary.

*Petals:* structures that serve to attract pollinators to help increase the plant's reproductive success.

Below is a quick display that lists many of the major evolutionary trends observed during the phylogenetic development of plants.

**Remember these evolutionary trends seen in plants!**
- Dominant gametophyte generation → dominant sporophyte generation
- Nonvascular → vascular
- Seedless → seeds
- Motile sperm → pollen
- Naked seeds → seeds in flowers

# Kingdom Fungi

Nearly all fungi are multicellular and are built from filamentous structures called **hyphae.** These hyphae form meshes of branching filaments known as a **mycelium,** which function as mouthlike structures for the fungus, absorbing food. Many fungi contain **septae,** which divide the hyphae filaments into different compartments. The septa have pores, which allow organelles and other structures to flow from compartment to compartment. Fungi that do not contain septae are called **coenocytic fungi.** Fungus walls are built using the polysaccharide **chitin.** As was discussed in Chapter 9, Cell Division, the fungus life cycle is predominately haploid. The only time they are diploid is as the 2*n* zygote.

The following is a list of fungus-related organisms that you should know:

1. *Zygomycota.* These *coenocytic* and *land-dwelling* fungi have very few septa and reproduce sexually. A classic example of a zygomycete is bread mold.
2. *Basidiomycota.* These club-shaped fungi are known for their haploid basidiospores and love of decomposing wood. Famous members include mushrooms and rusts.
3. *Ascomycota.* Many members of this group of saprobic fungi live as part of the symbiotic relationship called **lichen.** These fungi produce sexual **ascospores,** which are contained in sacs. Famous ascomycetes you may have heard of are yeasts and mildews. These are discussed again in Chapter 19, Laboratory Review.
4. *Lichens.* These are formed by a *symbiotic association* of photosynthetic organisms grouped together with fungal hyphae (usually an *ascomycete*). The algae member of this group tends to be *cyanobacteria* or *chlorophyta* and provides the food (sugar from photosynthesis). The fungus provides protection and drink (water).
5. *Molds.* These are *asexual, quick-growing* fungi known as *deuteromycota* or the "imperfect fungi." If you check any college refrigerator, you can find many fine samples of this organism.
6. *Yeasts.* These are *unicellular* fungi that can be asexual *or* sexual. One member of this group, *Candida,* is known to cause yeast infections in humans.

# Kingdom Animalia

Animals are the final kingdom to be discussed in this chapter. There are some characteristics that separate animals from other organisms:

| ADAPTATION | DESCRIPTION |
| --- | --- |
| Cell wall | Animals lack cell walls. |
| Mode of reproduction | Sexual reproduction is the norm (although there are several animals capable of asexual reproduction). |
| Dominant life cycle stage | The diploid stage is usually the dominant generation in the life cycle. |
| Motile | Most animals are mobile. |
| Nutritional class | Animals are multicellular heterotrophs. |
| Storage of energy | Animals store carbohydrates as glycogen, not starch as is seen in plants. |
| Special embryological events | Most animals undergo a process in which specialized tissue layers (endoderm, mesoderm, ectoderm) form during a process known as **gastrulation.** |
| Nervous and muscle tissue | Animals (with the exception of sponges) have specialized nervous and muscle tissue. |
| Cellular junctions | Animal cells contain tight junctions and gap junctions. |

As is the case with all of the other kingdoms in this chapter, you do not need to become the master of animal phylogeny and taxonomy. But it is definitely useful to know the general evolutionary history of the animal kingdom and how it diversified so quickly over time (Figure 13.1).

Many people believe that the original common ancestor that started the whole process of animal evolution was most likely the **choanoflagellate.** During the evolutionary progression from choanoflagellate to the present, there have been *four* major branchpoints on which you should focus. Let's take a look at all the important changes that have allowed such diversity of life.

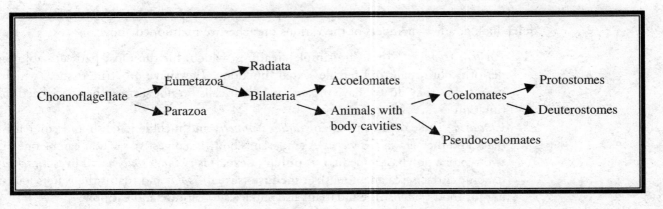

**Figure 13.1  The animal phylogenetic tree.**

The first major branchpoint occurred after the development of multicellularity from choanoflagellates. Off this branch of the tree emerged two divisions:

1. *Parazoa:* sponges; these organisms have no true tissues.
2. *Eumetazoa:* all the other animals with true tissue.

After this split into parazoa and eumetazoa, the second major branchpoint in animal evolutionary history occurred: the subdivision of eumetazoa into two further branches on the basis of body symmetry. The eumetezoans were subdivided into

1. *Radiata:* those that have radial symmetry, which means that they have a single orientation. This can be a top, a bottom, or a front and back. This branch includes jellyfish, corals, and hydras.
2. *Bilateria:* those that have bilateral symmetry, which means that they have a top and a bottom (dorsal/ventral) as well as a head and a tail (anterior/posterior).

The next major split in the phylogenetic tree for animal development involved the split of bilateral organisms into two further branches—one of which subdivides into two smaller branches:

1. *Acoelomates:* animals with no blood vascular system and lacking a cavity between the gut and outer body wall. An example of a member of this group is the flatworm.
2. Animals *with* a vascular system and a body cavity.
   - *Pseudocoelomates:* animals that have a fluid-filled body cavity that is *not* enclosed by mesoderm. Roundworms are a member of this branch.
   - *Coelomates:* a **coelom** is a fluid-filled body cavity found between the body wall and gut that has a lining. It comes from the mesoderm.

The final major branchpoint comes off from the coelomates. It branches into two more divisions:

1. *Protostomes:* a bilateral animal whose first embryonic indentation eventually develops into a *mouth*. Prominent members of this society include *annelids, arthropods,* and *mullusks*.
2. *Deuterostomes:* a branch that includes *chordates* and *echinoderms*. The first indentation for their embryos eventually develops into the *anus*.

These two divisions differ in their embryonic developmental stages. As already mentioned, the protostomes' first embryonic indent develops into the mouth, whereas for the dueterostome, it becomes the anus. Another difference is the *angle* of the cleavages that occur during the early cleavage division of the embryo. A third difference is the tissue from which the coelom divides.

That concludes the evolutionary development portion of this chapter. Now let's take a quick look at a few members of the various branches we mentioned above.

1. *Porifera* (*sponges*). These are simple creatures, which, for the most part, are able to perform both male and female sexual functions. They have no "true tissue," which means that they do *not* have organs, and their cells do not seem to be specialized in function.
2. *Cnidaria.* These organisms are of *radial symmetry* and include jellyfish and coral animals, and they *lack* a *mesoderm*. A cnidarian's body is a digestive sac that can be one of two types: a polyp or a medusa. A **polyp** (asexual) is *cylinder shaped* and lives *attached* to some surface (sea anemones). A **medusa** (sexual) is *flat* and roams the waters looking for food (jellyfish). Cnidarians use tentacles to capture and eat prey.

3. *Platyhelminthes.* These are *flatworms,* members of the *acoelomate* club. They have *bilateral symmetry* and a touch of *cephalization.* There are three main types of flatworms you should be familiar with:
   - *Flukes:* parasitic flatworms that alternate between sexual and asexual reproduction life cycles.
   - *Planarians:* free-living carnivores that live in water.
   - *Tapeworms:* parasitic flatworms whose adult form lives in vertebrates, including us (humans).

4. *Rotifera.* These are also members of the *pseudocoelomate* club; they have *specialized organs,* a full digestive tract, and are very tiny.

5. *Nematoda.* These are *roundworms,* found in moist environments. They have a *psuedocoelomate* body plan. Trichinosis, a disease found in humans, is caused by a roundworm that infects meat products, usually pork. Humans ingesting infected meat can become affected with this disease.

6. *Mollusca.* These creatures are members of the *protostome* division and include such species as snails, slugs, octopuses, and squids. They are *coelomates* with a full digestive system. **Bivalves,** such as clams and oysters, are mollusks that have hinged shells that are divided into two parts.

7. *Annelida.* These are segmented worms such as earthworms and leeches.

8. *Arthropoda.* This is the most heavily represented group on the planet. These creatures are *segmented, contain a hard exoskeleton* constructed out of *chitin,* and have *specialized appendages.* Some well-known members include spiders, crustaceans, and insects. One interesting tidbit about arthropods is that, like humans, some members of this group, when born, are miniature versions of their adult selves that grow in size to resemble adults. Others look completely different from adults and exist in a larva form in their youth. At some point, the larvae undergo a metamorphosis and change to the expected adult form.

9. *Echinodermata.* These are *sea stars.* These coelomates are of the dueterostome body plan. One neat characteristic of echinoderms is the presence of a **water vascular system,** which is a series of tubes and canals within the organism, that plays a role in ingestion of food, movement of the organism, and gas exchange.

10. *Chordata.* This group includes **invertebrates** (animals lacking backbones), and **vertebrates** (animals with backbones). Just in case you are asked to identify some vertebrates on a multiple-choice question, here are some members—fish, amphibians, reptiles, birds, and mammals. There are four features common to chordates you should know:
    - *Dorsal hollow nerve cord:* forms the nervous system and becomes the brain and spinal cord in some.
    - *Notochord:* long support rod that is replaced by bone in most (mesodermal in origin).
    - *Pharyngeal gill slits:* slit-containing structure, which functions in respiration and feeding, present only in the embryonic stage of most chordates.
    - *Tail:* extension past the anus that is lost by birth in many species.

# › Review Questions

1. Which of the following is thought to be the common ancestor to plants?

   A. Chemoautotrophs
   B. Choanoflagellates
   C. Chordata
   D. Chlorophytes

2. Which of the following pairs of organisms is most closely interrelated?

   A. Sponge and halophile
   B. Jellyfish and coral
   C. Oyster and conifer
   D. Lichen and roundworm

3. Which of the following was an evolutionary adaptation vital to the survival of the bryophytes?

   A. The switch from the gametophyte to the sporophyte as the dominant generation of the life cycle
   B. The development of branched sporophytes
   C. The birth of pollination
   D. The packaging of gametes into gametangia

4. Which of the following is the most specific category of classification?

   A. Class
   B. Family
   C. Order
   D. Division

5. Which of the following is *not* associated with flowers?

   A. Carpel
   B. Stigma
   C. Style
   D. Hypha

6. Which of the following was the latest to branch off the animal phylogenetic tree?

   A. Radiata
   B. Acoelomates
   C. Eumetazoa
   D. Deuterostomes

For questions 7–10, please use the following answer choices:

   A. Kingdom Animalia
   B. Kingdom Fungi
   C. Kingdom Protista
   D. Kingdom Monera

7. Thermoacidophiles are grouped into this kingdom that consists of single-celled organisms lacking nuclei and membrane-bound organelles.

8. Arthropods are grouped into this kingdom whose members are multicellular heterotrophs that have the diploid stage as their dominant generation in the life cycle.

9. This kingdom is divided into plant-like, animal-like, and fungus-like divisions.

10. Molds, or deuteromycota, are grouped into this kingdom that consists of mostly multicellular organisms that are constructed out of hypha.

# › Answers and Explanations

1. **D**—Chlorophytes are green algae that are the common ancestors of land plants. Chemoautotrophs are monerans that produce energy from inorganic substances. Choanoflagellates are the organisms thought to be the starting point for the animal kingdom's phylogenetic tree. Chordata includes the invertebrates and vertebrates.

2. **B**—Jellyfish and coral are both cnidarians of the animal kingdom.

3. **D**—Since the bryophytes were the first plants to brave the land, they were still somewhat dependent on water and also needed protection for their gametes. The gametangia provided a safe haven for the gametes where fertilization and zygote development could occur. Answer choices A and B were adaptations made by seedless vascular plants. Choice C was an adaptation made by the gymnosperms.

4. **B**—**K**araoke **p**layers **c**an **o**rder **f**ree **g**rape **s**oda or **K**ing **P**hillip **c**ame **o**ver **f**or **g**ood **s**paghetti (enough said).

5. **D**—Hyphae are associated with fungi. The other parts are all associated with flowers.

6. **D**—Take a look at Figure 13.1 for this one; the deuterostomes were indeed the last to branch off.

7. **D**

8. **A**

9. **C**

10. **B**

# › Rapid Review

Quickly review the following terms:

*Taxonomy*: Classification of organisms based upon the presence or absence of shared characteristics: kingdom → phylum (division) → class → order → family → genus → species.

*Five-kingdom system*: Monera → Protista → Plantae → Fungi → Animalia.

*Six-kingdom system*: Archaebacteria → Eubacteria → Protista → Plantae → Fungi → Animalia.

### Kingdom Monera

*Autotrophs* (producers) versus *heterotrophs* (consumers).

*Obligate aerobes* (require $O_2$) versus *obligate anaerobes* (*no* $O_2$) versus *facultative anaerobes* (either or).

*Archaebacteria*: halophiles (salt), methanogens (methane-producers), thermoacidophiles (hot and acidic).

*Eubacteria*: bacteria classified according to movement, shape, nutritional methods.

*Endosymbiotic theory*: eukaryotes originated from a symbiotic partnership of prokaryotic cells.

### Kingdom Protista

*Plant like protists*: photosynthetic algae; all contain chlorophyll *a*.

*Animal-like protists*: heterotrophic protists (protozoa).

*Fungus like protists*: absorptive protists that resemble fungi.

## Kingdom Plantae

*Chlorophytes*: green algae that are the common ancestor of land plants.

*Bryophytes*: first land plants; two important adaptations—waxy cuticle (stop water loss), gametangia:

- *Gametangia*: protective structures to aid survival of gametes on land.
- *Mosses*: important bryophyte, dominant life cycle generation is a **haploid gametophyte.**

*Seedless vascular plants*: came after bryophytes and had two further changes:

- Switch from haploid gametophyte to diploid sporophyte as dominant generation.
- Development of branched sporophytes.

*Ferns*: important member, **homosporous** (bisexual gametophytes).

*Gymnosperm*: came after seedless vascular plants and had three evolutionary adaptations:

- Further increase in dominance of sporophyte generation.
- Birth of pollination.
- Evolution of the seed.

*Conifers*: plants whose reproductive structure is a cone.

*Angiosperm*: flowering plants that came after gymnosperms divided into **monocots** and **dicots.**

## Kingdom Fungi

Multicellular, built from hyphae, which can be separated by septae. Fungus walls are constructed from **chitin.**

Life cycle is predominately **haploid.**

## Kingdom Animalia

Important characteristics: no cell walls, $2n$ is dominant, mobile, multicellular, heterotrophic, gastrulation.

Four major branchpoints (Figure 13.1).

Common ancestor: **choanoflagellate.**

Important members (in order of split from phylogenetic tree): sponges (parazoa), jellyfish (Radiata), flatworms (Acoelomates), roundworms (Pseudocoelomate nematodes), arthropods (protostomes), humans (Chordates).

Skim the information by each subdivision of this kingdom earlier in this chapter for more information.

# CHAPTER 14

# Plants

**IN THIS CHAPTER**

**Summary:** This chapter discusses the anatomy of plants, the mechanisms of root and shoot growth, plant hormones, tropisms, and the mechanism of water and nutrient movement from roots to shoots and back.

**Key Ideas**

✪ Roots are the portions of the plant that are below ground; shoots are the portions of the plant that are above ground.

✪ There are three plant tissue systems to know: ground, vascular, and dermal.

✪ Two important plant vascular structures: xylem and phloem.

✪ Regions of plant growth: root cap, zone of cell division, zone of elongation, and zone of maturation.

✪ Five important plant hormones: abscisic acid, auxin, cytokinins, ethylene, and gibberellins.

✪ Three important tropisms: gravitropism, phototropism, and thigmotropism.

## Introduction

This chapter begins with a quick tour of the anatomy of plants, starting with the roots and moving to the shoots. In these two sections, the mechanisms of root and shoot growth will be examined and the important players will be identified. From there we will turn our focus to plant hormones and tropisms. A discussion on photoperiodism follows, and the chapter concludes with a look at the mechanism by which water and nutrients travel through plants from roots to shoots and back.

# Anatomy of Plants

The anatomy of a plant in its most simplistic form can be divided into the roots and the shoots. **Roots** are the portions of the plant that are below the ground, while **shoots** are the portions of the plant that are above the ground. The roots wind their way through the terrain, working as an anchor to keep the plants in place. In addition, the roots work as gatherers, absorbing the water and nutrients vital to a plant's survival.

## Tissue Systems

There are *three* plant tissue systems to know: ground, vascular, and dermal.

**BIG IDEA 2.D.2**

*Homeostatic mechanisms (e.g., plants obtaining $CO_2$ and eliminating $O_2$) reflect common ancestry and divergence due to adaptation to different environments.*

### Ground Tissue

The ground tissue, which makes up most of the body of the plant, is found between the dermal and vascular systems and is subdivided into three cell types: **collenchyma cells,** live cells that provide flexible and mechanical support—often found in stems and leaves; **parenchyma cells,** the most prominent of the three types, with many functions—parenchyma cells found in leaves are called *mesophyll cells,* and allow $CO_2$ and $O_2$ to diffuse through intercellular spaces (owing to the presence of large vacuoles, these cells play a role in storage and secretion for plants); and **sclerenchyma cells,** which protect seeds and support the plant.

### Vascular Tissue

Plant vascular tissue comes up often on the AP Biology exam. The two characters you need to be familiar with are the xylem and the phloem.

*Joscelyn (12th grader): "Know these two and what their driving forces are."*

*Xylem.* This structure has multiple functions. It is a support structure that strengthens the plant and functions as a passageway for the transport of water and minerals from the soil. One interesting (and sad) note about xylem cells is that most of them are dead and are simply there as cell walls that contain the minerals and water being passed along the plant. Xylem cells can be divided into two categories: **vessel elements** and **tracheid cells.** They both function in the passage of water, but vessel elements move water more efficiently because of structural differences that are not pertinent to this exam. ☺

*Phloem.* This structure also functions as a "highway" for plants, assisting in the movement of sugars from one place to another. Unlike the xylem, the functionally mature cells of the phloem, *sieve-tube elements,* are alive and well.

### Dermal Tissue

Dermal tissue provides the protective outer coating for plants. It is the skin, or **epidermis.** This coating attempts to keep the bad guys (infectious agents) out, and the good guys (water and nutrients) in. Within the epidermis are cells called **guard cells,** which control the opening and closing of gaps called *stomata* that are vital to the process of photosynthesis as was discussed back in Chapter 8, Photosynthesis.

# Roots

**BIG IDEA 2.A.3**

*The high surface area of root hairs helps plants exchange matter with the environment.*

## Root Systems

How do plants get their nutrients? Through the hard work of roots, whose tips absorb nourishment for the plant (minerals and water) via root hairs. Most of the water and minerals are absorbed by plants at the root tips, which have **root hairs** extending from their surface. These hairs create a larger surface area for absorption in much the same way as the **brush border** does in the human intestines—improving the efficiency of nutrient and water acquisition.

A root is not just a root, for not all root structures are the same. In Chapter 13, Taxonomy and Classification, two types of angiosperm plants were mentioned: dicots and monocots. Dicots are known for having a taproot system, while monocots are associated with fibrous roots. The **taproot** (e.g., carrot) **system** branches in a way similar to the human lungs; the roots start as one thick root on entrance into the ground, and then divide into smaller and smaller branches called **lateral roots** underneath the surface, which serve to hold the plant in place. **Fibrous roots** provide plants with a very strong anchor in the ground without going very deep into the soil. The root system can be summarized as follows:

Dicots → taproot → thick entry root → division into smaller branches

Monocots → fibrous root → shallow entry into ground → strong anchor effect

## Root Structure

Let's take a look at the structure of a root moving from outside to inside. The root is lined by the **epidermis,** whose cells give rise to the root hairs that plants must thank for their ability to absorb water and nutrients. Moving farther in, we come to the cortex, the majority of the root that functions as a starch storage receptacle. The innermost layer of the cortex is composed of a cylinder of cells known as the **endodermis.** These cells are important to the plant because the walls between these cells create an obstacle known as the **casparian strip,** which blocks water from passing. This is one of the mechanisms by which plants control the flow of water. Moving in through the endodermis, we come to the **vascular cylinder,** which is composed of a collection of cells known as the *pericycle.* The lateral roots of the plant are made from the pericycle, and hold the vascular tissue of the root—our friends from earlier, the xylem and phloem.

## Root Growth

Plants grow as long as they are alive as a result of the presence of **meristemic cells.** Early on in the life of a plant, after a seed matures, it sits and waits until the time is right for germination. At this point, water is absorbed by the embryo, which begins to grow again. When large enough, it busts through the seed coat, beginning its journey to planthood. At the start of this journey, the growth is concentrated in the actively dividing cells of the **apical meristem.** Growth in this region leads to an increase in the length of a plant: **primary plant growth.** Later on growth occurs in cells known as the **lateral meristems,** which extend all the way through the plant. This growth leads to an increase in the width of a plant and is known as **secondary plant growth.**

### Regions of Growth

*Root cap:* protective structure that keeps roots from being damaged during push through soil.

*Zone of cell division:* section of root where cells are actively dividing.

*Zone of elongation:* next section up along the root, where cells absorb $H_2O$ and increase in length to make the plant taller.

*Zone of maturation:* section of root past the zone of elongation where the cells differentiate to their finalized form (phloem, xylem, parenchyma, epidermal, etc).

# The Shoot System

Now that we have discussed roots—the part of the plant that is *in* the ground—let's take a look at shoots (leaves and stems), the parts of the plant that are *out of* the ground.

### Structure of a Leaf

Leaves are protected by the waxy **cuticle** of the epidermis, which functions to decrease the transpiration rate. Inside the epidermis lies the ground tissue of the leaf, the mesophyll, which is involved in the ever-so-important process of photosynthesis. There are two important layers to the mesophyll: the **palisade mesophyll** and the **spongy mesophyll.** Most of the photosynthesis of the leaf occurs in the palisade mesophyll, where there are *many* chloroplasts. Inside a bit farther is the spongy mesophyll whose cells provide $CO_2$ to the cells performing photosynthesis. Important structures to successful photosynthesis are **stomata,** which are controlled by the guard cells that line the walls of the epidermis. Extending a bit farther inside the leaf, we find the *xylem,* the supplier of water to photosynthesizing cells, and the *phloem,* which carries *away* the products of photosynthesis. In $C_4$ plants, a second type of cell called a *bundle sheath cell* surrounds the vascular tissue to make the use of $CO_2$ more efficient and allow the stomata to remain closed during the hot daytime hours. These cells prevent excessive transpiration.

### Structure of Stems

Again, let's travel from the outside in and discuss the basic structure. The epidermis for the stem provides protection and is covered by **cutin,** a waxy protective coat. The cortex of a stem contains the parenchyma, collenchyma, and schlerenchyma cells mentioned earlier in this chapter. You'll notice that there is no endodermis in the stem because this portion of the plant is not involved in the *absorption* of water. As a result, the next structure we see as we move inward is the vascular cylinder and our friends the xylem and phloem.

A term to know is the **vascular cambium,** which extends along the entire length of the plant and gives rise to secondary xylem and phloem. Over time, the stem of a plant will increase in width because of the secondary xylem produced each year.

Another term to know is the **cork cambium,** which produces a thick cover for stems and roots. This covering replaces the epidermis when it dries up and falls off the stem during secondary growth, forming a protective barrier against infection and physical damage.

The growth of plants is not a continuous process in seasonal environments. There are periods of dormancy in between phases of growth. Have you ever seen the rings of a tree after it has been cut down? These rings produced each year are a window into the past, and give insight into the amount of rain a tree has encountered in a given year. The wider the ring, the more water it saw.

# Plant Hormones

Hormones perform the same general function for plants that they do for humans—they are signals that can travel long distances to affect the actions of another cell. There are five main plant hormones you should study for this exam.

1. *Abscisic acid.* This is the "babysitter" hormone. It makes sure that seeds do not germinate too early, inhibits cell growth, and stimulates the closing of the stomata to make sure the plant maintains enough water.
2. *Auxin.* This is a popular AP Biology exam plant hormone selection. Auxin is a hormone that performs several functions—it leads to the elongation of stems, and plays a role in phototropism and gravitropism, which we will discuss a bit later.
3. *Cytokinins.* Hormones that promote cell division and leaf enlargement. They also seem to have an element of the "fountain of youth" in them, as they seem to slow

down the aging of leaves. Supermarkets use synthetic cytokinins to keep their veggies fresh.

**BIG IDEA 3.B.2**

*The ethylene signal causes changes in production of different enzymes.*

4. *Ethylene.* This hormone initiates fruit ripening and causes flowers and leaves to drop from trees (associated with aging).
5. *Gibberellins.* Another hormone group that assists in stem elongation. When you think gibberellins, think "grow." It is thought to induce the growth of dormant seeds, buds, and flowers.

# Plant Tropisms

A **tropism** is growth that occurs in response to an environmental stimulus such as sunlight or gravity. The three tropisms you should familiarize yourself with are gravitropism, phototropism, and thigmotropism.

1. *Gravitropism.* This is a plant's growth response to gravitational force. Two of the hormones mentioned earlier play a role in this movement: **auxin** and **gibberellins.** A plant placed on its side will show gravitropic growth in which the cells on the upward-facing side will not grow as much as those on the downward side. It is believed that the relative concentrations of these hormones in the various areas of the plant are responsible for this imbalanced growth of the plant.

**BIG IDEA 2.E.2**

*In plants, physiological events involve interactions between environment (light) and internal molecular signals.*

2. *Phototropism.* This is a plant's growth response to light. Auxin is the hormone in charge here. Auxin works its magic in the zone of elongation. While the mechanics of the phototropism process may not be vital to this exam, it is still quite interesting to know. When a plant receives light on all sides, auxin is distributed equally around the zone of elongation and growth is even. When one half of a plant is in the sun, and the other is in the shade, auxin (almost as if it feels bad for the shady portion) focuses on the darker side. This leads to unequal growth of the stem with the side receiving less light growing faster—causing the movement of the plant *toward* the light source.
3. *Thigmotropism.* This is a plant's growth response to contact. One example involves vines, which wind around objects with which they make contact as they grow.

How in the world did we figure out that auxin played such a large role in phototropism? A series of experiments performed by two scientists proved vital to the understanding of this process. Grass seedlings are surrounded by a protective structure known as the **coleoptile.** Peter Boysen-Jensen performed an experiment in which a gelatin block permeable to chemical signals was placed in between this coleoptile structure and the body of a grass seedling. When the piece of grass was exposed to light on one side, it grew toward the light. When a barrier impermeable to chemical signals was placed in between the two structures instead, this growth toward light did not occur. Another scientist, F. W. Went, came onto the scene and took Jensen's experiment a step further. Went wanted to show that it was indeed a chemical and not the coleoptile tip itself that was responsible for the phototropic response. He cut off the tip and exposed it to light while the tip was resting on an agar block that would collect any chemicals that diffused out. The block was then placed on the body of a tipless grass seedling sitting in a dark room. Even in the absence of light, a block placed more toward the right side of a seedling caused the seedling to bend to the left. A block placed more toward the left side of a seedling caused the seedling to bend to the right. Because there was no further light stimulation causing the growth, the agar block must indeed have contained a chemical that induced a phototropic response. This chemical was given the name *auxin.*

# Photoperiodism

**BIG IDEA 2.E.1**

*Timing of specific events is important in the development of an organism.*

Like all of us, plants have a biological clock that maintains a **circadian rhythm**—a physiologic cycle that occurs in time increments that are roughly equivalent to the length of a day. The month of June has the longest days of the year—the most sunlight. The month of December has the shortest days of the year—the least sunlight. How is it that plants, which are so dependent on light, are able to survive through these varying conditions? This is thanks to **photoperiodism,** the response by a plant to the change in the length of days. One commonly discussed example of photoperiodism involves flowering plants (angiosperms). A hormone known as **florigen** is thought to assist in the blooming of flowers. An important pigment to the process of flowering is **phytochrome,** which is involved in the production of florigen. Because plants differ in the conditions required for flowering to occur, different amounts of florigen are needed to initiate this process from plant to plant.

One interesting application of photoperiodism involves the distinction between **short-day plants** and **long-day plants,** which flower only if certain requirements are met:

| PLANT TYPE | EXAMPLE | FLOWERING REQUIREMENTS | FLOWERS DURING |
|---|---|---|---|
| Short-day plants | Poinsettias | Exposure to a night *longer* than a certain number of hours (e.g., 10 hours) | End of summer to end of winter |
| Long-day plants | Spinach | Exposure to a night *shorter* than a certain number of hours (e.g., 8 hours) | Late spring to early summer |

# Go with the Flow: Osmosis, Capillary Action, Cohesion-Tension Theory, and Transpiration

Osmosis drives the absorption of water and minerals from the soil by the root tips. Water then moves deeper into the root until it reaches the endodermis. Once there, because of the casparian strip, it can only travel through the selective endodermal cells that choose which nutrients and minerals they let through to the vascular cylinder beyond. The casparian strip essentially lets only those with a backstage pass through. Potassium has a backstage pass and can go into the vascular cylinder . . . sodium does not and gets denied. Once the water gets to the xylem, it has reached the $H_2O$ superhighway and is ready to go all over the plant.

There are a few driving forces responsible for the movement of a plant's water supply. The three main forces we will cover here are osmosis, capillary action, and cohesion-tension theory. Of those three, the cohesion-tension theory pulls the most weight.

## Osmosis

Osmosis is the driving force that moves water from the soil into xylem cells. How in the world does the plant keep the concentration gradient such that it promotes the movement of water in the appropriate direction? There are two contributing factors: (1) the water is constantly moving away from the root tips creating the space for more water to enter, and (2) osmosis is defined as the passive diffusion of water down its concentration gradient across selectively permeable membranes. It flows from a region with a high water concentration to a region with a low water concentration. There is a higher mineral concentration inside the vascular cylinder, which drives water into the xylem contained in this cylinder by a force known as **root pressure.**

### Capillary Action

*Capillary action* is the force of adhesion between water and a passageway that pulls water up along the sides. Along with osmosis, this mechanism is a minor contributor to the movement of water up the xylem due to the counteracting force of gravity.

### Cohesion-Tension Theory and Transpiration

This process is the major mover of water in the xylem. Transpiration creates a negative pressure in the leaves and xylem tissue due to the evaporative loss of water. Water molecules display molecular attraction (cohesion) for other water molecules, in effect creating a single united water molecule that runs the length of the plant. Imagine that you tie a bunch of soda cans to a rope. If you are standing in a tree, and pull up on the cans at the top of the rope, the cans at the bottom will follow—not really because they are loyal to the other cans, but because they are connected to them, they are bonded. This is similar to the movement of water through the xylem. When water evaporates off the surface of the leaf, the water is pulled up through the xylem toward the leaves—transpiration is the force pulling water through the plant.

## The Changing of the Guard: Regulating Stomata Activity

The stomata are structures vital to the daily workings of a plant. When closed, photosynthesis is halted because water and carbon dioxide are inaccessible. When open, mesophyll cells have access to water and carbon dioxide. But with every reward, there is always a risk. When the stomata are open, the plant could dry out as a result of excessive transpiration. This process of opening and closing the stomata must therefore be very carefully controlled. Guard cells are the ones for the job. They surround and tightly regulate the actions of the stomata. When water flows into neighboring guard cells (leading to an increase in turgor pressure), a structural change occurs that causes the opening of the stomata. When the water flows out of the guard cells (a decrease in turgor pressure), the stomata will close. It is by this mechanism that guard cells control the opening and closing of the stomata.

## "Move Over, Sugar": Carbohydrate Transport Through Phloem

The transport of carbohydrates through the phloem is called **translocation.** After their production, carbohydrates, the all-important product of photosynthesis, are dumped into the phloem (the sugar superhighway) near the site of their creation, to be distributed throughout the plant. The movement of the sugar into the phloem creates a driving force because it establishes a concentration gradient. This gradient leads to the passive diffusion of water into the phloem, causing an increase in the pressure of these cells. This pressure drives the movement of sugars and water through the phloem. As the sugars arrive at various destination sites, the sugar is consumed by plant cells, causing a reversal in the driving force for water that pushes water out of the phloem. As water exits the phloem, the increased pressure disappears and all is good once again.

## ❯ Review Questions

1. Which of the following is *not* a time when most stomata tend to be open?

   A. When $CO_2$ concentrations are low inside the leaf
   B. When temperatures are low
   C. When the concentration of water inside the plant is low
   D. During the day

For questions 2–5, please use the following answer choices:

   A. Abscisic acid
   B. Cytokinins
   C. Ethylene
   D. Gibberellins

2. This hormone is used by supermarkets for its "fountain of youth" effect.

3. This hormone initiates fruit ripening and works hard during the autumn months.

4. This hormone prevents seeds from germinating prematurely.

5. This hormone is known to induce growth in dormant seeds, buds, and flowers.

6. A vine is observed to wrap around a tree as it grows in the forest. This is an example of

   A. gravitropism.
   B. phototropism.
   C. thigmotropism.
   D. photoperiodism.

7. This portion of the root of a plant is responsible for the visual perception of growth:

   A. Zone of cell division
   B. Vascular cylinder
   C. Zone of elongation
   D. Endodermis

For questions 8–10, please use the following answers:

   A. Sieve-tube elements
   B. Vessel elements
   C. Guard cells
   D. Collenchyma cells

8. These cells are responsible for controlling the opening and closing of the stomata.

9. These cells are the more efficient of the two types of xylem cells.

10. These cells are live cells that function as structural support for a plant.

11. The unequal growth of the stem of a plant in which the side in the shade grows faster than the side in the sun is an example of

    A. gravitropism.
    B. phototropism.
    C. thigmotropism.
    D. photoperiodism.

## › Answers and Explanations

1. **C**—When the concentration of water inside the plant is low, the stomata close in an effort to minimize transpiration.

2. **B**

3. **C**

4. **A**

5. **D**

6. **C**—Thigmotropism is a plant's growth in response to touch. Phototropism is growth in response to light, and gravitropism is growth in response to gravitational force. Photoperiodism is the response by a plant to the change in the length of days.

7. **C**

8. **C**

9. **B**

10. **D**

11. **B**—Phototropism, a plant's growth response to light, is controlled by auxin. This hormone is produced in the apical meristem and sent to the zone of elongation to initiate growth toward the sun.

## › Rapid Review

The following terms and topics are important in this chapter:

*Anatomy of plants*: tissue systems are divided into *ground, vascular,* and *dermal.*

*Ground tissue*: the body of the plant is divided into three cell types:

- *Collenchyma cells*: provide flexible and mechanical support; found in stems and leaves.
- *Parenchyma cells*: play a role in storage, secretion, and photosynthesis in cells.
- *Sclerenchyma cells*: protect seeds and support the plant.

*Vascular tissue*: *xylem* (transports water and minerals) and *phloem* (transports sugar).

*Dermal tissue*: protective outer coating for plants: *epidermis.*

### Roots

*Types*: **taproot system** (dicots)—system that divides into lateral roots that anchor the plant; **fibrous root system** (monocots)—anchoring system that does not go deep down into soil.

*Structure*: epidermis → endodermis (casparian strip) → vascular cylinder → xylem/phloem.

*Growth*: occurs for lifetime of the plant thanks to **meristem** cells:

- *Primary growth*: increased *length* of a plant (occurs in region of apical meristems).
- *Secondary growth*: increased *width* of a plant (occurs in region of lateral meristems, limited in monocots).
- *Three main growth regions*: zone of *cell division* (cells divide), zone of *elongation* (cells elongate), zone of *maturation* (cells mature to specialized form).

### Stems (Shoots)

*Structure*: epidermis (cutin) → cortex (ground tissue) → vascular cylinder → xylem/phloem.

*Vascular cambium*: gives rise to secondary xylem/phloem; runs entire length of plant.

*Cork cambium*: produces protective covering that replaces epidermis during secondary growth.

### Leaves (Shoots)

*Structure*: epidermis (cuticle) → mesophyll (photosynthesis) → vascular bundles → xylem/phloem.

*C$_4$ plants*: leaves contain another cell type, **bundle sheath cells,** which assist in respiration in hot and dry regions.

*Stomata*: structure, controlled by **guard cells,** that when open allows $CO_2$ in, and $H_2O$ and $O_2$ out.

*Plant hormones*: **abscisic acid** (inhibits cell growth, helps close stomata), **auxin** (stem elongation, gravitropism, phototropism), **cytokinins** (promotes cell division, leaf enlargement, slows aging of leaves), **ethylene** (ripens fruit and causes leaves to fall), **gibberellins** (stem elongation, induces growth in dormant seeds, buds, flowers).

*Plant tropisms*: **gravitropism** (a plant's growth in response to gravity—auxin, gibberellins), **phototropism** (plant's growth in response to light—auxin), **thigmotropism** (plant's growth in response to touch).

*Photoperiodism*: response of a plant to the change in length of days; remember **florigen** and **phytochrome.**

*Driving force for $H_2O$ movement in plants*: transpiration is the major driving force that draws $H_2O$ up the xylem because of the cohesive nature of water molecules. Osmosis and capillary action are minor contributors.

*Driving force for sugar movement in plants*: sugar, when created, is dumped into the phloem, creating a concentration gradient that draws water in, increasing the pressure that drives the sugar through the phloem.

# CHAPTER 15

# Human Physiology

## IN THIS CHAPTER

**Summary:** This chapter takes you on a tour of the human body and discusses how the various systems of the human body function on a daily basis.

**Key Ideas**

✪ Study this chapter well—human physiology comes up often on the AP exam.

✪ Passage of blood flow through the heart: vena cava → right atrium → right ventricle → lungs → left atrium → left ventricle → aorta → body and back.

✪ The functional unit of the lung is the alveolus.

✪ Four major thermoregulatory processes: conduction, convection, evaporation, and radiation.

✪ The CNS consists of the brain and spinal cord. The PNS is broken down into the sensory and motor divisions.

✪ Three main types of muscle: skeletal, cardiac, and smooth.

✪ Study the names, origins, and functions of the various hormones that appear in this chapter—this is a common subject for multiple-choice questions.

✪ Learn about the difference between nonspecific and specific immunity.

## Introduction

**BIG IDEA 4.B.2**
*Within multicellular organisms, specialization of organs contributes to overall function.*

Welcome to the tour of the human body. During this tour, we will discuss how our bodies work. We will be making eight stops, lunch will not be served, and we don't want to hear any requests for bathroom breaks (although we will be learning about things of that nature). Buckle up—here we go.

# Circulatory System

### Heart

Welcome to the heart. The human heart is a four-chambered organ whose function is to circulate blood by rhythmic contraction. The heart pumps oxygenated blood from the left ventricle out to the aorta (Figure 15.1). From there it travels through **arteries** to feed the organs, muscles, and other tissues of the body. The blood returns to the heart via the **veins.** The superior and inferior vena cavae return deoxygenated blood from the body to the heart. The blood reenters the heart through the right atrium, passes through to the right ventricle, and from there to the lungs to exchange carbon dioxide for more oxygen. At this point, the blood has made a complete cycle through the body. The blood is at its most oxygenated stage just after leaving the lungs as it enters the left side of the heart and travels into the aorta. The blood is in its least oxygenated stage as it reenters the right atrium of the heart.

Deoxygenated blood arrives via vena cavae into right atrium

Oxygenated blood returns to heart via pulmonary veins

Right atrium (blood is least oxygenated here)

Left atrium (blood is most oxygenated here)

Right ventricle

Left ventricle

Aorta (sends blood to rest of body)

To lungs via pulmonary artery

**Figure 15.1    Oversimplified diagram of the heart and blood flow.**

Structure–function relationships come up often on the AP Biology exam, and the circulatory system provides a good example you could add to an essay on the topic. The left ventricle of the heart is the thickest and most muscular part of the heart, and the most pressure is exerted on it. Why does this make sense functionally? Because the left ventricle is the portion of the heart that needs to pump the blood into the aorta and to the rest of the body. The left ventricle is structurally designed to fit its function. The right ventricle is smaller and less muscular because it only pumps blood a short distance to the lungs for gas exchange (the picking up of oxygen and the release of $CO_2$).

### Blood

As we continue on our journey, if you look off to your right, you will see some of the blood and its components passing us now. If you look closely, you will see little *red blood cells*, which carry oxygen, traveling in the bloodstream. Thanks to a molecule termed **hemoglobin,** the red blood cells are able to carry and deliver oxygen throughout the body to hardworking organs and tissues. Iron is a major component of hemoglobin. If you do not have enough iron in your diet, your ability to deliver oxygen via the blood can be compromised, and you may develop **anemia.**

Blood is able to flow so efficiently because it contains primarily water. The liquid portion of the blood, the **plasma,** contains minerals, hormones, antibodies, and nutritional materials. Another common component seen in the bloodstream is the **platelet,** which is involved in the clotting of blood. You might ask, "What are the white cells flowing around?" The white blood cells are the protection system for our body. We will be seeing those up close when we talk about the immune system.

The **lymphatic system** is worth a brief mention here because it is an important part of the circulatory system. When blood flows through the capillaries of the body, proteins and fluid leak out during the exchange. The lymphatic system functions as the route by which these poor lost souls find their way back into the bloodstream. The lymphatic system also functions as a protector for the body because of the presence of structures known as **lymph nodes,** which are full of white blood cells that live to fight infection. If your neck sometimes swells when you are sick with the flu, for instance, it is probably the multiplication of white blood cells in the lymph nodes of your neck.

### Diseases of the Cardiovascular System

Two diseases that you should be familiar with for the exam are *hypertension* and *arteriosclerosis*. *Hypertension* is high blood pressure and is a major cause of strokes and heart attacks. *Arteriosclerosis* is a big word that means hardening of the arteries. These hardened arteries become narrower and are a prime risk factor for death by embolism—the breaking off of a piece of tissue that lodges in an artery, blocking the flow of blood to vital tissues.

# Respiratory System

We are going to head down to the lungs now. Please stay close because it will get a little loud in these windy tunnels. Air comes into the body through the mouth and the nose. We are currently in the nasal passages, and along with the air that came into the nose, we are being warmed and moistened in the *nasal cavity* before we head down toward the **pharynx** region, where the air and food passages cross. We will come back to this area again later on in the tour when we take the road that food uses to get from the mouth to the stomach. During inhalation, the air goes through a structure called the *glottis* into the **larynx** (human voicebox). From there, the air moves into the **trachea,** which contains rings of cartilage that help it maintain its shape. Each trachea is the tunnel that leads the air into the *thoracic cavity*. If you look outside your windows, you will notice some tiny arms waving at us as we go by. They are the **cilia,** which beat in rhythmical waves to carry foreign particles (like our tour bus) and mucus away from the respiratory tract.

> **BIG IDEA 2.A.3**
> *The increased surface area of alveoli helps in gas exchange with the environment.*

We are now at a fork in the road. Here the trachea divides into two separate tunnels: the two **bronchi,** which are also held open by cartilage rings, one going to the left lung, and one going to the right lung. Each bronchus divides into smaller branches, which divide into even smaller branches, which divide into tunnels called **bronchioles.** These bronchioles branch repeatedly until they conclude as tiny air pockets containing **alveoli.**

In Figure 15.2, notice how thin the walls of the alveoli are. They are usually a single cell in thickness, are covered by a thin film of water, and are surrounded by a dense bed of capillaries. You might have questioned earlier exactly where the exchange of $O_2$ and $CO_2$ actually occurs—this is the place. The alveoli are considered to be the primary functional unit of the lung. Oxygen enters the alveolus the same way we just did—it dissolves in the water lining of the wall and diffuses across the cells into the bloodstream. At the same time, the $CO_2$, which is carried by the blood, primarily in the form of bicarbonate ($HCO_3^-$), passes out of the blood in a similar manner. The $O_2$ moves easily into the bloodstream

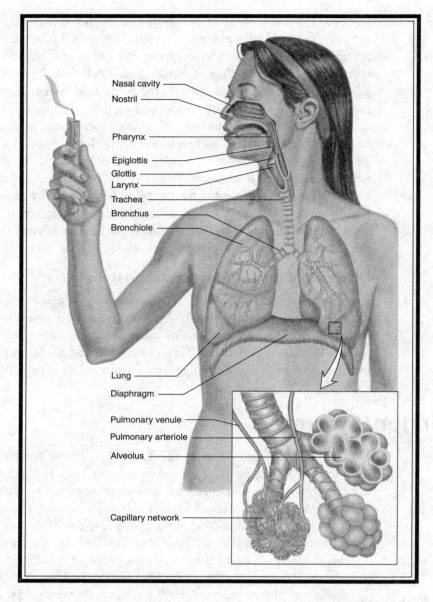

**Figure 15.2   The human lungs, with close-up view of alveoli, bronchi, and bronchioles.** (*From* Biology, *8th ed., by Sylvia S. Mader,* © *1985, 1987, 1990, 1993, 1996, 1998, 2001, 2004 by the McGraw Hill Companies, Inc. Reproduced with permission of The McGraw-Hill Companies.*)

because it is moving down its concentration gradient. Once there, it travels with the blood to the rest of the body.

Before we move on to the digestive system, we should discuss the mechanism by which breathing actually occurs. The rib cage and the diaphragm play important roles in the breathing process. Inhalation causes the volume of the thoracic cavity to increase. As a result, the air pressure in the chest falls below that of the atmosphere, and air flows into the body. This is accompanied by a contraction of the rib-cage muscles and the diaphragm, allowing for the increase in thoracic volume. After the air exchange occurs, the muscles relax, causing the diaphragm to move up against the lungs, reducing the thoracic volume. This causes the pressure in the lungs to exceed that of the atmosphere—driving the air containing $CO_2$ out of the body.

# Digestive System

Okay, folks, it is time to take the tour of the digestive system. Hang on tight—we are going to take a shortcut to the mouth as we are exhaled back through the system. Here we go: bronchioles, bronchi, trachea, larynx, pharynx, and mouth!

Here we sit in the oral cavity. This is where the digestion of food begins. Food is, of course, tasted in the oral cavity, and the teeth that help us chew (masticate) are performing a task called **mechanical digestion.** The liquid sloshing up against the windows of the bus is *saliva,* which contains enzymes such as **amylase** that help dissolve some of the food. Amylase breaks down the starches in our diet into simpler sugars like maltose, which are fully digested further down in the intestines. The saliva also acts as a lubricant to help the food move along the digestive pathway.

We need to carefully avoid the **tongue,** which functions to move food around while we chew and helps to arrange it into a ball that we swallow called a *bolus.* The tongue pushes the food toward the crossroad we visited during the tour of the respiratory system. You may notice that this time, as the swallowing occurs, we do not go through the glottis toward the lungs, but instead into the **esophagus,** which connects the throat to the stomach. The force created by the rhythmical contraction of the smooth muscle of the esophagus (currently pushing us toward the stomach) is called **peristalsis.**

After passing through the **esophageal sphincter,** which acts like a valve or trapdoor, food enters into the stomach, where more digestion will occur. The sphincter is usually closed in order to keep food from returning back up the esophagus to the mouth. In the stomach, the digestion occurs by a churning action that mixes the food and breaks it into smaller pieces. Folks, we would recommend that you do not step out of the bus here because the pH is way down in the 1.5–2.5 range, which provides *quite* an acidic environment. If you look closely along the edges of the stomach, you will see many glands. Some of these glands secrete gastric juice, composed of hydrochloric acid (HCl) and digestive enzymes, which helps in digestion and lowers the pH. The major enzyme of the stomach is **pepsin,** which breaks proteins down into smaller polypeptides that are handled by the intestines. The glands here secrete **pepsinogen**—the precursor to pepsin. Pepsinogen is activated into pepsin by HCl. Pepsin is picky and will function only in a particular range of pH values. This is a good thing because if it were active all the time, it would digest things it is not supposed to digest. Other glands secrete mucus to help line the stomach. It is this mucus that helps prevent the wall of the stomach from being digested along with the food.

Now we move on to the *small intestine.* To get to the small intestine, we need to pass through the Panama Canal of the body: the **pyloric sphincter.** For those of you interested in useful AP exam trivia, the small intestine is where most of the digestion and absorption occur. The terrain is a bit different in this organ. The walls are arranged into folds and ridges, which have more waving structures, this time called *villi,* similar to the cilia we saw in the respiratory tract. The walls in the small intestine contain something called a **brush border,** which is composed of a large amount of microvilli that increases the surface area of the small intestine to improve absorption efficiency. Digested nutrients absorbed in the small intestine are dumped into various veins that merge to form the hepatic portal vessel, which leads to the liver. The liver then gets first crack at the newly absorbed nutrients before they are sent to the rest of the body. As the food moves into the small intestine, it brings with it an acidity that promotes the secretion of numerous enzymes from the *pancreas* and the local glands. (***Important note to remember:*** hormones are vital to the turning on and off of the digestive glands.)

Those of you on the left side of the bus have a good view of the pancreatic duct as it expels **lipase, amylase, trypsin,** and **chymotrypsin.** Lipase is the major fat-digesting enzyme

> **BIG IDEA 2.A.3**
> *Villi create high surface area, helping in exchange of nutrients with the environment.*

of the body. It receives some help in the handling of the fat from a product made in the liver called **bile.** Bile contains bile salts, phospholipids, cholesterol, and bile pigments such as bilirubin. The bile is stored in the *gallbladder* and is dumped into the small intestine upon the arrival of food. The bile salts help digest the fat by *emulsifying* it into small droplets contained in water. (Emulsification is a physical change—bile does not contain any enzymes.) Amylase continues the breakdown of carbohydrates into simpler sugars. *Maltase, lactase,* and *sucrase* break maltose, lactose, and sucrose, respectively, into monosaccharides. Trypsin and chymotrypsin work together to handle the digestion of the peptides in our diet. Trypsin cuts peptide bonds next to arginine and lysine; chymotrypsin cuts bonds by phenylalanine, tryptophan, and tyrosine. Like pepsin, these two proteolytic enzymes are secreted as inactive forms: trypsinogen and chymotrypsinogen. Trypsinogen is activated first to become trypsin, which, in turn, activates chymotrypsin. Some of you might ask "If the proteolytic enzymes only cut at certain sites, how do we finish digesting the proteins?" Trypsin and chymotrypsin are examples of *enteropeptidases.* It is the **exopeptidases** that complete the digestion of proteins by hydrolyzing all the amino acids of the remaining fragments.

After the small intestine comes the large intestine (which includes the cecum, colon, and rectum). The two meet up in the lower right corner of the abdomen. The colon has three main parts: the *ascending, transverse,* and *descending colon.* There are two major functions for this part of the system—the primary function is to reabsorb water and electrolytes. A second function is to serve as a passageway for the waste material as it moves toward the rectum. The food enters the large intestine, travels up the ascending colon, across the transverse colon, down the descending colon into the rectum, where it is stored until it gets eliminated . . . but we don't need to go there. We've seen enough for now.

# Control of the Internal Environment

**BIG IDEA 2.D.2**
*Homeostatic mechanisms reflect common ancestry.*

The next stop on our tour is the kidney (see Figure 15.3 for an overview of the human excretory system). The kidneys lie on the posterior wall of the abdomen. The renal artery and vein bring blood to and from the kidney, respectively. Kidneys are divided into two major regions: an outer region called the **cortex,** and an inner region called the **medulla.** These two regions are full of **nephrons,** the functional units of the kidney. The medulla is divided into structures called *renal pyramids,* which dump urine into the *major and minor calyces.* From here, the urine is sent toward the *bladder* via the *ureter.* When contracted to urinate, the bladder sends the urine through the *urethra* to the outside world.

We've pulled the bus right up to one of over a million nephrons in each kidney. The nephron is composed of a *renal corpuscle, proximal convoluted tubule, loop of Henle, distal convoluted tubule,* and *collecting duct system.* If you look closely, you will see that the renal corpuscle is made up of **glomerular capillaries** surrounded by *Bowman's capsule.*

## Osmoregulation and Excretion

The blood that enters via the renal artery is sent to the various nephrons by the branching of the renal artery into smaller and smaller vessels that culminate in the capillaries of the glomerulus. The *blood pressure* is the force that leads to the movement of solutes such as water, urea, and salts into the lumen of Bowman's capsule from the glomerular capillaries. From here, the fluids pass down the proximal tubule, through the loop of Henle, and into the distal tubule, which dumps into the collecting duct. The various collecting ducts of the kidney collectively merge into the renal pelvis, which leads via the ureter to the bladder.

As we mentioned moments ago, fluid moves from the capillaries into the lumen of the nephron as a result of the force of blood pressure. During this process of **filtration,** the capillaries are able to let small particles through the pores of their endothelial linings,

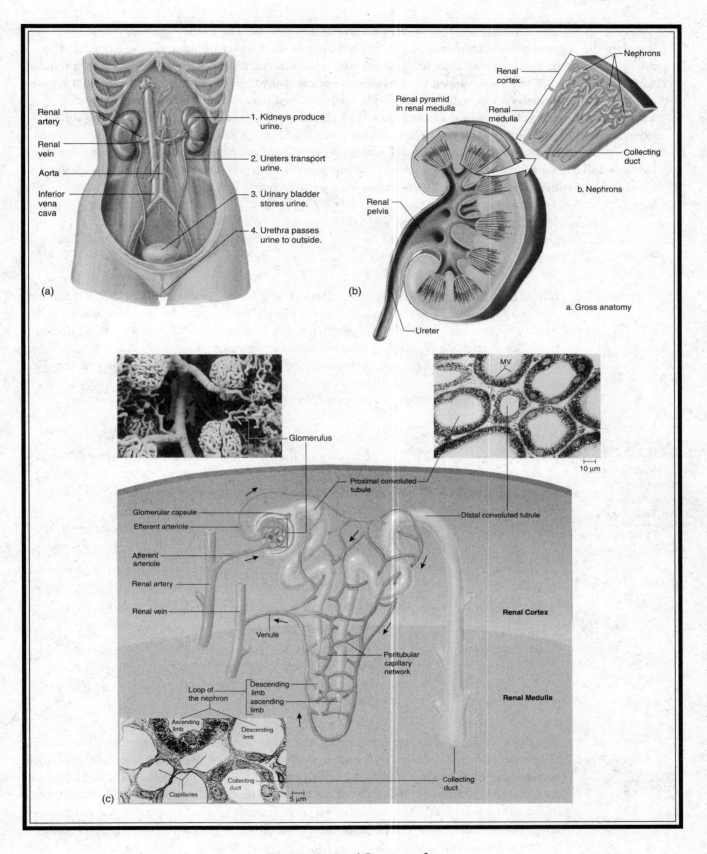

(a)

1. Kidneys produce urine.
2. Ureters transport urine.
3. Urinary bladder stores urine.
4. Urethra passes urine to outside.

Renal artery
Renal vein
Aorta
Inferior vena cava

(b)

Nephrons
Renal cortex
Renal medulla
Collecting duct

Renal pyramid in renal medulla

Renal pelvis

Ureter

b. Nephrons

a. Gross anatomy

Glomerulus

MV

10 µm

Proximal convoluted tubule

Glomerular capsule
Efferent arteriole
Afferent arteriole
Renal artery
Renal vein

Venule

Distal convoluted tubule

Peritubular capillary network

Renal Cortex

Loop of the nephron

Descending limb
ascending limb

Ascending limb
Descending limb

Capillaries

Collecting duct

Renal Medulla

Collecting duct

5 µm

(c)

**Figure 15.3**  (*Continued*)
**For legend see the following section.**

**Figure 15.3** **The human excretory system on four size scales. (a) The kidneys produce urine and regulate the composition of the blood. Urine is conveyed to the urinary bladder via the ureter and to the outside via the urethra. Branches of the aorta, the renal arteries convey blood to the kidneys; renal veins drain blood from the kidneys into the posterior vena cava. (b) Urine is formed in two distinct regions of the kidney: the outer renal cortex and inner renal medulla. It then drains into a central chamber, the renal pelvis, and into the ureters. (c) Excretory tubules (nephrons and collecting ducts) and associated blood vessels pack the cortex and medulla. The human kidney has about a million nephrons, representing about 80 km of tubules. Cortical nephrons are restricted mainly to the renal cortex. Juxtamedullary nephrons have a long, hairpinlike portion that extends into the renal medulla. Several nephrons empty into each collecting duct, which drains into the renal pelvis.**
*(Adapted from* Biology, *8th ed., by Sylvia S. Mader,* © *1985, 1987, 1990, 1993, 1996, 1998, 2001, 2004 by the McGraw Hill Companies, Inc. Reproduced with permission of The McGraw-Hill Companies.)*

but large molecules such as proteins, platelets, and blood cells tend to remain in the vessel. As the filtrate progresses along the tubule, plasma solutes such as urea are added by the process of *secretion,* a selective process that helps to create a solute gradient. It is important to realize that much of what is dumped into the tubule originally is *reabsorbed*—nearly all the sugars, water, and organic nutrients. The combination of reabsorption and secretion help the nephron to control what gets released in the urine. The following chart outlines in detail what happens in the various parts of the nephron:

> **BIG IDEA 2.C.1**
> *Animals use feedback mechanisms (e.g., ADH) to maintain internal conditions.*

| | |
|---|---|
| Proximal tubule | Reabsorbs 75 percent of NaCl and water of filtrate. Nutrients such as glucose and amino acids are reabsorbed unless their concentration is higher than the absorptive capacity. Glucose in urine is an indicator of diabetes, for this reason. |
| Descending loop of Henle | Freely permeable to $H_2O$ but not NaCl. Assists in control of water and salt concentrations. |
| Ascending loop of Henle | Freely permeable to NaCl but not water. Assists in control of salt concentration. |
| Distal tubule | Regulates concentration of $K^+$ and NaCl. Helps control pH by reabsorbing $HCO_3^-$ and secreting $H^+$. |
| Collecting duct | Determines how much water is actually lost in urine. The osmotic gradient created in the earlier regions of the nephron allows the kidney control in the final concentration of the urine. |

The body controls the concentration of the urine according to the needs of the system. When dehydrated, the body can excrete a small volume of hypertonic concentrated urine (little water in the urine; it is dark yellow). But in times of excessive fluid, the body will excrete a large volume of hypotonic dilute urine to conserve the necessary salts (lots of water in the urine; it is clear). This is controlled by hormones and is discussed in more detail in a later section, but briefly: **ADH** (antidiuretic hormone) is released by the pituitary gland; it increases permeability of the collecting duct to water, leading to more concentrated urine. **Aldosterone,** released from the adrenal gland, acts on the distal tubules to cause the reabsorption of more $Na^+$ and water to increase blood volume and pressure.

## Thermoregulation

A fairly constant body temperature is important for many living organisms. The process by which this temperature is maintained is known as **thermoregulation.** A major organ involved in thermoregulation is the skin, which also plays a role in excretion through sweating. Four major thermoregulatory processes are conduction, convection, evaporation, and radiation. **Conduction** is the process by which heat moves from a place of higher temperature to a place of lower temperature. For example, let's say that two people are sleeping in the same bed, and that person A is cold all the time. Person A would not make it through the night if it were not for this process. Since person B tends to be warmer than person A, person A takes advantage of conduction by pulling the heat from person B's body to hers. **Convection** is heat transfer caused by airflow. Thinking about my baseline warmth (similar to that of person B), if it were not for our air conditioners in the summer, we would probably not be here today to write this book. But we curse convection in the winter as the cold wind removes heat from our bodies, making it feel that much colder outside. **Evaporation** is the process by which water leaves our bodies in the form of water vapor: sweat. Why do humid days feel so much warmer than nonhumid days? Because humidity increases the amount of water in the air, decreasing the driving force for water to leave our bodies. **Radiation** is the loss of heat through ejection of electromagnetic waves.

Before moving on to the nervous system, we must mention two more terms: endotherm and ectotherm. An **endotherm** is an organism whose body temperature is not dramatically affected by the surrounding temperature. We humans are endothermic creatures. Sure, a cold day can feel really cold, but at least it does not dramatically lower the human body temperature. **Ectothermic animals** are organisms whose body temperatures *are* affected by the surrounding temperature. Fish, reptiles, and amphibians are good examples of ectothermic organisms.

# Nervous System

> **BIG IDEA 3.E.2**
> *Animals have a nervous system that detects signals, transmits information, and produces responses.*

The nervous system is divided into two systems: the **central nervous system** (CNS) and the **peripheral nervous system** (PNS). The CNS contains the brain and the spinal cord. The PNS can be broken down into a sensory and a motor division. The sensory division carries information *to* the CNS while the motor division carries information *away* from the CNS. The motor division can be further broken down in the **somatic nervous system** (SNS), also known as the voluntary nervous system, and the **autonomic nervous system** (ANS). As indicated by its name, the SNS controls the voluntary contraction of muscles, while the ANS controls the involuntary activities of the body: smooth muscle, cardiac muscle, and glands. The ANS is divided into the **sympathetic** and **parasympathetic** divisions.

Before delving into the various divisions of the nervous system, it is important to look at the mechanics of nerve cell transmissions (Figure 15.4). The functional unit of the nervous system is the *neuron* (nerve cell). Outside to the left of the bus is a nerve cell from the CNS. There are three main parts to a nerve cell: the cell body, the dendrite, and the axon. The **cell body** is the main body of the neuron. The **dendrite** is one of many short, branched processes of a neuron that help bring the nerve impulses toward the cell body. The **axon** is the longer extension that leaves from the neuron and carries the impulse away from the cell body toward the target cell. Some CNS nerve cells, as well as most PNS neurons, are **myelinated neurons,** which means that they have a layer of insulation around the axon, allowing for faster transmission. It is the cable Internet of the body.

**Figure 15.4   The components of a nerve cell (neuron).**

The nerve cells can be divided into three main classes: sensory neurons, motor neurons, and interneurons. **Sensory neurons** receive and communicate information from the sensory environment. **Interneurons** function to make synaptic connections with other neurons. Located in the CNS, they tie together sensory input and motor output and are the intermediaries of the operation. **Motor neurons** take the commands of the CNS and put them into action as motor outputs. This relationship is the basis for the *reflex arc,* which is the basic unit of response in the CNS. A sensory neuron sends an impulse to the spinal cord, which is transmitted via a series of interneurons to a motor neuron whose impulse causes a muscular contraction.

Whoa! Did you see that spark zip past just now? That was a perfect example of a nerve impulse. The membranes of these neurons all around us are full of pumps and special gated ion channels that allow the cell to change its membrane potential in response to certain stimuli. The opening of sodium channels causes the potential to become less negative, and the cell is **depolarized.** If the threshold potential is reached (electrical potential that, when reached, initiates an action potential), an action potential is triggered, which is the nerve impulse that we just saw zip by. *Action potentials* are quick changes in cell potential due to well-controlled opening and closing of ion channels. The cell also contains potassium channels that open slowly in response to depolarization. After a short period of time, the sodium channel closes, and potassium rushes out of the cell causing **repolarization** of the cell and lowering of the potential back down to its initial. Let's move farther down this axon to see where this impulse is going.

Here we are at the end of the axon, sometimes called the **synaptic knob.** This is where calcium gates are opened in response to the changing potential, which causes vesicles to release substances called **neurotransmitters** into the synaptic gap between the axon and the target cell. These neurotransmitters diffuse across the gap, causing a new impulse in the target cell. Two of the most common neurotransmitters used in the body are acetylcholine and norepinephrine. Substances called cholinesterases function to clear the neurotransmitters from the synaptic gap after an action potential by binding to the neurotransmitters and recycling them back to the neuron.

The ANS regulates involuntary activities in the body. As mentioned earlier, it is subdivided into the parasympathetic and sympathetic divisions. For the most part, the parasympathetic response is one that promotes energy conservation: slower heart rate, decreased blood pressure, and bronchial muscle and urinary bladder constriction. The sympathetic response is one that prepares us for "fight or flight"—increased heart rate, dilated bronchial muscles, increased blood pressure, and digestive slowdown.

The CNS consists of the brain and spinal cord. The brain is divided into various sections that control the different regions of our bodies (Figure 15.5). The **cerebellum** is in charge of coordination and balance. The **medulla oblongata** is the control center for involuntary activities such as breathing. The **hypothalamus** is the thermostat and

**BIG IDEA 4.A.4**
*Organisms exhibit complex properties due to interactions between constituent parts.*

**BIG IDEA 3.D.2**
*Cells communicate with each other using chemical signals (e.g., neurotransmitters).*

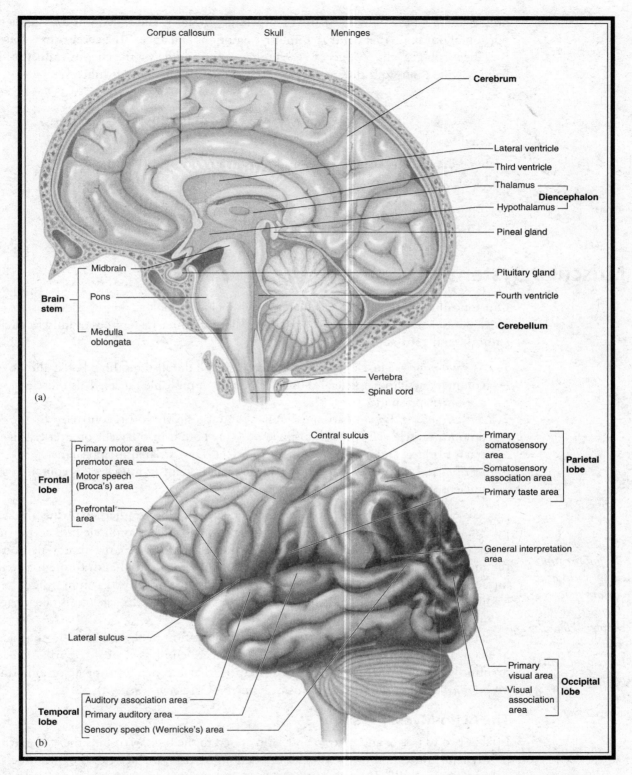

**Figure 15.5   Major structures of the human brain. (a) Of the brain's three ancestral regions, the forebrain is massively developed and contains the most sophisticated integrating centers. One of its subdivisions, the telencephalon, consists mainly of the cerebrum (cerebral hemispheres), which extends over and around most other brain centers. The diencephalon contains the thalamus and hypothalamus. The other two ancestral regions, the midbrain and hindbrain, make up the brian stem. (b) This rear view shows the bilateral nature of the brain components. The cerebral hemispheres, corpus callosum (large fiber tracts connecting the hemispheres), and basal ganglia are parts of the telencephalon.** *(From Biology, 8th ed., by Sylvia S. Mader, © 1985, 1987, 1990, 1993, 1996, 1998, 2001, 2004 by the McGraw Hill Companies, Inc. Reproduced with permission of The McGraw-Hill Companies.)*

hunger-meter of the body, regulating temperature, hunger, and thirst. The **amygdala** is the portion of our brain that controls impulsive emotions and anger. The **cerebrum** is split into two "hemispheres" that connect to each other in the middle via the **corpus callosum.** Each half is divided into four different lobes, each specializing in various functions:

| Lobes of the Brain and Their Functions | |
| --- | --- |
| Frontal lobe | Speech, motor cortex. |
| Parietal lobe | Speech, taste, reading, somatosensory. |
| Occipital lobe | Vision. |
| Temporal lobe | Hearing and smell. |

# Muscular System

Our tour of the muscle types of the body will include a look at the types of muscles and a quick demonstration of muscle contraction. There are three main types of muscle: **skeletal, smooth,** and **cardiac:**

1. *Skeletal muscle.* Muscle type that works when you do pushups, lift a book, and do other voluntary activities. Skeletal muscle cells contain multiple nuclei. This muscle type has a *striated* appearance.
2. *Smooth muscle.* Involuntary muscle that contracts slowly and is controlled by the ANS. Smooth muscle cells contain a single nucleus. Found in the walls of arteries, digestive tract, bladder, and elsewhere. Smooth muscle is not striated in appearance.
3. *Cardiac muscle.* Involuntary muscle of the heart. Cardiac muscle cells contain a single nucleus. Cardiac muscle cells are striated in appearance.

Muscle cells are activated by the mechanism described earlier involving the action potentials and ion channels. When an action potential reaches a muscle cell, acetylcholine is released at the **neuromuscular junction**—the space between the motor neuron and the muscle cell. This neurotransmitter depolarizes the muscle cell and, through a series of intracellular reactions, causes the release of large amounts of stored calcium inside the cell, leading to muscle contraction. Muscle contraction stops when the calcium is taken back up by the sarcoplasmic reticulum of the cell.

Folks, we are going to be treated to a demonstration of skeletal muscle contraction. Skeletal muscle consists of fiber bundles, which are composed of myofibrils. What are myofibrils? Good question. They are structures that are made up of a combination of *myofilaments* called *thin filaments* (*actin*) and *thick filaments* (*myosin*).

*CT teacher: "Know the functional units of the various systems discussed in this chapter. How the structure of these functional units relates to their function could be a nice essay."*

## The Actin-Myosin "Tango"

It takes two to tango, and myosin and actin are up to the task. Myosin is the lead partner of this dynamic duo and powers muscle contraction. Myosin, the heart of the thick fibers, has a "head" and a "tail." The tails of the numerous myosin molecules unite to form the "thick filament" seen in Figure 15.6. The heads of the myosin molecules stick out from the thick filament and serve as the contact point with the actin. The head can exist in two forms: low and high energy. A relaxed muscle begins with the myosin heads in the low-energy form, attached to ATP. If the ATP is converted into ADP and phosphate, the myosin changes to the higher-energy form and is ready to dance. Myosin smoothly approaches its beloved partner, actin. When ready, the myosin and actin attach to each other, forming the "cross-bridge." As they get ready to slide, myosin loses its ADP and phosphate, releasing

= Thin filament (actin)

= Thick filament (myosin)

**Figure 15.6   Actin-myosin interaction: (a) relaxed muscle; (b) contracted muscle.**

its energy, and causing it to elegantly tilt its head to one side . . . sliding the beautiful actin toward the center of the sarcomere (Figure 15.6b). The two part ways when myosin again binds to ATP, bringing us back to where we started (Figure 15.6a).

# :::Applause:::

Control mechanisms are often mentioned on the AP Biology exam and make good essay material. It would be really annoying and awkward if our muscles were contracting all the time. So, it makes sense that there must be some way to control the contraction. Myosin is only able to dance with actin if a regulatory protein, known as **tropomyosin,** is not blocking the attachment site on actin. The key to the removal of tropomyosin is the presence of calcium ions. Tropomyosin is also bound to *another* regulatory protein known as troponin. Calcium causes these two to do their own little dance and shuffle away from the actin-myosin binding site. This allows the actin-myosin dance to occur and muscle contraction to follow. When the calcium is gone, the dance is complete, and the filaments separate from each other.

What causes this calcium release seen in muscle contraction? This brings us back to the neuromuscular junction mentioned not too long ago. Nervous impulses from motor neurons cause the release of acetylcholine into the neuromuscular junction. Acetylcholine binds to the muscle cell and initiates a series of reactions that culminates in the dumping of calcium from its storage facility—the sarcoplasmic reticulum. This calcium finds troponin, binds to it, and lets the dance begin.

# Endocrine System

**BIG IDEA 3.B.2**
*A variety of intercellular and intracellular signals mediate gene expression.*

Endocrine signaling occurs when cells dump **hormones** into the bloodstream to affect cells in other parts of the body. Hormones are chemicals produced by glands such as the pituitary and distributed by the circulatory system to signal faraway target cells. Here we are at the pituitary gland. As you can see, it is not very big at all—it is the size of a pea and is divided into an anterior and a posterior division. The anterior pituitary gland is also called the adenohypophysis, and it produces six hormones: **TSH, STH, ACTH, LH, FSH,** and **prolactin;** the posterior pituitary gland, also known as the *neurohypophysis,* releases only two hormones: **ADH** and **oxytocin** (see definitions of these acronyms in the Glossary at the end of the book).

The two lobes of the pituitary gland differ in the way they deliver their hormones. If you look closely, you will see that there is a short stalk that connects the anterior portion of the pituitary gland to the brain. This stalk, called the **hypothalamus,** controls the output of hormones by the pituitary gland. The anterior pituitary is linked to the hypothalamus via the bloodstream. When the concentration of a particular anterior pituitary hormone is too low in the circulation, the hypothalamus will send releasing factors via the bloodstream that stimulate the production of the needed hormone. The posterior lobe of the pituitary gland is different—it is derived from neural tissue. Because of this, its connection to the hypothalamus is neural. ADH and oxytocin are produced by the nerve cell bodies that are located in the hypothalamus, where they are packaged into secretory granules and sent down the axons to be stored in the posterior pituitary. The posterior pituitary gland releases the hormones when appropriately stimulated by a nervous impulse from the hypothalamus. The following is a breakdown of the hormones you should be familiar with for the exam:

Hormones of the *anterior pituitary* are

*CT teacher: "Have a good general understanding of these hormones and their functions."O*

| | |
|---|---|
| FSH | Follicle-stimulating hormone. A gonadotropin—stimulates activities of the testes and ovaries. In females, it induces the development of the ovarian follicle, which leads to the production and secretion of estrogen. In males, it stimulates the production of sperm. |
| LH | Luteinizing hormone. A gonadotropin—stimulates ovulation, formation of corpus luteum, and synthesis of estrogens and progesterone in females. In males, it stimulates the production of testosterone. |
| TSH | Thyroid-stimulating hormone. Works to stimulate the synthesis and secretion of thyroid hormones in the thyroid gland, which in turn regulate the rate of metabolism in the body. |
| STH (or HGH) | Somatotropic hormone (or human growth hormone). Stimulates protein synthesis and general growth in the body. |
| ACTH | Stimulates the secretion of adrenal cortical hormones, which work to maintain electrolytic homeostasis and help to cope with chronic stress. |
| Prolactin | Controls lactogenesis—production of milk by the breasts. Decreases the synthesis and release of GnRH (gonadotropin-releasing hormone), inhibiting ovulation. |

Hormones of the *posterior pituitary* are

| | |
|---|---|
| ADH | Stimulates reabsorption of water by the collecting ducts of the kidney. |
| Oxytocin | Stimulates uterine contraction and milk ejection for breastfeeding. |

Hormones of the *adrenal gland* are

| | |
|---|---|
| Cortisol | Stress hormone released in response to physiological challenges. Increases the blood glucose level in response to chronic stress. |
| Aldosterone | Regulates blood sodium concentration and blood volume by controlling the renal excretion of sodium. |
| Epinephrine | Raises blood glucose level, increases metabolic activity—"fight or flight" hormone. Also known as *adrenaline*. |

**BIG IDEA 3.D.1**
*Activity within individual cells supports function for an entire organism (e.g., epinephrine stimulation of glycogen breakdown).*

*Pancreatic* hormones are

| | |
|---|---|
| Insulin | Secreted in response to high blood glucose levels to promote glycogen formation. Lowers blood sugar. |
| Glucagon | Stimulates conversion of glycogen into glucose. Raises blood sugar. |

The *parathyroid* hormone (PTH) increases serum concentration of $Ca^{2+}$, assisting in the process of bone maintenance.

*Sex* hormones are

| | |
|---|---|
| Progesterone | Regulates menstrual cycle and pregnancy. |
| Estrogen | Stimulates development of secondary sex characteristics in women. Secreted in ovaries. Induces the release of LH, including the LH surge of the menstrual cycle. With progesterone, helps maintain the endometrium during pregnancy. |
| Testosterone | Stimulates secondary sex characteristics and the production of sperm in men. Secreted in testes. |

**BIG IDEA 3.D.2**
*Cells communicate with each other from a distance via hormones.*

*Thyroid* hormones are

| | |
|---|---|
| Calcitonin | Lowers blood calcium. Works antagonistically to PTH. |
| Thyroxine | Stimulates metabolic activities. |

The thymus hormone is *thymosin,* a hormone involved in the development of the T cells of the immune system.

The pineal gland hormone is *melatonin,* a hormone that is known to be involved in our biological rhythms (circadian). It is released at night.

How is the hormone secretion process of the body regulated? The two main types of regulation with which you should be familiar are negative feedback and positive feedback. **Negative feedback** occurs when a hormone acts to directly or indirectly inhibit further secretion of the hormone of interest. A good example of negative feedback involves insulin, which is secreted by the pancreas. When the blood glucose gets too high, the pancreas is stimulated to produce insulin, which causes cells to use more glucose. As a result of this activity, the blood glucose level declines, halting the production of insulin by the pancreas. **Positive feedback** occurs when a hormone acts to directly or indirectly cause increased secretion of the hormone. An example of this feedback mechanism is the LH surge that occurs prior to ovulation in females. Estrogen is released as a result of the action of FSH, and travels to the anterior pituitary to stimulate the release of LH, which acts on the ovaries to stimulate further secretion of estrogen.

## Homeostasis

*NYC teacher:
"This could make
a nice subques-
tion to an essay.
Understand these
relationships."*

**BIG IDEA 2.C.1**
*Animals use feed-
back to maintain
homeostasis.*

Homeostasis is the maintenance of balance. Hormones can work antagonistically to maintain homeostasis in the body. Two examples we will talk about are insulin/glucagon and calcitonin/PTH:

1. *Insulin/glucagon.* Both are hormones of the pancreas and have opposing effects on blood glucose. Let's say that you eat a nice sugary snack that pushes the blood glucose above its desired level. This results in the release of insulin from the pancreas to stimulate the uptake of glucose from the blood to the liver to be stored as glycogen. It also causes other cells of the body to take up glucose to be used for energy. Sometimes if you go a long time between meals, your blood glucose can dip *below* the desired level. This sets glucagon into action and causes its release from the pancreas. Glucagon acts on the liver to stimulate the removal of glycogen from storage to produce glucose to pump into the bloodstream. When the glucose level gets back to the appropriate level, glucagon release ceases. This back-and-forth dance works to keep the glucose concentration in our bodies relatively stable over time.

2. *Calcitonin/PTH.* Like glucose, the body has a desired blood calcium ($Ca^{2+}$) level it tries to maintain. If it drops below this level, PTH is released by the parathyroid gland and works to increase the amount of $Ca^{2+}$ in circulation in three major ways: it (a) releases of $Ca^{2+}$ from bones, (b) increases absorption of $Ca^{2+}$ by the intestines, and (c) increases reabsorption of $Ca^{2+}$ by the kidneys. If the blood $Ca^{2+}$ level gets too high, the thyroid gland releases calcitonin, which pretty much performs the three *opposite* responses to PTH's work: it (a) puts $Ca^{2+}$ *into* bone, (b) decreases absorption of $Ca^{2+}$ by the intestines, and (c) decreases reabsorption of $Ca^{2+}$ by the kidneys.

One last distinction we want to make before we move on is to touch on the difference between protein hormones and steroid hormones.

**Protein hormones** are too large to move into cells and thus bind to receptors on the surface of cells. In response to the binding of a protein hormone, a change occurs in the receptor that leads to the activation of molecules inside the cell, called **second messengers,** which serve as intermediaries, activating other proteins and enzymes that carry out the mission. The second messenger to know for this exam is cyclic adenosine monophasphate (cAMP), involved in *numerous* signal cascade pathways. Protein hormones activate cAMP through a multi-step process that begins with protein–hormone activation of relay proteins such as **G proteins.** These proteins are able to directly activate a compound known as *adenyl cyclase,* which in turn produces cAMP.

Since we discussed regulatory mechanisms earlier, it is important to point out that there are G proteins that function to *inhibit* cAMP and work antagonistically to hormones that activate cAMP.

**Steroid hormones** are lipid-soluble molecules that pass through the cell membrane and combine with cytoplasmic proteins. These complexes pass through to the nucleus to interact with chromosomal proteins and directly affect transcription in the nucleus of cells.

# Immune System

*CT teacher:
"Concentrate on
the various cell
types and the dif-
ference between
specific and non-
specific defense."*

What we are about to witness is an absolute treat. We just got word from the central office that the body we are touring has just received a **vaccination.** A vaccine is given to a patient in an effort to prime the immune system for a fight against a specific invader. This truly is a rare opportunity for us to see the immune system in action.

We have reentered the general bloodstream circulation of the body in an attempt to find some activity. While we are in transit, we will explain some basic immune system terms to you.

**BIG IDEA 2.D.3**
*Organisms are affected by disruptions to their homeostasis (e.g., pathogens).*

**BIG IDEA 2.C.2**
*Organisms respond to changes in their environment (e.g., infections).*

**BIG IDEA 2.D.4**
*Animals have a variety of chemical defenses against infections that affect homeostasis.*

**BIG IDEA 3.D.2**
*Helper T cells communicate with other cells through direct contact.*

The immune system is a two-tiered defense mechanism. It consists of **nonspecific immunity** and **specific immunity.** Nonspecific immunity is exactly how it sounds—it is the nonspecific prevention of the entrance of invaders into the body. Saliva contains an enzyme called **lysozyme** that can kill germs before they have a chance to take hold. Lysozyme is also present in our tears, providing a nonspecific defense mechanism for our eyes. The skin covering the entire body is a nonspecific defense mechanism—it acts as a physical barrier to infection. The mucous lining of our trachea and lungs prevent bacteria from entering cells and actually assists in the expulsion of bacteria by ushering the bacteria up and out with a cough. Finally, remember how we told you that you did not want to get out of the bus in the stomach? That is also the case for bacteria—it is a dangerous place for them as well. The acidity of the stomach can wipe out a lot of potential invaders.

A nonspecific cellular defense mechanism is headed up by cells called **phagocytes.** These cells, *macrophages* and *neutrophils,* roam the body in search of bacteria and dead cells to engulf and clear away. Some assistance is offered to their cause by a protein molecule called **complement.** This protein makes sure that molecules to be cleared have some sort of identification displaying the need for phagocyte assistance. Complement coats these cells, stimulating phagocytes to ingest them. Cells involved in mechanisms that need cleanup assistance, such as platelets, have the ability to secrete chemicals that attract macrophages and neutrophils to places such as infection sites to help in the elimination of the foreign bacteria. They are nonspecific because they are not seeking out particular garbage . . . they are just looking for something to eat.

A prime example of a nonspecific cellular response is inflammation. Let's say that you pick up a tiny splinter as you grab a piece of wood. Within our tissues lie cells known as mast cells. These cells contain the signal **histamine** that calls in the cavalry and initiates the inflammation response. Entrance of the splinter damages these mast cells, causing them to release histamine, which migrates through the tissue toward the bloodstream. Histamine causes increased permeability and blood flow to the injured tissue. The splinter also causes the release of signals that call in our nonspecific phagocytic cell friends, which come to the site of the injury to clear away any debris or pathogens within the tissue. The redness and warmth associated with inflammation occur because of the increase in blood flow to the area that occurs in this process.

The immune system also contains defense mechanisms, which are quite specific. One such defense mechanism involves a type of white blood cell called **lymphocytes.** There are two main flavors of lymphocytes: B cells and T cells. These cells are made in the bone marrow of the body and come from cells called **stem cells.** B cells mature in the bone marrow, and T cells mature in the thymus. B cells can differentiate into plasma cells and memory B cells, and the two main types of T cells are helper T cells and cytotoxic T cells. Cytotoxic T cells are the main players involved in cell-mediated immunity. **Helper T cells,** which assist in the activation of B cells, recognize foreign antigens on the surface of phagocytic cells and bind to these cells. After binding, they multiply to produce a bunch of T cells that pump out chemical signals, which bring in the B cells to respond.

We have arrived at the vaccination site in the left arm, and things are definitely heating up here. An **antigen** is a molecule that is foreign to our bodies and causes the immune system to respond. What is occurring right now is the process called the **primary immune response.** Every B cell has a specific (randomly generated) antigen recognition site on its surface. B cells patrol the body looking for a particular invader. When a B cell meets and attaches to the appropriate antigen, it becomes activated, and the B cell undergoes mitosis and differentiation into the two types of cells mentioned earlier: **plasma cells** and **memory cells.** The plasma cells are the factories that produce antibodies that function in the elimination of any cell containing on its surface the antigen that it has been summoned to kill. These antibodies, when released, bind to the antigens, immobilizing them and marking them for the macrophages to engulf and eliminate. This type of immune response falls under the category of **humoral immunity**—immunity involving antibodies.

> **BIG IDEA 4.C.1**
> *Molecular variations in $F_{ab}$ enable cells to recognize a wider range of antigens.*

Someone had a question? How do antibodies recognize the antigen they are designed for? Excellent question. Antibodies are protein molecules with two functional regions. One end is called the *fragment antigen binding region* or $F_{ab}$—this is what allows an antibody to recognize a specific antigen. It is designed by the plasma cell to have an $F_{ab}$ that binds to the antigen of interest. The other end, which binds to effector cells, is called the $F_c$ region. There are five types of $F_c$ regions, one for each of the five types of antibodies: IgA, IgD, IgE, IgM, and IgG. Each antibody type serves a slightly different function and is present in different areas of the body. When the antibodies bind to an antigen, complement gets involved, and this combination of antibodies and complement leads to the elimination of the invader.

We see a hand raised in the back. Yes, you are correct that we neglected to mention the memory cells. Very good. Memory cells contain the basis for the body's **secondary immune response** to invaders. Memory cells are stored instructions on how to handle a particular invader. When an invader returns to our body, the memory cells recognize it, produce antibodies in rapid succession, and eliminate the invader very quickly. The secondary immune response is much more efficient than the primary response. This is why few people are infected by sicknesses such as chicken pox after they have had them once already—their memory cells protect them. One important fact that does come up on the exam is that the secondary immune response produces a *much* larger concentration of antibodies than does the primary response.

Well, this is too good to be true . . . we just got word that this body was just recently infected by a virus. This will allow us to look at the other side of the immune response: **cell-mediated immunity.** This type of immunity involves *direct* cellular response to invasion as opposed to antibody-based defense. The virus that infected this poor sap made it past the humoral immunity system because it entered into the host's cells. This brings the cytotoxic T cells into play. The cells infected by the virus are forced to produce viral antigens, some of which show up on the surface of the cell. The cytotoxic T cells recognize these cells and wipe them out.

You might wonder how these T cells avoid killing *all* cells. All the cells of the body, except for red blood cells, have on their surface antigens called **class I histocompatibility antigens** (major histocompatibility complex [MHC]). The MHC I antigens for each person are slightly different, and the immune system accepts as friendly any cell that has the identical match for this antigen. Anything with a different MHC is foreign. This is the reason that organ donation often fails—the donor and the recipient have incompatible MHCs. There are also **class II histocompatibility antigens,** which are found on the surface of the immune cells of the body. These antigens play a role in the interaction between the cells of the immune system.

Well, we'd like to thank you for joining us on our tour of the body. We've seen a lot of things today and—whoa! We've been hit by something—and hit hard! Oh, dear. . . . Folks, we don't want you to be alarmed, but it appears that our rival tour company has played a bit of a practical joke on us. Apparently as we were observing the B cell's interaction with the vaccine, they attached a series of antigens and complement proteins to the surface of our bus. That loud noise you just heard was the sound of a macrophage taking us in . . . oh, dear, this is bad. Oh, no . . . folks, brace yourselves! The macrophage is about to ———— (transmission ended).

## › Review Questions

1. In what form is most of the carbon dioxide of the body transported in the bloodstream?

   A. Complexed with hemoglobin
   B. As $CO_2$
   C. As $HCO_3^-$
   D. As CO

For questions 2–5, use the following answer choices:

   A. LH
   B. Estrogen
   C. Aldosterone
   D. TSH

2. This hormone is involved in the regulation of the body's metabolic rate.

3. This gonadotropin induces ovulation in females.

4. This hormone is involved in the regulation of the body's sodium concentration.

5. This hormone is vital to the maintenance of the endometrium during pregnancy.

6. The major emulsifier of fats in the digestive system is

   A. lipase.
   B. amylase.
   C. trypsin.
   D. bile salts.

7. Which cell type keeps humans from being infected by the same organism twice?

   A. Plasma cell
   B. Memory cell
   C. Macrophage
   D. Neutrophil

8. Which of the following muscle sites does not contain smooth muscle?

   A. Aorta
   B. Bladder
   C. Esophagus
   D. Quadriceps

9. Which of the following is the functional unit of the respiratory system?

   A. Bronchus
   B. Bronchioles
   C. Alveolus
   D. Larynx

10. Which of the following regions of the brain controls breathing?

    A. Cerebellum
    B. Medulla
    C. Cerebrum
    D. Hypothalamus

11. Which of the following is the major digestive enzyme of the stomach?

    A. Trypsin
    B. Chymotrypsin
    C. Pepsin
    D. Amylase

12. Which of the following is *not* an example of nonspecific immunity?

    A. Lysosyme of saliva
    B. Skin
    C. Mucous lining of the lungs and trachea
    D. Plasma cells

13. Which of the following is true about the filtrate of the glomerulus?

    A. It contains little or no glucose.
    B. It contains little or no protein.
    C. It contains little or no sodium.
    D. It contains little or no urea.

14. Which of the following is not a hormone secreted by the anterior pituitary?

    A. TSH
    B. FSH
    C. ADH
    D. LH

**15.** Which of the following scenarios would be *least* likely to initiate a response from the sympathetic nervous system of the body?

    A. Getting called on in class by the teacher when you do not know the answer

    B. Seeing a cop while you are driving too fast on the highway

    C. Walking through the woods and seeing a bear in the near distance

    D. Waking from a midafternoon nap as sunlight strikes your face

## ❯ Answers and Explanations

**1. C**—Most of the carbon dioxide traveling through the bloodstream of the body is in the form of the bicarbonate ion—$HCO_3^-$. Oxygen is the one that likes to complex with hemoglobin. You should try to avoid answer choice D when possible; carbon monoxide is poisonous.

**2. D**—The thyroid gland is important to the maintenance of the body's metabolic rate. An increase in TSH leads to an increase in thyroxin (thyroid hormone), which leads to an increase in the metabolic rate of the body.

**3. A**—The LH surge brought about by the combined effect of FSH and LH during the menstrual cycle leads to ovulation in females. This is essentially the release of an egg from its holding pattern in the ovary that allows it to move toward the uterus.

**4. C**—Aldosterone is released by the adrenal gland in an effort to maintain appropriate levels of sodium in the body. Its main site of action is the kidney.

**5. B**—Estrogen and progesterone work together to maintain the endometrium, which is the site of attachment for the growing fetus during pregnancy. Without these two hormones, the endometrium sloughs off and is lost.

**6. D**—Lipase is the major fat-*digesting* enzyme of our body. Bile salts help digest the fat by *emulsifying* it into small droplets contained in water. Amylase digests carbohydrates. Trypsin and chymotrypsin break down polypeptides.

**7. B**—Memory cells are produced after the body first reacts to a foreign invader. The next time the body is exposed to that invader, it can respond much more quickly and efficiently. Plasma cells produce the antibodies designed to wipe out the antigens. Macrophages and neutrophils are both types of phagocytes, which generally roam around looking for nonspecific garbage to pick up and destroy.

**8. D**—The quadriceps is the only muscle type on this list that is not a smooth muscle. It is a skeletal muscle involved in voluntary movements.

**9. C**—The alveolus is the functional unit of the lung. It is the true site of gas exchange during the respiratory process. The trachea, larynx, bronchus, and bronchioles are all tubes that the air passes through on its way to this exchange center.

**10. B**—The medulla oblongata controls the involuntary actions of the body, including respiration. The cerebellum controls balance, and the cerebrum is in charge of higher thinking. The hypothalamus monitors the concentration of many substances throughout the body, and determines when certain hormones of the pituitary should be released or cut down on.

**11. C**

**12. D**—Plasma cells are designed to produce antibodies that combat a particular antigen. They are a great example of *specific* immunity. All the other answer choices are examples of nonspecific immunity.

**13. B**—The filtrate in the glomerulus contains almost everything that is in the blood plasma except for large proteins, which are unable to fit through the pores. Glucose does pass into the filtrate but is usually reabsorbed if present in normal concentrations in the blood. Sodium and potassium are always present in the filtrate. Urea is one of the major waste products that the excretory system is attempting to eliminate, so it is definitely present in the filtrate.

**14. C**—ADH is secreted by the posterior pituitary.

**15. D**—A sympathetic response is one that comes in a time of fight or flight. It is designed to get you ready for action. All the other choices are things that rev you up, whereas waking from a nap as sunlight strikes your face is a rather passive and tranquil experience that doesn't usually make you want to flee the scene or fight a great battle.

## ❭ Rapid Review

The following terms are important in this chapter:

*Circulatory system*: blood flow—left side of heart → aorta → via arteries to organs, muscles → into the venous system of the body (vena cava) → right side of heart → lungs (pick up $O_2$ and release $CO_2$) → left side of heart.

*Respiratory pathway*: nose/mouth → pharynx → larynx → trachea → bronchi → bronchioles → alveoli (functional unit of the lungs; this is where gas exchange occurs).

*Digestive system*: digestion begins in mouth, continues in the stomach, and completes in the intestines.

- *Amylase*: enzyme that breaks down starches in the diet (mouth and small intestine).

- *Pepsin*: main digestive enzyme of the stomach that breaks down proteins.

- *Lipase*: major fat digesting enzyme of the body (small intestine).

- *Trypsin* and *chymotrypsin*: major protein digesting endopeptidases of the small intestine.

- *Bile*: contains phospholipids, cholesterol, and **bile salts** (major emulsifier of fat).

- *Maltase, lactase,* and *sucrase*: carbohydrate digesting enzymes of the small intestines.

- Most of the digestion and absorption of food occurs in the small intestine.

- Function of the large intestine is to reabsorb water and to pack the indigestible food into feces.

*Excretory system*: kidneys lie on the posterior wall of the abdomen. Kidney is divided into the cortex and the **medulla.** The functional unit of the kidney is the **nephron.** The medulla is divided into renal pyramids, which dump the urine produced into the minor and major calyces → renal pelvis → bladder via the ureter → out of the body via the urethra.

- Most of what is filtered out of the glomerulus is reabsorbed—nearly all the sugar, vitamins, water, and nutrients. If sugar appears in urine, it is because there is too much in the blood (diabetes).

- Two important hormones of the excretory system are **ADH** (controls water absorption) and **aldosterone** (controls sodium reabsorption).

**Muscular System**

| MUSCLE TYPE | STRIATED? | NUCLEI? | CONTROL? | WHERE IS IT FOUND? |
|---|---|---|---|---|
| Skeletal | Yes | Multiple | Voluntary | Biceps, triceps, etc. |
| Smooth | No | Single | Involuntary | Digestive tract, bladder, arteries |
| Cardiac | Yes | Single | Involuntary | Heart |

### Endocrine System

Anterior pituitary hormones

- *FSH*: stimulates production of eggs or sperm.
- *LH*: stimulates ovulation, increases estrogen/progesterone release.
- *TSH*: increases release of thyroid hormone.
- *STH*: increases growth.
- *ACTH*: increases secretion of adrenal cortical hormones.
- *Prolactin*: controls lactogenesis, decreases secretion of GnRH.

Pancreatic hormones

- *Insulin*: increases glycogen formation.
- *Glucagon*: increases glycogen breakdown.

*Parathyroid hormone* (PTH) increases blood $Ca^{2+}$ involved in bone maintenance.

Posterior pituitary hormones

- *ADH*: stimulates $H_2O$ reabsorption in kidneys.
- *Oxytocin*: stimulates uterine contraction and milk ejection.

Adrenal gland hormones

- *Aldosterone*: regulates blood sodium concentration.
- *Cortisol*: chronic stress hormone.

Sex hormones

- *Progesterone*: involved in menstrual cycle and pregnancy.
- *Estrogen*: made in ovaries; increases release of LH (LH surge); develops female secondary sex characteristics.
- *Testosterone*: (testes): stimulates sperm production; develops male secondary sex characteristics.

*Negative feedback*: hormone acts to directly, or indirectly, inhibit further release of the hormone of interest.

*Positive feedback*: hormone acts to directly, or indirectly, cause increased secretion of the hormone.

*Nervous system*: divided into two parts: **central nervous system** (CNS) and **peripheral nervous system** (PNS).

- *SNS*: controls skeletal muscles and voluntary actions.

- *ANS*: controls involuntary activities of body.

- *ANS*: *sympathetic* (prepare for fight): increased heart rate, increased blood pressure, digestive slowdown, dilate bronchial muscles; *parasympathetic* (conserve energy): decreased heart rate, decreased blood pressure, bladder constriction.

- Brain: **cerebellum** (coordination/balance); **medulla** (involuntary actions such as breathing); **hypothalamus** (regulates hunger, thirst, temperature); **amygdala** (emotion control center).

Immune system:

- *Nonspecific immunity*: nonspecific prevention of entrance of invaders into the body (skin, mucus).

- *Specific immunity*: multilayered defense mechanism: (1) first line of defense—phagocytes, macrophage, neutrophils, complement; (2) second line of defense: B cells (plasma/memory), T cells (helper/cytotoxic).

- *Primary immune response*: antigen invader → B cell meets antigen → B cell differentiates into plasma cells and memory cells → plasma cells produce antibodies → antibodies eliminate antigen (**humoral immunity**).

- *Secondary immune response*: antigen invader → memory cells recognize antigen and pump out antibodies much quicker than primary response → antibodies eliminate antigen.

- *Cell-mediated immunity*: involves T cells and direct cellular response to invasion. Defense against **viruses.**

# CHAPTER 16

# Human Reproduction

## IN THIS CHAPTER

**Summary:** This chapter discusses differences between the sexes, reproductive anatomy in humans, and how a sperm meets up with an egg to produce an embryo. The chapter concludes with a discussion of reproductive hormones.

**Key Ideas**

KEY IDEA

○ Primary sex characteristics are the internal structures that assist in the process of procreation.

○ Secondary sex characteristics are the noticeable physical characteristics that differ between males and females.

○ Understand the concepts and the basics of embryology, but learn the specific details only if you have time.

○ Take the time to learn which germ layer produces which structures (endoderm, mesoderm, and ectoderm).

○ Four extraembryonic structures necessary to the healthy development of an embryo: yolk sac, chorion, allantois, and amnion.

○ Factors in cellular differentiation: cytoplasmic distribution, induction, and homeotic genes.

## Introduction

Finally, the racy chapter you have all been waiting for: human reproduction! The topic was introduced in Chapter 9 in our discussion of cell division—meiosis and mitosis. This chapter begins by examining the differences between the sexes. A discussion of reproductive anatomy and the wild ride that a sperm must take to fertilize the female egg will follow. Then we will review the formation of gametes and the development of the embryo. Embryology is excessively detailed and not something you should get hung up on. You will want to know some details about development, but like glycolysis, the big picture is key. The AP Biology exam is not an embryology exam. Finally, the chapter concludes with a discussion of hormones and their effects on the reproductive system.

# Sex Differences

What are the biologic differences between a man and a woman? For the purposes of *this* exam, you should keep in mind that one of the first distinctions is that boys have a Y chromosome in the nuclei of their cells, and girls do not. Another major difference lies in the sex characteristics. **Primary sex characteristics** are the structures that assist in the vital process of procreation. Among these are the testes, ovaries, and uterus. **Secondary sex characteristics** are the noticeable physical characteristics that differ between males and females such as facial hair, deepness of voice, breasts, and muscle distribution. These characteristics come into play as indicators of reproductive maturity to those of the opposite sex.

# Anatomy

Since males tend to be a bit impatient, we will cover male anatomy first. The male sexual anatomy is designed for the delivery of sperm to the female reproductive system. Let's follow the journey of a sperm from the beginning to the end.

### Sperm's "Wild Ride"

Here we stand in the **testis.** The male has two testes, located in a sac called the scrotum. This is the sperm factory—a portion of the testis called the **seminiferous tubules** is where the sperm are actually made. We return later to look at how these sperm are created. Notice in the other corner of the testis the structures called the **interstitial cells.** These are the structures that produce the hormones involved in the male reproductive system. Remember that the testis is the site of sperm and hormone production in the male reproductive system.

We are going to move along the production line to the **epididymis**—the coiled structure that extends from the testes. The epididymis is where the sperm completes its maturation and waits until it is called on to do its duty. From here, when called into action, the sperm moves through a tunnel called the **vas deferens.** Each epididymis connects to the **urethra** via this tunnel. The urethra is the passageway through which the sperm exits during ejaculation. Yes . . . that is indeed the same tunnel that the urine uses to get out . . . good observation in back.

We're not done yet—let's look at some other important players in this process (see also Figure 16.1). we are sure you have all heard about the **prostate gland** and how prostate cancer is currently one of the major cancers among men. But do you know what the prostate gland does? Here we are standing by this fine structure whose function in the male reproductive system is to add a basic (pH > 7) liquid to the mix to help neutralize any urine that may remain in the common urethral passage. It also helps to combat the acidity of the vaginal region of the female toward which the sperm is heading.

Follow us, everyone, more to see, more to see. . . . Here, on either side of us, are the structures called the **seminal vesicles.** These characters play an important role in the success of the sperm on its way to the female ovum. When the male ejaculates, the seminal vesicles dump fluids into the vas deferens to send along with the sperm. Think of the seminal vesicle as a convenience store. It provides three important goods to the sperm: energy by adding fructose; power to progress through the female reproductive system by adding *prostaglandins* (which stimulates uterine contraction); and mucus, which helps the sperm swim more effectively.

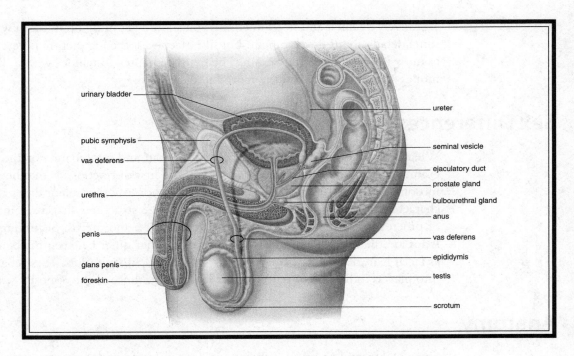

**Figure 16.1   The human male reproductive system.** (*From* Biology, *8th ed., by Sylvia S. Mader,* © *1985, 1987, 1990, 1993, 1996, 1998, 2001, 2004 by the McGraw Hill Companies, Inc. Reproduced with permission of The McGraw-Hill Companies.*)

The sperm is ready to enter the female reproductive system at this point, but before we observe the sperm as it does so, we want to take a quick tour of the female reproductive structures.

We begin in the **ovary,** the site of egg production. Females have two ovaries—one on either side of the body. The egg leaves the ovary before it has fully matured and enters a structure called the **oviduct.** The oviduct is also known as the **fallopian tube**—you may be more familiar with that term. Eggs travel through here from the ovary to the **uterus.** When fertilized by an incoming sperm in the fallopian tube, after several days' transit from the tube to the uterus, the egg usually attaches itself to the inner wall of the uterus, which is known as the **endometrium.** The uterus connects to the vaginal opening via a narrowed portion called the **cervix.** As we pass through the cervical area, we now find ourselves in the vagina, and it is here that the sperm enters the female reproductive system.

As the sperm enters, it must survive the different environment that the female body presents (Figure 16.2). Its task is to find its way to the fallopian tube, where it must meet the egg and penetrate its outer surface to achieve successful fertilization. The sperm works its way through the vaginal region, up through the cervix, through the uterus, and into the fallopian tube. Here, if the timing is appropriate, there will be a willing and waiting egg that is hoping to meet with a sperm to produce a new diploid zygote. After successful fertilization, the new happy couple moves down to the uterus and builds a nice house in the endometrium where it will develop into an embryo and remain until it is ready to be born.

## The Formation of Gametes

In Chapter 9, we discussed cell division and mentioned the process by which gametes are formed. Remember that the mechanics of gamete formation are different in women and men.

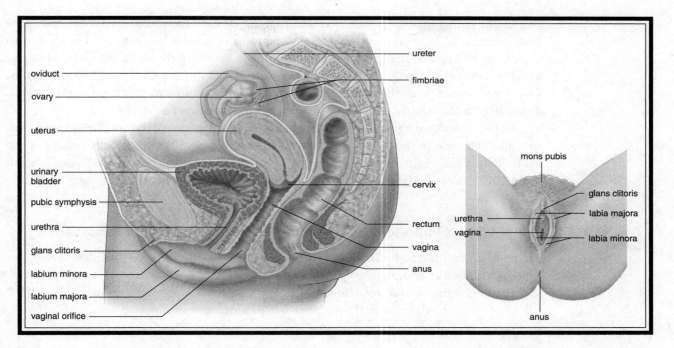

**Figure 16.2    The human female reproductive system.** (*From* Biology, *8th ed., by Sylvia S. Mader,* © *1985, 1987, 1990, 1993, 1996, 1998, 2001, 2004 by the McGraw Hill Companies, Inc. Reproduced with permission of The McGraw-Hill Companies.)*

### Oogenesis

In women, the process of gamete formation is called **oogenesis** (Figure 16.3), which begins quite early—as the embryo develops. Mitotic division turns fetal cells into cells known as **primary oocytes,** which begin the process of meiosis and progress until prophase I; then the wait begins. The primary oocyte sits halted in prophase I until the host female enters puberty a number of years later. This is where the menstrual cycle begins. Each month,

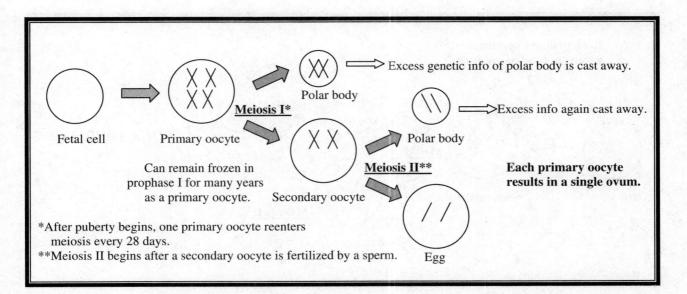

**Figure 16.3    Oogenesis.**

one of the primary oocytes frozen in the first act of meiosis returns to action and completes meiosis I. As we saw earlier, this phase produces a polar body, which has almost no cytoplasm and half of the genetic information of the parent cell, and a **secondary oocyte,** which has half the genetic information of the parent cell but the majority of its cytoplasm. This asymmetrical meiosis occurs because the developing embryo will need enough food, organelles, mitochondria, and other such structures for proper development.

As the menstrual cycle continues, ovulation frees the secondary oocyte to travel into the fallopian tube to make its way down to the uterus. Fertilization usually occurs in the oviduct. If a successful fertilization occurs, the secondary oocyte enters meiosis II, again producing a polar body, as well as an egg that combines with the sperm to form a zygote.

> ### What Is Important to Remember About This Oogenesis Business?
>
> 1. It doesn't all happen at once for the ova. A primary oocyte could sit in the ovary for 40 years before completing the first stage of meiosis.
> 2. The beginning of each menstrual cycle causes a primary oocyte to resume meiosis I.
> 3. Oocytes undergo meiosis II only after fertilization with the sperm.

### Spermatogenesis

For men, the process is less time-intensive. Let's face it, guys . . . we are lazy. Less effort is better. Less time makes sense and leaves us more time and energy to watch sports and play video games. Males produce gametes through a process called **spermatogenesis** (Figure 16.4). Unlike females, males do not begin forming gametes until puberty. Spermatogenesis occurs in our old friends, the seminiferous tubules. Here, **primary spermatocytes** are produced by mitotic division. These primary spermatocytes undergo meiosis I to produce two **secondary spermatocytes,** which undergo meiosis II to produce four **spermatids,** which are immature sperm. After production, they enter the epididymis, where their waiting game begins and the maturation completes.

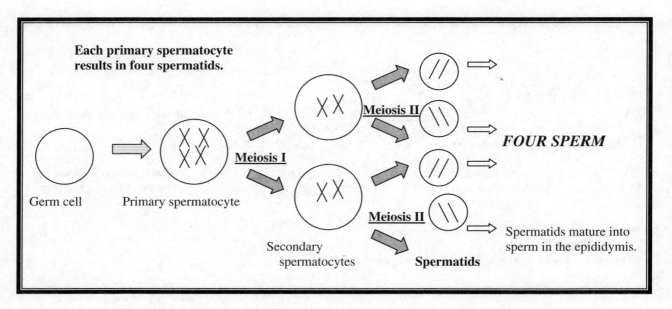

**Figure 16.4 Spermatogenesis.**

# Embryonic Development

**Embryology,** the study of embryonic development, is a detailed and complex field. Fortunately, you are not taking an AP exam in embryology. Stick to the basics here and do not let the complex details bog you down. Follow along with the pretty pictures, and the review questions at the end of this chapter will give you a good indication of the level of detail required for success on the embryology questions of the AP Biology exam.

## Cleavage

Embryonic development begins as soon as the egg is fertilized to produce a diploid zygote ($2n$). This zygote then divides mitotically many times without increasing the zygote's overall size. During these **"cleavage" divisions** (Figure 16.5), cytoplasm is distributed unevenly to the daughter cells but genetic information is distributed equally. This disparity exists because different cells will later produce different final products and the uneven distribution of cytoplasm plays a role in that process.

These cleavage divisions take a while in humans. The first three divisions take three days to complete. After the fourth division, the one cell has become 16 cells and is now called a **morula.** As it undergoes its next round of cell divisions, fluid fills the center of the morula

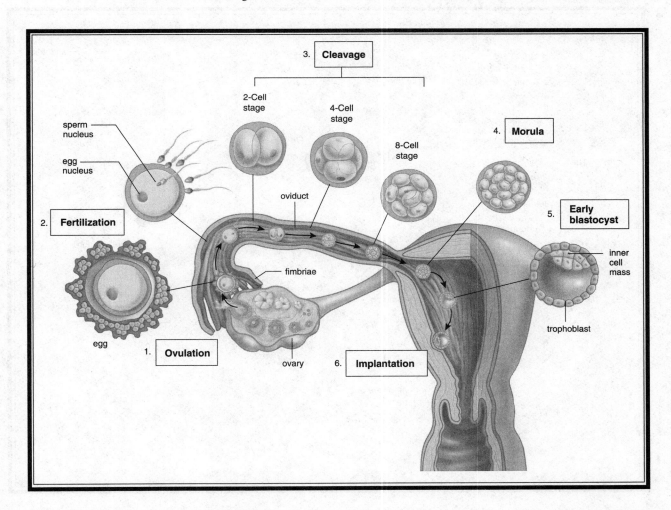

**Figure 16.5    Embryonic cleavage divisions.** (*From* Biology, *8th ed., by Sylvia S. Mader,* © *1985, 1987, 1990, 1993, 1996, 1998, 2001, 2004 by the McGraw Hill Companies, Inc. Reproduced with permission of The McGraw-Hill Companies.*)

to create the hollow-looking structure known to embryologists as the **blastula.** The fluid-filled cavity in the blastula is known as the blastocoel. Up to this point, much of the dividing has occurred as the zygote moves toward the uterus through the fallopian tube. By the time the blastula has formed, it has reached the uterus and has implanted on the wall. The blastula contains two parts: an **inner cell mass,** which later becomes the embryo, and a **trophoblast,** which becomes the placenta for the developing fetus and aids in attachment to the endometrium. The trophoblast also produces *human chorionic gonadotropin* (hCG), which maintains the endometrium by ensuring the continued production of progesterone and estrogen. The trophoblast later gives rise to the chorion, which we will discuss later.

## Gastrulation

Okay, here's where the discussion of embryology gets a little bit tricky. The next major stage of embryonic development after cleavage is **gastrulation** (also called *morphogenesis*). During gastrulation, cells separate into three primary layers called *germ layers,* which eventually give rise to the different tissues of an adult.

Let's look at this process in a bit more detail. (See also Figure 16.6.) After the blastocyst attaches to the uterine wall, the inner cell mass divides into two major cell masses:

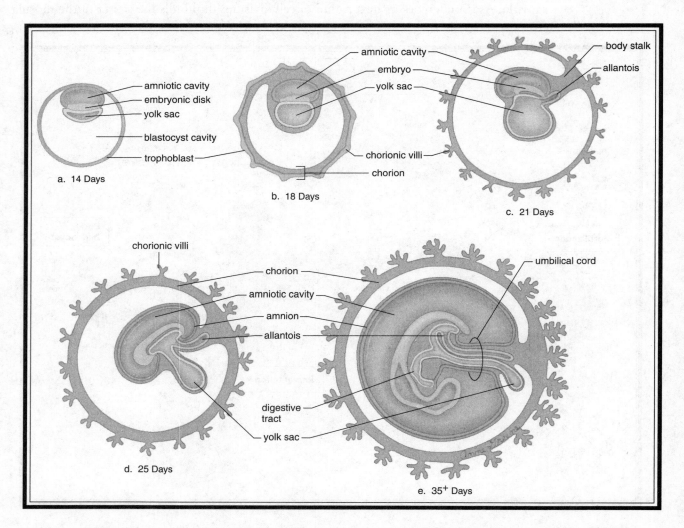

**Figure 16.6   Components in the gastrulation process.** (*From* Biology, *8th ed., by Sylvia S. Mader, © 1985, 1987, 1990, 1993, 1996, 1998, 2001, 2004 by the McGraw Hill Companies, Inc. Reproduced with permission of The McGraw-Hill Companies.*)

the **epiblast** and the **hypoblast.** The hypoblast gives rise to the yolk sac, which produces the embryo's first blood cells. In birds and reptiles, the yolk sac provides nutrients to the embryo. In humans, the **placenta** fills this role.

The epiblast develops into the three germ layers of the embryo: the **endoderm,** the **mesoderm,** and the **ectoderm.**

> *Endoderm:* inner germ layer; gives rise to the inner lining of the gut and the digestive system, liver, thyroid, lungs, and bladder.
>
> *Mesoderm:* intermediate germ layer; gives rise to muscle, the circulatory system, reproductive system, excretory organs, bones, and connective tissues of the gut and exterior of the body.
>
> *Ectoderm:* outer germ layer; gives rise to nervous system and skin, hair, and nails.

*Lindsay (12th grade): "Take the time to learn these. Know which layer produces what. It's worth a point on the exam."*

**BIG IDEA 2.E.1**
*The timing and coordination of specific events are necessary for normal development.*

The separation of cells into the three primary germ layers sets the stage for cellular differentiation by which different cells develop into different structures with different functions. As far as this specific structural and functional differentiation is concerned, keep your focus on the basic development of the nervous system.

The human nervous system derives primarily from the ectoderm, but the mesoderm contributes a structure known as the **notochord,** which serves to support the body. In vertebrates, this is present only in the embryo. The cells of the ectoderm that lie above the notochord form the **neural plate,** which becomes the **neural groove,** which eventually becomes the **neural tube.** This neural tube later gives rise to the central nervous system. One other term you should be familiar with in the development of the mammalian embryo is the **somite,** which gives rise to the muscles and vertebrae in mammals.

There are four extraembryonic structures necessary for the healthy development of the embryo:

1. *Yolk sac:* derived from the hypoblast; site of early blood cell creation in humans. Source of nutrients for bird and reptile embryos.
2. *Chorion:* formed from the trophoblast; the outer membrane of the embryo. Site of implantation onto the endometrium. Contributes to formation of the **placenta** in mammals.
3. *Allantois:* mammalian waste transporter. Later it becomes the **umbilical cord,** which carries oxygen, food, and wastes (including $CO_2$) back and forth from placenta to embryo.
4. *Amnion:* formed from epiblast. Surrounds fluid-filled cushion that protects the developing embryo. Present in birds, lizards, and humans, to name only a few.

## How Do Cells Know What to Do?

How do the various cells of the developing embryo differentiate into cells with different functions if they come from the same parent cell? As mentioned earlier, not every cell receives the same amount of cytoplasm during the cleavage divisions. It is thought that this asymmetric distribution of cytoplasm plays a role in the differentiation of the daughter cells. Cells containing different organelles or other cytoplasmic components are able to perform different functions. Two other factors, induction and homeotic genes, contribute to cellular differentiation.

**Induction** is the influence of one group of cells on the development of another through physical contact or chemical signaling. Just in case you are asked to write an essay on induction, it is good to know a bit about the experiments of the German embryologist Hans Spemann. His experiments revealed that the notochord induces cells of the dorsal ectoderm to develop into the neural plate. When cells from the notochord of an embryo are transplanted to a different place near the ectoderm, the neural plate will develop in the new location. The cells from the notochord region act as "project directors," telling the ectoderm where to produce the neural tube and central nervous system.

**BIG IDEA 3.B.2**

*Signal transmission by homeotic genes mediates cell function.*

**Homeotic genes** regulate or "direct" the body plan of organisms. For example, a fly's homeotic genes help determine how its segments will develop and which appendages should grow from each segment. Scientists interfering with the development of these poor creatures have found that mutations in these genes can lead to the production of too many wings, legs in the wrong place, and other unfortunate abnormalities. The DNA sequence of a homeotic gene that tells the cell where to put things is called the **homeobox.** It is similar from organism to organism and has been found to exist in a variety of organisms—birds, humans, fish, and frogs.

### Factors in Cellular Differentiation

| | |
|---|---|
| Cytoplasmic distribution | Asymmetry contributes to differentiation, since different areas have different amounts of cytoplasm, and thus perhaps different organelles and cytoplasmic structures. |
| Induction | One group of cells influences another group of cells through physical contact or chemical signaling. |
| Homeotic genes | Regulatory genes that determine how segments of an organism will develop. |

## The Influence of Hormones

In Chapter 15 we discussed the hormones that will be included in the AP exam. A few of those play a critical role in human sexual development and reproduction. The hormones involved include LH, FSH, estrogen, progesterone, and testosterone. You do not need to know every detail, just the big picture. As proper etiquette requires, ladies first. Let's talk about the hormones involved in the female reproductive system.

**BIG IDEA 2.C.1**

*Organisms use feedback mechanisms.*

Estrogen and progesterone continually circulate in the female bloodstream, and the hypothalamus monitors these levels to determine when to release certain hormones. For example, when the concentrations of estrogen and progesterone are low, the hypothalamus secretes GnRH, which travels to the anterior pituitary gland to induce the release of FSH and LH. (Just to remind you, FSH is follicle-stimulating hormone, LH is luteinizing hormone, and GnRH is gonadotropin-releasing hormone.) FSH induces the development of the follicle that contains the primary oocyte during its development. It also causes the follicular cells to release estrogen, which triggers the hypothalamus to dump more GnRH into the system. This GnRH acts on the anterior pituitary to produce the **LH surge** that initiates **ovulation**—the release of a secondary oocyte from the ovary.

This LH surge causes further release of estrogen and progesterone from the follicular cells, which have now become a structure called the corpus luteum. The corpus luteum induces the thickening of the endometrium, the site of future fertilized egg attachment. At this point in the cycle, the levels of estrogen and progesterone elevate enough to make the hypothalamus cut off production of GnRH so that the LH and FSH levels drop back down. (This decrease in production of LH and FSH, due to high levels of estrogen and progesterone, is called **negative feedback.**) Here lies a fork in the road for the female reproductive system. If fertilization has occurred in the fallopian tube, and if the blastocyst attaches successfully to the uterine wall, hCG will be secreted, which works to keep the corpus luteum alive. As a result, the levels of estrogen and progesterone remain high and keep the endometrium intact.

If a blastocyst does not implant, production of estrogen or progesterone from the corpus luteum will cease, causing the destruction of the endometrium.

This cycle of hormonal activity is known as the *menstrual cycle*. A woman repeats this cycle, on an average, every 28 days. This cycle is disrupted when a sperm fertilizes the egg and successful implantation occurs. During pregnancy, hormone levels in the body change as a result of the presence of the corpus luteum, which maintains constant levels of estrogen and progesterone. This halts ovulation for the remainder of the pregnancy. If a sperm does not fertilize the egg, however, negative feedback reduces the levels of LH and FSH and leads to the deterioration of the endometrium, which then sloughs off during the menstrual cycle. When the levels of hormones circulating in the blood drop low enough, the cycle will begin again with the release of LH and FSH, culminating in the next menstrual cycle.

In males, as in females, GnRH causes the pituitary to release LH and FSH. The LH causes the continual production of testosterone in men. FSH and testosterone work together to assist the maturation of sperm produced during spermatogenesis. The baseline levels of testosterone are vital to the development of secondary sex characteristics in men.

## › Review Questions

For questions 1–4, please use the following answer selections:

   A. Morula
   B. Somite
   C. Trophoblast
   D. Hypoblast

1. After the fourth cleavage division, the one cell has become 16 cells and is now given this name.

2. Gives rise to the yolk sac of the developing embryo.

3. Forms the placenta for the developing fetus.

4. Gives rise to the muscles and vertebrae in mammals.

5. Which of the following is not a structure involved in the ejaculation of sperm?

   A. Epididymis
   B. Seminal vesicles
   C. Cervix
   D. Vas deferens

6. Which of the following hormones feeds back to cause the LH surge of the menstrual cycle?

   A. Estrogen
   B. Progesterone
   C. FSH
   D. LH

7. Which of the following structures is *not* derived from the endoderm of a developing embryo?

   A. Liver
   B. Thyroid
   C. Heart
   D. Bladder

For questions 8–11, please use the following answer selections:

   A. FSH
   B. LH
   C. Testosterone
   D. hCG

8. This hormone ultimately triggers ovulation in females.

9. This hormone is produced in the interstitial cells.

10. This hormone is responsible for maintenance of the corpus luteum during early pregnancy.

11. This hormone works with testosterone to assist in maturation of the sperm produced during spermatogenesis.

**12.** Which structure is usually the site of fertilization in humans?

    A. Cervix
    B. Uterus
    C. Oviduct
    D. Ovary

**13.** Which of the following explains the mechanism by which the neural plate develops in human embryos?

    A. Induced fit
    B. Homeotic gene determination
    C. Induction
    D. Negative feedback

## › Answers and Explanations

**1. A**

**2. D**

**3. C**

**4. B**

**5. C**—The cervix is the only structure listed here that is a part of the female reproductive anatomy. The epididymis is the site of sperm storage and maturation while it awaits ejaculation. The seminal vesicles are the convenience store, providing the sperm with the necessary materials to survive its journey from ejaculation to fertilization. The vas deferens is the tunnel connecting the epididymis to the urethra.

**6. A**—At the beginning of each menstrual cycle, GnRH is released from the hypothalamus and travels to the anterior pituitary gland to induce the release of FSH and LH. FSH induces the development of the follicle and causes the follicle to release estrogen, which triggers the hypothalamus to dump more GnRH into the system. This GnRH acts on the anterior pituitary to produce the LH surge, which triggers ovulation. The estrogen feeds back to the hypothalamus to induce the release of large amounts of LH that ultimately lead to increased production of even more estrogen.

**7. C**—The heart is part of the circulatory system and is derived from the mesoderm.

**8. B**

**9. C**

**10. D**

**11. A**

**12. C**—The oviduct, or the fallopian tube, is where fertilization normally occurs in humans. The uterus is where implantation and development of the embryo normally occur. The embryo usually implants on the wall of the uterus—the endometrium. The cervix is the narrow pathway from the uterus to the vaginal opening. The ovary is the site of egg production.

**13. C**—Remember induction. It is a concept loved by the AP Biology exam writers. *Induction* is the ability of cells to influence the development of other cells by either physical contact or chemical signals. *Homeotic genes* are genes that determine how segments of an organism will develop. *Induced fit* is how enzymes and substrates interact. *Negative feedback* is the reduction in production of a substance due to high levels already present in circulation.

# › Rapid Review

Quickly review the following terms:

*Primary sex characteristics*: sexual organs that assist in reproduction.

*Secondary sex characteristics*: physical characteristics that differ between men and women.

Male anatomy:

- Two **testes** enclosed in the *scrotum*—site of sperm and testosterone production, which occurs in the **seminiferous tubules.**

- **Interstitial cells,** which produce testosterone involved in male reproduction.

- **Epididymis,** a coiled structure where sperm completes maturation.

- **Vas deferens,** a tunnel that connects epididymis to urethra, where sperm and urine are ejected.

- **Prostate gland,** a gland that adds basic liquid to neutralize urine acidity so that sperm don't die on the way out.

- **Seminal vesicles,** glands that produce fluid to help sperm in various ways (adds energy, power, help with swimming).

Female anatomy:

- *Ovary*: site of egg, estrogen, and progesterone production; eggs move from here through the *fallopian tube* (**oviduct**) to the **uterus,** which is where a fertilized egg attaches to the **endometrium.**

- *Cervix*: narrowed portion of the uterus that connects the uterus and vagina.

Formation of gametes:

- *Oogenesis*: formation of eggs; starts in embryonic development and doesn't finish for each egg until that egg matures during a menstrual cycle (hence, an egg could wait 40 years to finish maturation).

- *Meiosis II*: oocytes undergo this process only after fertilization by a sperm in the oviduct.

- *Spermatogenesis*: one primary spermatocyte produces four spermatids, which mature in the epididymis.

*Embryology* (the study of embryonic development):

- *Cleavage divisions*: mitotic divisions that occur as soon as a zygote is formed; these divisions don't increase the overall size of the zygote; cytoplasm distributed unevenly, genetic information distributed evenly.

- *Morula*: what we call the zygote when it has become 16 cells.

- *Blastula*: when a zygote has become 32 cells—by this time it is implanted in the endometrial wall.

- *Gastrulation*: cells separate into three germ layers, which give rise to different adult tissues.

    *Endoderm*: gives rise to inner layer; lining of gut and digestive system, liver, lungs.

    *Mesoderm*: gives rise to intermediate layer; muscle, circulation, bones, reproductive system.

    *Ectoderm*: gives rise to outer layer; nervous system, skin, hair, nails.

Factors in cellular differentiation:

1. *Cytoplasmic distribution*: different amounts of cytoplasm signal different structures.

2. *Induction*: ability of one group of cells to influence another.

3. *Homeotic genes*: regulate or direct the body plan of organisms.

*Hormones* play a major role in directing reproductive development and reproduction:

- *FSH*: stimulates oogenesis in females and spermatogenesis in males. Creates follicle that surrounds the primary oocyte during development.

- *LH*: stimulates the ovulation and production of estrogen and progesterone in females; stimulates production of testosterone and sperm in males. Surge in this hormone triggers ovulation (release of secondary oocyte from ovary).

- *GnRH*: causes pituitary to release LH and FSH.

- *Progesterone and estrogen*: female sex hormones involved in reproduction.

- *Testosterone*: male sex hormone involved in reproduction.

# CHAPTER 17

# Behavioral Ecology and Ethology

**IN THIS CHAPTER**

**Summary:** This chapter focuses on the interaction between animals and their environments (ecology) and introduces you to some of the basic terms used in behavioral ecology and ethology.

**Key Ideas**

❂ Learn the bold-faced terms in this chapter well because they show up often on the multiple-choice portion of the exam.

❂ Types of animal learning: associative learning, fixed-action pattern, habituation, imprinting, insight learning, observational learning, and operant conditioning.

❂ Three major types of animal movement: kinesis, migration, and taxis.

❂ Behavioral patterns/concepts to know: agonistic behaviors, altruistic behaviors, coefficient of relatedness, dominance hierarchies, foraging, inclusive fitness, optimal foraging, reciprocal altruism, and territoriality.

❂ Types of animal communication: chemical, visual, auditory, and tactile.

## Introduction

*CT teacher: "This chapter has a lot of multiple-choice-type questions in it. Learn the general concepts. . . ."*

Behavioral ecology and ethology both involve the study of animal behavior. **Behavioral ecology** focuses on the interaction between animals and their environments, and usually includes an evolutionary perspective. For example, a behavioral ecologist might ask, "Why do two bird species that live in the same environment eat two different types of seeds?" **Ethology** is a narrower field, focused particularly on animal behavior and less on ecological analysis. Historically, ethology has involved a lot of experimental work, which has given us insight into the nature of animal minds.

This chapter introduces you to some of the basic terms and concepts used in behavioral ecology and ethology.

# Types of Animal Learning

**Associative learning** is the process by which animals take one stimulus and associate it with another. Ivan Pavlov demonstrated **classical conditioning,** a type of associative learning, with dogs. As will come to be a pattern in this chapter, some poor animals were tampered with to help us understand an important biological principle. Pavlov taught dogs to anticipate the arrival of food with the sound of a bell. He hooked up these dogs to machines that measured salivation. He began the experiments by ringing a bell just moments before giving food to the dogs. Soon after this experiment began, the dogs were salivating at the sound of the bell before food was even brought into the room. They were conditioned to associate the noise of the bell with the impending arrival of food; one stimulus was substituted for another to evoke the same response.

A **fixed-action pattern** (FAP) is an innate, preprogrammed response to a stimulus. Once this action has begun, it will not stop until it has run its course. For example, male stickleback fish are programmed to attack any red-bellied fish that come into their territory. Males do not attack fish lacking this red coloration; it is specifically the color that stimulates aggressiveness. If fake fish with red bottoms are placed in water containing these stickleback fish, there's bound to be a fight! But if fake fish lacking a red bottom are dropped in, all is peaceful.

**Habituation** is the loss of responsiveness to unimportant stimuli. For example, as one of us started working on this book, he had just purchased a new fish tank for his office and was struck by how audible the sound of the tank's filter was. As he sits here typing tonight about two months later, he does not even hear the filter unless he *thinks* about it; he has become habituated to the noise. There are many examples of habituation in ethology. One classic example involves little ducklings that run for cover whenever birdlike objects fly overhead. If one were to torture these poor baby ducks and throw bird-shaped objects over their heads, in the beginning they would head for cover each time one flew past them, but over time as they learned that the fake birds did not represent any real danger, they would habituate to the mean trick and eventually not react at all. One side note is that ethologists who study wild animals usually have to habituate their study subjects to their presence before recording any behavioral data.

**Imprinting** is an innate behavior that is learned during a critical period early in life. For example, when geese are born, they imprint on motion that moves away from them, and they follow it around accepting it as their mother. This motion can be the baby's actual mother goose, it can be a human, or it can be an object. Once this imprint is made, it is irreversible. If given an essay about behavioral ecology, and imprinting in particular, the work of Konrad Lorenz would be a nice addition to your response. He was a scientist who became the "mother" to a group of young geese. He made sure that he was around the baby geese as they hatched and spent the critical period with them creating that mother–baby goose bond. These geese proceeded to follow him around everywhere and didn't recognize their real mother as their own.

**Insight learning** is the ability to do something right the first time with no prior experience. It requires reasoning ability—the skill to look at a problem and come up with an appropriate solution.

**Observational learning** is the ability of an organism to learn how to do something by watching another individual do it first, even if they have never attempted it themselves.

An example of this involves young chimpanzees in the Ivory Coast, who watch their mothers crack nuts with rock tools before learning the technique themselves.

**Operant conditioning** is a type of associative learning that is based on trial and error. This is different from classical conditioning because in operant conditioning, the association is made between the animal's *own* behavior and a response. This is the type of conditioning that is important to the aposometrically colored organisms that we discuss in Chapter 18 on ecology. For example, a brightly colored lizard with a chemical defense mechanism (it can spray predators in an attempt to escape) relies on this type of conditioning for survival. The coloration pattern is there in the hope that the predator will, in a trial-and-error fashion, associate the coloration pattern with an uncomfortable chemical-spraying experience that it had in the past. This association might make the predator think twice before attacking in the future and provide the prey with enough time to escape.

# Animal Movement

There are three major types of animal movement that you should familiarize yourself with for the AP exam: kinesis, migration, and taxis.

**KEY IDEA**

*Kinesis.* This is a seemingly random change in the *speed* of a movement in response to a stimulus. When an organism is in a place that it enjoys, it slows down, and when in a bad environment, it speeds up. Overall this leads to an organism spending more time in favorable environments. In Chapter 19, Laboratory Review, an example of kinesis involving pill bugs is discussed. These bugs prefer damp environments to dry ones, and when placed into a contraption that gives them the choice of being on the dry or damp side, they move quickly toward the damp side (where the speed of their movement slows).

> **BIG IDEA 2.E.3**
> Behaviors (such as migration) are regulated by various mechanisms and are important to natural selection.

*Migration.* This is a cyclic movement of animals over long distances according to the time of year. Birds are known to migrate south, where it is warmer, for the winter. It is amazing that these animals know where to go.

*Taxis.* These are cars taken by people who need transportation. Hmm . . . actually, *taxis,* the biological term, is a reflex movement toward or away from a stimulus. We always think about summer evenings, sitting on the porch with the bug light near by, watching the poor little moths fly *right* into the darn thing because of the taxis response. They are drawn to the light at night (**phototaxis**).

## Behave Yourselves, You Animals!

There are several typical behavior patterns that you should familiarize yourself with before the exam.

**KEY IDEA**

1. **Agonistic behavior.** Behavior that results from conflicts over resources. It often involves intimidation and submission. The battle is often a matter of who can put on the most threatening display to scare the other one into giving up, although the displays can also be quite subtle. Agonistic behaviors can involve food, mates, and territory, to name only a few. Participants in these displays do not tend to come away injured because most of these interactions are just that: displays.
2. **Altruistic behavior.** An *altruistic* action is one in which an organism does something to help another, even if it comes at its own expense. An example of this behavior involves bees. Worker bees are sterile, produce no offspring, and play the role of hive defenders,

sacrificing their lives by stinging intruders that pose a threat to the queen bee. (Sounds to us like they need a better agent.) Another example involves vampire bats that vomit food for group mates that did not manage to find food.

3. **Coefficient of relatedness.** This statistic represents the average proportion of genes that two individuals have in common. Siblings have a coefficient of relatedness (COR) of 0.5 because they share 50 percent of their genes. This coefficient is an interesting statistic because it can be expected that an animal that has a high COR with another animal will be more likely to act in an altruistic manner toward that animal.

4. **Dominance hierarchies.** A dominance hierarchy among a group of individuals is a ranking of power among the members. The member with the most power is the "alpha" member. The second-in-command, the "beta" member, dominates everyone in the group except for the alpha. It pretty much rocks to be at the top of the dominance hierarchy because you have first dibs (choice) on *every*thing (food, mates, etc.). The dominance hierarchy is not necessarily permanent—there can always be some shuffling around. For example, in chimpanzees, an alpha male can lose his alpha status and become subordinate to another chimp if power relationships change. One positive thing about these hierarchies is that since there is an order, known by all involved, it reduces the energy wasted and the risk from physical fighting for resources. Animals that know that they would be attacked if they took food before a higher-ranking individual wait until it is their turn to eat so as to avoid conflict. Keep in mind that dominance hierarchies are a characteristic of group-living animals.

5. **Foraging.** A word that describes the feeding behavior of an individual. This behavior is not as random as it may seem as animals tend to have something called a **search image** that directs them toward their potential meal. When searching for food, few fish look for a particular food; rather, they are looking for objects of a particular size that seem to match the size of what they usually eat. This is a search image. In an aquarium at mealtime, if you watch the fish closely, you will see them zoom around taking food into their mouths as they swim. Unfortunately, sometimes the "food" they ingest is the bathroom output of another fish that happens to be the same size as the food and is floating nearby. Simply because the fish dropping is the appropriate size and fits the search image, the fish may take it into its mouth for a second before emphatically spitting it out.

6. **Inclusive fitness.** This term represents the overall ability of individuals to pass their genes on to the next generation. This includes their ability to pass their *own* genes through reproduction as well as the ability of their relatives to do the same. Reproduction by relatives is included because related individuals share many of the same genes. Therefore, helping relatives to increase the success of passage of their genes to the next generation increases the inclusive fitness of the helper. The concept of inclusive fitness can explain many cases of altruism in nature.

7. **Optimal foraging.** Natural selection favors animals that choose foraging strategies that take into account costs and benefits. For example, food that is rich in nutrients but far away may cost too much energy to be worth the extra trip. There are many potential costs to traveling a long distance for some food—the animal itself could be eaten on the way *to* the food, and the animal could expend more energy than it would gain *from* the food. You *know* that you have displayed optimal foraging behavior before. "Hey, do you want to go to Wendy's?" "Uhh . . . not really, it's a really long drive . . . let's go to Bill's Burgers down the road instead."

8. **Reciprocal altruism.** Why should individuals behave altruistically? One reason may be the hope that in the future, the companion will return the favor. A baboon may defend

an unrelated companion in a fight, or perhaps a wolf will offer food to another wolf that shares no relation. Animals rarely display this behavior since it is limited to species with stable social groups that allow for exchanges of this nature. The bats described earlier represent a good example of reciprocal altruism.

9. **Territoriality.** Territorial individuals defend a physical geographic area against other individuals. This area is defended because of the benefits derived from it, which may include available mates, food resources, and high-quality breeding sites. An individual may defend a territory using scent marking, vocalizations that warn other individuals to stay away, or actual physical force against intruders. Animal species vary in their degree of territoriality (in fact, some species are *not* territorial), and both males and females may exhibit territorial behavior.

# Animal Communication

Animals communicate in many ways. Communication need not always be vocal, and we will discuss the various communication mechanisms in this next section: visual, auditory, chemical, and tactile.

**BIG IDEA 3.D.1**
*Communication can involve signals from other organisms or the environment.*

*Chemical communication.* Mammals and insects use chemical signals called **pheromones,** which in many species play a pivotal role in the mating game. Pheromones can be powerful enough to attract mates from miles away.

*Visual communication.* We mentioned a few visual communication examples earlier, such as agonistic displays. Another example of a visual display is a male peacock's feather splay, which announces his willingness to mate.

*Auditory communication.* This mode of communication involves the use of sound in the conveying of a message. In many parts of the United States, if one sits on one's porch on a summer night, one hears the song of night frogs and crickets. These noises are often made in an effort to attract mates.

*Tactile communication.* This mode of communication involves touch in the conveying of a message and is often used as a greeting (handshake in humans). A major form of primate tactile communication involves grooming behavior.

**BIG IDEA 3.E.1**
*Individuals can act on information and communicate it to others.*

Bees provide an example of communication that involves chemical, tactile, and auditory components. The beehive is a dark and crowded place, and when a worker bee returns after having found a good food source, how in the world is it going to get the attention of all of the co-workers? Unfortunately, intercom systems in hives are yet to be developed. What these bees do instead is a little dance; a dance in a tight circle accompanied by a certain wag signifies to the co-workers "Hey guys . . . food source is *right* down the street." But if the food is farther away, the bee changes the dance to one that provides directional clues as well. The bee will instead perform a different combination of funky moves. This dance provides distance and directional information to the other workers and helps them find the faraway source. The ever so pleasant chemical component to this process is the regurgitation of the food source to show the other bees what kind of food they are chasing. Imagine if humans did that . . . "Dude, I just found the greatest burger place like two miles from here . . . (burp) here . . . try this burger . . . it's delightful!"

# › Review Questions

1. When horses hear an unusual noise, they turn their ears toward the sound. This is an example of

   A. a fixed-action pattern.
   B. habituation.
   C. associative learning.
   D. imprinting.

2. Why do animal behaviorists have to account for a habituation period when undertaking an observational study?

   A. They have to make sure that the study animals do not imprint on them.
   B. They have to wait until their presence no longer affects the behavior of the animals.
   C. The animals need a period of time to learn to associate the observer with data collection.
   D. Before insight learning can be observed, the animals must practice.

3. Which of the following is an example of an agonistic behavior?

   A. A subordinate chimpanzee grooms a dominant chimpanzee.
   B. Two lionesses share a fresh kill.
   C. A female wolf regurgitates food for her nieces and nephews.
   D. A blackbird approaches and takes the feeding position of another blackbird, causing it to fly away.

4. In which of the following dyads do we expect *not* to see any altruistic behavior?

   A. Two sisters who are allies
   B. Two half-brothers
   C. Two individuals migrating in opposite directions
   D. Two group members who have frequent conflicts and reconciliations

5. Which of the following is not a requirement for reciprocal altruism to occur?

   A. Ability to recognize the other individual
   B. Long lifespan
   C. Opportunity for multiple interactions
   D. High coefficient of relatedness

6. A female tamarin monkey licks her wrists, rubs them together, and then rubs them against a nearby tree. What kind of communication is this probably an example of?

   A. Chemical
   B. Visual
   C. Auditory
   D. Territorial

For questions 7–10, please use the following answers:

   A. Habituation
   B. Imprinting
   C. Associative learning
   D. Operant conditioning

7. This type of learning is the lack of responsiveness to unimportant stimuli that do not provide appropriate feedback.

8. Trial-and-error learning important to animals displaying aposometric coloration.

9. Process by which animals associate one stimulus with another.

10. Innate behavior that is learned during a critical period in life.

## › Answers and Explanations

1. **A**—This is a fixed-action pattern—an innate behavior that is a programmed response to a stimulus that appears to be carried out without any thought by the organisms involved.

2. **B**—If the scientist does not allow for a period of habituation, the behavioral observations will be inaccurate since the behavior of the animal will be altered by the presence of the scientist.

3. **D**—An agonistic behavior is a contest of intimidation and submission where the prize is a desired resource. In this case, the resource is the feeding position.

4. **C**—Altruistic behavior cannot be expected from two migrating individuals for a couple of reasons: (1) there is no reason for either of them to believe that they will see the other in the future, taking the "If I help them now, perhaps they will help me sometime in the future" element out of play; and (2) if they are migrating in different directions, it is reasonably likely that they are probably not related, which takes the "I'll help because it'll increase the chance that more of my genes get passed along" element out of play.

5. **D**—Reciprocal altruism need not occur between related individuals.

6. **A**

7. **A**

8. **D**

9. **C**

10. **B**

## › Rapid Review

Quickly review the following terms:

*Behavioral ecology*: study of interaction between animals and their environments.

*Ethology*: study of animal behavior.

### Types of Animal Learning

- *Fixed-action pattern*: preprogrammed response to a stimulus (stickleback fish).
- *Habituation*: loss of responsiveness to unimportant stimuli or stimuli that provide no feedback.
- *Imprinting*: innate behavior learned during critical period early in life (baby ducks imprint to mama ducks).
- *Associative learning*: one stimulus is associated with another (classical conditioning—Pavlov).
- *Operant conditioning*: trial-and-error learning (aposometric predator training).
- *Insight learning*: ability to reason through a problem the first time through with no prior experience.
- *Observational learning*: learning by watching someone else do it first.

### Types of Animal Movement

- *Kinesis*: change in the speed of movement in response to a stimulus. Organisms will move faster in bad environments and slower in good environments.
- *Migration*: cyclic movement of animals over long distances according to the time of year.
- *Taxis*: reflex movement toward or away from a stimulus.

## Animal Behaviors

- *Agonistic behavior*: conflict behavior over access to a resource. Often a matter of which animal can mount the most threatening display and scare the other into submission.
- *Dominance hierarchies*: ranking of power among the members of a group; subject to change. Since members of the group know the order, less energy is wasted in conflicts over food and resources.
- *Territoriality*: defense of territory to keep others out.
- *Altruistic behavior*: action in which an organism helps another at its own expense.
- *Reciprocal altruism*: animals behave altruistically toward others who are *not* relatives, hoping that the favor will be returned sometime in the future.
- *Foraging*: feeding behavior of an individual. Animals have a search image that directs them to food.
- *Optimal foraging*: natural selection favors those who choose foraging strategies that maximize the differential between costs and benefits. If the effort involved in obtaining food outweighs the nutritive value of the food, forget about it.
- *Inclusive fitness*: the ability of individuals to pass their genes not only through the production of their own offspring, but also by providing aid to enable closely related individuals to produce offspring.
- *Coefficient of relatedness*: statistic that represents the average proportion of genes two individuals have in common. The higher the value, the more likely they are to altruistically aid one another.

## Communication

- *Chemical*: communication through the use of chemical signals, such as pheromones.
- *Visual*: communication through the use of visual cues, such as the tail feather displays of peacocks.
- *Auditory*: communication through the use of sound, such as the chirping of frogs in the summer.
- *Tactile*: communication through the use of touch, such as a handshake in humans.

# CHAPTER 18

# Ecology in Further Detail

**IN THIS CHAPTER**

**Summary:** This chapter covers the main concepts of ecology, including population growth, biotic potential, life history strategies, and predator–prey relationships. This chapter also discusses concepts such as succession, trophic levels, energy and biomass pyramids, biomes, and biogeochemical cycles.

### Key Ideas

- ✪ Three main types of dispersion patterns: clumped, uniform, and random.
- ✪ Two main types of population growth: exponential (J-shaped) and logistic (S-shaped.)
- ✪ Two primary life history strategies: *K*-selected and *R*-selected populations.
- ✪ Three main symbiotic relationships: commensalism, mutualism, and parasitism.
- ✪ Defense mechanisms: aposematic coloration, Batesian mimicry, cryptic coloration, deceptive markings, and Müllerian mimicry.
- ✪ Biomes that come up on the AP exam: desert, savannah, taiga, temperate deciduous forest, temperate grassland, tropical forest, tundra, and water.
- ✪ Have a general understanding of the biogeochemical cycles (carbon, nitrogen, and water).

## Introduction

*Ecology* is the study of the interaction of organisms and their environments. This chapter covers the main concepts of ecology, including population growth, biotic potential, life history "strategies," and predator–prey relationships. The chapter will also look at within-community and between-community (intra- and intercommunity) interactions. Finally we will talk about succession, trophic levels, energy pyramids, biomass pyramids, biomes, and biogeochemical cycles.

# Population Ecology and Growth

Like many fields of biology, ecology contains hierarchies of classification. A **population** is a collection of individuals of the same species living in the same geographic area. A collection of populations of species in a geographic area is known as a **community.** An **ecosystem** consists of the individuals of the community and the environment in which it exists. Ecosystems can be subdivided into abiotic and biotic components: **biotic components** are the living organisms of the ecosystem, while **abiotic components** are the *nonliving* players in an ecosystem, such as weather and nutrients. Finally, the **biosphere** is the entire life-containing area of a planet—all communities and ecosystems.

Three more terms for you: (1) the **niche** of an organism, which consists of all the biotic and abiotic resources used by the organism; (2) **population density,** which describes how many individuals are in a certain area; and (3) **distribution,** which describes how populations are dispersed over that area. There are three main types of dispersion patterns that you should know (see also Figure 18.1):

1.  *Clumped:* The individuals live in packs that are spaced out from each other, as in schools of fish or herds of cattle.
2.  *Uniform:* The individuals are evenly spaced out across a geographic area, such as birds on a wire sitting above the highway—notice how evenly spaced out they are.
3.  *Random:* The species are randomly distributed across a geographic area, such as a tree distribution in a forest.

**Figure 18.1   Distribution patterns: (a) clumped; (b) uniform; (c) random.**

**Population ecology** is the study of the size, distribution, and density of populations and how these populations change with time. It takes into account all the variables we have mentioned already and many more. The size of the population, symbolized $N$, indicates how many individuals of that species are in a given area. **Demographers** study the theory and statistics behind population growth and decline. The following is a list of demographic statistics you should be familiar with for the AP Biology exam:

| | |
|---|---|
| **Birth rate** | Offspring produced per time period. Highest among those in the middle of the age spectrum. |
| **Death rate** | Number of deaths per time period. Highest among those at two extremes of the age spectrum. |

Figure 18.2   A typical age structure chart.

| | |
|---|---|
| **Sex ratio** | Proportion of males and females in a population. |
| **Generation time** | Time needed for individuals to reach reproductive maturity. |
| **Age structure** | Statistic that compares the relative number of individuals in the population from each age group (Figure 18.2). |
| **Immigration rate** | Rate at which individuals relocate into a given population. |
| **Emigration rate** | Rate at which individuals relocate out of a given population. |

*Liz (college freshman): "Know how to read these charts."*

All these statistics together determine the size and growth rate of a given population. Obviously, a higher birth rate and a lower death rate will give a faster rate of population growth. A high female sex ratio could lead to an increase in the number of births in a population (more females to produce offspring). A short generation time allows offspring to be produced at a faster rate. An age structure that consists of more individuals in the middle of their reproductive years will grow at a faster rate than one weighted toward older people.

## Population Growth and Size

**Biotic potential** is the maximum growth rate of a population given unlimited resources, unlimited space, and lack of competition or predators. This rate varies from species to species. The **carrying capacity** is defined as the maximum number of individuals that a population can sustain in a given environment.

If biotic potential exists, then why isn't every inch of this planet covered with life? Because of the environment in which we live, numerous **limiting factors** exist that help control population sizes. A few examples of limiting factors include predators, diseases, food supplies, and waste produced by organisms. There are two broad categories of limiting factors:

*Density-dependent factors.* These limiting factors rear their ugly heads as the population approaches and/or passes the carrying capacity. Examples of density-dependent limiting factors include food supplies, which run low; waste products, which build up; and population-crowding-related diseases such as the bubonic plague, which just stink.

*Density-independent factors.* These limiting factors have nothing to do with the population size. Examples of density-independent limiting factors include floods, droughts, earthquakes, and other natural disasters and weather conditions.

There are two main types of population growth:

1. *Exponential growth:* the population grows at a rate that creates a J-shaped curve. The population grows as if there are no limitations as to how large it can get (biotic potential).
2. *Logistic growth:* the population grows at a rate that creates an S-shaped curve similar to the initial portion of Figure 18.3. Limiting factors are the culprits responsible for the S shape of the curve, putting a cap on the size to which the population can grow.

Take a look at Figure 18.3. As the population size increases exponentially from point *A* to point *C*, there seem to be enough natural resources available to allow the growth rate to be quite high. At some point, however, natural resources, such as food, will start to run out. This will lead to competition between the members of the population for the scarce food. Whenever there is competition, there are winners and losers. Those who win survive; those who lose do not. Notice that the population rises above the carrying capacity. How can this be? This is short-lived, as the complications of being overpopulated (lack of food, disease from increased population density, buildup of waste) will lead to a rise in the death rate that pushes the population back down to the carrying capacity or below. When it drops below the carrying capacity, resources replenish, allowing for an increase in the birth rate and decline in the death rate. What you are looking at in Figure 18.3 is the phenomenon known as a **population cycle.** Often, as seen in the figure, when the population size dips below the carrying capacity, it will later come back to the capacity and even surpass it.

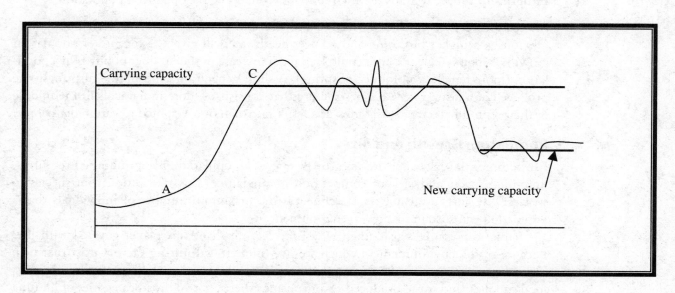

**Figure 18.3   Carrying capacity.**

However, another possibility shown in this figure is that when a population dips below the carrying capacity due to some major change in the environment, when all is said and done, it may equilibrate at a new, lower carrying capacity.

# Life History Strategies

You should be familiar with two primary life history "strategies," which represent two extremes of the spectrum:

K-*selected populations:* populations of a roughly constant size whose members have low reproductive rates. The offspring produced by these *K*-selected organisms require extensive postnatal care until they have sufficiently matured. Humans are a fine example of a *K*-selected population.

R-*selected populations:* populations that experience rapid growth of the J-curve variety. The offspring produced by *R*-selected organisms are numerous, mature quite rapidly, and require very little postnatal care. These populations are also known as **opportunistic populations** and tend to show up when space in the region opens up as a result of some environmental change. The opportunistic population grows fast, reproduces quickly, and dies quickly as well. Bacteria are a good example of an *R*-selected population.

## Survivorship Curves

**Survivorship curves** (Figure 18.4) are another tool used to study the population dynamics of species. These curves show the relative survival rates for population members of different ages.

*Type I* individuals live a long life until an age is reached where the death rate in the population increases rapidly, causing the steep downward end to the type I curve. Examples of type I organisms include humans and other large mammals.

*Type II* individuals have a death rate that is reasonably constant across the age spectrum. Examples of type II species include lizards, hydra, and other small mammals.

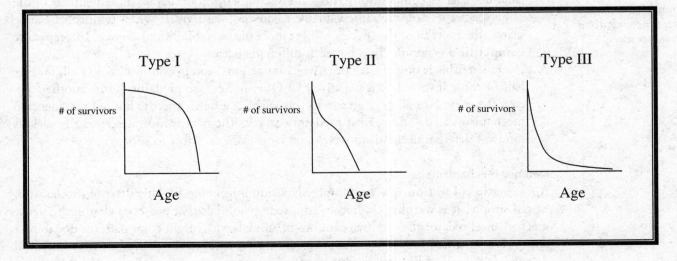

**Figure 18.4   Survivorship curves.**

*Type III* individuals have a steep downward curve for those of young age, representing a death rate that flattens out once a certain age is reached. Examples of type III organisms include many fishes, oysters, and other marine organisms.

# Community and Succession

## Community

Most species exist within a community. Because they share a geographic home, they are bound to interact. These interactions range from positive to neutral to negative.

*Del (12th grade): "Know this for the multiple-choice questions. I should have. . . ."*

### Forms of Species Interaction

1. *Symbiosis.* A symbiotic relationship is one between two different species that can be classified as one of three main types: commensalism, mutualism, or parasitism.

   A. *Commensalism.* One organism benefits while the other is unaffected. Commensalistic relationships are rare, and examples are hard to find. Cattle egrets feast on insects that are aroused into flight by cattle grazing in the insects' habitat. The birds benefit because they get food, but the cattle do not appear to benefit at all.

   B. *Mutualism.* Both organisms reap benefits from the interaction. One popular example of a mutualistic relationship is that between acacia trees and ants. The ants are able to feast on the yummy sugar produced by the trees, while the trees are protected by the ants' attack on any potentially harmful foreign insects. Another example involves a lichen, which is a collection of photosynthetic organisms (fungus and algae) living as one. The fungus component pulls its weight by helping to create an environment suitable for the lichen's survival, while the algae component supplies the food for the fungus. Without each other's contribution, they are doomed.

   C. *Parasitism.* One organism benefits at the other's expense. A popular example of a parasitic relationship involves tapeworms, which live in the digestive tract of their hosts. They reap the benefits of the meals that their host consumes by stealing the nutrients and depriving the host of nutrition. Another less well-known example of parasitism involves myself and my younger brother's Playstation 2 console.

2. *Competition.* Both species are harmed by this kind of interaction. The two major forms of competition are intraspecific and interspecific competition. **Intraspecific competition** is *within*-species competition. This kind of competition occurs because members of the same species rely on the same valuable resources for survival. When resources become scarce, the most fit of the species will get more of the resource and survive. **Interspecific competition** is competition between different species.

3. *Predation.* This is one of the "negative" interactions seen in communities (well, for one half of those involved, it is negative.) ☺ One species, the predator, hunts another species, the prey. Not all prey give in to this without a fight, and the hunted may develop mechanisms to defend against predatory attack. The next section describes the various kinds of defense mechanisms developed by prey in an effort to survive.

**BIG IDEA 2.D.1**

*Everything from cells to ecosystems is affected by interactions involving the exchange of matter and energy.*

**BIG IDEA 4.A.5**

*Communities are composed of populations that interact in complex ways.*

### Defense Mechanisms

**Aposematic coloration** is a very impressive-sounding name for this defense mechanism. Stated simply, it is warning coloration adopted by animals that possess a chemical defense mechanism. Predators have grown cautious of animals with bright color patterns due to past encounters in which prey of a certain coloration have sprayed the predator with a chemical defense. It is kind of like the blinking red light seen in cars with elaborate alarm systems.

Burglars notice the red light and may think twice about attempting to steal that car because of the potential for encountering an alarm system.

In **Batesian mimicry,** an animal that is harmless copies the appearance of an animal that is dangerous to trick predators. An example of this is a beetle whose colors closely resemble those of bees. Predators may fear that the beetle is a bee and avoid confrontation.

In **cryptic coloration,** those being hunted adopt a coloring scheme that allows them to blend in to the colors of the environment. It is like camouflage worn by army soldiers moving through the jungle. The more you look like the terrain, the harder you are to see.

Some animals have patterns called **deceptive markings,** which can cause a predator to think twice before attacking. For example, some insects may have colored designs on their wings that resemble large eyes, causing individuals to look more imposing than they truly are.

In **Müllerian mimicry,** two species that are aposematically colored as an indicator of their chemical defense mechanisms mimic each other's color scheme in an effort to increase the speed with which their predators learn to avoid them. The more often predators see dangerous prey with this coloration, the faster the negative association is made.

Looking at Figure 18.5, we can see how the predator–prey dance plays out. When the prey population starts to decrease because of predation, there is a reactionary reduction in the predator population. Why does this happen? Because the predators run low on a valuable resource necessary to their survival—their prey. Notice in the figure that as the predator population declines, an increase in the population of the prey begins to appear because more of those prey animals are able to survive and reproduce. As the prey population density rises, the predators again have enough food available to sustain a higher population, and their population density returns to a higher level again. Unless disturbed by a dramatic environmental change, this cyclical pattern continues.

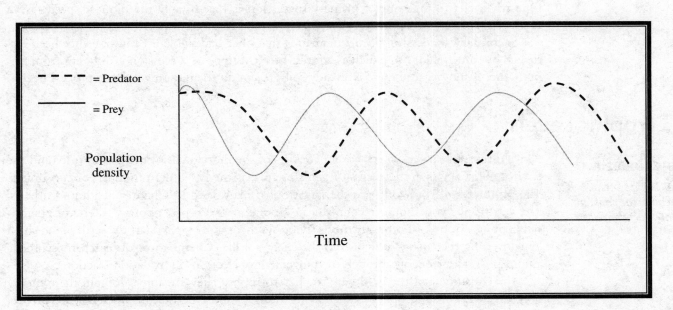

**Figure 18.5   Predator–prey population curves.**

**Coevolution** is mutual evolution between two species and is often seen in predator–prey relationships. For example, imagine that the hunted prey adapts a new character trait that allows it to better elude the predator. In order to survive, the predator must evolve so that it can catch its victim and eat.

## Succession

When something happens to a community that causes a shift in the resources available to the local organisms, it sets the stage for the process of **succession**—the shift in the local composition of species in response to changes that occur over time. As time passes, the community goes through various stages until it arrives at a final stable stage called the **climax community.** Two major forms of succession you should know about are primary and secondary succession.

**Primary succession** occurs in an area that is devoid of life and contains no soil. A **pioneer species** (usually a small plant) able to survive in resource-poor conditions takes hold of a barren area such as a new volcanic island. The pioneer species does the grunt work, adding nutrients and other improvements to the once uninhabited volcanic rock until future species take over. As the plant species come and go, adding nutrients to the environment, animal species are drawn in by the presence of new plant life. These animals contribute to the development of the area with the addition of further organic matter (waste). This constant changing of the guard continues until the **climax community** is reached and a steady-state equilibrium is achieved. **Bare-rock succession** involves the attachment of lichen to rocks, followed by the step-by-step arrival of replacement species up to the climax community. **Pond succession** is kicked off when a shallow, water-filled hole is created. As time passes, animals arrive on the scene as the pioneer species deposit debris, encouraging the growth of vegetation on the pond floor. Over time, plants develop whose roots are underwater and whose leaves are above the water. As these plants begin to cover the entire area of the pond, the debris continues to build up, transforming the once empty pond into a marsh. When enough trees fill into the area, the marsh becomes a swamp. If the conditions are appropriate, the swamp can eventually become a forest or grassland, completing the succession process. One trivia fact to take out of primary succession is that usually the pioneer species is an *R*-selected species, while the later species tend to be *K*-selected species.

**Secondary succession** occurs in an area that once had stable life but has since been disturbed by some major force such as a forest fire. This type of succession is different from primary succession because there is already soil present on the terrain when the process begins.

> **BIG IDEA 4.C.4**
> The diversity of species within an ecosystem may influence the stability of that ecosystem.

# Trophic Levels

> **BIG IDEA 2.A.1**
> All living systems require the constant input of energy.

As we discussed earlier, an ecosystem consists of the individuals of the community and the environment in which they exist. Organisms are classified as either producers or consumers. The producers of the world are the autotrophs mentioned in Chapter 8, Photosynthesis. The autotrophs you should recognize can be one of two types: photosynthetic or chemosynthetic autotrophs. **Photoautotrophs** (photosynthetic autotrophs) start the earth's food chain by converting the energy of light into the energy of life. **Chemoautotrophs** (chemosynthetic autotrophs) release energy through the movement of electrons in oxidation reactions.

The consumers of the world are the heterotrophs. They are able to obtain their energy only through consumption of other living things. One type of consumer is a **herbivore,** which feeds on plants for nourishment. Another consumer, the **carnivore,** obtains energy and nutrients through the consumption of other animals. A third consumer, the **detritivore,** obtains its energy through the consumption of dead animals and plants. A special subcategory of this type of consumer includes decomposers, which also consume dead animal and plant matter, but then release nutrients back into the environment. The decomposer subcategory includes fungi, bacteria, and earthworms.

Here comes another hierarchy for you to remember. The distribution of energy on the planet can be subdivided into a hierarchy of energy levels called **trophic levels.** Take a look

**Figure 18.6    Energy pyramid, indicating decrease in energy level.**

**BIG IDEA 4.B.3**

*Interactions between populations influence patterns of species distribution.*

at the energy pyramid in Figure 18.6. The primary producers make up the first trophic level. The next trophic level consists of the organisms that consume the primary producers: the herbivores. These organisms are known as **primary consumers.** The primary consumers are consumed by the **secondary consumers,** or primary carnivores, that are the next trophic level. These primary carnivores are consumed by the secondary carnivores to create the next trophic level. This is an oversimplified yet important basic explanation of how trophic levels work. Usually there are only four or five trophic levels to a food chain because energy is lost from each level as it progresses higher.

The energy pyramid is not the only type of ecological pyramid that you might encounter on the AP Biology exam. Be familiar with a type of pyramid known as a *biomass pyramid* (Figure 18.7), which represents the cumulative weight of all of the members at a given

**Figure 18.7    Biomass pyramid.**

trophic level. These pyramids tend to vary from one ecosystem to another. Like energy pyramids, the base of the biomass pyramid represents the primary producers and tends to be the largest.

There is also the **pyramid of numbers,** which is based on the *number* of individuals at each level of the biomass chain. Each box in this pyramid represents the number of members of that level. The highest consumers in the chain tend to be quite large, resulting in a smaller number of those individuals spread out over an area.

Two more terms to cover before moving on to the biomes are **food chains** and **food webs.** A *food chain* is a hierarchical list of who snacks on who. For example, bugs are eaten by spiders, who are eaten by birds, who are eaten by cats. A *food web* provides more information than a food chain—it is not so cut and dry. Food webs recognize that, for example, bugs are eaten by more than only spiders. Food webs can be regarded as overlapping food chains that show all the various dietary relationships.

> **BIG IDEA 4.A.6**
>
> *Interactions among organisms and with their environment result in movement of matter and energy.*

# Biomes

The various geographic regions of the earth that serve as hosts for ecosystems are known as **biomes.** Read through the following list so that you will be able to sprinkle some biome knowledge into an essay on ecological principles.

> **BIG IDEA 4.B.4**
>
> *Distribution of local and global ecosystems changes over time.*

1. *Deserts.* The driest land biome of the group, **deserts** experience a wide range of temperature from day to night and exist on nearly every continent. Deserts that do not receive adequate rainfall will not have any vegetative life. However, plants such as cacti seem to have adjusted to desert life and have done quite nicely in this biome, given enough water. Much of the wildlife found in deserts is nocturnal and conserves energy and water during the heat of the day. This biome shows the greatest daily fluctuation in temperature due to the fact that water moderates temperature.
2. *Savanna.* **Savanna** grasslands, which contain a spattering of trees, are found throughout South America, Australia, and Africa. Savanna soil tends to be low in nutrients, while temperatures tend to run high. Many of the grazing species of this planet (herbivores) make savannas their home.
3. *Taiga.* This biome, characterized by lengthy cold and wet winters, is found in Canada and has gymnosperms as its prominent plant life. **Taigas** contain coniferous forests (pine and other needle-bearing trees).
4. *Temperate deciduous forests.* A biome that is found in regions that experience cold winters where plant life is dormant, alternating with warm summers that provide enough moisture to keep large trees alive. **Temperate deciduous forests** can be seen in the northeastern United States, much of Europe, and eastern Asia.
5. *Temperate grasslands.* **Temperate grasslands** are found in regions with cold winters. The soil of this biome is considered to be among the most fertile of all. This biome receives less water than tropical savannas.
6. *Tropical forests.* Found all over the planet in South America, Africa, Australia, and Asia, **tropical forests** come in many shapes and sizes. Near the equator, they can be rainforests, whereas in lowland areas that have dry seasons, they tend to be dry forests. Rainforests consist primarily of tall trees that form a thick cover, which blocks the light from reaching the floor of the forest (where there is little growth). Tropical rainforests are known for their rapid recycling of nutrients and contain the greatest diversity of species.
7. *Tundras.* The **tundra** biome experiences extremely cold winters during which the ground freezes completely. The upper layer of the ground is able to thaw during the summer months, but the land directly underneath, called the **permafrost,** remains

frozen throughout the year. This keeps plants from forming deep roots in this soil and dictates what type of plant life can survive. The plant life that tends to predominate is short shrubs or grasses that are able to withstand difficult conditions.

8. *Water biomes.* Both freshwater and marine **water biomes** occupy the majority of the surface of the earth.

The general distribution of biomes on the earth's surface is shown in Figure 18.8.

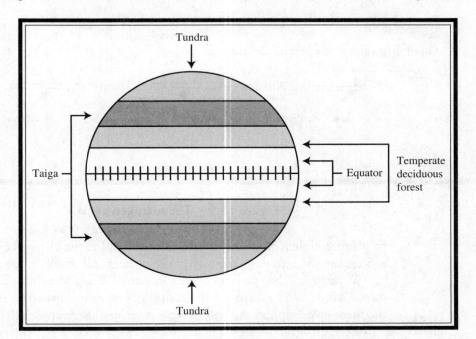

**Figure 18.8   General distribution of biomes on the earth's surface. (The other land biomes such as grassland and desert are interspersed in temperate and tropical regions with water as the limiting factor.)**

# Biogeochemical Cycles

One last topic to briefly cover before we wave goodbye to ecology is that of **biogeochemical cycles.** These cycles represent the movement of elements, such as nitrogen and carbon, from organisms to the environment and back in a continuous cycle. Do not attempt to become a master of these cycles, but you should understand the basics.

*Carbon cycle.* Carbon is the building block of organic life. The **carbon cycle** begins when carbon is released to the atmosphere from volcanoes, aerobic respiration ($CO_2$), and the burning of fossil fuels (coal). Most of the carbon in the atmosphere is present in the form of $CO_2$. Plants contribute to the carbon cycle by taking in carbon and using it to perform photosynthetic reactions, and then incorporating it into their sugars. The carbon is ingested by animals, who send the carbon back to the atmosphere when they die.

*Nitrogen cycle.* Nitrogen is an element vital to plant growth. In the **nitrogen cycle** (Figure 18.9), plants have nitrogen to consume thanks to the existence of organisms that perform the thankless task of **nitrogen fixation**—the conversion of $N_2$ to $NH_3$ (ammonia). The only source of nitrogen for animals is the plants they consume. When these organisms die, their remains become a source of nitrogen for the remaining members of the environment. Bacteria and fungi (decomposers) chomp at these organisms and break down any nitrogen remains. The $NH_3$ in the environment is converted by bacteria into $NO_3$ (nitrate), and this $NO_3$ is taken up

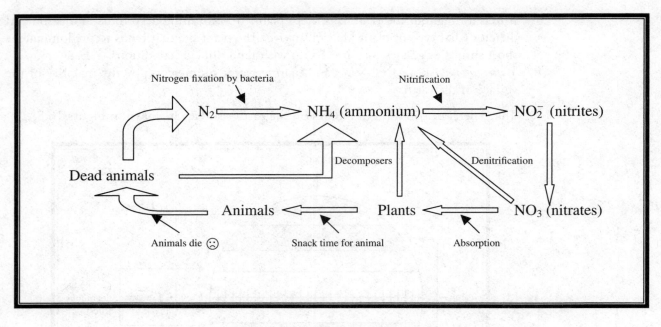

**Figure 18.9  The nitrogen cycle.**

by plants and then eventually by animals to complete the nitrogen cycle. **Denitrification** is the process by which bacteria themselves use nitrates and release $N_2$ as a product.

*Water cycle.* The earth is covered in water. A considerable amount of this water evaporates each day and returns to the clouds. Eventually, this water is returned to the earth in the form of precipitation. This process is termed the **water cycle.**

## ❯ Review Questions

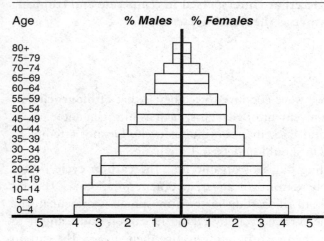

1. How would you describe the population depicted in the age structure graph shown here?

   A.  Growing rapidly
   B.  Growing slowly
   C.  Not growing at all
   D.  Experiencing slow negative growth

2. Carbon is most commonly present in the atmosphere in what form?

   A.  $CCl_4$
   B.  $CO$
   C.  $CO_2$
   D.  $CH_2$

3. Which of the following is a density-dependent limiting factor?

   A.  Flood
   B.  Drought
   C.  Earthquake
   D.  Famine

**4.** The process by which bacteria themselves use the nitrate of the environment, releasing $N_2$ as a product, is called

    A. nitrogen fixation.
    B. abiotic fixation.
    C. denitrification.
    D. chemosynthetic autotrophism.

For question 5, please use the following curve:

**5.** At what point on the graph does the decline in rabbit population act as a limiting factor to the survival of the foxes, leading to a decline in their population size?

    A. A
    B. B
    C. C
    D. D

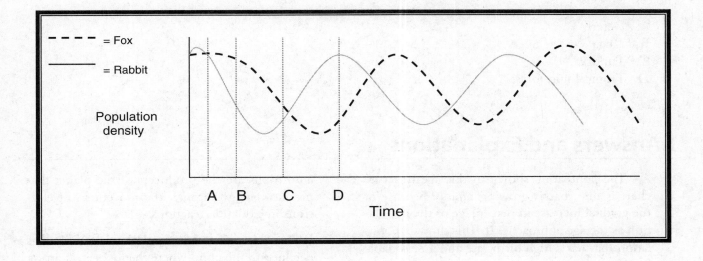

**6.** A collection of all the individuals of an area combined with the environment in which they exist is called a/an

    A. population.
    B. community.
    C. ecosystem.
    D. biosphere.

For questions 7–10, please use the following answer choices:

    A. Aposematic coloration
    B. Batesian mimicry
    C. Müllerian mimicry
    D. Cryptic coloration

**7.** A beetle that has the coloration of a yellow jacket is displaying which defense mechanism?

**8.** A moth whose body color matches that of the trees in which it lives is displaying which defense mechanism?

**9.** Two different lizard species, each possessing a particular chemical defense mechanism and sharing a similar body coloration, are displaying which defense mechanism?

**10.** A lizard with a chemical defense mechanism has a bright-colored body as a warning to predators that it is one tough customer is displaying which defense mechanism?

**11.** Which of the following is *not* a characteristic of a *K*-selected population?

    A. Populations tend to be of a relatively constant size.
    B. Offspring produced tend to require extensive postnatal care.
    C. Primates are classified as *K*-selected organisms.
    D. Offspring are produced in large quantities.

12. Which of the following would have the survivorship curve shown in the following diagram?

    A. Humans
    B. Lizards
    C. Oysters
    D. Fish

For questions 13–16, please use the following answer choices:

    A. Desert
    B. Taiga
    C. Tundra
    D. Tropical rain forest

13. This biome is known for having the most diverse variety of species.

14. This biome is the driest of the land biomes.

15. The predominate plant life of this biome is short shrubs or grasses.

16. This biome is known for its cold, lengthy, and snowy winters and the presence of coniferous forests.

## › Answers and Explanations

1. **A**—The population shown in this age structure chart is one that is growing rapidly because of the gradual increase in percentage of the population as the age approaches 0. This shows a population that has a high birth rate and a reasonable life expectancy.

2. **C**—$CO_2$ is the dominant form of carbon present in the atmosphere.

3. **D**—Density-dependent limiting factors show up as the population approaches and/or passes the carrying capacity. Examples of density-dependent limiting factors include availability of food resources, waste buildup, and density-induced diseases. The other three choices are examples of density-independent factors, which affect population size regardless of how large or small it may be.

4. **C**—*Denitrification* is defined as the process by which bacteria themselves use nitrates and release nitrogen gas as a product. Bacteria also perform the necessary task of nitrogen fixation, which takes atmospheric nitrogen and converts it to $NH_3$. They later take this $NH_3$ and convert it to nitrate, which plants require for photosynthetic success. (*Abiotic fixation* is a term that we made up because it sounded cool.) Chemiosynthetic autotrophs are the producers of the planet that produce energy through the movement of electrons in oxidation reactions.

5. **B**—At this point, the population of rabbits has declined to the point where the foxes are starting to feel the reduction in their food supply. The fox survival curve soon begins its decline, which leads to the revival of the rabbits.

6. **C**—An *ecosystem* consists of all the individuals in the community and the environment in which they exist. A *population* is a collection of individuals of the same species living in the same area. A *community* is a collection of all the different populations of the various species in a geographic area. A *biosphere* is the collection of all the life-containing areas of the planet.

7. **B**—An animal that is harmless copies the appearance of an animal that *is* dangerous as a defense mechanism to make predators think twice about attacking.

8. **D**—Cryptic coloration is the animal kingdom's version of army clothes. Their coloration matches that of their environment so they can blend in and hide from their predators.

9. **C**—Two species that are aposematically colored as an indicator of their chemical defense mechanism mimic each other's color scheme in an effort to increase the speed with which their predators learn to avoid them. This, of course, requires a predator that can learn based on experience.

10. **A**—This defense mechanism is warning coloration adopted by animals that possess a chemical defense mechanism. Ideally, predators will learn to avoid the species, helping the prey survive longer.

11. **D**—*K*-selected populations tend to be populations of a roughly constant size, with low reproductive rates and whose offspring require extensive postnatal care until they have sufficiently matured. *R*-selected populations tend to produce many offspring per birth.

12. **B**—Lizards follow a type II survivorship curve as illustrated in the diagram in review question 12. Humans (answer A) follow a type I curve, while oysters and fish (answers C and D) follow a type III survivorship curve.

13. **D**

14. **A**

15. **C**

16. **B**

## › Rapid Review

The following terms are important in this chapter:

*Population*: collection of individuals of the same species living in the same geographic area.

*Community*: collection of populations of species in a geographic area.

*Ecosystem*: community + environment.

*Biosphere*: communities + ecosystems of planet.

*Biotic components*: living organisms of ecosystem.

*Abiotic components*: nonliving players in ecosystem.

*Dispersion patterns*: **clumped dispersion** (animals live in packs spaced from each other—cattle), **uniform distribution** (species are evenly spaced out across an area, e.g., birds on a wire), **random distribution** (species are randomly distributed across an area, e.g., trees in a forest).

*Biotic potential*: maximum growth rate for a population.

*Carrying capacity*: maximum number of individuals that a population can sustain in a given environment.

*Limiting factors*: factors that keep population size in check: **density-dependent** (food, waste, disease), **density-independent** (weather, natural disasters).

*Population growth*: **exponential growth** (J-shaped curve, unlimited growth), **logistic growth** (S-shaped curve, limited growth).

*Life history strategies*: ***K*-selected populations** (constant size, low reproductive rate, extensive postnatal care—humans); ***R*-selected populations** (rapid growth, J-curve style, little postnatal care, reproduce quickly, die quickly—bacteria).

*Survivorship curves*: show survival rates for different-aged members of a population:

- *Type I*: live long life, until age is reached where death rate increases rapidly—humans, large mammals.

- *Type II*: constant death rate across the age spectrum—lizards, hydra, small mammals.
- *Type III*: steep downward death rate for young individuals that flattens out at certain age—fish, oysters.

### Forms of Species Interaction

- *Parasitism*: one organism benefits at another's expense (tapeworms and humans).
- *Commensalism*: one organism benefits while the other is unaffected (cattle egrets and cattle).
- *Mutualism*: both organisms reap benefits from the interaction (acacia trees and ants, lichen).
- *Competition*: both species are harmed by the interaction (**intraspecific** vs. **interspecific**).
- *Predation*: one species, the predator, hunts the other, the prey.

### Defense Mechanisms

- *Cryptic coloration*: coloring scheme that allows organism to blend into colors of environment.
- *Deceptive markings*: patterns that cause an animal to appear larger or more dangerous than it really is.
- *Aposematic coloration*: warning coloration adopted by animals that possess a chemical defense mechanism.
- *Batesian mimicry*: animal that is harmless copies the appearance of an animal that is dangerous.
- *Müllerian mimicry*: two aposemetrically colored species have a similar coloration pattern.

*Primary succession*: occurs in area devoid of life that contains no soil; **pioneer species** come in, add nutrients, and are replaced by future species, which attract animals to the area, thus adding more nutrients; constant changing of guards until the **climax community** is reached and a steady-state equilibrium is achieved.

*Secondary succession*: occurs in area that once had stable life but was disturbed by major force (fire).

### Biomes: The Special Facts

We recommend that you read the biome material in the chapter for more detail.

- *Desert*: driest land biome.
- *Taiga*: lengthy cold, wet winters; lots of conifers.
- *Temperate grasslands*: most fertile soil of all.
- *Tundra*: permafrost, cold winters, short shrubs.
- *Savanna*: grasslands, home to herbivores.
- *Deciduous forest*: cold winters/warm summers.
- *Tropical forest*: greatest diversity of species.
- *Water biomes*: freshwater and marine biomes of earth.

*Trophic levels*: hierarchy of energy levels on a planet; energy level decreases from bottom to top (Figure 18.7); primary producers (bottom) → primary consumers (herbivores) → secondary consumers → tertiary consumers → decomposers.

# CHAPTER 19

# Laboratory Review

**IN THIS CHAPTER**

**Summary:** This chapter covers the 13 laboratory experiments that are included in the AP Biology curriculum.

**Key Ideas**

✪ Hands-on lab work and understanding the process of science are central parts of AP Biology. Translation—LEARN THESE WELL!

✪ Read the summaries found here and review the work that you did on the labs during the year.

✪ If you missed one of these labs in class, or just do not feel comfortable with the material even after reading this chapter, ask your teacher to go over the lab with you.

## Introduction

In this chapter we take a look at each of the 13 lab experiments that are included in the AP Biology curriculum. We summarize the major objectives from each experiment and the major skills and conclusions that you should remember. This chapter is important, so do not just brush it aside if lab experiments are not your cup of tea. Experimental (data) analysis will be heavily emphasized on the exam, in both the multiple-choice and the essay sections. Of course, the questions will not be an exact duplication of the experiment, but they will test your understanding of the objectives and main ideas that are discussed in this chapter. So, only 13 experiments separate us and the end of the review material for this exam.

All of the investigations in this chapter have multiple parts, including the opportunity for you to go crazy and create your own investigation. We have no idea what kind of mad-scientist experiment you might design, so we will instead focus on the more straightforward portions of these labs, including a summary of what the key ideas are from each investigation.

# Investigation 1: Artificial Selection

**BIG IDEA 1**
*Evolution*

This lab focuses on the role of *differential reproduction* in natural selection, meaning some organisms in a population reproduce more than others and leave more offspring. But instead of it being "natural" selection, it's "artificial" because *you* get to choose which organisms are allowed to reproduce!

## Basic Setup

For natural selection to occur, first there needs to be variation in a population, right? Well, look closely at the Wisconsin Fast Plants that you'll be working with. Do you see any trait that you could easily measure (e.g., leaf color, hairiness, height)? Are there any variations in this particular trait? It should not be something that is a clear-cut yes or no, but rather a trait that exhibits a range. Now you get to make selection decisions! You will choose the top (or bottom) 10 percent of your plants with this trait, and those lucky few are the ones allowed to reproduce. You will transfer pollen between this pool of "winners" and, once the seeds develop, plant and grow your second generation of plants. Once again, you will measure your chosen trait in this second population.

## Results

In this experiment you are essentially choosing which genes are passed to the next generation. By artificially selecting, say, only the purplest of the plants, you are ensuring that the next generation will have inherited those "purpley" genes. You will hopefully observe an increase (or decrease, depending on your investigation) of your chosen trait in the second population of plants. This is called *directional selection*. Considering that one of the requirements of this class is your ability to graph and analyze data, it would probably be an excellent idea for you to create a bar graph to compare the quantity of your trait between these two generations. Are the means significantly different?

Don't forget to keep this a controlled experiment! Did you measure the trait of your first-generation plants when they were nine days old? Remember to measure the second generation *at the same age, using the same method.*

## Key Skills

- Graph your data.
- Explain how natural selection acts on phenotypes.
- Use data to show how a measurable trait is changing in your plant population.

# Investigation 2: Mathematical Modeling: Hardy-Weinberg

**BIG IDEA 1**
*Evolution*

This investigation lets you build upon what you learned from Investigation 1: the idea of natural selection and how it changes a population. If you truly wanted to see if a population was evolving, you would track the frequency of alleles and how they change from generation to generation. To do so, you first need to determine what your population's alleles look like *right now*, before any funky evolutionary stuff happens. This information can then be used as a point of comparison to see if the allelic frequencies are indeed changing in your population. The Hardy-Weinberg equilibrium is used to describe a population that is in stasis, or not evolving. Your goal in this lab is to model how allele frequencies change in a generation of some imaginary population, and you will do this using a computer model.

## Basic Setup

On the AP Biology exam, will you have to open up a spreadsheet file and correctly enter a formula? No. Will you have to understand how to use the Hardy-Weinberg equilibrium and how to correctly analyze the data obtained? You bet! The idea to understand is how the fitness of an allele affects its frequency in a population. For example, there are two alleles for a given gene: A and a. If a population is in Hardy-Weinberg equilibrium (i.e., not evolving), and the frequency of both alleles is 0.5 (meaning one half of the alleles in this population's gene pool is the dominant A form, whereas the other half is in the recessive a form), then it will remain that way for gazillions of generations. But how could you make that ratio change? That, my friend, is evolution, and that is the point of this lab. Using tools such as computer programs and spreadsheets, you can model how a hypothetical gene pool changes from generation to generation.

## Results

Though the bulk of this lab was dedicated to creating your spreadsheet, the real investigation begins when you get to tweak your non-evolving population. The equations you have to know for this experiment are $p + q = 1$ and $p^2 + 2pq + q^2 = 1$. Chapter 12 lists the five conditions required for the existence of Hardy-Weinberg equilibrium:

1. No mutations
2. No gene flow
3. No genetic drift (large population size)
4. No natural selection (so that the traits are neutral; none gives an advantage or disadvantage)
5. Random mating

If any of these five conditions does not hold true, then the population will experience microevolution, and the frequencies of the alleles will be subject to change.

Using your computer model, you can design an experiment to measure the effect of selection, heterozygote advantage, and genetic drift:

- *Selection.* Imagine that an individual homozygous recessive for a condition does not survive to reproduce. Because the aa offspring would not survive to reproduce, this will cause a shift in allele frequencies to include more A children and fewer a children.
- *Heterozygote advantage.* This is a situation in which being heterozygous for a condition provides some benefit (e.g., sickle cell allele in malarial regions). In this case, the allele will still decrease, but not as fast as in the selection example.
- *Genetic drift.* Imagine that 60 percent of your hypothetical population were killed in some horrific environmental disaster. This would leave the remaining 40 percent to continue breeding and passing on genes to the next generation. The random nature in which organisms are eliminated can lead to a shift in the allele frequency and the $p$ and $q$ will probably change depending on the genotype of those who are left behind.

There are two questions to ponder as you finish this experiment:

1. *Why is it so difficult to eliminate a recessive allele?* It is difficult because the allele remains in the population, hidden as part of the heterozygous condition, safe from selection, which can act only against genes that are expressed. So, although the $q$ for a population may decline, it will not disappear completely because of the $pq$ individuals.

2. *Why does heterozygote advantage protect recessive genes from being eliminated?* Those who are heterozygous for the condition are receiving some benefit. For example, those who have sickle trait are protected against malaria. This positive benefit for heterozygous individuals helps keep the recessive condition alive in the population.

### Key Skills

- Use data from a changing population and analyze it using the Hardy-Weinberg equation.
- Explain how data from using this equation demonstrates genetic drift and the effects of selection.

# Investigation 3: Comparing DNA Sequences to Understand Evolutionary Relationships with BLAST

**BIG IDEA 1**
*Evolution*

Say you found a brand-new fossilized creature buried in your backyard, and you want to find its closest living relative. Or maybe you identified a single gene that causes disease in hedgehogs and you want to know if that same gene is found in humans. This lab focuses on the use of BLAST (Basic Local Alignment Search Tool) as a tool to answer such questions. In addition, it incorporates the use of cladograms. A cladogram is a visual representation of the evolutionary relatedness of a species. In this investigation, you will use BLAST to generate the information needed to construct a cladogram.

### Basic Setup

Given a genetic sequence, you are required to use the online BLAST software to compare it to other gene sequences already in their gigantic database. Results will show a ranking of the most closely related organisms (and what percentage of their base pairs actually match up). Just as in the previous lab, you won't have a computer available to you during the AP exam, so no, you won't have to actually know how to use BLAST while taking the test. You will, however, most likely need to analyze data obtained from a hypothetical BLAST query and, from those results, generate a cladogram depicting evolutionary relatedness.

### Results

By determining the percent similarity of an unknown gene with those from other organisms, you should be able to then place your unknown creature within a cladogram to show evolutionary relatedness. For example, say you had a table showing the percent similarity of "gene X" in humans versus four other species (see Table 19.1).

If you drew a cladogram showing the evolutionary relationship, it would look something like Figure 19.1.

**Table 19.1   Percent similarity between gene X in humans and other species.**

| SPECIES | GENE PERCENT SIMILARITY COMPARED TO HUMANS |
|---------|--------------------------------------------|
| A       | 98%                                        |
| B       | 91%                                        |
| C       | 70%                                        |
| D       | 52%                                        |

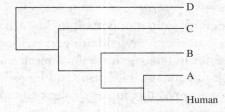

**Figure 19.1    Cladogram for percent similarity between gene X in humans and other species. The closer two species reside on a clade, the closer they are genetically related.**

### Key Skills

- Explain the relationship between genetic sequences and evolutionary relatedness.
- Draw and/or analyze a cladogram that shows evolutionary relationships.

# Investigation 4: Diffusion and Osmosis

**BIG IDEA 2**

*Cellular Processes: Energy, Communication, and Homeostasis*

This investigation draws on information covered in Chapter 6, Cells. If you feel uncomfortable with this material, take a few moments to flip back to Chapter 6 and scan through the information about diffusion, osmosis, and cell transport. In summary, osmosis occurs from an area of high water potential to an area of low water potential. In a given solution, the higher the solute concentration, the lower that solution's water potential.

## Part 1: Surface Area and Cell Size

### Basic Setup for Part 1

Besides turning your fingers blue, this lab will demonstrate the relationship between surface area and volume and how this ratio affects diffusion rates in a cell. Your cell model is a block of agar that contains an indicator dye that changes color when the pH drops. You're given a chunk of this blue agar to carve into three different block sizes, each with differing surface area–to–volume ratios (SA:V). Each block is dropped into a solution, and as the liquid diffuses into the agar, the pH causes a change in agar color. This enables you to easily track the amount of time it takes for diffusion to be completed.

### Results for Part 1

It's all about a large surface area–to–volume ratio. The block with the biggest SA:V ratio wins the race. For example, say you have three sizes of agar blocks:

block 1 = 1 cm × 1 cm × 1 cm
block 2 = 2 cm × 2 cm × 2 cm
block 3 = 1 cm × 1 cm × 8 cm

You should be able to calculate both the volume ($cm^3$) and the surface area ($cm^2$) for each of these blocks. (Remember: formulas will be provided for you on the AP exam!)

| BLOCK | VOLUME ($cm^3$) | SURFACE AREA ($cm^2$) | SA:V |
|-------|-----------------|------------------------|------|
| 1 | 1 | 6 | 6 |
| 2 | 8 | 24 | 3 |
| 3 | 8 | 34 | 4.25 |

Notice that even though blocks 2 and 3 have the same volume, their surface areas are different. This results in diffusion taking longer in block 2 than it does in block 3.

### Key Concept

- A high SA:V ratio is important for any cell that relies on a high diffusion rate. If you were a tiny bacterium, your health and well-being would be dependent on quickly getting good stuff in (glucose for cellular respiration!) and bad stuff out (metabolic waste). The linings of your small intestine and lungs have many folds in order to create the highest surface area possible in the smallest amount of space and thereby facilitate diffusion of food monomers or oxygen molecules.

## Part 2: Modeling Diffusion and Osmosis

### Basic Setup for Part 2

Now you get to create a model of a cell using dialysis tubing. Just like a real cell, the tubing is selectively permeable to water and some solutes. The point of this lab investigation is to use different solutions to model how water potential influences osmosis.

### Results for Part 2

Say you filled your dialysis bag with a 1 Molar (1 M) sucrose solution, weighed it, and placed it in a beaker of 1 M NaCl solution. After 30 minutes, you weigh the bag again and—voilà!—it got lighter! That means it lost some water, right? Can you use water potential to show why that makes sense? Recall that you can calculate the solute potential for a solution with this equation:

$$\Psi_S = iCRT, \text{ where } i = \text{ionization constant and } C = \text{molarity}$$

The molarities are equal for both of these solutions, so the ionization constant is the deciding factor. NaCl ionizes and sucrose does not! So for NaCl, i = 2, whereas for sucrose i = 1. Therefore, the NaCl solution has a higher solute potential; or, in other words, it is a hypertonic solution compared to your dialysis tubing "cell." Therefore, water will diffuse out of the bag into the surrounding NaCl solution.

### Key Concepts

- Osmosis occurs from an area of high water potential to low water potential.
- A cell's environment allows you to make predictions about molecular movement through cell membranes.

## Part 3: Observing Osmosis in Living Cells

### Basic Setup for Part 3

Here you get to work with pretty, color-coded (unlabeled) sucrose solutions ranging from 0.0 M up to 1.0 M, and use potato cores to figure out the relative concentrations of these solutions. To take it one step further, you can then calculate percent change in weight of your potato cores and determine the water potential of the potato tissue. Remember that the bigger the difference in water potential between a cell and the solution, the bigger the movement of water (either into or out of the cells).

### Results for Part 3

Once you calculate the potatoes' percent change in weight for each of the unknown solutions, you can arrange them from most negative to most positive. A supernegative percent change in weight indicates a significant loss of water; a highly hypertonic solution increases water loss from cells. The more negative the number, the higher the molarity of the solution! The same is true for superpositive percent change in weight. That means the potato cores gained a lot of water, which happens in a hypotonic solution. The greater the weight gain, the lower the molarity of the solution.

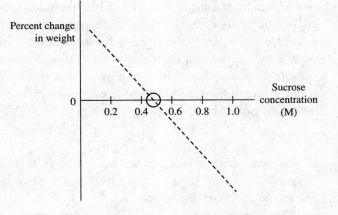

**Figure 19.2    Potato core change in weight.**

What if you wanted to determine the actual water potential (molarity) of the potato? It's easy, once you remember that if the water potential of the solution equals that of the cells, there is no net change in weight. If you graph your percent changes in weight, you can estimate the potato's water potential (see Figure 19.2).

The point where the line crosses the *x*-axis indicates the molarity when there would be no net change in weight. Therefore, 0.5 M is the approximate molarity (or, in this case, water potential) of your potato!

One final thought about your data: Although we often focus on quantitative (numerical) measurements in our labs, qualitative observations are still very important. When you removed your potato cores from the solution, did they feel different? Floppy and bendy? That would suggest that the cells lost water because they were in a hypertonic solution (the higher molarities). Was the potato core rigid, and would it snap if you bent it? That would suggest that it was in a hypotonic (low molarity) solution and water flowed into the cells, increasing their turgor pressure.

### Key Concepts (for All Three Procedures)

- A high surface area–to–volume ratio increases diffusion rates.
- A cell that relies on diffusion would evolve to have a high SA:V ratio.
- Water diffuses from an area of high to low water potential.

**KEY IDEA**

# Investigation 5: Photosynthesis

**BIG IDEA 2**

*Cellular Processes: Energy, Communication, and Homeostasis*

Photosynthesis is a complex (and possibly confusing) metabolic process through which autotrophs generate glucose by first converting the sun's light energy into the chemical form that all living cells use (ATP). If you wish to design a lab to track the rate of photosynthesis, how would you do it? Measure glucose production? Carbon dioxide use? Maybe focus on the light reaction's reduction of the electron carrier NAD+ into its reduced form (NADH) as in the DPIP lab? Well, some of the best experiments are the simplest, so let's watch little pieces of a leaf float in water as oxygen is produced as a by-product of photosynthesis.

### Basic Setup

This is a cool way to measure photosynthetic rates, based on the amount of oxygen produced. Little leaf disks are put in a large syringe with some slightly soapy water (this helps break surface tension). The little disks float on top of the water, which introduces the challenging part of the lab: getting them to sink. A vacuum must be created in the syringe to pull out the atmospheric gases from the spongy mesophyll layer in the leaf tissue. This takes a bit of trial and error, but once it is accomplished, the disks will slowly drift to the bottom of the syringe. The contents of the syringe are dumped into a cup filled with a sodium bicarbonate solution and put under light. As more photosynthesis occurs, more oxygen is produced:

$$6CO_2 + 6H_2O \rightarrow C_6H_{12}O_6 + 6O_2$$

If you look closely, you can see tiny bubbles forming on your leaf disks! Once enough oxygen is produced (and caught within the internal leaf space), the little disks will begin to rise to the top very slowly.

Here's a question: if your leaf pieces are photosynthesizing, where are they getting the necessary carbon dioxide? When sodium bicarbonate ionizes in water, it provides an alternative source of carbon dioxide for the plant.

### Results

The investigative part of the lab allows you to explore variables that you think might influence photosynthesis in your leaf disks. Do the levels of $CO_2$ effect photosynthesis? How about amount of light? Regardless of your choice of variable, perform the same leaf disk analysis and compare the amount of time it takes for half of your disks to rise ($ET_{50}$, or estimated time it takes 50 percent of the disks to float) in both your control and experimental groups.

### Key Concepts

- A lot of photosynthesis means a lot of oxygen production.
- Light increases the rate of photosynthesis.
- Carbon dioxide was provided by dissolved sodium bicarbonate.

# Investigation 6: Cellular Respiration

**BIG IDEA 2**

*Cellular Processes: Energy, Communication, and Homeostasis*

If you would like to see how different environmental conditions affect an organism's respiration rate, this is the lab for you! In this investigation you will use a respirometer (or microrespirometer) to track the respiration rate of seeds. Based on the equation for cellular respiration, $C_6H_{12}O_6 + 6O_2 \rightarrow 6CO_2 + 6H_2O$, how would you measure respiration rates?

There are, in fact, three ways to measure respiration:

1. *Oxygen consumption:* how much $O_2$ is actually consumed
2. *Carbon dioxide production:* how much $CO_2$ is actually produced
3. *Energy released during respiration:* how much energy is released

### Basic Setup

This experiment examines germinating peas by measuring the volume of gas that surrounds the peas at certain intervals in an effort to determine the rate of respiration. Two gases contribute to the volume around the pea: $O_2$ and $CO_2$. How can we use the amount of oxygen consumed during respiration as our measuring point if $CO_2$ is present as well? Something needs to be done with the $CO_2$ released during respiration. Otherwise we would not get a true representation of how much the volume is changing as a result of oxygen consumption. The $CO_2$ would skew the numbers by making it appear as if less $O_2$ were being consumed.

The $CO_2$ problem can be handled by adding potassium hydroxide, which reacts with $CO_2$ to produce $K_2CO_3$. This reaction allows us to limit the number of variables that could be affecting the volume around our beloved peas to

1. Change in the volume of oxygen
2. Change in the temperature ($PV = nRT$)
3. Change in the pressure of the surrounding atmosphere

Aerobic respiration requires and uses oxygen. So, one would expect the volume of oxygen around the pea to decline as respiration occurs. The reactions of interest for this experiment occur in a tubelike device known as a **respirometer**. To calculate the change in volume that occurs with these peas, one first has to measure the initial volume around the peas. A control group must then be set up that consists of peas that are not currently germinating and will have a rate of respiration lower than that of germinating seeds. This will give the experimenter a baseline with which to compare the respiration rate of the germinating seeds. Since temperature and pressure are also able to affect the volume around the peas, it is important to set up another control group that can calculate the change in volume that is due to temperature and pressure as opposed to respiration. Any changes in this control group should be subtracted from the changes found in the germinating seeds to determine how much of the volume change is actually due to oxygen consumption and respiration.

Just a side thought: Can you imagine how awkward it could have been if one of Mendel's lab partners had decided to run this experiment? I can see it now: Mendel walks into the lab and asks, "Has anyone seen my peas? After seven long years, I've nearly completed my research. Just need to tally up that last generation of peas. . . . Very exciting. . . . Hmm. . . . I thought my peas were sitting here on this desk by my respirometer."

## Results

1. Germinating seeds consume *more* oxygen than do nongerminating seeds. This makes sense, because they have more reactions going on.
2. Seeds germinating at a lower temperature consume *less* oxygen than do seeds germinating at a higher temperature.
3. You can determine how much oxygen is consumed by watching how much water is drawn into the pipettes as the experiment proceeds. (Refer to your classroom lab manual if you are confused by the pipette portion of this lab.) This water is drawn in as a result of the drop in pressure caused by the consumption of oxygen during respiration.

## Key Concepts

- A respirometer measures respiration rates by tracking the amount of oxygen being used in cellular respiration.
- Warm conditions usually speed up cellular respiration; cold slows it down.

# Investigation 7: Cell Division: Mitosis and Meiosis

**BIG IDEA 3**

*Genetics and Information Transfer*

This experiment draws on information found in Chapter 9, Cell Division.

## Part 1: Onion Roots Treated with a Mitosis-Inducing Chemical

### Basic Setup for Part 1

Your goal is to see if there is a greater number of cells undergoing mitosis in root cells treated with lectin, a chemical that induces mitosis. Either you or your teacher will prepare slides of these root cells, and you will then count the number of cells either in interphase or in mitosis. Since you need a point of comparison, you will do similar counts with root cells that have not been treated with this chemical (the control).

**Results for Part 1**

So, how are you supposed to estimate how much time cells on a slide in front of you spend in either mitosis or interphase? Say, for example, that you record your findings and get the following breakdown: For your control, of 300 cells examined, 268 are in interphase and 32 cells are in one of the stages of mitosis (prophase, metaphase, anaphase, or telophase). This would mean that the cell spent 89.3 percent of its time in interphase. At any moment in time, 89.3 percent of the cells are in interphase. Here's how to get that number. Take the number of cells in interphase, 268, and divide that by the number of cells examined, 300. The result is 0.893. Move the decimal point two places to the right to get the percentage, 89.3 percent. By the same logic, these data also show that 10.7 percent are in mitosis. For comparison, let's say the chemically treated slide had 210 cells in interphase and 40 in mitosis (for a total of 250 cells examined).

Now, once you count your mitotic versus interphase cells for both treated and untreated roots, you need to use chi-square analysis to check if the difference is significant:

$$x^2 = \sum \frac{(o-e)^2}{e}$$

Do not panic! Even though that equation may seem intimidating, it's really not that bad. First, determine how many of your treated cells would be in mitosis *if the chemical didn't have any effect.* In other words, if 10.7 percent of your control cells were stuck in mitosis, you'd expect that same percentage in your treated group: (250 treated cells) × (0.107) = ~27 cells in mitosis. That leaves the remaining 223 cells in interphase (if you didn't expect that mitosis-inducing chemical to do its job). So now you use chi-square analysis to compare what you actually saw in your chemically treated cells (40 in mitosis and 210 in interphase) to see if there are, in fact, significantly more cells stuck in mitosis. In other words, your null hypothesis is that the treatment did not make a difference. If you find that the chi-square value is greater than the critical value, you reject this null hypothesis in favor of the experimental hypothesis (the chemical likely *did* make a difference). See Table 19.2.

As you can see, your chi-square value is 0.758 + 6.26 = 7.02. To determine your critical value, you must choose a *p* value (usually 0.05) and the degrees of freedom. The degrees of freedom (df) equals the number of groups minus one. In this lab, there are two groups, interphase and mitosis; therefore, df = 2 − 1, or 1. Based on the chi-square table (which will be provided for you on the AP exam), your degrees of freedom equals 3.38. Since your calculated chi-square value (7.02) was bigger than 3.38, you can reject the null hypothesis that said the treatment made *no* difference. The chemical did increase the number of cells in mitosis.

**Table 19.2  Chi-Square Table for Investigation 7.**

|  | # OBSERVED (o) | # EXPECTED (e) | (o − e) | (o − e)² | (o − e)²/e |
|---|---|---|---|---|---|
| Interphase cells | 210 | 223 | −13 | 169 | 0.758 |
| Mitosis cells | 40 | 27 | 13 | 169 | 6.26 |

**Key Skill**

- Analyze data using chi-square analysis. You can be sure that the AP exam will have at least one question asking you to do this. This lab is excellent practice for such a question.

## Part 2: Meiosis and Crossover in *Sordaria*

### Basic Setup and Results for Part 2

The title to this section makes *Sordaria* sound like some posh vacation spot in Europe. In reality it is a haploid ascomycete fungus. Anyway, the final portion of this experiment looks at the crossover that occurs during meiosis of this fungus and briefly discusses how recombination maps can be created using such data. Meiosis in *Sordaria* results in the formation of eight haploid **ascospores,** each of which can develop into a new haploid fungus. Crossover in *Sordaria* can be observed by making hybrids between wild-type and mutant strains. Wild-type *Sordaria* have black ascospores, and mutants have different colored ascospores (e.g., tan). When mycelia of these two strains come together and undergo meiosis, and if no crossover occurs, the asci that develop will contain four black and four tan ascospores in a 4:4 pattern. If crossover occurs, the ratio will change to either 2:2:2:2 or 2:4:2.

Chapter 10, Heredity, discusses gene maps constructed from crossover frequencies. You would construct the map here by first determining the percentage of asci that showed crossover. Referring to Figure 19.3, count the number of 2:2:2:2 and 2:4:2 asci and divide that sum into the total number of offspring. This result multiplied by 100 will give the crossover percentage. This number can then be used to determine how far away the gene is from the centromere. The crossover percentage is divided by 2 to determine this distance because a crossover involves only half the spores in each ascus.

**Key Skill**

- Explain how meiosis and crossing over leads to increased genetic diversity.

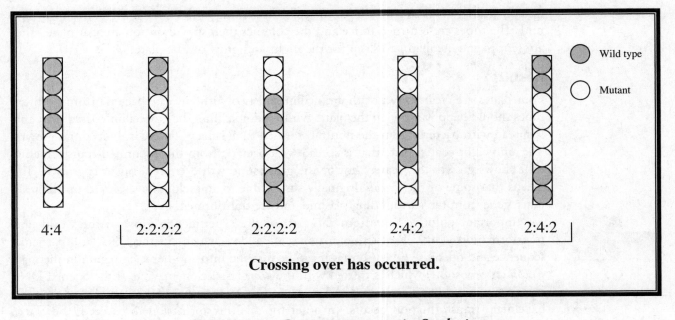

**Figure 19.3 Crossover patterns in *Sordaria*.**

# Investigation 8: Biotechnology: Bacterial Transformation

**BIG IDEA 3**
*Genetics and Information Transfer*

This experiment deals with material from Chapter 11, Molecular Genetics. This is the kind of experiment that can make you feel like a biotech junkie. Here, you use plasmids to move DNA from one cell to another cell—**transformation.** You get to play with restriction enzymes, *E. coli* (*Escherichia coli*—eww), and gel electrophoresis.

Full understanding of this experiment requires a basic knowledge of

1. What vectors are and how they are made
2. What gel electrophoresis is and how it works
3. What a restriction enzyme is and why it is so important to the field of biotechnology

You will find all this information waiting for you in Chapter 11. We are not going to cave in and explain to you now what those things are. That is something you should do on your own.

OK, we'll tell you now. . . . *Escherichia coli* (usually abbreviated *E. coli*) is a bacteria that is present in everyone's intestinal tract. It grows in the laboratory as well and contains extrachromosomal DNA circles called **plasmids.** This experiment deals with the process of *transformation:* the uptake of foreign DNA from the surrounding environment. This is made possible by the presence of proteins on the surface of cells that snag pieces of DNA from around the cell; these DNA pieces are from closely related species.

The goal of this experiment is to take a bacterial strain that has ampicillin resistance, and transfer the gene for this resistance to a strain that dies when exposed to ampicillin. After attempting to transform the bacteria, the experimenter can check to see if it was successful by growing the potentially transformed bacteria on a plate containing ampicillin. If it grows as if all is well, the transformation has succeeded. If nothing grows, something has gone wrong.

## Basic Setup

A colony of *E. coli* is added to each of two test tubes. In one tube a solution is added that contains a plasmid that carries the ampicillin-resistance gene; the other tube receives no such plasmid. The waiting game follows, and after 15 minutes on ice, the two tubes are quickly heated in an effort to shock the cells into taking in the foreign DNA from the plasmid. The tubes are returned to ice and the colonies then spread out on an agar plate. They are sent to the incubator to sleep for the night and grow on the plate.

## Results

Four plates are created: two with ampicillin and two without. The bacteria from both test tubes should happily grow on the plates without ampicillin. The ampicillin-coated plate that is spread with bacteria from the nontransformed tube is bare—there is, indeed, no growth. The ampicillin-coated plate that is spread with bacteria from the attempted-transformation tube shows growth . . . it may not be the greatest growth ever seen, but it is growth. This means that some of the *E. coli* originally susceptible to ampicillin have picked up the resistance gene from the surrounding plasmid and are transformed.

KEY IDEA

Important point to take from this part of the experiment: "How in the world does transformation work?" Restriction enzymes are added, which cut the DNA at a particular sequence and open the DNA so that it can be inserted into another such region in the main *E. coli* chromosome, which is treated with the *same* restriction enzyme. If the opened DNA from the plasmid happens to find and attach to DNA of the *E. coli* that is added to the tube, hallelujah, transformation occurs. In order for this transformation to succeed, the *E. coli* must be **competent,** which means ready to accept the foreign DNA from the environment.

This competence is ensured by treating the cells with calcium or magnesium. Don't worry too much about how this competence business really works. Just know that bacteria must be competent for transformation to occur.

### Key Concepts

- DNA works the same for all cells, both eukaryotic and prokaryotic.
- By adding a gene (changing an organism's genotype), you can change how it looks (its phenotype).
- Environmental factors can affect gene expression! If lactose is present, *E. coli*'s lac operon will turn on.

# Investigation 9: Biotechnology: Restriction Enzyme Analysis of DNA

**BIG IDEA 3**
*Genetics and Information Transfer*

The three activities in this lab all work together to analyze and compare DNA sequences. For example, after cutting DNA samples from two different people with the same restriction enzymes, you would see that the RFLP patterns produced by gel electrophoresis are different. Do you have no idea what that last sentence even means? Read on . . .

## Activity 1: Restriction Enzymes

Restriction enzymes are special because they are very picky about their job—they cut DNA at very specific sequences, called *restriction sites*. Many restriction sites are a 4- to 10-nucleotide base pair (bp) palindrome, a sequence that reads the same from either direction. If a restriction enzyme cuts exactly in the center of the restriction site, it will create blunt ends; if it cuts the backbone in two places, the pieces will have single-stranded overhanging "sticky" ends with exposed hydrogen bonds. If you cut two different DNA sequences with the same restriction enzyme, and if sticky ends are created, you could use ligase to then glue two sequences together, even if the DNA was not originally from the same organism! That is called a recombinant DNA molecule, and it is the basis of many biotechnological wonders. For example, if you isolate the human insulin gene with a restriction enzyme, and use that same enzyme to cut open a bacterial plasmid, you could glue the human gene into the plasmid. That's how therapeutic insulin is produced today (thank you, *E. coli*).

## Activity 2: DNA Mapping Using Restriction Enzymes

Say you wanted to identify somebody based on his or her DNA. You hear about it all the time, but how is it actually done? Using those restriction enzymes we just talked about, you can cut up a sample of DNA and look at the sizes of the distinct little pieces you have created (this requires gel electrophoresis—more on that in a bit). Everyone has a unique pattern of different lengths of DNA fragments. Restriction mapping is a way to create an organism's unique genetic "fingerprint." These unique DNA fragments are called restriction fragment length polymorphisms (RFLPs). But how do you arrange these little pieces in such a way that you can compare the DNA of two or more people? Once again, read on . . .

## Activity 3: Gel Electrophoresis

Another important biotechnological tool is gel electrophoresis. Gel electrophoresis is a lab technique used to separate DNA on the basis of size. When there is an electric current running from one end of the gel to the other, the fragments of DNA dumped into the wells at the head of the gel will migrate to the other side, with the smaller pieces moving the fastest. The more voltage there is running through the gel, the *faster* the DNA will migrate. The longer the voltage is run through the gel, the *farther* the DNA will migrate. The more DNA cut by the same restriction enzymes you put into each well, the *thicker* the bands will be on the gel. If you reverse the flow of the current on the gel, the DNA will migrate in the opposite direction. The DNA just wants to go toward the positive charge . . . optimists, we suppose.

> **Important Facts About Electrophoresis**
> 1. DNA migrates from negative to positive charges.
> 2. Smaller DNA travels faster than larger DNA.
> 3. The DNA migrates only when the current is running.
> 4. The more voltage that runs through the gel, the faster the DNA migrates.
> 5. The more time the current runs through the gel, the farther the DNA goes.

### Key Concepts

- Understand how to use restriction enzymes and gel electrophoresis to create genetic profiles.
- The pattern made by RFLP using gel electrophoresis will look different for each individual.

## Investigation 10: Energy Dynamics

**BIG IDEA 4**
*Interactions*

You will create a simple model of an ecosystem, with a single producer (plant) and a single consumer (caterpillars). Producers are so important because they capture the sun's energy and convert it into a form that can be used by us nonphotosynthetic organisms (consumers). The term **gross productivity** refers to the total amount of energy captured by producers. The **net productivity** is the amount of that energy that is actually stored by the plant (and thus is available for consumers to munch on).

As you may recall, the second law of thermodynamics says that energy transfer is never 100 percent efficient. This lab demonstrates that fact by tracking energy as it travels through a food chain. Specifically, how much of a plant's energy is actually used by the caterpillars who eat it? How much is applied to the caterpillar's growth, and how much is burned up in cellular respiration? Also, be aware that this lab has the best procedure direction of the entire year: you get to mass the frass (more on that in a bit).

### Basic Setup

You will determine the total weight of all your caterpillars at the beginning of the investigation and then, after they feed for three days, weigh them again. Their change in mass was fueled by the plants they ate. The question is what percentage of that plant's energy was actually turned into caterpillar mass? If you determine the plant energy consumed by each larva, and also take into consideration the amount of their food that wasn't actually used (caterpillar poop, also called "frass"), then you're left with the amount of the producer's energy that was used for the caterpillar's metabolism. Furthermore, if you knew the amount of plant energy consumed by the larva, and subtracted from that both the energy lost in the poop and energy used for the caterpillar's increase in mass, what you're left with is the energy used in respiration.

## Results

You should find that, no, energy transfer isn't perfect. All of that plant's energy was not, in fact, transferred to and used by the caterpillars.

## Key Concepts

- Understand how this lab relates to the idea of how living organisms use free energy.
- Biomass is the mass of living tissue minus any water weight.

# Investigation 11: Transpiration

**BIG IDEA 4**
*Interactions*

This experiment takes the concepts found in Chapter 6 of the text and applies them to the material in Chapter 14, Plants. You might want to review the material on plant anatomy and vascular tissue before you begin.

Here is just a quick reminder of how water moves from the soil to the leaves and branches of a plant. Three minor players in the transport of water are capillary action, osmosis, and root pressure. Water is drawn into the xylem (the water superhighway for the plant) by osmosis. The osmotic driving force is created by the absorption of minerals from the soil, increasing the solute concentration within the xylem. Once in the xylem, root pressure aids in pushing the water a small way up the superhighway. The main driving force for the movement of water in a plant from root to shoot is transpiration. When water evaporates from the plant, it causes an upward tug on the remaining water in the xylem, pulling it toward the shoots. The cohesive nature of water molecules contributes to this transpiration-induced driving force of water through the xylem of the plants. Water molecules like to stick together, and when one of their kind is pulled in a certain direction, the rest seem to follow.

This experiment examines various environmental factors that affect the rate of transpiration: air movement, humidity, light intensity, and temperature. The rate of transpiration increases with increased air movement, decreased humidity, increased light intensity, and increased temperature. It is not hard to remember that increased temperature leads to increased transpiration—think about how much more you sweat when it is hot. It also makes sense that decreased humidity would lead to an increase in the rate of transpiration. When it is less humid, there is less moisture in the air, and thus there is more of a driving force for water to leave the plant. Imagine that you are standing with a 40-watt bulb shining on your neck, and then a 100-watt bulb shining on your neck. The higher-wattage bulb will probably cause you to sweat more. The same thing with plants: the higher the intensity of the light, the more transpiration that occurs. Air movement is less obvious. If there is good airflow, then evaporated water on leaves is removed more quickly, increasing the driving force for more water to transpire from the plant.

## Basic Setup

One easy and straightforward way to measure water loss is by measuring the entire plant's mass every day for about a week. This "whole plant" method requires you to tightly seal a plastic sandwich bag around the root ball so the only water loss is through the leaves. Furthermore, if the poor plant is even *thinking* about flowering, you need to ensure that it does not do so (pull off any flowers or buds). Once you understand this basic setup, the real fun begins: inquiry! Think of some variables that may affect transpiration from your poor plants. Sun? Wind? It's up to you. One plant will be your control, and every other plant will be assigned a single variable. Take the weights of your little guys as soon as they're all ready to go; this will be your *time zero* weights. Then measure the weights again 24 hours later, for as many days as your teacher indicates. Remember that if a leaf falls off during this experiment, it has to stay with the plant for subsequent weighings. When your data collection is over, you need to determine the best way to compare results between treatments. Just looking at the total change in weight doesn't really get you anywhere; it's hard to compare if the initial plant weights were different to begin with. Calculating percent change would help. But what if you need to determine the total surface area ($cm^2$) of your leaves? The idea of outlining each and every leaf on a piece of grid paper makes even the most dedicated AP Biology student weep, so here's a suggestion: Calculate the surface area for only one lucky little leaf, and then weigh it. Now you have a conversion ratio (SA/g) you can use to determine the (approximate) surface area for all the leaves. All you need to do is determine how much all those leaves weigh. Easy!

Another method of measuring water loss is by using a device called a potometer. This tracks transpiration from only part of a plant that has been inserted into a water-filled tube with a pipette stuck on the other end. As water evaporates from the leaves, the water is pulled down the pipette, allowing you to track changes in volume.

## Results

Ideally, any treatment that increased water loss through either more photosynthesis (e.g., light) or more evaporation from the leaf surfaces (e.g., wind) would decrease your plant's weight. On the flip side, if you slow down transpiration by creating a humid environment (e.g., misting your plant) or slow down photosynthesis (e.g., stick the poor plant in the dark), you would expect water loss to be slowed.

### Key Concepts

- The higher the leaf surface area, the greater the rate of transpiration.
- The more stomata, the more water loss.
- An increase in water potential of the environment would slow evaporation; a decrease in water potential would increase evaporation.

# Investigation 12: Fruit Fly Behavior

**BIG IDEA 4**
*Interactions*

This experiment draws on information found in Chapter 17, Behavioral Ecology and Ethology. This experiment is basically an exercise in messing with fruit flies' heads. You get to stick them in a choice chamber and explore environmental factors that either attract or repel them.

## Basic Setup

First, get to know your flies. For example, males have a darker abdomen whereas females' abdomens are pale and rounder. Next, you get to create something called a choice chamber. In this experiment the chamber consists of two plastic bottles with their bottoms cut off and joined together with tape. Each end of the chamber will have one of the substances you decide to test. You can also use the chamber to investigate the flies' response to other variables, such as light or gravity. No matter what you're interested in, wrangle about 25 of those little creatures in there and let them get used to their new digs. Place a cotton ball with a few drops of water in the cap at one end (control) and a few drops of the substance you're testing at the other end. The flies will exhibit positive chemotaxis if they move toward the substance you're testing, negative chemotaxis if they move away from it.

## Results

It is not important that you take away from this experiment that fruit flies enjoy the scent of one type of substance over another. What is important is that you recognize how to set up an experiment such as this one involving the choice chamber to measure chemotaxis in animals.

## Key Skills

- Design a controlled experiment to determine environmental factors that either attract or repel your fruit flies.
- Analyze your data to identify the effect of environmental factors on your flies' behavior.

# Investigation 13: Enzyme Activity

**BIG IDEA 4**
*Interactions*

This experiment draws on information from Chapter 5, Chemistry. The experiment is designed to practice the calculation of the rate of enzyme-catalyzed reactions through the measurement of the products produced. In this particular experiment, the enzyme **peroxidase** is used to convert hydrogen peroxide to water and oxygen, and the products are measured to assist in the determination of the rate of reaction. If you do not feel comfortable with your knowledge of enzyme-substrate interactions, refer to Chapter 5 before continuing this section.

### The Nitty-Gritty About Experiment 2

The reaction of interest in this experiment is as follows:

$$2H_2O_2 \rightarrow 2H_2O + O_2$$

This reaction does indeed occur without the assistance of peroxidase, but it occurs at a slow rate. When our friend peroxidase is added to the mix, the reaction occurs at a much faster clip. Take a look at the enzymatic activity curve in Figure 19.4. Notice the constant rate of reaction in the first six minutes of the experiment.

However, after the sixth minute, the rate slows, as if the enzyme has become tired. This is because as the reaction proceeds, the number of substrate molecules remaining declines, which means that fewer enzyme-substrate interactions can occur. When calculating the **rate of reaction,** it is the constant linear portion of the curve that matters. That is the accepted rate value for the enzyme. Do not attempt to factor in the slowing portion of the curve.

### Basic Setup

In this particular experiment, turnip peroxidase is added to a beaker that holds $H_2O_2$ and is allowed to react for a certain period of time. After the reaction stops, the amount of $O_2$

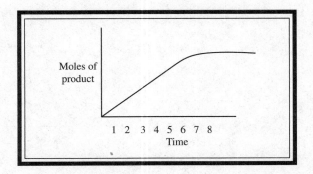

**Figure 19.4   Enzyme-activity curve.**

produced is measured using the color indicator guaiacol. Guaiacol readily grabs and binds to oxygen, forming tetraguaiacol, a brown chemical. The greater the amount of oxygen produced, the darker brown your solution becomes. The relative amount of oxygen is determined by comparing the color of the tube to a turnip peroxidase color chart (a previously made series of dilutions of the oxygen-guaiacol reaction). Once you're comfortable with the experimental setup, you will investigate at what pH peroxidase works its best.

### Results

You'll have six test tubes, each with a different pH buffer. Once the reaction has proceeded long enough to produce a nice color spectrum among all the different pH solutions, record the color for each tube. Once you use your lab manual's turnip peroxidase color chart to help you quantify the relative amounts of oxygen produced, you can graph your data as color intensity versus pH. Peroxidase is found in many different forms with optimum pHs ranging from 4 to 11 depending on the source. Turnip peroxidase, for example, tends to work best at pH 5.

### Key Concepts

- The reaction rate can be affected by four major factors: pH, temperature, substrate concentration, and enzyme concentration.
- The rate of reaction can be found by measuring either the appearance of product or the disappearance of reactant. Either measure can provide insight into the effectiveness of an enzyme's presence.
- When calculating the rate of reaction, remember that the rate is actually the portion of the graph with a constant slope.
- To determine the ideal pH at which an enzyme functions, run the enzyme reaction at a series of different pH values and measure the various reaction rates.

# › Review Questions

1. If a dialysis bag with a solute concentration of 0.6 M is placed into a beaker with a solute concentration of 0.4 M, in which direction will water flow?

   A. Water will flow from the dialysis bag to the beaker.
   B. Water will flow from the beaker into the dialysis bag.
   C. Water will first flow out of the bag, and then back into the bag.
   D. The solution is already in equilibrium, and water will not move at all.

2. What is the rate of reaction for the enzyme–substrate interaction shown in the graph below?

   A. 6 μmol/min (micromoles per minute)
   B. 5 μmol/min
   C. 4 μmol/min
   D. 3 μmol/min

3. In an experiment involving *Sordaria,* an ascomycete fungus, it was found that of 450 offspring produced, 58 yielded a 2:2:2:2 ratio and 32 a 2:4:2 ratio. Approximately how far apart is the gene from the centromere?

   A. 10.0 map units
   B. 15.0 map units
   C. 20.0 map units
   D. 25.0 map units

4. A plant would show the highest rate of transpiration under which of the following conditions?

   A. High humidity
   B. Low temperature
   C. High light intensity
   D. Low air movement

5. Which of the following will result in a quicker rate of DNA migration on an electrophoresis gel?

   A. Increase in temperature of the gel
   B. Increase in amount of DNA added to the well
   C. Reversal of charge of gel, switching positive and negative sides
   D. Increase in current flowing through the gel

6. A lab experiment is set up in which the participants are heterozygous individuals (Aa). After the $F_1$ generation is produced, 40 percent of the participants are randomly removed from the experiment and the remaining 60 percent are left to continue breeding. This experiment would be used to show what phenomenon?

   A. Natural selection
   B. Genetic drift
   C. Gene flow
   D. Mutation

7. You are studying a population of pea plants with flower colors ranging from white to dark pink. You selected only those plants with the darkest pink flowers to use in cross-pollination. Once you plant the seeds and grow your new generation of pea plants, what would you expect to see?

   A. The relative numbers of flower colors would remain unchanged.
   B. You would see disruptive selection.
   C. Your results would show directional selection.
   D. The relative numbers of white flowers would increase.

8. Which of the following would indicate you successfully transformed your *E. coli* culture with the plasmid containing the gene for ampicillin resistance?

   A. The ampicillin-containing agar plates would show growth from your control culture (*E. coli* without the plasmid), but not your transformed culture.
   B. The ampicillin-containing agar plates would show growth from your transformed culture, but not the control.
   C. The transformed culture would not grow on the agar-only plates.
   D. Both the transformed *E. coli* and the untransformed *E. coli* would grow on the plain agar plates.

## › Answers and Explanations

1. **B**—The water will flow into the dialysis bag because the solute concentration in the bag is higher than that of the beaker. This creates an osmotic driving force that moves water into the bag in an effort to equalize the discrepancy in solute concentrations.

2. **D**—The rate of reaction can be approximated by calculating the slope of the straight portion of the graph. In this case it is 15 μmol of product produced in 5 minutes for an approximate rate of 3 μmoles/min.

3. **A**—The distance between the gene and the centromere in *Sordaria* is determined by adding up the number of crossovers that occur and dividing that by the number of offspring produced. This quotient should be multiplied by 100, and that product represents the percent of the offspring that experienced crossover. This percentage should be divided by 2 to obtain the distance from the centromere to the gene of interest.

4. **C**—The factors that increase the rate of transpiration are high light intensity, high temperature, low humidity, and high airflow.

5. **D**—The more current you put through the gel, the faster the DNA will migrate. Adding more DNA will result in thicker bands. Reversing the positive and negative ends will swap the direction in which the DNA migrates. Running the gel for a longer amount of time will increase the distance that the DNA fragments travel, and increasing the temperature really won't have too much of an effect.

6. **B**—This is an example of genetic drift, in which a random chunk of the population is eliminated resulting in a potential change in the frequencies of the alleles being studied.

7. **C**—If you allow only the plants with the dark-pink flower genes to reproduce, those are the genes that will be passed on to the next generation. This will shift the average flower color towards the darker end of the spectrum, an example of directional selection.

8. **B**—By successfully transforming your *E. coli*, you are giving it the gene that enables it to survive in the presence of ampicillin (something the bacteria are unable to do otherwise). Therefore, you have successfully transformed your culture if it grows on ampicillin-containing agar, but the control culture without the plasmid dies.

# › Rapid Review

*Investigation 1: Artificial Selection*

- To demonstrate evolution in a plant population, choose which traits are selected for and cross-pollinate only between those selected plants. Once the offspring (seeds) are planted and grown, check this trait to see if it is more prevalent in the new population.

- This is an example of directional selection, when members of a population at one end of a spectrum are selected for, whereas the trait at the other end of the spectrum becomes rarer.

*Investigation 2: Mathematical Modeling: Hardy-Weinberg*

- The Hardy-Weinberg equation is used to check the frequencies of alleles in a population that is not evolving. This "snapshot" of the population is used as a point of comparison, to see if evolution does occur (and changes the allelic frequencies).

- For a given gene, there is the $p$ allele and the $q$ allele. Therefore, $p + q = 1$.

- For that same gene, organisms can be homozygous dominant ($pp$), homozygous recessive ($qq$), or heterozygous ($pq$ or $qp$). Therefore, $p^2 + 2pq + q^2 = 1$.

- By altering any of the five conditions required for a non-evolving Hardy-Weinberg population, you can cause a change in your population's gene pool.

*Investigation 3: Comparing DNA Sequences to Understand Evolutionary Relationships with BLAST*

- BLAST is a computer program used to compare specific genes from different organisms.

- The more similar the nucleotide base sequence between two genes, the closer the evolutionary relationship.

- A cladogram is a visual representation of the evolutionary relatedness of a species.

*Investigation 4: Diffusion and Osmosis*

- Water flows from **hypotonic** (low solute) to **hypertonic** (high solute).

- To measure diffusion and osmosis, take dialysis bags containing solutes of varying concentrations, place them into beakers containing solutions of various concentrations, and record the direction of flow during each experiment.

*Investigation 5: Photosynthesis*

- To experimentally determine the photosynthetic rate of various plants in various environments, first remove the air from leaf disk samples and add the samples to water containing sodium bicarbonate (a source of carbon dioxide). They will sink to the bottom of the cup.

- As the leaf tissue photosynthesizes, oxygen is released, causing the disks to rise to the surface. Expose different plant samples to different environmental conditions, measure how much photosynthesis occurs ($ET_{50}$), and then compare.

*Investigation 6: Cell Respiration*

- To experimentally determine the rate of respiration in peas, use a respirometer to calculate the change in volume that occurs around the peas. Set up (1) a control group of nongerminating peas that will have a lower baseline respiration rate, (2) a control group that measures the change in oxygen due to pressure and temperature changes, and (3) an experimental group that contains the group whose respiration rate you want to measure.

### Investigation 7: Cell Division: Mitosis and Meiosis

- To determine experimentally the percentage of cells in a particular stage of the cell cycle, examine an onion root slide and count the number of cells per stage. Divide the number in each stage by the total number of cells to determine the relative percentages.

- To determine how far a gene for an ascomycete fungus is from its centromere, cross a wild-type strain with a mutant and examine the patterns among the ascospores. A ratio of 4:4 means no crossover occurred, whereas ratios of 2:2:2:2 or 2:4:2 indicate crossing over did occur. Total number of crossover divided by total number of offspring equals the percent crossover. Divide this by 2 to get distance from the centromere.

### Investigation 8: Biotechnology: Bacterial Transformation

- To run a transformation, add ampicillin-sensitive bacteria to two tubes, and to only one of the two, add a plasmid containing both the gene you would like to transform and the gene for ampicillin resistance. The other tube is the control. Ice the two tubes for 15 minutes, then quickly heat-shock the cells into picking up foreign DNA. Ice the tubes again, spread the bacteria out on ampicillin-coated plates, and incubate overnight. If transformation occurs, your bacteria will grow on the ampicillin plate.

### Investigation 9: Biotechnology: Restriction Enzyme Analysis of DNA

- Gel electrophoresis can be used in court to determine if an individual committed a crime or if an individual is the parent of a particular child. Each person has a particular DNA fingerprint. When that individual's DNA is cut with restriction enzymes and run on an electrophoresis gel, it will show a unique pattern that only that person has. By matching a person's DNA fingerprint with that of the child of interest or the evidence from the crime scene, proper identifications can be made.

### Investigation 10: Energy Dynamics

- A simple model system can be used to track how much energy is transferred from a single producer (plant) to a single consumer (caterpillars).

- By weighing the amount of plant eaten by the caterpillars (and the amount of the plant excreted), it is possible to calculate the percent of the plant's energy that was either incorporated into the caterpillar's body or used in cellular respiration.

- These are methods for estimating the efficiency of transfer of energy from producer to consumer.

### Investigation 11: Transpiration

- To design an experiment to test the effects of various environmental factors on the rate of transpiration, measure the amount of water that evaporates from the surface of plants over a certain amount of time under normal conditions. You can do this using the whole-plant method or by using a piece of equipment known as a potometer, a device that measures water loss by plants. Compare the normal rate with the rates obtained when the temperature, humidity, airflow, or light intensity is altered. If you run an experiment of this nature, it is important to measure the surface area of the leaves involved because larger surface areas can transpire more water more quickly.

*Investigation 12: Fruit Fly Behavior*

- To study kinesis of an insect such as a fruit fly, create a contraption known as a choice chamber, which is designed to study which of two substances an organism prefers. For example, one-half of the choice chamber may contain banana extract, the other distilled water. Place the organism of interest into the choice chamber and record how many of that organism are on each side of the chamber every 30 seconds. This procedure can also be performed for a choice chamber that has differing temperatures, humidities, light intensities, salinities, and other parameters.

*Investigation 13: Enzyme Activity*

- Enzyme reaction rate is affected by pH, temperature, substrate concentration, and enzyme concentration.

- To test the rate of reactivity of an enzyme and the difference it makes compared to the speed of the normal reaction, run the reaction without an enzyme, then run it with your enzyme, and compare.

- To determine the ideal pH (or temperature) for an enzyme, run the reaction at varying pH values (or temperatures) and compare.

# STEP 5

# Build Your Test-Taking Confidence

AP Biology Practice Exam 1
AP Biology Practice Exam 2

# Answer Sheet for AP Biology Practice Exam 1

## PART A: MULTIPLE-CHOICE QUESTIONS

1. (A) (B) (C) (D)
2. (A) (B) (C) (D)
3. (A) (B) (C) (D)
4. (A) (B) (C) (D)
5. (A) (B) (C) (D)
6. (A) (B) (C) (D)
7. (A) (B) (C) (D)
8. (A) (B) (C) (D)
9. (A) (B) (C) (D)
10. (A) (B) (C) (D)
11. (A) (B) (C) (D)
12. (A) (B) (C) (D)
13. (A) (B) (C) (D)
14. (A) (B) (C) (D)
15. (A) (B) (C) (D)
16. (A) (B) (C) (D)
17. (A) (B) (C) (D)
18. (A) (B) (C) (D)
19. (A) (B) (C) (D)
20. (A) (B) (C) (D)
21. (A) (B) (C) (D)

22. (A) (B) (C) (D)
23. (A) (B) (C) (D)
24. (A) (B) (C) (D)
25. (A) (B) (C) (D)
26. (A) (B) (C) (D)
27. (A) (B) (C) (D)
28. (A) (B) (C) (D)
29. (A) (B) (C) (D)
30. (A) (B) (C) (D)
31. (A) (B) (C) (D)
32. (A) (B) (C) (D)
33. (A) (B) (C) (D)
34. (A) (B) (C) (D)
35. (A) (B) (C) (D)
36. (A) (B) (C) (D)
37. (A) (B) (C) (D)
38. (A) (B) (C) (D)
39. (A) (B) (C) (D)
40. (A) (B) (C) (D)
41. (A) (B) (C) (D)
42. (A) (B) (C) (D)

43. (A) (B) (C) (D)
44. (A) (B) (C) (D)
45. (A) (B) (C) (D)
46. (A) (B) (C) (D)
47. (A) (B) (C) (D)
48. (A) (B) (C) (D)
49. (A) (B) (C) (D)
50. (A) (B) (C) (D)
51. (A) (B) (C) (D)
52. (A) (B) (C) (D)
53. (A) (B) (C) (D)
54. (A) (B) (C) (D)
55. (A) (B) (C) (D)
56. (A) (B) (C) (D)
57. (A) (B) (C) (D)
58. (A) (B) (C) (D)
59. (A) (B) (C) (D)
60. (A) (B) (C) (D)
61. (A) (B) (C) (D)
62. (A) (B) (C) (D)
63. (A) (B) (C) (D)

## PART B: GRID-IN QUESTIONS

# AP Biology Practice Exam 1: Section I

## PART A: MULTIPLE-CHOICE QUESTIONS

Time—1 hour and 30 minutes (for Parts A and B)

For the multiple-choice questions that follow, select the best answer
and fill in the appropriate letter on the answer sheet.

1. Which of the following characteristics would allow you to distinguish a prokaryotic cell from an animal cell?

   A. Ribosomes
   B. Cell membrane
   C. Chloroplasts
   D. Cell wall

2. Which of the following is the source of oxygen produced during photosynthesis?

   A. $H_2O$
   B. $H_2O_2$
   C. $CO_2$
   D. $CO$

3. An organism exposed to wild temperature fluctuations shows very little, if any, change in its metabolic rate. This organism is most probably a

   A. ectotherm.
   B. endotherm.
   C. thermophyle.
   D. ascospore.

4. Which of the following is a frameshift mutation?

   A. CAT HAS HIS → CAT HAS HIT
   B. CAT HAS HIS → CAT HSH ISA
   C. CAT HAS HIS → CAT HIS HAT
   D. CAT HAS HIS → CAT WAS HIT

5. A researcher conducts a survey of a biome and finds 35 percent more species than she has found in any other biome. Which biome is she most likely to be in?

   A. Tundra
   B. Tiaga
   C. Tropical rainforest
   D. Temperate deciduous forest

6. On the basis of the following crossover frequencies, determine the relative location of these four genes:

   | | | |
   |---|---|---|
   | m & n | → | 15% |
   | p & f | → | 20% |
   | n & f | → | 30% |
   | m & f | → | 45% |
   | n & p | → | 10% |

   A. f    p    m    n
   B. m    n    f    p
   C. m    n    p    f
   D. n    m    p    f

7. A man contracts the same flu strain for the second time in a single winter season. The second time he experiences fewer symptoms and recovers more quickly. Which cells are responsible for this rapid recovery?

   A. Helper T cells
   B. Cytotoxic T cells
   C. Memory cells
   D. Plasma cells

8. Which of the following are traits that are affected by more than one gene?

   A. Heterozygous traits
   B. Pleiotropic traits
   C. Polygenic traits
   D. Blended alleles

9. A lizard lacking a chemical defense mechanism that is colored in the same way as a lizard that has a defense mechanism is displaying

   A. aposometric coloration.
   B. cryptic coloration.
   C. Batesian mimicry.
   D. Müllerian mimicry.

10. Crossover would most likely occur in which situation?

    A. Two genes (1 and 2) are located right next to each other on chromosome A.
    B. Gene 1 is located on chromosome A, and gene 2 is on chromosome B.
    C. Genes 1 and 2 are located near each other on the X chromosome.
    D. Gene 1 is located on chromosome A; gene 2 is located far away but on the same chromosome.

11. Imagine an organism whose $2n = 96$. Meiosis would leave this organism's cells with how many chromosomes?

    A. 192
    B. 96
    C. 48
    D. 24

12. A student conducts an experiment to test the efficiency of a certain enzyme. Which of the following protocols would probably not result in a change in the enzyme's efficiency?

    A. Bringing the temperature of the experimental setup from 20°C to 50°C
    B. Adding an acidic solution to the setup
    C. Adding substrate but not enzyme
    D. Placing the substrate and enzyme in a container with double the capacity

13. You observe a species that gives birth to only one offspring at a time and has a relatively long lifespan for its body size. Which of the following is probably *also* true of this organism?

    A. It lives in a newly colonized habitat.
    B. It is an aquatic organism.
    C. It requires relatively high parental care of offspring.
    D. The age at which the offspring themselves can give birth is relatively young.

14. Which of the following is an example of a detritivore?

    A. Cactus
    B. Algae
    C. Bat
    D. Fungus

15. In a certain population of squirrels that is in Hardy-Weinberg equilibrium, black color is a recessive phenotype present in 9 percent of the squirrels, and 91 percent are gray. What percentage of the population is homozygous dominant for this trait?

    A. 21 percent
    B. 30 percent
    C. 49 percent
    D. 70 percent

16. Refer to question 15 for details on the squirrel population. Which of the following conditions is required to keep this population in Hardy-Weinberg equilibrium?

    A. Random mating
    B. Genetic drift
    C. Mutation
    D. Gene flow

17. A reaction that includes energy as one of its reactants is called a(n)

    A. exergonic reaction.
    B. hydrolysis reaction.
    C. endergonic reaction.
    D. redox reaction.

18. To which of the following labeled trophic levels would a herbivore most likely be assigned?

    A. A
    B. B
    C. C
    D. D

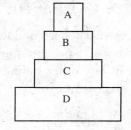

19. A population undergoes a shift in which those who are really tall and those who are really short decrease in relative frequency compared to those of medium size, due to a change in the availability of resources. This is an example of

A. directional selection.
B. stabilizing selection.
C. disruptive selection.
D. sympatric speciation.

20. Which of the following statements is correct?

A. Water flows from hypertonic to hypotonic.
B. Germinating seeds use less oxygen than do nongerminating seeds.
C. The rate of transpiration decreases with an increase in air movement.
D. Smaller DNA fragments migrate more rapidly than do larger DNA fragments on gel electrophoresis.

21. Which of the following is not a form of interspecies interaction?

A. Commensalism
B. Succession
C. Mutualism
D. Parasitism

22. Sickle cell anemia is a disease caused by the substitution of an incorrect nucleotide into the DNA sequence for a particular gene. The amino acids are still added to the growing protein chain, but the symptoms of sickle cell anemia result. This is an example of a

A. frameshift mutation.
B. missense mutation.
C. nonsense mutation.
D. thymine dimer mutation.

For questions 23–26, please refer to the following structures:

23. This represents the backbone of a structure that is vital to the construction of many cells and is used to produce steroid hormones.

24. This structure plays a vital role in energy reactions.

25. This structure is a purine found in DNA.

26. This structure was synthesized in the ribosome.

For questions 27–30, please refer to the following answers:

A. Glycolysis
B. Chemiosmosis
C. Fermentation
D. Calvin cycle

27. When oxygen becomes unavailable, this process regenerates $NAD^+$, allowing respiration to continue.

28. This process leads to the net production of two pyruvate, two ATP, and two NADH.

29. This process couples the production of ATP with the movement of electrons down the electron transport chain by harnessing the driving force created by a proton gradient.

30. This process has as its products $NADP^+$, ADP, and sugar.

For questions 31–34, please refer to the following answers:

A. Desert
B. Tundra
C. Taiga
D. Deciduous forests

**31.** This biome has cold winters and is known for its pine forests.

**32.** This biome is the driest of the land biomes and experiences the greatest daily temperature fluctuations.

**33.** This biome contains trees that drop their leaves during the winter months.

**34.** This biome contains plants whose roots cannot go deep due to the presence of a permafrost.

Questions 35–36: A behavioral endocrinologist captures male individuals of a territorial bird species over the course of a year to measure testosterone (T) levels. In this population, males may play one of two roles: (1) they may stay in their natal group (the group they were born in) and help raise their younger siblings, or (2) they may leave the natal group to establish a new territory. Use this information and the two histograms that follow to answer the following questions.

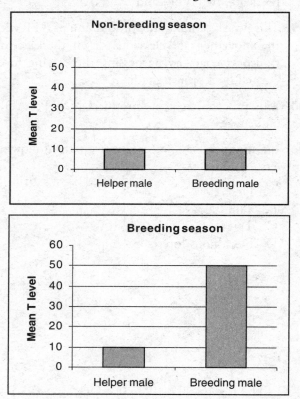

**35.** Testosterone level in this population may be an example of

A. adaptive radiation.
B. an adaptation.
C. divergent selection.
D. development.

**36.** What can you infer about the role of testosterone in reproduction in this species?

A. It is detrimental to breeding.
B. It aids adult males only.
C. It ensures that all males reproduce equally.
D. It aids in breeding.

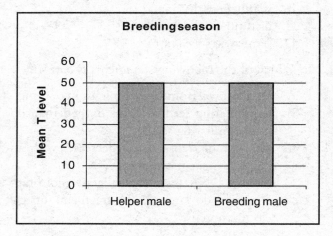

**37.** Which of the following is the best explanation of the results presented in the preceding graph, collected from the same population in a different year?

A. The so-called helper males are actually breeding.
B. The population has stopped growing.
C. Females are equally attracted to adult and helper males.
D. Testosterone level is affected by many processes.

Questions 38–41: A researcher grows a population of ferns in her laboratory. She notices, after a few generations, a new variant that has a distinct phenotype. When she tries to breed the original phenotype with the new one, no offspring are produced. When she breeds the new variants, however, offspring that look like the new variant result.

**38.** What originally caused the change in the variant?

A. Karyotyping
B. Balance polymorphism
C. Mutation
D. Polyploidy

**39.** What kind of speciation does this example illustrate?

    A. Allopatric
    B. Sympatric
    C. Isolated
    D. Polyploidy

**40.** Which of the following could possibly characterize the new variant?
    A. Adaptive radiation
    B. Divergent selection
    C. Equilibrium
    D. Polyploidy

**41.** Which of the following is likely to exhibit the process described earlier?

    A. Fallow deer
    B. Fruit flies
    C. Grass
    D. Spotted toads

For questions 42–44, please refer to the following answers:

Evidence  A   B   C   D

**42.** The DNA placed in this electrophoresis gel separates as a result of what characteristic?

    A. pH
    B. Charge
    C. Size
    D. Polarity

**43.** If this gel were used in a court case as DNA evidence taken from the crime scene, which of the following suspects appears to be guilty?

    A. Suspect A
    B. Suspect B
    C. Suspect C
    D. Suspect D

**44.** Which two suspects, while not guilty, could possibly be identical twins?

    A. A and B
    B. A and C
    C. B and C
    D. B and D

Questions 45–48: The frequency of genotypes for a given trait are given in the accompanying graph. Answer the following questions using this information:

| AA | Aa | aa |
|----|----|----|
| 36% | 45% | ?% |

**45.** What is the frequency of the recessive homozygote?

    A. 15 percent
    B. 19 percent
    C. 25 percent
    D. 40 percent

**46.** What would be the approximate frequency of the heterozygote condition if this population were in Hardy-Weinberg equilibrium?

    A. 20 percent
    B. 45 percent
    C. 48 percent
    D. 72 percent

**47.** Is this population in Hardy-Weinberg equilibrium?

    A. Yes
    B. No
    C. Cannot tell from the information given
    D. Maybe, if individuals are migrating

**48.** Which of the following processes may be occurring in this population, given the allele frequencies?

   A. Directional selection
   B. Homozygous advantage
   C. Hybrid vigor
   D. Allopatric speciation

Questions 49–51: An eager AP Biology student interested in studying osmosis and the movement of water in solutions took a dialysis bag containing a 0.5 M solution and placed it into a beaker containing a 0.6 M solution.

**49.** After the bag has been sitting in the beaker for a while, what would you expect to have happened to the bag?

   A. There will have been a net flow of water out of the bag, causing it to decrease in size.
   B. There will be have been a net flow of water into the bag, causing it to swell in size.
   C. The bag will be the exact same size because no water will have moved at all.
   D. The solute will have moved out of the dialysis bag into the beaker.

**50.** If this bag were instead placed into a beaker of distilled water, what would be the expected result?

   A. There will be a net flow of water out of the bag, causing it to decrease in size.
   B. There will be a net flow of water into the bag, causing it to swell in size.
   C. The bag will remain the exact same size because no water will move at all.
   D. The solute will flow out of the dialysis bag into the beaker.

**51.** Which of the following is true about water potential?

   A. It drives the movement of water from a region of lower water potential to a region of higher water potential.
   B. Solute potential is the only factor that determines the water potential.
   C. Pressure potential combines with solute potential to determine the water potential.
   D. Water potential *always* drives water from an area of lower pressure potential to an area of higher pressure potential.

Questions 52–54 all use the following pedigree, but are independent of each other:

**52.** If the pedigree is studying an autosomal recessive condition for which the alleles are A and a, what was the probability that a child produced by parents A and B would be heterozygous?

   A. 0.0625
   B. 0.1250
   C. 0.2500
   D. 0.5000

**53.** Imagine that a couple (C and D) go to a genetic counselor because they are interested in having children. They tell the counselor that they have a family history of a certain disorder and they want to know the probability of their firstborn having this condition. What is the probability of the child having the autosomal recessive condition?

   A. 0.0625
   B. 0.1250
   C. 0.2500
   D. 0.3333

**54.** Imagine that a couple (C and D) have a child (E) that has the autosomal recessive condition being traced by the pedigree. What is the probability that their second child (F) will have the autosomal recessive condition?

   A. 0.0625
   B. 0.1250
   C. 0.2500
   D. 0.5000

For questions 55–56, please refer to the following diagram:

**55.** The bold line that point *C* intersects is known as the

A. biotic potential.
B. carrying capacity.
C. limiting factor.
D. maximum attainable population.

**56.** On the basis of what happens at the end of this chart, what is the most likely explanation for the population decline after point *E*?

A. The population became too dense and it had to decline.
B. There was a major environmental shift that made survival impossible for many.
C. Food became scarce, leading to a major famine.
D. The population had become too large.

Population of wild turkeys

Time

Questions 57 and 58: The solutions in the two arms of this U-tube are separated by a membrane that is permeable to water and sodium chloride, but not to sucrose. Side A is filled with a solution of 0.6 M sucrose and 0.2 M sodium chloride (NaCl), and side B is filled with a solution of 0.2 M sucrose and 0.3 M NaCl. Initially, the volume on both sides is the same.

**57.** At the beginning of the experiment,

A. Side A is hypertonic to side B.
B. Side A is hypotonic to side B.
C. Side A is isotonic to side B.
D. Side A is hypotonic to side B with respect to sucrose.

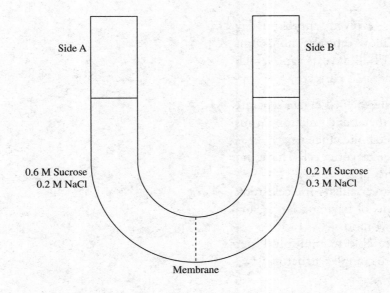

Side A

Side B

0.6 M Sucrose
0.2 M NaCl

0.2 M Sucrose
0.3 M NaCl

Membrane

**58.** If you examine side A after a couple of days, you will see

   A. an increase in the concentration of NaCl and sucrose and an increase in water level.

   B. a decrease in the concentration of NaCl, an increase in water level, and no change in the concentration of sucrose.

   C. no net change.

   D. an increase in the concentration of NaCl and an increase in the water level.

**59.** Tay-Sachs is a disease caused by a recessive allele. Individuals with the genetic disorder usually do not survive more than a few years, and thus are not able to reproduce and pass on the gene. What would explain how this allele and its associated disease is preserved in the population?

   A. Heterozygous individuals will show no symptoms.

   B. Spontaneous mutation converts the dominant allele to the recessive form.

   C. Occasionally the gene will instead increase the fitness of the individual.

   D. Tay-Sachs is asymptomatic in people who are homozygous recessive.

**60.** A new plant was discovered and determined to have an unusually low number of stomata on the undersides of its leaves. For what environment would this plant most likely be best adapted?

   A. Cold and rainy

   B. Humid and sunny

   C. Hot and humid

   D. Hot and dry

**61.** The first simple cells evolved approximately 3.5 billion years ago, followed by the more complex eukaryotic cells 2.1 billion years ago. Which of the following statements is correct?

   A. Eukaryotic organelles helped create separate environments for metabolic reactions, thus increasing their metabolic efficiency.

   B. Prokaryotic and eukaryotic cells have no structural similarities.

   C. The organelles in larger eukaryotic cells took care of the problems of having a larger surface area–to–volume ratio.

   D. Eukaryotic cells are able to multiply faster based on their more complex structure.

**62.** Easily produced genetic variation is key to the rapid evolution of viral and microbial populations. Furthermore, pathogens that need to escape the immune system rely on this variation to generate new surface antigens that go unrecognized by the host's immune system. Which of the following is an example of this antigenic variation?

   A. HIV, which can remain integrated into the host genome for many years

   B. The flu virus, which changes its envelope proteins

   C. MRSA, which has become resistant to many antibiotics

   D. Multiple sclerosis, which attacks the cells of the nervous system

**63.** Two species of hamster (X and Y) are in the genus *Cricetulus*, whereas a third species (Z) is instead part of genus *Mesocricetus*. Which of the following phylogenetic trees shows the correct evolutionary relatedness?

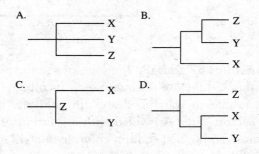

## PART B: GRID-IN QUESTIONS

Calculate the correct answer and enter it on the top line of the grid-in area with each number/symbol in a separate column. Then fill in the correct circle below each number/symbol you entered (only one filled-in circle per column).

1. In a certain species of plant, the allele to produce green melons (G) is dominant over the allele to produce yellow melons (g). A student performed a cross between a plant that produced green melons and a plant that produced yellow melons. When the student observed the next generation, the 94 seeds that were produced from the cross matured into 53 plants with green melons and 41 plants with yellow melons. Calculate the chi-squared value for the null hypothesis that the green-melon parent was heterozygous for the melon-color gene.

2. In a population of grasshoppers, the allele for tan color is dominant to the allele for green color. A drastic increase in rainfall leads to selection against the tan phenotype. When the rainy season ends, 23 percent of the remaining grasshoppers have the green phenotype. If this population is now in Hardy-Weinberg equilibrium, what will the frequency of the tan allele be in the next generation?

3. The bacteria that cause pimples can be grown in the lab using a suitable nutrient broth, where they will eventually achieve exponential growth. Using the graph that follows, calculate the mean rate of growth, in millions of bacteria per hour, during their exponential phase.

4. What is the water potential for a solution that is 0.1 M at 20°C? The solution is in an open container. The equation for water potential is:

water potential ($\Psi$) = pressure potential ($\Psi_P$) + solute potential ($\Psi_S$)

The equation for solute potential is:

$$\Psi_S = -iCRT$$

where:

   i = ionization constant (assume that it is 1)
   C = molar concentration
   R = pressure constant (R = 0.0831 liter MPa/mole K)
   T = temperature in Kelvin (assume a room temperature of 293 K)

5. Determine the surface area–to–volume ratio for a cube that has a side length of 2.5 cm. The volume of a cube = $(l)(w)(h)$. The surface area = 6 × area of a single side.

6. If $C_iV_i = C_fV_f$, where $i$ is the initial solution concentration and $f$ is the final concentration, how many milliliters of a 0.5 M glucose solution would you need in order to make 250 milliliters of a 0.1 M glucose solution?

Time (hours)

# AP Biology Practice Exam 1: Section II

## FREE-RESPONSE QUESTIONS

Time—1 hour and 30 minutes

(The first 10 minutes is a reading period. Do not begin writing until the 10-minute period has passed.)
Questions 1 and 2 are long free-response questions that should require about 20 minutes each.
Questions 3–8 are short-response questions that should require about 6 minutes each.
Outline form is not acceptable. Answers should be in essay form.

1. A murder trial court case ended up ruling against the defendant because of DNA evidence found at the crime scene and analyzed in the forensics lab.

   A. Describe how a gel electrophoresis experiment works and is set up, why things move the way they do, and why the gel would be able to prove, beyond a shadow of a doubt, that the defendant was indeed guilty as charged.
   B. Gel electrophoresis is also used to determine court paternity cases. Describe how a gel could be used to prove whether an individual is the father of a particular baby. Include all the pertinent experimental laboratory procedures in your description.

2. Speciation, the process by which new species are formed, can occur by many mechanisms. Explain how *three* of the following are involved in the process of species formation.

   A. Geographic barriers
   B. Polyploidy
   C. Balanced polymorphism
   D. Reproductive isolation

3. Life on Earth is made possible because of certain unique characteristics of water. Choose **two** characteristics of water.

   A. For each characteristic that you choose, identify and define the property.
   B. Describe one example of how the property affects the functioning of living organisms.

4. Evolution is the change in allele frequencies in a population over time. This can occur through a variety of mechanisms, three of which are listed below.

   • Natural selection
   • Genetic drift
   • Mutation

   A. Define **two** of the three forces of evolution listed above and give an example.
   B. You are studying a population of field mice that includes individuals with light and dark brown coats. Every six months you perform capture/recapture experiments to census the proportion of light and dark individuals. The following numbers indicate the percentage of dark-coat individuals caught in each successive census over the course of five years:

   96, 94, 95, 91, 93, 95, 74, 73, 77, 76

Explain which of the three processes of evolution is most consistent with this data, and give a hypothetical explanation for the observed changes in phenotypic frequencies in this mouse population.

5. Homeostasis, or the maintenance of a steady-state environment, is a characteristic of all living organisms. For each of the following physiological parameters describe how homeostasis is maintained:

   A. Blood glucose levels
   B. Body temperature
   C. Blood calcium levels

6. Membranes are vital to the transport of substances into and out of cells. Three important forms of cellular transport include:

   A. Active transport
   B. Endocytosis and exocytosis
   C. Facilitated diffusion

   For each of the forms listed above, explain how the organization of the cell membranes functions in the movement of specific molecules across membranes and explain the significance of each type of transport to a specific cell.

7. Skin is coated with sebum, an oily substance that slows water loss and inhibits growth of some microorganisms.

   A. Briefly explain how sebum is able to perform its function.
   B. Explain why lungs are more vulnerable to infection than skin. Include the idea of surface area in your answer.

8. The complete oxidation of a mole of glucose produces 686 kcal of free energy. The oxidation of a mole of glucose in a cell generates a maximum of 38 moles of ATP. Each mole of ATP stores about 7.3 kcal of energy. The efficiency of the ATP energy yield from the complete aerobic respiration of glucose is about 40 percent.

   A. Using the laws of thermodynamics, explain what happens to the rest of the energy.
   B. How do humans benefit from this energy loss?
   C. Why would hibernating animals possess an adaptation to reduce efficiency of cellular respiration even further?

# › Answers and Explanations for AP Biology Practice Exam 1

## PART A: MULTIPLE-CHOICE QUESTIONS

1. **D**—Cell walls are present in prokaryotes but not eukaryotic animal cells. Ribosomes and cell membranes are present in both of them. Chloroplasts and large central vacuoles are not seen in either of them. Animal cells have small vacuoles.

2. **A**—The oxygen released by plants is produced during the light reactions of photosynthesis. The main inputs to the light reactions are water and light. Water is the source of the oxygen.

3. **B**—Endotherms are organisms whose metabolic rates do not respond to shifts in environmental temperature.

4. **B**—A frameshift mutation is one in which the reading frame for the protein construction machinery is shifted. It is a deletion or addition of nucleotides in a number that is *not* a multiple of 3. Often this can lead to premature stop codons, which lead to nonfunctional proteins.

5. **C**

6. **C**—We can see from the data that m and f have the highest crossover frequency. They must therefore be farthest apart of any pair along the chromosome. This leaves only answer choice C.

7. **C**—Memory B cells are able to recognize foreign invaders if they come back into our systems and lead to a more rapid and efficient attack on the invader.

8. **C**—Polygenic traits are traits that require the input of multiple genes to determine the phenotype. Skin color is a classic example of a polygenic trait; three genes combine to provide the various shades of skin tone seen in humans.

9. **C**—This is a classic example of Batesian mimicry.

10. **D**—Crossover is most likely to occur between two genes that are located far away from each other on the same chromosome.

11. **C**—Meiosis reduces the number of chromosomes in an individual by half: $96 \div 2 = 48$.

12. **D**—The volume of the container is not a major factor that affects enzyme efficiency.

13. **C**—The original question describes an organism that can be classified as a *K*-selected population. Individuals of this class tend to have fairly constant size, low reproductive rates, and offspring that require extensive care.

14. **D**—A detritivore is an organism that includes the subcategory of decomposers. Fungi are decomposers.

15. **C**—If 9 percent of the population is homozygous recessive, this means that $q^2 = 0.09$, and that the square root of $q^2 = 0.30 = q$. This means that $p = 0.70$ since $p + q = 1$. Thus, the percentage of the population that is homozygous dominant: $p^2 = (0.7)^2 = 0.49$ or 49 percent.

16. **A**—All the other answer choices are violations of the Hardy–Weinberg equilibrium.

17. **C**—Exergonic reactions give off energy, and hydrolysis reactions are reactions that use water to break apart a compound. Redox reactions are reactions that involve the movement of electrons.

18. **D**—Herbivores tend to be the primary consumers of trophic pyramids, and thus would take up the first level up from the bottom.

19. **B**—Stabilizing selection tends to eliminate the extremes of a population, directional selection is a shift toward one of the extremes, and disruptive selection is the camel-hump selection in which the two extremes are favored over the middle. Sympatric speciation is the formation of new species due to an inability to reproduce that is not caused by geographic separation.

20. **D**—This is a lab experiment question based on the material in Chapter 19. We threw it in here just to remind you that you should not ignore the concepts of this very important chapter. You will be asked about these concepts on the exam.

21. **B**—Succession is an ecological process in which landforms evolve over time in response to the environmental conditions. Commensalism is when one organism benefits while the other is unaffected. Mutualism is when both organisms

reap benefits from the interaction. Parasitism is when one organism benefits at the other's expense.

22. **B**

23. **A**—Cholesterol is one of the lipids that serves as the starting point for the synthesis of sex hormones.

24. **C**

25. **D**—Purines have a double-ring structure; pyrimidines, a single-ring one.

26. **B**—The ribosome is the site of protein synthesis.

27. **C**

28. **A**

29. **B**

30. **D**

31. **C**

32. **A**

33. **D**

34. **C**

35. **B**—Testosterone level is an adaptive trait in this population, one that has been molded by natural selection (or possibly sexual selection; we cannot determine this from the question) to aid in reproduction. Adaptive radiation is a process by which many speciation events occur in a newly exploited environment and does not apply here. This is not an example of divergent selection because both breeding and nonbreeding males have low testosterone levels during at least one part of the year; if the two male types always differed in testosterone level, this population could eventually split into two populations. Development and sperm production may be related to testosterone but are not addressed in this experiment.

36. **D**—Since testosterone levels are increased only during the breeding season, we can infer that testosterone has some role in breeding. Since reproductive males express higher testosterone levels only during the breeding season, we hypothesize that testosterone is beneficial, as opposed to detrimental, to breeding.

37. **A**—Since testosterone seems to be linked with reproduction, we infer from the new data that the "nonbreeding" males are actually breeding

and therefore have elevated testosterone levels. Females, population growth, and number of offspring produced are not considered in this example. Finally, although testosterone does affect many physiological processes, none of these are discussed or illustrated in this example.

38. **C**—Although several processes can affect the frequency of a new phenotype or genotype, once it is in place, the original genetic change must have been the result of a mutation (probably a chromosomal aberration).

39. **B**—No physical barrier separated the two populations; this is therefore an example of sympatric, not allopatric speciation. The other answer choices are not types of speciation.

40. **D**—Polyploidy is the only answer that can describe an *individual*. All the others are processes or states that describe *population* events. Polyploidy is the duplication of whole chromosomes that leads to speciation because the new variety can no longer breed with the original.

41. **C**—Polyploidy is much more common in plants; mutations such as the duplication of whole chromosomes are usually lethal to animals.

42. **C**—Gel electrophoresis separates DNA on the basis of size. Smaller samples travel a greater distance down the gel compared to larger samples.

43. **B**—His DNA fingerprint seems to exactly match that of the evidence DNA sample.

44. **B**—A and C seem to share the exact same restriction fragment cut of their DNA. Perhaps they are messing with our heads and added the DNA from the same individual twice.

45. **B**—$100 - 45 - 36 = 19$ percent.

46. **C**—36 percent of the population is AA. Taking the square root of 0.36, we find the frequency of the A allele to be 0.6. This means that the a allele's frequency must be $1 - 0.6$, or 0.4. From these numbers, we can calculate the *expected* Hardy–Weinberg heterozygous frequency is $2pq = 2(A)(a) = 2(0.6)(0.4) = 48.0$ or 48 percent.

47. **B**—The expected heterozygous probability does not match up with the actual. This population is not in Hardy–Weinberg equilibrium.

48. **B**—The homozygous frequency is higher than expected; one explanation for this is that the homozygotes are being selected for.

49. **A**—Water will flow *out* of the bag because the solute concentration of the beaker is hypertonic compared to the dialysis bag. Osmosis passively drives water from a hypotonic region to a hypertonic region.

50. **B**—Water would now flow *into* the bag because the solute gradient has been reversed. Now the beaker is hypotonic compared to the dialysis bag. Water thus moves into the bag.

51. **C**—Water potential = pressure potential + solute potential. Water passively moves from regions with high water potential toward those with lower water potential.

52. **D**—The mother (person B) must be heterozygous Aa because she and her husband (aa) have produced children that have the double recessive condition. This means that person B (the mother) must have contributed an a and that the cross is Aa × aa—and the probability is ½.

53. **D**—To answer this question, we must first determine the probability that person D is heterozygous. We know she is not aa because she does not have the condition. Since we know that the father *has* the condition, we know for certain that his genotype is aa. Both of mother D's parents must be heterozygous since neither of them have the condition, but they have produced a child with the condition. The probability that mother D is heterozygous Aa is ⅔. The probability that a couple with the genotypes Aa × aa have a double recessive child is ½. The probability that these two will have a child with the condition is ½ × ⅔ = ⅓ = 0.3333.

54. **D**—If the couple has a child (person E) with the recessive condition, then we know for certain that mother D must be heterozygous. It is definitely an aa × Aa cross, leaving a 50 percent chance that their child will be aa.

55. **B**

56. **B**

57. **A**—The total solute potential for side A is 1.0 MPa (remember that for NaCl, i = 2), and the total solute potential for side B is 0.8 MPa. Therefore, side A has a higher concentration of solute (hypertonic).

58. **D**—Water will move from a hypotonic solution (side B) toward a hypertonic solution (side A). Sodium will diffuse from a region of more sodium (side B) to a region of less sodium (side A).

59. **A**—Heterozygous individuals carry the recessive gene but are themselves healthy.

60. **D**—Low numbers of stomata help to reduce water loss, helpful in hot and dry regions.

61. **A**—Prokaryotic and eukaryotic cells *do* have similar structures, the organelles in eukaryotic cells took care of having a *smaller* surface area–to–volume ratio, and eukaryotic cells are not able to multiply faster.

62. **B**—Changing envelope proteins are created because of genetic variation in the genes that code for these proteins.

63. **D**—This cladogram shows a closer relationship between X and Y.

|   | A | a |
|---|---|---|
| A | AA | Aa |
| a | Aa | aa |

## PART B: GRID-IN QUESTIONS

1. **1.53**—If the green-melon parents were Gg, you would expect a cross with a yellow-melon plant (gg) to produce 50 percent Gg and 50 percent gg offspring. What you actually observed was 53 green and 41 yellow. Based on a total number of 94 offspring, your expected half-and-half ratios would be 47 of each color.

| | # OBSERVED (o) | # EXPECTED (e) | (o − e) | (o − e)$^2$ | (o − e)$^2$/e |
|---|---|---|---|---|---|
| green-melon plant | 53 | 47 | 6 | 36 | 0.766 |
| yellow-melon plant | 41 | 47 | −6 | 36 | 0.766 |

The chi-square value is 1.53 (less than the critical value of 3.84), so the null hypothesis is accepted.

2. **0.52**

tan = $p$; green = $q$

green phenotype = $q^2$ = 0.23; frequency of green allele = $\sqrt{0.23}$ = 0.48

Since $p + q = 1$, the tan allele ($p$) = 1 − 0.48 = 0.52.

**3. 1.27**—Logarithmic growth takes place during the time where the slope is the greatest, approximately between 12 and 30 hours. During that time (18 hours), the bacterial population started at 10 million and increased to 33 million (a difference of 23 million). Therefore, 23 million divided by 18 hours gives a rate of 1.27 million bacteria per hour.

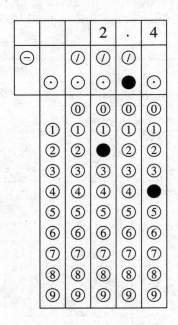

**4. −2.4**—The solute potential is −(1) × (0.1 M) × (0.00831 MPa/mole K) × (293 K) = −0.24 MPa. The pressure potential is zero because the solution is in an open container. Therefore (−0.24) + 0 = −0.24 MPa.

**5. 2.4**

SA = 6 × (2.5 cm × 2.5 cm) = 37.5 cm$^2$
V = (2.5 cm)$^3$ = 15.6 cm$^3$
SA/V = 37.5/15.6 = 2.4

**6. 50**

(0.5 M)(V$_i$) = (0.1 M)(250 mL)
V$_i$ = 50 mL

# › **Free-Response Grading Outline**

1. Gel electrophoresis question (10 points)

   A. Electrophoresis experiment (maximum 5 points)
      - Mentioning that smaller particles travel faster. (1 point)
      - Mentioning that the fragments of DNA are placed into wells at the head of the gel to begin their migration to the other side. (1 point)
      - Mentioning that the DNA migrates only as electric current is passed through the gel. (1 point)
      - Mentioning that the DNA migrates from negative charge to positive charge. (1 point)
      - Mentioning that when DNA samples from different individuals are cut with restriction enzymes, they show variations in the band patterns on gel electrophoresis known as *restriction fragment length polymorphisms* (RFLPs). (1 point)
      - Mentioning that DNA is specific to each individual, and when it is mixed with restriction enzymes, different combinations of RFLPs will be obtained from person to person. (1 point)
      - Definition of a DNA fingerprint as the combination of an individual's RFLPs inherited from each parent. (1 point)
      - Mentioning that if an individual's electrophoresis pattern identically matches that of the crime scene evidence, the DNA has spoken and shown the individual to be the perpetrator, since the probability of two people having an identical set of RFLPs is virtually non-existent. (1 point)

   B. Paternity (maximum 5 points)
      - Mentioning that DNA samples would need to be taken from the disputed child and the potential parents involved. (1 point)
      - Definition of a restriction enzyme as an enzyme that cuts DNA at a particular sequence and creates open fragments of DNA called "sticky ends." (1 point)
      - Mentioning that the DNA from all the different individuals involved must be cut by the same restriction enzyme(s) so that the RFLPs created can be compared with each other. (1 point)
      - Mentioning that each sample of DNA must be placed into a different well at the top of the gel plate. (1 point)
      - Mentioning that the DNA will migrate from negative charge to positive charge, once the current is applied, to create an RFLP pattern specific for each individual—this is a look at the DNA fingerprint of an individual. (1 point)
      - Mentioning that some sort of dye should be added to the DNA samples that will allow for proper viewing of the bands after the current is disconnected. (1 point)
      - Mentioning that one of the two DNA cuts from the child's fingerprint should match up with one of the two DNA cuts from the father's fingerprint and one from the mother's fingerprint as well, because the child inherits one chromosome of each homologous pair from the mother and one from the father. (1 point)

2. Speciation question (here, you can obtain 4 points from a couple of the answers; if 4 points are obtained for an answer, a maximum of 3 points can be obtained from each of the other 2 answers)

   A. Geographic barriers (maximum 4 points)
      - Mentioning how geographic barriers can lead to reproductive isolation of members from the same species. (½ point)
      - Mentioning that if these geographically separated species are moved into regions that have different environments, natural selection might favor different characteristics from the same species in the different environments. (1 point)
      - Mentioning that this is an example of allopatric speciation—interbreeding ceases because some sort of barrier separates a single population into two. (1 point)
      - Definition of divergent evolution as the evolution of two species farther apart from each other as they are exposed to different environmental challenges. (1 point)

- Mentioning the Galapagos finches as an example of geographic barriers leading to reproductive isolation and divergent evolution. (½ point)
- Mentioning that if after a long period of time, these divergent species come back together and are unable to reproduce, they have become a new species. (1 point)

B. Polyploidy (maximum 4 points)
- Definition of polyploidy as a condition in which an individual has more than the normal number of sets of chromosomes. (1 point)
- Description of how polyploidy initially occurs—an accident during cell division could double the chromosome number in the offspring, producing a tetraploid ($4n$) organism. (1 point)
- Alternate description of how polyploidy could initially occur—the breeding of two individuals from different species leads to a hybrid that is usually sterile and contains chromosomes that are not able to pair up during meiosis because they are not homologous. (1 point)
- Definition of an autopolyploid—organism with more than two chromosome sets all from the same species. (½ point)
- Definition of an allopolyploid—organism with more than two chromosome sets that come from more than one species. (½ point)
- Mentioning that although an individual may be healthy, it cannot reproduce with nonpolyploidic members of its species. (1 point)
- Mentioning that polyploidic individuals are able to mate only with other individuals who have the same polyploidic chromosomal makeup. (1 point)

C. Balanced polymorphism (maximum 3 points)
- Definition of balanced polymorphism—some characters have two or more phenotypic variants, such as tulip color. (1 point)
- Mention of the fact that if one phenotypic variant leads to increased reproductive success, directional selection will eventually eliminate all other varieties because

only those who have the particular phenotypic variant of choice will survive to be able to reproduce, and thus only their genes will be passed along. (1 point)
- Mentioning that this requirement for a particular variant of the trait in order to survive reproductively isolates individuals of the same species from each other, opening the door for sympatric speciation. (1 point)
- Mentioning that if the balanced polymorphism causes the two variants to diverge enough to no longer be able to interbreed, speciation has occurred. (1 point)
- Citing an example of balanced polymorphism. (1 point)

D. Reproductive isolation (maximum 4 points)
- Mentioning that any barrier that prevents two species from producing offspring can be categorized as reproductive isolation. (½ point)
- Definition of prezygotic barriers as reproductive barriers that make the fertilization of the female ovum impossible. (1 point)
- Mentioning, as an example of prezygotic barriers, any of the following (½ point each, up to 1 point total for prezygotic barrier examples): (a) *habitat isolation*—two species live in different habitats (they just don't see each other, so they cannot reproduce); (b) *temporal isolation*—two species mate at either different times of the year or different times of the day (either way, they are isolated from each other because they do not mate at the same time); (c) *behavioral isolation*—two species have different mating behaviors that do not mix well (members of the other species do not understand the actions of the other as mating signals—a simple communication breakdown ☺); (d) *mechanical isolation*—mating may actually be attempted, but the physical sexual structures do not function together properly (they are incompatible).
- Definition of postzygotic barriers as reproductive barriers that prevent a properly formed hybrid between two species from reproducing themselves. (1 point)

- Mentioning, as an example of postzygotic barriers, any of the following (½ point each, up to 1 point total for postzygotic barrier examples): (a) *hybrid breakdown*—sometimes the first generation of hybrids produced are able to reproduce with each other, but after that the wheels come off and the next generation is infertile; (b) *reduced hybrid viability*—the two different species are able to mate physically and the hybrid zygote is formed, but problems arise during the development of the hybrid that lead to prenatal death of the individual; (c) *reduced hybrid fertility*—the two different species are able to mate physically and produce a viable offspring, but the offspring is infertile.

3. Life on earth is made possible because of certain unique characteristics of water. (maximum 4 points for entire question)

   A. Properties of water (maximum 2 points)
      - Mentioning that hydrogen bonding holds water molecules together (cohesion). (1 point)
      - Mentioning that water has high specific heat (water changes its temperature less than most substances when it absorbs or loses a certain amount of heat). (1 point)
      - Mentioning that the solid form of water is less dense than its liquid form. (1 point)
      - Mentioning water acts as a solvent for so many substances. (1 point)

   B. Effects on living organisms (maximum 2 points)
      - Mentioning that hydrogen bonding allows for flow of water through plants (xylem). (1 point)
      - Mentioning that water's high specific heat means large bodies of water store heat and leads to milder climates in coastal areas. (1 point)
      - Noting that water's unusual density means ice floats. If it sank, all bodies of water would freeze solid from the bottom up, and sustainable life on earth would not be possible. (1 point)
      - Mentioning that water's ability as a solvent allows for many reactions to occur in the cell. (1 point)

4. Evolution is the change in allele frequencies in a population over time. (maximum 4 points for entire question)

   A. Definition and examples (maximum 2 points)
      - Defining natural selection. (maximum 1 point)
        a. Mentioning it is the process by which certain alleles increase in frequency in a population because of the survival or reproduction benefit they give to those individuals who possess them. (½ point)
        b. Possible example: sickle cell allele persists in populations where malaria is present (having sickle-shaped red blood cells makes you less likely to contract malaria). (½ point)
        c. Defining genetic drift. (maximum 1 point)
        d. Describing how random processes can change allele frequencies. (½ point)
        e. Possible example: allele frequencies in a new population are dependent on which alleles are present in the founders of that population (founder effect). (½ point)
      - Defining mutation.
        a. Mentioning that changes in DNA create genetic variation and new alleles. (½ point)
        b. Mentioning that evolution by "neutral mutations" can occur even if the new alleles are not acted on by natural selection. (½ point)
        c. Possible example: eye color gene mutates to a different color without any change in vision or behavior as a result of the mutation. (½ point)

   B. Explanation of data (maximum 2 points)
      - Mentioning the changes could not be the gradual process of natural selection because they occurred rapidly between two censuses. (1 point)
      - Indicating that the changes could be caused by genetic drift. (1 point)
      - Indicating that the changes could be caused by some environmental event (flood, fire) that randomly killed many dark-coated mice. (1 point)

5. Homeostasis, or the maintenance of a steady-state environment, is a characteristic of all living organisms. (maximum 4 points for entire question)

   A. Blood glucose levels (maximum 1½ points)
      • Mentioning insulin/glucagon is released from the pancreas. (½ point)
      • Mentioning insulin stimulates uptake of glucose from the blood to the liver. (½ point)
      • Mentioning insulin causes glucose to be stored as glycogen in the liver. (½ point)
      • Mentioning insulin signals body cells to take up glucose for energy use. (½ point)
      • Mentioning glucagon stimulates the liver to release glucose into the bloodstream. (½ point)

   B. Body temperature (maximum 1½ points)
      • Describing how body insulation (hair, fat, feathers) reduces heat loss. (½ point)
      • Mentioning that vasodilation results in increased blood flow and increased heat loss. (½ point)
      • Mentioning that vasoconstriction results in decreased blood flow and decreased heat loss. (½ point)
      • Mentioning that sweating results in evaporative cooling. (½ point)
      • Mentioning that shivering generates energy. (½ point)

   C. Blood calcium levels (maximum 1½ points)
      • Mentioning that parathyroid hormone (PTH) is released by the parathyroid gland. (½ point)
      • Mentioning that PTH increases the amount of calcium in circulation. (½ point)
      • Mentioning that PTH causes release of calcium from bones. (½ point)
      • Mentioning that PTH leads to increased absorption of calcium by the intestines and kidneys. (½ point)
      • Mentioning that calcitonin is released by the thyroid gland. (½ point)
      • Mentioning that calcitonin decreases the amount of calcium in circulation. (½ point)

      • Mentioning that calcitonin promotes reabsorption of calcium by the bones. (½ point)
      • Mentioning that calcitonin leads to decreased absorption of calcium by the kidneys and intestines. (½ point)

6. Membranes are vital to the transport of substances into and out of cells. (maximum 4 points for entire question)

   A. Active transport (maximum 1½ points)
      • Describing active transport as the movement of a particle against its concentration gradient (from low concentration to high concentration), which requires input of energy. (½ point)
      • Mentioning that it allows the cell to concentrate substances within the cell membrane. (½ point)
      • Mentioning that it is performed by protein pumps in the membrane. (½ point)
      • Possible example: sodium-potassium pump moves potassium into the cell and sodium out of the cell. (½ point)

   B. Endocytosis and exocytosis (maximum 2 points)
      • Mentioning that endocytosis brings a substance into a cell by enclosing it within a membrane-created vesicle. (½ point)
      • Mentioning that the vesicle then fuses with lysosome (contains hydrolytic enzymes). (½ point)
      • Possible example: phagocytes (white blood cells) of the immune system engulf foreign invaders. (½ point)
      • Mentioning that receptor-mediated endocytosis uses proteins embedded in a membrane that contains receptors for specific molecules. (½ point)
      • Mentioning that exocytosis expels waste substances for export by enclosing these substances in a vesicle that fuses with the membrane. (½ point)
      • Possible examples: cells expelling waste or a pancreatic cell exporting insulin protein into the bloodstream. (½ point)

   C. Facilitated diffusion (maximum 1½ points)
      • Describing facilitated diffusion as the diffusion of particles with the assistance

of membrane transport proteins. (½ point)
- Mentioning that transport proteins are specific and have a binding site for the specific molecule of interest. (½ point)
- Mentioning that it does not require energy. (½ point)
- Mentioning that osmosis occurs from a hypotonic solution to a hypertonic solution. (½ point)

7. Skin is coated with sebum, an oily substance that slows water loss and inhibits growth of some microorganisms. (maximum 4 points for entire question)

A. How sebum works (maximum 2 points)
- Mentioning that sebum (or any oily substance) is composed of lipids. (1 point)
- Mentioning that lipids are hydrophobic (repel water). (1 point)
- Mentioning that sebum creates a hydrophobic barrier on skin that slows water loss. (1 point)

B. Why lungs are more vulnerable to infection (maximum 2 points)
- Mentioning that lungs provide a moist environment, ideal for microbial growth. (1 point)
- Mentioning that lungs have a highly folded surface (high surface area). (1 point)
- Mentioning that a higher surface area provides more opportunities for invasion. (1 point)

8. The complete oxidation of a mole of glucose produces 686 kcal of free energy. (maximum 4 points for entire question)

A. Loss of energy (maximum 3 points)
- Mentioning that energy cannot be created or destroyed but only transformed from one form to another (first law of thermodynamics). (1 point)
- Mentioning that every energy transformation results in some energy loss as heat (second law of thermodynamics). (1 point)
- Mentioning that the remaining 60 percent energy from glucose oxidation is lost as heat. (1 point)

B. Benefits from loss of energy (maximum 1 point)
- Mentioning that humans use some of the heat to maintain body temperature. (1 point)

C. Adaptation of hibernating animals (maximum 2 points)
- Mentioning that hibernating animals don't need a lot of ATP because they are inactive. (1 point)
- Mentioning that they must still maintain internal body heat. (1 point)
- Mentioning that lower efficiency means heat generation without much ATP being produced. (1 point)

# Scoring and Interpretation
# AP BIOLOGY PRACTICE EXAM 1

**Multiple-Choice Questions:**

number of correct answers: _____
number of incorrect answers: _____
number of blank answers: _____

**Grid-In Questions:**

number of correct answers: _____
number of incorrect answers: _____
number of blank answers: _____

_____ + _____ = _____
multiple-choice            grid-in                     Section I
number correct             number correct              raw score

**Free-Response Questions:**

1. ____ / 10      3. ____ / 4      6. ____ / 4
2. ____ / 10      4. ____ / 4      7. ____ / 4
                  5. ____ / 4      8. ____ / 4

Add up the total points accumulated in the eight questions and multiply the sum by 1.57 to obtain the free-response raw score: _____ × 1.57 = _____
free-response points                                Section II raw score

## CALCULATE YOUR SCORE

Now combine the raw scores from the multiple-choice and free-response sections to obtain your new raw score for the entire practice exam. Use the ranges listed below to determine your grade for this exam. Don't worry about how we arrived at the following ranges, and remember that they are rough estimates on questions that are not actual AP exam questions . . . do not read too much into them.

| Raw Score | Approximate AP Score |
|-----------|----------------------|
| 83–138    | 5                    |
| 63–82     | 4                    |
| 48–62     | 3                    |
| 26–47     | 2                    |
| 0–25      | 1                    |

# Answer Sheet for AP Biology Practice Exam 2

## ANSWER SHEET FOR MULTIPLE-CHOICE QUESTIONS

1 Ⓐ Ⓑ Ⓒ Ⓓ　　22 Ⓐ Ⓑ Ⓒ Ⓓ　　43 Ⓐ Ⓑ Ⓒ Ⓓ
2 Ⓐ Ⓑ Ⓒ Ⓓ　　23 Ⓐ Ⓑ Ⓒ Ⓓ　　44 Ⓐ Ⓑ Ⓒ Ⓓ
3 Ⓐ Ⓑ Ⓒ Ⓓ　　24 Ⓐ Ⓑ Ⓒ Ⓓ　　45 Ⓐ Ⓑ Ⓒ Ⓓ
4 Ⓐ Ⓑ Ⓒ Ⓓ　　25 Ⓐ Ⓑ Ⓒ Ⓓ　　46 Ⓐ Ⓑ Ⓒ Ⓓ
5 Ⓐ Ⓑ Ⓒ Ⓓ　　26 Ⓐ Ⓑ Ⓒ Ⓓ　　47 Ⓐ Ⓑ Ⓒ Ⓓ
6 Ⓐ Ⓑ Ⓒ Ⓓ　　27 Ⓐ Ⓑ Ⓒ Ⓓ　　48 Ⓐ Ⓑ Ⓒ Ⓓ
7 Ⓐ Ⓑ Ⓒ Ⓓ　　28 Ⓐ Ⓑ Ⓒ Ⓓ　　49 Ⓐ Ⓑ Ⓒ Ⓓ
8 Ⓐ Ⓑ Ⓒ Ⓓ　　29 Ⓐ Ⓑ Ⓒ Ⓓ　　50 Ⓐ Ⓑ Ⓒ Ⓓ
9 Ⓐ Ⓑ Ⓒ Ⓓ　　30 Ⓐ Ⓑ Ⓒ Ⓓ　　51 Ⓐ Ⓑ Ⓒ Ⓓ
10 Ⓐ Ⓑ Ⓒ Ⓓ　　31 Ⓐ Ⓑ Ⓒ Ⓓ　　52 Ⓐ Ⓑ Ⓒ Ⓓ
11 Ⓐ Ⓑ Ⓒ Ⓓ　　32 Ⓐ Ⓑ Ⓒ Ⓓ　　53 Ⓐ Ⓑ Ⓒ Ⓓ
12 Ⓐ Ⓑ Ⓒ Ⓓ　　33 Ⓐ Ⓑ Ⓒ Ⓓ　　54 Ⓐ Ⓑ Ⓒ Ⓓ
13 Ⓐ Ⓑ Ⓒ Ⓓ　　34 Ⓐ Ⓑ Ⓒ Ⓓ　　55 Ⓐ Ⓑ Ⓒ Ⓓ
14 Ⓐ Ⓑ Ⓒ Ⓓ　　35 Ⓐ Ⓑ Ⓒ Ⓓ　　56 Ⓐ Ⓑ Ⓒ Ⓓ
15 Ⓐ Ⓑ Ⓒ Ⓓ　　36 Ⓐ Ⓑ Ⓒ Ⓓ　　57 Ⓐ Ⓑ Ⓒ Ⓓ
16 Ⓐ Ⓑ Ⓒ Ⓓ　　37 Ⓐ Ⓑ Ⓒ Ⓓ　　58 Ⓐ Ⓑ Ⓒ Ⓓ
17 Ⓐ Ⓑ Ⓒ Ⓓ　　38 Ⓐ Ⓑ Ⓒ Ⓓ　　59 Ⓐ Ⓑ Ⓒ Ⓓ
18 Ⓐ Ⓑ Ⓒ Ⓓ　　39 Ⓐ Ⓑ Ⓒ Ⓓ　　60 Ⓐ Ⓑ Ⓒ Ⓓ
19 Ⓐ Ⓑ Ⓒ Ⓓ　　40 Ⓐ Ⓑ Ⓒ Ⓓ　　61 Ⓐ Ⓑ Ⓒ Ⓓ
20 Ⓐ Ⓑ Ⓒ Ⓓ　　41 Ⓐ Ⓑ Ⓒ Ⓓ　　62 Ⓐ Ⓑ Ⓒ Ⓓ
21 Ⓐ Ⓑ Ⓒ Ⓓ　　42 Ⓐ Ⓑ Ⓒ Ⓓ　　63 Ⓐ Ⓑ Ⓒ Ⓓ

## PART B: GRID-IN QUESTIONS

# AP Biology Practice Exam 2: Section I

## PART A: MULTIPLE-CHOICE QUESTIONS

Time—1 hour and 30 minutes (for Parts A and B)

For the multiple-choice questions to follow, select the best answer
and fill in the appropriate letter on the answer sheet.

1. A baby duck runs for cover when a large object is tossed over its head. After this object is repeatedly passed overhead, the duck learns there is no danger and stops running for cover when the same object appears again. This is an example of

    A. imprinting.
    B. fixed-action pattern.
    C. agonistic behavior.
    D. habituation.

2. In a population of giraffes, an environmental change occurs that favors individuals that are tallest. As a result, more of the taller individuals are able to obtain nutrients and survive to pass along their genetic information. This is an example of

    A. directional selection.
    B. stabilizing selection.
    C. sexual selection.
    D. disruptive selection.

3. The relatives of a group of pelicans from the same species that separated from each other because of an unsuccessful migration are reunited 150 years later and find that they are unable to produce offspring. This is an example of

    A. allopatric speciation.
    B. sympatric speciation.
    C. genetic drift.
    D. gene flow.

4. A cell is placed into a hypertonic environment and its cytoplasm shrivels up. This demonstrates the principle of

    A. diffusion.
    B. active transport.
    C. facilitated diffusion.
    D. plasmolysis.

5. Which of the following is a biotic factor that could affect the growth rate of a population?

    A. Volcanic eruption
    B. Glacier melting
    C. Destruction of the ozone layer
    D. Sudden reduction in the animal food resource

6. Which of the following is not a way to form recombinant DNA?

    A. Translation
    B. Conjugation
    C. Specialized transduction
    D. Transformation

7. Chemiosmosis occurs in
    I. Mitochondria
    II. Nuclei
    III. Chloroplasts

    A. I only
    B. II only
    C. III only
    D. I and III

8. Which of the following theories is based on the notion that mitochondria and chloroplasts evolved from prokaryotic cells?

    A. Fluid mosaic model
    B. Endosymbiotic model
    C. Taxonomic model
    D. Respiration feedback model

9. Which of the following is *not* known to be involved in the control of cell division?

    A. Cyclins
    B. Protein kinases
    C. Checkpoints
    D. Fibroblast cells

10. Which of the following statements about post-transcriptional modification is incorrect?

    A. A poly-A tail is added to the 3′ end of the mRNA.
    B. A guanine cap is added to the 5′ end of the mRNA.
    C. Introns are removed from the mRNA.
    D. Posttranscriptional modification occurs in the cytoplasm.

11. In a certain pond, there are long-finned fish and short-finned fish. A horrific summer thunderstorm leads to the death of a disproportionate number of long-finned fish to the point where the relative frequency of the two forms has drastically shifted. This is an example of

    A. gene flow.
    B. natural selection.
    C. genetic drift.
    D. stabilizing selection.

12. Which of the following cells is most closely associated with phagocytosis?

    A. Neutrophils
    B. Plasma cells
    C. B cells
    D. Memory cells

13. Which of the following statements about photosynthesis is *incorrect*?

    A. $H_2O$ is an input to the light-dependent reactions.
    B. $CO_2$ is an input to the Calvin cycle.
    C. Photosystems I and II both play a role in the cyclic light reactions.
    D. $O_2$ is a product of the light-dependent reactions.

14. If a couple has had three sons and the woman is pregnant with their fourth child, what is the probability that child 4 will *also* be male?

    A. ½
    B. ¼
    C. ⅛
    D. ¹⁄₁₆

15. Which of the following is an *incorrect* statement about gel electrophoresis?

    A. DNA migrates from positive charge to negative charge.
    B. Smaller DNA travels faster.
    C. The DNA migrates only when the current is running.
    D. The longer the current is running, the farther the DNA will travel.

16. You are told that in a population of guinea pigs, 4 percent are black (recessive) and 96 percent are brown. Which of the following is the frequency of the heterozygous condition?

    A. 16 percent
    B. 32 percent
    C. 40 percent
    D. 48 percent

17. Which of the following is known to be involved in the photoperiodic flowering response of angiosperms?

    A. Auxin
    B. Cytochrome
    C. Phytochrome
    D. Gibberellins

18. Which of the following tends to be highest on the trophic pyramid?

    A. Primary consumers
    B. Herbivores
    C. Primary carnivores
    D. Primary producers

19. A form of species interaction in which one of the species benefits while the other is unaffected is called

    A. parasitism.
    B. mutualism.
    C. commensalism.
    D. symbiosis.

20. The transfer of DNA between two bacterial cells connected by sex pili is known as

    A. specialized transduction.
    B. conjugation.
    C. transformation.
    D. generalized transduction.

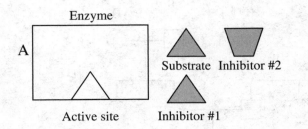

For questions 21–22, please use the preceding diagram:

21. If inhibitor 1 is able to bind to the active site and block the attachment of the substrate to the enzyme, this is an example of

    A. noncompetitive inhibition.
    B. competitive inhibition.
    C. a cofactor.
    D. a coenzyme.

22. Which of the following is *not* a change that would affect the efficiency of the enzyme shown above?

    A. Change in temperature
    B. Change in pH
    C. Change in salinity
    D. Increase in the concentration of the enzyme

23. Which of the following points on the preceding energy chart represents the activation energy of the reaction involving the enzyme?

    A. A
    B. B
    C. C
    D. D

For questions 24–27, please use the following answers:

    A. Aposomatic coloration
    B. Batesian mimicry
    C. Deceptive markings
    D. Cryptic coloration

24. Those being hunted adopt a coloring scheme that allows them to blend in to the colors of the environment.

25. An animal that is harmless copies the appearance of an animal that is dangerous as a defense mechanism to make predators think twice about attacking.

26. Warning coloration adopted by animals that possess a chemical defense mechanism.

27. Some animals have patterns that can cause a predator to think twice before attacking.

Questions 28–31 refer to the following choices:

    A. Enhancer
    B. Repressor
    C. Operator
    D. Promoter

28. Short sequence by promoter that assists transcription by interacting with regulatory proteins.

29. Protein that prevents the binding of RNA polymerase to the promoter site.

30. Transcription-affecting DNA region that may be located thousands of basepairs away from the promoter.

31. Basepair sequence that signals the start site for gene transcription.

Questions 32–35 refer to the following choices:

    A. Divergent evolution
    B. Convergent evolution
    C. Parallel evolution
    D. Coevolution

32. Two unrelated species evolve in a way that makes them more similar.

33. Similar evolutionary changes occurring in two species that can be related or unrelated.

34. The tandem back-and-forth evolution of closely related species, which is exemplified by predator-prey relationships.

35. Two related species evolve in a way that makes them less similar.

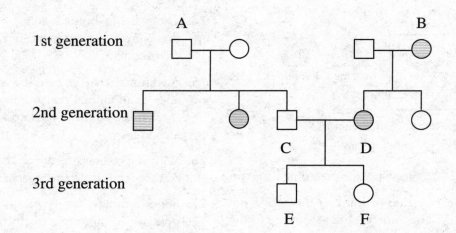

1st generation

2nd generation

3rd generation

Questions 36–39 refer to the preceding pedigree.

**36.** What kind of inheritable condition does this pedigree appear to show?

A. Autosomal dominant
B. Autosomal recessive
C. Sex-linked dominant
D. Sex-linked recessive

**37.** What is the probability that couple C and D will produce a child that has the condition?

A. 0
B. 0.125
C. 0.250
D. 0.333

**38.** Which of the following conditions could show the same kind of pedigree results?

A. Cri-du-chat syndrome
B. Turner syndrome
C. Albinism
D. Hemophilia

**39.** If child E does in fact have the condition, what is the probability that child F will also have it?

A. 0
B. 0.250
C. 0.500
D. 0.750

Questions 40–42: An experiment involving fruit flies produced the following results:

Vestigial wings are wild type, crumpled wings are mutant.

Gray body is dominant, black body is mutant.

525 vestigial, gray-bodied flies    V = vestigial
555 crumpled, black-bodied flies    v = crumpled
75 crumpled, gray flies    G = gray
45 vestigial, black-bodied flies    g = black

**40.** From the data presented above, one can conclude that these genes are

A. sex-linked.
B. epistatic.
C. holandric.
D. linked.

**41.** What is the crossover frequency of these genes?

A. 10 percent
B. 20 percent
C. 30 percent
D. 35 percent

**42.** How many map units apart would these genes be on a linkage map?

A. 5 map units
B. 10 map units
C. 20 map units
D. 30 map units

Questions 43–45: A laboratory procedure involving plants presents you with the data found in the following 2 charts:

| Pigment | $R_f$ |
| --- | --- |
| Beta carotene | 1.251 |
| Chlorophyll *a* | 1.015 |
| Chlorophyll *b* | 0.985 |
| Xanthophyll | 1.125 |

**Transpiration Rate → 1.0 = Control Rate (All Leaves Have the Same Surface Area)**

| PLANT | $T^*$10°C | $T$ 15°C | $T$ 20°C | HUMIDITY 20% | HUMIDITY 15% | HUMIDITY 10% | WIND 5 MPH[†] | WIND 10 MPH | WIND 15 MPH |
|---|---|---|---|---|---|---|---|---|---|
| A | 1.042 | 1.105 | 1.211 | 1.121 | 1.130 | 1.205 | 1.001 | 1.025 | 1.100 |
| B | 0.600 | 0.800 | 1.000 | 0.851 | 0.910 | 0.950 | 0.760 | 0.785 | 0.810 |
| C | 1.240 | 1.245 | 1.251 | 1.411 | 1.519 | 1.550 | 1.214 | 1.240 | 1.301 |

*Temperature
†Miles per hour

**43.** From the transpiration rate data, it appears that transpiration rate rises as

A. temperature ↑, wind speed ↓, humidity ↓
B. temperature ↑, wind speed ↑, humidity ↓
C. temperature ↑, wind speed ↑, humidity ↑
D. temperature ↓, wind speed ↑, humidity ↑

**44.** According to the $R_f$ values given in the preceding smaller table, which pigment would migrate the fastest on chromatography paper?

A. Xanthophyll
B. Chlorophyll *a*
C. Chlorophyll *b*
D. Beta carotene

**45.** From the transpiration rate data presented in the preceding larger table, which of the following plants appears to be most resistant to transpiration?

A. Plant A
B. Plant B
C. Plant C
D. Plants B and C are similarly resistant

Questions 46–48: A population of rodents is studied over the course of 100 generations to examine changes in dental enamel thickness. Species that are adapted to eat food resources that require high levels of processing have thicker enamel than do those that eat softer, more easily processed foods. Answer the following questions using this information and the curves that follow.

**46.** How is average enamel thickness changing in this population?

A. There is no real change.
B. The color and size are changing.
C. It is increasing.
D. It is decreasing.

**47.** You randomly pick one data point from all three sets of data (all three generations), and the individual's enamel thickness score is 15. Which of the following can be inferred?

A. The individual comes from generation 1.
B. The individual comes from generation 50.
C. The individual comes from generation 100.
D. The individual could be from any of these generations.

**48.** What inference can you make about this species' diet?

A. Its food resources are getting softer and easier to process.
B. Its food resources are getting harder and more difficult to process.
C. The population is growing.
D. The population is shrinking.

**Original**          **50th generation**          **100th generation**

Questions 49–52: A student sets up a lab experiment to study the behavior of slugs. She sets up a large tray filled with soil that measures 1 square meter and has four sets of conditions, one in each quadrant:

| Low salinity, high temperature | Low salinity, low temperature |
|---|---|
| High salinity, high temperature | High salinity, low temperature |

She places 20 slugs in the tray, 5 in each quadrant. Use this information to answer the following questions:

**49.** What is this lab setup called?

 A. A gel sheet
 B. A choice chamber
 C. A potometer
 D. An incubation chamber

**50.** After 5 minutes, there are 5 slugs in each quadrant. Which of the following is not a viable explanation for this finding?

 A. The slugs haven't had time to move yet.
 B. The slugs have no preference for temperature or salinity conditions.
 C. The slugs can't move from one area of the tray to another.
 D. The slugs do not like to live in high-temperature areas.

**51.** After 20 minutes, 20 slugs are in the high-temperature, low-salinity quadrant. What kind of animal behavior has this experiment displayed?

 A. Kinesis
 B. Taxis
 C. Survival
 D. Feeding

**52.** A classmate has set up a similar experiment in the following manner:

| Low salinity, low temperature |
|---|
| High salinity, high temperature |

Of the 20 slugs that she puts in her tray, 18 move to the high-salinity, high-temperature section within one hour, while the other 2 move to the low-salinity, low-temperature section. She concludes that slugs prefer conditions of high salinity and temperature. What is wrong with this conclusion?

 A. She didn't specify what the two temperatures or salinities were.
 B. The slugs may not have been able to move where they wanted.
 C. Crowding may have affected the behavior of the slugs, causing the 2 others to move to the other section.
 D. She is measuring two variables at once with no control, and therefore can't conclude anything about slug tastes.

**53.** Viral transduction is the process by which viruses carry bacterial DNA from one bacterial cell to another. In what way does this process play a role in bacterial evolution?

 A. By making the bacterial cell more resistant to predators
 B. By directly creating new species of bacteria
 C. By increasing genetic variation of the bacteria
 D. By selecting for viruses better able to infect bacteria

**54.** ADH is a hormone secreted by the kidneys that reduces the amount of water excreted in the urine. ADH is released in times of dehydration. This is an example of

 A. innate behavior.
 B. maintaining homeostasis.
 C. failure to respond to the environment.
 D. positive feedback.

For questions 55–57 refer to the information and graph that follows.

Five dialysis bags, made from a semipermeable membrane that is impermeable to glucose, were filled with various concentrations of glucose and placed in separate beakers containing 0.5 M glucose solution. The bags were weighed every 10 minutes and the percent change in mass for each bag was graphed:

**55.** Which line represents the bag that contained a solution isotonic to the 0.5 M solution?

A. A
B. B
C. C
D. D

**56.** Which line represents that bag with the highest initial concentration of glucose?

A. A
B. B
C. C
D. D

**57.** Which line or lines represent bags that contain a solution that is hypertonic at 50 minutes?

A. A and B
B. B
C. C
D. D and E

**58.** A mutation in a bacterial enzyme changed a previously polar amino acid into a nonpolar amino acid. This amino acid was located at a site distant from the enzyme's active site. How might this mutation alter the enzyme's substrate specificity?

A. By changing the enzyme's pH optimum
B. By changing the enzyme's location in the cell
C. By changing the shape of the protein
D. An amino acid change away from the active site cannot alter the enzyme's substrate specificity.

Use the following picture of DNA to answer questions 59 and 60:

template strand        5' _____ 3'
complementary strand   3' _____ 5'

**59.** Based on the preceding picture, which direction would RNA polymerase move?

A. 3' → 5' along the template strand
B. 3' → 5' along the complementary strand
C. 5' → 3' along the template strand
D. 5' → 3' along the complementary strand

**60.** If the DNA segment is a transcriptional unit, where would the promoter be located?

A. To the left of the complementary strand
B. To the right of the template strand
C. To the left of the template strand
D. To the right of the complementary strand

**61.** A single gene from five related species of leafhopper was compared, and the nucleotide differences between the genes are as shown in the table:

**Nucleotide Differences**

| Species | 1 | 2 | 3 | 4 | 5 |
|---------|---|---|---|---|---|
| 1 | — | 1 | 8 | 19 | 7 |
| 2 | | — | 8 | 20 | 9 |
| 3 | | | — | 19 | 2 |
| 4 | | | | — | 18 |
| 5 | | | | | — |

Which of the following phylogenetic trees best shows the correct evolutionary relationship between the leafhoppers?

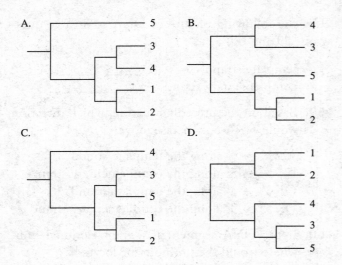

**62.** What is the common ancestor for B and E?

    A. 1

    B. 2

    C. 3

    D. 4

**63.** Which two species are most closely related?

    A. A and E

    B. A and B

    C. B and C

    D. D and E

Answer questions 62 and 63 based on the following cladogram:

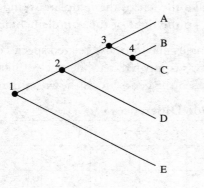

# PART B: GRID-IN QUESTIONS

Calculate the correct answer and enter it on the top line of the grid-in area with each number or symbol in a separate column. Then fill in the correct circle below each number or symbol you entered (only one filled-in circle per column).

1. Twenty people decide to start a new population, totally isolated from anyone else. Two of the individuals are heterozygous for a recessive allele, which in homozygotes causes cystic fibrosis. Assuming this population is in Hardy-Weinberg equilibrium, what fraction (expressed as a decimal) of people in this new population will have cystic fibrosis?

2. A certain mutation found in fruit flies (*Drosophila melanogaster*) is hypothesized to be autosomal recessive. The experimenter crossed two *Drosophila* flies that were heterozygous for the trait. The next generation produced 70 wild-type males, 65 wild-type females, 36 males with the mutation, and 40 mutant females. Calculate the chi-squared value for the null hypothesis that the mutation is autosomal recessive.

3. If the pH of a solution is calculated using the equation $pH = -\log[H^+]$, what is the pH of a solution with a hydrogen ion concentration of $1.33 \times 10^{-8}$?

4. A cell is in equilibrium with its surroundings. The molarity of the surrounding solution at 20°C is 0.8 M. Calculate the solute potential of the surrounding solution.

   The equation for solute potential is $\Psi_s = -i\,CRT$ where

   i = ionization constant (assume that it is 1)
   C = molar concentration
   R = pressure constant (R = 0.0831 liter MPa/ mole K)
   T = temperature in kelvins (room temperature is 293 K)

5. Treatment of tomato plants with a growth hormone yielded the following weights of tomatoes: 100 g, 86 g, 123 g, 98 g, 104 g, 71 g. What is the average weight of a tomato after treatment?

6. After seven days of growth, a plant's weight was 14.3 grams. The percent biomass of that plant was determined to be 23.1 percent. What amount of energy (in kcal) is stored in the plant, if the amount of stored energy = (g biomass) × 4.35 kcal?

# AP Biology Practice Exam 2: Section II

## FREE-RESPONSE QUESTIONS

Time—1 hour and 30 minutes

(The first 10 minutes is a reading period. Do not begin writing until the 10-minute period has passed.)
Questions 1 and 2 are long free-response questions that should require about 20 minutes each.
Questions 3–8 are short-response questions that should require about 6 minutes each.
Outline form is not acceptable. Answers should be in essay form.

1. The immune system is the body's defense against foreign invaders and is divided into specific and nonspecific immunity, and humoral and cell-mediated immunity. Answer three of the following four questions:

   A. Describe the primary immune response and how an invading antigen is met, dealt with, and eliminated. Describe the cells involved and how they are created.

   B. Describe the mechanism by which the immune system deals with viruses, invaders that make it *inside* our *cells.*

   C. Define nonspecific immunity, and list three examples of nonspecific defense mechanisms in humans.

   D. Define the term *vaccination*, and describe how a vaccination works.

2. You just started working at a local laboratory and are usually given the grunt-work lab assignments to perform. Design and describe how you would do the following experiments:

   A. Describe how you would design an experiment to prove the theory that photosynthesis requires both light and chloroplasts. Describe what equipment you would use, what your control would be, and how your expected outcome would support your hypothesis.

   B. You are told that you need to determine how the following factors affect the rate of transpiration in plants: temperature, humidity, light intensity, and air movement. Describe how you would perform an experiment that could accomplish that task, and give your prediction of the expected results. Be sure to describe your experimental setup.

3. The phenotype for scale color in gila monsters is determined by a specific locus. The dominant allele (black) is represented by G and the recessive allele (brown) is represented by g. The cross between a male gila monster with black scales and a female gila monster with brown scales produced the following $F_1$ generation:

   • Black-scaled gila monsters: 52
   • Brown-scaled gila monsters: 55
   • White-scaled gila monsters: 1

   The black-scaled females and brown-scaled males from the $F_1$ generation were then crossed to produce the following $F_2$ generation:

   • Black-scaled gila monsters: 53
   • Brown-scaled gila monsters: 54
   • White-scaled gila monsters: 0

   A. Based on the data presented here, determine the P-generation genotypes. Provide Punnett squares that support your answer.

   B. The white-scaled female in the $F_1$ generation resulted from a mutational change. Explain what a mutation is and discuss a type of mutation that might have produced the white-scaled female in the $F_1$ generation.

4. The idea of surface area is an important concept in biology. Explain how surface area plays a critical role in the digestive system.

5. The following table includes data from scan samples conducted on a fictional mammal called a googabear every 10 minutes over the course of 42 hours. At each scan, it was noted whether the googabear was active or inactive. The percentage of active (feeding, moving, engaging in social behavior) and inactive (resting or sleeping) scans recorded for each time period are shown in the table. Describe the pattern of activity for the googabear and discuss possible reasons for this pattern.

| TIME | 0600–1200 | 1200–1800 | 1800–2400 | 0000–0600 | 0600–1200 | 1200–1800 | 1800–2400 |
|------|-----------|-----------|-----------|-----------|-----------|-----------|-----------|
| % active | 83 | 75 | 22 | 5 | 93 | 89 | 15 |
| % inactive | 17 | 25 | 88 | 95 | 7 | 11 | 85 |

6. In earth's early history, the evolution of photosynthesis in simple cells occurred before the evolution of more complex cells. Briefly describe the significance of photosynthesis being present first.

7. What evidence supports the theory that chloroplasts and mitochondria are evolved from prokaryotic cells?

8. You are asked to estimate if a certain species of plant could live in a salt marsh. You collect the following data:

- The overall $\Psi$ of the soil ($\Psi_{soil}$): −2.2 MPa
- Solute concentration of plant cell contents: 0.08 M (assume i = 1, and 12°C
- Pressure potential of the plant cells: −1.2 MPa
- R = 0.00831 liter MPa/mole K

Do you think the plant could grow in this environment? Why or why not? Show your work.

## › Answers and Explanations for Practice Exam 2

### PART A: MULTIPLE-CHOICE QUESTIONS

1. **D**—Habituation is the loss of responsiveness to unimportant stimuli or stimuli that do not provide appropriate feedback. This is a prime example of habituation.

2. **A**—Directional selection occurs when members of a population at one end of a spectrum are selected against, while those at the other end are selected for. Taller giraffes are being selected for; shorter giraffes are being selected against.

3. **A**—When interbreeding ceases because some sort of barrier separates a single population into two (an area with no food, a mountain, etc.), the two populations evolve independently, and if they change enough, then, even if the barrier is removed, they cannot interbreed. This is allopatric speciation.

4. **D**—Chapter 19, despite being last, is a very important chapter. The experiments are very well represented on the AP Biology exam, and you should read this chapter carefully and learn how to design and interpret experiments.

5. **C**

6. **A**

7. **D**

8. **B**—The endosymbiotic theory proposes that mitochondria and chloroplasts evolved through the symbiotic relationship between prokaryotic organisms.

9. **D**—Fibroblast *growth factor* is said to be involved, but fibroblast cells are not.

10. **D**—Posttranscriptional modification actually occurs in the nucleus.

11. **C**—Genetic drift is a change in allele frequencies that is due to chance events. When drift dramatically reduces population size, it is called a "bottleneck."

12. **A**—Neutrophils are phagocytic cells of the immune system. They roam the body looking for rubbish to clear.

13. **C**—Only photosystem I is involved in the cyclic reactions. Photosystem II is not.

14. **A**—Genetics has no memory . . . it will be ½ forever.

15. **A**—DNA migrates from a negative charge to a positive charge. The rest are true.

16. **B**—$0.04 = q^2$. Therefore, the square root of $0.04 = q = 0.20$ and $p + q = 1$. So $p + 0.20 = 1$. Therefore, $p = 0.80$, and $2pq$ is the frequency of the heterozygote condition: $2(0.20)(0.80) = 0.320 = 32$ percent.

17. **C**—Phytochrome is an important pigment to the process of flowering. Of its two forms, the active form, $P_{fr}$, is responsible for the production of the hormone florigen, which is thought to assist in the blooming of flowers.

18. **C**—Primary carnivores > primary consumers = herbivores > primary producers.

19. **C**—The example to know is the cattle egrets that feast on insects aroused into flight by cattle grazing in the insects' habitat. The birds benefit because they get food, but the cattle do not appear to benefit at all.

20. **B**—Conjugation is the sexual reproduction of bacteria.

21. **B**—In competitive inhibition, an inhibitor molecule resembling the substrate binds to the active site and physically blocks the substrate from attaching.

22. **C**—This is the only factor that is not a major factor affecting enzyme efficiency.

23. **B**—The activation energy of a reaction is the amount of energy needed for the reaction to occur. Notice that the activation energy for the enzymatic reaction is much lower than the non-enzymatic reaction.

24. **D**

25. **B**

26. A

27. C

28. C

29. B

30. A

31. D

32. B

33. C

34. D

35. A

36. **B**—It is not autosomal dominant because in order for the second generation on the left to have those two individuals with the condition, one parent would need to display the condition as well. It is probably not sex-linked because it seems to appear as often in females as in males. Autosomal recessive seems to be the best fit for this disease.

37. **D**—One first needs to determine the probability that person C is heterozygous (Bb). We know that person D is double recessive because she has the condition. We know that the parents for person C must be Bb and Bb because neither of them has the condition, but they produced children with the condition. The probability of person C being heterozygous is ⅔, because a monohybrid cross of his parents (Bb × Bb) gives the following Punnett square:

|   | **B** | **b** |
|---|---|---|
| **B** | BB | Bb |
| **b** | Bb | bb |

Since you know that he doesn't have the condition, he cannot be bb. This leaves just three possible outcomes, two of which are Bb. A cross must then be done between the father (person C) Bb and the mother (person D) bb. The chance of their child being bb is 50 percent or ½. This means that the chance of these two having a child with the condition is ⅔ × ½ or ⅓.

38. **C**—Albinism is the only autosomal recessive condition on this list.

39. **C**—It is ½, because finding out that one of their children has the condition lets us know that the father (person C) is *definitely* Bb. This changes the probability of ⅔ to 1, meaning that the probability of the two having another child with this condition is simply the result of the Punnett square of Bb × bb, or ½.

40. **D**—When you see a ratio like the one in this problem—7:7:1:1 (approximately)—the genes are probably linked. The reason the crumpled, gray, and vestigial black flies exist at all is because crossover must have occurred.

41. **A**—To determine the crossover frequency in a problem like this, simply add up the total number of crossovers (75 + 45 = 120) and divide that sum by the total number of offspring (120 + 555 + 525 = 1200). This results in 120/1200 or 10 percent.

42. **B**—One map unit is equal to a 1 percent recombination frequency.

43. **B**—The data in the table show you that this answer is the correct choice.

44. **D**—The larger the value of $R_f$ for a bunch of pigments dissolved in a particular chromatography solvent, the faster the pigments will migrate. Beta carotene has the highest $R_f$ value.

45. **B**—Across the board it seems to have the lowest rate of transpiration. You can make this leap because, as mentioned on top of the larger chart, all the leaves have the same surface area, allowing you to compare their transpiration values.

46. **C**—The average enamel thickness started at 10, increased to 12, and then increased to 15. It is therefore increasing overall.

47. **D**—The average enamel thickness does not describe the range of possible values; an individual with a thickness of 15 could reasonably come from any of the three generations (if we took into account probability, we could say that the individual most likely came from the 100th generation because this population has the highest frequency of individuals with this thickness; however, the question does not ask for probabilities).

48. **B**—Because thicker enamel in this species indicates foods that are more difficult to process, the answer is B.

49. **B**—Experimental setups where individuals are given a choice as to where to move are called "choice chambers."

50. **D**—All the answers except D are possible, and are important things to consider when setting up an experiment. For example, it is important to allow your study animals enough time to move and/or get used to their new surroundings and conditions before drawing conclusions about their behavior. D is not a good answer because half of the slugs started in a high-temperature area and haven't moved.

51. **A**—Kinesis is the movement of animals in response to current conditions; animals tend to move until they find a favorable environment, at which point their movement slows.

52. **D**—It is important to try to measure only one variable at once. The 18 slugs may have moved to the higher-temperature, higher-salinity conditions because they need high temperatures to survive, even if they dislike high salinity, and vice versa. The original experiment circumvents this problem by giving a choice for all the possible combinations of variables.

53. **C**—New genes are introduced into the bacterium through viral transduction.

54. **B**—When the body has too little water, ADH works to increase the amount of water available. This drive to maintain a stable condition is an example of homeostasis.

55. **C**—Line C showed no net change in weight, indicating the concentration of the solution inside the bag was the same (isotonic) as the solution in the beaker.

56. **A**—The most water would diffuse into the most hypertonic solution; line A shows the biggest increase in weight.

57. **B**—Line B still shows an increase in weight at 50 minutes, whereas line A has leveled out and is isotonic at 50 minutes.

58. **C**—Even though an amino acid doesn't have direct contact with the substrate, it still plays a role in the overall shape of the enzyme.

59. **A**—As RNA polymerase adds new nucleotides to the 3′ end of the new strand, it is moving toward the 5′ end of the (antiparallel) template strand.

60. **B**—The promoter would be located upstream from where transcription would begin.

61. **C**—There are few nucleotide differences between species 1 and 2, indicating they would reside close to one another on the cladogram. The same holds true for species 3 and 5. There are large numbers of differences between species 4 and all others, indicating it would be positioned on its own branch.

62. **A**—Both B and E branches originate from point 1.

63. **C**—Species B and C reside the closest to one another.

## PART B: GRID-IN QUESTIONS

1. **.0025**—For this specific gene in this specific population, there are a total of 40 alleles, two of which are the recessive cf allele ($2/40 = 0.05 = q$). Since you need to be homozygous recessive to have cystic fibrosis, $(q) \times (q) = q^2 = (0.05)^2 = .0025$. In other words, 25 out of 10,000 people (0.25 percent) will have cystic fibrosis.

|  | . | 0 | 0 | 2 | 5 |
|---|---|---|---|---|---|

2. **13.33**—If both parents were heterozygous and if this trait is indeed recessive, you would expect the next generation to show 75 percent normal-looking flies and 25 percent of the flies with the recessive trait. Based on a total of 211 flies, that would mean you would expect 158 normal flies and 53 recessive flies. Your observed numbers were, instead, 135 normal flies and 76 recessive flies.

|  | # OBSERVED (O) | # EXPECTED (e) | (o − e) | (o − e)² | (o − e)²/e |
|---|---|---|---|---|---|
| wild-type flies | 135 | 158 | −23 | 529 | 3.35 |
| recessive flies | 76 | 53 | 23 | 529 | 9.98 |

Since your chi-squared value (13.33) is higher than the critical value of 6.64 (based on 1 degree of freedom), you have to reject your hypothesis. Something other than an autosomal recessive trait is going on.

|  | 1 | 3 | . | 3 | 3 |
|---|---|---|---|---|---|

**3. 7.88**—pH = $-\log(1.33 \times 10^{-8})$ = 7.88

**5. 97**—Add the weight of all tomatoes and divide by the number of tomatoes. The average is 97 grams.

**4. −19.5**—$\Psi_s$ = −(1)(0.8 M)(0.0831 L bars/mole K)(294 K) = −19.5 MPa

**6. 14.4**—The computation is shown below:

(14.3 g)(0.231) = 3.30 g biomass

(3.30 g biomass)(4.35 kcal) = 14.4 kcal

# › Free-Response Grading Outline

1. Immune system question (here, the student can obtain 4 points from two of the answers; if 4 points are awarded for an answer, a maximum of 3 points can be obtained for each of the remaining answers)

   A. (maximum 4 points)
   - Definition of an antigen as a molecule foreign to the body. (½ point)
   - Mentioning that the primary immune response is an example of humoral immunity. (½ point)
   - Description of a B cell and how each B cell has a specific antigen recognition site on its surface that will match up with only *one* antigen. (1 point)
   - When B cells meet and attach to the appropriate antigen, they become activated and undergo mitosis and differentiation into two types of cell. (1 point)
   - The two types of cell are the memory cells and plasma cells. (½ point)
   - Definition of plasma cells as the cells that produce the specific antibodies. (½ point)
   - Definition of memory cells as the cells that head up the secondary immune response. (½ point)
   - Description of how an antibody recognizes a particular antigen, including the fact that antibodies have two functional regions: $F_{ab}$, which binds to the antigen; and $F_c$, which binds to the effector cells, and later comes in and cleans up the trash left behind. (1 point)
   - Mentioning that complement is the one that binds to the antigen–antibody complex and aids in the quicker removal of the complex from the body. (½ point)

   B. (maximum 3 points)
   - Mentioning that this portion of the immune system is known as *cell-mediated immunity*. (½ point)
   - Mentioning that the major player involved here is the cytotoxic T cell. (1 point)
   - Mentioning that the cells infected by a virus are forced to produce viral antigens, some of which show up on the surface of the cell, and that it is these antigens that cytotoxic T cells recognize and attack. (1 point)
   - Mentioning that all cells of the human body (except red blood cells) have class I histocompatibility antigens (MHC I) on their surfaces. (1 point)
   - Further discussion of MHC—mentioning that MHC I antigens are slightly different for each person and the immune system accepts any cell that has the identical MHC I as friendly, and any cell that has a different form of MHC on its surface as an enemy. (1 point)

   C. (maximum 4 points)
   - Definition of nonspecific immunity as the nonspecific prevention of the entrance of invaders into the human body. (1 point)
   - Examples (each example is worth 1 point)
     a. Lysozyme in the saliva can kill germs before they have the chance to take hold.
     b. The skin covering the body is a major form of nonspecific protection against invasion.
     c. The mucous membrane lining the trachea and lungs prevent bacteria from entering cells and actually assist in the expulsion of bacteria by ushering them up and out with a cough.
     d. The low pH of the stomach (acidity) is a nonspecific defense mechanism because it is able to kill a lot of bacteria that enter the body that cannot handle such an acidic environment.

   D. (maximum 4 points)
   - Definition of a vaccination as something given to an individual in an effort to prime the immune system to be prepared to fight a specific sickness if confronted again in the future. (1 point)

- Recognition that a vaccination is the injection of an antigen into the system (human body). (½ point)
- Description of how the reception of an antigen by a B cell causes B-cell differentiation into memory and plasma cells. (½ point)
- Mentioning that at the time of the vaccination, the plasma cells will produce antibodies to wipe out the small dose of antigen presented during the vaccination, and that the memory cells will remember the antigen and be ready to react later if necessary. (1 point)
- Definition of a secondary immune response. Memory cells are stored instructions on how to handle a particular invader. When the invader returns to the body, the memory cells recognize it and produce antibodies in rapid fashion. (1 point)
- Mentioning that the secondary immune response is faster and more efficient than the primary immune response. (½ point)
- Mentioning that the principle of a successful vaccination rests on the belief that the secondary immune response will succeed and wipe out the sickness if the individual is exposed in the future. (½ point)

2. Plant laboratory question

A. (maximum 5 points)
- Mentioning that the products of the light reactions of photosynthesis are ATP, NADPH, and oxygen. (½ point)
- Mentioning that in this experiment, the $NADP^+$ would be replaced by a compound known as DPIP. (½ point)
- Mentioning that normally this compound DPIP has a nice blue color, but when reduced, it changes to a colorless solution. (½ point)
- Mentioning that a machine called a *spectrophotometer* will be used to measure the amount of light that can pass through various samples. (½ point)

- Description of the experiment.
  a. Set aside three beakers—one with boiled chloroplasts, two with unboiled chloroplasts. (1 point)
  b. Take initial reading on spectrophotometer to determine how much light passes through the unboiled chloroplasts *before* the experiment begins. (½ point)
  c. Take one sample (unboiled chloroplasts) and measure how much photosynthesis occurs while it sits in a dark environment. After a certain amount of time, use the spectrophotometer to measure how much light can pass through the solution. (1 point)
  d. Take a second sample (unboiled chloroplasts) and measure how much photosynthesis occurs when it is exposed to light. After a certain amount of time, use the spectrophotometer to measure how much light can pass through the solution. (1 point)
- Mentioning that they would now compare the two samples to see the effect of light on photosynthesis. (1 point)
- Take a third sample (boiled chloroplasts) and expose it to light, and after a certain period of time, measure how much light can pass through the solution. (1 point)
- Mentioning that they would now compare the third sample and the second sample to see the effect of the presence or absence of chloroplasts on photosynthesis. (1 point)

B. (maximum 5 points)
- Definition of transpiration as the evaporative water loss from plants. (1 point)
- Mentioning that they will use a potometer to measure the amount of water loss from plants. (1 point)
- Mentioning that the surface area of a leaf is important to the measurement of transpiration rate in an experiment of this nature. (½ point)

- Description of experiment.
  a. Begin by measuring the amount of water that evaporates from the surface of a plant over a certain amount of time under normal conditions. Use this as the control. (1 point)
  b. Change the temperature, humidity, light intensity, and air movement that the plant is exposed to by 5-degree increments, and measure the amount of transpiration that occurs at the various temperatures. (1 point for each variable mentioned up to a maximum of 2 points)
  c. Mention that these values will be compared to the control to determine the effect of temperature, humidity, light intensity, and air movement. (½ point for each variable mentioned up to a maximum of 1 point)
- Mentioning that transpiration increases with an increase in temperature, decrease in humidity, increase in light intensity, and increased air movement. (1 point for each, up to a maximum of 2 points)

3. The phenotype for scale color in gila monsters is determined by a specific locus. (maximum 4 points for entire question)

   A. P-generation genotypes (maximum 2 points)
      - Creating the correct Punnett square, as shown here (1 point):

|     | g   | g   |
| --- | --- | --- |
| G   | Gg  | Gg  |
| g   | gg  | gg  |

      - Mentioning that genotype of P-generation = Gg (heterozygous) crossed with gg (homozygous recessive). (1 point)

   B. Explanation for mutation (maximum 3 points)
      - Mentioning that mutation is a random event that causes change in allele frequencies. (1 point)

- Possible explanation: scale-color gene is tied to another gene that controls pigment distribution (gene at one locus alters phenotypic expression of a gene at another locus). (1 point)
- Using the term *epistasis* correctly. (1 point)
- Possible explanation: point mutation occurred as DNA responsible for the production of protein that determines scale color was undergoing replication. (1 point)

4. The idea of surface area is an important concept in biology. Explain how surface area plays a critical role in the digestive system. (maximum 4 points for entire question)
   - Mentioning that majority of absorption occurs in small intestine. (1 point)
   - Mentioning that numerous folds and ridges increase surface area. (1 point)
   - Mentioning that brush border and microvilli increase surface area. (1 point)
   - Mentioning that large surface area leads to greater absorption of nutrients. (1 point)
   - Mentioning that chewing (mastication) breaks up food into smaller pieces. (1 point)
   - Mentioning that higher surface area gives greater access to salivary amylase. (1 point)

5. The following table includes data from scan samples conducted on a fictional mammal called a googabear every 10 minutes over the course of 42 hours. (maximum 4 points for entire question)
   - Mentioning that googabears are more active from 6 a.m. until 6 p.m. (during daylight hours). (1 point)
   - Mentioning that they decrease activity from 6 p.m. to 6 a.m. (when it is dark). (1 point)
   - Mentioning that googabears' food source is available during daylight. (1 point)
   - Mentioning that googabear predators are nocturnal (out at night), so it is safest for googabears to remain hidden at night. (1 point)
   - Mentioning that googabears rely on collective body heat at night (huddling); activity of huddled group is low. (1 point)

6. In earth's early history, the evolution of photosynthesis in simple cells occurred before the evolution of more complex cells. (maximum 4 points for entire question)
   - Mentioning that photosynthesis releases oxygen as a by-product. (1 point)
   - Mentioning that photosynthesis led to an increase in atmospheric oxygen. (1 point)
   - Mentioning that the presence of more oxygen in the atmosphere allowed the evolution of cellular respiration. (1 point)
   - Mentioning that oxygen allowed cells to generate more energy and grow larger and more complex. (1 point)
   - Mentioning that the first photosynthetic cells were prokaryotic. (1 point)
   - Mentioning that eukaryotic cells could not evolve until there was a higher level of atmospheric oxygen. (1 point)

7. What evidence supports the theory that chloroplasts and mitochondria are evolved from prokaryotic cells? (maximum 4 points for entire question)
   - Mentioning that chloroplasts and mitochondria have their own DNA. (1 point)
   - Mentioning that chloroplast and mitochondrial DNA consist of a single, circular molecule (like bacterial DNA). (1 point)
   - Mentioning that chloroplast and mitochondrial DNA are not associated with histones (like bacterial DNA). (1 point)
   - Mentioning that chloroplasts and mitochondria replicate by a process similar to prokaryotes. (1 point)
   - Mentioning that the inner membranes of both organelles have enzymes homologous to those found in prokaryotes. (1 point)

8. You are asked to estimate if a certain species of plant could live in a salt marsh. (maximum 4 points for entire question)
   - Calculate $\Psi_{plant\ cell}$:
     $\Psi$ = pressure potential + solute potential solute potential of plant cell = $\Psi_s$ = $-iCRT$ = $-(1)(0.08\ M)(.00831)(273 + 12)$ = $-0.189$ MPa (1 point)
     $\Psi$ = $-1.2$ MPa (pressure potential) + $-0.189$ MPa (solute potential) = $-1.39$ MPa (1 point)
   - Mentioning that the plant cell's water potential ($-1.39$ MPa) is higher than that of the soil ($-2.2$ MPa). (1 point)
   - Mentioning that water would flow out of the plant cell (hypotonic) into soil (hypertonic). (1 point)
   - Mentioning that the plant cell would not survive. (1 point)

# Scoring and Interpretation
# AP BIOLOGY PRACTICE EXAM 2

## Multiple-Choice Questions:

number of correct answers: _____
number of incorrect answers: _____
number of blank answers: _____

_____ + _____ = _____
multiple-choice        grid-in        Section I
number correct        number correct        raw score

## Grid-In Questions:

number of correct answers: _____
number of incorrect answers: _____
number of blank answers: _____

## Free-Response Questions:

1. ____ / 10    3. ____ / 4    6. ____ / 4
2. ____ / 10    4. ____ / 4    7. ____ / 4
               5. ____ / 4    8. ____ / 4

Add up the total points accumulated in the eight questions and multiply the sum by 1.57 to obtain the free-response raw score: _____ × 1.57 = _____
                    free-response points               Section II raw score

## CALCULATE YOUR SCORE

Now combine the raw scores from the multiple-choice and free-response sections to obtain your new raw score for the entire practice exam. Use the ranges listed below to determine your grade for this exam. Don't worry about how we arrived at the following ranges, and remember that they are rough estimates on questions that are not actual AP exam questions . . . do not read too much into them.

| Raw Score | Approximate AP Score |
| --- | --- |
| 83–138 | 5 |
| 63–82 | 4 |
| 48–62 | 3 |
| 26–47 | 2 |
| 0–25 | 1 |

# 5 Minutes to a 5

## 180 Activities and Questions in

## 5 Minutes a Day

# INTRODUCTION

Welcome to *5 Minutes to a 5: 180 Questions and Activities!* This bonus section is another tool for you to use as you work toward your goal of achieving a 5 on the AP exam in May. It includes 180 AP questions and activities that cover the most essential course materials and are meant to be completed in conjunction with the *5 Steps* book.

One of the secrets to excelling in your AP class is spending a bit of time each day studying the subject/s. The questions and activities offered here are designed to be done one per day, and each should take 5 minutes or so to complete (although there might be exceptions. Depending on the exam – some exercises may take a little longer, some – a little less.) You will encounter stimulating questions to make you think about a topic in a big way, some very subject-specific activities which cover the main book's chapters; some science subjects will offer at-home labs, and some humanities subjects will offer ample chunks of text to be read on one day, with questions and activities for follow-up on the following day/s. There will also be suggestions for relevant videos for you to watch and/or websites to visit. Most questions and activities are linked to the specific chapters of your book, so that you are constantly fortifying your knowledge.

Remember – approaching this section for 5 minutes a day is much more effective than binging a week's worth in one sitting! So, if you practice all the extra exercises in this section and reinforce the main content of this book – we are certain you will build the skills and confidence needed to succeed on your exam. Good luck!

—Editors of McGraw-Hill Education

Check off each activity as it is completed.

| | | | | | | | |
|---|---|---|---|---|---|---|---|
| 1. ❑ | 46. ❑ | 91. ❑ | 136. ❑ |
| 2. ❑ | 47. ❑ | 92. ❑ | 137. ❑ |
| 3. ❑ | 48. ❑ | 93. ❑ | 138. ❑ |
| 4. ❑ | 49. ❑ | 94. ❑ | 139. ❑ |
| 5. ❑ | 50. ❑ | 95. ❑ | 140. ❑ |
| 6. ❑ | 51. ❑ | 96. ❑ | 141. ❑ |
| 7. ❑ | 52. ❑ | 97. ❑ | 142. ❑ |
| 8. ❑ | 53. ❑ | 98. ❑ | 143. ❑ |
| 9. ❑ | 54. ❑ | 99. ❑ | 144. ❑ |
| 10. ❑ | 55. ❑ | 100. ❑ | 145. ❑ |
| 11. ❑ | 56. ❑ | 101. ❑ | 146. ❑ |
| 12. ❑ | 57. ❑ | 102. ❑ | 147. ❑ |
| 13. ❑ | 58. ❑ | 103. ❑ | 148. ❑ |
| 14. ❑ | 59. ❑ | 104. ❑ | 149. ❑ |
| 15. ❑ | 60. ❑ | 105. ❑ | 150. ❑ |
| 16. ❑ | 61. ❑ | 106. ❑ | 151. ❑ |
| 17. ❑ | 62. ❑ | 107. ❑ | 152. ❑ |
| 18. ❑ | 63. ❑ | 108. ❑ | 153. ❑ |
| 19. ❑ | 64. ❑ | 109. ❑ | 154. ❑ |
| 20. ❑ | 65. ❑ | 110. ❑ | 155. ❑ |
| 21. ❑ | 66. ❑ | 111. ❑ | 156. ❑ |
| 22. ❑ | 67. ❑ | 112. ❑ | 157. ❑ |
| 23. ❑ | 68. ❑ | 113. ❑ | 158. ❑ |
| 24. ❑ | 69. ❑ | 114. ❑ | 159. ❑ |
| 25. ❑ | 70. ❑ | 115. ❑ | 160. ❑ |
| 26. ❑ | 71. ❑ | 116. ❑ | 161. ❑ |
| 27. ❑ | 72. ❑ | 117. ❑ | 162. ❑ |
| 28. ❑ | 73. ❑ | 118. ❑ | 163. ❑ |
| 29. ❑ | 74. ❑ | 119. ❑ | 164. ❑ |
| 30. ❑ | 75. ❑ | 120. ❑ | 165. ❑ |
| 31. ❑ | 76. ❑ | 121. ❑ | 166. ❑ |
| 32. ❑ | 77. ❑ | 122. ❑ | 167. ❑ |
| 33. ❑ | 78. ❑ | 123. ❑ | 168. ❑ |
| 34. ❑ | 79. ❑ | 124. ❑ | 169. ❑ |
| 35. ❑ | 80. ❑ | 125. ❑ | 170. ❑ |
| 36. ❑ | 81. ❑ | 126. ❑ | 171. ❑ |
| 37. ❑ | 82. ❑ | 127. ❑ | 172. ❑ |
| 38. ❑ | 83. ❑ | 128. ❑ | 173. ❑ |
| 39. ❑ | 84. ❑ | 129. ❑ | 174. ❑ |
| 40. ❑ | 85. ❑ | 130. ❑ | 175. ❑ |
| 41. ❑ | 86. ❑ | 131. ❑ | 176. ❑ |
| 42. ❑ | 87. ❑ | 132. ❑ | 177. ❑ |
| 43. ❑ | 88. ❑ | 133. ❑ | 178. ❑ |
| 44. ❑ | 89. ❑ | 134. ❑ | 179. ❑ |
| 45. ❑ | 90. ❑ | 135. ❑ | 180. ❑ |

Which of the following statements is incorrect?

**A.** An element is made of one specific type of atom.

**B.** An ion is an atom with a net electric charge due to the loss or gain of one or more protons. *electrons* *An ion can also have a positive charge*

**C.** A compound is composed of two or more elements in a fixed ratio.

**D.** An element is defined by the number of protons.

Bacteriorhodopsin is a protein composed of seven transmembrane sections that form a channel through the bacterial cell membrane. Which statement **best** describes the primary structure of bacteriorhodopsin?

**A.** The outer region of the channel is composed mostly of acidic amino acids.

**B.** The alpha-helical structure of the hydrophobic region lies embedded within the interior of the cell membrane.

**C.** Hydrophobic amino acids line the outside of the channel, closest to the cell membrane; hydrophilic amino acids face inward toward the open channel.

**D.** The primary structure of bacteriorhodopsin has very little effect on its function as a hydrogen-ion channel.

**Day 3**

The structural building block of the cell membrane is the phospholipid.

**A.** Generally describe the structure of a phospholipid.

**B.** Explain how the *amphipathic* nature of a phospholipid is critical to its function as the building block of cell membranes. *Amphipathic* means that the molecule has both hydrophilic and hydrophobic parts.

The tertiary structure of a protein is held together by interactions between the side chains ("R groups") of the amino acids. The amino acids asparagine (asn) and serine (ser) form a hydrogen bond between their side groups. This can occur in side chains that have a hydrogen atom attached to either an oxygen or a nitrogen atom. The following diagram shows only the R groups of the amino acids serine and asparagine forming a hydrogen bond within a larger polypeptide:

Which of the following pairs of amino acids would also form a hydrogen bond between their R groups?

**A.** Tyrosine + glutamine

**B.** Glycine + lysine

**C.** Glutamine + methionine

**D.** Methionine + phenylalanine

What level of protein structure is created by hydrogen bonding at regular intervals along the polypeptide backbone?

**A.** Primary

**B.** Secondary

**C.** Tertiary

**D.** Quaternary

# Day 6

Effects of varying carbon sources and temperature on cellulose production.

| **Carbon Sources** (15 ml of medium + 1 ml culture, 3 day incubation) | |
| --- | --- |
| Condition | Mass of Cellulose (g) |
| No Glucose (neg. control) | 0.026 |
| Maltose | 0.120 |
| Galactose | 0.029 |
| Lactose | 0.030 |
| **Temperature** (15 ml of medium + 1 ml culture) | |
| Temperature | Mass of Cellulose (g) |
| 4° C | 0.001 |
| 22° C | 0.052 |
| 30° C | 0.105 |
| 37° C | 0.041 |

A student wanted to study the conditions that would affect cellulose production by the bacterium *Acetobacter xylinum*. In the experiment, *A. xylinum* was incubated with different carbon sources and at different temperatures. Based on the results above, which variables would yield the highest cellulose production by *A. xylinum*?

**A.** No glucose and 22°C

**B.** Maltose and 22°C

**C.** Lactose and 30°C

**D.** Maltose and 30°C

5 Minutes to a 5

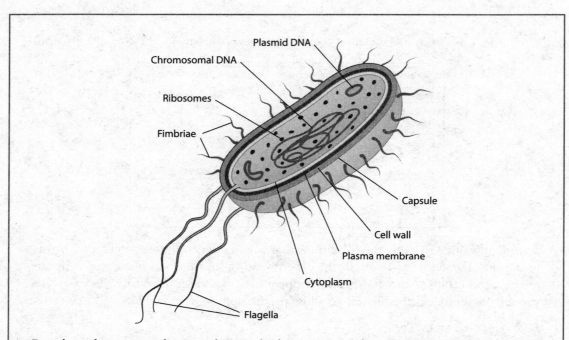

Based on the picture above, indicate which structure is found in most prokaryotes but is found in very few eukaryotes.

**A.** Ribosome

**B.** Plasmid DNA

**C.** Cell wall

**D.** Flagella

Which of the following statements **best** explains why prokaryotic cells evolved before eukaryotic cells?

**A.** There are more prokaryotic cells on Earth than eukaryotic cells.

**B.** Prokaryotic cells can only generate energy through anaerobic respiration.

**C.** Prokaryotic cells have developed mutualistic relationships with animals.

**D.** The endosymbiotic theory proposes that chloroplasts and mitochondria were once autonomous prokaryotic cells.

Which of the following is **not** an advantage a cell gains by having organelles?

**A.** A cell gains the ability to concentrate enzymes and reactants in a small volume, thus increasing the rate of reaction.

**B.** Enzymes for biochemical pathways can be embedded in membranes in their correct sequences, such as the electron carrying proteins of the light reactions.

**C.** Microenvironments can be created, such as pHs, greatly different from the cytosol.

**D.** The complexity of the cell is lowered, thus making it easier for substances to pass freely through the cell.

The liver is the site for alcohol detoxification, whereas adipocytes store fat. Which organelle would be found in larger amounts in the liver cell, compared to the adipocyte?

**A.** Smooth endoplasmic reticulum

**B.** Golgi apparatus

**C.** Cytoskeleton

**D.** Mitochondria

Which of the following **best** describes how the organelles of a eukaryotic cell work together when creating a protein?

**A.** The proteins translated in the nucleus are processed by the rough endoplasmic reticulum, which then export the proteins to their final destination.

**B.** The Golgi apparatus synthesizes proteins and either exports them out of the cell or sends them to the rough endoplasmic reticulum for further processing.

**C.** Proteins synthesized by the ribosomes on the rough endoplasmic reticulum are moved by vacuoles to the Golgi apparatus for processing.

**D.** The smooth endoplasmic reticulum creates proteins, packages them in vacuoles, and sends them to the Golgi apparatus for processing and transport to the final destination.

5 Minutes to a 5

Bacteria can adjust the composition of their cell membranes by changing the relative amounts of unsaturated versus saturated fatty acids. Which of the following statements correctly describes the bacterial membrane?

**A.** An increase of unsaturated fatty acids would decrease the fluidity of the membrane.

**B.** Fatty acids with double bonds help to reduce fluidity.

**C.** Bacteria living in cold climates would need to decrease the ratio of saturated to unsaturated fatty acids.

**D.** Changes in fatty acid composition would affect only one side of the phospholipid bilayer.

Cell membranes regulate the flow of substances into and out of the cell. Not all molecules are equally soluble. Which of the following is a **false** statement regarding passage across a cell membrane?

**A.** Small, uncharged, polar molecules can pass through.

**B.** Small, hydrophobic molecules can pass through.

**C.** Charged particles such as ions are repelled.

**D.** Only oxygen and carbon dioxide can easily pass through; all other substances require a transport protein.

There are occasional reports of accidental IV administration of sterile water instead of a saline solution. What are the risks to the patient in such circumstances?

**A.** The increased volume of the blood will stress the arteries, potentially resulting in an aneurysm.

**B.** The dilution of blood glucose will signal the liver to increase hydrolysis of glucose from stored glycogen.

**C.** The hormone aldosterone will send a signal to the kidneys to increase the amount of sodium in the blood serum.

**D.** The water will create hypotonic conditions, leading to swelling of the red blood cells.

# Day 15

Cystic fibrosis is a genetic disorder caused by a mutated cystic fibrosis transmembrane conductance regulator (CFTR) protein. This protein is important for controlling the exchange of materials in the gas-exchange and digestive systems. The defective protein is no longer able to properly move chloride ions from the inside of the cell to the outside. Because of this, water balance is negatively affected, leading to a buildup of thick mucus secretions outside of the cells. Victims of CF suffer from lung infections and digestion difficulties. Which statement **best** describes the physiological problem faced by those with CF?

**A.** A faulty CFTR protein is unable to create a hypertonic environment on the outside of the cell.

**B.** Without a functioning CFTR protein, water cannot be transported across the membrane.

**C.** The CFTR protein is required to establish a higher concentration of chloride ions on the inside of the cell.

**D.** When the movement of the chloride ions is compromised, the cell cannot create a hypotonic environment on the outside of the cell, thus creating conditions for a thick mucus layer.

# Day 16

When a cell responds to a chemical signal, the signal itself is often unable to pass through the cell membrane. The signal, however, must activate some sort of cellular response *inside* the cell. This movement of a message into the cell is called *signal reception*. Describe how a message can move into a cell without the chemical messenger itself passing through the cell membrane.

When the haploid form of the yeast *Saccharomyces cerevisiae* mates, it must fuse with another haploid cell. The two haploid mating types of *S. cerevisiae* are designated as either an α (alpha) cell or an **a** cell; in order to increase diversity in the offspring, an α cell will only fuse with an **a** cell. In order to accomplish this, a cell must sense when a cell of the other mating type is nearby. This is accomplished by secreting extracellular signals: α cells secrete α factors and **a** cells secrete **a** factors. These mating pheromones signal the presence of an **a** cell to neighboring α cells (and vice versa). When these chemical signals bind to the other cell type, it elicits a response of the cell rearranging its cytoskeleton so it "moves" toward the opposite cell type. Once the two cells touch, they fuse and create a diploid cell. Create a simple illustration and description of the three steps of *signal transduction* using the model of an α and an **a** *S. cerevisiae* cell.

## Day 18

One type of transmembrane receptor that plays a prominent role in cell signaling is the G protein-coupled receptor (GPCR). Once this receptor binds the ligand it activates an associated G protein that is tethered to the inside of the cell membrane. The activated G protein releases the receptor and slides across the membrane until it reaches its target enzyme, thus activating it. The activated enzyme leads to the cellular response that the initial signal called for.

If a cell with the G protein-coupled receptor suffered a mutation that reduced the ability of the G protein to release the GPCR, which of the following would result?

**A.** The enzyme would remain in its inactive form, thus leading to an increase in the cellular response.

**B.** The signaling molecule would be unable to bind to the GPCR.

**C.** The activated G protein would be unable to alter the enzyme's shape and activity.

**D.** The cellular response would be triggered in the absence of the signal molecule.

5 Minutes to a 5

‹ 343

A biochemist is running an enzyme-catalyzed reaction in a flask. An inhibitor was accidentally added to the flask, greatly slowing the reaction. Depending on the type of inhibitor—competitive or non-competitive—the addition of more substrate will have a different effect on the reaction. Create a graph with three plots (no inhibitor; competitive inhibitor; noncompetitive inhibitor) showing how the reaction rate changes with increasing concentration of substrate.

5 Minutes to a 5

ATP is the energy currency of all cells and its hydrolysis is used to "power" reactions. Which of the following is the **best** explanation of how, exactly, ATP uses its energy to drive other chemical reactions?

**A.** ATP is used to create a phosphorylated intermediate that is more unstable, and thus more reactive.

**B.** When the third phosphate group is cleaved off of ATP, the energy diffuses through space and creates favorable conditions for other reactions to occur.

**C.** When ATP is created, the energy that is released is absorbed by nearby reactants.

**D.** The hydrolysis of the third phosphate group requires energy and takes it from the reaction it is coupled with.

The diagram above shows the biosynthetic pathways for the amino acids valine, isoleucine, and leucine. It is an example of both positive and negative feedback controlling the activity of the enzyme threonine deaminase. Which of the following is a true statement about the activity of threonine deaminase?

**A.** An increase in the production of isoleucine would lead to an increase in threonine deaminase activity.

**B.** An increase of valine would lead to an increase of α-ketobutyrate production.

**C.** A decrease of isoleucine would lead to a decrease of α-ketobutyrate production.

**D.** A decrease of valine would increase the activity of threonine deaminase.

5 Minutes to a 5

What is the metabolic outcome when a person's exertion level exceeds their respiratory rate, leading to a shortage of oxygen in muscle tissue?

**A.** The electron transport chain will increase its rate of substrate-level phosphorylation to keep up with ATP demand.

**B.** ATP production will stop.

**C.** Lactic acid concentration will increase in the muscle tissue.

**D.** The only ATP produced will be through oxidative phosphorylation.

One method of measuring cellular respiration is to use a respirometer. A respirometer allows changes in gas volume to be measured as the organism sealed inside it undergoes cellular respiration. During cellular respiration, oxygen gas is used at the same rate carbon dioxide is produced. What must be taken into consideration in order to accurately compare the respiration rate of a cricket versus a mouse?

**A.** The amount of gas exchanged must be adjusted per gram of organism.

**B.** In order to accurately measure the volume of oxygen used, the carbon dioxide must be removed from the respirometer.

**C.** The temperature must remain the same for both the mouse and the cricket.

**D.** All of the above

5 Minutes to a 5

If the same experiment as the previous question was going to be performed on a plant, which of the following things must be taken into consideration?

**A.** Plants only photosynthesize and do not undergo cellular respiration.

**B.** In order to measure cellular respiration, the plant must be kept in the dark.

**C.** The experiment would fail because a plant is unable to survive once it is removed from the soil.

**D.** A plant only uses carbon dioxide and does not produce it.

**Day 25**

Most organisms require oxygen to release energy from food through the process of cellular respiration; some anaerobic organisms can only harvest energy in the absence of oxygen. Additionally, there are some microorganisms that use oxygen if it's available but can generate energy in the absence of oxygen, too. These are called facultative anaerobes. A researcher wanted to investigate the bacterium *Streptococcus thermophiles*, a facultative anaerobe. The bacteria were grown in test tubes, some of which were sealed, so no oxygen was available. The other test tubes had a stream of air bubbling through the growth media.

Bacterial Growth at Different Glucose Concentrations

| Concentration of Glucose (mg/100 mL) | Concentration of Bacteria (millions/mL) | | | |
|---|---|---|---|---|
| | Exp. A | | Exp. B | |
| | Test tube | Without Air | Test tube | With Air |
| 15 | 1A | 42 | 1B | 180 |
| 30 | 2A | 98 | 2B | 450 |
| 60 | 3A | 161 | 3B | 720 |
| 120 | 4A | 220 | 4B | 1100 |
| 240 | 5A | 410 | 5B | 2300 |

Compare test tubes 4A and 4B. How many times greater was the growth when air was present?

A. 0.2

B. 2.2

C. 4.66

D. 5

Review the experiment from Day 25. What hypothesis **best** explains why there are many more bacteria per milligram of glucose in the B test tubes than in the A test tubes?

**A.** When oxygen is absent, *Streptococcus thermophiles* is more efficient at generating ATP from glucose, thus more bacteria were able to grow.

**B.** The test tubes with air bubbling through them provided a greater surface area on which the bacteria could grow.

**C.** When oxygen is present, cellular respiration is a more efficient means for extracting energy from glucose, thus more bacteria were able to grow.

**D.** The higher the concentration of glucose, the quicker the bacteria were able to reproduce.

A culture of *Saccharomyces cerevisiae* yeast was studied to determine the optimal temperature for fermentation. A glucose, water, and yeast solution was sealed in an enclosed flask. Any carbon dioxide gas released through fermentation would exit through a glass tube attached to a graduated pipette. As fermentation occurs, the $CO_2$ would push a colored drop of water through the pipette, thus measuring volume of carbon dioxide produced (mL).

The following table shows carbon dioxide accumulation (mL) at different temperatures over five different time periods.

| TIME (MINUTES) | 5°C | 10°C | 35°C | 50°C |
|---|---|---|---|---|
| 2 | 0 | 0.3 | 0.6 | 0.2 |
| 4 | 0 | 0.8 | 1.8 | 0.5 |
| 6 | 0.1 | 1.5 | 3.3 | 0.6 |
| 8 | 0.2 | 2.2 | 4.5 | 1.2 |
| 10 | 0.3 | 3.1 | 6.1 | 1.3 |

**A.** Graph the $CO_2$ accumulation for the four temperatures.

**B.** Calculate the rates of $CO_2$ accumulation for both 10°C and 35°C between 4 and 8 minutes.

**C.** Determine how much greater the rate of fermentation is at 35°C compared to 10°C.

**5 Minutes to a 5**

Why is lactic acid produced when a muscle cell temporarily switches from cellular respiration to fermentation?

**A.** Pyruvic acid is reduced in order to oxidize the NADH and re-create NAD+ to keep glycolysis running.

**B.** Once oxidative phosphorylation comes to a halt, lactic acid is required for ATP production through substrate-level phosphorylation.

**C.** Lactic acid is a normal product of the glycolytic pathway in muscle cells, regardless of oxygen concentration.

**D.** The Krebs cycle comes to a halt, thus allowing a build-up of lactic acid, the carbon compound that participates in the first reaction of the Krebs cycle.

Below is a graph charting the approximate amounts of dissolved oxygen in a lake throughout a 24-hour period. Explain the overall dissolved oxygen fluctuation the lake experiences throughout this timeframe.

# Day 30

Photosynthesis can be divided into two sets of reactions: light-dependent reactions and light-independent reactions. Summarize the purpose of these two sets of reaction and how they are dependent upon one another.

The bacterium *Halobacterium* carries out photosynthesis using the purple pigment bacteriorhodopsin. Bacteriorhodopsin is a protein composed of seven trans-membrane sections that form a channel through the bacterial cell membrane. There is a molecule called retinal loosely bound to an amino acid near the opening to the interior of the cell. When retinal absorbs sunlight, it releases the amino acid and instead binds to a hydrogen ion. Retinal then moves to the outermost region of bacteriorhodopsin, attaches to a different amino acid, and releases the hydrogen ion into the outside environment. This leads to an eventual accumulation of hydrogen ions outside of the cell. ATP synthase can use the difference in hydrogen-ion concentration between the inside and the outside of the cell to power ATP synthesis.

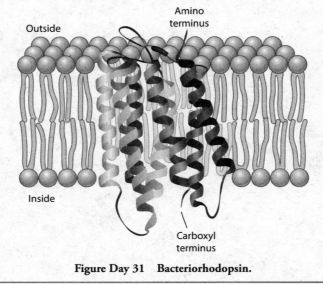

**Figure Day 31    Bacteriorhodopsin.**

5 Minutes to a 5

Which statement regarding photosynthesis of *Halobacterium* versus photosynthesis in a plant cell is correct?

**A.** Unlike chlorophyll, bacteriorhodopsin is not highly adapted to its function in photosynthesis.

**B.** Both systems require a mobile secondary molecule (e.g., retinal) to physically shuttle the hydrogen ion across the membrane.

**C.** Both *Halobacterium* and a plant rely on chemiosmosis to drive ATP production.

**D.** In *Halobacterium,* the energy to drive the movement of hydrogen ions is from light, whereas in a plant, the energy is derived from the splitting of water.

Rubisco is the enzyme responsible for the first step of the Calvin cycle in photosynthesis. It catalyzes the reaction of fixing a molecule of atmospheric carbon dioxide onto a molecule of ribulose 1,5-bisphosphate (RuBP). When plants close their stomata in times of water conservation, they experience a shortage of carbon dioxide and the oxygen produced is unable to leave the plant tissue. These conditions lead to rubisco accidentally fixing oxygen onto RuBP instead of carbon dioxide ("photorespiration"). Considering that natural selection tends to select for the "most fit" option, which would be a possible explanation as to how this mistake-prone enzyme would evolve?

**A.** Prior to the evolution of photosynthesis, there was very little oxygen in the atmosphere; rubisco did not have the selective pressure of atmospheric oxygen to contend with.

**B.** The products of photorespiration can still be used by the Calvin cycle.

**C.** Natural selection cannot act on enzymes and biochemical pathways.

**D.** When photosynthesis first evolved, the cell membranes of the photosynthesizing cells were impermeable to atmospheric oxygen.

$C_4$ plants have evolved specializations that help reduce inefficiencies caused by photorespiration. An enzyme in the mesophyll cells fixes carbon dioxide with greater efficiency than rubisco. The $CO_2$ is then shuttled farther into the leaf, where it is transferred to the Calvin cycle (and rubisco) away from atmospheric oxygen. The graph below shows the difference in fixation efficiency between C3 ("standard" photosynthesis) and C4 plants. Label the two plots as either C3 or C4, and use the data for 20 percent oxygen to calculate how much more efficient the C4 plant is compared to the C3 plant.

A. Write the balanced chemical equation for photosynthesis.

B. If the water molecules contained radioactive oxygen, where would they end up on the product side of the equation? Explain.

By using a suspension of chloroplasts in the presence of a blue dye (2,6-dichlorophenol-indophenol, or DPIP), the rate of photosynthesis can be tracked using a simple color change. A chloroplast suspension is created so that the thylakoids are broken apart and the natural electron transport chains no longer function normally. When this suspension is mixed with DPIP, the dye turns from blue to clear when reduced by electrons and hydrogens. Which of the following **best** describes the role of DPIP in the experiment?

**A.** The dye attaches to chlorophyll molecules and absorbs photons of light, turning colorless.

**B.** The DPIP is reduced by the energized electron from photosystem II.

**C.** The DPIP absorbs the light and funnels the energy to reaction-center chlorophyll a. This role as electron carrier causes DPIP to turn from blue to colorless.

**D.** The DPIP replaces NADP+ from photosystem I.

The figure below shows the relative amount of DNA in a cell as it progresses through two rounds of cellular division. For each of the stages (labeled I–V) indicate what stage of the cell cycle applies, based on the concentration of DNA.

5 Minutes to a 5

This drawing shows dividing onion root cells. Based on this figure, answer the following question.

Arrange cells 2, 11, 21, 22, and 33 in the correct order, demonstrating the stages of mitosis.

**A.** 11, 22, 2, 21, 33

**B.** 22, 11, 21, 33, 2

**C.** 2, 21, 22, 11, 33

**D.** 21, 22, 2, 33, 11

5 Minutes to a 5

Colchicine is a chemical that acts as a mitotic inhibitor by blocking spindle formation. If this sample had been treated with colchicine, which cell represents the FIRST step of mitosis to be blocked?

**A.** 12

**B.** 15

**C.** 23

**D.** 29

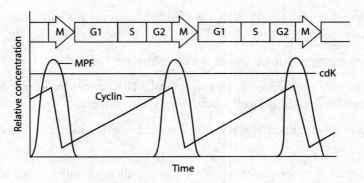

Based on the above graph, which of the following statements about the changes in chemical signal concentration is correct?

**A.** As the concentration of cyclin increases, the concentration of MPF drops.

**B.** The concentration of Cdk varies throughout the cell cycle.

**C.** The concentration of cyclin is highest in $G_1$.

**D.** Accumulation of MPF is highest near the $G_2$ checkpoint.

Review the graph from Day 39. What is a good reason for the rapid enzyme-catalyzed degradation of cyclin?

**A.** MPF cannot properly form unless the concentration of cyclin is below that of Cdk.

**B.** A breakdown of cyclin means a reduction of MPF concentration. If MPF concentration remained high, the cell would continually divide.

**C.** If cyclin levels remained high, the cell would not be able to properly synthesize Cdk.

**D.** In order for MPF to properly signal progression through mitosis, the levels of cyclin must be decreasing.

# Day 41

The diploid chromosome number for a chicken is 78. What would the haploid number of chromosomes be in the chicken's gametes?

A. 18

B. 34

C. 39

D. 78

Which of the following occurs in meiosis but **not** in mitosis?

**A.** Attachment of spindle fibers to the kinetochore

**B.** Replication of DNA prior to the start of cell division

**C.** Separation of sister chromatids at anaphase

**D.** Pairing of homologous chromosomes at the metaphase plate

*Sordaria fimicola* is a fungus that reproduces by forming structures called asci. Each ascus contains eight spores. The color of the spores (either black or tan) is determined by a single gene. The asci of the parental generation contain spores with a pattern of four black in a row and four tan in a row (4:4). The occurrence of crossing over and recombination during meiosis can be observed by looking at the spore color pattern in the asci of the offspring. If crossing over occurred, the spore color patterns will be different:

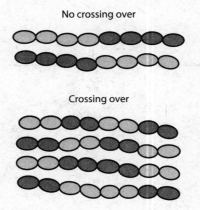

Crossover frequency can be used to map the location of the spore color gene on the chromosome. The farther the gene is located from the centromere, the higher the chances of crossover occurring. Based on the drawing of *Sordaria* below, determine the percentage of asci showing crossover, and then calculate the color gene locus.

To calculate the gene locus (in map units), divide the crossover percent by two. A map unit is a relative measure of the distance between the gene and the centromere.

| NUMBER OF 4:4 ASCI (NO CROSSOVER) | NUMBER OF ASCI WITH CROSSOVER | TOTAL NUMBER OF ASCI | PERCENTAGE OF ASCI SHOWING CROSSOVER | GENE-TO-CENTROMERE DISTANCE (% CROSSOVER / 2) |
|---|---|---|---|---|
|  |  |  |  |  |

**Alternation of generations**

1 (in reproductive cells)

Haploid cells

2

Haploid individual

Diploid individual

Diploid zygote

Haploid gametes

4

Fertilization

3

The diagram above shows the process of alternation of generations in a fern. Which of the following labels are correct for boxes 1–4?

**A.** Meiosis, mitosis, mitosis, mitosis

**B.** Mitosis, meiosis, mitosis, meiosis

**C.** Meiosis, meiosis, meiosis, mitosis

**D.** Mitosis, meiosis, meiosis, mitosis

5 Minutes to a 5

Which of the following statements about heredity is true?

A. An individual's genotype is the physical manifestation of a genetic trait.

B. An individual with matching alleles for a given trait is said to be heterozygous for that trait.

C. For any given gene, there can only be two different alleles.

D. An individual's phenotype is the physical expression of the trait associated with a particular gene.

When Mendel crossed pure-breeding purple-flowered and white-flowered pea plants, the offspring ($F_1$) all had the dominant phenotype (purple). When the $F_1$ offspring were crossed, the resulting $F_2$ generation showed a purple to white (recessive) ratio of 3:1. Explain these results and why they suggested a "particulate" model of inheritance instead of the "blending" hypothesis.

When an individual with a dominant phenotype is crossed with an individual with a recessive phenotype, 6 of their 11 offspring show the recessive phenotype. What is the genotype of the first parent?

**A.** AA

**B.** Aa

**C.** aa

**D.** AA or Aa

# Day 48

If the probability of a chicken having a rose-shaped comb is ¾ and the probability of that same chicken having white feathers is ¼, then what is the probability of the chicken having both a rose-shaped comb and white feathers?

A. ¾

B. ⅜

C. ½

D. ³⁄₁₆

A geneticist was attempting to cross a spotted beetle with a striped beetle. She predicted a phenotypic outcome of four beetles with only stripes, three beetles with only spots, and nine beetles with both stripes and spots.

When the cross was performed and she counted the offspring, she found 40 with only stripes, 31 with only spots, and 75 with both stripes and spots. According to the chi-square test, did she get the predicted outcome?

Huntington's disease is a neurodegenerative disorder that affects muscle coordination. The disease is caused by an autosomal dominant mutation. Which of the following is a correct description of the inheritance pattern of Huntington's disease?

**A.** The Huntington's allele is carried on the X chromosome and tends to effect more males than females.

**B.** If two individuals with Huntington's disease had a baby, the baby would have a 100 percent chance of also having Huntington's disease.

**C.** An individual with Huntington's disease might only have a single allele for the disease.

**D.** A person could unknowingly be a carrier for the Huntington allele.

Down syndrome is a diseased caused by nondisjunction of chromosome 21, leading to a person with three copies of chromosome 21. Which of the following statements about Down syndrome is *false*?

**A.** It is a result of the improper segregation of chromosomes during meiosis.

**B.** It is the result of an abnormal number of chromosomes in the offspring.

**C.** It is a mistake that occurs during the M phase of the cell cycle.

**D.** The sister chromatids are not properly separated during mitosis.

**5 Minutes to a 5**

A geneticist observed a dihybrid cross (aabb × AaBb) and instead of the expected 1:1:1:1 ratio, he saw the following numbers:

- 64 AaBb

- 444 Aabb

- 453 aaBb

- 52 aabb

What would be the **best** explanation for these unexpected results?

**A.** These numbers represent simple statistical variation and do not suggest a genetic anomaly.

**B.** The genes for A and B are located on the same chromosome and could not assort independently.

**C.** A mutation occurred, changing the dominant B allele to its recessive b form.

**D.** Being phenotypically dominant or recessive for both traits was a lethal condition and the zygote would not survive.

A woman with AB-negative blood has a child with a man of blood type B-positive (heterozygous for both blood type and the Rh factor). What are the odds that their child will have type A-positive blood?

Yellow (Y) and black (B) coat color in cats is a sex-linked trait. A heterozygous female is called a calico. The possible genotypes and their phenotypes are given below:

Females:  $X^Y X^Y$ = yellow          Males:  $X^Y Y$ = yellow

$X^B X^Y$ = calico                    $X^B Y$ = black

$X^B X^B$ = black

A calico cat has a litter of eight kittens: one yellow male, two black males, two yellow females, and three calico females. What is the probable color of the father of this litter?

DNA is a double-stranded polymer that is the universal hereditary material of cells. All proteins required by a cell are coded for by the DNA's genes. When a given gene is expressed (turned into a protein), only one of the two DNA strands is transcribed by RNA polymerase into a molecule of mRNA, and in turn, read by a ribosome for protein synthesis. This is called the *template strand*. For another gene, the template strand may instead be the other strand of DNA. Regardless, the template strand contains the necessary sequence of bases; the other strand has a complementary base sequence and would not produce the correct sequence of amino acids. Why, then, would DNA bother being double stranded? Why not hold the code for all genes on a single template strand?

Chromosomes are a mixture of DNA and special proteins called histones. In order to isolate a pure sample of DNA, a researcher mixes the DNA suspension with protease, an enzyme that digests proteins. To determine the purity of the treated sample, the researcher compared the ratio of nitrogen to phosphorus of her preparation. What would be the predicted N/P ratio based on the structure of DNA? Assume the representative sample of DNA contains equal ratios G, C, A, and T. How would the researcher know if the sample was contaminated with protein?

5 Minutes to a 5

# Day 57

RNA and DNA are both macromolecules necessary for cellular function, reproduction, and transmission of genetic traits. These two molecules, though similar in structure, have significant differences that help to define their functions. Make a chart comparing the similarities and the differences in the structures of DNA and RNA.

5 Minutes to a 5

RNA has numerous functions in the cell. Describe the four functions RNA has in a cell.

When DNA replicates, new nucleotides are added by DNA polymerase to the growing chain. Once the nucleotide is incorporated into the DNA strand, it is composed of deoxyribose, a nitrogenous base, and a single phosphate group. Each nucleotide comes from a free-floating nucleoside triphosphate (same as a nucleotide, but with three phosphate groups). Why is it significant that when a nucleoside triphosphate is attached to the growing strand, two phosphate groups are removed?

What is the proper order of the following events in the expression of a eukaryotic gene?

**1.** Translation

**2.** RNA processing

**3.** Transcription

**4.** Modification of protein

**A.** 1, 2, 3, 4

**B.** 3, 2, 1, 4

**C.** 4, 2, 3, 1

**D.** 2, 3, 4, 1

The following is a eukaryotic transcription unit ("bp" stands for base pairs):

| Exon 1 | Intron 1 | Exon 2 | Intron 2 | Exon 3 |
|--------|----------|--------|----------|--------|
| 100 bp | 75 bp | 50 bp | 70 bp | 25 bp |

Eukaryotic gene transcription includes extensive pre-mRNA processing. Introns are removed, exons are spliced together, a 5′-guanine cap is attached, and a poly-A tail is also attached. Assuming the poly-A tail consists of 200 adenines, how many base pairs would the fully processed mRNA be?

**Day 62**

3′ – G G A T A G C T G C T T C C T T G T A G A – 5′
5′ – C C T A T C G A C G A A G G A A C A T C T – 3′  ← Template strand

Given the above segment of DNA, show the products of transcription and translation. Do not forget the importance of polarity of DNA, and how a ribosome knows where to start translation.

A researcher noticed that two differently structured proteins were translated from the same mouse gene. Which mechanism below could **best** account for this?

**A.** A mutation altered the gene in some cells but not others.

**B.** Exons from the same gene could be spliced in different ways to make different mRNAs.

**C.** The two proteins have different functions in the cell.

**D.** Different transcription factors were involved in the transcription of the two mRNAs.

Cystic fibrosis is a genetic disorder caused by a mutated cystic fibrosis transmembrane conductance regulator (CFTR) protein. This protein is important for controlling the exchange of materials in the gas-exchange and digestive systems. The defective protein is no longer able to properly move chloride ions from the inside of the cell to the outside. Because of this, water balance is negatively affected, leading to a buildup of thick mucus secretions outside of the cells. Victims of CF suffer from lung infections and digestion difficulties. There are many classifications of CFTR mutations. Which of the following would result in a truncated (shortened) protein?

**A.** Defective post-translational processing and transport

**B.** Premature stop codon

**C.** Reduction in channel opening probability

**D.** Splicing defect during mRNA processing

The *lac* operon allows bacteria to express the genes for lactose digestion only when the substrate (lactose) is present in the environment. The operon's regulatory gene (*lacI*) produces a repressor in the active form that binds to the operator and stops transcription of the genes for lactose digestion. When lactose is available in the environment (as signaled by the present of allolactose, an isomer of lactose), allolactose binds to the repressor and inactivates it. The lactose-utilizing enzymes are now transcribed: LacZ digests lactose, LacY transports lactose into the cell, and LacA (whose function is still unclear).

Which of the following is a **false** statement about the bacterial lac operon?

**A.** The accumulation of allolactose leads to increased expression of LacY, which in turn increases the rate of lactose/allolactose intake, an example of positive feedback.

**B.** LacZ metabolizes allolactose and decreases its availability to LacI. This leads to repression of the operon in a negative feedback loop.

**C.** A mutation in the *lacI* gene would lead to an inability to properly regulate the lac operon.

**D.** Activation of the LacI repressor requires binding to the inducer allolactose.

5 Minutes to a 5

Review the function and structure of a bacterial operon. Which of the following is the **best** definition of an operator?

**A.** A non-coding sequence that controls the access of RNA polymerase

**B.** A DNA-binding protein that regulates gene expression

**C.** A cluster of genes and their controlling elements

**D.** A specific small molecule that inactivates the repressor

Transcription factors are proteins that play an important role in gene expression by mediating the binding of RNA polymerase to the promoter. For even more precise control over gene expression, eukaryotic cells depend on specific transcriptional factors called activators. These proteins bind to a specific region in the DNA called the enhancer region, which is itself made up of a mix-and-match combination of DNA sequences called control elements. The combination of about 10 different control elements make up a gene's enhancer region (a lock); in order for high-level expression of a given gene, the cell must have the correct combination of activator proteins to bind at each of the gene's specific control elements (the key). Based on the following simplified example, which statement is correct?

5 Minutes to a 5

**A.** The cell must be a pancreatic cell because the available activators target and "unlock" the insulin gene.

**B.** Control elements "orange" and "silver" would correctly cause differential gene expression of the cerumen gene.

**C.** Neither gene will be transcribed until activators for all eight different control elements are present.

**D.** The cerumen gene will be expressed at high levels because the correct combination of activators will bind the enhancer region.

Gene expression is regulated at many steps along the pathway from gene to functional protein. Based on the following stages, explain how the cell has a chance to regulate the expression of a gene's protein product:

- Chromatin modification

- Transcription

- RNA processing

- Translation

- Protein modification

Day 69

Why is gene regulation important for bacteria?

**A.** It allows bacteria to make quick metabolic changes in response to environmental changes.

**B.** It helps to prevent the cell from wasting energy and resources.

**C.** The cell is able to alter its biochemical pathways to suit the available substrate.

**D.** All of the above

# Day 70

Cancer is a possible result when a cell no longer responds properly to signals of the cell cycle. Which of the following is **least** likely to cause a cell to become cancerous?

**A.** Hyperactive Ras protein, which issues unnecessary signals from a growth factor receptor responsible for stimulating the cell cycle

**B.** Progression into $G_2$ after incorrectly replicating the chromosomes

**C.** Inability of the cell to heed density-dependent inhibition

**D.** Duplication of the p53 gene (and thus amplification of the protein product) would further stop the cell cycle.

The process of cell differentiation allows a fertilized egg cell (zygote) to divide and change into what will become the different tissues of a multicellular organism. Cells that make up these tissues create different proteins, have different functions, and can look extremely different. What explains how an undifferentiated cell is able to change into such different cells types?

**A.** Early in the developmental pathway, a cell will differentiate and lose any genes not related to its specific function.

**B.** When a cell begins to differentiate, only the genes related to that cell's final function are expressed; other unnecessary genes are not targeted by RNA polymerase.

**C.** Different cell types produce the all the same proteins, but only the proteins related to the cells particular function will create a positive feedback loop and further affect the cell's mature morphology.

**D.** When a cell begins to differentiate and turn into a certain cell type, it will only use RNA polymerase molecules that specifically target promoters of genes involved in the tissue's function.

Apoptosis is the process of a cell dying in response to a genetic signal. Which of the following is **not** a function of apoptosis in a developing organism?

**A.** Removal of excess tissue between developing digits in order to form independent fingers and toes

**B.** When a cell dies, apoptosis protecting neighboring cells from potentially damaging materials released from the dying cell

**C.** The immune system responding to a virally infected cell, destroying it before the infection can spread

**D.** The signal for apoptosis targets invading bacterial cells, inducing their self-destruction and removal

Using the following items, create a simple diagram outlining the process of cloning through nuclear transplantation:

- Somatic cell donor

- Egg donor

- Early embryo

- Removal of nucleus

- Organism being cloned

- Surrogate mother

- Nucleus injected into cell

Day 74

Viruses are not considered to be alive, even though they exhibit qualities that suggest otherwise. Make a list of characteristics that support the argument that viruses are living and a list of characteristics that suggest they are not.

5 Minutes to a 5

The Hershey-Chase experiment is outlined in the following diagram:

Which of the following statements is **not** an accurate description of their experiment?

**A.** If radioactive phosphorus was detected outside the cell after centrifugation, that suggests the genetic material was DNA.

**B.** The element sulfur was chosen to label protein because sulfur is not found in DNA.

**C.** If the radioactivity remained in the cell after centrifugation, the polymer containing that radioactive element must be the genetic material.

**D.** Carbon could not be used as a radioactive label because it is found in both protein and DNA.

5 Minutes to a 5

Getting a seasonal flu vaccination is an excellent way to protect oneself during the course of a flu epidemic. It is, however, necessary to get a new vaccination for each of the following flu seasons. Explain how this is an example of evolution.

The DNA of a virus was sequenced and found to contain 17 percent guanine. What is the percentage of adenine?

The human genome is composed of many types of DNA sequences. List the following types of DNA sequences in order from **largest** percentage to **smallest** percentage:

**1.** Introns

**2.** Protein coding regions

**3.** Transposons

**4.** Sequences for gene regulation

**A.** 3, 1, 4, 2

**B.** 2, 1, 4, 3

**C.** 2, 3, 1, 4

**D.** 4, 3, 1, 2

Day 79

Which of the following statements about homeotic genes (also called *Hox* genes) is/are correct?

A. Homeotic genes include a DNA sequence called the homeobox that is similar in everything from invertebrates to vertebrates.

B. Homeotic genes that control anterior (nearer the front) and posterior (farther back) structures of the body occur in the same sequences in fruit flies and mice.

C. Homeotic genes determine the developmental fates of groups of cells in a growing embryo.

D. All of the above

What significant insights could be discovered by comparing the genomes of a spider monkey, a human, and a crustacean?

5 Minutes to a 5

## Day 81

Variation is the foundation for natural selection. Describe how variation is achieved through formation of gametes and sexual reproduction.

A biologist measured antibiotic resistance in the human population over 8 years. How does this graph demonstrate evidence of evolution?

**A.** At or around year 4 the bacteria responded to the presence of the antibiotic and intentionally developed a means by which the cells could withstand the antibiotic.

**B.** Over multiple generations, the ability to resist antibiotics was selected for and increased in the bacterial population.

**C.** The negative slope of the graph suggests a decrease in the presence of antibiotic-resistant bacteria.

**D.** The percentage of antibiotic-resistance was greatest for the first five years but tapered off after antibiotics was no longer a selective pressure.

**Day 83**

Explain how the very distantly related organisms, the hummingbird and the hummingbird hawk-moth, can look so similar.

The process of evolution is supported by an overwhelming amount of scientific evidence, yet arguments against evolution's validity remain. One invalid argument is based on the idea of "irreducible complexity." This pseudoscientific argument claims that the process of natural selection cannot occur because of the incremental adaptations required to create a final elaborate structure with interlocking parts, such as the mammalian eye or the bacterial flagella. The argument says that a complex structure could not function properly without all its smaller structures intact; for example, the eye would not function without the lens, retina, cornea, etc.—all in finalized, perfected forms. Therefore it would be impossible for incremental modifications over millennia to select for and shape this final structure. (What evolutionary benefit would an intermediately formed and not fully functional eye provide an animal?) Refute this faulty argument and explain how a complex structure such as the bacterial flagellum or the mammalian eye can form through the gradual process of natural selection.

5 Minutes to a 5

| SPECIES COMPARED | DNA SEQUENCE DIFFERENCES (%) |
|---|---|
| Chimpanzee vs. bonobo | 0.7 |
| Human vs. chimpanzee | 1.6 |
| Human vs. gorilla | 2.3 |
| Gorilla vs. chimpanzee | 2.3 |

Molecular comparisons of living species help establish the pattern of their evolutionary relationships. The table above quantifies the DNA differences between closely related species. Which of the following cladograms correctly shows the evolutionary relationship between these four species?

**A.** A

**B.** B

**C.** C

**D.** D

When creating a phylogenic tree, there is often more than one possible construct that can be created to explain the evolutionary relatedness of the organisms in question. Usually the best phylogenic tree is the one that best reflects the principle of **maximum parsimony** (the simplest explanation is the best explanation). Based on this principle, explain which of the following phylogenetic trees is preferable:

5 Minutes to a 5

Based on the following table of derived characteristics, create a cladogram depicting plant evolution. A "0" indicates that the organism lacks the trait; a "1" indicates that the organism possesses the derived characteristic (vascular tissue, flowers, or seeds).

| PLANT | VASCULAR TISSUE | FLOWERS | SEEDS |
| --- | --- | --- | --- |
| Pine trees | 1 | 1 | 0 |
| Mosses | 0 | 0 | 0 |
| Flowering plants | 1 | 1 | 1 |
| Ferns | 1 | 0 | 0 |

5 Minutes to a 5

If beetles, earwigs, and flies belong to the same class (*Insecta*) but to different orders, and if aphids, water striders, and leaf hoppers belong to the same order (*Hemiptera*) but to different families, which of the following pairs of organisms would be expected to show the greatest degree of similarity?

**A.** Beetles and earwigs

**B.** Beetles and flies

**C.** Flies and leaf hoppers

**D.** Water striders and aphids

5 Minutes to a 5

The greater prairie chicken was an unfortunate example of the bottleneck effect. Based on the data below, explain the bottleneck effect and its impact on the greater prairie chicken population in Illinois.

| YEAR | POPULATION SIZE | NUMBER OF ALLELES PER LOCUS | PERCENTAGE OF EGGS HATCHED |
|---|---|---|---|
| 1930–1960 | 25,000 | 5.2 | 93 |
| 1993 | Less than 50 | 3.7 | Less than 50 |

In an experiment, a population of the plant *Brassica rapa* (field mustard) was studied before and after drought conditions. Flowering time is controlled by a gene that shows allelic variation. During times of drought, plants that flower early in the spring (before heat becomes dangerous) are favored. The number of days it took for the field mustard to first flower was recorded using seeds from plants that were not exposed to drought conditions. The plant population was then subjected to drought conditions for 10 generations; seeds from this population were then grown and the days to first flowering was recorded and compared to the original population.

| DAYS TO FIRST FLOWERING | INITIAL DISTRIBUTION (%) | DISTRIBUTION AFTER DROUGHT CONDITIONS (%) |
|---|---|---|
| 17–21 | 5 | 55 |
| 22–39 | 75 | 40 |
| 40–62 | 20 | 5 |

Which of the following is the **best** explanation of the recorded data?

**A.** The allele for early flowering increased the plants' fitness during dry conditions.

**B.** Dry conditions caused the gene for flowering time to mutate into an early flowering form.

**C.** The allele for late flowering was more beneficial to the plants during drought and was selected for.

**D.** Herbivores selectively ate late-flowering plants during drought conditions.

Draw a graph (frequency of individuals versus phenotype) for each of the following modes of selection and choose which one **best** represents the data from Day 90 of a population of *Brassica rapa* (field mustard) before and after drought conditions.

**A.** Stabilizing selection

**B.** Disruptive selection

**C.** Directional selection

Albinism is a genetic trait that is only expressed in individuals with two of the recessive alleles. The worldwide frequency of albinism is 1 in 17,000. What is the frequency of the allele for albinism?

**A.** 0.0000588

**B.** 0.00767

**C.** 0.0153

**D.** 0.992

As described in the question for Day 92, albinism is only expressed in homozygous recessive individuals. If the worldwide frequency of albinism is 1 in 17,000, what is the frequency of people who are heterozygous for albinism?

**A.** 0.00761

**B.** 0.0152

**C.** 0.152

**D.** 0.300

Within a population of butterflies, the color brown is dominant over the color white; 60 percent of all butterflies are brown. Given this information, calculate the following:

**A.** The percentage of butterflies in the population that is heterozygous

**B.** The frequency of homozygous dominant individuals

Andalusian chickens have two alleles for feather color: black and white. The alleles show an incompletely dominant inheritance pattern, and heterozygous individuals have slate-blue plumage. In a flock of 1,000 chickens, 85 have black plumage. Determine the frequency of each allele and each genotype in the population.

Adaptive radiation is the process of rapid diversification when an ancestral species occupy a new ecological niche. Which of the following factors would **not** facilitate adaptive radiation?

**A.** Bottleneck effect

**B.** Uninhabited niches

**C.** Evolutionary adaptations

**D.** Migration to an isolated region with few predators

**Day 97**

A species is a group of organisms able to produce viable, fertile offspring. Explain what is necessary in order to create a new species from an existing ancestral population.

Speciation can occur with or without a geographical barrier occurring between populations of the existing species. Which of the following statements is correct?

**A.** Allopatric speciation does not require geographic separation between subsets of a population.

**B.** Speciation without a geographical barrier is possible if sexual selection is prevalent, such as when females select males based on their appearance.

**C.** If a river changes course and divides a population that is then unable to cross the river, this would result in sympatric speciation.

**D.** It is impossible for speciation to occur unless one subset of the population is physically isolated from the ancestral population.

# Day 99

The age of a newly discovered fossilized skull is determined through carbon radiometric dating. The ratio of carbon-14 to carbon-12 was $\frac{1}{16}$ that of present-day skulls. If carbon-14 has a half-life of 5,730 years, what is the age of the fossil?

Why are islands good places to observe examples of adaptive radiation?

Every type of cell must contain DNA as its hereditary genetic material. Which of the following statements is **not** true regarding bacterial DNA?

**A.** The bacterial chromosome is a single loop of DNA.

**B.** Bacteria can have "extra" pieces of DNA that are not required for survival and can replicate independently of the chromosome.

**C.** The bacterial chromosome is composed of a mixture of DNA and histone proteins.

**D.** The bacterial chromosome is attached to the plasma membrane instead of being contained within a nucleus.

Just like the more complex eukaryotic cells, bacteria must divide in order to reproduce. The process of cell division, however, is simpler in a prokaryotic cell. List both the **similarities** and **differences** between cell division in prokaryotes ("binary fission") versus eukaryotes.

The pBLU plasmid contains the genes for ampicillin resistance and beta-galactosidase production. The *amp^r* gene allows *Escherichia coli* to grow in the presence of the antibiotic ampicillin; β-galactosidase is an enzyme that hydrolyzes the substrate X-gal, producing an insoluble blue pigment. *E. coli* colonies are normally white; *E. coli* expressing β-galactosidase in the presence of X-gal will be colored blue. pBLU can be used as a vector to introduce the human insulin gene into *E. coli*. Using a restriction enzyme that cuts and inserts the insulin gene into a gene on the plasmid will inactivate that plasmid gene.

**pBlu Plasmid Map**

Xmal 3155   HinDIII 3190
Smal 3155   Sphl 3184
Kpnl 3151   Sall 3172
Asp 718 3151   Xbal 3166
EcoRI 3139   BamHI 3160

**Key:**

**AMP** = ampicillin resistance gene
**Beta-galactosidase** = gene coding for the b-galactosidase enzyme
**Unique sites** = the restriction enzymes shown cut the plasmid
 in only one place
**EcoRV 2028** = the restriction anzyme EcoRV cuts at nucleotide number 2028

Which of the following restriction enzymes should be used in order to isolate *E.coli* that contain the insulin gene?

**A.** Choose a restriction enzyme within the *amp$^r$* gene and plate the transformed bacteria on nutrient agar containing ampicillin. White colonies that grow on the agar plate carry the insulin gene.

**B.** Choose a restriction enzyme that cuts within the β-galactosidase gene and plate on nutrient agar containing ampicillin and X-gal. Blue colonies that grow on the agar plate carry the insulin gene.

**C.** Use two restriction enzymes, one that cuts within the *amp$^r$* gene and one that cuts within the β-galactosidase gene. Plate the bacteria on plain nutrient agar. Any colony growing on the agar plate contains the insulin gene.

**D.** Use a restriction enzyme that cuts within the β-galactosidase gene. Grow on nutrient agar that contains ampicillin and X-gal. Any white colonies that grow on the agar plate carry the insulin gene.

Review the use of pBLU as a vector to introduce a gene of interest into *Escherichia coli*. What is the role of ampicillin in this procedure?

**A.** Ampicillin is necessary for bacterial growth.

**B.** Ampicillin screens for *E. coli* that has been transformed with the plasmid.

**C.** Ampicillin is the substrate for β-galactosidase.

**D.** Ampicillin reduces the chances of outside contamination.

Until the 1970s, all prokaryotes were categorized together under one kingdom: Monera. Once microbiologists began comparing genetic sequences, however, they concluded that some prokaryotes were more closely related to eukaryotes than to bacteria and belonged in a domain of their own (Archaea). The remaining prokaryotes were now members of domain Bacteria, and all eukaryotic cells were part of domain Eukarya. Fill in the following table comparing characteristics of the three domains of life.

|  | BACTERIA | ARCHAEA | EUKARYA |
|---|---|---|---|
| Membrane-bound nucleus | Absent | ? | Present |
| Organelles | ? | Absent | Present |
| Peptidoglycan (a structure carbohydrate polymer) in cell walls | Present | Absent | ? |
| Circular chromosome | Present | Present | ? |
| Growth at extreme temperatures (i.e., greater than 100°C) | ? | Some species | ? |

Review the general characteristics of the three domains of life. Only members of domain Archaea are able to grow at extreme temperatures. What does this suggest about the ancestral origins of Archaea?

Which of the following is **not** addressed by the endosymbiotic theory?

**A.** The evolutionary origins of all the organelles in a eukaryotic cell

**B.** The presence of DNA in mitochondria and chloroplasts

**C.** The evolution of prokaryotic cells before eukaryotic cells

**D.** Symbiotic relationship in which one organism lives inside another

The study of the evolutionary relationship of protists is complex, uncertain, and oftentimes controversial. One phylogenetic hypothesis uses "supergroups" to try and categorize eukaryotes. One supergroup, Unikonts, is an amazingly diverse group of organisms:

Unikonts

Gymnamoebas

Slime molds

Nucleariids

Fungi

Choanoflagellates

Animals

Which of the following statements correctly describes the evolutionary relationship of Unikonts?

**A.** Fungi and animals are as closely related as slime molds and gymnamoebas.

**B.** Choanoflagellates are the most likely closest living protist relatives of animals.

**C.** Nucleariids have a longer evolutionary history than slime molds.

**D.** The most recent common ancestor of fungi and animals is older than that of gymnamoebas and choanoflagellates.

The diagram above depicts the life cycle of a fungus. Which of the following is a **similarity** between the life cycles of a fungus and a human?

**A.** Gametes are formed by mitosis, not meiosis.

**B.** The only diploid stage is the zygote.

**C.** The only haploid stage is the zygote.

**D.** The gametes are haploid.

# Day 110

There is evidence that suggests plant colonization of land was facilitated by a mutualistic relationship with fungi (mycorrhiza). How would this symbiotic relationship expedite the movement of plants onto land?

Further colonization of land required adaptations that allowed plants to become more able to survive, thrive, and reproduce in drier conditions. Given the following adaptations and plant groups, create a cladogram of plant evolution.

**Adaptations:** flowers, pollen, seeds, vascular tissue

**Plant groups:** ferns, flowering plants, mosses, conifers

Which of the following is **not** a beneficial adaptation a plant acquires by producing seeds?

**A.** Water is no longer necessary for embryo germination.

**B.** Embryos are protected from desiccation (drying out).

**C.** Plant offspring can "travel" farther as animals eat the seeds and move them away from the parent plant (via feces).

**D.** Water is no longer acquired for fertilization.

Giant kelp is often mistakenly thought to be a plant. Explain why kelp and seaweed are protists and **not** plants.

# Day 114

Which of the following is a unique and defining characteristic of kingdom Animalia?

**A.** Muscle tissue

**B.** Hormones

**C.** Movement

**D.** Light detection

Based on the cladogram depicting the evolution of vertebrates, which of the following labels is correct?

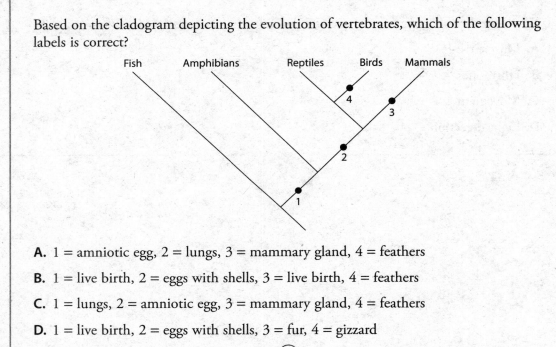

**A.** 1 = amniotic egg, 2 = lungs, 3 = mammary gland, 4 = feathers

**B.** 1 = live birth, 2 = eggs with shells, 3 = live birth, 4 = feathers

**C.** 1 = lungs, 2 = amniotic egg, 3 = mammary gland, 4 = feathers

**D.** 1 = live birth, 2 = eggs with shells, 3 = fur, 4 = gizzard

5 Minutes to a 5

An animal's body plan can refer to its symmetry: either radial symmetry or bilateral symmetry. How does an animal's symmetry reflect its movement in the environment?

Which of the following animal groups has the greatest number of species?

**A.** Deuterostomes

**B.** Lophotrochozoans

**C.** Ecdysozoans

**D.** Arthropods

The Cambrian explosion was a time of adaptive radiation of animals into aquatic environments. Another significant event in animal evolution would be the movement onto land. What challenges would be faced by a species' movement from an aquatic habitat into a terrestrial environment? Give general examples of how these challenges could be overcome.

The discovery of *Tiktaalik roseae*, a lobe-finned fish with basic wrist bones and indication of primitive lungs, was evidence that tetrapods evolved from lobe-finned fish. Why did *Tiktaalik* provide this evidence for evolution?

**A.** *Tiktaalik* would have most likely eaten the same food as a tetrapod from the same geographic region.

**B.** Both *Tiktaalik* and early tetrapods lived in the water.

**C.** *Tiktaalik* had morphological characteristics similar to that of fish, but lacked any characteristics similar to early tetrapods.

**D.** Tiktaalik was a lobe-finned fish that also possessed characteristics of early tetrapods.

**5 Minutes to a 5**

The following graphs show the metabolic rate and body temperature of an endotherm at different environmental temperatures. The thermoneutral zone is the span of temperature in which the metabolic rate is low and independent of environmental temperature. The upper limit of the thermoneutral zone is the upper critical temperature, above which the animal begins to expend energy to lose heat (panting or sweating), which increases its metabolic rate. The lower critical temperature is when the animal must produce metabolic heat to compensate for the cold environmental conditions.

**A.** What is this animal's thermoneutral zone?

**B.** At what temperatures does the animal lose the battle to maintain a constant body temperature?

The vascular tissue of a plant consists of xylem (water transport) and phloem (sugar transport). The vascular tissue permeates throughout the tissues of the leaves and stems but is constrained within a protected cylinder in the very middle of a root. Why would natural selection favor such positioning of the vascular tissue in the shoots versus the roots?

Draw a simple plant. Label the three organs (leaf, stem, root) and show the location of the three tissue systems within each organ (dermal, ground, vascular). Indicate the primary purpose for each of the organs and each of the tissues.

Which of the following is **not** a purpose of root hairs?

**A.** Increased surface area

**B.** Increased absorption

**C.** Increased stability

**D.** Water and mineral collection

The process of natural selection favors biological forms that best suit their functions. The structure of a leaf is best suited to its function as the major photosynthetic organ of a plant. Looking at the cross section of a leaf below, explain how the internal arrangement of the tightly packed column-shaped palisade mesophyll layer and loosely packed spongy mesophyll layer are best suited for their functions of gathering light and carbon dioxide for photosynthesis.

Palisade mesophyll

Spongy mesophyll

Guard cell

Stomata

5 Minutes to a 5

A lateral root is a secondary root that extends horizontally from the primary root of the plant. Lateral roots help to anchor the plant and contribute to water and nutrient uptake. When a lateral root forms, it extends outward, not from the outermost epidermal layer of the root, but from the tissues within the deeper vascular cylinder. Explain why the lateral root doesn't emerge from the cells of the epidermal layer.

Many processes aid in the movement of water up the xylem of a plant. Which of the following does **not** contribute to this transport?

**A.** Higher water potential is at the top of the plant.

**B.** Cohesion of water molecules creates a linked "chain" up the plant.

**C.** Water evaporates from the top of the plant and enters through the roots of the plant.

**D.** Water molecules hold on to the sides of the xylem cells through adhesion.

The stomata on plant leaves are small pores through which water can be lost. Stomata are closed when the guard cells surrounding the stomata lose water and become flaccid. Which of the following would **not** contribute to reducing water loss from plant leaves?

**A.** Potassium ions are transported from the surrounding fluid into the guard cells.

**B.** Osmosis occurs the direction from the inside to the outside of the cell.

**C.** The water potential of the guard cells is high compared to the surrounding fluid.

**D.** Aquaporins facilitate the movement of water out of the guard cells.

Water potential is the physical property that predicts the directions in which water will flow. Water potential plays an important role in the movement of water and dissolved solutes throughout plant tissues. Water will move from a region of high to low water potential. Water potential ($\Psi$) is affected by both the solute concentration ($\Psi_S$) and the pressure ($\Psi_P$) exerted on the cell as shown in the following equation:

$$\Psi = \Psi_P + \Psi_S$$

where adding solute or decreasing pressure will both work toward lowering overall water potential.

If the soil surrounding root cells have a water potential of −0.18 MPa (MPa = megapascal, a unit of pressure) and the root tissue has a water potential of −0.28 MPa, which of the following statements is **correct**?

A. If salt was applied to the soil surrounding the plant, the water potential in the soil would increase.

B. A decrease of pressure inside the root xylem would lead to an increase of water potential within the root tissue.

C. Assuming the pressures are the same, there is more solute in the root tissue than the surrounding soil.

D. Water will move from the root tissue into the surrounding soil.

If a plant cell immersed in water has a $\Psi_S$ of −0.5 MPa and a $\Psi$ of 0 MPa, what is the cell's $\Psi_P$?

A sugar source in a plant produces sugars, whereas a sugar sink uses (or stores) those sugars. Explain how the organs of source/sink could change, depending on season.

**Day 131**

Reproduction in angiosperms is defined by three characteristics: flowers, double fertilization, and fruit. The first trait, flowers, is a key step in the evolution of plants. Which of the following statements correctly explains how a flower is related to the other two terms?

**A.** A flower is formed through the process of one sperm fertilizing an egg, and the fruit is formed from a second fertilization of a second egg. This process is called "double fertilization."

**B.** The flower is the reproductive organ of the plant, in which the two sperm from a pollen grain will fertilize a single egg. This process is double fertilization.

**C.** When a fruit inside of a flower is pollinated through double fertilization, one egg is fertilized to create an ovule and a second egg becomes the embryo.

**D.** An egg within the flower is fertilized by a sperm to produce the embryo, and the second sperm will be used to produce the food for the embryo. This is the process of double fertilization.

**Day 132**

Once double fertilization occurs, what is the fate of the egg cell, the ovule, and the ovary? Use a "simple" fruit as the model for your answer.

Which of the following vegetables is actually a fruit?

**A.** Carrot

**B.** Bell pepper

**C.** Broccoli

**D.** Cabbage

# Day 134

Flowers are the reproductive structure of a plant. Flowers that have both stamens and carpels are called "perfect flowers." Some plant species have flowers that are either male (staminate) or female (carpellate), and depending on the species, each individual plant can either house both the male and female flowers (monoecious) or a single "gender" of flower (dioecious). Which of the following statements is correct?

**A.** Plants with imperfect flowers are never able to self-pollinate.

**B.** Within a random population of dioecious plants, only approximately half would produce fruits.

**C.** A species of plant with perfect flowers contain both staminate and carpellate flowers on a single plant.

**D.** A berry bush is a carpellate plant.

**Day 135**

Seedless fruits (such as seedless grapes) are frequently available at grocery stores. They are considered to be easier and more convenient to eat. How, then, can a seedless grape plant reproduce if it doesn't produce seeds?

5 Minutes to a 5

In 1880, Charles and Francis Darwin created an experiment that led to the discovery of plant hormones. Which of the following statements correctly describes their conclusions?

**A.** A plant must receive sun along the entire length of the coleoptile in order to stimulate production of the hormone.

**B.** A chemical produced at the tip of the plant is unable to diffuse throughout the tissues.

**C.** Cell elongation occurs on the illuminated side of the coleoptile.

**D.** A chemical produced at the tip affects growth throughout the entire plant.

Auxin stimulates cell elongation and growth. The acid growth hypothesis is a model to explain the mechanism behind this physiological response. Using the following word bank, fill in the blanks in the following description of the acid growth hypothesis. *Not all words in the word bank will be used.*

Word bank:

acidic, basic, contract, covalent, hydrogen, decreased/decreases, elongate, increased/increases, proton, turgor, voltage

_____ pumps move H+ ions across a cell membrane. When auxin is present, it stimulates these pumps, and H+ is moved from the inside of the cell out of the cell. When there is a differential concentration of H+ across a membrane, this creates a _____ (membrane potential). The pH in the cell wall is also _____. When the cell wall becomes _____, enzymes called *expansins* are activated. They break the _____ bonds between cellulose fibers, making the cell wall more pliable. An increase in the membrane potential also enhances ion uptake into the cell. This in turn _____ water potential, and osmotic uptake of water increases _____ pressure in the cell. This increase in pressure (along with a looser cell wall) allows the cell to _____.

Senescence is the programmed death of certain cells in a plant. One familiar example of this process is leaf abscission. A layer of dead cells develop near the base of the petiole and hydrolytic enzymes destroy the cell walls. The leaf soon falls off the tree. Why would natural selection create such a process, considering that leaves are the primary source for photosynthesis?

As mentioned in the question for Day 136, Charles and Francis Darwin discovered the plant hormone auxin when studying the directional growth of plants exposed to light. Further investigation focused on finding the specific wavelength of light that is best at signaling for this curvature. Based on the graph below, hypothesize which photoreceptors might be receiving light to initiate this growth response.

One of the qualities of all living things is their ability to respond to their environment. Other than light, what other stimuli do plants respond to? Explain why each particular response would increase a plant's fitness.

The kidneys play an important role in maintaining homeostasis by regulating blood composition. The production of urine by the kidneys and its excretion from the body helps to remove unwanted chemicals and ions from the blood.

| COMPARISON OF SUBSTANCES IN THE BLOOD AND URINE | | |
|---|---|---|
| | PERCENTAGE IN BLOOD (ENTERING THE KIDNEY) | PERCENTAGE IN URINE (LEAVING KIDNEY) |
| Water | 91.5% | 96.0% |
| Glucose | 0.1% | 0.0% |
| Protein | 7.0% | 0.0% |
| Urea | 0.03% | 2.70% |
| Sodium | 0.33% | 0.29% |
| Potassium | 0.02% | 0.24% |

Protein molecules are not normally found in urine. Explain why.

**A.** The body rarely has too high a concentration of protein in the blood and thus does not need to excrete excess protein in the urine.

**B.** Seven percent protein in the blood is not high enough to warrant removal into the urine.

**C.** In order for proteins to be excreted, there needs to be an equal or greater amount of urea present in the blood.

**D.** Proteins are too large and are not filtered out of the blood.

Review the data from Day 141. Based on the data for sodium, what would happen to the sodium content in the urine of a person who increases his or her intake of sodium chloride?

**A.** It would remain the same because the body works to maintain homeostasis of the chemical composition of the urine.

**B.** It would go up because the concentration of salt in the blood would be higher and the excess salt would be excreted in the urine.

**C.** It would go down because kidneys maintain proper salt concentration in the blood via a positive feedback loop.

**D.** Kidneys do not play a role in sodium regulation.

Summarize the processes that take place between blood and urine, and identify the structures where they occur.

**A.** The capillaries of the glomerulus filter out water and small particles into the Bowman's capsule. As the filtrate passes along the tubules, further solutes are added to be passed out of the collecting duct as urine, and most of the water and sugars are reabsorbed back into the blood.

**B.** After solutes are moved from the blood into the tubule, the urine collects in the Bowman's capsule before it is moved into the collecting tubule for excretion.

**C.** Proteins, sugars, and other dissolved ions are filtered through the glomerulus, which passes through the Loop of Henle where more proteins are secreted. The collecting duct allows one last chance for sodium chloride reabsorption back into the blood.

**D.** Nitrogenous compounds, small ions, and water are actively transported from the glomerulus into the Bowman's capsule. As the filtrate passes along the tubules, water and salts passively flow between the blood and the urine, depending on the need for homeostasis.

Day 144

How does blood glucose regulation by insulin and glucagon provide an ideal example for maintaining homeostasis by negative feedback?

Antidiuretic hormone (ADH) is produced by the pituitary gland and helps protect against excessive water loss in the urine by signaling the nephrons in the kidney to increase the reabsorption of water. A special transport protein called an aquaporin facilitates the movement of water from the urine back into the bloodstream by creating channels through which water can flow. ADH signals for a temporary increase in the number of aquaporin proteins in the nephron. Based on this information, what would an increase of ADH do to:

**A.** urine volume?

**B.** blood osmolarity?

Digestion of food begins in the mouth as the teeth grind up food into smaller pieces. This ground-up food then passes down the esophagus and into the stomach where it is further macerated by muscular contractions of the stomach. After combining with digestive juices, the mixture passes into the small intestine to be further digested by enzymes. Which of the following statements is **not** correct?

**A.** Breaking up food into smaller pieces is an example of mechanical digestion; the increase in surface area helps the enzymes perform their chemical digestion.

**B.** Enzymes in the stomach work best at a high pH, otherwise they may denature or not function properly.

**C.** The enzymes of the digestive system have an optimal temperature of 37°C (body temperature).

**D.** Different enzymes are needed to digest the different macromolecules such as protein, carbohydrates, nucleic acids, and fats.

The disaccharide lactose is broken down by the enzyme lactase into the monomers glucose and galactose:

$$\text{lactose} + \text{water} \rightarrow \text{glucose} + \text{galactose}$$

Lactose intolerance is an inability to digest lactose because the person no longer has a functioning lactase enzyme. If lactose is not digested, it can change the water balance in the colon; too much lactose means more water is drawn into the colon by osmosis. This can lead to diarrhea. Improper digestion of lactose causes what type of environment inside the colon?

A. Isotonic

B. Hypotonic

C. Hypertonic

D. Turgid

Which of the following is a correct depiction of the reaction catalyzed by lactase?

Vertebrate digestive systems are a product of evolutionary adaptations to ensure the form of the system best matches its function (what food will be digested). The alimentary canals of a carnivore and an herbivore have the same organs, yet differ in their size:

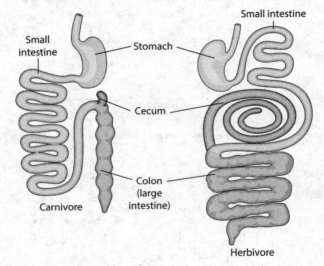

Which of the following statements does **not** reflect these structural differences?

**A.** The herbivore has a more substantial mutualistic relationship with symbiotic bacteria in the cecum to help with cellulose digestion.

**B.** In the herbivore the small intestine is shorter than the small intestine in the carnivore. This suggests that the majority of digestion in the herbivore occurs farther down the digestive tract.

**C.** The long small intestine of the carnivore facilitates digestion and nutrient absorption.

**D.** The longer colon of the herbivore suggests that the majority of nutrient absorption already occurred higher up in the alimentary canal.

5 Minutes to a 5

When a person exercises, their respiration rate increases to speed up removal of carbon dioxide from the bloodstream. If their respiration rate was unable to keep up, explain the effects on their blood pH, using the equation below:

$$H_2O + CO_2 \rightleftharpoons H^+ + HCO_3^-$$

The vessels of the circulatory system reflect structures that best fit their particular functions. Arteries that carry blood from the heart have thick, elastic walls. The pliable veins bring blood back to the heart after circulation throughout the body and contain one-way valves. Capillaries are the sites of gas exchange in the tissues and are exceedingly narrow with thin walls. Justify that the structures of these three vessels best fit their functions.

5 Minutes to a 5

The fruit fly *Drosophila melanogaster* is a model organism for many scientific experiments, and it is often necessary to anesthetize the fly in order to study it closely. One method is to use dry ice, which releases gaseous carbon dioxide ($CO_2$) as it sublimates. An increase in blood $CO_2$ concentration leads to a decrease in blood pH, because carbon dioxide reacts with water to form carbonic acid. Which of the following is **not** a possible side effect of this form of anesthesia?

**A.** The increased concentration of carbon dioxide would reduce oxidative phosphorylation in the tissues.

**B.** The blood pH would become acidic due to lack of oxygen.

**C.** The carbon dioxide could cause accelerated heart rate.

**D.** ATP production would increase due to tissues switching to fermentation.

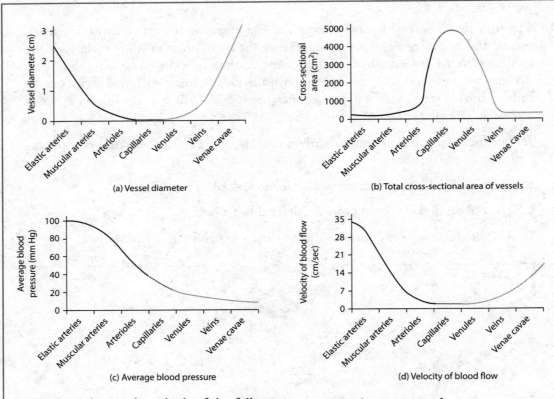

(a) Vessel diameter

(b) Total cross-sectional area of vessels

(c) Average blood pressure

(d) Velocity of blood flow

Based on the graphs, which of the following statements is **not** correct?

**A.** Vessel diameter is directly proportional to the cross-sectional area.

**B.** As the cross-sectional area of the vessels increase, the velocity of blood flow decreases.

**C.** Blood pressure is highest in the elastic arteries.

**D.** Velocity of blood flow increases as the blood begins to travel back to the heart.

The immune system consists of two types of response: innate immunity and adaptive immunity. Compare these two types of immunity in regard to

**1.** Speed of response

**2.** Specificity

**3.** What is providing protection

The immune system will target and attack anything that is not "self," including protein markers on the surface of red blood cells. If a patient with type A− blood needs a transfusion, which of the following could be safely given?

**A.** O+ and O−

**B.** A− and O−

**C.** A+ and A−

**D.** O− and A+

Draw a graph depicting time (*x*-axis) versus antibody concentration (*y*-axis) of a primary and secondary humoral response. Explain how this relates to improved health through vaccinations.

T cells are part of the cell-mediated immune response. Which of the following statements about cytotoxic T cell function is **not** correct?

**A.** Cytotoxic T cells target extracellular pathogens.

**B.** Cytotoxic T cells, unlike B cells, must come into direct contact with their intended target.

**C.** Cancerous body cells are targeted by cytotoxic T cells.

**D.** Cytotoxic T cells must have the antigen "presented" by an infected cell along with a marker of "self" called MHC.

The bacterium meningococcus type B is a dangerous pathogen that causes inflammation of the membranes covering the brain and spinal cord. This bacterium has the ability to bind certain proteins circulating in the blood and mimic the cells of the host. How would this similarity provide the bacterium with a selective advantage?

Tetrodotoxin is a potent neurotoxin carried by symbiotic bacteria in certain aquatic species such as the pufferfish. The toxin blocks sodium channels in neurons.

Which of the following is an accurate statement about the effect of tetrodotoxin on axons?

**A.** It blocks the potassium channels when a neuron undergoes hyperpolarization.

**B.** It disrupts the depolarization step of a firing neuron.

**C.** It interrupts depolarization because potassium channels are blocked.

**D.** It blocks the ability of a neuron to release neurotransmitters into the synaptic cleft.

5 Minutes to a 5

Once an action potential reaches the end of a neuron, the signal must be relayed to the adjacent (postsynaptic) neuron. In order for this signal to jump the synaptic cleft it must be converted into a chemical signal (from an electrical signal). Explain this process.

Describe the basic pathway that information flows throughout a nervous system when a person hears a flying hawk's call and turns toward the sound. How does this informational pathway differ from the pathway of that person's pupils contracting when they look up into the bright sky?

The bacterial genus *Clostridium* is the source of two of the most potent toxins on Earth: botulinum toxin and tetanus toxin. *Clostridium botulinum* is a food-borne pathogen that produces a toxin that binds presynaptic terminals and blocks release of the neurotransmitter acetylcholine. *Clostridium tetani* is a soil bacterium whose toxin blocks the release of inhibitory neurotransmitters. Which of the following statements does **not** correctly describe these toxins' modes of action?

**A.** The tetanus toxin causes constant contraction of the muscles.

**B.** Botulinum toxin interferes with the action potential of a neuron.

**C.** The two toxins have opposite effects on neuron signaling.

**D.** Botulinum poisoning can result in respiratory failure because the diaphragm is unable to contract.

Using the graph below, draw a plot of the membrane potential (*y*-axis) during an action potential (*x*-axis). A neuron's resting potential is about −70 mV, and it peaks at +35 mV. Label the significant stages of a neuron firing.

The graph below is a growth curve of yeast cells growing in yeast-malt broth at 24°C. At what point is the population growth rate the highest?

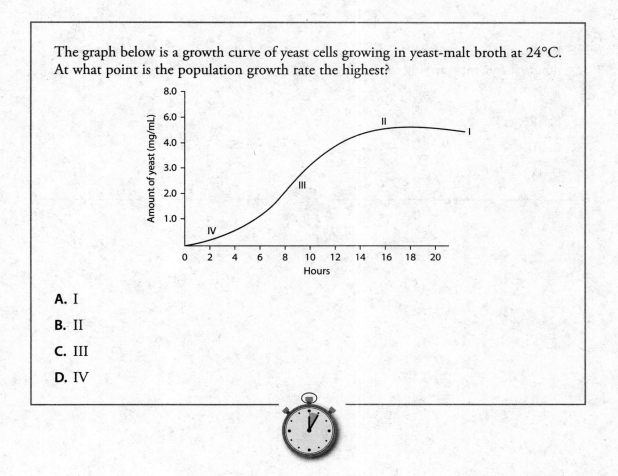

**A.** I

**B.** II

**C.** III

**D.** IV

5 Minutes to a 5

Review the graph of yeast growth from Day 164. At what point did the yeast population first reach its carrying capacity?

**A.** I

**B.** II

**C.** III

**D.** IV

5 Minutes to a 5

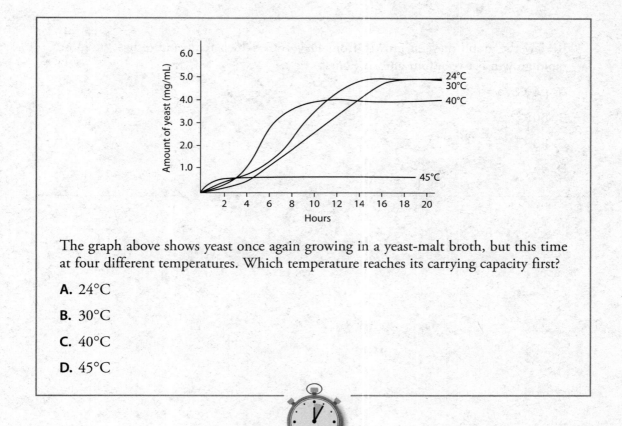

The graph above shows yeast once again growing in a yeast-malt broth, but this time at four different temperatures. Which temperature reaches its carrying capacity first?

**A.** 24°C

**B.** 30°C

**C.** 40°C

**D.** 45°C

Day 167

Review the graph of yeast growth from Day 166. Which temperature has the most rapid growth between four and six hours?

A. 24°C

B. 30°C

C. 40°C

D. 45°C

Each female cane toad can produce up to 30,000 eggs per year. Create a graph showing the most likely survivorship curve for these hatchling frogs. On the same graph, compare this to the survivorship curve of humans.

Negative feedback plays an important role in maintaining homeostasis in the body (e.g., blood glucose regulation). Negative feedback is also important in population dynamics. How does negative feedback play a role in density-dependent inhibition of population growth?

**A.** When individuals are born, the population density rises and increases the odds of more births.

**B.** As the population decreases, it causes an increase in the birthrate.

**C.** When individuals die, the number of births increases in order to maintain the population density.

**D.** When the population increases and the density reaches a critical level, the accumulation of "product" (individuals) will slow the birth rate, thus reducing the population.

5 Minutes to a 5

In order to study the population size of aquatic snail, the researcher employs a method called "mark-recapture," which is when captured individuals are marked, released, and identified upon recapturing. The proportion of marked individuals that are recaptured is the same as the proportion of marked individuals in the entire population. Given the data below, estimate the total number of snail in the population. Give your answer to the nearest whole number.

|  | NUMBER OF MARKED INDIVIDUALS | TOTAL NUMBER INDIVIDUALS |
|---|---|---|
| Recapture group | 18 | 94 |
| Entire population | 200 | ? |

Batesian mimicry is a biological relationship in which a harmless prey species (the mimic) is protected by their resemblance to another species (the model). The harmless mimic (which is palatable to the predator) resembles the toxic model species, thus reaping the benefit of the warning colorations or markings without actually itself being toxic or dangerous. Explain how this relationship could be considered parasitic from the model's perspective.

Some species of ground squirrels communicate through warning barks that signal the presence of a predator. This warning will signal other squirrels to hide in their burrows, whereas the squirrel who gave the warning bark has put itself at increased risk. What is this an example of?

**A.** Altruistic behavior, because the squirrel does something to help another, even if it comes at its own expense.

**B.** Territoriality, because the squirrel issuing the warning bark is defending a geographic area against other squirrels.

**C.** Agonistic behavior, because the squirrel is giving a threatening display to scare away the predator.

**D.** Dominance hierarchies, because the squirrel issuing the warning bark is the "alpha" squirrel.

Review the description of ground squirrel communication from Day 172. Which of the following ground squirrels is most likely to give an altruistic alarm call?

**A.** A male with no kin nearby

**B.** A female with no kin nearby

**C.** A male with kin nearby

**D.** A female with kin nearby

Fill in the following table with the correct interaction: **commensalism, competition, mutualism, parasitism**. Not all spaces will have an answer.

| | | EFFECT ON ORGANISM 2 | | |
| --- | --- | --- | --- | --- |
| | | **HARM** | **BENEFIT** | **NO EFFECT** |
| Effect on organism 1 | **Harm** | | | |
| | **Benefit** | | | |
| | **No effect** | | | |

In an experiment, the distribution of two species of sea anemone was studied. Species A was distributed in great numbers higher up on coastal rocks, so that the entire population was covered with water only during high tide. Species B's niche was the portion of the rocks that remained underwater even during low tide. The investigator hypothesized that the niche of species A was a function of interspecies competition. Describe what the investigator could do to test this hypothesis.

Predator and prey populations are closely interrelated, a classic example being the lynx and the hare. Draw a graph generally showing how these two populations cycle up and down in response to one another. Correctly label the *x*-axis and the *y*-axis.

*Ecological succession* is the term used to describe the ecological changes that occur after a disturbance. Which type of succession plays the most important role after wildfires destroy acres of forest land?

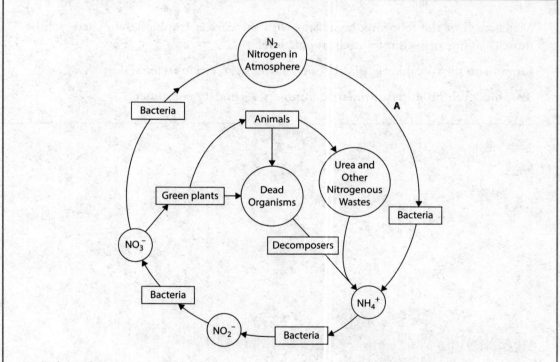

Based on the nitrogen cycle shown above, explain the significance of step A.

Match each of the following organisms with the correct trophic level. There will be more than one organism for each trophic level.

**Organism:** phytoplankton, grasshopper, hawk, tiger, cyanobacteria, deer

**Trophic level:** producers, primary consumers, secondary consumers

**Day 180**

---

**Review Questions**

Question 1: If $H_2O$ is the formula for water, what is the formula for ice?

Question 2: What did one cell say to her sister cell when she stepped on her toe?

Question 3: Explain the pick-up line: "I wish I was adenine, then I could get paired with U."

Question 4: Bonus question (fill in the blanks): Biology is the only science in which _____ means the same thing as _____.

# Answers

## Day 1

**B**

## Day 2

**C**—The primary structure of a protein is the sequence of amino acids that make the polypeptide. This transmembrane protein must span the hydrophobic interior of the membrane; the portion of the protein extending beyond into the cytoplasm or out into the external environment will be in contact with water. The amino acids that make up the region of the protein that spans the membrane must be hydrophobic and the amino acids that extend beyond must be hydrophilic.

## Day 3

**A**—The phospholipid is composed of a phosphate head group and two fatty acids tails.

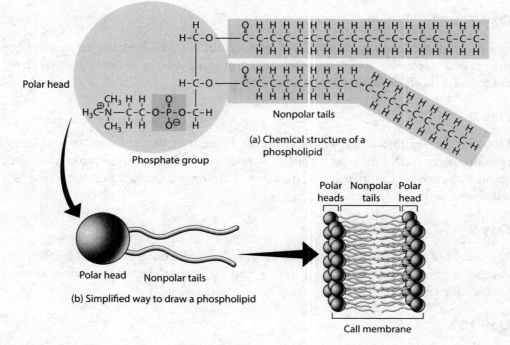

(a) Chemical structure of a phospholipid

(b) Simplified way to draw a phospholipid

**B**—The phosphate head group is charged and hydrophilic (loves water); the non-polar fatty acid tails are hydrophobic (hate water). As a result, the molecules will spontaneously arrange themselves in water so that the hydrophobic tails of the two layers face each other (hidden from water) and the hydrophilic heads face outward toward water.

## Day 4

**A**—The answer is "a" because the two R groups can form a hydrogen bond (between the hydroxyl "—OH" and carboxyl "—C═").

## Day 5

**B**—The secondary structure of a protein is a regular pattern of folding caused by hydrogen bonding among the protein backbone.

## Day 6

**D**—The sugar maltose yielded the most cellulose, as did the temperature 30°C.

## Day 7

**B**—Plasmids are "extra" pieces of DNA that are not required for bacterial survival but may confer a selective advantage (such as the production of a toxin). All other items are found in both prokaryotic and eukaryotic cells.

## Day 8

**D**—The endosymbiotic theory addresses the hypothesis that chloroplasts and mitochondria were small prokaryotic cells that, once taken in by a larger prokaryotic cell, formed a permanent mutualistic relationship. This formed the first organelles (the first eukaryotic cell).

## Day 9

**D**—Answer D is incorrect because the complexity of the cell is increased by the presence of organelles. Substances can diffuse and move more freely in smaller, simpler prokaryotic cells.

## Day 10

**A**—The smooth endoplasmic reticulum is responsible for detoxification (thus found in higher numbers in the organ responsible for toxin removal).

## Day 11

**C**—Ribosomes synthesize proteins. If the ribosomes are floating freely, those proteins remain in the cell. If the ribosomes are stuck on the rough endoplasmic reticulum, the proteins are immediately sent to the Golgi for processing and exported out of the cell.

## Day 12

**C**—An increase in the percentage of unsaturated fatty acids (contain double bonds) would increase the fluidity. Bacteria in cold conditions would have stiffer, less flexible membranes; an increase in unsaturated fatty acids would help increase fluidity.

## Day 13

**D**—Many small, nonpolar molecules (such as hydrocarbons, along with carbon dioxide and oxygen) can dissolve in the lipid bilayer and easily cross without the aid of membrane proteins. Even small, uncharged, polar molecules can pass—answer (A)—through slowly without aid from a transport protein.

## Day 14

**D**—The other answer choices aren't true.

## Day 15

**A**—Without a functioning transmembrane protein, chloride ions cannot move to the outside of the cell. A high concentration of ions is needed to create a hypertonic environment.

## Day 16

The chemical signal is "heard" by the cell once the signal (ligand) binds to the appropriate cell surface receptor. The receptor is a transmembrane protein that has an extracellular portion and an intracellular portion; once the receptor binds the signal, the protein changes shape on the inside of the cell. This change transmits the message into the cell without the chemical messenger itself passing into the cell.

## Day 17

α - Cell with surface receptors for the a - factor

a - cell with surface receptors for the α - factor

a - factor

α - factor

(1)   Signal <u>reception</u> : The α and a factors bind them appropriate receptors.

(2)   <u>Transduction</u> of message into the cell: Once the receptor attaches to the signal (a - or α - factor) it changes shape on the inside of the cell. This triggers a series of reactions that both amplify and move the message to its intracellular target.

(3)   <u>Response</u> : The cells rearrange their cytoskeletons and grow projections towards opposite cell type.

## Day 18

**C**—In order for the response to manifest, the activated G protein must serve as an intermediate to shuttle the message from the membrane receptor (GPCR) to the enzyme. If the G protein is "stuck," it cannot transmit the message to the enzyme.

## Day 19

The competitive inhibitor is competing with the substrate for the enzyme's active site. The more substrate added, the greater the chance that the correct molecule (the substrate) will attach to the active site instead of the inhibitor. But in the case of the noncompetitive inhibitor, flooding the reaction with substrate cannot overcome the effects of the inhibitor. This is because the noncompetitive inhibitor is binding at a location *other* than the active site (thus it isn't directly "competing" with the substrate).

## Day 20

**A**—The hydrolysis of ATP (exergonic) is "coupled" with an endergonic reaction by transferring the third phosphate group from ATP to the reactant. This "phosphory-lated intermediate" is made unstable and is more likely to react.

## Day 21

**B**—When valine increases, so does the activity of the enzyme threonine deaminase (and thus an increase of its product, $\alpha$-ketobutyrate). Isoleucine, on the other hand, has the opposite effect: the more isoleucine present, the stronger the inhibition of the enzyme (and a subsequent decease of its product).

## Day 22

**C**—When oxygen becomes a limiting factor, the Krebs cycle and the electron transport chain shut down, leaving only glycolysis running in the muscle tissue. This switch to fermentation (creating ATP in absence of oxygen) produces lactic acid as a by-product.

## Day 23

**D**—A is true because in order to compare respiration rates of two differently sized organisms, the variable of size must be removed by instead considering respiration rate per gram. B is true because any oxygen gas removed via respiration would be replaced by the carbon dioxide product. C is also true because temperature affects respiration rate, and two different temperatures would introduce another variable.

## Day 24

**B**—Plant cells have both mitochondria and chloroplasts (and thus undergo both photosynthesis and cellular respiration). In order to accurately measure the rate of cellular respiration by either oxygen consumption or carbon dioxide production, photosynthesis must be halted (otherwise oxygen would be released and carbon dioxide used, making it difficult to track respiration).

## Day 25

**D**—growth without air = 220
growth with air = 1100
1100/220 = 5

## Day 26

**C**—Cellular respiration (energy production in the presence of oxygen) includes glycolysis, Krebs cycle, and the electron transport chain. This yields the maximum amount of ATP. Without oxygen, the cell must rely on fermentation, when only glycolysis is running.

## Day 27

**A.**

**B.** The rate of a reaction is the same as the slope: (change in gas volume)/(minutes). The rate of reaction for 10°C is determined by finding the gas volume at 4 minutes (0.8 mL) and 8 minutes (2.2 mL):

$$(2.2 \text{ mL} - 0.8 \text{ mL}) / (8 \text{ min} - 4 \text{ min}) = 1.4/4 = 0.35$$

The rate of reaction for 35°C is determined by finding the gas volume at 4 minutes (1.8 mL) and 8 minutes (4.5 mL):

$$(4.5 \text{mL} - 1.8 \text{ mL}) / (8 \text{ min} - 4 \text{ min}) = 2.7/4 = 0.68$$

**C.** The fermentation rate at 35°C is 1.9 times greater than at 10°C.

## Day 28

**A**—In the absence of oxygen, neither the Krebs cycle nor the electron transport chain is running. The only energy pathway that functions in anaerobic conditions is glycolysis. The NADH created during glycolysis, however, cannot drop off the electrons/H+ at the electron transport chain. If NAD+ cannot be recycled, glycolysis will stop. Therefore, fermentation is a way to oxidize NADH back into NAD+ by transferring the hydrogens and electrons onto pyruvate (reducing it into lactic acid).

## Day 29

During the daylight hours, photosynthesis occurs (algae, cyanobacteria) at a rapid rate. The amount of oxygen produced through photosynthesis is greater than the amount of oxygen consumed through cellular respiration. When darkness falls, however, photosynthesis comes to a halt, leaving only cellular respiration to remove the dissolved oxygen from the water.

## Day 30

The light-independent reactions (also called the Calvin cycle) produce glucose ($C_6H_{12}O_6$) from carbon dioxide (six molecules of $CO_2$). In order to do so, the Calvin cycle needs a source of energy to form many new covalent bonds and a source of hydrogens and electrons to reduce the $CO_2$. Both of these requirements (ATP for new bond formation and NADPH as a source of hydrogens and electrons) are provided by the light-dependent reactions.

## Day 31

**C**—Chemiosmosis is the process of using the diffusion of a chemical down its concentration gradient to "power" another biological mechanism. In both of these cases, the flow of ions is being used to spin the turbine of ATP synthase.

## Day 32

**A**—When the enzyme rubisco first evolved; there was very little oxygen gas in the atmosphere. Rubisco had to "fix" atmospheric carbon dioxide onto the molecule RuBP, and since carbon dioxide was the main organic molecule in the atmosphere, the enzyme did not have to discern the difference between latching onto carbon dioxide versus oxygen. Now that oxygen is at a much higher concentration, rubisco can't tell if it accidentally "grabs" $O_2$ instead of $CO_2$.

## Day 33

Plot A is the C4 plant and plot B is the C3 plant. At levels of 20 percent carbon dioxide, the C4 plant is able to take up about 53 $\mu mol \ m^{-2} \ sec^{-1}$ whereas the C3 plant takes up 15 $\mu mol \ m^{-2} \ sec^{-1}$. The C4 plant is about 3.5 times more efficient.

## Day 34

**A.** $6\ CO_2 + 6\ H_2O \rightarrow C_6H_{12}O_6 + 6\ O_2$

**B.** The radioactive oxygen from the water will be released as $O_2$ (it would *not* end up in the glucose). This is because in photosystem II of the light reactions, lost electrons are replaced by splitting water; water-derived oxygen is released as gas into the atmosphere.

## Day 35

**D**—DPIP plays the role of substitute electron acceptor and replaces NADP+ at the end of photosystem I. DPIP is reduced by the excited electrons from the chlorophyll and changes from blue to colorless.

## Day 36

I and V are the stages with the lowest amount of DNA possible (thus the "normal" amount that is present). Stages I and V are during $G_1$, a cell at rest, not actively dividing. Stage II shows a ramping-up of DNA, which means S phase (DNA replication). Stage III is when the DNA is at its maximum: after replication, but before the sister chromatids are separated (the cell is at $G_2$). Once the cell progresses into stage IV, the amount of DNA is reduced because mitosis has begun. Mitosis concludes once the DNA is separated into the two daughter cells and the cell once again enters $G_1$ (V).

## Day 37

**A**—First, the chromosomes condense and the nuclear envelope begins to break down. Next, the chromosomes line up in the middle with either sister chromatid straddling the metaphase plate. Shortly thereafter the sister chromatids are pulled towards the opposite poles of the cell, and finally the chromosomes unwind and the nuclear envelope reforms.

## Day 38

**C**—The spindle apparatus is needed in order to form spindle fibers to attach to chromatids. Without spindle fibers, the chromatids will not be maneuvered to the center of the cell. Cell number 23 would not occur because the chromatids have been moved to the center of the cell.

## Day 39

**D**—The MPF line is the highest on the *y* axis (meaning concentration of MPF) right after $G_2$.

## Day 40

**B**—MPF levels are dependent upon cyclin levels. As cyclin concentration drops, MPF cannot maintain its previous levels and thus also decreases in concentration.

## Day 41

**C**—Diploid number refers to both sets of homologous chromosomes; haploid indicates only one set. Therefore if the diploid number is 78, the haploid number is half that (39).

## Day 42

**D**—Meiosis separates homologous chromosomes; mitosis does not. Therefore the alignment of homologous on the metaphase plate (necessary for their eventual separation in anaphase I) would only occur in meiosis.

## Day 43

C = crossover
NC = no crossover

| NUMBER OF 4:4 ASCI (NO CROSSOVER) | NUMBER OF ASCI WITH CROSSOVER | TOTAL NUMBER OF ASCI | PERCENTAGE OF ASCI SHOWING CROSSOVER | GENE-TO-CENTROMERE DISTANCE (% CROSSOVER / 2) |
|---|---|---|---|---|
| 10 | 14 | 24 | 58% | 29 map units |

## Day 44

**A**—Any step that goes [diploid →haploid] is the result of meiosis. Once a cell is haploid, it cannot undergo reduction division (meiosis) again because it only has a single set of chromosome. When a haploid cell divides, it can only divide by mitosis.

## Day 45

**D**—Genotype refers to the genetic composition of an organism; phenotype refers to how those genes are expressed, physically. A gene comes in different forms, called alleles. A gene can have multiple alleles, though each cell can only have two of those alleles (diploid). If the alleles contained within that cell are the same, it's referred to as homozygous. If the alleles are different, it is heterozygous.

## Day 46

Prior to Mendel's work, the prevailing theory of inheritance was the "blending" hypothesis that parental traits, once combined in offspring, would mix together such as colors do: a purple-flowered parent and a white-flowered parent would create all lavender offspring. What Mendel discovered, however, was that the inherited traits remained separate and pure ("particulate"), and though they could seemingly disappear for a generation (as was the case for all the heterozygous $F_1$ offspring who displayed the dominant purple phenotype), only to reappear in a later generation, due to the inherited "discrete particles" (which we now know are genes) ability to stay true.

## Day 47

**B**—The first parent has the dominant phenotype, which means it is either AA or Aa. Considering that half the offspring are recessive (aa), the first parent can only be heterozygous (Aa).

## Day 48

**D**—The rule of multiplication states that the chances of two independent events occurring together can be determined by multiplying their individual odds of occurrence:

$$\tfrac{3}{4} \times \tfrac{1}{4} = \tfrac{3}{16}.$$

## Day 49

The predicted ratios are as follows:

$$\text{Stripes} = \tfrac{4}{16} = 0.25$$
$$\text{Spots} = \tfrac{3}{16} = 0.19$$
$$\text{Both} = \tfrac{9}{16} = 0.56$$

Therefore, based on the predicted ratios, the geneticist expects to see the follow distribution (based on a total number of 146 offspring):

$$146 \times 0.25 = 36.5 \text{ striped}$$
$$146 \times 0.19 = 27.7 \text{ spotted}$$
$$146 \times 0.56 = 81.8 \text{ both striped and spotted}$$

These numbers, along with the observed data, are recorded in the chi-square table below:

| PHENOTYPES | OBSERVED (O) | EXPECTED (E) | O-E | (O-E)$^2$ | (O-E)$^2$/E |
|---|---|---|---|---|---|
| Stripes | 40 | 36.5 | 3.5 | 12.3 | 0.34 |
| Spots | 31 | 27.7 | 3.3 | 10.9 | 0.39 |
| Both | 75 | 81.8 | −6.8 | 46.2 | 0.56 |

$$\chi^2 = \Sigma[(o-e)^2/e] = 0.34 + 0.39 + 0.56 = 1.29$$

The $\chi^2$ value must be compared to a critical value, as obtained from the chi-square table:

**CHI-SQUARE TABLE**

| P VALUE | DEGREES OF FREEDOM | | | | | | | |
|---|---|---|---|---|---|---|---|---|
| | 1 | 2 | 3 | 4 | 5 | 6 | 7 | 8 |
| 0.05 | 3.84 | 5.99 | 7.82 | 9.49 | 11.07 | 12.59 | 14.07 | 15.51 |
| 0.01 | 6.64 | 9.21 | 11.34 | 13.28 | 15.09 | 16.81 | 18.48 | 20.09 |

Based on a $p$ value of 0.05 and 2 degrees of freedom (df = # of phenotypes − 1), the critical value is 5.99. Since the chi-square value is less than the critical value (1.29 > 5.99), the geneticist **did** get the predicted outcome.

## Day 50

**C**—The term *autosomal* refers to a gene that does not reside on the X chromosome (not sex-linked). Because the gene for Huntington's disease is dominant, a person with only one allele for this trait would express the disease (therefore could not be a carrier, which means the person would have the gene but not express the trait). Two individuals with the disease would not necessarily have a 100 percent chance of an afflicted baby because they could both be heterozygous.

## Day 51

**D**—Nondisjunction occurs when the homologous chromosomes are not separated during anaphase I of meiosis or the sister chromatids are not separated (either during mitosis or anaphase II of meiosis). In order for Down syndrome to occur, the nondisjunction event must occur during meiosis I, so that both homologous of chromosome 21 end up in a single gamete.

## Day 52

**B**—Normally, a cross of aabb × AaBb would create a 1:1:1:1 ratio because the "A/a" and "B/b" genes are on separate chromosomes and can assort independently, like shuffling cards in a deck. However, if these genes are stuck together on the same chromosome, you would see two of the genotypes with a much higher number, and two genotypes underrepresented (because crossing over was necessary for this genetic combination to occur).

## Day 53

Woman = AB-negative = $I^A I^B$ $Rh^- Rh^-$

Man = B-positive (heterozygous) = $I^B i$ $Rh^+ Rh^-$

Blood type Punnett square:

| | $I^A$ | $I^B$ |
|---|---|---|
| $I^B$ | $I^A I^B$ | $I^B$ |
| i | $I^A i$ | $I^B i$ |

Odds of their child having type A blood = ¼

Answers ↑

Rh-factor Punnett square:

|       | Rh⁻     | Rh⁻     |
|-------|---------|---------|
| Rh⁺   | Rh⁺ Rh⁻ | Rh⁺ Rh⁻ |
| Rh⁻   | Rh⁻ Rh⁻ | Rh⁻ Rh⁻ |

Odds of their child having Rh-positive blood = ½

Odds of their child having both type A blood and Rh-positive (rule of multiplication) = ¼ × ½ = ⅛.

## Day 54

Female: $X^B X^Y$
Male: ?
Kittens:

$$X^Y Y = \text{yellow male (1)}$$
$$X^B Y = \text{black male (2)}$$
$$X^Y X^Y = \text{yellow female (2)}$$
$$X^B X^Y = \text{calico female (3)}$$

In order for a cross to generate the kittens listed above, the male is most likely $X^Y Y$:

|       | $X^B$     | $X^Y$     |
|-------|-----------|-----------|
| $X^Y$ | $X^B X^Y$ | $X^Y X^Y$ |
| Y     | $X^B Y$   | $X^Y Y$   |

## Day 55

If genes were all coded properly on one strand, then that cell would indeed be able to transcribe the correct mRNA molecules and produce the correct proteins. The problem occurs when that single cell needs to reproduce. In order for a cell to properly copy itself, it needs to create an *exact* copy of its DNA to send to the daughter cell. This ensures the daughter cell will have the same, properly coded suite of genes for translation. If DNA was single stranded, however, the process of DNA replication would create a second daughter strand of DNA that was *complementary* to the first. The daughter cell would not have the proper base sequence in its genes. So it is necessary that DNA be double stranded in order to provide all daughter cells with *exactly* the same DNA (and thus the ability to create all the same proteins).

## Day 56

For each of four nucleotides A, C, G, and T, there are a total of 15 nitrogen atoms (at 14 amu each) and 4 phosphorus atoms (at 31 amu each):

$$N \ 15 \times 14 = 210$$
$$P \ 4 \times 31 = 124$$
$$\text{Ratio N/P} = 210/124 = 1.69$$

If the sample was contaminated with protein, the ratio would be higher because protein contains N (but no P).

## Day 57

**SIMILARITIES**

- Polymers
- Monomer = nucleotide
- Monomers linked via a sugar-phosphate backbone
- Monomer consists of three parts: 5-carbon sugar, phosphate group, nitrogenous base
- Both contain three common nitrogenous bases: guanine, cytosine, adenine

| DIFFERENCES | DNA | RNA |
|---|---|---|
| Sugar | • Deoxyribose | • Ribose |
| Nitrogenous bases | • Contains bases adenine, cytosine, guanine, and thymine<br>• Guanine pairs with cytosine; adenine pairs with thymine | • Contains bases adenine, cytosine, guanine, and uracil<br>• Guanine pairs with cytosine; adenine pairs with uracil |
| Overall structure | • Forms a double-stranded helix | • Single stranded (though can fold around and hydrogen bond with itself) |

## Day 58

1. Messenger RNA (mRNA)—the "intermediate" message that moves instructions for protein synthesis from the DNA in the nucleus out into the cytoplasm for ribosomes to translate.

2. Transfer RNA (tRNA)—clover-shaped molecules of RNA that bind certain amino acids, as dictated by their specific anticodon. They transfer the amino acids over to the ribosome for translation of the mRNA.

3. Ribosomal RNA (rRNA)—molecules of RNA embedded within ribosomes. The rRNA catalyzes the linking of amino acids.

4. Micro RNA (miRNA)—small, non-protein coding pieces of RNA. Plays a role in gene expression, specifically RNA silencing (stopping mRNA from being translated by a ribosome).

## Day 59

A nucleoside triphosphate is similar to ATP in that both contain three high-energy phosphate groups, and hydrolysis of one or more of those phosphates release energy. In the case of DNA replication, the energy released by the removal of two phosphate groups from a nucleoside triphosphate is used to attach the monomer to the growing chain.

## Day 60

**B**—A gene is first copied into an mRNA intermediate (transcription), and then the mRNA is processed: introns removed, exons spliced together, and the addition of a 3'-cap and poly-A tail. The mRNA is then ready for translation by a ribosome, which leads to the protein being modified for its final function.

## Day 61

1 guanine cap + 100 bp (exon 1) + 50 bp (exon 2) + 25 bp (exon 3) + 200 adenines = 376 bp

## Day 62

mRNA = 5' – AG <u>AUG</u> UUC CUU CGU CGA UAG G – 3'

protein = (start codon) met – phe – leu – arg – arg (stop codon)

## Day 63

**B**—One gene is capable of coding for multiple proteins. The presence of exons and introns makes it possible to create multiple mRNA from a single gene, thanks to mRNA processing and the ability to mix-and-match exons.

## Day 64

**B**—When a mutation creates an early stop codon, the ribosome halts protein synthesis before it should. This leads to a shortened protein product.

## Day 65

**D**—D is false because the lac operon is *inducible*, meaning the repressor is by default stopping transcription of *lacZ*, *lacY*, and *lacA*. Binding of allolactose to the repressor *inactivates* the repressor.

## Day 66

**A**—An operator is a sequence within the promoter where the repressor binds, thus blocking access by RNA polymerase. It is not a protein that binds DNA (the operator is a DNA sequence itself).

## Day 67

**D**—In order for the gene to be expressed at high levels, the correct activators that match the corresponding control elements in the enhancer region must be present. The colors of activators present match the control elements before the cerumen gene. The "orange" and "silver" control elements are found before both genes, so they could not cause differential gene expression.

## Day 68

- **Chromatin modification:** In order for genes to be accessed by RNA polymerase, the tightly packed chromatin must relax. Acetylation of histone proteins help to loosen the chromatin and enable transcription. Methylation, on the other hand, has the opposite effect and suppresses transcription.

- **Transcription:** General transcription factors help the binding of RNA polymerase at a low level. Activators, transcription factors specific to a given gene, bind the enhancer region and help increase RNA polymerase binding and initiation of transcription at a high level.

- **RNA processing:** Alternate splicing of introns and exons will produce different mature mRNA transcripts.

- **Translation:** Binding of ribosomes to mRNA can be effected by regulating the "lifespan" of mRNA sequences. Micro RNA (miRNA) functions in this capacity by either destroying the mRNA molecule or blocking a ribosome's ability to bind it.

- **Protein modification:** A protein may need to be chemically modified, folded, or transported to a specific location before it is functional.

## Day 69

D

## Day 70

D—Answer D would actually increase the chances of stopping a cancerous cell because amplification of the p53 protein would further stop the cell cycle.

## Day 71

B—When a cell begins the process of differentiation, certain transcription factors are activated, leading to a specific set of genes being expressed because RNA polymerase knows to "target" these promoters. These genes further regulate the expression of other genes that are linked to specific cell and tissue functions.

## Day 72

D—The process of apoptosis can only be triggered in "self" cells of the organism.

## Day 73

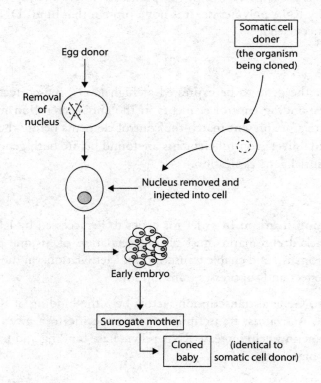

## Day 74

| VIRUSES ARE ALIVE | VIRUSES ARE NOT ALIVE |
|---|---|
| • Contain nucleic acid as a genetic code<br>• Can reproduce and create offspring<br>• Need materials and energy<br>• Can evolve and change | • Cannot reproduce independently (obligate intracellular parasite)<br>• Do not undergo metabolic processes without help of a cell<br>• Not made of cells |

## Day 75

**A**—The genetic material must be found *within* the cell.

## Day 76

The influenza virus mutates very quickly. When a person gets infected by the flu, his or her immune system fights off the infection because antibodies specific to that virus are able to destroy and remove the virus. Because of natural selection, however, any virus particles that happened to have a genetic mutation that enabled them to avoid detection by the immune system would then survive, reproduce, and possibly reappear as the following year's flu strain.

## Day 77

33 percent adenine

The percentage of cytosine must equal the percentage of guanine (Chargaff's rules), so the total amount of C and G = 34 percent. The remaining 66 percent (100 − 34 = 66) of the genome is composed of adenine and thymine, which must both be in equal amounts, at 33 percent each.

## Day 78

**D**

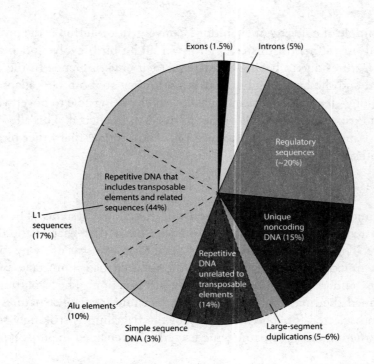

## Day 79

**D**

## Day 80

Because a human and a spider monkey are both primates, there should be significant similarities when comparing their genomes. Any differences would have arisen in a relatively recent time period, when the lineages diverged. These differences would account for the distinguishing characteristics of spider monkeys (or humans). Comparing the crustacean to the primates would also provide significant insight. Any genes that are shared between such seemingly disparate groups would have arisen a very long time ago, and their conservation through macroevolutionary events would reflect their importance.

## Day 81

When the gametes (egg and sperm) are formed through meiosis, the homologous chromosomes are assorted randomly into the two daughter cells during meiosis I. This is due to the random alignment of maternal/paternal homologous on the metaphase plate during metaphase I (Law of Independent Assortment). Furthermore, when the homologous chromosomes first come together through synapsis, crossing over occurs, creating further recombination of alleles. Finally, there are a staggering number of different combinations of sperm + egg between two individuals.

## Day 82

**B**—Answer A is incorrect because there is no "intention" in the process of natural selection; it is based on an organism randomly containing an allele that happens to increase survivability for a given environment. Answers C and D are incorrect in their descriptions of the slope/shape of the graph.

## Day 83

This is an example of convergent evolution. Convergent evolution is the process where two unrelated organisms (in this case, an insect and a bird) evolve independently to have similar features due to having to adapt to their environments. In the case of the hummingbird and the hummingbird hawk-moth, they are both best adapted to their food source (long-stemmed and perch-free flowers) by being able to hover while drinking nectar and using their long bill/proboscis to reach the nectar. This allows both the hummingbird and the hawk-moth to feed on a food source that other birds, butterflies, and moths are unable to access.

## Day 84

These small modifications occur to preexisting functional systems. The preexisting functional systems, however, may have a purpose other than that of the final, complex structure. The bacterial flagellum, in its final form, consists of many interlocking proteins that function together and power the rotating flagellum; take away any of those proteins and the flagellar propeller doesn't function. The evolutionary pathway that formed the final flagellum, however, had intermediate structures that were functional and selected-for. The basal body of the flagellum is strikingly similar to a needle-like structure on some pathogenic bacteria that enabled the injection of toxins

Answers ↑

into eukaryotic cells. This needle has many structural elements in common with the flagellum but is missing some proteins that make the flagellum work. Thus the final flagellum is not "irreducibly complex"; it simply has a function of its own.

The mammalian eye also evolved through incremental stages, and each of these stages provided an evolutionary advantage. A pigmented spot of photoreceptor cells among the epithelial layer would provide an early animal an advantage for sensing light. A random mutation that created a small depression around these photoreceptor cells would provide an evolutionary advantage of better sensing the light's source. Offspring born with deeper depressions would be even more fit, more likely to survive, and more likely to pass on their genetic variation to their offspring. Visual precision increased as an aperture was incrementally selected, and eventually a protective layer of transparent cells and eventually a crude lens. Any stop along this evolutionary pathway to the fully formed mammalian eye provided a selective advantage to the lucky organism that happened to have the mutation.

## Day 85

**B**—The smaller the difference in the DNA, the closer the common ancestor (which is depicted by a closer branching point). The chimp and the bonobo have little differences in their DNA, so they reside close to one another on the cladogram. Answers A, B, and C are possible, yet only one is considered the best cladogram. According to the data, a gorilla is as closely related (based on DNA similarities) to a human as it is to a chimp. Answer C suggests a gorilla is more closely related to a human (wrong), and answer A shows the common ancestor between a gorilla and a human to be much older than the common ancestor between gorilla and chimp. Answer B correctly shows that the common ancestor (branch point) that leads to gorilla has both chimp and human emerging from the other path.

## Day 86

Tree #2 is the preferred (and simplest) explanation. Each trait (A, B, C, and D) arose once along the evolutionary pathway, and thus has fewer evolutionary events than tree #1. Trait A arose before the first divergence, and thus organisms 1, 2, and 3 all have trait A. Trait B arose after that first divergence, and organisms 1 and 2 share that derived characteristic; organism 3 does not. Tree #1 shows that both organism 1 and organism 2 have trait B, but this characteristic was derived twice, as independent events. Because of this added complexity, it is not as parsimonious as tree #1.

## Day 87

## Day 88

**D**—Organisms grouped within the smallest, most specific classification level are the most closely related. The classification categories from largest (most inclusive) to smallest (most specific) are: domain, kingdom, phylum, class, order, family, genus, species. Water striders and aphids are members of the same order, making them the closest relatives.

## Day 89

The number of prairie chickens was drastically reduced in the 1990s. As a consequence, there was less genetic variation in the remaining population (bottleneck). This reduction in genetic variability compromised the health of the prairie chickens, as seen in the huge reduction of eggs that produced viable hatchlings.

## Day 90

**A**—After the selective environmental factor of drought conditions, the percentage of early flowering plants increased. There was an increased survival of plants that were able to flower earlier (and reproduce faster) in dry conditions. These plants were able to pass on their alleles to the next generation. Answer B is incorrect because natural selection works on already present alleles (a mutation occurring in one individual would not be found within the gametes, and thus not passed down to the next generation). The late-flowering allele was not beneficial (the percentage declined), so answer C is wrong. And there is no reason to think herbivores selectively ate late-flowering plants (answer D).

## Day 91

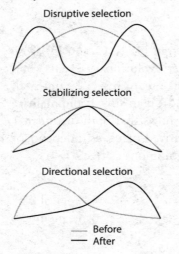

**A**—The data are an example of directional selection.

## Day 92

**B**—Albinism (homozygous recessive) = $1/17,000 = q^2$

$q = 0.00767$

## Day 93

**B**—If $q = 0.00767$, then $p = (1 - 0.00767) = 0.992$

Heterozygous individuals $= 2pq = 2(0.00767)(0.992) = 0.0152$

## Day 94

If 60 percent are brown (BB or Bb), the remaining 40 percent must be white (bb).

$bb = q^2 = 0.4$

$q = 0.63$

Since $p + q = 1$, then $p$ must be $1 - 0.63 = 0.37$

**A.** The percentage of butterflies in the population that are heterozygous =

$2pq = 2 (0.37) (0.63) = 0.47 = 47\%$

**B.** The frequency of homozygous dominant individuals $= p^2 = (0.37)^2 = 0.14 = 14\%$

## Day 95

In order for the feathers to appear black, the chicken must be homozygous for the black allele:

$$85/1000 = 0.085 = p^2 \text{ (homozygous black)}$$

$$p = 0.29 \text{ (black allele)}$$

$$q = 1 - p = 1 - 0.29 = 0.71 \text{ (white allele)}$$

$$q^2 = 0.50 \text{ (homozygous white)}$$

$$2pq = 2 (0.29) (0.71) = 0.412 \text{ (heterozygous slate-blue)}$$

## Day 96

**A**—Only the bottleneck effect would counteract rapid diversification of species, in that it has the opposite effect of reducing the genetic variation for a small population.

## Day 97

An ancestral population must be somehow divided and isolated, blocking gene flow between the newly created factions. This allows two separate gene pools to develop and differentiate due to natural selection. Reproductive isolation is the biological barrier that helps to keep these gene pools separate and distinct by preventing members of the two species from again interbreeding and producing viable, fertile offspring. Reproductive isolation can be established by either preventing fertilization (prezygotic) or preventing development after fertilization (postzygotic). Prezygotic barriers prevent a sperm and egg from forming a zygote; postzygotic barriers prevent the hybrid zygote from ever developing into a viable, fertile adult.

## Day 98

**B**—Answer A is false because allopatric speciation does require a physical barrier between subsets of a population. Answer C is also false because it describes allopatric speciation (not sympatric). Answer D is wrong because sympatric speciation indeed occurs without a physical barrier between populations.

## Day 99

This method of determining the age of a fossil is based on the ratio of the radioactive isotope carbon-14 to its most common isotope, carbon-12. The half-life of a radioactive isotope refers to the time it takes for half of the amount to decay. The isotope carbon-14, for example, has a half-life of 5,730 years. When an organism dies, it takes 5,730 years for half of a sample of carbon-14 to decay into nitrogen-14. The amount of carbon-12, however, stays constant. By measuring the ratio of carbon-14 to carbon-12 in a fossil, the approximate age of the fossil can be determined. If the fossil had $\frac{1}{16}$ of the amount of carbon-14, it had aged four half-lives worth of years:

$$\frac{1}{2} \times \frac{1}{2} \times \frac{1}{2} \times \frac{1}{2} = \frac{1}{16}$$

4 half-lives $\times$ 5,730 years for each half-year = 22,920 years old

## Day 100

Islands provide ideal conditions for the process of rapid diversification of new forms of species from an ancestral species ("adaptive radiation"). Islands provide geographical isolation and diverse environmental conditions for natural selection to create new species from the ancestral population. The ideal example is the Galapagos Islands, a closely-clustered group of islands each of which has a distinct environment (flora, rainfall, soil conditions, etc.). Any ancestral species that arrived from the mainland would be exposed to the specific selective pressure of that island and evolve accordingly.

## Day 101

**C**—Prokaryotic DNA lacks histone proteins.

## Day 102

### Similarities:

- The DNA must first be replicated before division occurs.

- Both cell types must increase their volume before pinching in half.

### Differences:

- There is only a single, circular chromosome in prokaryotic cells.

- The prokaryotic chromosome must be anchored to the cell membrane; no spindle formation.

- There is no complex cell cycle in binary fission: no mitosis and no replication of organelles (prokaryotic cells do not have organelles).

- Binary fission is much faster (reproductive rate of bacteria faster, for the most part).

## Day 103

**D**—Choosing a restriction enzyme that cuts within the *amp*$^r$ gene would render the bacterium unable to survive in the presence of the antibiotic (and remove the ability to screen/select bacteria with the plasmid). If the enzyme cuts within the β-galactosidase gene, there would be no blue pigment produced in the presence of X-gal.

## Day 104

**B**—The presence of ampicillin in the agar kills any *E. coli* that has not been transformed (i.e., do not contain the plasmid with the *amp*$^r$ gene). This ensures that only transformed bacteria are growing on the agar plate (selecting/screening for transformed bacteria).

## Day 105

|  | BACTERIA | ARCHAEA | EUKARYA |
|---|---|---|---|
| Membrane-bound nucleus | Absent | Absent | Present |
| Organelles | Absent | Absent | Present |
| Peptidoglycan (a structure carbohydrate polymer) in cell walls | Present | Absent | Absent |
| Circular chromosome | Present | Present | Absent |
| Growth at extreme temperatures (i.e., greater than 100°C) | No | Some species | No |

## Day 106

The name Archaea ("archaic") hints to the origins of these prokaryotes: many resemble those cells which first colonized Earth 3.5 billion years ago. These early cells were subjected to extreme conditions (temperature, pH, no atmospheric oxygen, salinity, etc.) and thus had to evolve to survive in extreme environments. Their ancestors today, the *extremophiles*, include prokaryotic cells that inhabit inhospitable niches such as hydrothermal vents, sulfur-rich volcanic springs, and the Great Salt Lake.

## Day 107

**A**—The endosymbiotic theory states that mitochondria and chloroplasts were once autonomous prokaryotic cells that were engulfed by other, larger prokaryotic cells (to the mutual benefit of both cells). This would explain why these two organelles have their own DNA (separate from the cells nuclear DNA) and why they can divide independently of the cell. The endosymbiotic theory only addresses the origins of chloroplasts and mitochondria (and not the other organelles of the eukaryotic cell).

## Day 108

**B**—Answer B is correct because they share the most recent common ancestor on the cladogram. Answer A is incorrect because slime molds and gymnamoebas have a more recent common ancestor than fungi and animals. Answer C is incorrect because the slime mold clade originated before that of the nucleariid clade. Answer D is incorrect because the common ancestor of gymnamoebas and choanoflagellates was one of the earliest branch-points.

## Day 109

**D**—Answer A is incorrect because human gametes are formed by meiosis (unlike fungi). Answer B is incorrect because humans' adult stage is also diploid (along with the zygote), and answer C is incorrect because fungi have multiple haploid stages.

## Day 110

The biggest challenge faced by plants is desiccation. The move from water onto land required plants to obtain their water through absorption into roots. A mutualistic relationship between fungal hyphae that penetrate within plant cells could help the plant better exploit soil resources. The mutualistic association of plant roots and a fungus is called a mycorrhiza.

## Day 111

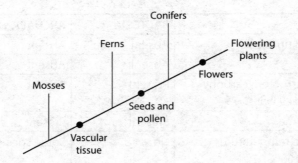

## Day 112

**A**—Answer A is not a beneficial adaptation because water is still the most important environmental cue that signals the time for germination. Once enough water is absorbed by the seed (imbibition), a suite of metabolic pathways are switched on and the dormant embryo begins to grow.

## Day 113

Multicellular protists such as seaweed are able to photosynthesize like plants, but the likeness ends there. Seaweed is unable to live outside of water. It is made of undifferentiated cells and does not have the organs of a true plant. Plants have differentiated cell types (vascular tissue, dermal tissue, ground tissue) and organs (roots, stems, leaves).

## Day 114

**A**—Only animals have true muscle tissue (along with nervous tissue). Plants also have hormones, other organisms (e.g., some protists, bacteria) are able to move, and some animals (e.g., corals) are sessile and cannot move. Many other organisms are able to sense and detect light.

## Day 115

C

## Day 116

A radially symmetrical animal such as a sea jelly or an anemone tend to move in a "planktonic" manner (just drifting with the current) or not move at all (sessile). Radial symmetry is ideal because animals with this symmetry can meet their environment equally from all sides. A bilateral animal moves in a very intentional, directional manner. Bilateral symmetry corresponds to a clustering of the sensory organs in their anterior (front) end, including a brain in the head. This allows them to best coordinate complex movements in response to their environment.

## Day 117

**C**—Deuterostomes include hemichordates (e.g., marine worms), echinoderms (e.g., sea stars and urchins), and chordates. Though this group includes all vertebrates (the chordates), it is not the most populated. Even though the lophotrochozoan group includes a hugely diverse group of animals (e.g., flatworms, rotifers, mollusks and annelids), it is not the most abundant on the planet. The vast majority of known species are arthropods, which includes insects, crustaceans, and arachnids. This is not the correct answer, however, because the clade of ecdysozoans includes arthropods *plus* all roundworms.

## Day 118

The transition to terrestrial life would mean a decreased dependence on water. Natural selection would favor structures that reduce water loss through evaporation. The exoskeletons of arthropods or the keratin-infused scales of reptiles, for example, prevented water loss and provided support. These adaptions would also help protect against ultraviolent radiation (which would have otherwise been filtered out by the water). Animals would also need to become more efficient at processing and conserving water for digestion and metabolism. The complete digestive tract that many animals possessed after the Cambrian explosion would vastly increase efficiency of digestion and nutrient acquisition. Land animals must deal with movement outside of water. The muscles and nervous system that also formed during the Cambrian explosion would be further selected for and modified to better aid in fighting gravity during tetrapod locomotion. Of course, obtaining atmospheric oxygen would mean the development of internal surfaces for gas exchange, such as the tracheal system of insects and the lungs of vertebrates.

## Day 119

**D**—Answers A–C do not provide enough physical evidence that would successfully suggest *Tiktaalik* was the linking ancestor between fish and tetrapods.

## Day 120

**A.** 27°C–35°C

**B.** Between 0°C–1°C at the low end and 33°C–34°C at the high end. This is indicated by deviation from 37°C on the graph of body temperature versus environmental temperature.

## Day 121

The leaves most load products of photosynthesis into the phloem for transport throughout the plant (and water must similarly be provided from the roots). This process is facilitated if the vascular system branches throughout the tissues within easy reach of the photosynthetic machinery. The roots, however, must protect the vascular tissue from any toxins or otherwise harmful substances that could move from the soil into the root. If the xylem was within easy reach of any substances that diffused from the soil, the plant would have very little chance to screen and select which substances would be allowed into the vascular system (and thus throughout the entire plant). By keeping the xylem protected within the central cylinder of the roots, there is a greater opportunity for active screening of soluble chemicals. Furthermore, the vascular cylinder in the root is surrounded by a waxy layer called the Casparian strip, which provides further protection from dissolved soil substances.

## Day 122

Leaf
(Photosynthesis)

Stem
(support)

Roots
(absorption of
minerals and $H_2O$)

■ Dermal tissue (protection)

■ Vascular tissue (nutrient and $H_2O$ transport)

■ Ground tissue (cells specialized for storage and support)

## Day 123

C—Root hairs are tiny outgrowths of the epidermal cells of plant roots. These microscopic, hair-like roots vastly increase the surface area, thus aiding in absorption of water and minerals from the soil. They are way too small to provide stability to the plant.

## Day 124

The palisade layer is at the top of the leaf, and its tightly-packed arrangement is best for exposing as many chloroplasts as possible to the sunlight shining down onto the top of the leaf. The spongy layer, however, needs to have open airspaces to allow the carbon dioxide gas to move pass through the stomata, throughout the leaf tissue, and up into the palisade layer.

## Day 125

Any root must be tethered to the vascular system of the plant. The phloem and xylem in roots are protected within a vascular bundle deep within the center of the root. In order for new lateral roots to be "linked" to the vascular system, growth must originate from this vascular cylinder, and not from the outermost epidermal layer.

## Day 126

**A**—Answer A does not contribute to this transport because osmosis occurs from a region of high water potential to lower water potential. Water evaporates from the top of the plant (lowering water potential) and water comes into the plant at the roots (increasing water potential).

## Day 127

**A**—Answer A would lower the water potential inside the guard cells, leading to water also moving into the guard cells. This causes the guard cells to swell and open the stomata. All other answers lead to a loss of water from the guard cells (causing them to close over the stomata).

## Day 128

**C**—Answer A is incorrect because adding solute decreases water potential. Decreasing pressure lowers water potential; answer B is also incorrect. Answer C is correct because the root tissue has a lower water potential (which means the presence of more solute). Water will therefore move from the soil into the root (which means answer D is wrong).

## Day 129

The cell's $\Psi_P$ is 0.5 MPa, because it has to cancel out the $\Psi_S = -0.5$ MPa, so overall:

$$\Psi = \Psi_P + \Psi_S = 0$$

## Day 130

When a carrot plant begins growth, the shoots are the source of sugars (through photosynthesis) whereas the root is the sink, using the energy for root development and sugar storage. As the season progresses, the root grows and develops into the carrot root we consume. If, however, the plant is left in the soil, the root will switch to being a sugar source, releasing the energy for the top of the plant to then use (sink) for the energy-costly process of flowering.

## Day 131

**D**—The flower houses the ovary; the ovary contains an egg cell and two polar nuclei. Each pollen grain yields two sperm, one of which will fertilize the egg to produce the embryo, the other of which will fertilize the two polar nuclei to create the endosperm (food source for embryo). This is "double fertilization."

## Day 132

Once the egg cell is fertilized it becomes the embryo, which is protected within the ovule, which becomes the seed. The outermost layer is the ovary, which becomes the fruit (which contains the seed).

## Day 133

**B**—A pepper is a fruit, a product of a flower of the pepper plant. A carrot is a root, broccoli is a flower, and cabbages are leaves.

## Day 134

**B**—Answer A is incorrect because plants with imperfect flowers can self-pollinate if they are monoecious and each plant has both carpellate and staminate flowers. Answer B is correct because dioecious species of plants have either staminate or carpellate flowers. Only the female carpellate flowers would turn into fruit once fertilized. Answer C is wrong because each individual perfect flower has both stamen and carpel, and answer D is wrong because berries are ovaries and must come from either carpellate imperfect flowers or perfect flowers.

## Day 135

Some plants can reproduce asexually through cloning. Seedless grapes are grown from cuttings taken from existing plants. This eliminates the need for sexual reproduction, creation of embryos, and formation of seeds.

## Day 136

**D**—When the tip of the coleoptile senses light, a hormone is produced that diffuses throughout the tissues, down the body of the plant. This hormone (named "auxin") causes elongation of cells on the dark side of the plant. When these cells elongate, it pushes the body of the plant toward the light source.

## Day 137

**Proton** pumps move H+ ions across a cell membrane. When auxin is present, it stimulates these pumps, and H+ is moved from the inside of the cell out of the cell. When there is a differential concentration of H+ across a membrane, this creates a **voltage** (membrane potential). The pH in the cell wall is also **decreased**. When the cell wall becomes **acidic**, enzymes called *expansins* are activated. They break the **hydrogen** bonds between cellulose fibers, making the cell wall more pliable. An increase in the membrane potential also enhances ion uptake into the cell. This in turn **decreases** water potential, and osmotic uptake of water increases turgor pressure in the cell. This increase in pressure (along with a looser cell wall) allows the cell to **elongate**.

## Day 138

The loss of leaves prevents trees from desiccation (drying out) during seasons of water stress. Even though there is a subsequent decrease in photosynthesis (and thus growth), it is more important to protect against the unavailability of water for the plant.

## Day 139

The curvature response is greatest when the light is between ~400 and ~500 nm. This suggests that blue-light photoreceptors are responsible for sensing light for a growth response.

## Day 140

**Gravitropism** (growth in response to gravity). A plant's shoot grows upward (against gravity) and its roots grow downward (toward gravity). The growth of shoots against gravity ensures that a plant reaches toward the light. This is called *negative gravitropism*. The roots, on the other hand, must grow as far down as possible in order to reach water sources. This is called *positive gravitropism*.

   **Thigmomorphogenesis** (directional growth in response to touch and other mechanical forces, such as wind). Trees growing in very windy environments grow squatter, thicker trunks to help them withstand the pressures of blowing wind. Some vines and plants with tendrils are able to grow in the direction of physical contact to allow them to wrap around support structures.

## Day 141

**D**—The filtration step of excretion is dependent upon size; small molecules (water, glucose, ions) are able to pass through the glomerulus into the Bowman's capsule, whereas large molecules (proteins) are unable to squeeze through.

## Day 142

**B**—Kidneys play a huge role in maintaining balanced salt levels in the blood. An increase in salt concentration would elicit an increase in salt excretion in the urine (negative feedback).

## Day 143

**A**

## Day 144

Maintaining homeostasis means keeping some condition within a small, ideal parameter. The amount of glucose in the bloodstream must remain constant and not swing too far in either extreme (hypoglycemia or hyperglycemia). Immediately after a person eats a big meal there is a lot of free glucose in the bloodstream. This signals a release of the hormone insulin, which triggers cells to take in and oxidize the glucose (cellular respiration) or signals the liver to take up free glucose and store it as glycogen (a polymer of glucose). This is negative feedback because when a condition becomes too high (high blood glucose) the response is to counteract that condition (remove glucose from the bloodstream). The same is true on the opposite end of the spectrum; if a person has not eaten, his or her blood glucose may be too low. In this example of negative feedback, the condition is below the set parameter and the body releases another hormone (glycogen) to counteract the low blood glucose by hydrolyzing it from the glycogen stores in the liver, releasing glucose into the bloodstream, thus reestablishing the homeostatic condition.

## Day 145

**A.** Urine volume would decrease because water is removed from the urine and moved back into the bloodstream).

**B.** Blood osmolarity would decrease because the salt concentration in the blood would essentially be diluted by the water reabsorbed back into the bloodstream.

## Day 146

**B**—The stomach creates a very acidic environment (which means a low pH). Therefore enzymes in the stomach work best at a low pH and may denature if the pH becomes too high (basic).

## Day 147

**C**—A higher concentration of solute (in this case, lactose) per volume of water creates a hypertonic environment. *Hypotonic* means that there is less solute, and *isotonic* means the solute concentration is equal on both sides of the membrane/barrier.

## Day 148

**A**—The reaction is the hydrolysis of lactose (shown in answers A and C), but answer C is incorrect because enzymes are not destroyed in the reaction.

## Day 149

**D**—Answer D does not reflect these structural differences because a longer colon actually suggests a need to continue digestion and absorption of nutrients. Cellulose is being processed by mutualistic bacteria at this point.

## Day 150

The reaction is reversible, and if the carbon dioxide builds up (due to a too-slow respiration rate), it will result in a build-up of hydrogen ions, dropping blood pH and increasing its acidity.

## Day 151

Arteries leading from the pumping heart must withstand the highest blood pressure of the circulatory system. Their thick, elastic walls help protect them from the resulting high blood pressure. Veins, on the other hand, bring blood back to the heart and are relatively far away from the pumping force. They must compensate for low blood pressure with their one-way valves (to prevent backflow). Capillaries are tiny with very thin walls to help facilitate diffusion of oxygen from the blood into the surrounding tissues (and the diffusion of carbon dioxide from the tissues into the bloodstream). Their small, branching network increases the surface area available for the transport of these gases.

## Day 152

**D**—Answer A is a possible side effect because an increase in the amount of carbon dioxide correlates with a reduction in oxygen (and oxygen is required for the electron transport chain to run). Answer B is also a possible side effect because an increase in carbon dioxide acidifies the blood (meaning a lowering of blood pH). Answer C is a possible side effect because an increase in carbon dioxide (and resulting decrease of blood pH) sends a signal to the brain to increase respiration (breathing) and increase heart rate. Answer D is not a possible side effect because when cells switch to fermentation (as they do in low-oxygen conditions), the rate of ATP production is significantly reduced.

## Day 153

**A**—Although the individual diameter of each capillary is tiny, there are so many of them that combined, their total cross-sectional area is immense.

## Day 154

|  | SPEED OF RESPONSE | SPECIFICITY | WHAT IS PROVIDING PROTECTION |
|---|---|---|---|
| Innate immunity | Fast | Recognizes broad range of pathogens; does not "remember" being previously exposed to a pathogen | Skin, mucous membranes, inflammatory response, general phagocytic cells |
| Adaptive immunity | Slower | Responds to specific pathogens ("antigens"); "remembers" previous exposure and will mount an improved response upon second exposure | B cells (which produce antibodies) and T cells (which target intracellular pathogens) |

## Day 155

**B**—There are two different surface proteins to consider: the blood type marker (A, B, and O) and the Rh protein ("+" indicates it is present on RBC, "−" indicates it is absent). A person with A− blood has an immune system that would not respond against the A antigen ("self") nor would it respond against type O blood (which is lacking the surface protein). The patient's immune system, however, would respond against the Rh factor. The only safe option is answer B (types A− and O−).

## Day 156

After the initial exposure it takes a while for the correct B-cell to be triggered for clonal selection and ramp up antibody production. After the initial infection is cleared, a population of those specific B cells remains in the circulatory system ("memory cells"). Upon second exposure to the same pathogen, the memory cells respond quickly; antibodies are produced faster and in higher numbers. Vaccines work in this very way. A vaccination challenges a person's immune system with a specific pathogen. Though the pathogen is a weakened version of the actual pathogen, it is enough to goad the immune system into responding (primary immune response). After the vaccination, there is now a population of memory cells ready to respond quickly in a secondary immune response in case the "real" pathogen is encountered.

## Day 157

**A**—Answer A is not a correct statement because cytotoxic T cells target intracellular pathogens (such as viral infections), foreign tissues, and cancerous body cells. B cells and their antibodies target extracellular pathogens.

## Day 158

By mimicking the host, the bacterium appears as "self" and thus avoids detection by the immune system.

## Day 159

**B**—A resting neuron has a higher concentration of sodium ions on the outside of the cell and a higher concentration of potassium ions on the inside of the cell. In order for an action potential to arise in a neuron, sodium channels must open and allow sodium ions to flow into the neuron, thus generating a positive charge inside the cell (the action potential).

## Day 160

Once the action potential reaches the end of the presynaptic neuron, the positive membrane potential opens calcium channels. The influx of calcium ions causes vesicles containing neurotransmitters to fuse with the presynaptic membrane and dump the chemical neurotransmitter into the synaptic cleft. The neurotransmitter then binds to ion channels on the postsynaptic neuron's membrane and triggers them to open; sodium flows in, potassium flows out, thus propagating an action potential in the second neuron.

## Day 161

When a person hears a hawk's scream, sensors in the ears transmit the sound information to the brain. Interneurons of the brain process the sound, enabling the person to recognize it as a hawk's cry. In response, motor neurons transmit signals to the muscles of the neck allowing the head to turn toward the source of the sound and look up into the sky. This differs from the pupil response because eye dilation is an automatic reflex response. Once a signal is received (bright light hitting photoreceptors on the retina), the signal skips any "processing" in the central nervous system and instead elicits an immediate response (sphincter muscle fibers contract and decrease pupil size). This is called a "reflex arc."

## Day 162

**B**—Botulinum toxin does not interfere with the action potential within an individual neuron (the positive wave generated by an influx of sodium ions). Instead, it interferes with communication between neurons by blocking the release of the chemical neurotransmitter that ferries the information between adjacent neurons.

## Day 163

A = Sodium channels are opened because of a stimulus; sodium flows in and causes depolarization (increase of positive charge within the neuron).

B = Peak of the membrane potential

C = Sodium channels close and potassium channels open, allowing K+ to flow out. This reestablishes the negative charge inside the cell.

D = Membrane's permeability to K+ is higher than at rest, resulting in hyperpolarization.

E = Potassium channels eventually close; membrane potential returns to normal.

Even though at this stage the membrane potential is back to resting state, the neuron cannot fire again until sodium-potassium pumps return the ions to their initial location (K+ on the inside; Na+ on the outside).

## Day 164

**C**—The highest growth rate is the greatest slope of the graph: change in amount of yeast ($\Delta Y$) divided by the corresponding change in time ($\Delta X$). The slope is greatest at point III on the graph.

## Day 165

**B**—The carrying capacity of a population is when the amount of yeast levels out and maintains a constant concentration. This "level" carrying capacity is reached at point II in the graph.

## Day 166

**D**—The 45°C plot reaches its plateau (carrying capacity) soonest, after approximately 1.5 hours of growth.

## Day 167

**C**—The most rapid growth is indicated by the slope of the graph. Between four and six hours, the plot for 40°C has the steepest growth (fastest growth rate).

## Day 168

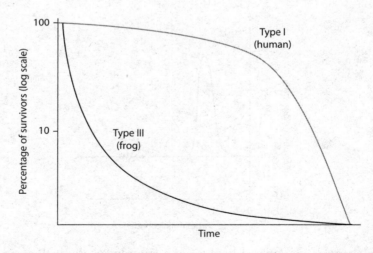

The frogs have a type 3 curve because very few of the young survive, whereas humans tend to have a very low death rate during early and middle life (until a steep decline during older age groups).

## Day 169

**D**—Negative feedback in a population occurs when an increase in population density produces an effect (competition, disease, overcrowding) that in turn decreases the population's numbers. Answer A is incorrect because it is actually describing an example of positive feedback. Answers B and C are incorrect because they both describe decreasing populations (not a density-dependent inhibition situation). Answer D is correct because it describes an increasing population reaching a critical concentration when it will "feedback" and cause a drop in the birth rate.

## Day 170

To answer this question, create a ratio of recaptured/entire population for the number of marked individuals:

$$18/200 = 0.09$$

This ratio is assumed to be the same for the total number of individuals:

$$94/x = 0.09 \quad \ldots \quad 94 = 0.09x \quad \ldots \quad x = 94/0.09$$

$x = 1,044$ individuals in entire population

## Day 171

When the predators eat the model prey, the toxicity reinforces the coloration-warning relationship. When the mimic is eaten, however, there is no toxic negative reinforcement, thus degrading the "coloration = dangerous" signal.

## Day 172

**A**

## Day 173

**D**—Even though the female may put her own life at risk, her alarm call will help the survival of her relatives, and thus her genes.

## Day 174

| Effect on organism 1 | | EFFECT ON ORGANISM 2 | | |
|---|---|---|---|---|
| | | **HARM** | **BENEFIT** | **NO EFFECT** |
| Effect on organism 1 | **Harm** | Competition | Parasitism | – |
| | **Benefit** | Parasitism | Mutualism | Commensalism |
| | **No effect** | – | Commensalism | – |

## Day 175

If this was interspecies competition, species B is the "winner" because it occupied the ideal niche for a sea anemone (the area on the rocks that remains underwater). The hypothesis would be supported if after removing all individuals of species B in a given location, species A subsequently moved in to fill in the now-unoccupied niche.

**Day 176**

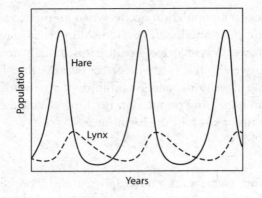

**Day 177**

Primary succession occurs in a virtually lifeless area, where there is no soil. An example of primary succession would be colonization of an area obliterated by a lava flow. The only life initially present would be bacteria. Even though after a wildfire there is a severe reduction of the previous biodiversity, there is still an established soil ecosystem; recolonization of the area will occur soon thereafter. This is an example of secondary succession, when an existing community has been cleared but the soil is still intact.

**Day 178**

Step "A" shows nitrogen fixation by prokaryotic cells. This step is very important because it converts unavailable atmospheric nitrogen gas into a form that can be used by plants. This is the major pathway for nitrogen to enter an ecosystem.

**Day 179**

Producers use the sun's energy to create glucose: phytoplankton, cyanobacteria

Primary consumers (herbivore) eat producers: grasshopper, deer

Secondary consumers (along with tertiary and quaternary consumers) are carnivores: hawk, tiger

**Day 180**

**Answer of Review Questions**

Answer 1: $(H_2O)^3$ (water "cubed")

Answer 2: "Mitosis!"

Answer 3: In transcription, RNA polymerase pairs up uracil nucleotides with the complementary DNA nucleotide adenine.

Answer 4: multiplication, division

# BIBLIOGRAPHY

Futuyma, Douglas J. *Evolutionary Biology*. 3d ed. Sunderland, MA: Sinauer Associates, Inc., 1998.

Kotz, John C., Paul M. Treichel, and John Townsend. *Chemistry and Chemical Reactivity*. 8th ed. Stamford, CT: Brooks/Cole, 2011.

Reece, Jane B., Lisa A. Urry, and Michael L. Cain. *Campbell Biology*. 9th ed. San Francisco: Benjamin Cummings, 2011.

Starr, Cecie, Christine Evers, and Lisa Starr. *Biology: Concepts and Applications*. 8th ed. San Francisco: Brooks/Cole, 2011.

Strauss, Eric, and Marylin Lisowski. *Biology: The Web of Life*. Teacher's ed. Menlo Park, CA: Addison-Wesley Longman, 1998.

Wilbraham, Antony C. *Chemistry*. 5th ed. New York: Pearson, 2000.

# WEBSITES

Here is a list of websites that contain information and links that you might find useful to your preparation for the AP Biology exam:

- http://www.campbellbiology.com
- http://www.collegeboard.com
- http://www.africangreyparrott.com/teach.html
- http://faculty.washington.edu/herronjc/ SoftwareFolder/AlleleA1.html
- http://blast.ncbi.nlm.nih.gov

**abiotic components** The *nonliving* players in an ecosystem, such as climate and nutrients.

**abscisic acid** Plant hormone that inhibits cell growth, prevents premature germination, and stimulates closing of the stomata.

**achondroplasia** Autosomal dominant form of dwarfism seen in one out of 10,000 people.

**ACTH** See **adrenocorticotropic hormone.**

**active site** Part of the enzyme that interacts with the substrate in an enzyme–substrate complex.

**active transport** The movement of a particle across a selectively permeable membrane *against* its concentration gradient. This movement requires the input of energy, which is why it is termed "active" transport.

**adaptation** A trait that, if altered, affects the fitness of the organism. Adaptations are the result of natural selection and can include not only physical traits such as eyes and fingernails but also the intangible traits of organisms, such as lifespan.

**adaptive radiation** A rapid series of speciation events that occur when one or more ancestral species invades a new environment.

**ADH** See **antidiuretic hormone.**

**adrenocorticotropic hormone (ACTH)** A hormone that stimulates the secretion of adrenal cortical hormones, which work to maintain electrolytic homeostasis in the body.

**aerobic respiration** Energy-producing reactions in animals that involve three stages: glycolysis, the Krebs cycle, and oxidative phosphorylation. Requires oxygen.

**age structure** Statistic that compares the relative number of individuals in the population from each age group.

**agonistic behavior** Behavior that results from a conflict of interest between individuals; often involves intimidation and submission.

**alcohol** Organic compound that contains a hydroxyl (—OH) functional group.

**alcohol fermentation** Occurs in fungi, yeast, and bacteria. Pyruvate is converted in two steps to ethanol, regenerating two molecules of $NAD^+$.

**aldehyde** Carbonyl group in which one R is a hydrogen and the other is a carbon chain. Hydrophilic and polar.

**aldosterone** Released from the adrenal gland, this hormone acts on the distal tubules to cause the reabsorption of more $Na^+$ and water. This increases blood volume and pressure.

**allantois** Transports waste products in mammals to the placenta. Later it is incorporated into the umbilical cord.

**allele** A variant of a gene for a particular character.

**allopatric speciation** Interbreeding ceases because some sort of barrier separates a single population into two (an area with no food, a mountain, etc.). The two populations evolve independently, and if they change enough, then, even if the barrier is removed, they cannot interbreed.

**alternation of generations** Plant life cycle, so named because during the cycle, plants sometimes exist as a diploid organism and at other times as a haploid organism.

**altruistic behavior** Behavior pattern that reduces the overall fitness of one organism while increasing the fitness of another.

**alveoli** Functional unit of the lung where gas exchange occurs.

**amines** Compounds containing amino groups.

**amino acid** A compound with a carbon center surrounded by an amino group, a carboxyl group, a hydrogen, and an R group that provides an amino acid's unique chemical characteristics.

**aminoacyl tRNA synthetase** Enzyme that makes sure that each tRNA molecule picks up the appropriate amino acid for its anticodon.

**amino group** A functional group that contains —$NH_2$ and that acts as a base; an example is an amino acid.

**amnion** Structure formed from epiblast that encloses the fluid-filled cavity that helps cushion the developing embryo.

**amygdala** The portion of the human brain that controls impulsive emotions and anger.

**amylase** Enzyme that breaks down the starches in the human diet to simpler sugars such as maltose, which are fully digested farther down in the intestines.

**anaerobic respiration** Energy-producing reactions, known as *fermentation,* that do not involve oxygen. It begins with glycolysis and concludes with the formation of $NAD^+$.

**anemia** Illness in which a lack of iron causes red blood cells to have a diminished capacity for delivering oxygen.

**aneuploidy** The condition of having an abnormal number of chromosomes.

**angiosperm** Flowering plant divided into monocots and dicots (monocotyledons and dicotyledons).

**anion** Ion with a negative charge that contains more electrons than protons.

**anterior pituitary gland** Structure that produces six hormones: TSH, STH (or HGH), ACTH, LH, FSH, and prolactin.

**anther** Pollen-producing portion of a plant.

**antheridia** Male gametangia in bryophytes and ferns designed to produce flagellated sperm that swim to meet up with the eggs produced by the female gametangia.

**anticodon** Region present at a tRNA attachment site; a three-nucleotide sequence that is perfectly complementary to a particular codon.

**antidiuretic hormone (ADH)** A hormone produced in the brain and stored in the pituitary gland; it increases the permeability of the collecting duct to water, leading to more concentrated urine content.

**antigen** A molecule that is foreign to our bodies and causes our immune systems to respond.

**apical meristem** Region at the tips of roots and shoots where plant growth is concentrated and many actively dividing cells can be found.

**apoplast pathway** Movement of water and nutrients through the nonliving portion of cells.

**aposematic coloration** Warning coloration adopted by animals that possess a chemical defense mechanism.

**archaebacteria** One of two major prokaryotic evolutionary branches. These organisms tend to live in extreme environments and include halophiles, methanogens, and thermoacidophiles.

**archegonium** Female gametangia in bryophytes, ferns, and gymnosperms.

**archezoa** Eukaryotic organism that allegedly most closely resembles prokaryotes.

**arteries** Structures that carry blood away from the heart.

**artificial selection** When humans become the agents of natural selection (breeding of dogs).

**ascospores** Haploid meiotic products produced by certain fungi.

**A site** Region on protein synthesis machinery that holds the tRNA carrying the next amino acid.

**associative learning** Process by which animals take one stimulus and associate it with another.

**atom** The smallest form of an element that still displays its unique properties.

**ATP synthase** Enzyme that uses the flow of hydrogens to drive the phosphorylation of an adenosine diphosphate molecule to produce adenosine triphosphate.

**auditory communication** Communication that involves the use of sound in the conveying of a message.

**autonomic nervous system (ANS)** A subdivision of the peripheral nervous system (PNS) that controls the involuntary activities of the body: smooth muscle, cardiac muscle, and glands. The ANS is divided into the sympathetic and parasympathetic divisions.

**autosomal chromosome** One that is not directly involved in determining gender.

**autotroph** An organism that is self-nourishing. It obtains carbon and energy without ingesting other organisms.

**auxin** Plant hormone that leads to elongation of stems and plays a role in phototropism and gravitropism.

**axon** A longer extension that leaves a neuron and carries the impulse away from the cell body toward target cells.

**balanced polymorphism** When there are two or more phenotypic variants maintained in a population.

**bare-rock succession** The attachment of lichen to rocks, followed by the step-by-step arrival of replacement species.

**Barr bodies** Inactivated genes on X chromosomes.

**Batesian mimicry** An animal that is harmless copies the appearance of an animal that is dangerous as a defense mechanism to make predators think twice about attacking.

**behavioral ecology** Science that studies the interaction between animals and their environments from an evolutionary perspective.

**bile** Substance that contains bile salts, phospholipids, cholesterol, and bile pigments such as bilirubin, is stored in the gallbladder, and is dumped into the small intestine on the arrival of the food.

**bile salts** Help to mechanically digest fat by emulsifying it into small droplets contained in water.

**binary fission** Mechanism by which prokaryotic cells divide. The cell elongates and pinches into two new daughter cells.

**binomial system of classification** System created by Linnaeus in which each species is given a two-word name: Genus + species (e.g., *Homo sapiens*).

**biogeochemical cycles** Cycles that represent the movement of elements, such as nitrogen and carbon, from organisms to the environment and back in a continuous cycle.

**biomass pyramid** *Biomass* represents the cumulative weight of all of the members at a given trophic level.

**biome** The various geographic regions of the earth that serve as hosts for ecosystems.

**biosphere** The entire life-containing area of a planet— all ecosystems and communities.

**biotic components** Living organisms of an ecosystem.

**biotic potential** The maximum growth rate for a population given unlimited resources, unlimited space, and lack of competition or predators.

**birth rate** Offspring produced per a specific time period.

**bivalves** Mollusks with hinged shells such as oysters and clams.

**blastula** As a morula undergoes its next round of cell divisions, fluid fills its center to create this hollow-looking structure.

**"blending" hypothesis** Theory that the genes contributed by two parents mix as if they are paint colors and the exact genetic makeup of each parent can never be recovered; the genes are as inseparable as blended paint.

**bottleneck** A dramatic reduction in population size that increases the likelihood of genetic drift.

**bronchi** Tunnels that branch off the trachea that lead into the individual lungs and divide into smaller branches called bronchioles.

**bronchioles** Tiny lung tunnels that branch repeatedly until they conclude as tiny air pockets containing alveoli.

**brush border** Large numbers of microvilli that increase the surface area of the small intestine to improve absorption efficiency.

**bryophytes** The first land plants to evolve from the chlorophytes. Members of this group include mosses, liverworts, and hornworts.

**bundle sheath cells** Cells that are tightly wrapped around the veins of a leaf. They are the site for the Calvin cycle in $C_4$ plants.

**$C_4$ photosynthesis** Photosynthetic process that alters the way in which carbon is fixed to better deal with the lack of $CO_2$ that comes from the closing of the stomata in hot, dry regions.

**$C_4$ plant** Plant that has adapted its photosynthetic process to more efficiently handle hot and dry conditions.

**Calvin cycle** A name for the light-independent (dark) reactions of photosynthesis.

**CAM (crassulacean acid metabolism) photosynthesis** Plants close their stomata during the day, collect $CO_2$ at night, and store the $CO_2$ in the form of acids until it is needed during the day for photosynthesis.

**capsid** A protein shell that surrounds genetic material.

**carbohydrate** Organic compound used by the cells of the human body in energy-producing reactions and as structural material. The three main types of carbohydrates are monosaccharides, disaccharides, and polysaccharides.

**carbon cycle** The movement of carbon from the atmosphere to living organisms and back to the environment in a continuous cycle.

**carbon fixation** The attachment of the carbon from $CO_2$ to a molecule that is able to enter the Calvin cycle, assisted by rubisco.

**carbonyl group** A functional group that is hydrophilic and polar. It has a central carbon connected to R groups on either side. If both Rs are carbon chains, it is a ketone. If one R is a hydrogen and the other a carbon chain, it is an aldehyde.

**carboxyl group** An acidic functional group (COOH). This functional group shows up along with amino groups in amino acids.

**cardiac muscle** Involuntary muscle of the heart that is striated in appearance and contains multiple nuclei.

**carnivore** A consumer that obtains energy and nutrients through consumption of other animals.

**carotenoid** A photosynthetic pigment.

**carrying capacity** The maximum number of individuals a population can sustain in a given environment.

**casparian strip** Obstacle that blocks the passage of water through the endodermis of plants.

**catalase** Enzyme that assists in the conversion of hydrogen peroxide to water and oxygen. Found in peroxisomes.

**catalysts** Molecules that speed up reactions by lowering the activation energy of a reaction.

**cation** Ion with a positive charge that contains more protons than electrons.

**cell body** The main body of the neuron.

**cell cycle** A cycle that consists of four stages: $G_1$, S, $G_2$, and M. $G_1$ and $G_2$ are growth stages, S is the part of the cell cycle in which the DNA is duplicated, and the M phase stands for mitosis—the cell division phase.

**cell-mediated immunity** This type of immunity involves *direct* cellular response to invasion as opposed to antibody-based defense.

**cell plate** Plant cell structure constructed in the Golgi apparatus composed of vesicles that fuse together along the middle of the cell, completing the separation process.

**cellular slime molds** Protists with a unique eating strategy. When plenty of food is available, they eat alone. When food is scare, they clump together and form a unit.

**cellulose** Polysaccharide composed of glucose used by plants to form cell walls.

**cell wall** Wall that functions to shape and protect cells. Present in plant but not animal cells.

**central nervous system (CNS)** The CNS is made up of the brain and the spinal cord. The CNS controls skeletal muscles and voluntary movement.

**cephalization** The concentration of sensory machinery in the anterior end of a bilateral organism.

**cerebellum** Portion of brain in charge of coordination and balance.

**cerebrum** Portion of the brain that controls functions such as speech, hearing, sight, and motor control. Divided into two hemispheres and four lobes per hemisphere.

**cervix** The uterus connects to the vaginal opening via this narrowed region.

**CF** See **cystic fibrosis.**

**character** A heritable feature, such as flower color, that varies among individuals.

**checkpoints** Stop points throughout the cell cycle where the cell verifies that there are enough nutrients and raw materials to progress to the next stage of the cycle.

**chemical communication** Mammals and insects communicate through the use of chemical signals called *pheromones.*

**chemiosmosis** The coupling of the movement of electrons down the electron transport chain with the formation of ATP using the driving force provided by a proton gradient. Seen in both photosynthesis and respiration.

**chemoautotrophs** Autotrophs that produce energy through oxidation of inorganic substances.

**chitin** Polysaccharide that is an important part of the exoskeletons of arthropods such as insects, spiders, and shellfish.

**chlorophyll** A photosynthetic pigment.

**chlorophytes** Green algae that are probably the common ancestors of land plants.

**chloroplast** The site of photosynthesis and energy production in plant cells and algae.

**choanoflagellate** Accepted to be the common ancestor of the animal kingdom.

**choice** Refers to the selection of mates by one sex (in mammals, it is usually females who exercise choice over males).

**choice chamber** Chamber used in scientific experiments to study kinesis.

**cholesterol** Steroid that is an important structural component of cell membranes and serves as a precursor molecule for steroid sex hormones.

**chorion** Formed from the trophoblast, it is the outer membrane of the embryo and the site of implantation onto the endometrium. It contributes to formation of the placenta in mammals.

**chromatin** The raw material that gives rise to the chromosomes (genetic material is uncoiled).

**chromosomal translocations** Condition in which a piece of one chromosome is attached to another, nonhomologous chromosome.

**chromosome duplication** Error in chromosomal replication that results in the repetition of a genetic segment.

**chromosome inversion** Condition in which a piece of a chromosome separates and reattaches in the opposite direction.

**chronic myelogenous leukemia** A cancer affecting white blood cell precursor cells. In this disease, a portion of chromosome 22 has been swapped with a piece of chromosome 9.

**chymotrypsin** Enzyme that cuts protein bonds in the small intestine.

**cilia** Structures that beat in rhythmical waves to carry foreign particles and mucus away from the lungs.

**circadian rhythm** A physiologic cycle that occurs in time increments that are roughly equivalent to the length of a day.

**class I histocompatibility antigens** The surface of all the cells of the human body, except for red blood cells, have these antigens, which are slightly different for each individual. The immune system accepts any cell that has the identical match for this antigen as friendly. Anything with a different major histocompatibility complex is foreign.

**class II histocompatibility antigens** Antigens found on the surface of the immune cells of the body. These antigens play a role in the interaction between the cells of the immune system.

**classical conditioning** Type of associative learning that Ivan Pavlov demonstrated with his experiments involving salivation in dogs.

**cleavage divisions** Developing embryo divides; cytoplasm is distributed unevenly to the daughter cells while the genetic information is distributed equally.

**cleavage furrow** Groove formed in animal cells between the two daughter cells; this groove pinches together to complete the separation of the two cells after mitosis.

**climax community** Final stable stage at the completion of a succession cycle.

**clumped dispersion** Scenario in which individuals live in packs that are spaced out from each other.

**codominance** Both alleles express themselves fully in a heterozygous organism.

**codon** A triplet of nucleotides that codes for a particular amino acid.

**coefficient of relatedness** Statistic that represents the average proportion of genes that two individuals have in common.

**coelom** Fluid-filled body cavity found between the body wall and the gut that has a lining and is derived from the mesoderm.

**coelomates** Animals that contain a true coelum.

**coenocytic fungi** Fungi that do not contain septae.

**coevolution** The mutual evolution between two species, which is exemplified by predator–prey relationships.

**coleoptile** Protective structure found around a grass seedling.

**collenchyma cells** Live plant cells that provide flexible and mechanical support.

**commensalism** One organism benefits from the relationship while the other is unaffected.

**community** A collection of populations of species in a given geographic area.

**competent** Describes a cell that is ready to accept foreign DNA from the environment.

**competition** Both species involved are harmed by this kind of interaction. The two major forms of competition are intraspecific and interspecific competition.

**competitive inhibition** Condition in which an inhibitor molecule resembling the substrate binds to the active site and physically blocks the substrate from attaching.

**complement** A protein that coats cells that need to be cleared, stimulating phagocytes to ingest them.

**compounds** Two or more elements combined to form an entity.

**conduction** Process by which heat moves from a place of higher temperature to a place of lower temperature.

**conifers** Gymnosperm plants whose reproductive structure is a cone.

**conjugation** The transfer of DNA between two bacterial cells connected by appendages called *sex pili*.

**conservative DNA replication** The original double helix of DNA does not change at all; it is as if the DNA is placed on a copy machine and an exact duplicate is made. DNA from the parent appears in only one of the two daughter cells.

**convection** Heat transfer caused by airflow.

**convergent characters** Characters are convergent if they look the same in two species, even though the species do *not* share a common ancestor.

**convergent evolution** Two unrelated species evolve in a way that makes them *more* similar. They both respond the same way to some environmental challenge, bringing them closer together.

**cork cambium** Area that produces a thick cover for stems and roots. It produces tissue that replaces dried-up epidermis lost during secondary growth.

**cork cells** Cells produced by the cork cambium that die and form a protective barrier against infection and physical damage.

**corpus callosum** Bridge that connects the two hemispheres of the brain.

**cortex** Outer region of the kidney or adrenal gland.

**cortisol** Stress hormone released in response to physiological challenges.

**cotyledon** Structure that provides nutrients for a developing angiosperm plant.

**cri-du-chat syndrome** This syndrome occurs with a deletion in chromosome 5 that leads to mental retardation, unusual facial features, and a small head. Most die in infancy or early childhood.

**crossover** Also referred to as "crossing over." When the homologous pairs match up during prophase I of meiosis, complementary pieces from the two homologous chromosomes wrap around each other and are exchanged between the chromosomes. This is one of the mechanisms that allows offspring to differ from their parents.

**cryptic coloration** Those being hunted adopt a coloring scheme that allows them to blend in to the colors of the environment.

**cuticle** Waxy covering that protects terrestrial plants against water loss.

**cutin** Waxy coat that protects plants.

**cyclic light reactions** Pathway that produces only ATP and uses only photosystem I.

**cyclin** Protein that accumulates during interphase; vital to cell cycle control.

**cystic fibrosis (CF)** A recessive disorder that is the most common lethal genetic disease in the United States. A defective version of a gene on chromosome 7 results in the excessive secretion of a thick mucus, which accumulates in the lungs and digestive tract. Left untreated, children with CF die at a very young age.

**cytokinesis** The physical separation of the newly formed daughter cells during meiosis and mitosis. Occurs immediately after telophase.

**cytokinin** Plant hormone that promotes cell division and leaf enlargement, and slows down the aging of leaves.

**cytoskeleton** Provides support, shape, and mobility to cells.

**death rate** Number of deaths per time period.

**deceptive markings** Patterns that can cause a predator to think twice before attacking. For example, some insects may have colored designs on their wings that resemble large eyes, making individuals look more imposing than they are.

**decomposer** See **detritivore**.

**dehydration reaction** A reaction in which two compounds merge, releasing $H_2O$ as a product.

**deletion** A piece of the chromosome is lost in the developmental process.

**demographers** Scientists who study the theory and statistics behind population growth and decline.

**dendrite** One of many short, branched processes of a neuron that help send the nerve impulses toward the cell body.

**denitrification** The process by which bacteria use nitrates and release $N_2$ as a product.

**density-dependent inhibition** When a certain density of cells is reached, cell growth will slow or stop. This is because there are not enough raw materials for the growth and survival of more cells.

**density-dependent limiting factors** Factors related to population size that come into play as population size approaches or passes the carrying capacity. Examples of density-dependent limiting factors include food, waste, and disease.

**density-independent limiting factors** Factors that limit population growth that have nothing to do with the population size, such as natural disasters and weather.

**depolarization** The electric potential becomes less negative inside the cell, allowing an action potential to occur.

**desert** The driest land biome on earth, which experiences a wide range of temperatures from day to night and exists on nearly every continent.

**detritivore** Also known as *decomposer*. A consumer that obtains its energy through the consumption of dead animals and plants.

**dicot** (dicotyledon) An angiosperm plant that has two cotyledons.

**diffusion** The movement of molecules down their concentration gradients without the use of energy. It is a passive process during which molecules move from a region of higher concentration to a region of lower concentration.

**dihybrid cross** The crossing of two different characters (BbRr × BbRr). A dihybrid cross between heterozygous gametes gives a 9:3:3:1 phenotype ratio in the offspring.

**diploid (2*n*)** An organism that has two copies of each type of chromosome. In humans, this refers to the pairs of homologous chromosomes.

**diplomonads** A phylum that is associated with the archezoan eukaryotes.

**directional selection** Occurs when members of a population at one end of a spectrum are selected against and/or those at the other end are selected for.

**disaccharide** A sugar consisting of two monosaccharides bound together. Common disaccharides include sucrose, maltose, and lactose.

**dispersive DNA replication** A theory that suggests that every daughter strand contains *some* parental DNA, but it is dispersed among pieces of DNA not of parental origin.

**disruptive selection** Selection is disruptive when individuals at the two extremes of a spectrum of variation do better than the more common forms in the middle.

**distribution** Describes the way populations are dispersed over a geographic area.

**divergent evolution** Two related species evolve in a way that makes them less similar, sometimes causing speciation.

**division** The classification category that replaces the phylum in plant classification.

**DNA methylation** The addition of $CH_3$ groups to the bases of DNA, rendering DNA inactive.

**DNA polymerase** The main enzyme in DNA replication that attaches to primer proteins and adds nucleotides to the growing DNA chain in a 5′-to-3′ direction.

**DNA replication** The process by which DNA is copied. This process occurs during the S phase of the cell cycle to ensure that every cell produced during mitosis or meiosis receives the proper amount of DNA.

**dominance hierarchy** A ranking of power among the members of a group of individuals.

**double helix** The shape of DNA—two strands held together by hydrogen bonds.

**Down syndrome** A classic aneuploid syndrome affecting one of every 700 children born in the United States. It most often involves a trisomy of chromosome 21, and leads to mental retardation, heart defects, short stature, and characteristic facial features.

**Duchenne muscular dystrophy** Sex-linked disorder caused by the absence of an essential muscle protein that leads to progressive weakening of the muscles combined with a loss of muscle coordination.

**ecosystem** All the individuals of a community and the environment in which it exists.

**ectoderm** Outer germ layer that gives rise to the nervous system, skin, hair, and nails.

**ectothermic animal** Animal whose basic metabolic rates increase in response to increases in temperature.

**Edwards syndrome** The presence of trisomy 18, which occurs in one out of every 10,000 live births and affects almost every organ of the body.

**electron transport chain (ETC)** The chain of molecules, located in the mitochondria, that passes electrons along during the process of chemiosmosis to regenerate $NAD^+$ to form ATP. Each time an electron passes to another member of the chain, the energy level of the system drops.

**element** The simplest form of matter.

**embryology** The study of embryonic development.

**emigration rate** Rate at which individuals relocate *out of* a given population.

**endergonic reaction** A reaction that requires *input* of energy to occur. A + B + energy → C.

**endocytosis** Process by which substances are brought into cells by enclosure into a membrane-created vesicle that surrounds the substance and escorts it into the cell.

**endoderm** Inner germ layer that gives rise to the inner lining of the gut, digestive system, liver, thyroid, lungs, and bladder.

**endodermis** Cells that line the innermost layer of the cortex in plants that give rise to the casparian strip.

**endometrium** Inner wall of the uterus to which the embryo attaches.

**endopeptidases** Enzymes that initiate the digestion of proteins by hydrolyzing all the polypeptides into small amino acid groups.

**endosymbiotic theory** Proposes that groups of prokaryotes associated in symbiotic relationships to form eukaryotes (mitochondria and chloroplasts).

**endothermic animal** Animal whose body temperature is relatively unaffected by external temperature.

**enhancer** DNA region, also known as a "regulator," that is located thousands of bases away from the promoter that influences transcription by interacting with specific transcription factors.

**enzymes** Catalytic proteins that are picky, interacting only with particular substrates. However, the enzymes can be reused and react with more than one copy of their substrate of choice and have a major effect on a reaction.

**epiblast** Develops into the three germ layers of the embryo: the endoderm, the mesoderm, and the ectoderm.

**epidermis (plants)** The protective outer coating of plants.

**epididymis** The coiled region that extends from the testes. This is where the sperm completes its maturation and waits until it is called on to do its duty.

**episomes** Plasmids that can be incorporated into a bacterial chromosome.

**epistasis** A gene at one locus alters the phenotypic expression of a gene at another locus. A dihybrid cross involving epistatic genes produces a 9:4:3 phenotype ratio.

**esophageal sphincter** Valvelike trapdoor between the esophagus and the stomach.

**esophagus** Structure that connects the throat to the stomach.

**estrogen** Hormone made (secreted) in ovaries that stimulates development of sex characteristics in women and induces the release of luteinizing hormone (LH) before the LH surge.

**ETC** See **electron transport chain.**

**ethology** The study of animal behavior.

**ethylene** Plant hormone that initiates the ripening of fruit and the dropping of leaves and flowers from trees.

**eubacteria** One of two major prokaryotic evolutionary branches. Categorized according to their mode of nutritional acquisition, mechanism of movement, shape, and other characteristics.

**eukaryotic cell** Complex cell that contains a nucleus, which functions as the control center of the cell, directing DNA replication, transcription, and cell growth. Organisms can be unicellular or multicellular and contain many different membrane-bound organelles.

**evaporation** Process by which a liquid changes into a vapor form. Functions in thermoregulation for humans when water leaves our bodies in the form of water vapor—sweat.

**evolution** Descent with modification. Evolution happens to populations, not individuals, and describes change in allele frequencies in populations with time.

**excision repair** Repair mechanism for DNA replication in which a section of DNA containing an error is cut out and the gap is filled by DNA polymerase.

**exergonic reaction** A reaction that *gives off* energy as a product. A + B → energy + C.

**exocytosis** Process by which substances are exported out of the cell. A vesicle escorts the substance to the plasma membrane, fuses with the membrane, and ejects its contents out of the cell.

**exons** Coding regions produced during transcription that are glued back together to produce the mRNA that is translated into a protein.

**exopeptidases** Enzymes that complete the digestion of proteins by hydrolyzing all the amino acids of any remaining fragments.

**exponential growth** A population grows at a rate that creates a J-shaped curve.

**extreme halophiles** Archaebacteria that live in environments with high salt concentrations.

**$F_1$** The first generation of offspring, or the first "filial" generation in a genetic cross.

**$F_2$** The second generation of offspring, or the second "filial" generation in a genetic cross.

**facilitated diffusion** The diffusion of particles across a selectively permeable membrane with the assistance of transport proteins that are specific in what they will carry and have a binding site designed for molecules of interest. This process requires no energy.

**facultative anaerobe** Organisms that can survive in oxygen-rich or oxygen-free environments.

**fallopian tube** See **oviduct.**

**fats** Lipids, made by combining glycerol and fatty acids, used as long-term energy stores in cells. They can be saturated or unsaturated.

**fatty acid** Long carbon chain that contains a carboxyl group on one end that combines with glycerol molecules to form lipids.

**fermentation** Anaerobic respiration pathway that occurs in absence of oxygen. Produces less ATP than aerobic respiration.

**ferredoxin** Molecule that donates the electrons to $NADP^+$ to produce NADPH during the light reactions of photosynthesis.

**fibrous root system** Root system found in monocots that provides the plant with a very strong anchor without going very deep into the soil.

**filtration** Capillaries allow small particles through the pores of their endothelial linings, but large molecules such as proteins, platelets, and blood cells tend to remain in the vessel.

**fixed-action pattern** An innate behavior that seems to be a programmed response to some stimulus.

**florigen** Hormone thought to assist in the blooming of flowers.

**fluid mosaic model** Model that states that the membrane is made of a phospholipid bilayer with proteins of various lengths and sizes, interspersed with cholesterol.

**fluke** Parasitic flatworm that alternates between sexual and asexual reproductive cycles.

**follicle-stimulating hormone (FSH)** A gonadotropin that stimulates activities of the testes and ovaries. In females, it induces the development of the ovarian follicle, leading to the production and secretion of estrogen, and in males it stimulates the production of sperm.

**food chain** A hierarchical list of who snacks on who. For example, bugs are eaten by spiders, who are eaten by birds, who are eaten by cats.

**food web** Can be regarded as overlapping food chains that show all the various dietary relationships in an environment.

**foraging** The behavior of actively searching for and eating a particular food resource.

**fossil record** The physical manifestation of species that have gone extinct (e.g., bones and imprints).

**F-plasmid** Plasmid that contains the genes necessary for the production of a sex pillus.

**frameshift mutations** Deletion or addition of DNA nucleotides that does not add or remove a multiple of three nucleotides. Usually produces a nonfunctional protein unless it occurs late in protein production.

**frequency-dependent selection** Alleles are selected for or against depending on their relative frequency in a population.

**FSH** See **follicle-stimulating hormone.**

**functional groups** The groups responsible for the chemical properties of organic compounds.

**$G_1$ phase** The first growth phase of the cell cycle, which produces all the necessary raw materials for DNA synthesis.

**$G_2$ phase** The second growth phase of the cell cycle, which produces all the necessary raw materials for mitosis.

**gametangia** Protective covering that provides a safe haven for the fertilization of the gametes and the development of the zygote in bryophytes, ferns, and some gymnosperms.

**gametes** Sex cells produced during meiosis in the human life cycle.

**gametophyte** A haploid multicellular organism.

**gastrulation** Cells separate into three primary layers called *germ layers,* which eventually give rise to the different tissues of an adult.

**gene flow** The change in frequencies of alleles as genes from one population are incorporated into those from another.

**generalized transduction** Transduction caused by the accidental placement of host DNA into a phage instead of viral DNA during viral reproduction. This host DNA may find its way into another cell where crossover could occur.

**generation time** Time needed for individuals to reach reproductive maturity.

**genetic code** Code that translates codons found on mRNA strands into amino acids.

**genetic drift** A change in allele frequencies that is due to chance events.

**genotype** An organism's genetic makeup for a given trait. A simple example of this could involve eye color, where B represents the allele for brown and b represents the allele for blue. The possible genotypes include homozygous brown (BB), heterozygous brown (Bb), and homozygous blue (bb).

**genus** Taxonomic group to which a species belongs.

**gibberellin** Plant hormone that assists in stem elongation and induces growth in dormant seeds, buds, and flowers.

**glomerular capillaries** The early portion of the nephron where the filtration process begins.

**glucagon** Hormone that stimulates conversion of glycogen into glucose.

**glycerol** Three-carbon molecule that combines with fatty acids to produce a variety of lipids.

**glycogen** Storage polysaccharide made of glucose molecules used by animals.

**glycolysis** Occurs in the cytoplasm of cells and is the beginning pathway for both aerobic and anaerobic respiration. During glycolysis, a glucose molecule is broken down through a series of reactions into two molecules of ATP, NADH, and pyruvate.

**glycoprotein** Protein that has been modified by the addition of a sugar.

**Golgi apparatus** Organelle that modifies proteins, lipids, and other macromolecules by the addition of sugars and other molecules to form glycoproteins. The products are then sent to other parts of the cell.

**G-proteins** Proteins vital to signal cascade pathways. These proteins directly activate molecules such as adenyl cyclase to assist in a reaction.

**gradualism** The theory that evolutionary change is a steady, slow process.

**grana** Flattened channels and disks arranged in stacks found in the thylakoid membrane.

**gravitropism** A plant's growth response to gravitational force. Auxin and gibberellins are involved in this response.

**gross productivity** The difference over time between the dissolved oxygen concentrations of the light and dark bottles calculated in primary productivity experiments.

**growth factors** Assist in the growth of structures.

**guard cells** Cells within the epidermis of plants that control the opening and closing of the stomata.

**gymnosperm** First major seed plant to evolve. Heterosporous plant that *usually* transports its sperm through the use of pollen. Conifers are the major gymnosperm to know.

**habituation** Loss of responsiveness to unimportant stimuli that do not provide appropriate feedback.

**haploid (*n*)** An organism that has only one copy of each type of chromosome.

**Hardy-Weinberg equilibrium** A special case where a population is in stasis, or not evolving.

**helicase** Enzyme that unzips DNA, breaking the hydrogen bonds between the nucleotides and producing the replication fork for replication.

**helper T cell** Immune cells that assist in activation of B cells.

**hemoglobin** Molecule that allows red blood cells to carry and deliver oxygen throughout the body to hardworking organs and tissues.

**hemophilia** Sex-linked disorder caused by the absence of a protein vital to the clotting process. Individuals with this condition have difficulty clotting blood after even the smallest of wounds.

**herbivore** Consumer that obtains energy and nutrients through consumption of plants.

**heterosporous plant** Plant that produces two types of spores, male and female.

**heterotroph** An organism that must consume other organisms to obtain nourishment. They are the consumers of the world.

**heterotroph theory** Theory that posits that the first organisms were heterotrophs (organisms that cannot produce their own food).

**heterozygote advantage** The situation, such as sickle cell anemia in malarial regions, in which being heterozygous for a condition provides some benefit.

**heterozygous (hybrid)** An individual is heterozygous (or a hybrid) for a gene if the two alleles are different (Bb).

**histamine** Chemical signal responsible for initiation of the inflammation response of the immune system.

**holandric trait** A trait inherited via the Y chromosome.

**homeobox** DNA sequence of a homeotic gene that tells the cell where to put body structures.

**homeotic genes** Genes that regulate or "direct" the body plan of organisms.

**homologous characters** Traits are said to be homologous if they are similar because their host organisms arose from a common ancestor.

**homologous chromosomes** Chromosomes that resemble one another in shape, size, function, and the genetic information they contain. They are not identical.

**homosporous plant** Plants that produce a single spore type that gives rise to bisexual gametophytes.

**homozygous (pure)** An individual is homozygous for a gene if both of the given alleles are the same (BB or bb).

**honest indicators** Sexually selected traits that are the result of female choice and signal genetic quality.

**hormones** Chemicals produced by glands such as the pituitary and used by the endocrine system to signal distant target cells.

**host range** The range of cells that a virus is able to infect. For example, HIV infects the T cells of our body.

**humoral immunity** Immunity involving antibodies and circulating fluids.

**Huntington's disease** An autosomal dominant degenerative disease of the nervous system that shows itself when a person is in their 30s or 40s and is both irreversible and fatal.

**hybrid vigor** Refers to the fact that hybrids may have increased reproductive success compared to inbred strains. This is due to the fact that inbreeding increases the likelihood that two deleterious, recessive alleles will end up in the same offspring.

**hydrolysis reaction** A reaction that breaks down compounds by the addition of $H_2O$.

**hydrophilic** Water-loving.

**hydroxyl group** A hydrophilic and polar functional group (—OH) that is present in compounds known as *alcohols.*

**hypercholesterolemia** Recessive disorder (hh) that causes cholesterol levels to be many times higher than normal and can lead to heart attacks in children as young as two years old.

**hypertonic** Characterizes a solution that has a higher solute concentration than does a neighboring solution.

**hypha** Filament found in fungi made of chitin that separates fungi into multicellular compartments.

**hypoblast** Forms the yolk sac, which produces the embryo's first blood cells.

**hypothalamus** The thermostat and "hunger meter" of the body, regulating temperature, hunger, and thirst.

**hypotonic** Characterizes a solution that has a lower solute concentration than a neighboring solution.

**immigration rate** Rate at which individuals relocate *into* a given population.

**imprinting** Innate behavior that is learned during a critical period early in life.

**inclusive fitness** An individual's fitness gain that is a direct result of his or her contribution to the reproductive effort of closely related kin. This results from the fact that close kin share copies of identical genes.

**incomplete dominance** Blending inheritance. The heterozygous genotype produces an intermediate phenotype rather than the dominant phenotype; neither allele dominates the other.

**induced-fit model** Theory that suggests that when an enzyme and a substrate bind together, the enzyme is *induced* to alter its shape for a tighter active-site/substrate attachment, which places the substrate in a favorable position to react more quickly.

**inducer** Molecule that binds to and inactivates a repressor.

**induction** The ability of one group of cells to influence the development of another. This influence can be through physical contact or chemical signaling.

**inner cell mass** Portion of the blastula that develops into the embryo.

**inorganic compounds** For the most part, compounds containing no carbon. There are some exceptions such as carbon dioxide, carbon monoxide, and others.

**insight learning** The ability to do something correctly the first time even with no prior experience.

**insulin** Hormone secreted in response to high blood glucose levels to promote glycogen formation.

**integral proteins** Proteins that are implanted within the bilayer and can extend part way or all the way across the membrane.

**intermediate filaments** Substances constructed from a class of proteins called keratins; function as reinforcement for the shape and position of organelles in a cell.

**intermediate inheritance** An individual heterozygous for a trait (Yy) shows characteristics not exactly like those of *either* parent. The phenotype is a "mixture" of both of the parents' genetic input.

**interneurons** Function to make synaptic connections with other neurons. They work to integrate sensory input and motor output.

**interphase** The first three stages of the cycle, $G_1$, S, and $G_2$. Accounts for approximately 90 percent of the cell cycle.

**interspecific competition** Competition between different species that rely on the same resources for survival.

**interstitial cells** The structures that produce the hormones involved in the male reproductive system.

**intraspecific competition** *Within*-species competition that occurs because members of the same species rely on the same valuable resources for survival.

**introns** Noncoding regions produced during transcription that are cut out of the mRNA.

**invertebrate** Animal without a backbone.

**ion** An atom with a positive or negative charge.

**isotonic solution** Solution that has the same solute concentration as surrounding solutions.

**karyotype** A chart that organizes chromosomes in relation to number, size, and type.

**ketone** Carbonyl group in which both Rs are carbon chains; hydrophilic and polar.

**kinesis** A random change in the speed of movement in response to a stimulus. Organisms speed up in places they don't like and slow down in places they do like.

**kingdom** The broadest of the classification groups.

**Klinefelter syndrome (XXY)** Syndrome in which individuals have male sex organs but are sterile and display several feminine body characteristics.

**Krebs cycle** Energy-producing reaction that occurs in the matrix of the mitochondria, in which pyruvate is broken down completely to $H_2O$ and $CO_2$ to produce 3 NADH, 1 $FADH_2$, and 1 ATP.

*K*-selected populations Populations of a roughly constant size whose members have low reproductive rates. The offspring produced by *K*-selected organisms require extensive postnatal care.

**lac operon** Operon that aids in control of transcription of lactose metabolizing genes.

**lactic acid fermentation** Occurs in human muscle cells when oxygen is unavailable. Pyruvate is directly reduced to lactate by NADH to regenerate the NAD$^+$ needed for the resumption of glycolysis.

**lagging strand** The discontinuous strand produced during DNA replication.

**larynx** Passageway from the pharynx to the trachea. Commonly called the "voicebox."

**lateral meristems** Cells that extend all the way through the plant from roots to shoots and provide the secondary growth that increases the girth of a plant.

**lateral roots** Roots that serve to hold a plant in place in the soil.

**law of dominance** When two opposite pure-breeding varieties (homozygous dominant vs. homozygous recessive) of an organism are crossed, all the offspring resemble one parent. This is referred to as the "dominant" trait. The variety that is hidden is referred to as the "recessive" trait.

**law of independent assortment** Members of each pair of factors are distributed independently when the gametes are formed. In other words, inheritance of one particular trait or characteristic does not interfere with inheritance of another trait (in unlinked genes). For example, if an individual is BbRr for two genes, gametes formed during meiosis could contain BR, Br, bR, or br. The B and b alleles assort *independently* of the R and r alleles.

**law of multiplication** Law that states that to determine the probability that two random events will occur in succession, you simply multiply the probability of the first event by the probability of the second event.

**law of segregation** Every organism carries pairs of factors, called *alleles*, for each trait, and the members of the pair segregate out (separate) during the formation of gametes. For example, if an individual is Bb for eye color, during gamete formation one gamete would receive a B and the other made from that cell would receive a b.

**leading strand** The continuous strand produced during DNA replication.

**LH** See **luteinizing hormone.**

**LH surge** Giant release of LH that triggers ovulation—the release of a secondary oocyte from the ovary.

**lichen** A symbiotic collection of organisms (fungus and algae) living as one.

**life cycle** Sequence of events that make up the reproductive cycle of an organism.

**limiting factors** Environmental factors that keep population sizes in check (predators, diseases, food supplies, and waste).

**linkage map** A genetic map put together using crossover frequencies.

**linked genes** Genes along the same chromosome that tend to be inherited together because the chromosome is passed along as a unit.

**lipase** The major fat-digesting enzyme of the human body.

**lipids** Hydrophobic organic compounds used by cells as energy stores or building blocks. Three important lipids are fats, steroids, and phospholipids.

**logistic growth** A population grows at a rate that creates an S-shaped curve.

**long day plants** Plants, such as spinach, which flower if exposed to a night that is shorter than a critical period.

**luteinizing hormone (LH)** A gonadotropin that stimulates ovulation and formation of a corpus luteum, as well as the synthesis of estrogen and progesterone.

**lymphatic system** Important part of the circulatory system that functions as the route by which proteins and fluids that have leaked out of the bloodstream can return to circulation. The lymphatic system also functions as a protector for the body because of the presence of lymph nodes.

**lymph nodes** Structures found in the lymphatic system that are full of white blood cells, which live to fight infection. These nodes often swell up during infection as a sign of the body's fight against the infectious agent.

**lymphocyte** White blood cell. There are two main types of lymphocyte: B cells and T cells. These cells are formed in the bone marrow of the body and arise from stem cells.

**lysogenic cycle** The virus falls dormant and incorporates its DNA into the host DNA as an entity called a *provirus.* The viral DNA is quietly reproduced by the cell every time the cell reproduces itself, and this allows the virus to stay alive from generation to generation without killing the host cell.

**lysosome** Membrane-bound organelle that specializes in digestion and contains enzymes that break down proteins, lipids, nucleic acids, and carbohydrates.

**lysozyme** An enzyme, present in saliva and tears, that can kill germs before they have a chance to take hold.

**lytic cycle** The cell actually produces many viral offspring, which are released from the cell, killing the host cell in the process.

**macroevolution** The big picture of evolution, which includes the study of evolution of groups of species over very long periods of time.

**macronucleus** A nucleus present in some protists (Ciliophora) and which controls the everyday activities of organisms.

**macrospores** Female gametophytes produced by heterosporous plants.

**map unit** Also termed *centigram*. Unit used to geographically relate the genes on the basis of cross-over frequencies. One map unit is equal to a 1 percent recombination frequency.

**matter** Anything that has mass and takes up space.

**mechanical digestion** The physical breakdown of food that comes from chewing.

**medulla** Inner region of the kidney.

**medulla oblongata** The control center for involuntary activities such as breathing.

**medusa** A cnidarian that is flat and roams the waters looking for food (e.g., jellyfish).

**melatonin** Hormone that is known to be involved in our biological rhythms (circadian).

**memory cells** Stored instructions on how to handle a particular invader. When an invader returns to the body, the memory cells recognize it, produce antibodies in rapid fashion, and eliminate the invader very quickly.

**meristemic cells** Cells that allow plants to grow indeterminately.

**mesoderm** Intermediate germ layer that gives rise to muscle, the circulatory system, the reproductive system, excretory organs, bones, and connective tissues of the gut and exterior of the body.

**mesophyll** Interior tissue of a leaf.

**mesophyll cells** Cells that contain many chloroplasts and host the majority of photosynthesis.

**methanogens** Archaebacteria that produce methane as a by-product.

**microevolution** Evolution at the level of species and populations.

**microfilaments** Substances built from actin that play a major role in muscle contraction.

**micronucleus** A nucleus present in some protists (Ciliophora) and which functions in conjugation.

**microspores** Male gametophytes produced by heterosporous plants.

**microtubules** Substances constructed from tubulin; play a lead role in the separation of cells during cell division; are also important components of cilia and flagella.

**migration** This is a cyclic movement of animals over long distances according to the time of year.

**mismatch repair** Process during DNA replication by which DNA polymerase replaces an incorrectly placed nucleotide with proper nucleotide.

**missense mutation** Substitution of the wrong nucleotides into the DNA sequence. These substitutions still result in the addition of amino acids to the growing protein chain during translation, but they can sometimes lead to the addition of *incorrect* amino acids to the chain.

**mitochondrion** Double-membraned organelle that specializes in the production of ATP; host organelle for the Krebs cycle (matrix) and oxidative phosphorylation (cristae).

**mitotic spindle** Apparatus constructed from microtubules that assists in the physical separation of the chromosomes during mitosis.

**monocot** (monocotyledon) Angiosperm with a single cotyledon.

**monohybrid cross** A cross that involves a single character in which both parents are heterozygous (Bb × Bb). A monohybrid cross between heterozygous gametes gives a 3:1 phenotype ratio in the offspring.

**monosaccharide** The simplest form of a carbohydrate. The most important monosaccharide is glucose, which is used in cellular respiration to provide energy for cells.

**morula** A structure formed during the cleavage divisions of the zygote.

**motor neurons** Nerve cells that take the commands from the central nervous system (CNS) and put them into action as motor outputs.

**M phase mitosis** This is the stage during which the cell separates into two new cells.

**Müllerian mimicry** Two species that are aposematically colored as an indicator of their chemical defense mechanism; they mimic each other's color scheme in an effort to increase the speed with which predators learn to avoid them.

**mutant phenotypes** Characters that are not the wild-type strain in fruit flies and other organisms.

**mutation** A random event that can cause changes in allele frequencies. It is *always* random with respect to which genes are affected, although the changes in allele frequencies that occur as a result of the mutation may not be.

**mutualism** Scenario in which two organisms benefit from an interaction or relationship.

**mycelium** Meshes of branching filaments formed from hyphae that function as mouthlike structures for fungi.

**myelinated neurons** Neurons with a layer of insulation around the axon, allowing for faster transmission. They form the cable Internet of the body.

**natural selection** The process by which characters or traits are maintained or eliminated in a population based on their contribution to the differential survival and reproductive success of their "host" organisms.

**negative feedback** Occurs when a hormone acts to directly or indirectly inhibit further secretion of the hormone of interest.

**nephron** The functional unit of the kidney.

**net productivity** Difference between the concentration of dissolved oxygen for the initial and light bottle in a primary productivity experiment.

**neural plate** Structure that becomes the neural groove, which eventually becomes the neural tube. This neural tube later gives rise to the central nervous system.

**neural tube** Embryonic structure that gives rise to the central nervous system.

**neuromuscular junction** The space between the motor neuron and the muscle cell.

**neurotransmitter** Chemical released by neurons that functions as a messenger, causing a nearby cell to react and continue the nervous impulse.

**niche** Term used to describe all the biotic and abiotic resources used by the organism.

**nitrogen cycle** The shuttling of nitrogen from the atmosphere, to living organisms, and back to the atmosphere in a continuous cycle.

**nitrogen fixation** The conversion of $N_2$ to $NH_3$ (ammonia).

**nitrogenous bases** Monomers such as adenine, guanine, cytosine, thymine, and uracil out of which DNA and RNA are constructed.

**noncompetitive inhibition** Condition in which an inhibitor molecule binds to an enzyme away from the active site, causing a change in the shape of the active site so that it can no longer interact with the substrate.

**noncyclic light reactions** Pathway that produces ATP, NADPH, and $O_2$. Uses both photosystem I and II.

**nondisjunction** The improper separation of chromosomes during meiosis, which leads to an abnormal number of chromosomes in offspring. Examples include Down syndrome, Turner syndrome, and Klinefelter's syndrome.

**nonsense mutation** Substitution of the wrong nucleotides into the DNA sequence. These substitutions lead to premature stoppage of protein synthesis by the early placement of a stop codon. This type of mutation usually leads to a nonfunctional protein.

**nonspecific immunity** The nonspecific prevention of the entrance of invaders into the body.

**notochord** Structure that serves to support the body. Found in the embryos of chordates.

**nucleic acid** Macromolecule composed of nucleotides, sugars, and phosphates that serves as genetic material of living organisms (DNA and RNA).

**nucleoid** Region of a prokaryotic cell that contains the genetic material.

**nucleolus** Eukaryotic structure in which ribosomes are constructed.

**nucleus** The control center of eukaryotic cells that is the storage site of the genetic material (DNA). It is the site of replication, transcription, and posttranscriptional modification of RNA.

**obligate aerobe** Organism that requires oxygen for respiration.

**obligate anaerobe** Organism that only survives in oxygen-free environments.

**observational learning** The ability of an organism to learn how to do something by watching another individual do it first.

**oil** Type of lipid.

**Okazaki fragments** The lagging DNA strand consists of these tiny pieces that are later connected by an enzyme, DNA ligase, to produce the completed double-stranded daughter DNA molecule.

**ontogeny** The development of an individual.

**oogenesis** Process by which female gametes are formed. Each meiotic cycle leads to the production of a single ovum, or egg.

**operant conditioning** Type of associative learning that is based on trial and error.

**operator** A short sequence near the promoter that assists in transcription by interacting with regulatory proteins (transcription factors).

**operon** A promoter/operator pair that services multiple genes.

**opportunistic populations** *R*-selected organisms that tend to appear when space in the region opens up due to some environmental change. They grow fast, reproduce quickly, and die quickly as well.

**optimal foraging** Theory that predicts that natural selection will favor animals that choose foraging strategies that maximize the differential between benefits and costs.

**organic compounds** Carbon-containing compounds. Important examples include carbohydrates, proteins, lipids, and nucleic acids.

**osmosis** The passive diffusion of water down its concentration gradient across selectively permeable membranes. It will flow from a region with a lower solute concentration (hypotonic) to a region with a higher solute concentration (hypertonic).

**outbreeding** Mating between unrelated individuals of the same species.

**ovary** The site of egg production. In animals, females often have two, one on either side of the body. Plants *usually* only have one ovary.

**oviduct** Known also as the *fallopian tube,* this is the site of fertilization and connects the ovary to the uterus. Eggs move through here from the ovary to the uterus (in animals only).

**ovulation** Stage of menstrual cycle in which the secondary oocyte is released from the ovary.

**oxaloacetate** Compound that plays an important role in $C_4$ photosynthesis of plants and the Krebs cycle in animals.

**oxidative phosphorylation** Aerobic process in which NADH and FADH$_2$ pass their electrons down the electron transport chain to produce ATP.

**oxytocin** Hormone that stimulates uterine contraction and milk ejection for breastfeeding.

**P$_1$** The parent generation in a genetic cross.

**palisade mesophyll** Host to many chloroplasts and much of the photosynthesis of a leaf.

**parallel evolution** Similar evolutionary changes occurring in two either related or unrelated species that respond in a similar manner to a similar environment.

**parasitism** Scenario in which one organism benefits at the other's expense.

**parasympathetic nervous system** Branch of autonomic nervous system that shuts down the body to conserve energy.

**parathyroid hormone (PTH)** Hormone that increases serum concentration of Ca$^{2+}$, assisting in the process of bone maintenance.

**parenchyma cells** Plant cells that play a role in photosynthesis (mesophyll cells), storage, and secretion.

**Patau syndrome** Presence of trisomy 13, which occurs in about one out of every 12,000–16,000 live births and causes serious brain and circulatory defects.

**pedigrees** Family trees used to describe the genetic relationships within a family. One use of a pedigree is to determine whether parents will pass certain conditions to their offspring.

**pepsin** The major enzyme of the stomach, which breaks down proteins into smaller polypeptides to be handled by the intestines.

**pepsinogen** The precursor to pepsin that is activated by active pepsin (a small amount of which normally exists in the stomach).

**peripheral nervous system (PNS)** The PNS can be broken down into a sensory and a motor division. The sensory division carries information *to* the CNS while the motor division carries information *away* from the CNS.

**peripheral proteins** Proteins, such as receptor proteins, not implanted in the bilayer, which are often attached to integral proteins of the membrane.

**peristalsis** The force created by the rhythmic contraction of the smooth muscle of the esophagus and intestines.

**permafrost** Frozen layer of soil just underneath the upper soil layer, found in the tundra biome.

**peroxisome** Organelle that functions to break down fatty acids, and detoxify.

**petals** Structures that serve to attract pollinators.

**PGAL** (phosphoglyceraldehyde) Molecule important to energy-producing reactions photosynthesis and respiration.

**phage** A virus that infects bacteria.

**phagocytes** Immune cells (macrophages and neutrophils) that use endocytosis to engulf and eliminate foreign invaders.

**pharynx** Tube through which both food and air pass after leaving the mouth.

**phenotype** The physical expression of the trait associated with a particular genotype. Some examples of the phenotypes for Mendel's peas were round or wrinkled, green or yellow, purple flower or white flower.

**phenylketonuria (PKU)** An autosomal recessive disease caused by a single gene defect that leaves a person unable to break down phenylalanine, which results in a by-product that can accumulate to toxic levels in the blood and cause mental retardation.

**pheromones** Chemical signals important to communication.

**phloem** Important part of plant vascular tissue that functions to transport sugars from their production site to the rest of the plant.

**phosphate group** An acidic functional group that is a vital component of molecules that serve as cellular energy sources: ATP, ADP, and GTP.

**phospholipid** Lipid with both a hydrophobic tail *and* a hydrophilic head; the major component of cell membranes with the hydrophilic phosphate group forming the outside portion and the hydrophobic tail forming the interior of the wall.

**photoautotrophs** Photosynthetic autotrophs that produce energy from light.

**photolysis** Process by which water is broken up by an enzyme into hydrogen ions and oxygen atoms. Occurs during the light reactions of photosynthesis.

**photoperiodism** The response by a plant to the change in the length of days.

**photophosphorylation** Process by which ATP is made during the light-dependent reactions of photosynthesis. It is the chloroplast equivalent of oxidative phosphorylation.

**photorespiration** Process by which oxygen competes with carbon dioxide and attaches to RuBP. Plants that experience photorespiration have a lowered capacity for growth.

**photosynthesis** The process by which plants generate energy from light and inorganic raw materials. This occurs in the chloroplasts and involves two stages: the light-dependent reactions and the light-independent reactions.

**photosystem** Cluster of light-trapping pigments involved in the process of photosynthesis.

**phototaxis** Reflex movement toward light at night.

**phototropism** A plant's growth in response to light. Auxin is the hormone involved with this process.

**phycobilin** Photosynthetic pigment.

**phylogeny** The evolutionary history of a species.

**phytochrome** Important pigment in the process of flowering. Leads to the production of florigen.

**pigment** A molecule that absorbs light of a particular wavelength.

**pioneer species** A species that is able to survive in resource-poor conditions and takes hold of a barren area such as a volcanic island. Pioneer species do the grunt work, adding nutrients and other improvements to the once-uninhabited volcanic rock until future species take over.

**PKU** See **phenylketonuria.**

**placenta** In humans, this structure provides the nutrients for the developing embryo.

**planarians** Free-living platyhelminthe carnivores that live in the water.

**plasma** The liquid portion of the blood that contains minerals, hormones, antibodies, and nutritional materials.

**plasma cells** The factories that produce antibodies that eliminate any cell containing on its surface the antigen that the plasma cell has been summoned to kill.

**plasma membrane** Selective barrier around a cell composed of a double layer of phospholipids that controls what is able to enter and exit a cell.

**plasmids** Extra circles of DNA in bacteria that contain just a few genes and have been useful in genetic engineering. Plasmids replicate independently of the main chromosome.

**plasmodial slime molds** Nonphotosynthetic heterotrophic funguslike protists. They eat and grow as a unified clumped unicellular mass known as a *plasmodium.*

**plasmodium** This word has two meanings in this book. It can be the causative agent of malaria, or it can be the clumped unicellular mass that fungi form under certain feeding conditions.

**plasmolysis** The shriveling of the cytoplasm of a cell in response to loss of water in hypertonic surroundings.

**platelet** Blood cell involved in the clotting of blood.

**pleiotropy** A single gene has multiple effects on an organism.

**PNS** See **peripheral nervous system.**

**polar** A molecule that has an unequal distribution of charge, which creates a positive and a negative side to the molecule.

**polar body** Castaway cell produced during female gamete formation that contains only genetic information.

**pollen** Sperm-bearing male gametophyte of gymnosperms and angiosperms.

**polygenic traits** Traits that are affected by more than one gene (e.g., eye color).

**polymerase chain reaction** Technique used to create large amounts of a DNA sequence in a short amount of time.

**polyp** Cylinder-shaped cnidarian that lives attached to a surface (e.g., sea anemone).

**polyploidy** A condition in which an individual has more than the normal number of sets of chromosomes.

**polysaccharide** A carbohydrate usually composed of hundreds or thousands of monosaccharides, which acts as a storage form of energy, and as structural material in and around cells. Starch and glycogen are storage polysaccharides; cellulose and chitin are structural polysaccharides.

**pond succession** Process by which a hole filled with water passes through the various succession stages until it has become a swamp, forest, or grassland.

**population** A collection of individuals of the same species living in the same geographic area.

**population cycle** When a population size dips below the carrying capacity, it will later come back to the capacity and even surpass it. However, the population could dip below the carrying capacity as a result of some major change in the environment and equilibrate at a new, lower carrying capacity.

**population density** The number of individuals per unit area in a given population.

**population ecology** The study of the size, distribution, and density of populations and how they change with time.

**positive feedback** Occurs when a hormone acts to directly or indirectly cause increased secretion of a hormone.

**posterior pituitary gland** Structure that produces only two hormones: ADH and oxytocin.

**potometer** Lab apparatus used to measure transpiration rates in plants.

**predation** Scenario in which one species, the predator, hunts another species, the prey.

**primary consumers** The consumers that obtain energy through consumption of the producers of the planet. Known as *herbivores.*

**primary immune response** When a B cell meets and attaches to the appropriate antigen, it becomes activated and undergoes mitosis and differentiation into plasma cells and memory cells.

**primary oocytes** Cells that begin the process of meiosis and progress until prophase I, where they sit halted until the host female enters puberty.

**primary plant growth** Increase in the length of a plant.

**primary productivity** Rate at which carbon-containing compounds are stored.

**primary sex characteristics** The sexual organs that assist in the vital process of procreation; include the testes, ovaries, and uterus.

**primary spermatocytes** Produced by mitotic division, these cells immediately undergo meiosis I to produce two secondary spermatocytes, which undergo meiosis II to produce four spermatids.

**primary structure** The sequence of the amino acids that make up a protein.

**primary succession** Succession that occurs in an area that is devoid of life and contains no soil.

**primer sites** DNA segments that signal where replication should originate.

**prion** Incorrectly folded form of a brain cell protein that works by converting other normal host proteins into misshapen proteins. Prion diseases tend to cause dementia, muscular control problems, and loss of balance.

**progesterone** Hormone involved in menstrual cycle and pregnancy.

**prokaryotic cell** A *simple* cell with no nucleus, or membrane-bound organelles; divides by binary fission and includes bacteria—both heterotrophic and autotrophic types.

**prolactin** Hormone that controls the production of milk and leads to a decrease in the synthesis and release of GnRH, thus inhibiting ovulation.

**promoter region** A recognition site that shows the polymerase where transcription should begin.

**prostate gland** Structure whose function in the male reproductive system is to add a basic (pH > 7) liquid to the mix to help neutralize the acidity of the urine that may remain in the common urethral passage.

**protein** Organic compound composed of chains of amino acids that function as structural components, transport aids, enzymes, and cell signals, among other things.

**protein hormones** Hormones too large to move inside a cell, and which bind to receptors on the surface of the cell instead.

**protein kinase** Protein that controls the activities of other proteins through the addition of phosphate groups.

**provirus** A virus genome that is integrated into the DNA of a host cell that can be transmitted from one generation to the next without causing lysis.

**pseudocoelomate** Animal that has a fluid-filled body cavity that is not enclosed by mesoderm.

**pseudopods** Extensions from protists (organisms of the kingdom Protist) that assist in collection of nutrients.

**P site** Region in protein synthesis machinery that holds the tRNA carrying the growing protein.

**PTH** See **parathyroid hormone.**

**punctuated equilibria model** Theorizes that evolutionary change occurs in rapid bursts separated by large periods of stasis (no change).

**purine** A nitrogenous base that contains a double ring structure (adenine, guanine).

**pyloric sphincter** The connection point between the stomach and the small intestine.

**pyramid of numbers** Pyramid based on the *number* of individuals at each level of the biomass chain. Each box in this pyramid represents the number of members of that level. The highest consumers in the chain tend to be quite large, resulting in a smaller number of those individuals spread out over a given area.

**pyrimidine** A nitrogenous base that contains a single ring structure (cytosine, thymine).

**$Q_{10}$ value** Statistic that shows how an increase in temperature affects the metabolic activity of an organism.

**quaternary structure** The arrangement of separate polypeptide "subunits" into a single protein. Seen only in proteins with more than one polypeptide chain.

**radiation** The loss of heat through ejection of electromagnetic waves.

**random distribution** Random distribution of species in a given geographic area.

**rate of reaction** Rate at which a chemical reaction occurs.

**reaction centers** Control centers made up of pigments.

**reciprocal altruism** Altruistic behavior performed with the expectation that the favor will be returned.

**recombinant DNA** DNA that contains DNA pieces from multiple sources.

**red blood cells** Cells in body that contain hemoglobin and serve as the oxygen delivery system in the body.

**red-green colorblindness** Sex-linked condition that leaves those afflicted unable to distinguish between red and green colors.

**redox reaction** A reduction–oxidation reaction involving the transfer of electrons.

**replication fork** Fork opened in DNA strand that allows DNA replication to occur.

**repolarization** The lowering of the potential back down to its initial level, stopping the transmission of neural signals at that point.

**repressor** Protein that prevents the binding of RNA polymerase to the promoter site.

**reproductive success** A measure of how many surviving offspring one produces relative to how many the other individuals in one's population produce.

**RER** See **rough endoplasmic reticulum.**

**respirometer** Machine that can be used to calculate the respiration rate of a reaction.

**restriction enzymes** Enzymes that cut DNA at specific nucleotide sequences. This results in DNA fragments with single-stranded ends called "sticky ends," which find and reconnect with other DNA fragments containing the same ends (with the assistance of DNA ligase).

**retrovirus** An RNA virus that carries an enzyme called *reverse transcriptase* that reverse-transcribes the genetic information from RNA into DNA. In the nucleus of the host, the newly transcribed DNA incorporates into the host DNA and is transcribed into RNA when the host cell undergoes normal transcription.

**reverse transcriptase** Enzyme carried by retroviruses that function to convert RNA to DNA.

**R$_f$** Variable that indicates the relative rate at which one molecule migrates compared to the solvent of a paper chromatograph.

**ribosomes** Host organelle for protein synthesis composed of a large subunit and a small subunit. Ribosomes are built in the nucleolus.

**RNA polymerase** Enzyme that runs transcription and adds the appropriate nucleotides to the 3′ end of the growing strand.

**RNA splicing** Process that removes introns from newly produced mRNA and then glues exons back together to produce the final product.

**root** Portion of the plant that is below the ground.

**root cap** Protective structure found around the apical meristem of a root that keeps it together as it pushes through the soil.

**root hairs** Hairs extending off the surface of root tips that increase the surface area for absorption of water and nutrients from the soil.

**root pressure** Driving force that contributes to the movement of water through the xylem of a plant.

**rough endoplasmic reticulum (RER)** Membrane-bound organelle with ribosomes on the cytoplasmic surface of the cell. Proteins produced by RER are often secreted and carried by vesicles to the Golgi apparatus for further modification.

**rRNA** Ribosomal RNA, which makes up a huge portion of ribosomes.

***R*-selected populations** Populations that experience rapid growth of the J-curve variety. The offspring produced by *R*-selected organisms are numerous, mature quite rapidly, and require very little postnatal care.

**rubisco** Enzyme that catalyzes the first step of the Calvin cycle in C$_3$ plants.

**saprobe** Organism that feeds off dead organisms.

**saturated fat** Fat that contains no double bonds. It is associated with heart disease and atherosclerosis.

**savanna** Grassland that contains a spattering of trees found all over South America, Australia, and Africa. Savanna soil tends to be low in nutrients, while temperatures tend to run high.

**sclerenchyma cells** Plant cells that function as protection and mechanical support.

**search image** Mental image that assists animals during foraging. It directs them to food of interest.

**secondary consumers** Consumers that obtain energy through consumption of the primary consumers.

**secondary immune response** Memory cells are the basis for this efficient response to invaders.

**secondary oocyte** An oocyte that has half the genetic information of the parent cell, but the majority of its cytoplasm.

**secondary plant growth** Growth that leads to an increase in plant girth.

**secondary sex characteristics** The noticeable physical characteristics that differ between males and females such as facial hair, deepness of voice, breasts, and muscle distribution.

**secondary spermatocyte** Cells formed during spermatogenesis that give rise to spermatids and eventually sperm.

**secondary structure** The three-dimensional arrangement of a protein caused by hydrogen bonding.

**secondary succession** Succession in an area that previously had stable plant and/or animal life but has since been disturbed by some major force such as a forest fire.

**second messenger** Molecule that serves as an intermediary, activating other proteins and enzymes in a chemical reaction.

**semiconservative DNA replication** Before the parent strand is copied, the DNA unzips, with each single strand serving as a template for the creation of a new double strand. One strand of DNA from the parent goes to one daughter cell; the second parent strand goes to the second daughter cell.

**seminal vesicles** Structures that dump fluids into the ejaculatory duct to send along with the sperm, providing three important advantages to the sperm: energy by adding fructose; power to progress through the female reproductive system by adding prostaglandin (which stimulates uterine contraction); and mucus, which helps the sperm swim more effectively.

**seminiferous tubules** Actual site of sperm production.

**sensory neurons** Nerve cells that receive and communicate information from the sensory environment.

**septae** Structures that divide the hypha filaments of fungi into different compartments.

**SER** See **smooth endoplasmic reticulum.**

**sex pili** bacterial appendage vital to process of conjugation.

**sex ratio** Proportion of males and females in a given population.

**sexual selection** The process by which certain characters are selected for because they aid in mate acquisition.

**shoots** Parts of a plant that are above the ground.

**short-day plants** Plants, such as poinsettias, that flower if exposed to nighttime conditions longer than a critical period of length.

**sickle cell anemia** A recessive disease caused by the substitution of a single amino acid in the hemoglobin protein of red blood cells, leaving hemoglobin less able to carry oxygen and also causing the hemoglobin to deform to a sickle shape when the oxygen content of the blood is low. The sickling causes pain, muscle weakness, and fatigue.

**sieve-tube elements** Functionally mature cells of the phloem that are alive.

**sink** Site of carbohydrate consumption in plants.

**skeletal muscle** Striated muscle that controls voluntary activities and contains multiple nuclei.

**smooth endoplasmic reticulum (SER)** Membrane-bound organelle involved in lipid synthesis, detoxification, and carbohydrate metabolism; has no ribosomes on its cytoplasmic surface.

**smooth muscle** Involuntary muscle that contracts slowly and is controlled by the autonomic nervous system (ANS).

**sodium–potassium pump** A mechanism that actively moves potassium *into* the cell and sodium *out of* the cell against their respective concentration gradients to maintain appropriate levels inside the cell.

**solute** A substance dissolved in a solution.

**somatotropic hormone (STH)** A hormone that stimulates protein synthesis and growth in the body.

**somite** Structure that gives rise to the muscles and vertebrae in mammals.

**source** Site of carbohydrate creation in plants.

**Southern blotting** Procedure used to determine if a particular sequence of nucleotides is present in a sample of DNA.

**specialized transduction** Transduction involving a virus in the lysogenic cycle that shifts to the lytic cycle. If it accidentally brings with it a piece of the host DNA as it pulls out of the host chromosome, this DNA could find its way into another cell.

**speciation** The process by which new species evolve.

**species** A group of interbreeding (or potentially interbreeding) organisms.

**specific immunity** Complicated multilayered defense mechanism that protects a host against foreign invasion.

**spectrophotometer** Machine used to determine how much light can pass through a sample.

**spermatids** Immature sperm that enter the epididymis, where their waiting game begins and maturation is completed.

**spermatogenesis** Process by which the male gametes are formed. Four haploid sperm are produced during each meiotic cycle. This does not begin until puberty, and it occurs in the seminiferous tubules.

**S phase** The DNA is copied so that each daughter cell has a complete set of chromosomes at the conclusion of the cell cycle.

**spongy mesophyll** Region of a plant where the cells are more loosely arranged, aiding in the passage of $CO_2$ to cells performing photosynthesis.

**sporophyte** The diploid multicellular stage of the plant life cycle.

**sporozoite** Small infectious form that apicomplexa protists take to spread from place to place.

**stabilizing selection** This describes selection for the mean of a population for a given allele; has the effect of reducing variation in a given population.

**stamen** Male structure of a flower that contains the pollen-producing anther.

**starch** Storage polysaccharide made of glucose molecules; seen in plants.

**start codon (AUG)** Codon that establishes the reading frame for protein formation.

**stem cells** Cells that give rise to the immune cells of the human body.

**steroid hormones** Lipid-soluble molecules that pass through the cell membrane and combine with cytoplasmic proteins. These complexes pass through to the nucleus to interact with chromosomal proteins and directly affect transcription in the nucleus.

**steroids** Lipids composed of four carbon rings. Examples include cholesterol, estrogen, progesterone, and testosterone.

**STH** See **somatotropic hormone.**

**sticky ends** Single-stranded DNA fragments formed when DNA is treated with restriction enzymes. These fragments find and reconnect with other fragments with the same ends.

**stigma** Flower structure that functions as the receiver of pollen.

**stomata** Structure through which $CO_2$ enters a plant, and water vapor and $O_2$ leave.

**stop codons (UGA, UAA, UAG)** Codons that stop the production of a protein.

**storage diseases** Diseases such as Tay-Sachs that are caused by the absence of a particular lysosomal hydrolytic enzyme.

**strain** Groups into which bacterial species are placed.

**stroma** The inner fluid portion of the chloroplast that plays host to the light-independent reactions of photosynthesis.

**style** Pathway in flower that leads to the ovary.

**substrates** Substances that enzymes act upon.

**succession** Shift in the local composition of species in response to changes that occur over time.

**sulfhydryl group** A functional group that helps stabilize the structure of many proteins.

**survivorship curves** A tool used to study the population dynamics of species.

**symbiosis** A relationship between two different species that can be classified as one of three main types: commensalism, mutualism, and parasitism.

**sympathetic nervous system** Branch of the autonomic nervous system that gets the body ready to move.

**sympatric speciation** Interbreeding ceases even though no physical barrier prevents it. Can occur as a result of polyploidy and balanced polymorphism.

**symplast pathway** Movement of water and nutrients through the living portion of plant cells.

**synaptic knob** The end of the axon. This is where calcium gates are opened in response to the changing potential, which causes vesicles to release substances called *neurotransmitters* (NTs) into the synaptic gap between the axon and the target cell. These NTs diffuse across the gap, causing a new impulse in the target cell.

**tactile communication** Communication that involves the use of touch in the conveying of a message.

**taiga** Biome characterized by lengthy, cold, and wet winters. This biome is found in Canada and has gymnosperms as its prominent plant life. This biome contains coniferous forests (pine and other needle-bearing trees).

**tapeworm** Parasitic flatworm whose adult form lives in vertebrates.

**taproot system** System of roots found in many dicots that starts as one thick root and divides into many smaller lateral roots, which serve as an anchor for the plant.

**TATA box** Group of nucleotides found in the promoter region that assists in binding of RNA polymerase to the DNA strand for transcription.

**taxis** The reflex movement toward or away from a stimulus.

**taxonomy** The field of biology that classifies organisms according to the presence or absence of shared characteristics in an effort to discover evolutionary relationships between species.

**Tay-Sachs disease** A fatal genetic storage disease that renders the body unable to break down a particular type of lipid.

**temperate deciduous forest** A biome that is found in regions that experience cold winters where plant life is dormant, alternating with warm summers that provide enough moisture to keep large trees alive.

**temperate grasslands** Found in regions with cold winter temperatures. The soil of this biome is considered to be among the most fertile of all.

**termination site** Region of DNA that tells the polymerase when transcription should conclude.

**territoriality** Scenario in which territorial individuals defend their territory against other individuals.

**tertiary structure** The 3D (three-dimensional) arrangement of a protein caused by interaction among the various R groups of the amino acids involved.

**test cross** Crossing of an organism of unknown dominant genotype with an organism that is homozygous recessive for the trait, resulting in offspring with observable phenotypes. Test crosses are used to determine the unknown genotype.

**testis** The site of sperm and testosterone production in animals; males have two testes, located in the scrotum.

**testosterone** Sex hormone produced in testes that stimulates the growth of male sex characteristics.

**thermoacidophiles** Archaebacteria that live in hot, acidic environments.

**thermoregulation** The process by which temperature is maintained.

**thigmotropism** A plant's growth in response to touch.

**thylakoid membrane system** Inner membrane that winds through the stroma of a chloroplast. Site of the light-dependent reactions of photosynthesis.

**thymine dimers** Thymine nucleotides located adjacent to one another on the DNA strand bind together when excess exposure to UV light occurs. This can negatively affect replication of DNA and assist in the creation of further mutations.

**thymosin** Hormone involved in the development of the T cells of the immune system.

**thyroid-stimulating hormone (TSH)** A hormone that stimulates the synthesis and secretion of thyroid hormones, which regulate the rate of metabolism in the body.

**thyroxin** Hormone released by the thyroid gland that functions in the control of metabolic activities in the body.

**tongue** Structure that functions to move food around while we chew and helps to arrange the food into a swallowable bolus.

**trachea** The tunnel that leads air into the thoracic cavity.

**tracheid cells** Xylem cells in charge of water transport in gymnosperm.

**tracheophytes** Vascular plants.

**transcription factors** Helper proteins that assist RNA polymerase in finding and attaching to the promoter region.

**transduction** The movement of genes from one cell to another by phages.

**transformation** The transfer of genetic material from one cell to another, resulting in a genetic change in the receiving cell.

**translocation** Movement of the ribosome along the mRNA in such a way that the A site becomes the P site and the next tRNA comes into the new A site carrying the next amino acid.

**translocation (plants)** Movement of carbohydrates through the phloem.

**transpiration** Process by which plants lose water by evaporation through their leaves.

**trichinosis** Disease found in humans caused by a round-worm that infects meat products.

**trophic levels** Hierarchy of energy levels that describe the energy distribution of a planet.

**trophoblast** Forms the placenta for the developing fetus, and aids in attachment to the endometrium. This structure also produces human chorionic gonadotropin (hCG), which maintains the endometrium by ensuring the continued production of progesterone.

**tropical forests** These forests consist primarily of tall trees that form a thick cover, which blocks the light from reaching the floor of the forest (where there is little growth). Tropical rainforests are known for their rapid recycling of nutrients and contain the greatest diversity of species.

**tropism** Plant growth that occurs in response to an environmental stimulus such as sunlight or gravity.

**tropomyosin** Regulatory protein known to block the actin–myosin binding site and prevent muscular contraction in the absence of calcium.

**trypsin** Enzyme that cuts protein bonds in the small intestine.

**TSH** See **thyroid-stimulating hormone.**

**tundra** This biome experiences extremely cold winters during which the ground freezes completely. Short shrubs or grasses that are able to withstand the difficult conditions dominate.

**Turner syndrome** Affects females who are missing an X chromosome.

**umbilical cord** Structure that transports oxygen, food, and waste ($CO_2$) between the embryo and the placenta.

**uniform distribution** Scenario in which individuals are evenly spaced out across a given geographic area.

**unsaturated fat** Fat that contains one or more double bonds; found in plants.

**uracil** The nucleotide that replaces thymine in RNA.

**urethra** Exit point for both urine and sperm from males and urine for females.

**uterus** Site of embryo attachment and development in mammals.

**vaccination** Inoculation of medicine into a patient in an effort to prime the immune system to be prepared to fight a specific sickness if confronted in the future.

**vacuole** A storage organelle that is large in plant cells but small in animal cells.

**vascular cambium** A cylinder of tissue that extends the length of the stem and root and gives rise to the secondary xylem and phloem.

**vascular cylinder** Structure in plants that is composed of cells that produce the lateral roots of the plant.

**vas deferens** Tunnel that connects the epididymis to the urethra.

**vector** Agent that moves DNA from one source to another.

**veins** Structures that return blood to the heart.

**vena cava system** System of veins that returns deoxygenated blood from the body to the heart to be reoxygenated in the lungs.

**vertebrate** Animal with a backbone.

**vessel elements** Xylem cells in charge of water transport in angiosperms. More efficient than tracheid cells.

**vestigial characters** Characters that are no longer useful, although they once were.

**viral envelope** Protective barrier that surrounds some viruses but also helps them attach to cells.

**viroids** Plant viruses that are only a few hundred nucleotides in length.

**virus** A parasitic infectious agent that is unable to survive outside a host organism. Viruses do not contain enzymes for metabolism or ribosomes for protein synthesis.

**visual communication** Communication through the use of the visual senses.

**water biomes** Both freshwater and marine biomes, which occupy the majority of the surface of the earth.

**water cycle** The earth is covered in water. A lot of this water evaporates each day and returns to the clouds. This water is then returned to the earth in the form of precipitation.

**water potential** The force that drives water to move in a given direction. Combination of solute potential and pressure potential.

**water vascular system** Series of tubes and canals within echinoderms that play a role in ingestion of food, movement, and gas exchange.

**wild-type phenotype** The normal phenotype for a characteristic in fruit flies and other organisms.

**within-sex competition** Competition for mates between members of the same sex.

**wobble** Nucleotides in the third position of an anticodon are able to pair with many nucleotides instead of just their normal partner.

**X-inactivation** During the development of the female embryo, one of the two X chromosomes in each cell remains coiled as a Barr body whose genes are not expressed. A cell expresses the alleles of the active X chromosome only.

**xylem** The "superhighway," or important part of the vascular tissue in plants, through which water and nutrients travel throughout the plant. Also functions as a support structure that strengthens the plant.

**yolk sac** Derived from the hypoblast, this is the site of early blood cell formation in humans and the source of nutrients for bird and reptile embryos.

**zone of cell division** Region at the tip of a root formed by the actively dividing cells of the apical meristem.

**zone of elongation** Cells of this region elongate tremendously during plant growth.

**zone of maturation** Region in the plant where cells differentiate into their final forms.

# Study Smarter and Manage Your Time Better

## Create Your Own Personal Study Schedule

**Download Your BONUS McGraw-Hill Education AP Planner App**

# *5 Steps to a 5: AP Biology 2018*
### *Now with extra AP practice questions*

Select your exam date

Create your own customized study schedule based on diagnostic test results

Get a complete, day-by-day study schedule with review and practice assignments

**AVAILABLE FOR iPHONE, iPAD, AND ANDROID™ DEVICES**

SEARCH **MCGRAW-HILL EDUCATION AP PLANNER APP**
IN THE iTUNES APP STORE OR GOOGLE PLAY FOR ANDROID™.